Groovy in Action

Groovy in Action

DIERK KÖNIG

WITH ANDREW GLOVER, PAUL KING
GUILLAUME LAFORGE, AND JON SKEET

MANNING

Greenwich
(74° w. long.)

For online information and ordering of this and other Manning books, please go to
www.manning.com. The publisher offers discounts on this book when ordered in quantity.
For more information, please contact:

    Special Sales Department
    Manning Publications Co.
    Cherokee Station
    PO Box 20386   Fax: (609) 877-8256
    New York, NY 10021   email: orders@manning.com

Manning Publications Co.
Cherokee Station   Copyeditor: Benjamin Berg
PO Box 20386   Typesetter: Denis Dalinnik
New York, NY 10021   Cover designer: Leslie Haimes

ISBN 1-932394-84-2

Printed in the United States of America
1 2 3 4 5 6 7 8 9 10 – MAL – 10 09 08 07 06

To the love of my life
—D.K.

brief contents

contents

foreword

I first integrated Groovy into a project I was working on almost two years ago. There is a long and rich history of using "scripting languages" as a flexible glue to stitch together, in different ways, large modular components from a variety of frameworks. Groovy is a particularly interesting language from this tradition, because it doesn't shy away from linguistic sophistication in the pursuit of concise programming, especially in the areas around XML, where it is particularly strong. Groovy goes beyond the "glue" tradition of the scripting world to being an effective implementation language in its own right. In fact, while Groovy is often thought of and referred to as a scripting language, it really is much more than that.

It is traditional for scripting languages to have an uneasy relationship with the underlying linguistic system in which the frameworks are implemented. In Groovy's case, they have been able to leverage the underlying Java model to get integration that is smooth and efficient. And because of the linguistic similarities between Java and Groovy, it is fairly painless for developers to shift between programming in one environment and the other.

Groovy in Action by Dierk König and his coauthors is a clear and detailed exposition of what is groovy about Groovy. I'm glad to have it on my bookshelf.

JAMES GOSLING
Creator of Java
Sun Microsystems, Inc.

preface

Fundamental progress has to do with the reinterpretation of basic ideas.

—Alfred North Whitehead

In recent years, we have witnessed major improvements in software development with Java—and beyond. It's easy to overlook these achievements when you're bogged down with daily development work. We work with elaborate tool support, have all kinds of frameworks for various domains, and have discovered new agile ways of organizing software development in teams. Each of these disciplines—tooling, frameworks, and methodology—has successfully pushed its limits. We are still waiting for two other important aspects of software development to contribute to bringing our trade forward: personal skills management and programming languages.

Language does matter. It determines how you perceive the world—and it determines *your world*. Your programming language determines how you think about software solutions and the way you think about the underlying problems. Your knowledge of programming languages is key to your personal skill portfolio as a software developer.

Source code is a means of communication: from you to the compiler, to other team members, and then back to you. There is both a technical and a human aspect in this communication. Classical programming languages focus on the technical aspect and are optimized for performance and resource consumption. Other languages focus on the human aspect, trying to reveal the programmer's intent in the code as clearly as possible. Many attempts have been made to bridge the two aspects, ranging from Literate Programming to Programming in Logic, none of which has taken the world by storm.

While Groovy is unlikely to dominate traditional languages, what distinguishes it from previous attempts is that it allows a smooth transition from machine-centric to human-centric coding. It builds on the basic idea of the Java platform with a new interpretation of code appearance. That means that on the bytecode level, Groovy *is* Java, allowing a seamless mix-and-match of the two languages. For example, unlike other projects that try to make scripting languages available on the Java platform, a literal string in Groovy is of the type `java.lang.String`. You get the best of both worlds.

As a direct consequence, Groovy fully leverages the availability of frameworks, with the Java standard library being the most important one. James Strachan and Bob McWhirter founded the Groovy project in 2003, recognizing that application development in Java is characterized by using multiple frameworks and gluing them together to form a product. They designed Groovy to streamline exactly this kind of work.

At the same time, Richard Monson-Haefel met James, who introduced him to Groovy. Richard immediately recognized Groovy's potential and suggested the submission of a Java Specification Request (JSR-241). To make a long story short, this JSR passed "without a hitch," as Richard puts it in his blog, thanks to additional support from Geir Magnusson, Jr. and the foresight of the folks at Sun Microsystems. They don't see Groovy as Java's rival but rather as a companion that attracts brilliant developers who might otherwise move to Ruby or Python and thus away from the Java platform. Since the JSR has been accepted, Groovy is the second standard language for the Java VM (besides the Java language itself).

The JSR process was the acid test for the Groovy community. It showed where contributors were pushing in different directions and it imposed more structure on the development than some were willing to accept. Development slowed down in late 2004. This was when some key people stepped in and took the lead: Guillaume Laforge and Jeremy Rayner organized what was later called *Groovy-One*. This led to a *Groovy Language Specification (GLS)*, a *Test Compatibility Kit (TCK)*, and a new parser generated from a descriptive grammar specification. They got the ball rolling again—a ball that has now become an avalanche.

From the beginning, it was clear that Groovy would need a book like *Groovy in Action* to introduce newcomers to the language, provide comprehensive documentation, and show what's possible with Groovy in order to trigger the reader's curiosity and imagination.

John Wilson started this venture and passed the baton to Scott Stirling, who in turn came across some contributions that I had made to the Groovy Wiki. He quickly convinced me to join the book effort. By that time, I was downloading every single bit of information that I could find about Groovy into my personal knowledge base to have it available offline. I jotted down personal notes about Groovy idioms that I found helpful. Putting all this into a book seemed natural, even if it was only for my personal purposes.

Unfortunately, Scott had to resign and I was left alone for half a year, pushing things forward as best I could. I was lucky enough to get support from Andrew and Guillaume, both well-known Groovy experts. Andrew runs the *Practically Groovy* online series and Guillaume is not only the Groovy project manager, he is the heart and soul of Groovy. From day one of this book project, I was aware that as I am not a native speaker, I would not be able to write a full-length book in English without serious help. This was the initial reason for asking Dr. Paul King and Jon Skeet to come on board. I could not have been luckier. It turned out that they not only plowed tirelessly through every sentence in this book, leaving no stone unturned, but clarified the book's arguments, made the text more accessible, and corrected errors and weaknesses. They also suggested more compelling examples, and, last but not least, contributed content. This book would never have come to fruition without their diligent and mindful work.

Even though we will probably never see the day that Richard envisions "when Groovy is used to control space flight and has solved world hunger," I would be pleased if Groovy, and this book, help to push our profession of software development one inch farther.

DIERK KÖNIG

acknowledgments

I'm very grateful for having had the opportunity to write this book. It has helped me sharpen my programming skills in both Groovy and Java. Thanks to my coauthors and editors, especially my development editor, Jackie Carter, I also learned a great deal about writing. Most of all, I enjoyed working with so many brilliant people!

I'm deeply indebted to our reviewing team: Jonas Trindler, Jochen Theodorou, Jeremy Rayner, Christopher DeBracy, Bob McWhirter, Sam Pullara, John Stump, Graeme Rocher, Jeff Cunningham, Bas Vodde, Guillaume Alleon, Doug Warren, Derek Lane, Scott Shaw, Norman Richards, Stuart Caborn, Glen Smith, John Wilson, and Martin C. Martin. The "most observant reviewer" award goes to Marc Guillemot!

Other friends helped with the book in one way or another: Denis Antonioli, Christian Bauer, Gerald Bauer, Tim Bray, Jesse Eichar, Benjamin Feiermann, James Gosling, Martin Huber, Stephan Huber, Andy Hunt, Vincent Massol, Richard Monson-Haefel, Johannes Link, Rolf Pfenninger, Franck Rasolo, Stefan Roock, Rene Schönfeldt, Tomi Schütz, Scott Stirling, Roman Strobl, Frank Westphal, John Wilson, Dr. Russel Winder, all Groovy folks, as well as participants in Manning's Early Access Program.

Special thanks to Jochen Theodorou, the technical lead of the Groovy project, and John Wilson, Groovy's grandmaster of dynamic programming, for always being available when we needed advice about Groovy's inner workings.

In addition, Jochen was the technical proofreader for the book, checking the code one last time, just before the book went to press. Finally, very special thanks to James Gosling for writing the foreword to *Groovy in Action*.

The book would never had made it to the shelves without the support and guidance of everyone at Manning Publications, especially our publisher Marjan Bace and our editor Jackie Carter. We would also like to thank the rest of the team at Manning: Benjamin Berg, Denis Dalinnik, Gabriel Dobrescu, Dottie Marsico, Mary Piergies, Iain Shigeoka, Hieu Ta, Tiffany Taylor, Karen Tegtmeyer, Katie Tennant, Ron Tomich, Helen Trimes, Lianna Wlasiuk, and Megan Yockey.

My family, and especially my parents, have always supported me when times were tough and—most importantly—encouraged me to pursue my ideas. Thank you so much.

about this book

Roadmap

Groovy in Action describes the Groovy language, presents the library classes and methods that Groovy adds to the standard Java Development Kit, and leads you through a number of topics that you are likely to encounter in your daily development work. The book is made up of these three parts:

- Part 1: The Groovy language
- Part 2: Around the Groovy library
- Part 3: Everyday Groovy

An introductory chapter explains what Groovy is and then part 1 starts with a broad overview of Groovy's language features, before going into more depth about scalar and collective datatypes. The language description includes an explanation of the closure concept that is ubiquitous in Groovy, describing how it relates to and distinguishes itself from control structures. Part 1 closes with Groovy's model of object-orientation and its Meta-Object Protocol, which makes Groovy the dynamic language that it is.

Part 2 begins the library description with a presentation of Groovy's builder concept, its various implementations, and their relation to template engines, along with their use in Groovlets for simple web applications. An explanation of the GDK follows, with Groovy's enhancements to the Java standard library. This is the "beef" of the library description in part 2. The Groovy library shines with simple but powerful support for database programming and XML handling, and we include a detailed exposition of both topics. Another big advantage of Groovy is its all-out seamless integration with Java, and we explain the options provided by the Groovy library for setting this into action.

If part 1 was a tutorial and part 2 a reference, part 3 is a cookbook. It starts with tips and tricks, warnings of typical pitfalls and misconceptions, and snippets and solutions for common tasks, and then it leads you through the organizational aspects of your daily work with Groovy. A big part of day-to-day programming work is unit testing, and we describe in detail how Groovy helps with that. Since many programmers work on the Windows platform, we describe how to leverage your Groovy knowledge through integration with COM and ActiveX components.

A final bonus chapter gives a glimpse of how to use Grails, the Groovy web application framework. Grails is a perfect example for understanding and appreciating Groovy. It fully exploits Groovy's dynamic capabilities for runtime injection of features while using the solid base of the Java enterprise platform and the performance and scalability of third-party libraries such as Spring and Hibernate to the fullest. Grails is worth studying on its own; we have included it in part 3 to demonstrate how mindful engineering can lead to new levels of productivity by standing on the shoulders of giants.

The book ends with a series of appendixes which are intended to serve as a quick reference.

Who should read this book?

This book is for everyone who wants to learn Groovy as a new agile programming language. Existing Groovy users can use it to deepen their knowledge; and both new and experienced programmers can use it as a black-and-white reference. We found ourselves going to our own book to look up details that we had forgotten. Newcomers to Groovy will need a basic understanding of Java since Groovy is completely dependent on it; Java basics are not covered in our book.

Topics have been included that will make reading and understanding easier, but are not mandatory prerequisites: patterns of object-oriented design, Ant, Maven, JUnit, HTML, XML, and Swing. It is beneficial—but not required—to have been exposed to some other scripting language. This enables you to connect what you read to what you already know. Where appropriate, we point out similarities and differences between Groovy and other scripting languages.

Code conventions

This book provides copious examples that show how you can make use of each of the topics covered. Source code in listings or in text appears in a `fixed-width font like this` to separate it from ordinary text. In addition, class and method names, object properties, and other code-related terms and content in text are presented using `fixed-width font`.

Occasionally, code is italicized, as in `reference.dump()`. In this case `reference` should not be entered literally but replaced with the content that is required, such as the appropriate reference.

Where the text contains the pronouns "I" and "we," the "we" refers to all the authors. "I" refers to the lead author of the respective chapter: Guillaume Laforge for chapters 11 and 15, Andrew Glover for chapter 14, and Dierk König for the remaining chapters.

Most of the code examples contain Groovy code. This code is very compact so we present it "as is" without any omissions. Unless stated otherwise, you can copy and paste it into a new file and run it right away. In rare cases, when this wasn't possible, we have used ... ellipsis.

Java, HTML, XML, and command-line input can be verbose. In many cases, the original source code (available online) has been reformatted; we've added line breaks and reworked indentation to accommodate the page space available in the book. In rare cases, when even this was not enough, line-continuation markers were added.

Code annotations accompany many of the listings, highlighting important concepts. In some cases, numbered cueballs link to additional explanations that follow the listing.

You can download the source code for all of the examples in the book from the publisher's website at www.manning.com/koenig.

Keeping up to date

The world doesn't stop turning when you finish writing a book, and getting the book through production also takes time. Therefore, some of the information in any technical book becomes quickly outdated, especially in the dynamic world of agile languages.

This book covers Groovy 1.0. Groovy will see numerous improvements, and by the time you read this, it's possible that an updated version will have become available. New Groovy versions always come with a detailed list of changes. It is unlikely that any of the core Groovy concepts as laid out in this book will change significantly before Groovy 2.0; and even then the emphasis is likely to be on *additional* concepts and features. This outlook makes the book a wise investment, even in a rapidly changing world.

We will do our best to keep the online resources for this book reasonably up to date and provide information about language and library changes as the project moves on. Please check for updates on the book's web page at www.manning.com/koenig.

Author Online

Purchase of *Groovy in Action* includes free access to a private web forum run by Manning Publications where you can make comments about the book, ask technical questions, and receive help from the authors and from other users. To access the forum and subscribe to it, point your web browser to www.manning.com/koenig. This page provides information on how to get on the forum once you are registered, what kind of help is available, and the rules of conduct on the forum. It also provides links to the source code for the examples in the book, errata, and other downloads.

Manning's commitment to our readers is to provide a venue where a meaningful dialog between individual readers and between readers and the authors can take place. It is not a commitment to any specific amount of participation on the part of the authors, whose contribution to the AO remains voluntary (and unpaid). We suggest you try asking the authors some challenging questions lest their interest stray!

The Author Online forum and the archives of previous discussions will be accessible from the publisher's website as long as the book is in print.

about the authors

DIERK KÖNIG holds degrees in business administration and computer science, and has worked with Java for 10 years as a professional software developer, mentor, and coach. He is an acknowledged reviewer and/or contributor to numerous books, including the classic *Extreme Programming Explained* (Kent Beck), *Test-Driven Development* (Kent Beck), *Agile Development in the Large* (Eckstein/Josuttis), *JUnit* (Johannes Link), *JUnit and Fit* (Frank Westphal), and *Refactorings* (Roock/Lippert).

Dierk publishes in leading German magazines on software development and speaks at international conferences. Recently, Skillsmatter London hosted his Groovy and Grails training course and related events. He has worked with Canoo Engineering AG, Basle, Switzerland, since 2000, where he is a founding partner and member of the executive board. Dierk founded the open-source Canoo WebTest project and has been its manager since 2001. His consulting and engineering activities are related largely to agile software development practices and test automation. He joined the Groovy project in 2004 and has worked as a committer ever since.

ANDREW GLOVER is an established expert in automated testing frameworks and tools. He is an author for multiple online publications, including IBM's *DeveloperWorks* and O'Reilly's ONJava and ONLamp portals. He is the co-author of *Java Testing Patterns*. Andrew is a frequent speaker at Java Users Groups around the country as well as a speaker for the No Fluff Just Stuff Software Symposium group. His interest in building quality into software with technologies that lower software bug counts, reduce integration and testing times, and improve overall code stability led him to found Vanward Technologies in 2001. Vanward was acquired by JNetDirect in 2005 and renamed Stelligent in 2006. He blogs actively about software quality at thediscoblog.com and testearly.com.

DR. PAUL KING'S career spans technical and managerial roles in a number of organizations, underpinned by deep knowledge of the information technology and telecommunications markets and a passion for the creation of innovative organizations. Throughout his career, Paul has provided technical and strategic consulting to hundreds of organizations in the U.S. and Asia Pacific. The early stages of Paul's career were highlighted by his contribution to various research fields, including object-oriented software development, formal methods, telecommunications, and distributed systems. He has had numerous publications at international conferences and in journals and trade magazines. He is an award-winning author and sought-after speaker at conferences.

Currently, Paul leads ASERT (Advanced Software Engineering, Research & Training), which is recognized as a world-class center of expertise in the areas of middleware technology, agile development, and Internet application development and deployment. ASERT has experience teaching thousands of students in more than 15 countries, and has provided consulting services and development assistance throughout Asia Pacific to high-profile startups and government e-commerce sites. In his spare time, Paul is a taxi driver and homework assistant for his seven children.

GUILLAUME LAFORGE has been the official Groovy project manager since the end of 2004, after having been a contributor and later a core committer on the project. He is also the specification lead for JSR-241, the ongoing effort to standardize the Groovy language through Sun's Java Community Process. Guillaume is Groovy's "public face" and often responds to interviews regarding Groovy and presents his project at conferences such as at JavaOne 2006, where he spoke about how scripting can simplify enterprise development. In his professional life, Guillaume is a software architect working at OCTO Technology, a French-based consultancy focusing on software and information systems architecture, as well as on agile methodologies.

JON SKEET is a recent convert to Groovy, but has been helping fellow software developers through community efforts for several years, primarily through newsgroups, his website of Java and C# articles, and, more recently, through his blog on software development practices. Jon has been a Microsoft Most Valuable Professional since 2003 for his contributions to the C# community, and enjoys seeing how the worlds of .NET and Java are constantly learning from each other. One day, perhaps there'll be a C# equivalent of Groovy. In the meantime, Jon is looking forward to the far-off day when he can teach pair-programming to his twin sons, who were born while this book was being written. By then, Jon fully expects that his eldest son, Tom, will know more about computing than his father does.

about the title

By combining introductions, overviews, and how-to examples, Manning's *In Action* books are designed to help learning and remembering. According to research in cognitive science, the things people remember are things they discover during self-motivated exploration.

Although no one at Manning is a cognitive scientist, we are convinced that for learning to become permanent, it must pass through stages of exploration, play, and, interestingly, retelling of what is being learned. People understand and remember new things, which is to say they master them, only after actively exploring them. Humans learn in action. An essential part of an *In Action* guide is that it is example-driven. It encourages the reader to try things out, play with new code, and explore new ideas.

There is another, more mundane, reason for the title of this book: our readers are busy. They use books to do a job or solve a problem. They need books that allow them to jump in and jump out easily and learn just what they want, just when they want it. They need books that aid them in action. The books in this series are designed for such readers.

about the cover illustration

The figure on the cover of *Groovy in Action* is a "Danzerina del Japon," a Japanese dancer, taken from a Spanish compendium of regional dress customs first published in Madrid in 1799. While the artist may have captured the "spirit" of a Japanese dancer in his drawing, the illustration does not accurately portray the looks, dress, or comportment of a Japanese woman or geisha of the time, compared to Japanese drawings from the same period. The artwork in this collection was clearly not researched first hand!

The book's title page states:

Coleccion general de los Trages que usan actualmente todas las Nacionas del Mundo desubierto, dibujados y grabados con la mayor exactitud por R.M.V.A.R. Obra muy util y en special para los que tienen la del viajero universal

which we translate, as literally as possible, thus:

General collection of costumes currently used in the nations of the known world, designed and printed with great exactitude by R.M.V.A.R. This work is very useful especially for those who hold themselves to be universal travelers

Although nothing is known of the designers, engravers, and workers who colored this illustration by hand, the "exactitude" of their execution is evident in this drawing. The "Danzerina del Japon" is just one of many figures in this colorful collection. Travel for pleasure was a relatively new phenomenon at the time and books such as this one were popular, introducing both the tourist as well as the armchair traveler to the exotic inhabitants, real and imagined, of other regions of the world

Dress codes have changed since then and the diversity by nation and by region, so rich at the time, has faded away. It is now often hard to tell the inhabitant of one continent from another. Perhaps, trying to view it optimistically, we have traded a cultural and visual diversity for a more varied personal life. Or a more varied and interesting intellectual and technical life.

We at Manning celebrate the inventiveness, the initiative, and the fun of the computer business with book covers based on the rich diversity of regional life two centuries ago, brought back to life by the pictures from this collection.

Your way to Groovy

> One main factor in the upward trend of animal life has been the power of wandering.
>
> —Alfred North Whitehead

Welcome to the world of Groovy.

You've heard of Groovy on blogs and mailing lists. Maybe you've seen a snippet here and there. Perhaps a colleague has pointed out a page of your code and claimed the same work could be done in just a few lines of Groovy. Maybe you only picked up this book because the name is catchy. Why should you learn Groovy? What payback can you expect?

Groovy will give you some quick wins, whether it's by making your Java code simpler to write, by automating recurring tasks, or by supporting ad-hoc scripting for your daily work as a programmer. It will give you longer-term wins by making your code simpler to *read*. Perhaps most important, it's fun to use.

Learning Groovy is a wise investment. Groovy brings the power of advanced language features such as closures, dynamic typing, and the meta object protocol to the Java platform. Your Java knowledge will not become obsolete by walking the Groovy path. Groovy will build on your existing experience and familiarity with the Java platform, allowing you to pick and choose when you use which tool—and when to combine the two seamlessly.

If you have ever marveled at the Ruby folks who can implement a full-blown web application in the afternoon, the Python guys juggling collections, the Perl hackers managing a server farm with a few keystrokes, or Lisp gurus turning their whole codebase upside-down with a tiny change, then think about the *language* features they have at their disposal. The goal of Groovy is to provide language capabilities of comparable impact on the Java platform, while obeying the Java object model and keeping the perspective of a Java programmer.

This first chapter provides background information about Groovy and everything you need to know to get started. It starts with the Groovy story: why Groovy was created, what considerations drive its design, and how it positions itself in the landscape of languages and technologies. The next section expands on Groovy's merits and how they can make life easier for you, whether you're a Java programmer, a script aficionado, or an agile developer.

We strongly believe that there is only one way to learn a programming language: by trying it. We present a variety of scripts to demonstrate the compiler, interpreter, and shells, before listing some plug-ins available for widely used IDEs and where to find the latest information about Groovy.

By the end of this chapter, you will have a basic understanding of what Groovy is and how you can experiment with it.

We—the authors, the reviewers, and the editing team—wish you a great time programming Groovy and using this book for guidance and reference.

1.1 *The Groovy story*

At GroovyOne 2004—a gathering of Groovy developers in London—James Strachan gave a keynote address telling the story of how he arrived at the idea of inventing Groovy.

Some time ago, he and his wife were waiting for a late plane. While she went shopping, he visited an Internet café and spontaneously decided to go to the Python web site and study the language. In the course of this activity, he became more and more intrigued. Being a seasoned Java programmer, he recognized that his home language lacked many of the interesting and useful features Python had invented, such as native language support for common datatypes in an expressive syntax and, more important, dynamic behavior. The idea was born to bring such features to Java.

This led to the main principles that guide Groovy's development: to be a feature rich and Java friendly language, bringing the attractive benefits of dynamic languages to a robust and well-supported platform.

Figure 1.1 shows how this unique combination defines Groovy's position in the varied world of languages for the Java platform.[1] We don't want to offend anyone by specifying exactly where we believe any particular other language might fit in the figure, but we're confident of Groovy's position.

Some languages may have a few more features than Groovy. Some languages may claim to integrate better with Java. None can currently touch Groovy when you consider both aspects together: Nothing provides a better combination of Java friendliness *and* a complete range of modern language features.

Knowing some of the aims of Groovy, let's look at what it *is*.

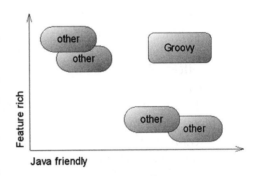

Figure 1.1 The landscape of JVM-based languages. Groovy is feature rich *and* Java friendly—it excels at both sides instead of sacrificing one for the sake of the other.

---

[1] http://www.robert-tolksdorf.de/vmlanguages.html lists close to 200 (!) languages targeting the Java Virtual Machine.

1.1.1 *What is Groovy?*

The Groovy web site (http://groovy.codehaus.org) gives one of the best definitions of Groovy: "Groovy is an agile dynamic language for the Java Platform with many features that are inspired by languages like Python, Ruby and Smalltalk, making them available to Java developers using a Java-like syntax."

Groovy is often referred to as a scripting language—and it works very well for scripting. It's a mistake to label Groovy purely in those terms, though. It can be precompiled into Java bytecode, be integrated into Java applications, power web applications, add an extra degree of control within build files, and be the basis of whole applications on its own—Groovy is too flexible to be pigeon-holed.

What we *can* say about Groovy is that it is closely tied to the Java platform. This is true in terms of both implementation (many parts of Groovy are written in Java, with the rest being written in Groovy itself) and interaction. When you program in Groovy, in many ways you're writing a special kind of Java. All the power of the Java platform—including the massive set of available libraries—is there to be harnessed.

Does this make Groovy just a layer of syntactic sugar? Not at all. Although everything you do in Groovy *could* be done in Java, it would be madness to write the Java code required to work Groovy's magic. Groovy performs a lot of work behind the scenes to achieve its agility and dynamic nature. As you read this book, try to think every so often about what would be required to mimic the effects of Groovy using Java. Many of the Groovy features that seem extraordinary at first—encapsulating logic in objects in a natural way, building hierarchies with barely any code other than what is *absolutely* required to compute the data, expressing database queries in the normal application language before they are translated into SQL, manipulating the runtime behavior of individual objects after they have been created—all of these are tasks that Java cannot perform. You might like to think of Groovy as being a "full color" language compared with the monochrome nature of Java—the miracle being that the color pictures are created out of lots of carefully engineered black and white dots.

Let's take a closer look at what makes Groovy so appealing, starting with how Groovy and Java work hand-in-hand.

1.1.2 *Playing nicely with Java: seamless integration*

Being Java friendly means two things: seamless integration with the Java Runtime Environment and having a syntax that is aligned with Java.

Seamless integration

Figure 1.2 shows the integration aspect of Groovy: It runs inside the Java Virtual Machine and makes use of Java's libraries (together called the Java Runtime Environment or *JRE*). Groovy is only a new way of creating *ordinary* Java classes—from a runtime perspective, Groovy *is* Java with an additional jar file as a dependency.

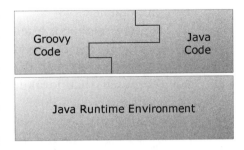

Figure 1.2   Groovy and Java join together in a tongue-and-groove fashion.

Consequently, calling Java from Groovy is a nonissue. When developing in Groovy, you end up doing this all the time without noticing. Every Groovy type is a subtype of `java.lang.Object`. Every Groovy object is an instance of a type in the normal way. A Groovy date *is* a `java.util.Date`, and so on.

Integration in the opposite direction is just as easy. Suppose a Groovy class `MyGroovyClass` is compiled into a *.class file and put on the classpath. You can use this Groovy class from within a Java class by typing

```
new MyGroovyClass();     // create from Java
```

In other words, instantiating a Groovy class is identical to instantiating a Java class. After all, a Groovy class *is* a Java class. You can then call methods on the instance, pass the reference as an argument to methods, and so forth. The JVM is blissfully unaware that the code was written in Groovy.

Syntax alignment

The second dimension of Groovy's friendliness is its syntax alignment. Let's compare the different mechanisms to obtain today's date in Java, Groovy, and Ruby in order to demonstrate what alignment *should* mean:

```
import java.util.*;          // Java
Date today = new Date();     // Java

today = new Date()           // a Groovy Script

require 'date'               # Ruby
today = Date.new             # Ruby
```

The Groovy solution is short, precise, and more compact than normal Java. Groovy does not need to import the `java.util` package or specify the `Date` type; moreover, Groovy doesn't require semicolons when it can understand the code without them. Despite being more compact, Groovy is fully comprehensible to a Java programmer.

The Ruby solution is listed to illustrate what Groovy avoids: a different packaging concept (`require`), a different comment syntax, and a different object-creation syntax. Although the Ruby way makes sense in itself (and may even be more consistent than Java), it does not align as nicely with the Java syntax and architecture as Groovy does.

Now you have an idea what Java friendliness means in terms of integration and syntax alignment. But how about feature richness?

1.1.3 *Power in your code: a feature-rich language*

Giving a list of Groovy features is a bit like giving a list of moves a dancer can perform. Although each feature is important in itself, it's how well they work together that makes Groovy shine. Groovy has three main types of features over and above those of Java: language features, libraries specific to Groovy, and additions to the existing Java standard classes (GDK). Figure 1.3 shows some of these features and how they fit together. The shaded circles indicate the way that the features use each other. For instance, many of the library features rely heavily on

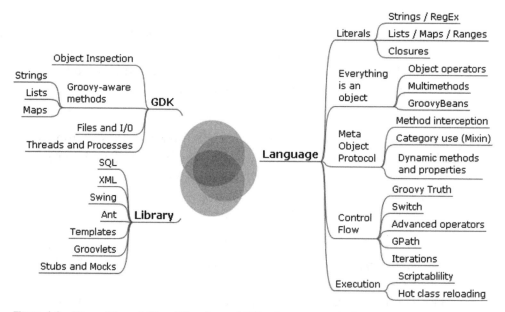

Figure 1.3   Many of the additional libraries and JDK enhancements in Groovy build on the new language features. The combination of the three forms a "sweet spot" for clear and powerful code.

language features. Idiomatic Groovy code rarely uses one feature in isolation—instead, it usually uses several of them together, like notes in a chord.

Unfortunately, many of the features can't be understood in just a few words. *Closures*, for example, are an invaluable language concept in Groovy, but the word on its own doesn't tell you anything. We won't go into all the details now, but here are a few examples to whet your appetite.

Listing a file: closures and I/O additions

Closures are blocks of code that can be treated as first-class objects: passed around as references, stored, executed at arbitrary times, and so on. Java's anonymous inner classes are often used this way, particularly with adapter classes, but the syntax of inner classes is ugly, and they're limited in terms of the data they can access and change.

File handling in Groovy is made significantly easier with the addition of various methods to classes in the `java.io` package. A great example is the `File.eachLine` method. How often have you needed to read a file, a line at a time, and perform the same action on each line, closing the file at the end? This is such a common task, it shouldn't be difficult—so in Groovy, it isn't.

Let's put the two features together and create a complete program that lists a file with line numbers:

```
def number=0
new File ('test.groovy').eachLine { line ->
    number++
    println "$number: $line"
}
```

The closure in curly braces gets executed for each line, and `File`'s new `eachLine` method makes this happen.

Printing a list: collection literals and simplified property access

`java.util.List` and `java.util.Map` are probably the most widely used interfaces in Java, but there is little language support for them. Groovy adds the ability to declare list and map literals just as easily as you would a string or numeric literal, and it adds many methods to the collection classes.

Similarly, the JavaBean conventions for properties are almost ubiquitous in Java, but the language makes no use of them. Groovy simplifies property access, allowing for far more readable code.

Here's an example using these two features to print the package for each of a list of classes. Note that the word *package* needs to be quoted because it's a keyword, but it can still be used for the property name. Although Java would allow a similar first line to declare an array, we're using a real list here—elements could be added or removed with no extra work:

```
def classes = [String, List, File]
for (clazz in classes)
{
    println clazz.'package'.name
}
```

In Groovy, you can even avoid such commonplace for loops by applying property access to a list—the result is a list of the properties. Using this feature, an equivalent solution to the previous code is

```
println( [String, List, File].'package'.name )
```

to produce the output

```
["java.lang", "java.util", "java.io"]
```

Pretty cool, eh?

XML handling the Groovy way: GPath with dynamic properties

Whether you're reading it or writing it, working with XML in Java requires a considerable amount of work. Alternatives to the W3C DOM make life easier, but Java itself doesn't help you in language terms—it's unable to adapt to your needs. Groovy allows classes to act as if they have properties at runtime even if the names of those properties aren't known when the class is compiled. GPath was built on this feature, and it allows seamless XPath-like navigation of XML documents.

Suppose you have a file called customers.xml such as this:

```
<?xml version="1.0" ?>
<customers>
  <corporate>
    <customer name="Bill Gates"         company="Microsoft" />
    <customer name="Steve Jobs"         company="Apple" />
    <customer name="Jonathan Schwartz" company="Sun" />
  </corporate>

  <consumer>
    <customer name="John Doe" />
    <customer name="Jane Doe" />
  </consumer>
</customers>
```

You can print out all the corporate customers with their names and companies using just the following code. (Generating the file in the first place with Groovy using a Builder would be considerably easier than in Java, too.)

```
def customers = new XmlSlurper().parse(new File('customers.xml'))
for (customer in customers.corporate.customer)
{
    println "${customer.@name} works for ${customer.@company}"
}
```

Even trying to demonstrate just a few features of Groovy, you've seen other features in the preceding examples—string interpolation with `GString`, simpler `for` loops, optional typing, and optional statement terminators and parentheses, just for starters. The features work so well with each other and become second nature so quickly, you hardly notice you're using them.

Although being Java friendly and feature rich are the main driving forces for Groovy, there are more aspects worth considering. So far, we have focused on the hard technical facts about Groovy, but a language needs more than that to be successful. It needs to *attract* people. In the world of computer languages, building a better mousetrap doesn't guarantee that the world will beat a path to your door. It has to appeal to both developers and their managers, in different ways.

1.1.4 Community-driven but corporate-backed

For some people, it's comforting to know that their investment in a language is protected by its adoption as a standard. This is one of the distinctive promises of Groovy. Since the passage of JSR-241, Groovy is the second standard language for the Java platform (the first being the Java language).

The size of the user base is a second criterion. The larger the user base, the greater the chance of obtaining good support and sustainable development. Groovy's user base is reasonably sized. A good indication is the activity on the mailing lists and the number of related projects (see http://groovy.codehaus.org/Related+Projects).

Attraction is more than strategic considerations, however. Beyond what you can measure is a gut feeling that causes you to enjoy programming *or not*.

The developers of Groovy are aware of this feeling, and it is carefully considered when deciding upon language features. After all, there is a reason for the name of the language.

GROOVY   "A situation or an activity that one enjoys or to which one is especially well suited (found his groove playing bass in a trio). A very pleasurable experience; enjoy oneself (just sitting around, grooving on the music). To be affected with pleasurable excitement. To react or interact harmoniously." [Leo]

Someone recently stated that Groovy was, "Java-stylish with a Ruby-esque feeling." We cannot think of a better description. Working with Groovy feels like a partnership between you and the language, rather than a battle to express what is clear in your mind in a way the computer can understand.

Of course, while it's nice to "feel the groove," you still need to pay your bills. In the next section, we'll look at some of the practical advantages Groovy will bring to your professional life.

1.2 What Groovy can do for you

Depending on your background and experience, you are probably interested in different features of Groovy. It is unlikely that anyone will require every aspect of Groovy in their day-to-day work, just as no one uses the whole of the mammoth framework provided by the Java standard libraries.

This section presents interesting Groovy features and areas of applicability for Java professionals, script programmers, and pragmatic, extreme, and agile programmers. We recognize that developers rarely have just one role within their jobs and may well have to take on each of these identities in turn. However, it is helpful to focus on how Groovy helps in the kinds of situations typically associated with each role.

1.2.1 Groovy for Java professionals

If you consider yourself a Java professional, you probably have years of experience in Java programming. You know all the important parts of the Java Runtime API and most likely the APIs of a lot of additional Java packages.

But—be honest—there are times when you cannot leverage this knowledge, such as when faced with an everyday task like recursively searching through all files below the current directory. If you're like us, programming such an ad-hoc task in Java is just too much effort.

But as you will learn in this book, with Groovy you can quickly open the console and type

```
groovy -e "new File('.').eachFileRecurse { println it }"
```

to print all filenames recursively.

Even if Java had an `eachFileRecurse` method and a matching `FileListener` interface, you would still need to explicitly create a class, declare a `main` method, save the code as a file, and compile it, and only then could you run it. For the sake of comparison, let's see what the Java code would look like, assuming the existence of an appropriate `eachFileRecurse` method:

```
public class ListFiles {                        // JAVA !!
    public static void main(String[] args) {
        new java.io.File(".").eachFileRecurse(      Imagine Java
            new FileListener() {                    had this
                public void onFile (File file) {
                    System.out.println(file.toString());
                }
            }
        );
    }
}
```

Notice how the intent of the code (printing each file) is obscured by the scaffolding code Java requires you to write in order to end up with a complete program.

Besides command-line availability and code beauty, Groovy allows you to bring dynamic behavior to Java applications, such as through expressing business rules, allowing smart configurations, or even implementing *domain specific languages*.

You have the options of using static or dynamic types and working with pre-compiled code or plain Groovy source code with on-demand compiling. As a developer, you can decide where and when you want to put your solution "in stone" and where it needs to be flexible. With Groovy, you have the choice.

This should give you enough safeguards to feel comfortable incorporating Groovy into your projects so you can benefit from its features.

1.2.2 *Groovy for script programmers*

As a script programmer, you may have worked in Perl, Ruby, Python, or other dynamic (non-scripting) languages such as Smalltalk, Lisp, or Dylan.

But the Java platform has an undeniable market share, and it's fairly common that folks like you work with the Java language to make a living. Corporate clients often run a Java standard platform (e.g. J2EE), allowing nothing but Java to be developed and deployed in production. You have no chance of getting your ultra-slick scripting solution in there, so you bite the bullet, roll up your sleeves, and dig through endless piles of Java code, thinking all day, "If I only had [*your language here*], I could replace this whole method with a single line!" We confess to having experienced this kind of frustration.

Groovy can give you relief and bring back the fun of programming by providing advanced language features where you need them: in your daily work. By allowing you to call methods on *anything*, pass blocks of code around for immediate or later execution, augment existing library code with your own specialized semantics, and use a host of other powerful features, Groovy lets you express yourself clearly and achieve miracles with little code.

Just sneak the groovy-all-*.jar file into your project's classpath, and you're there.

Today, software development is seldom a solitary activity, and your teammates (and your boss) need to know what you are doing with Groovy and what Groovy is about. This book aims to be a device you can pass along to others so they can learn, too. (Of course, if you can't bear the thought of parting with it, you can tell them to buy their own copies. We won't mind.)

1.2.3 *Groovy for pragmatic programmers, extremos, and agilists*

If you fall into this category, you probably already have an overloaded bookshelf, a board full of index cards with tasks, and an automated test suite that threatens to turn red at a moment's notice. The next iteration release is close, and there is anything but time to think about Groovy. Even uttering the word makes your pair-programming mate start questioning your state of mind.

One thing that we've learned about being pragmatic, extreme, or agile is that every now and then you have to step back, relax, and assess whether your tools are still *sharp* enough to cut smoothly. Despite the ever-pressing project schedules, you need to *sharpen the saw* regularly. In software terms, that means having the knowledge and resources needed and using the right methodology, tools, technologies, and languages for the task at hand.

Groovy will be an invaluable tool in your box for all automation tasks that you are likely to have in your projects. These range from simple build automation, continuous integration, and reporting, up to automated documentation, shipment, and installation. The Groovy automation support leverages the power of existing solutions such as Ant and Maven, while providing a simple and concise language means to control them. Groovy even helps with testing, both at the unit and functional levels, helping us test-driven folks feel right at home.

Hardly any school of programmers applies as much rigor and pays as much attention as we do when it comes to self-describing, intention-revealing code. We feel an almost physical need to remove duplication while striving for simpler solutions. This is where Groovy can help tremendously.

Before Groovy, I (Dierk) used other scripting languages (preferably Ruby) to sketch some design ideas, do a *spike*—a programming experiment to assess the feasibility of a task—and run a functional prototype. The downside was that I was never sure if what I was writing would *also* work in Java. Worse, in the end I had the work of porting it over or redoing it from scratch. With Groovy, I can do all the exploration work *directly* on my target platform.

EXAMPLE   Recently, Guillaume and I did a spike on *prime number disassembly.*[2] We started with a small Groovy solution that did the job cleanly but not efficiently. Using Groovy's interception capabilities, we unit-tested the solution and counted the number of operations. Because the code was clean, it was a breeze to optimize the solution and decrease the operation count. It would have been much more difficult to recognize the optimization potential in Java code. The final result can be used from Java as it stands, and although we certainly still have the option of porting the optimized solution to plain Java, which would give us another performance gain, we can defer the decision until the need arises.

The seamless interplay of Groovy and Java opens two dimensions of optimizing code: using Java for code that needs to be optimized for runtime performance, and using Groovy for code that needs to be optimized for flexibility and readability.

Along with all these tangible benefits, there is value in learning Groovy for its own sake. It will open your mind to new solutions, helping you to perceive new concepts when developing software, whichever language you use.

No matter what kind of programmer you are, we hope you are now eager to get some Groovy code under your fingers. If you cannot hold back from looking at some real Groovy code, look at chapter 2.

1.3 *Running Groovy*

First, we need to introduce you to the tools you'll be using to run and optionally compile Groovy code. If you want to try these out as you read, you'll need to have Groovy installed, of course. Appendix A provides a guide for the installation process.

There are three commands to execute Groovy code and scripts, as shown in table 1.1. Each of the three different mechanisms of running Groovy is demonstrated in the following sections with examples and screenshots. Groovy can also be "run" like any ordinary Java program, as you will see in section 1.4.2, and there also is a special integration with Ant that is explained in section 1.4.3.

We will explore several options of integrating Groovy in Java programs in chapter 11.

---

[2] Every ordinal number N can be uniquely disassembled into factors that are prime numbers: N = p1*p2*p3. The disassembly problem is known to be "hard." Its complexity guards cryptographic algorithms like the popular Rivest-Shamir-Adleman (RSA) algorithm.

Table 1.1 Commands to execute Groovy

Command	What it does
groovysh	Starts the groovysh command-line shell, which is used to execute Groovy code interactively. By entering statements or whole scripts, line by line, into the shell and giving the go command, code is executed "on the fly."
groovyConsole	Starts a graphical interface that is used to execute Groovy code interactively; moreover, groovyConsole loads and runs Groovy script files.
groovy	Starts the interpreter that executes Groovy scripts. Single-line Groovy scripts can be specified as command-line arguments.

1.3.1 Using groovysh for "Hello World"

Let's look at groovysh first because it is a handy tool for running experiments with Groovy. It is easy to edit and run Groovy iteratively in this shell, and doing so facilitates seeing how Groovy works without creating and editing script files.

To start the shell, run groovysh (UNIX) or groovysh.bat (Windows) from the command line. You should then get a command prompt like this:

```
Lets get Groovy!
================
Version: 1.0-RC-01-SNAPSHOT JVM: 1.4.2_05-b04
Type 'exit' to terminate the shell
Type 'help' for command help
Type 'go' to execute the statements

groovy>
```

The traditional "Hello World!" program can be written in Groovy with one line and then executed in groovysh with the go command:

```
groovy> "Hello, World!"
groovy> go

===> Hello, World!
```

The go command is one of only a few commands the shell recognizes. The rest can be displayed by typing help on the command line:

```
groovy> help
Available commands (must be entered without extraneous characters):
exit/quit    - terminates processing
help         - displays this help text
```

```
discard         - discards the current statement
display         - displays the current statement
explain         - explains the parsing of the current statement (currently
                  disabled)
execute/go      - temporary command to cause statement execution
binding         - shows the binding used by this interactive shell
discardclasses  - discards all former unbound class definitions
inspect         - opens ObjectBrowser on expression returned from
                  previous "go"
```

The `go` and `execute` commands are equivalent. The `discard` command tells Groovy to forget the last line typed, which is useful when you're typing in a long script, because the command facilitates clearing out the small sections of code rather than having to rewrite an entire script from the top. Let's look at the other commands.

Display command

The `display` command displays the last noncommand statement entered:

```
groovy> display
1> "Hello World!"
```

Binding command

The `binding` command displays variables utilized in a `groovysh` session. We haven't used any variables in our simple example, but, to demonstrate, we'll alter our "Hello World!" using the variable `greeting` to hold part of the message we print out:

```
groovy> greeting = "Hello"
groovy> "${greeting}, World!"
groovy> go

===> Hello, World!

groovy> binding
Available variables in the current binding
greeting = Hello
```

The `binding` command is useful when you're in the course of a longer `groovysh` session and you've lost track of the variables in use and their current values.

To clear the binding, exit the shell and start a new one.

Inspect command

The `inspect` command opens the *Groovy Object Browser* on the last evaluated expression. This browser is a Swing user interface that lets you browse through an object's native Java API and any additional features available to it via Groovy's

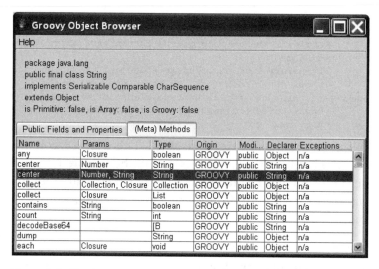

**Figure 1.4   The Groovy Object Browser when opened on an object of type
`String`, displaying the table of available methods in its bytecode and
registered Meta methods**

GDK. Figure 1.4 shows the Object Browser inspecting an instance of `String`. It
contains information about the `String` class in the header and two tables showing
available methods and fields.

Look at the second and third rows. A method with the name `center` is available
on a `String` object. It takes a `Number` parameter (second row) and an optional
`String` parameter (third row). The method's return type is a `String`. Groovy
defined this new public method on the `String` class.

If you are anything like us, you cannot wait to try that new knowledge in the
groovysh and type

```
groovy> 'test'.center 20, '-'
groovy> go

===> --------test--------
```

That's almost as good as IDE support!

For easy browsing, you can sort columns by clicking the headers and reverse the
sort with a second click. You can sort by multiple criteria by clicking column headers in sequence, and rearrange the columns by dragging the column headers.

Future versions of the Groovy Object Browser may provide even more sophisticated features.

1.3.2 *Using groovyConsole*

The groovyConsole is a Swing interface that acts as a minimal Groovy interactive interpreter. It lacks support for the command-line options supported by groovysh; however, it has a File menu to allow Groovy scripts to be loaded, created, and saved. Interestingly, groovyConsole is written in Groovy. Its implementation is a good demonstration of Builders, which are discussed in chapter 7.

The groovyConsole takes no arguments and starts a two-paned Window like the one shown in figure 1.5. The console accepts keyboard input in the upper pane. To run a script, either key in Ctrl+R, Ctrl+Enter or use the Run command from the Action menu to run the script. When any part of the script code is selected, only the selected text is executed. This feature is useful for simple debugging or *single stepping* by successively selecting one or multiple lines.

The groovyConsole's File menu has New, Open, Save, and Exit commands. New opens a new groovyConsole window. Open can be used to browse to a Groovy script on the file system and open it in the edit pane for editing and running. Save can be used to save the current text in the edit pane to a file. Exit quits the groovyConsole.

The Groovy Object Browser as shown in figure 1.4 is equally available in groovyConsole and also operates on the last evaluated expression. To open the browser, press Ctrl+I (for *inspect*) or choose Inspect from the Actions menu.

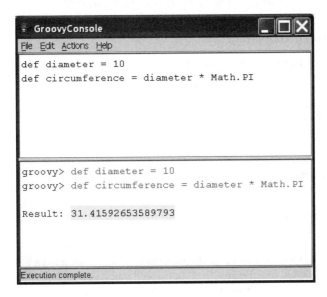

Figure 1.5
The groovyConsole with a simple script in the edit pane that calculates the circumference of a circle based on its diameter. The result is in the output pane.

That's it for groovyConsole. Whether you prefer working in groovysh or groovy-Console is a personal choice. Script programmers who perform their work in command shells tend to prefer the shell.

AUTHOR'S CHOICE I (Dierk) personally changed my habits to use the console more often for the sake of less typing through cut-and-paste in the edit pane.

Unless explicitly stated otherwise, you can put any code example in this book directly into groovysh or groovyConsole and run it there. The more often you do that, the earlier you will get a feeling for the language.

1.3.3 Using groovy

The groovy command is used to execute Groovy programs and scripts. For example, listing 1.1 shows the obligatory Fibonacci[3] number sequence Groovy program that prints the first 10 Fibonacci numbers. The Fibonacci number sequence is a pattern where the first two numbers are 1 and 1, and every subsequent number is the sum of the preceding two.

If you'd like to try this, copy the code into a file, and save it as Fibonacci.groovy. The file extension does not matter much as far as the groovy executable is concerned, but naming Groovy scripts with a .groovy extension is conventional. One benefit of using an extension of .groovy is that you can omit it on the command line when specifying the name of the script—instead of groovy MyScript.groovy, you can just run groovy MyScript.

Listing 1.1   Fibonacci.groovy

```
current = 1
next    = 1            loop
10.times {         ⟵┘  10 times
    print current + ' '
    newCurrent = next
    next = next + current
    current = newCurrent
}
println ''
```

---

[3] Leonardo Pisano (1170..1250), aka Fibonacci, was a mathematician from Pisa (now a town in Italy). He introduced this number sequence to describe the growth of an isolated rabbit population. Although this may be questionable from a biological point of view, his number sequence plays a role in many different areas of science and art. For more information, you can subscribe to the *Fibonacci Quarterly*.

Run this file as a Groovy program by passing the file name to the `groovy` command. You should see the following output:

```
> groovy Fibonacci
1 1 2 3 5 8 13 21 34 55
```

The `groovy` command has many additional options that are useful for command-line scripting. For example, expressions can be executed by typing `groovy -e "println 1+1"`, which prints 2 to the console. Section 12.3 will lead you through the full range of options, with numerous examples.

In this section, we have dealt with Groovy's support for simple ad-hoc scripting, but this is not the whole story. The next section expands on how Groovy fits into a code-compile-run cycle.

1.4 Compiling and running Groovy

So far, we have used Groovy in *direct* mode, where our code is directly executed without producing any executable files. In this section, you will see a second way of using Groovy: compiling it to Java bytecode and running it as regular Java application code within a Java Virtual Machine (JVM). This is called *precompiled* mode. Both ways execute Groovy inside a JVM eventually, and both ways compile the Groovy code to Java bytecode. The major difference is *when* that compilation occurs and whether the resulting classes are used in memory or stored on disk.

1.4.1 Compiling Groovy with groovyc

Compiling Groovy is straightforward, because Groovy comes with a compiler called `groovyc`. The `groovyc` compiler generates at least one class file for each Groovy source file compiled. As an example, we can compile Fibonacci.groovy from the previous section into normal Java bytecode by running `groovyc` on the script file like so:

```
> groovyc -d classes Fibonacci.groovy
```

In our case, the Groovy compiler outputs two Java class files to a directory named classes, which we told it to do with the `-d` flag. If the directory specified with `-d` does not exist, it is created. When you're running the compiler, the name of each generated class file is printed to the console.

For each script, `groovyc` generates a class that extends `groovy.lang.Script`, which contains a `main` method so that `java` can execute it. The name of the compiled class matches the name of the script being compiled.

More classes may be generated, depending on the script code; however, we don't really need to care about that because that is a Java platform topic. In essence, `groovyc` works the same way that `javac` compiles nested classes.

> **NOTE** The Fibonacci script contains the `10.times{}` construct that causes `groovyc` to generate a class of type *closure*, which implements what is inside the curly braces. This class is nested inside the Fibonacci class. You will learn more about closures in chapter 5. If you find this confusing, you can safely ignore it for the time being.

The mapping of class files to implementations is shown in table 1.2, with the purpose of each explained.

Table 1.2 Classes generated by `groovyc` for the Fibonacci.groovy file

Class file	Is a subclass of ...	Purpose
Fibonacci.class	groovy.lang. Script	Contains a `main` method that can be run with the `java` command.
Fibonacci$_run_ closure1.class	groovy.lang. Closure	Captures what has to be done 10 *times*. You can safely ignore it.

Now that we've got a compiled program, let's see how to run it.

1.4.2 Running a compiled Groovy script with Java

Running a compiled Groovy program is identical to running a compiled Java program, with the added requirement of having the embeddable groovy-all*.jar file in your JVM's classpath, which will ensure that all of Groovy's third-party dependencies will be resolved automatically at runtime. Make sure you add the directory in which your compiled program resides to the classpath, too. You then run the program in the same way you would run any other Java program, with the `java` command.[4]

```
> java -cp %GROOVY_HOME%/embeddable/groovy-all-1.0.jar;classes Fibonacci
1 1 2 3 5 8 13 21 34 55
```

Note that the .class file extension for the main class should not be specified when running with `java`.

---

[4] The command line as shown applies to Windows shells. The equivalent on Linux/Solaris/UNIX/Cygwin would be

```
java -cp $GROOVY_HOME/embeddable/groovy-all-1.0.jar:classes Fibonacci
```

All this may seem like a lot of work if you're used to building and running your Java code with Ant at the touch of a button. We agree, which is why the developers of Groovy have made sure you can do all of this easily in an Ant script.

1.4.3 Compiling and running with Ant

An Ant task is shipped with Groovy for running the `groovyc` compiler in an Ant build script. To use it, you need to have Ant installed.[5] We recommend version 1.6.2 or higher.

Listing 1.2 shows an Ant build script, which compiles and runs the Fibonacci.groovy script as Java bytecode.

Listing 1.2   build.xml for compiling and running a Groovy program as Java bytecode

```
<project name="fibonacci-build" default="run">

  <property environment="env"/>

  <path id="groovy.classpath">                              ❶ Path
    <fileset dir="${env.GROOVY_HOME}/embeddable/"/>             definition
  </path>

  <taskdef name    ="groovyc"                               ❷ taskdef
    classname    ="org.codehaus.groovy.ant.Groovyc"
    classpathref="groovy.classpath"/>

  <target name="compile"
    description="compile groovy to bytecode">
    <mkdir   dir="classes"/>
    <groovyc
      destdir="classes"                                    ❸ compile
      srcdir="."                                               target
      includes="Fibonacci.groovy"
      classpathref="groovy.classpath">
    </groovyc>
  </target>

  <target name="run" depends="compile"
    description="run the compiled class">
    <java classname="Fibonacci">                           ❹ run
      <classpath refid="groovy.classpath"/>                    target
      <classpath location="classes"/>
    </java>
  </target>
</project>
```

---

[5] Groovy ships with its own copy of the Ant jar files that could also be used for this purpose, but it is easier to explain with a standalone installation of Ant.

Store this file as build.xml in your current directory, which should also contain the Fibonacci.groovy script, and type ant at the command prompt.

The build will start at the ❹ run target, which depends on the ❸ compile target and therefore calls that one first. The compile target is the one that uses the groovyc task. In order to make this task known to Ant, the ❷ taskdef is used. It finds the implementation of the groovyc task by referring to the groovy. classpath in the ❶ path definition.

When everything compiles successfully in the ❸ compile target, the ❹ run target calls the java task on the compiled classes.

You will see output like this:

```
> ant
Buildfile: build.xml

compile:
    [mkdir] Created dir: …\classes
  [groovyc] Compiling 1 source file to …\classes
run:
    [java] 1 1 2 3 5 8 13 21 34 55

  BUILD SUCCESSFUL
Total time: 2 seconds
```

Executing ant a second time shows no compile output, because the groovyc task is smart enough to compile *only when necessary*. For a *clean* compile, you have to delete the destination directory before compiling.

The groovyc Ant task has a lot of options, most of which are similar to those in the javac Ant task. The srcdir and destdir options are mandatory.

Using groovyc for compilation can be handy when you're integrating Groovy in Java projects that use Ant (or Maven) for build automation. More information about integrating Groovy with Ant and Maven will be given in chapter 14.

1.5 *Groovy IDE and editor support*

If you plan to code in Groovy often, you should look for Groovy support for your IDE or editor of choice. Some editors only support syntax highlighting for Groovy at this stage, but even that can be useful and can make Groovy code more convenient to work with. Some commonly used IDEs and text editors for Groovy are listed in the following sections.

This section is likely to be out of date as soon as it is printed. Stay tuned for updates for your favorite IDE, because improved support for Groovy in the major Java IDEs is expected in the near future. Sun Microsystems recently announced

Groovy support for its NetBeans *coyote* project (https://coyote.dev.java.net/), which is particularly interesting because it is the first IDE support for Groovy that is managed by the IDE's own vendor itself.

1.5.1 *IntelliJ IDEA plug-in*

Within the Groovy community, work is ongoing to develop an open-source plug-in called GroovyJ. With the help of this plug-in and IDEA's built-in features, a Groovy programmer can benefit from the following:

- Simple syntax highlighting based on user preferences: GroovyJ currently uses Java 5's syntax highlighter, which covers a large proportion of the Groovy syntax. Version 1.0 will recognize the full Groovy syntax and allow customization of the highlighting through the Colors & Fonts panel, just as it is possible with the Java syntax.
- Code completion: To date, code completion is limited to word completion, leveraging IDEA's word completion based on an on-the-fly dictionary for the current editor only.
- Tight integration with IDEA's *compile*, *run*, *build*, and *make* configuration as well as output views.
- Lots of advanced editor actions that can be used as in Java.
- Efficient lookup for all related Java classes in the project or dependent libraries.
- Efficient navigation between files, including .groovy files.
- A Groovy file-type icon.

GroovyJ has a promising future, which is greatly dependent on its implementation of IDEA's *Program Structure Interface (PSI)* for the Groovy language. It will do so by specializing the Groovy grammar file and generating a specialized parser for this purpose. Because IDEA bases all its advanced features (such as refactoring support, inspections, navigation, intentions, and so forth) on the PSI, it seems to be only a matter of time before we will see these features for Groovy.

GroovyJ is an interesting project, mindfully led by Franck Rasolo. This plug-in is one of the most advanced ones available to Groovy at this point. For more information, see http://groovy.codehaus.org/GroovyJ+Status.

1.5.2 *Eclipse plug-in*

The Groovy plug-in for Eclipse requires Eclipse 3.1.1 or newer. The plug-in will also run in Eclipse 3.x-derived tools such as IBM Rational's Rational Application Developer and Rational Software Architect. As of this writing, the Groovy Eclipse plug-in supports the following features:

- Syntax highlighting for Groovy files
- A Groovy file decorator (icon) for Groovy files in the Package Explorer and Resources views
- Running Groovy scripts from within the IDE
- Auto-build of Groovy files
- Debugger integration

The Groovy Eclipse plug-in is available for download at http://groovy.codehaus.org/Eclipse+Plugin.

1.5.3 *Groovy support in other editors*

Although they don't claim to be full-featured development environments, a lot of all-purpose editors provide support for programming languages in general and Groovy in particular.

UltraEdit can easily be customized to provide syntax highlighting for Groovy and to start or compile scripts from within the editor. Any output goes to an integrated output window. A small sidebar lets you jump to class and method declarations in the file. It supports smart indentation and brace matching for Groovy. Besides the Groovy support, it is a feature-rich, quick-starting, all-purpose editor. Find more details at http://groovy.codehaus.org/UltraEdit+Plugin.

The *JEdit* plug-in for Groovy supports executing Groovy scripts and code snippets from within the editor. A syntax-highlighting configuration is available separately. More details are available here: http://groovy.codehaus.org/JEdit+Plugin.

Syntax highlighting configuration files for TextPad, Emacs, Vim, and several other text editors can be found on the Groovy web site at http://groovy.codehaus.org/Other+Plugins.

> **AUTHOR'S CHOICE** When programming small ad-hoc Groovy scripts, I (Dierk) personally use UltraEdit on Windows and Vim on Linux. For any project of some size, I use IntelliJ IDEA with the GroovyJ plug-in.

As Groovy matures and is adopted among Java programmers, it will continue to gain support in Java IDEs with features such as debugging, unit testing, and dynamic code-completion.

1.6 Summary

We hope that by now we've convinced you that you really want Groovy in your life. As a modern language built on the solid foundation of Java and with support from Sun, Groovy has something to offer for everyone, in whatever way they interact with the Java platform.

With a clear idea of why Groovy was developed and what drives its design, you should be able to see where features fit into the bigger picture as each is introduced in the coming chapters. Keep in mind the principles of Java integration and feature richness, making common tasks simpler and your code more expressive.

Once you have Groovy installed, you can run it both directly as a script and after compilation into classes. If you have been feeling energetic, you may even have installed a Groovy plug-in for your favorite IDE. With this preparatory work complete, you are ready to see (and try!) more of the language itself. In the next chapter, we will take you on a whistle-stop tour of Groovy's features to give you a better feeling for the shape of the language, before we examine each element in detail for the remainder of part 1.

Part 1

The Groovy language

Learning a new programming language is comparable to learning to speak a foreign language. You have to deal with new vocabulary, grammar, and language idioms. This initial effort pays off multiple times, however. With the new language, you find unique ways to express yourself, you are exposed to new concepts and styles that add to your personal abilities, and you may even explore new perspectives on your world. This is what Groovy did for us, and we hope Groovy will do it for you, too.

The first part of this book introduces you to the language basics: the Groovy syntax, grammar, and typical idioms. We present the language *by example* as opposed to using an academic style.

You may skim this part on first read and revisit it before going into serious development with Groovy. If you decide to skim, please make sure you visit chapter 2 and its examples. They are cross-linked to the in-depth chapters so you can easily look up details about any topic that interests you.

One of the difficulties of explaining a programming language by example is that you have to start somewhere. No matter where you start, you end up needing to use some concept or feature that you haven't explained yet for your examples. Section 2.3 serves to resolve this perceived deadlock by providing a collection of self-explanatory warm-up examples.

We explain the main portion of the language using its built-in datatypes and introduce expressions, operators, and keywords as we go along. By starting with some of the most familiar aspects of the language and building up your knowledge in stages, we hope you'll always feel confident when exploring new territory.

Chapter 3 introduces Groovy's typing policy and walks through the text and numeric datatypes that Groovy supports at the language level.

Chapter 4 continues looking at Groovy's rich set of built-in types, examining those with a collection-like nature: ranges, lists, and maps.

Chapter 5 builds on the preceding sections and provides an in-depth description of the *closure* concept.

Chapter 6 touches on logical branching, looping, and shortcutting program execution flow.

Finally, chapter 7 sheds light on the way Groovy builds on Java's object-oriented features and takes them to a new level of dynamic execution.

At the end of part 1, you'll have the whole picture of the Groovy language. This is the basis for getting the most out of part 2, which explores the Groovy library: the classes and methods that Groovy adds to the Java platform. Part 3, titled "Everyday Groovy," will apply the knowledge obtained in parts 1 and 2 to the daily tasks of your programming business.

Overture:
The Groovy basics

2

> *Do what you think is interesting, do something that you think is fun and worthwhile, because otherwise you won't do it well anyway.*
>
> —Brian Kernighan

This chapter follows the model of an overture in classical music, in which the initial movement introduces the audience to a musical topic. Classical composers wove euphonious patterns that, later in the performance, were revisited, extended, varied, and combined. In a way, overtures are the whole symphony *en miniature*.

In this chapter, we introduce you to many of the basic constructs of the Groovy language. First, though, we cover two things you need to know about Groovy to get started: code appearance and assertions. Throughout the chapter, we provide examples to jump-start you with the language; however, only a few aspects of each example will be explained in detail—just enough to get you started. If you struggle with any of the examples, revisit them after having read the whole chapter.

Overtures allow you to make yourself comfortable with the instruments, the sound, the volume, and the seating. So lean back, relax, and enjoy the Groovy symphony.

2.1 General code appearance

Computer languages tend to have an obvious lineage in terms of their look and feel. For example, a C programmer looking at Java code might not understand a lot of the keywords but would recognize the general layout in terms of braces, operators, parentheses, comments, statement terminators, and the like. Groovy allows you to start out in a way that is almost indistinguishable from Java and transition smoothly into a more lightweight, suggestive, idiomatic style as your knowledge of the language grows. We will look at a few of the basics—how to comment-out code, places where Java and Groovy differ, places where they're similar, and how Groovy code can be briefer because it lets you leave out certain elements of syntax.

First, Groovy is *indentation unaware,* but it is good engineering practice to follow the usual indentation schemes for blocks of code. Groovy is mostly unaware of excessive whitespace, with the exception of line breaks that end the current statement and single-line comments. Let's look at a few aspects of the appearance of Groovy code.

2.1.1 Commenting Groovy code

Single-line comments and multiline comments are exactly like those in Java, with an additional option for the first line of a script:

```
#!/usr/bin/groovy

// some line comment
```

```
/*
    some multi-
    line comment
*/
```

Here are some guidelines for writing comments in Groovy:

- The `#!` *shebang* comment is allowed only in the first line. The shebang allows Unix shells to locate the Groovy bootstrap script and run code with it.

- `//` denotes single-line comments that end with the current line.

- Multiline comments are enclosed in `/* … */` markers.

- Javadoc-like comments in `/** … */` markers are treated the same as other multiline comments, but support for *Groovydoc* is in the works at the time of writing. It will be the Groovy equivalent to Javadoc and will use the same syntax.

Comments, however, are not the only Java-friendly part of the Groovy syntax.

2.1.2 *Comparing Groovy and Java syntax*

Some Groovy code—but not all—appears exactly like it would in Java. This often leads to the false conclusion that Groovy's syntax is a superset of Java's syntax. Despite the similarities, neither language is a superset of the other. For example, Groovy currently doesn't support the classic Java *for(init;test;inc)* loop. As you will see in listing 2.1, even language semantics can be slightly different (for example, with the `==` operator).

Beside those subtle differences, the overwhelming majority of Java's syntax is *part* of the Groovy syntax. This applies to

- The general packaging mechanism
- Statements (including package and import statements)
- Class and method definitions (except for nested classes)
- Control structures (except the classic *for(init;test;inc)* loop)
- Operators, expressions, and assignments
- Exception handling
- Declaration of literals (with some twists)
- Object instantiation, referencing and dereferencing objects, and calling methods

The added value of Groovy's syntax is to

- Ease access to the Java objects through new expressions and operators
- Allow more ways of declaring objects literally
- Provide new control structures to allow advanced flow control
- Introduce new datatypes together with their operators and expressions
- Treat *everything* as an object

Overall, Groovy looks like Java with these additions. These additional syntax elements make the code more compact and easier to read. One interesting aspect that Groovy *adds* is the ability to leave things *out*.

2.1.3 *Beauty through brevity*

Groovy allows you to leave out some elements of syntax that are always required in Java. Omitting these elements often results in code that is shorter, less verbose, and more *expressive*. For example, compare the Java and Groovy code for encoding a string for use in a URL:

Java:
```
java.net.URLEncoder.encode("a b");
```

Groovy:
```
URLEncoder.encode 'a b'
```

Not only is the Groovy code shorter, but it expresses our objective in the simplest possible way. By leaving out the package prefix, parentheses, and semicolon, the code boils down to the bare minimum.

The support for optional parentheses is based on the disambiguation and precedence rules as summarized in the *Groovy Language Specification (GLS)*. Although these rules are unambiguous, they are not always intuitive. Omitting parentheses can lead to misunderstandings, even though the compiler is happy with the code. We prefer to include the parentheses for all but the most trivial situations. The compiler does not try to judge your code for readability—you must do this yourself.

In chapter 7, we will also talk about optional `return` statements.

Groovy automatically imports the packages `groovy.lang.*`, `groovy.util.*`, `java.lang.*`, `java.util.*`, `java.net.*`, and `java.io.*` as well as the classes `java.math.BigInteger` and `BigDecimal`. As a result, you can refer to the classes in these packages without specifying the package names. We will use this feature throughout the book, and we'll use fully qualified class names only for disambiguation or for pointing out their origin. Note that Java automatically imports `java.lang.*` but nothing else.

This section has given you enough background to make it easier to concentrate on each individual feature in turn. We're still going through them quickly rather than in great detail, but you should be able to recognize the general look and feel of the code. With that under our belt, we can look at the principal tool we're going to use to test each new piece of the language: assertions.

2.2 *Probing the language with assertions*

If you have worked with Java 1.4 or later, you are probably familiar with *assertions*. They test whether everything is right with the world as far as your program is concerned. Usually, they live in your code to make sure you don't have any inconsistencies in your logic, performing tasks such as checking invariants at the beginning and end of a method or ensuring that method parameters are valid. In this book, however, we'll use them to demonstrate the features of Groovy. Just as in test-driven development, where the tests are regarded as the ultimate demonstration of what a unit of code should do, the assertions in this book demonstrate the results of executing particular pieces of Groovy code. We use assertions to show not only what code can be run, but the result of running the code. This section will prepare you for reading the code examples in the rest of the book, explaining how assertions work in Groovy and how you will use them.

Although assertions may seem like an odd place to start learning a language, they're our first port of call, because you won't understand any of the examples until you understand assertions. Groovy provides assertions with the `assert` keyword. Listing 2.1 shows what they look like.

Listing 2.1 Using assertions

```
assert(true)
assert 1 == 1
def x = 1
assert x == 1
def y = 1 ; assert y == 1
```

Let's go through the lines one by one.

```
assert(true)
```

This introduces the `assert` keyword and shows that you need to provide an expression that you're asserting will be true.[1]

```
assert 1 == 1
```

This demonstrates that `assert` can take full expressions, not just literals or simple variables. Unsurprisingly, 1 equals 1. Exactly like Ruby and unlike Java, the `==` operator denotes *equality*, not *identity*. We left out the parentheses as well, because they are optional for top-level statements.

```
def x = 1
assert x == 1
```

This defines the variable x, assigns it the numeric value 1, and uses it inside the asserted expression. Note that we did not reveal anything about the *type* of x. The `def` keyword means "dynamically typed."

```
def y = 1 ; assert y == 1
```

This is the typical style we use when asserting the program status for the current line. It uses two statements on the same line, separated by a semicolon. The semicolon is Groovy's statement terminator. As you have seen before, it is optional when the statement ends with the current line.

Assertions serve multiple purposes:

- Assertions can be used to reveal the current program state, as we are using them in the examples of this book. The previous assertion reveals that the variable y now has the value 1.

- Assertions often make good replacements for line comments, because they reveal assumptions and verify them *at the same time*. The previous assertion reveals that for the remainder of the code, it is assumed that y has the value 1. Comments may go out of date without anyone noticing—assertions are always checked for correctness. They're like tiny unit tests sitting inside the real code.

> **REAL LIFE** A real-life experience of the value of assertions was writing this book. This book is constructed in a way that allows us to run the example code and the assertions it contains. This works as follows: There is a raw version of this book in MS-Word format that contains no code, but only placeholders

---

[1] Groovy's meaning of *truth* encompasses more than a simple boolean value, as you will see in section 6.7.

that refer to files containing the code. With the help of a little Groovy script, all placeholders are scanned and loaded with the corresponding file, which is evaluated and replaces the placeholder. For instance, the assertions in listing 2.1 were evaluated and found to be correct during the substitution process. The process stops with an error message, however, if an assertion fails.

Because you are reading a production copy of this book, that means the production process was not stopped and all assertions succeeded. This should give you confidence in the correctness of all the Groovy examples we provide. Not only does this prove the value of assertions, but it uses Scriptom (chapter 15) to control MS-Word and AntBuilder (chapter 8) to help with the building side—as we said before, the features of Groovy work best when they're used together.

Most of our examples use assertions—one part of the expression will do something with the feature being described, and another part will be simple enough to understand on its own. If you have difficulty understanding an example, try breaking it up, thinking about the language feature being discussed and what you would expect the result to be given

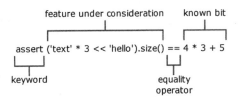

Figure 2.1   A complex assertion, broken up into its constituent parts

our description, and then looking at what *we've* said the result will be, as checked at runtime by the assertion. Figure 2.1 breaks up a more complicated assertion into the different parts.

This is an extreme example—we often perform the steps in separate statements and then make the assertion itself short. The principle is the same, however: There's code that has functionality we're trying to demonstrate and there's code that is trivial and can be easily understood without knowing the details of the topic at hand.

In case assertions do not convince you or you mistrust an asserted expression in this book, you can usually replace it with output to the console. For example, an assertion such as

```
assert x == 'hey, this is really the content of x'
```

can be replaced by

```
println x
```

which prints the value of x to the console. Throughout the book, we often replace console output with assertions for the sake of having self-checking code. This is not a common way of presenting code in books, but we feel it keeps the code and the results closer—and it appeals to our test-driven nature.

Assertions have a few more interesting features that can influence your programming style. Section 6.2.4 covers assertions in depth. Now that we have explained the tool we'll be using to put Groovy under the microscope, you can start seeing some of the real features.

2.3 Groovy at a glance

Like many languages, Groovy has a language specification that breaks down code into statements, expressions, and so on. Learning a language from such a specification tends to be a dry experience and doesn't move you far toward the goal of writing Groovy code in the shortest possible amount of time. Instead, we will present simple examples of typical Groovy constructs that make up most Groovy code: classes, scripts, beans, strings, regular expressions, numbers, lists, maps, ranges, closures, loops, and conditionals.

Take this section as a broad but shallow overview. It won't answer all your questions, but it will enable you to start experiencing Groovy *on your own*. We encourage you to experiment—if you wonder what would happen if you were to tweak the code in a certain way, try it! You learn best by experience. We promise to give detailed explanations in later *in-depth* chapters.

2.3.1 Declaring classes

Classes are the cornerstone of object-oriented programming, because they define the blueprint from which objects are drawn.

Listing 2.2 contains a simple Groovy class named Book, which has an instance variable title, a constructor that sets the title, and a getter method for the title. Note that everything looks much like Java, except there's no accessibility modifier: Methods are *public* by default.

Listing 2.2 A simple Book class

```
class Book {
    private String title

    Book (String theTitle) {
        title = theTitle
```

```
    }
    String getTitle(){
        return title
    }
}
```

Please save this code in a file named Book.groovy, because we will refer to it in the next section.

The code is not surprising. Class declarations look much the same in most object-oriented languages. The details and nuts and bolts of class declarations will be explained in chapter 7.

2.3.2 *Using scripts*

Scripts are text files, typically with an extension of .groovy, that can be executed from the command shell via

```
> groovy myfile.groovy
```

Note that this is very different from Java. In Groovy, we are executing the source code! An ordinary Java class is generated for us and executed behind the scenes. But from a user's perspective, it looks like we are executing plain Groovy source code.[2]

Scripts contain Groovy statements without an enclosing class declaration. Scripts can even contain method definitions outside of class definitions to better structure the code. You will learn more about scripts in chapter 7. Until then, take them for granted.

Listing 2.3 shows how easy it is to use the Book class in a script. We create a new instance and call the getter method on the object by using Java's *dot*-syntax. Then we define a method to read the title backward.

Listing 2.3 Using the Book class from a script

```
Book gina = new Book('Groovy in Action')

assert gina.getTitle()          == 'Groovy in Action'
assert getTitleBackwards(gina) == 'noitcA ni yvoorG'
```

---

[2] Any Groovy code can be executed this way as long as it can be *run*; that is, it is either a script, a class with a main method, a *Runnable*, or a *GroovyTestCase*.

```
String getTitleBackwards(book) {
    title = book.getTitle()
    return title.reverse()
}
```

Note how we are able to invoke the method `getTitleBackwards` before it is declared. Behind this observation is a fundamental difference between Groovy and other scripting languages such as Ruby. A Groovy script is fully constructed—that is, parsed, compiled, and generated—*before execution*. Section 7.2 has more details about this.

Another important observation is that we can use `Book` objects without explicitly compiling the `Book` class! The only prerequisite for using the `Book` class is that Book.groovy must reside on the classpath. The Groovy runtime system will find the file, compile it transparently into a class, and yield a new `Book` object. Groovy combines the ease of scripting with the merits of object orientation.

This inevitably leads to how to organize larger script-based applications. In Groovy, the preferred way is not meshing together numerous script files, but instead grouping reusable components in classes such as `Book`. Remember that such a class remains fully scriptable; you can modify Groovy code, and the changes are instantly available without further action.

Programming the `Book` class and the script that uses it was simple. It's hard to believe that it can be any simpler, but it *can*, as you will see next.

2.3.3 GroovyBeans

JavaBeans are ordinary Java classes that expose *properties*. What is a property? That's not easy to explain, because it is not a single entity on its own. It's a concept made up from a naming convention. If a class exposes methods with the naming scheme get*Name*() and set*Name*(name), then the concept describes *name* as a property of that class. The get- and set- methods are called *accessor* methods. (Some people make a distinction between *accessor* and *mutator* methods, but we don't.)

A *GroovyBean* is a JavaBean defined in Groovy. In Groovy, working with beans is much easier than in Java. Groovy facilitates working with beans in three ways:

- Generating the accessor methods
- Allowing simplified access to all JavaBeans (including GroovyBeans)
- Simplified registration of event handlers

Listing 2.4 shows how our `Book` class boils down to a one-liner defining the title property. This results in the accessor methods `getTitle()` and `setTitle(title)` being generated.

We also demonstrate how to access the bean the standard way with accessor methods, as well as the simplified way, where property access reads like direct field access.

Listing 2.4 Defining the `Book` class as a GroovyBean

```
class Book {
    String title          ◁─┐  Property
}                            │  declaration

def groovyBook = new Book()                         Property use
                                                    with explicit
groovyBook.setTitle('Groovy conquers the world')    method calls
assert groovyBook.getTitle() == 'Groovy conquers the world'

groovyBook.title = 'Groovy in Action'      Property use with
assert groovyBook.title == 'Groovy in Action'   Groovy shortcuts
```

Note that listing 2.4 is a fully valid script and can be executed *as is*, even though it contains a class declaration and additional code. You will learn more about this construction in chapter 7.

Also note that `groovyBook.title` is *not* a field access. Instead it is a shortcut for the corresponding accessor method.

More information about methods and beans will be given in chapter 7.

2.3.4 Handling text

Just like in Java, character data is mostly handled using the `java.lang.String` class. However, Groovy provides some tweaks to make that easier, with more options for string literals and some helpful operators.

GStrings

In Groovy, string literals can appear in single or double quotes. The double-quoted version allows the use of placeholders, which are automatically resolved as required. This is a *GString*, and that's also the name of the class involved. The following code demonstrates a simple variable expansion, although that's not all GStrings can do:

```
def nick = 'Gina'
def book = 'Groovy in Action'
assert "$nick is $book" == 'Gina is Groovy in Action'
```

Chapter 3 provides more information about strings, including more options for GStrings, how to escape special characters, how to span string declarations over multiple lines, and available methods and operators on strings. As you'd expect, GStrings are pretty neat.

Regular expressions

If you are familiar with the concept of *regular expressions*, you will be glad to hear that Groovy supports them *at the language level*. If this concept is new to you, you can safely skip this section for the moment. You will find a full introduction to the topic in chapter 3.

Groovy provides a means for easy declaration of regular expression patterns as well as operators for applying them. Figure 2.2 declares a pattern with the slashy // syntax and uses the =~ find operator to match the pattern against a given string. The first line ensures that the string contains a series of digits; the second line replaces every digit with an x.

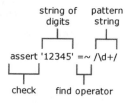

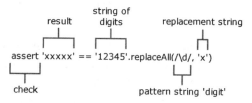

Figure 2.2   Regular expression support in Groovy through operators and slashy strings

Note that replaceAll is defined on java.lang.String and takes two string arguments. It becomes apparent that '12345' is a java.lang.String, as is the expression /\d/.

Chapter 3 explains how to declare and use regular expressions and goes through the ways to apply them.

2.3.5 Numbers are objects

Hardly any program can do without numbers, whether for calculations or, more often, for counting and indexing. Groovy *numbers* have a familiar appearance, but unlike in Java, they are first-class objects, *not* primitive types.

In Java, you cannot invoke methods on primitive types. If x is of primitive type int, you cannot write x.toString(). On the other hand, if y is an object, you cannot use 2*y.

In Groovy, both are possible. You can use numbers with numeric operators, and you can also call methods on number instances.

```
def x = 1
def y = 2
assert x + y == 3
assert x.plus(y) == 3
assert x instanceof Integer
```

The variables x and y are objects of type `java.lang.Integer`. Thus, we can use the `plus` method. But we can just as easily use the + operator.

This is surprising and a major lift to object orientation on the Java platform. Whereas Java has a small but ubiquitously used part of the language that isn't object-oriented at all, Groovy makes a point of using objects for everything. You will learn more about how Groovy handles numbers in chapter 3.

2.3.6 Using lists, maps, and ranges

Many languages, including Java, directly understand only a single collection type—an array—at the syntax level and have language features that only apply to that type. In practice, other collections are widely used, and there is no reason why the language should make it harder to use those collections than to use arrays. Groovy makes collection handling simple, with added support for operators, literals, and extra methods beyond those provided by the Java standard libraries.

Lists

Java supports indexing arrays with a square bracket syntax, which we will call the *subscript operator*. Groovy allows the same syntax to be used with *lists*—instances of `java.util.List`—which allows adding and removing elements, changing the size of the list at runtime, and storing items that are not necessarily of a uniform type. In addition, Groovy allows lists to be indexed outside their current bounds, which again can change the size of the list. Furthermore, lists can be specified as literals directly in your code.

The following example declares a list of Roman numerals and initializes it with the first seven numbers, as shown in figure 2.3.

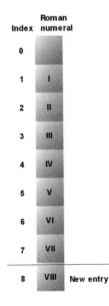

Figure 2.3
An example list where the content for each index is the Roman numeral for that index

The list is constructed such that each index matches its representation as a Roman numeral. Working with the list looks much like working with arrays, but in Groovy, the manipulation is more expressive, and the restrictions that apply to arrays are gone:

```
def roman = ['', 'I', 'II', 'III', 'IV', 'V', 'VI', 'VII']    ⟵┐
                                                        List of Roman
assert roman[4] == 'IV'   ⟵  List access                   numerals
roman[8] = 'VIII'   ⟵  List expansion
assert roman.size() == 9
```

Note that there was no list item with index 8 when we assigned a value to it. We indexed the list outside the current bounds. Later, in section 4.2, we will discuss more capabilities of the `list` datatype.

Simple maps

A *map* is a storage type that associates a key with a value. Maps store and retrieve the values by key, whereas lists retrieve the values by numeric index.

Unlike Java, Groovy supports maps at the language level, allowing them to be specified with literals and providing suitable operators to work with them. It does so with a clear and easy syntax. The syntax for maps looks like an array of

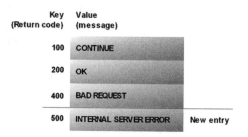

Figure 2.4   An example map where HTTP return codes map to their respective messages

key-value pairs, where a colon separates keys and values. That's all it takes.

The following example stores descriptions of HTTP[3] return codes in a map, as depicted in figure 2.4.

You see the map declaration and initialization, the retrieval of values, and the addition of a new entry. All of this is done with a single method call explicitly appearing in the source code—and even that is only checking the new size of the map:

```
def http = [
    100 : 'CONTINUE',
    200 : 'OK',
    400 : 'BAD REQUEST'    ]
```

---

[3] Hypertext Transfer Protocol, the protocol used for the World Wide Web. The server returns these codes with every response. Your browser typically shows the mapped descriptions for codes above 400.

```
assert http[200] == 'OK'

http[500] = 'INTERNAL SERVER ERROR'
assert http.size() == 4
```

Note how the syntax is consistent with that used to declare, access, and modify lists. The differences between using maps and lists are minimal, so it's easy to remember both. This is a good example of the Groovy language designers taking commonly required operations and making programmers' lives easier by providing a simple and consistent syntax. Section 4.3 gives more information about maps and the wealth of their Groovy feature set.

Ranges

Although *ranges* don't appear in the standard Java libraries, most programmers have an intuitive idea of what a range is—effectively a start point and an end point, with a notion of how to move from the start to the end point. Again, Groovy provides literals to support this useful concept, along with other language features such as the for statement, which understands ranges.

The following code demonstrates the range literal format, along with how to find the size of a range, determine whether it contains a particular value, find its start and end points, and reverse it:

```
def x   = 1..10
assert x.contains(5)
assert x.contains(15) == false
assert x.size()      == 10
assert x.from        == 1
assert x.to          == 10
assert x.reverse()   == 10..1
```

These examples are limited because we are only trying to show what ranges do *on their own*. Ranges are usually used in conjunction with other Groovy features. Over the course of this book, you'll see a lot of range usages.

So much for the usual datatypes. We will now come to *closures*, a concept that doesn't exist in Java, but which Groovy uses extensively.

2.3.7 *Code as objects: closures*

The concept of *closures* is not a new one, but it has usually been associated with functional languages, allowing one piece of code to execute an arbitrary piece of code that has been specified elsewhere.

In object-oriented languages, the *Method-Object pattern* has often been used to simulate the same kind of behavior by defining types whose sole purpose is to implement an appropriate single-method interface so that instances of those types can be passed as arguments to methods, which then invoke the method on the interface.

A good example is the `java.io.File.list(FilenameFilter)` method. The `FilenameFilter` interface specifies a single method, and its only purpose is to allow the list of files returned from the `list` method to be filtered while it's being generated.

Unfortunately, this approach leads to an unnecessary proliferation of types, and the code involved is often widely separated from the logical point of use. Java uses anonymous inner classes to address these issues, but the syntax is clunky, and there are significant limitations in terms of access to local variables from the calling method. Groovy allows closures to be specified inline in a concise, clean, and powerful way, effectively promoting the Method-Object pattern to a first-class position in the language.

Because closures are a new concept to most Java programmers, it may take a little time to adjust. The good news is that the initial steps of using closures are so easy that you hardly notice what is so new about them. The *aha-wow-cool* effect comes later, when you discover their real power.

Informally, a closure can be recognized as a list of statements within curly braces, like any other code block. It optionally has a list of identifiers in order to name the parameters passed to it, with an `->` arrow marking the end of the list.

It's easiest to understand closures through examples. Figure 2.5 shows a simple closure that is passed to the `List.each` method, called on a list `[1, 2, 3]`.

The `List.each` method takes a single parameter—a closure. It then executes that closure for each of the elements in the list, passing in that element as the argument to the closure. In this example, the main body of the closure is a statement to print out

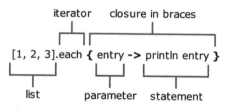

Figure 2.5 A simple example of a closure that prints the numbers 1, 2 and 3

whatever is passed to the closure, namely the parameter we've called `entry`.

Let's consider a slightly more complicated question: If *n* people are at a party and everyone clinks glasses with everybody else, how many clinks do you hear?[4]

---

[4] Or, in computer terms: What is the maximum number of distinct connections in a dense network of *n* components?

Figure 2.6 sketches this question for five people, where each line represents one clink.

To answer this question, we can use `Integer`'s `upto` method, which does *something* for every `Integer` starting at the current value and going *up to* a given end value. We apply this method to the problem by imagining people arriving at the party one by one. As people arrive, they clink glasses with everyone who is already present. This way, everyone clinks glasses with everyone else exactly once.

Listing 2.5 shows the code required to calculate the number of clinks. We keep a running total of the number of clinks, and when each guest arrives, we add the number of people already present (the guest number − 1). Finally,

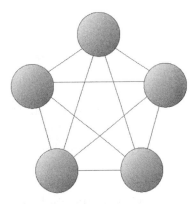

Figure 2.6 Five elements and their distinct connections, modeling five people (the circles) at a party clinking glasses with each other (the lines). Here there are 10 "clinks."

we test the result using Gauss's formula[5] for this problem—with 100 people, there should be 4,950 clinks.

Listing 2.5   Counting all the clinks at a party using a closure

```
def totalClinks = 0
def partyPeople = 100
1.upto(partyPeople) { guestNumber ->
    clinksWithGuest = guestNumber-1
    totalClinks += clinksWithGuest
}

assert totalClinks == (partyPeople*(partyPeople-1))/2
```

How does this code relate to Java? In Java, we would have used a loop like the following snippet. The class declaration and main method are omitted for the sake of brevity:

```
//Java
int totalClinks = 0;
for(int guestNumber = 1;
```

---

[5] Johann Carl Friedrich Gauss (1777..1855) was a German mathematician. At the age of seven, when he was a school boy, his teacher wanted to keep the kids busy by making them sum up the numbers from 1 to 100. Gauss discovered this formula and finished the task correctly and surprisingly quickly. There are different reports on how the teacher reacted.

```
            guestNumber <= partyPeople;
            guestNumber++) {
        int clinksWithGuest = guestNumber-1;
        totalClinks += clinksWithGuest;
    }
```

Note that guestNumber appears four times in the Java code but only two times in the Groovy version. Don't dismiss this as a minor thing. The code should explain the programmer's intention with the simplest possible means, and expressing behavior with two words *rather than four* is an important simplification.

Also note that the upto method encapsulates and hides the logic of how to walk over a sequence of integers. That is, this logic appears only *one time* in the code (in the implementation of upto). Count the equivalent for loops in any Java project, and you'll see the amount of structural duplication inherent in Java.

There is much more to say about the great concept of closures, and we will do so in chapter 5.

2.3.8 *Groovy control structures*

Control structures allow a programming language to control the flow of execution through code. There are simple versions of everyday control structures like if-else, while, switch, and try-catch-finally in Groovy, just like in Java.

In conditionals, *null* is treated like *false*; not-*null* is treated like *true*. The for loop has a for(i in x){*body*} notation, where x can be anything that Groovy knows how to iterate through, such as an iterator, an enumeration, a collection, a range, a map, or literally any object, as explained in chapter 6. In Groovy, the for loop is often replaced by iteration methods that take a closure argument. Listing 2.6 gives an overview.

Listing 2.6 Control structures

```
if (false) assert false      ◁——  if as one-liner

if (null)     ◁—┘  Null is false
{
                    ◁—┐  Blocks may start
    assert false    │  on new line
}
else
{
    assert true
}

def i = 0
while (i < 10) {    │  Classic
    i++             │  while
                    ▽
```

```
}                        ⌃ Classic
assert i == 10           │ while

def clinks = 0
for (remainingGuests in 0..9) {
    clinks += remainingGuests        for in
}                                    range
assert clinks == (10*9)/2

def list = [0, 1, 2, 3, 4, 5, 6, 7, 8, 9]
for (j in list) {                         for in
    assert j == list[j]                   list
}

list.each() { item ->
    assert item == list[item]        each method
}                                    with a closure

switch(3)  {
    case 1 : assert false; break
    case 3 : assert true;  break     Classic
    default: assert false            switch
}
```

The code in listing 2.6 should be self-explanatory. Groovy control structures are reasonably close to Java's syntax. Additionally, you will find a full introduction to Groovy's control structures in chapter 6.

That's it for the initial syntax presentation. You got your feet wet with Groovy and should have the impression that it is a nice mix of Java-friendly syntax elements with some new interesting twists.

Now that you know how to write your first Groovy code, it's time to explore how it gets executed on the Java platform.

2.4   *Groovy's place in the Java environment*

Behind the fun of Groovy looms the world of Java. We will examine how Groovy classes enter the Java environment to start with, how Groovy *augments* the existing Java class library, and finally how Groovy gets its groove: a brief explanation of the dynamic nature of Groovy classes.

2.4.1   *My class is your class*

"Mi casa es su casa." My home is your home. That's the Spanish way of expressing hospitality. Groovy and Java are just as generous with each other's classes.

So far, when talking about Groovy and Java, we have compared the appearance of the source code. But the connection to Java is much stronger. Behind the scenes, all Groovy code runs inside the *Java Virtual Machine* (*JVM*) and is therefore bound to Java's object model. Regardless of whether you write Groovy classes or scripts, they run as Java classes inside the JVM.

You can run Groovy classes inside the JVM two ways:

- You can use `groovyc` to compile *.groovy files to Java *.class files, put them on Java's classpath, and retrieve objects from those classes via the Java classloader.

- You can work with *.groovy files directly and retrieve objects from those classes via the Groovy classloader. In this case, no *.class files are generated, but rather *class objects*—that is, instances of `java.lang.Class`. In other words, when your Groovy code contains the expression `new MyClass()`, and there is a MyClass.groovy file, it will be parsed, a class of type `MyClass` will be generated and added to the classloader, and your code will get a new `MyClass` object as if it had been loaded from a *.class file.[6]

These two methods of converting *.groovy files into Java classes are illustrated in figure 2.7. Either way, the resulting classes have the same format as classic Java classes. Groovy enhances Java at the *source code level* but stays identical at the *byte-code level*.

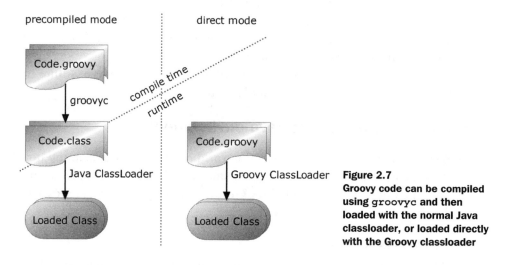

Figure 2.7
Groovy code can be compiled using `groovyc` **and then loaded with the normal Java classloader, or loaded directly with the Groovy classloader**

---

[6] We hope the Groovy programmers will forgive this oversimplification.

2.4.2 *GDK: the Groovy library*

Groovy's strong connection to Java makes using Java classes from Groovy and vice versa exceptionally easy. Because they are both the same thing, there is no gap to bridge. In our code examples, every Groovy object is instantly a Java object. Even the term *Groovy object* is questionable. Both are identical objects, living in the Java runtime.

This has an enormous benefit for Java programmers, who can fully leverage their knowledge of the Java libraries. Consider a sample string in Groovy:

```
'Hello World!'
```

Because this *is* a `java.lang.String`, Java programmers knows that they can use JDK's `String.startsWith` method on it:

```
if ('Hello World!'.startsWith('Hello')) {
  // Code to execute if the string starts with 'Hello'
}
```

The library that comes with Groovy is an extension of the JDK library. It provides some new classes (for example, for easy database access and XML processing), but it also adds functionality to existing JDK classes. This additional functionality is referred to as the *GDK*,[7] and it provides significant benefits in consistency, power, and expressiveness.

> **NOTE** Going back to plain Java and the JDK after writing Groovy with the GDK can often be an unpleasant experience! It's all too easy to become accustomed not only to the features of Groovy as a language, but also to the benefits it provides in making common tasks simpler within the standard library.

One example is the `size` method as used in the GDK. It is available on everything that is of some size: strings, arrays, lists, maps, and other collections. Behind the scenes, they are all JDK classes. This is an improvement over the JDK, where you determine an object's size in a number of different ways, as listed in table 2.1.

We think you would agree that the GDK solution is more consistent and easier to remember.

---

[7] This is a bit of a misnomer because *DK* stands for *development kit*, which is more than just the library; it should also include supportive tools. We will use this acronym anyway, because it is conventional in the Groovy community.

Table 2.1   Various ways of determining sizes in the JDK

Type	Determine the size in JDK via...	Groovy
Array	`length` field	`size()` method
Array	`java.lang.reflect.Array.getLength(array)`	`size()` method
String	`length()` method	`size()` method
StringBuffer	`length()` method	`size()` method
Collection	`size()` method	`size()` method
Map	`size()` method	`size()` method
File	`length()` method	`size()` method
Matcher	`groupCount()` method	`size()` method

Groovy can play this trick by funneling all method calls through a device called `MetaClass`. This allows a dynamic approach to object orientation, only part of which involves adding methods to existing classes. You'll learn more about `MetaClass` in the next section.

When describing the built-in datatypes later in the book, we also mention their most prominent GDK properties. Appendix C contains the complete list.

In order to help you understand how Groovy objects can leverage the power of the GDK, we will next sketch how Groovy objects come into being.

2.4.3   The Groovy lifecycle

Although the Java runtime understands compiled Groovy classes without any problem, it doesn't understand .groovy source files. More work has to happen behind the scenes if you want to load .groovy files dynamically at runtime. Let's dive under the hood to see what's happening.

Some relatively advanced Java knowledge is required to fully appreciate this section. If you don't already know a bit about classloaders, you may want to skip to the chapter summary and assume that magic pixies transform Groovy source code into Java bytecode at the right time. You won't have as full an understanding of what's going on, but you can keep learning Groovy without losing sleep. Alternatively, you can keep reading and not worry when things get tricky.

Groovy *syntax* is line oriented, but the *execution* of Groovy code is not. Unlike other scripting languages, Groovy code is not processed line-by-line in the sense that each line is interpreted separately.

Instead, Groovy code is fully parsed, and a class is generated from the information that the *parser* has built. The generated class is the binding device between Groovy and Java, and Groovy classes are generated such that their format is *identical* to Java bytecode.

Inside the Java runtime, classes are managed by a classloader. When a Java classloader is asked for a certain class, it loads the class from the *.class file, stores it in a cache, and returns it. Because a Groovy-generated class is identical to a Java class, it can also be managed by a classloader with the same behavior. The difference is that the Groovy classloader can also load classes from *.groovy files (and do parsing and class generation before putting it in the cache).

Groovy can *at runtime* read *.groovy files as if they were *.class files. The class generation can also be done *before* runtime with the groovyc compiler. The compiler simply takes *.groovy files and transforms them into *.class files using the same parsing and class-generation mechanics.

Groovy class generation at work

Suppose we have a Groovy script stored in a file named MyScript.groovy, and we run it via groovy MyScript.groovy. The following are the class-generation steps, as shown previously in figure 2.7:

1 The file MyScript.groovy is fed into the Groovy parser.

2 The parser generates an Abstract Syntax Tree (AST) that fully represents all the code in the file.

3 The Groovy class generator takes the AST and generates Java bytecode from it. Depending on the file content, this can result in multiple classes. Classes are now available through the Groovy classloader.

4 The Java runtime is invoked in a manner equivalent to running java MyScript.

Figure 2.8 shows a second variant, when groovyc is used instead of groovy. This time, the classes are written into *.class files. Both variants use the same class-generation mechanism.

All this is handled behind the scenes and makes working with Groovy feel like it's an interpreted language, which it isn't. Classes are always fully constructed before runtime and do not change while running.[8]

---

[8] This doesn't exclude *replacing* a class at runtime, when the .groovy file changes.

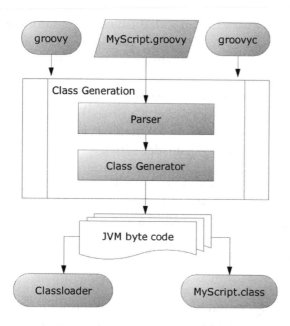

Figure 2.8
Flow chart of the Groovy bytecode
generation process when executed in
the runtime environment or compiled
into class files. Different options for
executing Groovy code involve different
targets for the bytecode produced, but
the parser and class generator are the
same in each case.

Given this description, you can legitimately ask how Groovy can be called a *dynamic* language if all Groovy code lives in the *static* Java class format. Groovy performs class construction and method invocation in a particularly clever way, as you shall see.

Groovy is dynamic

What makes dynamic languages so powerful is the ability to seemingly modify classes at runtime—for example to add new methods. But as you just learned, Groovy generates classes once and cannot change the bytecode after it has been loaded. How can you add a method without changing the class? The answer is simple but delicate.

The bytecode that the Groovy class generator produces is necessarily different from what the Java compiler would generate—not in *format* but in *content*. Suppose a Groovy file contains a statement like foo. Groovy doesn't generate bytecode that reflects this method call directly, but does something like[9]

```
getMetaClass().invokeMethod(this, "foo", EMPTY_PARAMS_ARRAY)
```

---

[9] The actual implementation involves a few more redirections.

That way, method calls are redirected through the object's MetaClass. This MetaClass can now do tricks with method invocations such as intercepting, redirecting, adding/removing methods at runtime, and so on. This principle applies to all calls from Groovy code, regardless of whether the methods are in other Groovy objects or are in Java objects. Remember: There is no difference.

> **TIP** The technically inclined may have fun running groovyc on some Groovy code and feeding the resulting class files into a decompiler such as Jad. Doing so gives you the Java code equivalent of the bytecode that Groovy generated.

A second option of dynamic code is putting the code in a string and having Groovy evaluate it. You will see how this works in chapter 11. Such a string can be constructed literally or through any kind of logic. But beware: You can easily get overwhelmed by the complexity of dynamic code generation.

Here is an example of concatenating two strings and evaluating the result:

```
def code = '1 + '
code += System.getProperty('os.version')
println code                              ⏎ Prints "1 + 5.1"
println evaluate(code)    ⟵  Prints "6.1"
```

Note that code is an ordinary string! It happens to contain '1 + 5.1', which is a valid Groovy expression (a *script*, actually). Instead of having a programmer write this expression (say, println 1 + 5.1), the program puts it together at runtime! The evaluate method finally executes it.

Wait—didn't we claim that line-by-line execution isn't possible, and code has to be fully constructed as a class? How can code then be *executed*? The answer is simple. Remember the left-hand path in figure 2.7? Class generation can transparently happen at runtime. The only news is that the class-generation input can also be a *string* like code rather than a *.groovy file.

The capability to evaluate an arbitrary string of code is the distinctive feature of scripting languages. That means Groovy can operate as a scripting language although it is a general-purpose programming language in itself.

2.5 Summary

That's it for our initial overview. Don't worry if you don't feel you've mastered everything we've covered—we'll go over it all in detail in the upcoming chapters.

We started by looking at how this book demonstrates Groovy code using assertions. This allows us to keep the features we're trying to demonstrate and the

results of using those features close together within the code. It also lets us automatically verify that our listings are correct.

You got a first impression of Groovy's code notation and found it both similar
to and distinct from Java at the same time. Groovy is similar with respect to defining classes, objects, and methods. It uses keywords, braces, brackets, and parentheses in a very similar fashion; however, Groovy's notation appears more
lightweight. It needs less scaffolding code, fewer declarations, and fewer lines of
code to make the compiler happy. This may mean that you need to change the
pace at which you read code: Groovy code says more in fewer lines, so you typically have to read more slowly, at least to start with.

Groovy is bytecode compatible with Java and obeys Java's protocol of full class
construction before execution. But Groovy is still fully dynamic, generating
classes transparently at runtime when needed. Despite the fixed set of methods
in the bytecode of a class, Groovy can modify the set of available methods as visible from a Groovy caller's perspective by routing method calls through the
MetaClass, which we will cover in depth in chapter 7. Groovy uses this mechanism
to enhance existing JDK classes with new capabilities, together named GDK.

You now have the means to write your first Groovy scripts. Do it! Grab the
Groovy shell (groovysh) or the console (groovyConsole), and write your own code.
As a side effect, you have also acquired the knowledge to get the most out of the
examples that follow in the upcoming in-depth chapters.

For the remainder of part 1, we will leave the surface and dive into the deep
sea of Groovy. This may be unfamiliar, but don't worry. We'll return to the sea
level often enough to take some deep breaths of Groovy code *in action*.

The simple
Groovy datatypes

3

Groovy supports a limited set of datatypes at the *language* level; that is, it offers means for literal declaration and specialized operators. This set contains the simple datatypes for strings, regular expressions, and numbers, as well as the collective datatypes for ranges, lists, and maps. This chapter covers the simple datatypes; the next chapter introduces the collective datatypes.

Before we go into details, you'll learn about Groovy's general approach to typing. With this in mind, you can appreciate Groovy's approach of treating everything as an object and all operators as method calls. You will see how this improves the level of object orientation in the language compared to Java's division between primitive types and reference types.

We then describe the natively supported datatypes individually. By the end of this chapter, you will be able to confidently work with Groovy's simple datatypes and have a whole new understanding of what happens when you write 1+1.

3.1 Objects, objects everywhere

In Groovy, everything is an object. It is, after all, an object-oriented language. Groovy doesn't have the slight "fudge factor" of Java, which is object-oriented apart from some built-in types. In order to explain the choices made by Groovy's designers, we'll first go over some basics of Java's type system. We will then explain how Groovy addresses the difficulties presented, and finally examine how Groovy and Java can still interoperate with ease due to automatic boxing and unboxing where necessary.

3.1.1 Java's type system—primitives and references

Java distinguishes between *primitive* types (such as int, double, char, and byte) and *reference* types (such as Object and String). There is a fixed set of *primitive* types, and these are the only types that have *value semantics*—where the value of a variable of that type is the actual number (or character, or true/false value). You cannot create your own value types in Java.

Reference types (everything apart from primitives) have *reference semantics*—the value of a variable of that type is only a *reference* to an object. Readers with a C/C++ background may wish to think of a reference as a pointer—it's a similar concept. If you change the value of a reference type variable, that has no effect on the object it was previously referring to—you're just making the variable refer to a different object, or to no object at all.

You cannot call methods on values of primitive types, and you cannot use them where Java expects objects of type java.lang.Object. This is particularly

painful when working with collections that cannot handle primitive types, such as
`java.util.ArrayList`. To get around this, Java has a *wrapper type* for each primi-
tive type—a reference type that stores a value of the primitive type in an object.
For example, the wrapper for `int` is `java.lang.Integer`.

On the other hand, operators such as `*` in `3*2` or `a*b` are *not* supported for
arbitrary reference types, but only for primitive types (with the exception of `+`,
which is also supported for strings). As an example of why this causes pain, let's
consider a situation where you have two lists of integers, and you want to come up
with a third list where the first element is the sum of the first elements of the
other two lists, and so on. The Java code would be something like this:

```
// Java code!
ArrayList results = new ArrayList();
for (int i=0; i < listOne.size(); i++)
{
    Integer first  = (Integer)listOne.get(i);
    Integer second = (Integer)listTwo.get(i);

    int sum = first.intValue()+second.intValue();
    results.add (new Integer(sum));
}
```

New features in Java 5 would make this simpler, but there would still be two types
(`int` and `Integer`) involved, which adds conceptual complexity. There are good
reasons for Java to follow this route: the heritage of C and performance optimization concerns. The Groovy answer puts more burden on the computer and less
on the programmer.

3.1.2 Groovy's answer—everything's an object

Groovy makes the previous scenario easier in so many ways they're almost hard
to count. However, for the moment we'll only look at why making everything an
object helps to keep the code compact and readable. Looking at the code block
in the previous section, you can see that the problem is in the last two lines of
the loop. To add the numbers, you must convert them from `Integer`s into `int`s.
In order to then store the result in another list, you have to create a new
`Integer`. Groovy adds the `plus` method to `java.lang.Integer`, letting you write
this instead:

```
results.add (first.plus(second))
```

So far, there's nothing that couldn't have been done in Java if the library designers had thought to include a `plus` method. However, Groovy allows operators to
work on objects, enabling the replacement of the last section of the loop body

```
// Java
int sum = first.intValue()+second.intValue();
results.add (new Integer(sum));
```

with the more readable Groovy solution[1]

```
results.add (first + second)
```

You'll learn more about what operators are available and how you can specify your own implementations in section 3.3.

In order to make Groovy fully object-oriented, and because at the JVM level Java does not support object-oriented operations such as method calls on primitive types, the Groovy designers decided to do away with primitive types. When Groovy needs to store values that would have used Java's primitive types, Groovy uses the wrapper classes already provided by the Java platform. Table 3.1 provides a complete list of these wrappers.

Table 3.1   Java's primitive datatypes and their wrappers

Primitive type	Wrapper type	Description
byte	java.lang.Byte	8-bit signed integer
short	java.lang.Short	16-bit signed integer
int	java.lang.Integer	32-bit signed integer
long	java.lang.Long	64-bit signed integer
float	java.lang.Float	Single-precision (32-bit) floating-point value
double	java.lang.Double	Double-precision (64-bit) floating-point value
char	java.lang.Character	16-bit Unicode character
boolean	java.lang.Boolean	Boolean value (true or false)

Any time you see what looks like a primitive literal value (for example, the number 5, or the Boolean value true) in Groovy source code, that is a reference to an instance of the appropriate wrapper class. For the sake of brevity and familiarity, Groovy allows you to declare variables as if they were primitive type variables.

---

[1] In fact, there is an idiomatic Groovy solution that replaces the full Java example with a two-liner. However, you need to learn a bit more before you can value such a solution.

Don't be fooled—the type used is really the wrapper type. Strings and arrays are not listed in table 3.1 because they are already *reference* types, not primitive types—no wrapper is needed.

While we have the Java primitives under the microscope, so to speak, it's worth examining the numeric literal formats that Java and Groovy each use. They are slightly different because Groovy allows instances of `java.math.BigDecimal` and `java.math.BigInteger` to be specified using literals in addition to the usual binary floating-point types. Table 3.2 gives examples of each of the literal formats available for numeric types in Groovy.

Table 3.2 Numeric literals in Groovy

Type	Example literals
`java.lang.Integer`	15, 0x1234ffff
`java.lang.Long`	100L, 200l[a]
`java.lang.Float`	1.23f, 4.56F
`java.lang.Double`	1.23d, 4.56D
`java.math.BigInteger`	123g, 456G
`java.math.BigDecimal`	1.23, 4.56, 1.4E4, 2.8e4, 1.23g, 1.23G

a. The use of the lowercase *l* as a suffix indicating Long is discouraged, as it can look like a 1 (number one). There is no difference between the uppercase and lowercase versions of any of the suffixes.

Notice how Groovy decides whether to use a `BigInteger` or a `BigDecimal` to hold a literal with a "G" suffix depending on the presence or absence of a decimal point. Furthermore, notice how `BigDecimal` is the default type of non-integer literals—`BigDecimal` will be used unless you specify a suffix to force the literal to be a `Float` or a `Double`.

3.1.3 Interoperating with Java—automatic boxing and unboxing

Converting a primitive value into an instance of a wrapper type is called *boxing* in Java and other languages that support the same notion. The reverse action—taking an instance of a wrapper and retrieving the primitive value—is called *unboxing*. Groovy performs these operations automatically for you where necessary. This is primarily the case when you call a Java method from Groovy. This automatic boxing and unboxing is known as *autoboxing*.

You've already seen that Groovy is designed to work well with Java, so what happens when a Java method takes primitive parameters or returns a primitive return type? How can you call that method from Groovy? Consider the existing method in the java.lang.String class: int indexOf (int ch).

You can call this method from Groovy like this:

```
assert 'ABCDE'.indexOf(67) == 2
```

From Groovy's point of view, we're passing an Integer containing the value 67 (the Unicode value for the letter *C*), even though the method expects a parameter of primitive type int. Groovy takes care of the unboxing. The method returns a primitive type int that is boxed into an Integer as soon as it enters the world of Groovy. That way, we can compare it to the Integer with value 2 back in the Groovy script. Figure 3.1 shows the process of going from the Groovy world to the Java world and back.

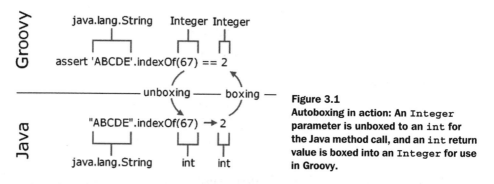

Figure 3.1
Autoboxing in action: An Integer parameter is unboxed to an int for the Java method call, and an int return value is boxed into an Integer for use in Groovy.

All of this is transparent—you don't need to do anything in the Groovy code to enable it. Now that you understand autoboxing, the question of how to apply operators to objects becomes interesting. We'll explore this question next.

3.1.4 *No intermediate unboxing*

If in 1+1 both numbers are objects of type Integer, are those Integers unboxed to execute the *plus* operation on primitive types?

No. Groovy is more object-oriented than Java. It executes this expression as 1.plus(1), calling the plus() method of the first Integer object, and passing[2] the

---

[2] The phrase "passing an object" is short for "passing a reference of an object." In Groovy and Java alike, objects are passed as references when they are arguments of a method call.

second `Integer` object as an argument. The method call returns a new `Integer` object of value 2.

This is a powerful model. Calling methods on objects is what object-oriented languages should do. It opens the door for applying the full range of object-oriented capabilities to those operators.

Let's summarize. No matter how literals (numbers, strings, and so forth) appear in Groovy code, they are always objects. Only at the border to Java are they boxed and unboxed. Operators are a shorthand for method calls. Now that you have seen how Groovy handles types when you tell it what to expect, let's examine what it does when you don't give it any type information.

3.2 *The concept of optional typing*

So far, we haven't used any typing in our sample Groovy scripts—or have we? Well, we haven't used any *explicit static* typing in the way that you're familiar with in Java. We assigned strings and numbers to variables and didn't care about the type. Behind the scenes, Groovy implicitly assumes these variables to be of static type `java.lang.Object`. This section discusses what happens when a type *is* specified, and the pros and cons of static and dynamic typing.

3.2.1 *Assigning types*

Groovy offers the choice of assigning types explicitly just as you do in Java. Table 3.3 gives examples of optional static type declarations and the dynamic type used at runtime. The `def` keyword is used to indicate that no particular type is demanded.

Table 3.3 Example Groovy statements and the resulting runtime type

Statement	Type of value	Comment
`def a = 1`	`java.lang.Integer`	Implicit typing
`def b = 1.0f`	`java.lang.Float`	
`int c = 1`	`java.lang.Integer`	Explicit typing using the Java primitive type names
`float d = 1`	`java.lang.Float`	
`Integer e = 1`	`java.lang.Integer`	Explicit typing using reference type names
`String f = '1'`	`java.lang.String`	

As we stated earlier, it doesn't matter whether you declare or cast a variable to be of type int or Integer. Groovy uses the reference type (Integer) either way. If you prefer to be concise, and you believe your code's readers understand Groovy well enough, use int. If you want to be explicit, or you wish to highlight to Groovy newcomers that you really are using objects, use Integer.

It is important to understand that regardless of whether a variable's type is explicitly declared, the system is *type safe*. Unlike untyped languages, Groovy doesn't allow you to treat an object of one type as an instance of a different type without a well-defined conversion being available. For instance, you could never treat a java.lang.String with value "1" as if it were a java.lang.Number, in the hope that you'd end up with an object that you could use for calculation. That sort of behavior would be dangerous—which is why Groovy doesn't allow it any more than Java does.

3.2.2 *Static versus dynamic typing*

The choice between static and dynamic typing is one of the key benefits of Groovy. The Web is full of heated discussions of whether static or dynamic typing is "better." In other words, there are good arguments for either position.

Static typing provides more information for optimization, more sanity checks at compile-time, and better IDE support; it also reveals additional information about the meaning of variables or method parameters and allows method overloading. Static typing is also a prerequisite for getting meaningful information from reflection.

Dynamic typing, on the other hand, is not only convenient for the lazy programmer who does some ad-hoc scripting, but also useful for relaying and duck typing. Suppose you get an object as the result of a method call, and you have to relay it as an argument to some other method call without doing anything with that object yourself:

```
def node = document.findMyNode()
log.info node
db.store node
```

In this case, you're not interested in finding out what the heck the actual type and package name of that node are. You are spared the work of looking them up, declaring the type, and importing the package. You also communicate: "That's just something."

The second usage of dynamic typing is calling methods on objects that have no guaranteed type. This is often called *duck typing*, and we will explain it in more detail in section 7.3.2. This allows the implementation of generic functionality with a high potential of reuse.

For programmers with a strong Java background, it is not uncommon to start programming Groovy almost entirely using static types, and gradually shift into a more dynamic mode over time. This is legitimate because it allows everybody to use what they are confident with.

> **NOTE** Experienced Groovy programmers tend to follow this rule of thumb: As soon as you *think* about the static type of a reference, declare it; when thinking "just an object," use dynamic typing.

Whether you specify your types statically or dynamically, you'll find that Groovy lets you do a lot more than you may expect. Let's start by looking at the ability to override operators.

3.3 Overriding operators

Overriding refers to the object-oriented concept of having types that specify behavior and subtypes that override this behavior to make it more specific. When a language bases its operators on method calls and allows these methods to be overridden, the approach is called *operator overriding*.

It's more conventional to use the term *operator overloading*, which means almost the same thing. The difference is that *overloading* suggests that you have multiple implementations of a method (and thus the associated operator) that differ only in their parameter types.

We will show you which operators can be overridden, show a full example of how overriding works in practice, and give some guidance on the decisions you need to make when operators work with multiple types.

3.3.1 Overview of overridable operators

As you saw in section 3.1.2, `1+1` is just a convenient way of writing `1.plus(1)`. This is achieved by class `Integer` having an implementation of the `plus` method.

This convenient feature is also available for other operators. Table 3.4 shows an overview.

You can easily use any of these operators with your own classes. Just implement the respective method. Unlike in Java, there is no need to implement a specific interface.

Table 3.4   Method-based operators

Operator	Name	Method	Works with
a + b	Plus	a.plus(b)	Number, string, collection
a – b	Minus	a.minus(b)	Number, string, collection
a * b	Star	a.multiply(b)	Number, string, collection
a / b	Divide	a.div(b)	Number
a % b	Modulo	a.mod(b)	Integral number
a++ ++a	Post increment Pre increment	a.next()	Number, string, range
a-- --a	Post decrement Pre decrement	a.previous()	Number, string, range
a**b	Power	a.power(b)	Number
a | b	Numerical or	a.or(b)	Integral number
a & b	Numerical and	a.and(b)	Integral number
a ^ b	Numerical xor	a.xor(b)	Integral number
~a	Bitwise complement	a.negate()	Integral number, string (the latter returning a regular expression pattern)
a[b]	Subscript	a.getAt(b)	Object, list, map, `String`, `Array`
a[b] = c	Subscript assignment	a.putAt(b, c)	Object, list, map, `StringBuffer`, `Array`
a << b	Left shift	a.leftShift(b)	Integral number, also used like "append" to `StringBuffers`, `Writers`, `Files`, `Sockets`, `Lists`
a >> b	Right shift	a.rightShift(b)	Integral number
a >>> b	Right shift unsigned	a.rightShiftUnsigned(b)	Integral number

switch(a) {
  case b:
}
	Classification	b.isCase(a)	Object, range, list, collection, pattern, closure; also used with collection c in `c.grep(b)`, which returns all items of c where `b.isCase(item)`

continued on next page

Table 3.4 Method-based operators *(continued)*

Operator	Name	Method	Works with
`a == b`	Equals	`a.equals(b)`	Object; consider `hashCode()`[a]
`a != b`	Not equal	`! a.equals(b)`	Object
`a <=> b`	Spaceship	`a.compareTo(b)`	`java.lang.Comparable`
`a > b`	Greater than	`a.compareTo(b) > 0`	
`a >= b`	Greater than or equal to	`a.compareTo(b) >= 0`	
`a < b`	Less than	`a.compareTo(b) < 0`	
`a <= b`	Less than or equal to	`a.compareTo(b) <= 0`	
`a as type`	Enforced coercion	`a.asType(typeClass)`	Any type

a. When overriding the `equals` method, Java strongly encourages the developer to also override the `hashCode()` method such that equal objects have the same hashcode (whereas objects with the same hashcode are not necessarily equal). See the API documentation of `java.lang.Object#equals`.

NOTE   Strictly speaking, Groovy has even more operators in addition to those in table 3.4, such as the dot operator for referencing fields and methods. Their behavior can also be overridden. They come into play in chapter 7.

This is all good in theory, but let's see how they work in practice.

3.3.2 Overridden operators in action

Listing 3.1 demonstrates an implementation of the *equals* == and *plus* + operators for a `Money` class. It is a low-level implementation of the *Value Object* pattern.[3] We allow money of the same form of currency to be added up but do not support multicurrency addition.

We implement `equals` such that it copes with null comparison. This is Groovy style. The default implementation of the *equals* operator doesn't throw any `NullPointerExceptions` either. Remember that == (or `equals`) denotes object *equality* (equal values), not *identity* (same object instances).

---

3 See http://c2.com/cgi/wiki?ValueObject.

Listing 3.1   Operator override

```
class Money {
    private int     amount
    private String  currency
    Money (amountValue, currencyValue) {
        amount   = amountValue
        currency = currencyValue
    }                                           ❶ Override ==
    boolean equals (Object other) {              operator
        if (null == other)                 return false
        if (! (other instanceof Money))    return false
        if (currency != other.currency)    return false
        if (amount   != other.amount)      return false
        return true
    }
    int hashCode() {
        amount.hashCode() + currency.hashCode()
    }                                           ❷ Implement
    Money plus (Money other) {                    + operator
        if (null           == other)     return null
        if (other.currency != currency) {
            throw new IllegalArgumentException(
                "cannot add $other.currency to $currency")
        }
        return new Money(amount + other.amount, currency)
    }
}

def buck = new Money(1, 'USD')
assert buck
assert buck          == new Money(1, 'USD')   ❸ Use overridden ==
assert buck + buck == new Money(2, 'USD')     ❹ Use overridden +
```

Overriding `equals` is straightforward, as we show at ❶. We also provide a `hashCode` method to make sure equal `Money` objects have the same hashcode. This is required by Java's contract for `java.lang.Object`. The use of this operator is shown at ❸, where one dollar becomes equal to any other dollar.

At ❷, the `plus` operator is not *overridden* in the strict sense of the word, because there is no such operator in `Money`'s superclass (`Object`). In this case, *operator implementing* is the best wording. This is used at ❹, where we add two `Money` objects.

To explain the difference between *overriding* and *overloading*, here is a possible overload for `Money`'s `plus` operator. In listing 3.1, `Money` can only be added to other `Money` objects. In case, we would like to add `Money` as

```
assert buck + 1 == new Money(2, 'USD')
```

We can provide the additional method

```
Money plus (Integer more) {
    return new Money(amount + more, currency)
}
```

that overloads the `plus` method with a second implementation that takes an `Integer` parameter. The Groovy method dispatch finds the right implementation at runtime.

> **NOTE**   Our `plus` operation on the `Money` class returns `Money` objects in both cases. We describe this by saying that `Money`'s `plus` operation is *closed* under its type. Whatever operation you perform on an instance of `Money`, you end up with another instance of `Money`.

This example leads to the general issue of how to deal with different parameter types when implementing an operator method. We will go through some aspects of this issue in the next section.

3.3.3 *Making coercion work for you*

Implementing operators is straightforward when both operands are of the same type. Things get more complex with a mixture of types, say

```
1 + 1.0
```

This adds an `Integer` and a `BigDecimal`. What is the return type? Section 3.6 answers this question for the special case of numbers, but the issue is more general. One of the two arguments needs to be promoted to the more general type. This is called *coercion*.

When implementing operators, there are three main issues to consider as part of coercion.

Supported argument types

You need to decide which argument types and values will be allowed. If an operator must take a potentially inappropriate type, throw an `IllegalArgumentException` where necessary. For instance, in our `Money` example, even though it makes sense to use `Money` as the parameter for the `plus` operator, we don't allow different currencies to be added together.

Promoting more specific arguments

If the argument type is a more specific one than your own type, promote it to *your* type and return an object of *your* type. To see what this means, consider how you might implement the `plus` operator if you were designing the `BigDecimal` class, and what you'd do for an `Integer` argument.

`Integer` is more specific than `BigDecimal`: Every `Integer` value can be expressed as a `BigDecimal`, but the reverse isn't true. So for the `BigDecimal.plus(Integer)` operator, we would consider promoting the `Integer` to `BigDecimal`, performing the addition, and then returning another `BigDecimal`—even if the result could accurately be expressed as an `Integer`.

Handling more general arguments with double dispatch

If the argument type is more general, call *its* operator method with *yourself* ("this," the current object) as an argument. Let *it* promote *you*. This is also called *double dispatch*,[4] and it helps to avoid duplicated, asymmetric, possibly inconsistent code. Let's reverse our previous example and consider `Integer.plus(BigDecimal operand)`.

We would consider returning the result of the expression `operand.plus(this)`, delegating the work to `BigDecimal`'s `plus(Integer)` method. The result would be a `BigDecimal`, which is reasonable—it would be odd for `1+1.5` to return an `Integer` but `1.5+1` to return a `BigDecimal`.

Of course, this is only applicable for *commutative*[5] operators. Test rigorously, and beware of endless cycles.

Groovy's conventional behavior

Groovy's general strategy of coercion is to return the most general type. Other languages such as Ruby try to be smarter and return the *least* general type that can be used without losing information from range or precision. The Ruby way saves memory at the expense of processing time. It also requires that the language promote a type to a more general one when the operation would generate an overflow of that type's range. Otherwise, intermediary results in a complex calculation could truncate the result.

Now that you know how Groovy handles types in general, we can delve deeper into what it provides for each of the datatypes it supports at the language level. We begin with the type that is probably used more than any other non-numeric type: the humble string.

---

[4] Double dispatch is usually used with overloaded methods: `a.method(b)` calls `b.method(a)` where `method` is overloaded with `method(TypeA)` and `method(TypeB)`.

[5] *Commutative* means that the sequence of operators can be exchanged without changing the result of the operation. For example, *plus* is usually required to be commutative (`a+b==b+a`) but *minus* is not (`a-b!=b-a`).

3.4 Working with strings

Considering how widely used strings are, many languages—including Java—provide few language features to make them easier to use. Scripting languages tend to fare better in this regard than mainstream application languages, so Groovy takes on board some of those extra features. This section examines what's available in Groovy and how to make the most of the extra abilities.

Groovy strings come in two flavors: plain strings and *GString*s. Plain strings are instances of `java.lang.String`, and GStrings are instances of `groovy.lang.GString`. GStrings allow placeholder expressions to be resolved and evaluated at runtime. Many scripting languages have a similar feature, usually called *string interpolation*, but it's more primitive than the GString feature of Groovy. Let's start by looking at each flavor of string and how they appear in code.

3.4.1 Varieties of string literals

Java allows only one way of specifying string literals: placing text in quotes "like this." If you want to embed dynamic values within the string, you have to either call a formatting method (made easier but still far from simple in Java 1.5) or concatenate each constituent part. If you specify a string with a lot of backslashes in it (such as a Windows file name or a regular expression), your code becomes hard to read, because you have to double the backslashes. If you want a lot of text spanning several lines in the source code, you have to make each line contain a complete string (or several complete strings).

Groovy recognizes that not every use of string literals is the same, so it offers a variety of options. These are summarized in table 3.5.

Table 3.5 Summary of the string literal styles available in Groovy

Start/end characters	Example	GString aware?	Backslash escapes?
Single quote	`'hello Dierk'`	No	Yes
Double quote	`"hello $name"`	Yes	Yes

Triple single quote (`'''`)	`'''------------`
	`Total: $0.02`
	`------------'''`
		No	Yes

continued on next page

Table 3.5 Summary of the string literal styles available in Groovy *(continued)*

Start/end characters	Example	GString aware?	Backslash escapes?
Triple double quote (""")	```"""first line second line third line"""```	Yes	Yes
Forward slash	```/x(\d*)y/```	Yes	Occasionally[a]

a. The main point of this type of literal is to avoid escaping, so the language avoids it where possible. There are remaining cases with \u for unicode support and \$ unless $ denotes the end of the pattern. See the Groovy Language Specification for the exact rules.

The aim of each form is to specify the text data you want with the minimum of fuss. Each of the forms has a single feature that distinguishes it from the others:

- The single-quoted form is never treated as a GString, whatever its contents. This is closely equivalent to Java string literals.

- The double-quoted form is the equivalent of the single-quoted form, except that if the text contains unescaped dollar signs, it is treated as a GString instead of a plain string. GStrings are covered in more detail in the next section.

- The triple-quoted form (or *multiline* string literal) allows the literal to span several lines. New lines are always treated as \n regardless of the platform, but all other whitespace is preserved as it appears in the text file. Multiline string literals may also be GStrings, depending on whether single quotes or double quotes are used. Multiline string literals act similar to HERE-documents in Ruby or Perl.

- The *slashy* form of string literal allows strings with backslashes to be specified simply without having to escape all the backslashes. This is particularly useful with regular expressions, as you'll see later. Only when a backslash is followed by a *u* does it need to be escaped[6]—at which point life is slightly harder, because specifying \u involves using a GString or specifying the Unicode escape sequence for a backslash.

---

6 This is slightly tricky in a slashy string and involves either using a GString such as /${'\\'}/ or using the Unicode escape sequence. A similar issue occurs if you want to use a dollar sign. This is a small (and rare) price to pay for the benefits available, however.

As we hinted earlier, Groovy uses a similar mechanism for specifying special characters, such as linefeeds and tabs. In addition to the Java escapes, dollar signs can be escaped in Groovy to allow them to be easily specified without the compiler treating the literal as a GString. The full set of escaped characters is specified in table 3.6.

Table 3.6 Escaped characters as known to Groovy

Escaped special character	Meaning
\b	Backspace
\t	Tab
\r	Carriage return
\n	Line feed
\f	Form feed
\\	Backslash
\$	Dollar sign
\uabcd	Unicode character U+abcd (where a, b, c and d are hex digits)
\abc[a]	Unicode character U+abc (where a, b, and c are octal digits, and b and c are optional)
\'	Single quote
\"	Double quote

a. Octal escapes are error-prone and should rarely be used. They are provided for the sake of compatibility. Problems occur when a string with an octal escape is changed. If the person changing the string doesn't notice the octal escape, a change that looks harmless can have unexpected consequences. For instance, consider "My age is\12Twenty" changing to "My age is \1220" via a search and replace of "Twenty" for "20". It sounds like a harmless thing to do, but the consequence is dramatic.

Note that in a double-quoted string, single quotes don't need to be escaped, and vice versa. In other words, `'I said, "Hi."'` and `"don't"` both do what you hope they will. For the sake of consistency, both still *can* be escaped in each case. Likewise, dollar signs can be escaped in single-quoted strings, even though they don't need to be. This makes it easier to switch between the forms.

Note that Java uses single quotes for *character* literals, but as you have seen, Groovy cannot do so because single quotes are already used to specify *strings*. However, you can achieve the same as in Java when providing the type explicitly:

```
char    a = 'x'
```

or

```
Character b = 'x'
```

The `java.lang.String` 'x' is coerced into a `java.lang.Character`. If you want to coerce a string into a character at other times, you can do so in either of the following ways:

```
'x' as char
```

or

```
'x'.toCharacter()
```

As a GDK goody, there are more `to*` methods to convert a string, such as `toInteger`, `toLong`, `toFloat`, and `toDouble`.

Whichever literal form is used, unless the compiler decides it is a GString, it ends up as an instance of `java.lang.String`, just like Java string literals. So far, we have only teased you with allusions to what GStrings are capable of. Now it's time to spill the beans.

3.4.2 *Working with GStrings*

GStrings are like strings with additional capabilities.[7] They are literally declared in double quotes. What makes a double-quoted string literal a GString is the appearance of placeholders. Placeholders may appear in a full `${expression}` syntax or an abbreviated `$reference` syntax. See the examples in listing 3.2.

Listing 3.2   Working with GStrings

```
me      = 'Tarzan'
you     = 'Jane'                              ❶ Abbreviated
line    = "me $me - you $you"                    dollar syntax
assert  line == 'me Tarzan - you Jane'

date = new Date(0)
out  = "Year $date.year Month $date.month Day $date.date"   ❷ Extended
assert out == 'Year 70 Month 0 Day 1'                          abbreviation

out = "Date is ${date.toGMTString()} !"       ❸ Full syntax with
assert out == 'Date is 1 Jan 1970 00:00:00 GMT !'    curly braces
```

---

[7] `groovy.lang.GString` isn't actually a subclass of `java.lang.String`, and couldn't be, because `String` is final. However, GStrings can usually be *used* as if they are strings—Groovy coerces them into strings when it needs to.

```
sql = """
SELECT FROM MyTable
   WHERE Year = $date.year
"""
assert sql == """
SELECT FROM MyTable
   WHERE Year = 70
"""
```
4 **In multiline GStrings**

```
out = "my 0.02\$"
assert out == 'my 0.02$'
```
5 **Literal dollar sign**

Within a GString, simple references to variables can be dereferenced with the dollar sign. This simplest form is shown at **1**, whereas **2** shows this being extended to use property accessors with the dot syntax. You will learn more about accessing properties in chapter 7.

The full syntax uses dollar signs and curly braces, as shown at **3**. It allows arbitrary Groovy expressions within the curly braces. The curly braces denote a *closure*.

In real life, GStrings are handy in templating scenarios. A GString is used in **4** to create the string for an SQL query. Groovy provides even more sophisticated templating support, as shown in chapter 8. If you need a dollar character within a template (or any other GString usage), you must escape it with a backslash as shown in **5**.

Although GStrings behave like `java.lang.String` objects for all operations that a programmer is usually concerned with, they are implemented differently to capture the fixed and the dynamic parts (the so-called *values*) separately. This is revealed by the following code:

```
me       = 'Tarzan'
you      = 'Jane'
line     = "me $me - you $you"
assert line == 'me Tarzan - you Jane'
assert line instanceof GString
assert line.strings[0] == 'me '
assert line.strings[1] == ' - you '
assert line.values[0]  == 'Tarzan'
assert line.values[1]  == 'Jane'
```

FOR THE GEEKS Each *value* of a GString is bound at declaration time. By the time the GString is converted into a `java.lang.String` (its `toString` method is called explicitly or implicitly[8]), each value gets written[9] to the string. Because the logic of how to write a value can be elaborate for certain value types, this behavior can be used in advanced ways. See chapter 13.

You have seen the Groovy language support for declaring strings. What follows is an introduction to the use of strings in the Groovy *library*. This will also give you a first impression of the seamless interplay of Java and Groovy. We start in typical Java style and gradually slip into Groovy mode, carefully watching each step.

3.4.3 *From Java to Groovy*

Now that you have your strings easily declared, you can have some fun with them. Because they are objects of type `java.lang.String`, you can call `String`'s methods on them or pass them as parameters wherever a string is expected, such as for easy console output:

```
System.out.print("Hello Groovy!");
```

This line is equally valid Java and Groovy. You can also pass a literal Groovy string in single quotes:

```
System.out.print('Hello Groovy!');
```

Because this is such a common task, the GDK provides a shortened syntax:

```
print('Hello Groovy!');
```

You can drop parentheses and semicolons, because they are optional and do not help readability in this case. The resulting Groovy style boils down to

```
print 'Hello Groovy!'
```

Looking at this last line only, you cannot tell whether this is Groovy, Ruby, Perl, or one of several other line-oriented scripting languages. It may not look sophisticated, but in a way it is. It shows *expressiveness*—the art of revealing intent in the simplest possible way.

Listing 3.3 presents more of the mix-and-match between core Java and additional GDK capabilities. How would you judge the expressiveness of each line?

---

[8] Implicit calls happen when a GString needs to be *coerced* into a `java.lang.String`.
[9] See `Writer.write(Object)` in section 8.2.4.

Listing 3.3   What to do with strings

```
greeting = 'Hello Groovy!'

assert greeting.startsWith('Hello')

assert greeting.getAt(0)  == 'H'
assert greeting[0]        == 'H'

assert greeting.indexOf('Groovy') >= 0
assert greeting.contains('Groovy')

assert greeting[6..11]   == 'Groovy'

assert 'Hi' + greeting - 'Hello' == 'Hi Groovy!'

assert greeting.count('o') == 3

assert 'x'.padLeft(3)       == '  x'
assert 'x'.padRight(3,'_')  == 'x__'
assert 'x'.center(3)        == ' x '
assert 'x' * 3              == 'xxx'
```

These self-explanatory examples give an impression of what is possible with strings in Groovy. If you have ever worked with other scripting languages, you may notice that a useful piece of functionality is missing from listing 3.3: changing a string in place. Groovy cannot do so because it works on instances of `java.lang.String` and obeys Java's *invariant* of strings being *immutable*.

Before you say "What a lame excuse!" here is Groovy's answer to changing strings: Although you cannot work on `String`, you can still work on `String-Buffer`![10] On a `StringBuffer`, you can work with the `<<` *left shift* operator for appending and the subscript operator for in-place assignments. Using the *left shift* operator on `String` returns a `StringBuffer`. Here is the `StringBuffer` equivalent to listing 3.3:

```
greeting = 'Hello'

greeting <<= ' Groovy'
```
① **Leftshift and assign at once**

---

[10] Future versions may use a `StringBuilder` instead. `StringBuilder` was introduced in Java 1.5 to reduce the synchronization overhead of `StringBuffer`s. Typically, `StringBuffer`s are used only in a single thread and then discarded—but `StringBuffer` itself is thread-safe, at the expense of synchronizing each method call.

```
assert greeting instanceof java.lang.StringBuffer

greeting << '!'      ←❷  Leftshift on StringBuffer

assert greeting.toString() == 'Hello Groovy!'

greeting[1..4] = 'i'    ←  Substring 'ello' becomes 'i'

assert greeting.toString() == 'Hi Groovy!'
```

> **NOTE**   Although the expression `stringRef << string` returns a `StringBuffer`,
> that `StringBuffer` is not automatically assigned to the *stringRef* (see
> ❶). When used on a `String`, it needs explicit assignment; on `String-`
> `Buffer` it doesn't. With a `StringBuffer`, the data in the existing object
> changed (see ❷)—with a `String` we can't change the existing data, so we
> have to return a new object instead.

Throughout the next sections, you will gradually add to what you have learned
about strings as you discover more language features. `String` has gained several
new methods in the GDK. You've already seen a few of these, but you'll see more
as we talk about working with regular expressions and lists. The complete list of
GDK methods on strings is listed in appendix C.

Working with strings is one of the most common tasks in programming, and for
script programming in particular: reading text, writing text, cutting words, replacing phrases, analyzing content, search and replace—the list is amazingly long.
Think about your own programming work. How much of it deals with strings?

Groovy supports you in these tasks with comprehensive string support. But
this is not the whole story. The next section introduces *regular expressions*, which
cut through text like a chainsaw: difficult to operate but extremely powerful.

3.5 *Working with regular expressions*

> *Once a programmer had a problem. He thought he could solve it with a regular expres-*
> *sion. Now he had two problems.*
>
> —from a fortune cookie

Suppose you had to prepare a table of contents for this book. You would need to
collect all headings like "3.5 Working with regular expressions"—paragraphs that
start with a number or with a number, a dot, and another number. The rest of the
paragraph would be the heading. This would be cumbersome to code naïvely:

iterate over each character; check whether it is a line start; if so, check whether it is a digit; if so, check whether a dot and a digit follow. Puh—lots of rope, and we haven't even covered numbers that have more than one digit.

Regular expressions come to the rescue. They allow you to *declare* such a *pattern* rather than programming it. Once you have the pattern, Groovy lets you work with it in numerous ways.

Regular expressions are prominent in scripting languages and have also been available in the Java library since JDK 1.4. Groovy relies on Java's *regex* (*regular expression*) support and adds three operators for convenience:

- The regex *find* operator =~
- The regex *match* operator ==~
- The regex *pattern* operator ~String

An in-depth discussion about regular expressions is beyond the scope of this book. Our focus is on Groovy, not on regexes. We give the shortest possible introduction to make the examples comprehensible and provide you with a jump-start.

Regular expressions are defined by *patterns*. A pattern can be anything from a simple character, a fixed string, or something like a date format made up of digits and delimiters, up to descriptions of balanced parentheses in programming languages. Patterns are declared by a sequence of symbols. In fact, the pattern description is a language of its own. Some examples are shown in table 3.7. Note that these are the raw patterns, not how they would appear in string literals. In other words, if you stored the pattern in a variable and printed it out, this is what you'd want to see. It's important to make the distinction between the pattern itself and how it's represented in code as a literal.

Table 3.7 Simple regular expression pattern examples

Pattern	Meaning
some text	Exactly "some text".
some\s+text	The word "some" followed by one or more whitespace characters followed by the word "text".
^\d+(\.\d+)? (.*)	Our introductory example: headings of level one or two. ^ denotes a line start, \d a digit, \d+ one or more digits. Parentheses are used for grouping. The question mark makes the first group optional. The second group contains the title, made of a dot for any character and a star for any number of such characters.
\d\d/\d\d/\d\d\d\d	A date formatted as exactly two digits followed by slash, two more digits followed by a slash, followed by exactly four digits.

A pattern like one of the examples in table 3.7 allows you to declare *what* you are looking for, rather than having to program *how* to find something. Next, you will see how patterns appear as literals in code and what can be done with them. We will then revisit our initial example with a full solution, before examining some performance aspects of regular expressions and finally showing how they can be used for classification in `switch` statements and for collection filtering with the `grep` method.

3.5.1 *Specifying patterns in string literals*

How do you put the sequence of symbols that declares a pattern inside a string?

In Java, this causes confusion. Patterns use lots of backslashes, and to get a backslash in a Java string literal, you need to double it. This makes for difficulty reading patterns in Java strings. It gets even worse if you need to match an actual backslash in your pattern—the pattern language escapes that with a backslash too, so the Java string literal needed to match the pattern a\b is "a\\\\b".

Groovy does much better. As you saw earlier, there is the *slashy* form of string literal, which doesn't require you to escape the backslash character and still works like a normal GString. Listing 3.4 shows how to declare patterns conveniently.

Listing 3.4 Regular expression GStrings

```
assert "abc" == /abc/
assert "\\d" == /\d/

def reference = "hello"
assert reference == /$reference/

assert "\$" == /$/
```

The slashy syntax doesn't require the dollar sign to be escaped. Note that you have the choice to declare patterns in either kind of string.

> **TIP** Sometimes the slashy syntax interferes with other valid Groovy expressions such as line comments or numerical expressions with multiple slashes for division. When in doubt, put parentheses around your pattern like (/pattern/). Parentheses force the parser to interpret the content as an expression.

Symbols

The key to using regular expressions is knowing the pattern symbols. For convenience, table 3.8 provides a short list of the most common ones. Put an earmark on this page so you can easily look up the table. You will use it a lot.

TIP   Symbols tend to have the same first letter as what they represent: for example, *d*igit, *s*pace, *w*ord, and *b*oundary. Uppercase symbols define the complement; think of them as a warning sign for *no*.

Table 3.8   Regular expression symbols (excerpt)

Symbol	Meaning
.	Any character
^	Start of line (or start of document, when in single-line mode)
$	End of line (or end of document, when in single-line mode)
\d	Digit character
\D	Any character except digits
\s	Whitespace character
\S	Any character except whitespace
\w	Word character
\W	Any character except word characters
\b	Word boundary
()	Grouping
$(x\|y)$	x or y, as in $(\texttt{Groovy}\|\texttt{Java}\|\texttt{Ruby})$
\1	Backmatch to group one: for example, find doubled characters with $(.)\backslash 1$
$x*$	Zero or more occurrences of x
$x+$	One or more occurrences of x
$x?$	Zero or one occurrence of x
$x\{m, n\}$	At least m and at most n occurrences of x
$x\{m\}$	Exactly m occurrences of x

continued on next page

Table 3.8 Regular expression symbols (excerpt) *(continued)*

Symbol	Meaning
`[a-f]`	Character class containing the characters *a, b, c, d, e, f*
`[^a]`	Character class containing any character except *a*
`(?is:x)`	Switches mode when evaluating *x*; i turns on `ignoreCase`, s means single-line mode

More to consider:

- Use grouping properly. The *expanding* operators such as *star* and *plus* bind closely; ab+ matches abbbb. Use `(ab)+` to match ababab.

- In normal mode, the expanding operators are *greedy*, meaning they try to match the longest substring that matches the pattern. Add an additional question mark after the operator to put them into *restrictive* mode. You may be tempted to extract the *href* from an HTML anchor element with this regex: `href="(.*)"`. But `href="(.*?)"` is probably better. The first version matches until the *last* double quote in your text; the latter matches until the *next* double quote.[11]

We have provided only a brief description of the regex pattern format, but a complete specification comes with your JDK. It is located in the Javadoc of class `java.util.regex.Pattern` and may change marginally between JDK versions. For JDK 1.4.2, it can be found online at http://java.sun.com/j2se/1.4.2/docs/api/java/util/regex/Pattern.html.

See the Javadoc to learn more about different evaluation modes, positive and negative lookahead, backmatches, and posix characters.

It always helps to test your expressions before putting them into code. There are online applications that allow interactive testing of regular expressions: for example, http://www.nvcc.edu/home/drodgers/ceu/resources/test_regexp.asp. You should be aware that not all regular expression pattern languages are exactly the same. You may get unexpected results if you take a regular expression designed for use in .NET and apply it in a Java or Groovy program. Although there aren't many differences, the differences that do exist can be hard to spot. Even if you

---

[11] This is only to explain the greedy behavior of regular expression, not to explain how HTML is parsed correctly, which would involve a lot of other topics such as ordering of attributes, spelling variants, and so forth.

take a regular expression from a book or a web site, you should still test that it works in your code.

Now that you have the pattern declared, you need to tell Groovy how to apply it. We will explore a whole variety of usages.

3.5.2 *Applying patterns*

Applied to a given string, Groovy supports the following tasks for regular expressions:

- Tell whether the pattern fully matches the whole string.
- Tell whether there is an occurrence of the pattern in the string.
- Count the occurrences.
- Do something with each occurrence.
- Replace all occurrences with some text.
- Split the string into multiple strings by cutting at each occurrence.

Listing 3.5 shows how Groovy sets patterns into action. Unlike most other examples, this listing contains some comments. This reflects real life and is not for illustrative purposes. The use of regexes is best accompanied by this kind of comment for all but the simplest patterns.

Listing 3.5   Regular expressions

```
twister = 'she sells sea shells at the sea shore of seychelles'

// twister must contain a substring of size 3
// that starts with s and ends with a
assert twister =~ /s.a/                    ❶ Regex find operator
                                             as usable in if      ❷ Find expression
finder = (twister =~ /s.a/)                                         evaluates to a
assert finder instanceof java.util.regex.Matcher                   matcher object

// twister must contain only words delimited by single spaces
assert twister ==~ /(\w+ \w+)*/            Regex match
                                           operator
WORD = /\w+/
matches = (twister ==~ /($WORD $WORD)*/)        Match expression
assert matches instanceof java.lang.Boolean     evaluates to a Boolean

assert (twister ==~ /s.e/) == false             Match is full, not
                                                partial like find
wordsByX = twister.replaceAll(WORD, 'x')
assert wordsByX == 'x x x x x x x x x x'
```

```
words = twister.split(/ /)        ⊲⎤  Split returns a
assert words.size() == 10            ⎦  list of words
assert words[0] == 'she'
```

❶ and ❷ have an interesting twist. Although the regex *find* operator evaluates to a `Matcher` object, it can also be used as a Boolean conditional. We will explore how this is possible when examining the "Groovy Truth" in chapter 6.

> **TIP** To remember the difference between the =~ *find* operator and the ==~ *match* operator, recall that *match* is more restrictive, because the pattern needs to cover the whole string. The demanded coverage is "longer" just like the appearance of its operator.

See your Javadoc for more information about the `java.util.regex.Matcher` object: how to walk through all matches and how to work with *groupings* at each match.

Common regex pitfalls

You do not need to fall into the regex trapdoors yourself. We have already done this for you. We have learned the following:

- When things get complex (note, this is *when*, not *if*), comment verbosely.
- Use the slashy syntax instead of the regular string syntax, or you will get lost in a forest of backslashes.
- Don't let your pattern look like a toothpick puzzle. Build your pattern from subexpressions like `WORD` in listing 3.5.
- Put your assumptions to the test. Write some assertions or unit tests to test your regex against static strings. Please don't send us any more flowers for this advice; an email with the subject "assertion saved my life today" will suffice.

3.5.3 *Patterns in action*

You're now ready to do everything you wanted to do with regular expressions, except we haven't covered "do something with each occurrence." *Something* and *each* sounds like a cue for a closure to appear, and that's the case here. `String` has a method called `eachMatch` that takes a regex as a parameter along with a closure that defines what to do on each match.

BY THE WAY The match is not a simple string but a list of strings, containing the whole match at position 0. If the pattern contains groupings, they are available as match[n] where *n* is group number *n*. Groups are numbered by the sequence of their opening parentheses.

The match gets passed into the closure for further analysis. In our musical example in listing 3.6, we append each match to a result string.

Listing 3.6   Working on each match of a pattern

```
myFairStringy = 'The rain in Spain stays mainly in the plain!!'

// words that end with 'ain': \b\w*ain\b
BOUNDS = /\b/
rhyme = /$BOUNDS\w*ain$BOUNDS/
found = ''
myFairStringy.eachMatch(rhyme) { match ->          ◁┐  string.eachMatch
    found += match[0] + ' '                         ❶ (pattern_string)
}
assert found == 'rain Spain plain '

found = ''                                          ❷  matcher.each
(myFairStringy =~ rhyme).each { match ->         ◁┘    (closure)
    found += match + ' '
}                                                       string.replaceAll  ❸
assert found == 'rain Spain plain '               (pattern_string, closure)

cloze = myFairStringy.replaceAll(rhyme){ it-'ain'+'___' }  ◁
assert cloze == 'The r___ in Sp___ stays mainly in the pl___!!'
```

There are two different ways to iterate through matches with identical behavior: use ❶ *String*.eachMatch(*Pattern*), or use ❷ *Matcher*.each(), where the Matcher is the result of applying the regex find operator to a string and a pattern. ❸ shows a special case for replacing each match with some dynamically derived content from the given closure. The variable it refers to the matching substring. The result is to replace "ain" with underscores, but only where it forms part of a rhyme.

In order to fully understand how the Groovy regular expression support works, we need to look at the java.util.regex.Matcher class. It is a JDK class that encapsulates knowledge about

- How often and at what position a pattern matches
- The groupings for each match

The GDK enhances the `Matcher` class with simplified array-like access to this information. This is what happens in the following (already familiar) example that matches all non-whitespace characters:

```
matcher = 'a b c' =~ /\S/

assert matcher[0]    == 'a'
assert matcher[1..2] == 'bc'
assert matcher.count == 3
```

The interesting part comes with *groupings* in the match. If the pattern contains parentheses to define groups, the matcher returns not a single string for each match but an array, where the full match is at index 0 and each extracted group follows. Consider this example, where each match finds pairs of strings that are separated by a colon. For later processing, the match is split into two groups, for the left and the right string:

```
matcher = 'a:1 b:2 c:3' =~ /(\S+):(\S+)/

assert matcher.hasGroup()
assert matcher[0] == ['a:1', 'a', '1']
```

In other words, what `matcher[0]` returns depends on whether the pattern contains groupings.

This also applies to the matcher's `each` method, which comes with a convenient notation for groupings. When the processing closure defines multiple parameters, the list of groups is distributed over them:

```
('xy' =~ /(.)(.)/).each { all, x, y  ->
    assert all == 'xy'
    assert x == 'x'
    assert y == 'y'
}
```

This matcher matches only one time but contains two groups with one character each.

> **NOTE**   Groovy internally stores the most recently used matcher (per thread). It can be retrieved with the static method `Matcher.getLastMatcher`. You can also set the index property of a matcher to make it look at the respective match with `matcher.index = x`. Both can be useful in some exotic corner cases. See `Matcher`'s API documentation for details.

`Matcher` and `Pattern` work in combination and are the key abstractions for regexes in Java and Groovy. You have seen `Matcher`, and we'll have a closer look at the `Pattern` abstraction next.

3.5.4 *Patterns and performance*

Finally, let's look at performance and the pattern operator ~*String*.

The pattern operator transforms a string into an object of type `java.util.regex.Pattern`. For a given string, this pattern object can be asked for a *matcher* object.

The rationale behind this construction is that patterns are internally backed by a so-called *finite state machine* that does all the high-performance magic. This machine is compiled when the pattern object is created. The more complicated the pattern, the longer the creation takes. In contrast, the *matching* process as performed by the machine is extremely fast.

The pattern operator allows you to split pattern-creation time from pattern-matching time, increasing performance by reusing the finite state machine. Listing 3.7 shows a poor-man's performance comparison of the two approaches. The precompiled pattern version is at least 20% faster (although these kinds of measurements can differ wildly).

Listing 3.7 Increase performance with pattern reuse.

```
twister = 'she sells sea shells at the sea shore of seychelles'
// some more complicated regex:
// word that starts and ends with same letter
regex = /\b(\w)\w*\1\b/

start = System.currentTimeMillis()
100000.times{                         Find operator with implicit
    twister =~ regex                  pattern construction
}
first = System.currentTimeMillis() - start

start = System.currentTimeMillis()    ❶ Explicit pattern
pattern = ~regex                          construction
100000.times{
    pattern.matcher(twister)          Apply the pattern on a String
}
second = System.currentTimeMillis() - start

assert first > second * 1.20
```

To find words that start and end with the same character, we used the \1 back-match to refer to that character. We prepared its usage by putting the word's first character into a group, which happens to be group 1.

Note the difference in spelling in ❶. This is not a =~ b but a = ~b. Tricky.

> **BY THE WAY** The observant reader may spot a language issue: What happens if you write a=~b without any whitespace? Is that the =~ *find* operator, or is it an assignment of the ~b pattern to a? For the human reader, it is ambiguous. Not so for the Groovy parser. It is greedy and will parse this as the *find* operator.
>
> It goes without saying that being explicit with whitespace is good programming style, even when the meaning is unambiguous for the parser. Do it for the next human reader, which will likely be you.

Don't forget that performance should usually come second to readability—at least to start with. If reusing a pattern means bending your code out of shape, you should ask yourself how critical the performance of that particular area is before making the change. Measure the performance in different situations with each version of the code, and balance ease of maintenance with speed and memory requirements.

3.5.5 *Patterns for classification*

Listing 3.8 completes our journey through the domain of patterns. The `Pattern` object, as returned from the *pattern* operator, implements an `isCase(String)` method that is equivalent to a full match of that pattern with the string. This classification method is a prerequisite for using patterns conveniently with the `grep` method and in `switch` cases.

The example classifies words that consist of exactly four characters. The pattern therefore consists of four dots. This is not an ellipsis!

Listing 3.8 Patterns in `grep()` and `switch()`

```
assert (~/..../).isCase('bear')

switch('bear'){
    case ~/..../ : assert true; break
    default      : assert false
}

beasts = ['bear','wolf','tiger','regex']

assert beasts.grep(~/..../) == ['bear','wolf']
```

> **TIP** Classifications read nicely in switch and grep. The direct use of classifier.isCase(candidate) happens rarely, but when it does, it is best read from right to left: "*candidate* is a case of *classifier*".

Regular expressions are difficult beasts to tame, but mastering them adds a new quality to all text-manipulation tasks. Once you have a grip on them, you'll hardly be able to imagine having programmed (some would say *lived*) without them. Groovy makes regular expressions easily accessible and straightforward to use.

This concludes our coverage of text-based types, but of course computers have always dealt with numbers as well as text. Working with numbers is easy in most programming languages, but that doesn't mean there's no room for improvement. Let's see how Groovy goes the extra mile when it comes to numeric types.

3.6 *Working with numbers*

The available numeric types and their declarations in Groovy were introduced in section 3.1.

You have seen that for decimal numbers, the default type is java.math. BigDecimal. This is a feature to get around the most common misconceptions about floating-point arithmetic. We're going to look at which type is used where and what extra abilities have been provided for numbers in the GDK.

3.6.1 *Coercion with numeric operators*

It is always important to understand what happens when you use one of the numeric operators.

Most of the rules for the addition, multiplication, and subtraction operators are the same as in Java, but there are some changes regarding floating-point behavior, and BigInteger and BigDecimal also need to be included. The rules are straightforward. The first rule to match the situation is used.

For the operations +, -, and *:

- If either operand is a Float or a Double, the result is a Double. (In Java, when only Float operands are involved, the result is a Float too.)
- Otherwise, if either operand is a BigDecimal, the result is a BigDecimal.
- Otherwise, if either operand is a BigInteger, the result is a BigInteger.
- Otherwise, if either operand is a Long, the result is a Long.
- Otherwise, the result is an Integer.

Table 3.9 depicts the scheme for quick lookup. Types are abbreviated by uppercase letters.

Table 3.9   Numerical coercion

+ - *	B	S	I	C	L	BI	BD	F	D
Byte	I	I	I	I	L	BI	BD	D	D
Short	I	I	I	I	L	BI	BD	D	D
Integer	I	I	I	I	L	BI	BD	D	D
Character	I	I	I	I	L	BI	BD	D	D
Long	L	L	L	L	L	BI	BD	D	D
BigInteger	BI	BI	BI	BI	BI	BI	BD	D	D
BigDecimal	BD	BD	BD	BD	BD	BD	BD	D	D
Float	D	D	D	D	D	D	D	D	D
Double	D	D	D	D	D	D	D	D	D

Other aspects of coercion behavior:

- Like Java but unlike Ruby, no coercion takes place when the result of an operation exceeds the current range, except for the power operator.
- For *division*, if any of the arguments is of type Float or Double, the result is of type Double; otherwise the result is of type BigDecimal with the maximum precision of both arguments, rounded half up. The result is normalized—that is, without trailing zeros.
- Integer division (keeping the result as an integer) is achievable through explicit casting or by using the intdiv() method.
- The *shifting* operators are only defined for types Integer and Long. They do not coerce to other types.
- The *power* operator coerces to the next best type that can take the result in terms of range and precision, in the sequence Integer, Long, Double.
- The *equals* operator coerces to the more general type before comparing.

Rules can be daunting without examples, so this behavior is demonstrated in table 3.10.

Table 3.10 Numerical expression examples

Expression	Result type	Comments
`1f*2f`	`Double`	In Java, this would be `Float`.
`(Byte)1+(Byte)2`	`Integer`	As in Java, integer arithmetic is always performed in at least 32 bits.
`1*2L`	`Long`	
`1/2`	`BigDecimal (0.5)`	In Java, the result would be the integer 0.
`(int)(1/2)`	`Integer (0)`	This is normal coercion of `BigDecimal` to `Integer`.
`1.intdiv(2)`	`Integer (0)`	This is the equivalent of the Java `1/2`.
`Integer.MAX_VALUE+1`	`Integer`	Non-*power* operators wrap without promoting the result type.
`2**31`	`Integer`	
`2**33`	`Long`	The *power* operator promotes where necessary.
`2**3.5`	`Double`	
`2G+1G`	`BigInteger`	
`2.5G+1G`	`BigDecimal`	
`1.5G==1.5F`	`Boolean (true)`	The `Float` is promoted to a `BigDecimal` before comparison.
`1.1G==1.1F`	`Boolean (false)`	1.1 can't be exactly represented as a `Float` (or indeed a `Double`), so when it is promoted to `BigDecimal`, it isn't equal to the exact `BigDecimal` 1.1G but rather 1.100000023841858G.

The only surprise is that there is no surprise. In Java, results like in the fourth row are often surprising—for example, (1/2) is always zero because when both operands of division are integers, only integer division is performed. To get 0.5 in Java, you need to write (1f/2).

This behavior is especially important when using Groovy to enhance your application with user-defined input. Suppose you allow super-users of your application to specify a formula that calculates an employee's bonus, and it gets specified as businessDone * (1/3). With Java semantics, this will be a bad year for the poor employees.

3.6.2 GDK methods for numbers

The GDK defines all applicable methods from table 3.4 to implement overridable operators for numbers such as `plus`, `minus`, `power`, and so forth. They all work without surprises. In addition, the `abs`, `toInteger`, and `round` methods do what you'd expect.

More interestingly, the GDK also defines the methods `times`, `upto`, `downto`, and `step`. They all take a closure argument. Listing 3.9 shows these methods in action: `times` is just for repetition, `upto` is for walking a sequence of increasing numbers, `downto` is for decreasing numbers, and `step` is the general version that walks until the end value by successively adding a step width.

Listing 3.9 GDK methods on numbers

```
def store = ''
10.times{          <--  Repetition
    store += 'x'
}
assert store == 'xxxxxxxxxx'

store = ''
1.upto(5) { number ->    <--  Walking up with
    store += number           loop variable
}
assert store == '12345'

store = ''
2.downto(-2) { number ->    <--  Walking
    store += number + ' '        down
}
assert store == '2 1 0 -1 -2 '

store = ''
0.step(0.5, 0.1 ){ number ->    <--  Walking with
    store += number + ' '            step width
}
assert store == '0 0.1 0.2 0.3 0.4 '
```

Calling methods on numbers can feel unfamiliar at first when you come from Java. Just remember that numbers are objects and you can treat them as such.

You have seen that in Groovy, numbers work the natural way and even guard you against the most common errors with floating-point arithmetic. In most cases, there is no need to remember all details of coercion. When the need arises, this section may serve as a reference.

The strategy of making objects available in unexpected places starts to become an ongoing theme. You have seen it with numbers, and section 4.1 shows the same principle applied to ranges.

3.7 *Summary*

The simple datatypes form a big portion of your everyday programming work with Groovy. After all, working with strings and numbers is the bread and butter of software development.

Making common activities more convenient is one of Groovy's main promises. Consequently, Groovy promotes even the simple datatypes to first-class objects and implements operators as method calls to make the benefits of object orientation ubiquitously available.

Developer convenience is further enhanced by allowing a variety of means for string literal declarations, whether through flexible GString declarations or with the slashy syntax for situations where extra escaping is undesirable, such as regular expression patterns. GStrings contribute to another of Groovy's central pillars: concise and expressive code. This allows the reader a clearer insight into the runtime string value, without having to wade through reams of string concatenation or switch between format strings and the values replaced in them.

Regular expressions are well represented in Groovy, again confirming its comfortable place among other scripting languages. Leveraging regular expressions is common in the scripting world, and a language that treated them as second-class citizens would be severely hampered. Groovy effortlessly combines Java's libraries with language support, retaining the regular expression dialect familiar to Java programmers with the ease of use found in scripting.

The Groovy way of treating numbers with respect to type conversion and precision handling leads to intuitive usage, even for non-programmers. This becomes particularly important when Groovy scripts are used for smart configurations of larger systems where business users may provide formulas—for example, to define share-valuation details.

Strings, regular expressions, and numbers alike profit from numerous methods that the GDK introduces on top of the JDK. The pattern is clear by now—Groovy is a language designed for the ease of those developing in it, concentrating on making repetitive tasks as simple as they can be without sacrificing the power of the Java platform.

You shall soon see that this focus on ease of use extends far beyond the simple types Java developers are used to having built-in language support for. The

Groovy designers are well aware of other concepts that are rarely far from a programmer's mind. The next chapter shows how intuitive operators, enhanced literals, and extra GDK methods are also available with Groovy's collective data types: ranges, lists, and maps.

The collective
Groovy datatypes

> *The intuitive mind is a sacred gift and the rational mind is a faithful servant. We have created a society that honors the servant and has forgotten the gift.*
>
> —Albert Einstein

The nice thing about computers is that they never get tired of repeatedly doing the same task. This is probably the single most important quality that justifies letting them take part in our life. Searching through countless files or web pages, downloading emails every 10 minutes, looking up all values of a stock symbol for the last quarter to paint a nice graph—these are only a few examples where the computer needs to repeatedly process an item of a data collection. It is no wonder that a great deal of programming work is about collections.

Because collections are so prominent in programming, Groovy alleviates the tedium of using them by directly supporting datatypes of a collective nature: ranges, lists, and maps. In accordance with what you have seen of the simple datatypes, Groovy's support for collective datatypes encompasses new lightweight means for literal declaration, specialized operators, and numerous GDK enhancements.

The notation that Groovy uses to set its collective datatypes into action will be new to Java programmers, but as you will see, it is easy to understand and remember. You will pick it up so quickly that you will hardly be able to imagine there was a time when you were new to the concept.

Despite the new notation possibilities, lists and maps have the exact same semantics as in Java. This situation is slightly different for ranges, because they don't have a direct equivalent in Java. So let's start our tour with that topic.

4.1 Working with ranges

Think about how often you've written a loop like this:

```
for (int i=0; i<upperBound; i++){
    // do something with i
}
```

Most of us have done this thousands of times. It is so common that we hardly ever think about it. Take the opportunity to do it now. Does the code tell you what it does or how it does it?

After careful inspection of the variable, the conditional, and the incrementation, we see that it's an iteration starting at zero and not reaching the upper bound, assuming there are no side effects on i in the loop body. We have to go through the description of *how* the code works to find out *what* it does.

Next, consider how often you've written a conditional such as this:

```
if (x >= 0 && x <= upperBound) {
    // do something with x
}
```

The same thing applies here: We have to inspect *how* the code works in order to understand *what* it does. Variable x must be between zero and an upper bound for further processing. It's easy to overlook that the upper bound is now inclusive.

Now, we're not saying that we make mistakes using this syntax on a regular basis. We're not saying that we can't get used to (or indeed haven't gotten used to) the C-style for loop, as countless programmers have over the years. What we're saying is that it's harder than it needs to be; and, more important, it's *less expressive* than it could be. Can you understand it? Absolutely. Then again, you could understand this chapter if it were written entirely in capital letters—that doesn't make it a good idea, though.

Groovy allows you to reveal the meaning of such code pieces by providing the concept of a *range*. A range has a left bound and a right bound. You can do *something* for *each* element of a range, effectively iterating through it. You can determine whether a candidate element falls inside a range. In other words, a range is an interval plus a strategy for how to move through it.

By introducing the new concept of ranges, Groovy extends your means of expressing your intentions in the code.

We will show how to specify ranges, how the fact that they are objects makes them ubiquitously applicable, how to use custom objects as bounds, and how they're typically used in the GDK.

4.1.1 *Specifying ranges*

Ranges are specified using the double dot .. range operator between the left and the right bound. This operator has a low precedence, so you often need to enclose the declaration in parentheses. Ranges can also be declared using their respective constructors.

The ..< range operator specifies a half-exclusive range—that is, the value on the right is not part of the range:

```
left..right
(left..right)
(left..<right)
```

Ranges usually have a lower left bound and a higher right bound. When this is switched, we call it a *reverse* range. Ranges can also be any combination of the types we've described. Listing 4.1 shows these combinations and how ranges can have bounds other than integers, such as dates and strings. Groovy supports ranges at the language level with the special *for-in-range* loop.

Listing 4.1 Range declarations

```
assert (0..10).contains(0)
assert (0..10).contains(5)
assert (0..10).contains(10)

assert (0..10).contains(-1) == false
assert (0..10).contains(11) == false

assert (0..<10).contains(9)
assert (0..<10).contains(10) == false

def a = 0..10
assert a instanceof Range
assert a.contains(5)

a = new IntRange(0,10)
assert a.contains(5)

assert (0.0..1.0).contains(0.5)

def today     = new Date()
def yesterday = today-1
assert (yesterday..today).size() == 2

assert ('a'..'c').contains('b')

def log = ''
for (element in 5..9){
    log += element
}
assert log == '56789'

log = ''
for (element in 9..5){
    log += element
}
assert log == '98765'

log = ''
(9..<5).each { element ->
    log += element
}
assert log == '9876'
```

Inclusive ranges

Half-exclusive ranges

❶ References to ranges

Explicit construction

❷ Date ranges

❸ String ranges

for-in-range loop

Loop with reverse range

❹ Half-exclusive, reverse, each with closure

Note that we assign a range to a variable in ❶. In other words, the variable holds a reference to an object of type `groovy.lang.Range`. We will examine this feature further and see what consequences it implies.

Date objects can be used in ranges, as in ❷, because the GDK adds the previous and next methods to date, which increase or decrease the date by one day.

BY THE WAY The GDK also adds *minus* and *plus* operators to java.util.Date, which increase or decrease the date by so many days.

The String methods previous and next are added by the GDK to make strings usable for ranges, as in ❸. The last character in the string is incremented/decremented, and over-/underflow is handled by appending a new character or deleting the last character.

We can walk through a range with the each method, which presents the current value to the given closure with each step, as shown in ❹. If the range is reversed, we will walk through the range backward. If the range is half-exclusive, the walking stops before reaching the right bound.

4.1.2 *Ranges are objects*

Because every range is an object, you can pass a range around and call its methods. The most prominent methods are each, which executes a specified closure for each element in the range, and contains, which specifies whether a value is within a range or not.

Being first-class objects, ranges can also participate in the game of operator overriding (see section 3.3) by providing an implementation of the isCase method, with the same meaning as contains. That way, you can use ranges as grep filters and as switch cases. This is shown in listing 4.2.

Listing 4.2 Ranges are objects

```
result = ''
(5..9).each{ element ->          Iterating
    result += element            through
}                                ranges
assert result == '56789'

assert (0..10).isCase(5)

age = 36
switch(age){
    case 16..20 : insuranceRate = 0.05 ; break
    case 21..50 : insuranceRate = 0.06 ; break      ❶  Ranges for
    case 51..65 : insuranceRate = 0.07 ; break          classification
    default: throw new IllegalArgumentException()
}
assert insuranceRate == 0.06
```

```
ages = [20,36,42,56]
midage = 21..50
assert ages.grep(midage) == [36,42]
```

❷ **Filtering with ranges**

The use with the `grep` method ❷ is a good example for passing around range objects: The `midage` range gets passed as a parameter to the `grep` method.

Classification through ranges as shown at ❶ is what we often find in the business world: interest rates for different ranges of allocated assets, transaction fees based on volume ranges, and salary bonuses based on ranges of business done. Although technical people prefer using functions, business people tend to use ranges. When you're modeling the business world in software, classification by ranges can be very handy.

4.1.3 *Ranges in action*

Listing 4.1 made use of date and string ranges. In fact, any datatype can be used with ranges, provided that both of the following are true:

- The type implements `next` and `previous`; that is, it overrides the `++` and `--` operators.

- The type implements `java.lang.Comparable`; that is, it implements `compareTo`, effectively overriding the `<=>` *spaceship* operator.

As an example, we implement a class `Weekday` in listing 4.3 that represents a day of the week. From the perspective of the code that uses our class, a `Weekday` has a value `'Sun'` through `'Sat'`. Internally, it's just an index between `0` and `6`. A little list maps indexes to weekday name abbreviations.

We implement `next` and `previous` to return the respective new `Weekday` object. `compareTo` simply compares the indexes.

With this preparation, we can construct a range of working days and work our way through it, reporting the work done until we finally reach the well-deserved weekend. Oh, and our boss wants to assess the weekly work report. A final assertion does this on his behalf.

Listing 4.3   Custom ranges: weekdays

```
class Weekday implements Comparable {
    static final DAYS = [
        'Sun', 'Mon', 'Tue', 'Wed', 'Thu', 'Fri', 'Sat'
    ]
    private int index = 0           ⎫ Construct by name
    Weekday(String day) {     ⎯⎯┘    and normalize index
```

```
        index = DAYS.indexOf(day)
    }
    Weekday next(){
        return new Weekday(DAYS[(index+1) % DAYS.size()])
    }
    Weekday previous(){
        return new Weekday(DAYS[index-1])          ◁──  Automatic
    }                                               ❶   underflow
    int compareTo(Object other){
        return this.index <=> other.index
    }
    String toString(){
        return DAYS[index]
    }
}

def mon = new Weekday('Mon')
def fri = new Weekday('Fri')

def worklog = ''                    │  Use the range
for (day in mon..fri){     ◁────────┘  for iteration
    worklog += day.toString() + ' '
}
assert worklog == 'Mon Tue Wed Thu Fri '
```

This code can be placed inside one script file, even though it contains both a class declaration and script code. The Weekday class is like an inner class to the script.

The implementation of previous at ❶ is a bit unconventional. Although next uses the modulo operator in a conventional way to jump from Saturday (index 6) to Sunday (index 0), the opposite direction simply decreases the index. The index −1 is used for looking up the previous weekday name, and DAYS[−1] references the last entry of the days list, as you will see in the next section. We construct a new Weekday('Sat'), and the constructor normalizes the index to 6.

Compared to the Java alternatives, ranges have proven to be a flexible solution. *For* loops and conditionals are not objects, cannot be reused, and cannot be passed around, but ranges can. Ranges let you focus on *what* the code does, rather than *how* it does it. This is a pure declaration of your intent, as opposed to fiddling with indexes and boundary conditions.

Using custom ranges is the next step forward. Look actively through your code for possible applications. Ranges slumber everywhere, and bringing them to life can significantly improve the expressiveness of your code. With a bit of practice, you may find ranges where you never thought possible. This is a sure sign that new language concepts can change your perception of the world.

You will shortly refer to your newly acquired knowledge about ranges when exploring the subscript operator on lists, the built-in datatype that we are going to cover next.

4.2 Working with lists

In a recent Java project, we had to write a method that takes a Java array and adds an element to it. This seemed like a trivial task, but we forgot how awkward Java programming could be. (We're spoiled from too much Groovy programming.) Java arrays cannot be changed in length, so you cannot add elements easily. One way is to convert the array to a `java.util.List`, add the element, and convert back. A second way is to construct a new array of size+1, copy the old values over, and set the new element to the last index position. Either takes some lines of code.

But Java arrays also have their benefits in terms of language support. They work with the subscript operator to easily retrieve elements of an array by index like `myarray[index]`, or to store elements at an index position with `myarray[index] = newElement`.

We will demonstrate how Groovy lists give you the best of both approaches, extending the features for smart operator implementations, method overloading, and using lists as Booleans. With Groovy lists, you will also discover new ways of leveraging the power of the Java Collections API.

4.2.1 Specifying lists

Listing 4.4 shows various ways of specifying lists. The primary way is with square brackets around a sequence of items, delimited with commas:

```
[item, item, item]
```

The sequence can be empty to declare an empty list. Lists are by default of type `java.util.ArrayList` and can also be declared explicitly by calling the respective constructor. The resulting list can still be used with the subscript operator. In fact, this works with any type of list, as we show here with type `java.util.LinkedList`.

Lists can be created and initialized at the same time by calling `toList` on ranges.

Listing 4.4 Specifying lists

```
myList = [1,2,3]

assert myList.size() == 3
assert myList[0]      == 1
assert myList instanceof ArrayList
```

```
emptyList = []
assert emptyList.size() == 0

longList = (0..1000).toList()
assert longList[555] == 555

explicitList = new ArrayList()
explicitList.addAll(myList)
assert explicitList.size() == 3
explicitList[0] = 10
assert explicitList[0] == 10

explicitList = new LinkedList(myList)
assert explicitList.size() == 3
explicitList[0] = 10
assert explicitList[0] == 10
```

❶ Fill from myList

We use the addAll(*Collection*) method from java.util.List at ❶ to easily fill the lists. As an alternative, the collection to fill from can be passed right into the constructor, as we have done with LinkedList.

For the sake of completeness, we need to add that lists can also be constructed by passing a Java array to Groovy. Such an array is subject to autoboxing—a list will be automatically generated from the array with its elements being autoboxed.

The GDK extends all arrays, collection objects, and strings with a toList method that returns a newly generated list of the contained elements. Strings are handled like lists of characters.

4.2.2 Using list operators

Lists implement some of the operators that you saw in section 3.3. Listing 4.4 contained two of them: the getAt and putAt methods to implement the subscript operator. But this was a simple use that works with a mere index argument. There's much more to the list operators than that.

The subscript operator

The GDK overloads the getAt method with range and collection arguments to access a range or a collection of indexes. This is demonstrated in Listing 4.5.

The same strategy is applied to putAt, which is overloaded with a *Range* argument, assigning a list of values to a whole sublist.

Listing 4.5 Accessing parts of a list with the overloaded subscript operator

```
myList = ['a','b','c','d','e','f']

assert myList[0..2]  == ['a','b','c']      getAt(Range)
assert myList[0,2,4] == ['a','c','e']      getAt(collection of indexes)

myList[0..2] = ['x','y','z']      putAt(Range)
assert myList == ['x','y','z','d','e','f']
                                   ❶ Removing
                                     elements
myList[3..5] = []
assert myList == ['x','y','z']

                    ❷ Adding elements
myList[1..1] = ['y','1','2']
assert myList == ['x','y','1','2','z']
```

Subscript assignments with ranges do not need to be of identical size. When the assigned list of values is smaller than the range or even empty, the list shrinks, as shown at ❶. When the assigned list of values is bigger, the list grows, as in ❷.

Ranges as used within subscript assignments are a convenience feature to access Java's excellent sublist support for lists. See also the Javadoc for `java.util.List#sublist`.

In addition to positive index values, lists can also be subscripted with negative indexes that count from the end of the list backward. Figure 4.1 show how positive and negative indexes map to an example list `[0,1,2,3,4]`.

Consequently, you get the last entry of a non-empty list with `list[-1]` and the next-to-last with `list[-2]`. Negative indexes can also be used in ranges, so `list[-3..-1]` gives you the last three entries. When using a *reversed* range, the resulting list is reversed as well, so `list[4..0]` is `[4,3,2,1,0]`. In this case, the result is a new list object rather than a *sublist* in the sense of the JDK. Even mixtures of positive and negative indexes are possible, such as `list[1..-2]` to cut away the first entry and the last entry.

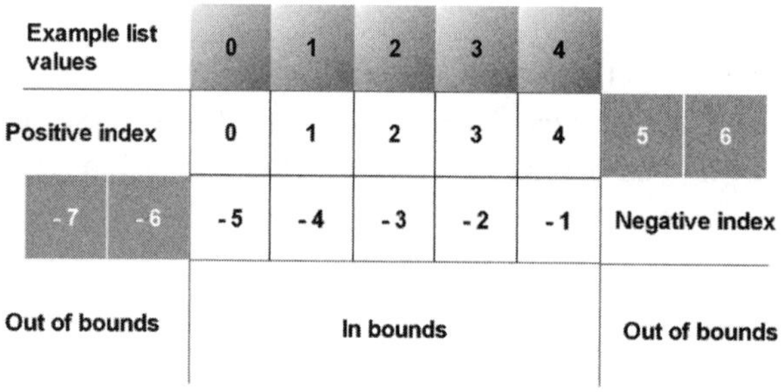

Example list values	0	1	2	3	4		
Positive index	0	1	2	3	4	5	6
Negative index	-7	-6	-5	-4	-3	-2	-1
	Out of bounds		In bounds				Out of bounds

Figure 4.1
Positive and negative indexes of a list of length five, with "in bounds" and "out of bounds" classification for indexes

TIP Ranges in List's subscript operator are IntRanges. Exclusive IntRanges are mapped to inclusive ones at construction time, before the subscript operator comes into play and can map negative indexes to positive ones. This can lead to surprises when mixing positive left and negative right bounds with exclusiveness; for example, IntRange (0..<-2) gets mapped to (0..-1), such that list[0..<-2] is effectively list[0..-1].

Although this is stable and works predictably, it may be confusing for the readers of your code, who may expect it to work like list[0..-3]. For this reason, this situation should be avoided for the sake of clarity.

Adding and removing items

Although the subscript operator can be used to change any individual element of a list, there are also operators available to change the contents of the list in a more drastic way. They are plus(Object), plus(Collection), leftShift(Object), minus (Collection), and multiply. Listing 4.6 shows them in action. The plus method is overloaded to distinguish between adding an element and adding all elements of a collection. The minus method only works with collection parameters.

Listing 4.6 List operators involved in adding and removing items

```
myList = []

myList += 'a'          ← plus(Object)
assert myList == ['a']

myList += ['b','c']    ← plus(Collection)
assert myList == ['a','b','c']

myList = []            | leftShift is like
myList <<  'a' << 'b'  ← append
assert myList == ['a','b']

assert myList - ['b'] == ['a']    ← minus(Collection)

assert myList * 2 == ['a','b','a','b']    ← Multiply
```

While we're talking about operators, it's worth noting that we have used the == operator on lists, happily assuming that it does what we expect. Now we see how it works: The equals method on lists tests that two collections have equal elements. See the Javadoc of java.util.List#equals for details.

Control structures

Groovy lists are more than flexible storage places. They also play a major role in organizing the execution flow of Groovy programs. Listing 4.7 shows the use of lists in Groovy's `if`, `switch`, and `for` control structures.

Listing 4.7   Lists taking part in control structures

```
myList = ['a', 'b', 'c']

assert myList.isCase('a')
candidate = 'a'
switch(candidate){                              ❶ Classify by
    case myList : assert true; break              containment
    default     : assert false
}
                                                ❷ Intersection
assert ['x','a','z'].grep(myList) == ['a']        filter

myList = []                       ❸ Empty lists
if (myList) assert false            are false

// Lists can be iterated with a 'for' loop
log = ''
for (i in [1,'x',5]){      ❹ for in Collection
    log += i
}
assert log == '1x5'
```

In ❶ and ❷, you see the trick that you already know from patterns and ranges: implementing `isCase` and getting a `grep` filter and a switch classification for free.

❸ is a little surprising. Inside a Boolean test, empty lists evaluate to `false`.

❹ shows looping over lists or other collections and also demonstrates that lists can contain mixtures of types.

4.2.3 Using list methods

There are so many useful methods on the `List` type that we cannot provide an example for all of them in the language description. The large number of methods comes from the fact that the Java interface `java.util.List` is already fairly wide (25 methods in JDK 1.4).

Furthermore, the GDK adds methods to the `List` interface, to the `Collection` interface, and to `Object`. Therefore, many methods are available on the `List` type, including all methods of `Collection` and `Object`.

Appendix C has the complete overview of all methods added to `List` by the GDK. The Javadoc of `java.util.List` has the complete list of its JDK methods.

While working with lists in Groovy, there is no need to be aware of whether a method stems from the JDK or the GDK, or whether it is defined in the `List` or `Collection` interface. However, for the purpose of describing the Groovy `List` datatype, we fully cover the GDK methods on lists and collections, but not all combinations from overloaded methods and not what is already covered in the previous examples. We provide only partial examples of the JDK methods that we consider important.

Manipulating list content

A first set of methods is presented in Listing 4.8. It deals with changing the content of the list by adding and removing elements; combining lists in various ways; sorting, reversing, and flattening nested lists; and creating new lists from existing ones.

Listing 4.8 Methods to manipulate list content

```
assert [1,[2,3]].flatten() == [1,2,3]

assert [1,2,3].intersect([4,3,1])== [3,1]
assert [1,2,3].disjoint([4,5,6])

list = [1,2,3]                     ❶ Treating a list
popped = list.pop()                  like a stack
assert popped == 3
assert list == [1,2]

assert [1,2].reverse() == [2,1]

assert [3,1,2].sort() == [1,2,3]

def list = [ [1,0], [0,1,2] ]      ❷ Comparing lists
list = list.sort { a,b -> a[0] <=> b[0] }    by first element
assert list == [ [0,1,2], [1,0] ]
                                   ❸ Comparing
                                     lists by size
list = list.sort { item -> item.size() }
assert list == [ [1,0], [0,1,2] ]

list = ['a','b','c']     ❹ Removing
list.remove(2)             by index
assert list == ['a','b']
list.remove('b')
assert list == ['a']     ❺ Removing
                           by value
```

```
list = ['a','b','b','c']
list.removeAll(['b','c'])
assert list == ['a']

def doubled = [1,2,3].collect{ item ->
    item*2
}
assert doubled == [2,4,6]

def odd = [1,2,3].findAll{ item ->
    item % 2 == 1
}
assert odd == [1,3]
```

❻ Transforming one list into another

❼ Finding every element matching the closure

List elements can be of arbitrary type, including other nested lists. This can be used to implement lists of lists, the Groovy equivalent of multidimensional arrays in Java. For nested lists, the `flatten` method provides a flat view of all elements.

An intersection of lists contains all elements that appear in both lists. Collections can also be checked for being `disjoint`—that is, whether their intersection is empty.

Lists can be used like *stacks*, with usual stack behavior on push and pop, as in ❶. The push operation is relayed to the list's << left-shift operator.

When list elements are `Comparable`, there is a natural sort. Alternatively, the comparison logic of the sort can be specified as a closure, as in ❷ and ❸. In the first example, we sort lists of lists by comparing their entry at index zero. The second example shows that a single argument can be used inside the closure for comparison. In this case, the comparison is made between the results that the closure returns when fed each of the candidate elements.

Elements can be removed by index, as in ❹, or by value, as in ❺. We can also remove all the elements that appear as values in the second list. These removal methods are the only ones in the listing that are available in the JDK.

The `collect` method, seen in ❻, returns a new list that is constructed from what a closure returns when successively applied to all elements of the original list. In the example, we use it to retrieve a new list where each entry of the original list is multiplied by two. With `findAll`, as in ❼, we retrieve a list of all items for which the closure evaluates to `true`. In the example, we use the modulo operator to find all odd numbers.

Two issues related to changing an existing list are removing duplicates and removing null values. One way to remove duplicate entries is to convert the list to a datatype that is free of duplicates: a Set. This can be achieved by calling a Set's constructor with that list as an argument.

```
def x = [1,1,1]
assert [1] == new HashSet(x).toList()
assert [1] == x.unique()
```

If you don't want to create a new collection but do want to keep working on your cleaned list, you can use the unique method, which ensures that the sequence of entries is not changed by this operation.

Removing null from a list can be done by keeping all non-nulls—for example, with the findAll methods that you have seen previously:

```
def x = [1,null,1]
assert [1,1] == x.findAll{it != null}
assert [1,1] == x.grep{it}
```

You can see there's an even shorter version with grep, but in order to understand its mechanics, you need more knowledge about closures (chapter 5) and "The Groovy truth" (chapter 6). Just take it for granted until then.

Accessing list content

Lists have methods to query their elements for certain properties, iterate through them, and retrieve accumulated results.

Query methods include a count of given elements in the list, min and max, a find method that finds the first element that satisfies a closure, and methods to determine whether every or any element in the list satisfies a closure.

Iteration can be achieved as usual, forward with each or backward with eachReverse.

Cumulative methods come in simple and sophisticated versions. The join method is simple: It returns all elements as a string, concatenated with a given string. The inject method is inspired by Smalltalk. It uses a closure to inject new functionality. That functionality operates on an intermediary result and the current element of the iteration. The first parameter of the inject method is the initial value of the intermediary result. In listing 4.9, we use this method to sum up all elements and then use it a second time to multiply them.

Listing 4.9   List query, iteration, and accumulation

```
def list = [1,2,3]

assert list.count(2) == 1
assert list.max() == 3
assert list.min() == 1

def even = list.find { item ->
    item % 2 == 0
}
assert even == 2

assert list.every { item -> item < 5}
assert list.any   { item -> item < 2}

def store = ''
list.each { item ->
    store += item
}
assert store == '123'

store = ''
list.reverseEach{ item ->
    store += item
}
assert store == '321'

assert list.join('-') == '1-2-3'

result = list.inject(0){ clinks, guests ->
    clinks += guests
}
assert result    == 0 + 1+2+3
assert list.sum() == 6

factorial = list.inject(1){ fac, item ->
    fac *= item
}
assert factorial == 1 * 1*2*3
```

Querying

Iteration

Accumulation

Understanding and using the `inject` method can be a bit challenging if you're new to the concept. Note that it is exactly parallel to the *iteration* examples, with `store` playing the role of the intermediary result. The benefit is that you do not need to introduce that extra variable to the outer scope of your accumulation, and your closure has no side effects on that scope.

The GDK introduces two more convenience methods for lists: `asImmutable` and `asSynchronized`. These methods use `Collections.unmodifiableList` and `Collections.synchronizedList` to protect the list from unintended content changes and concurrent access. See these methods' Javadocs for more details on the topic.

4.2.4 Lists in action

After all the artificial examples, you deserve to see a real one. Here it is: We will implement Tony Hoare's Quicksort[1] algorithm in listing 4.10. To make things more interesting, we will do so in a generic way; we will not demand any particular datatype for sorting. We rely on *duck typing*—as long as something walks like a duck and talks like a duck, we happily treat it as a duck. For our use, this means that as long as we can use the <, =, and > operators with our list items, we treat them as if they were comparable.

The goal of Quicksort is to be sparse with comparisons. The strategy relies on finding a good *pivot* element in the list that serves to split the list into two sublists: one with all elements smaller than the pivot, the second with all elements bigger than the pivot. Quicksort is then called recursively on the sublists. The rationale behind this is that you never need to compare elements from one list with elements from the other list. If you always find the perfect pivot, which exactly splits your list in half, the algorithm runs with a complexity of n*log(n). In the worst case, you choose a border element every time, and you end up with a complexity of n^2. In listing 4.10, we choose the middle element of the list, which is a good choice for the frequent case of preordered sublists.

Listing 4.10   Quicksort with lists

```
def quickSort(list) {
    if (list.size() < 2) return list
    def pivot  = list[list.size().intdiv(2)]
    def left   = list.findAll {item -> item <  pivot }
    def middle = list.findAll {item -> item == pivot }
    def right  = list.findAll {item -> item >  pivot }
    return (quickSort(left) + middle + quickSort(right))
}

assert quickSort([])      == []
assert quickSort([1])     == [1]
assert quickSort([1,2])   == [1,2]
```

❶ Classify by pivot

Recursive calls

---

[1] See http://en.wikipedia.org/wiki/Quicksort.

```
assert quickSort([2,1])              == [1,2]
assert quickSort([3,1,2])            == [1,2,3]                    ❷ Duck-
assert quickSort([3,1,2,2])          == [1,2,2,3]                    typed
assert quickSort([1.0f,'a',10,null])== [null, 1.0f, 10, 'a']  ←┐    items
assert quickSort('Karin and Dierk')  ==  ⎞   Duck-typed
'   DKaadeiiknnrr'.toList()               ❸   structure
```

In contrast to what we said earlier, we actually use not two but three lists in ❶. Use this implementation when you don't want to lose items that appear multiple times.

Our duck-typing approach is powerful when it comes to sorting different types. We can sort a list of mixed content types, as at ❷, or even sort a string, as at ❸. This is possible because we did not demand any specific type to hold our items. As long as that type implements size, getAt(*index*), and findAll, we are happy to treat it as a *sortable*. Actually, we used duck typing twice: for the items and for the structure.

BY THE WAY The sort method that comes with Groovy uses Java's sorting implementation that beats our example in terms of worst-case performance. It guarantees a complexity of n*log(n). However, we win on a different front.

Of course, our implementation could be optimized in multiple dimensions. Our goal was to be tidy and flexible, not to be the fastest on the block.

If we had to explain the Quicksort algorithm without the help of Groovy, we would sketch it in pseudocode that looks exactly like listing 4.10. In other words, the Groovy code itself is the best description of what it does. Imagine what this can mean to your codebase, when all your code reads like it was a formal documentation of its purpose!

You have seen lists to be one of Groovy's strongest workhorses. They are always at hand; they are easy to specify in-line, and using them is easy due to the operators supported. The plethora of available methods may be intimidating at first, but that is also the source of lists' power.

You are now able to add them to your carriage and let them pull the weight of your code.

The next section about maps will follow the same principles that you have seen for lists: extending the Java collection's capabilities while providing efficient shortcuts.

4.3 *Working with maps*

Suppose you were about to learn the vocabulary of a new language, and you set out to find the most efficient way of doing so. It would surely be beneficial to focus on those words that appear most often in your texts. So, you would take a collection of your texts and analyze the word frequencies in that text corpus.[2]

What Groovy means do you have to do this? For the time being, assume that you can work on a large string. You have numerous ways of splitting this string into words. But how do you count and store the word frequencies? You cannot have a distinct variable for each possible word you encounter. Finding a way of storing frequencies in a list is possible but inconvenient—more suitable for a brain teaser than for good code. Maps come to the rescue.

Some pseudocode to solve the problem could look like this:

```
for each word {
    if (frequency of word is not known)
        frequency[word] = 0
    frequency[word] += 1
}
```

This looks like the list syntax, but with strings as indexes rather than integers. In fact, Groovy maps appear like lists, allowing any arbitrary object to be used for indexing.

In order to describe the map datatype, we show how maps can be specified, what operations and methods are available for maps, some surprisingly convenient features of maps, and, of course, a map-based solution for the word-frequency exercise.

4.3.1 *Specifying maps*

The specification of maps is analogous to the list specification that you saw in the previous section. Just like lists, maps make use of the subscript operator to retrieve and assign values. The difference is that maps can use any arbitrary type as an argument to the subscript operator, where lists are bound to integer indexes. Whereas lists are aware of the sequence of their entries, maps are generally not. Specialized maps like `java.util.TreeMap` may have a sequence to their keys, though.

---

[2] Analyzing word frequencies in a text corpus is a common task in computer linguistics and is used for optimizing computer-based learning, search engines, voice recognition, and machine translation programs.

Simple maps are specified with square brackets around a sequence of items, delimited with commas. The key feature of maps is that the items are key-value pairs that are delimited by colons:

```
[key:value, key:value, key:value]
```

In principle, any arbitrary type can be used for keys or values. When using exotic[3] types for keys, you need to obey the rules as outlined in the Javadoc for `java.util.Map`.

The character sequence `[:]` declares an empty map. Maps are by default of type `java.util.HashMap` and can also be declared explicitly by calling the respective constructor. The resulting map can still be used with the subscript operator. In fact, this works with any type of map, as you see in listing 4.11 with type `java.util.TreeMap`.

Listing 4.11 Specifying maps

```
def myMap = [a:1, b:2, c:3]

assert myMap instanceof HashMap
assert myMap.size()  == 3
assert myMap['a']    == 1

def emptyMap = [:]
assert emptyMap.size() == 0

def explicitMap = new TreeMap()
explicitMap.putAll(myMap)
assert explicitMap['a'] == 1
```

In listing 4.11, we use the `putAll(Map)` method from `java.util.Map` to easily fill the example map. An alternative would have been to pass `myMap` as an argument to `TreeMap`'s constructor.

For the common case of having keys of type `String`, you can leave out the string markers (single or double quotes) in a map declaration:

```
assert ['a':1] == [a:1]
```

Such a convenience declaration is allowed only if the key contains no special characters (it needs to follow the rules for valid identifiers) and is not a Groovy keyword.

---

[3] *Exotic* in this sense refers to types whose instances change their `hashCode` during their lifetime. There is also a corner case with GStrings if their values write themselves lazily.

This notation can also get in the way when, for example, the content of a local variable is used as a key. Suppose you have local variable x with content 'a'. Because [x:1] is equal to ['x':1], how can you make it equal to ['a':1]? The trick is that you can force Groovy to recognize a symbol as an expression by putting it inside parentheses:

```
def x = 'a'
assert ['x':1] == [x:1]
assert ['a':1] == [(x):1]
```

It's rare to require this functionality, but when you need keys that are derived from local symbols (local variables, fields, properties), forgetting the parentheses is a likely source of errors.

4.3.2 Using map operators

The simplest operations with maps are storing objects in the map with a *key* and retrieving them back using that key. Listing 4.12 demonstrates how to do that. One option for retrieving is using the subscript operator. As you have probably guessed, this is implemented with map's getAt method. A second option is to use the key like a *property* with a simple dot-syntax. You will learn more about properties in chapter 7. A third option is the get method, which additionally allows you to pass a default value to be returned if the key is not yet in the map. If no default is given, null will be used as the default. If on a get(key, default) call the key is not found and the default is returned, the *key:default* pair is added to the map.

Listing 4.12 Accessing maps (GDK map methods)

```
def myMap = [a:1, b:2, c:3]

assert myMap['a']      == 1       Retrieve
assert myMap.a         == 1       existing
assert myMap.get('a')  == 1       elements
assert myMap.get('a',0) == 1

assert myMap['d']      == null    Attempt to retrieve
assert myMap.d         == null    missing elements
assert myMap.get('d')  == null

assert myMap.get('d',0) == 0      Supply a
assert myMap.d          == 0      default value

myMap['d'] = 1                    Simple
assert myMap.d == 1              assignments
myMap.d = 2                       in the map
assert myMap.d == 2
```

Assignments to maps can be done using the subscript operator or via the *dot-key* syntax. If the key in the *dot-key* syntax contains special characters, it can be put into string markers, like so:

```
myMap = ['a.b':1]
assert myMap.'a.b' == 1
```

Just writing myMap.a.b would not work here—that would be the equivalent of calling myMap.getA().getB().

Listing 4.13 shows how information can easily be gleaned from maps, largely using core JDK methods from java.util.Map. Using equals, size, containsKey, and containsValue as in listing 4.13 is straightforward. The method keySet returns a *set* of keys, a collection that is flat like a list but has no duplicate entries and no inherent ordering. See the Javadoc of java.util.Set for details. In order to compare the keySet against our list of known keys, we need to convert this list to a set. This is done with a small service method toSet.

The value method returns the list of values. Because maps have no idea how their keys are ordered, there is no foreseeable ordering in the list of values. To make it comparable with our known list of values, we convert both to a set.

Maps can be converted into a collection by calling the entrySet method, which returns a set of entries where each entry can be asked for its key and value property.

Listing 4.13 Query methods on maps

```
def myMap = [a:1, b:2, c:3]
def other = [b:2, c:3, a:1]

assert myMap == other        ◁— Call to equals

assert myMap.isEmpty()   == false
assert myMap.size()      == 3
assert myMap.containsKey('a')                           Normal JDK
assert myMap.containsValue(1)                           methods
assert myMap.keySet()         == toSet(['a','b','c'])
assert toSet(myMap.values()) == toSet([1,2,3])
assert myMap.entrySet() instanceof Collection

assert myMap.any   {entry -> entry.value > 2  }    ❶ Methods
assert myMap.every {entry -> entry.key   < 'd'}       added by GDK

def toSet(list){
    new java.util.HashSet(list)            Utility method used
}                                           for assertions
```

The GDK adds two more informational methods to the JDK map type: any and every, as in ❶. They work analogously to the identically named methods for lists: They return a Boolean value to tell whether *any* or *every* entry in the map satisfies a given closure.

With the information about the map, we can iterate over it in a number of ways: over the entries, or over keys and values separately. Because the sets that are returned from keySet and entrySet are collections, we can use them with the *for-in-collection* type loops. Listing 4.14 goes through some of the possible combinations.

Listing 4.14 Iterating over maps (GDK)

```
def myMap = [a:1, b:2, c:3]

def store = ''
myMap.each {entry ->                  Iterate over
    store += entry.key                entries
    store += entry.value
}
assert store.contains('a1')
assert store.contains('b2')
assert store.contains('c3')

store = ''
myMap.each {key, value ->             Iterate over
    store += key                      keys/values
    store += value
}
assert store.contains('a1')
assert store.contains('b2')
assert store.contains('c3')

store = ''
for (key in myMap.keySet()) {         Iterate over
    store += key                      just the keys
}
assert store.contains('a')
assert store.contains('b')
assert store.contains('c')

store = ''
for (value in myMap.values()) {       Iterate over
    store += value                    just the values
}
assert store.contains('1')
assert store.contains('2')
assert store.contains('3')
```

Map's each method uses closures in two ways: Passing one parameter into the closure means that it is an *entry*; passing two parameters means it is a key and a value. The latter is more convenient to work with for common cases.

NOTE   Listing 4.14 uses three assertions on the store string instead of a single one. This is because the sequence of entries is not guaranteed.

Finally, map content can be changed in various ways, as shown in listing 4.15. Removing elements works with the original JDK methods. New capabilities that the GDK introduces are as follows:

- Creating a subMap of all entries with keys from a given collection
- findAll entries in a map that satisfy a given closure
- find one entry that satisfies a given closure, where unlike lists there is no notion of a *first* entry, because there is no ordering in maps
- collect in a list whatever a closure returns for each entry, optionally adding to a given collection

Listing 4.15 Changing map content and building new objects from it

```
def myMap = [a:1, b:2, c:3]
myMap.clear()
assert myMap.isEmpty()

myMap = [a:1, b:2, c:3]
myMap.remove('a')
assert myMap.size() == 2

myMap = [a:1, b:2, c:3]                     ❶  Create a view onto
def abMap = myMap.subMap(['a','b'])            the original map
assert abMap.size() == 2

abMap = myMap.findAll    { entry -> entry.value < 3}
assert abMap.size() == 2
assert abMap.a        == 1

def found = myMap.find   { entry -> entry.value < 2}
assert found.key     == 'a'
assert found.value == 1

def doubled = myMap.collect { entry -> entry.value *= 2}
assert doubled instanceof List
assert doubled.every    {item -> item %2 == 0}
```

```
def addTo = []
myMap.collect(addTo)     { entry -> entry.value *= 2}
assert doubled instanceof List
assert addTo.every        {item -> item %2 == 0}
```

The first two examples (`clear` and `remove`) are from the core JDK; the rest are all GDK methods. Only the `subMap` method, at ❶, is particularly new here; `collect`, `find`, and `findAll` act as they would with lists, operating on map entries instead of list elements. The `subMap` method is analogous to `subList`, but it specifies a collection of keys as a filter for the view onto the original map.

In order to assert that the `collect` method works as expected, we recall a trick that we learned about lists: We use the `every` method on the list to make sure that every entry is even. The `collect` method comes with a second version that takes an addition collection parameter. It adds all closure results directly to this collection, avoiding the need to create temporary lists.

From the list of available methods that you have seen for other datatypes, you may miss our dearly beloved `isCase` for use with `grep` and `switch`. Don't we want to classify with maps? Well, we need to be more specific: Do we want to classify by the keys or by the values? Either way, an appropriate `isCase` is available when working on the map's `keySet` or `values`.

The GDK introduces two more methods for the map datatype: `asImmutable` and `asSynchronized`. These methods use `Collections.unmodifiableMap` and `Collections.synchronizedMap` to protect the map from unintended content changes and concurrent access. See these methods' Javadocs for more details on the topic.

4.3.3 *Maps in action*

In listing 4.16, we revisit our initial example of counting word frequencies in a text corpus. The strategy is to use a map with each distinct word serving as a key. The mapped value of that word is its frequency in the text corpus. We go through all words in the text and increase the frequency value of that respective word in the map. We need to make sure that we can increase the value when a word is hit the first time and there is no entry yet in the map. Luckily, the `get(key,default)` method does the job.

We then take all keys, put them in a list, and sort it such that it reflects the order of frequency. Finally, we play with the capabilities of lists, ranges, and strings to print a nice statistic.

The text corpus under analysis is Baloo the Bear's anthem on his attitude toward life.

Listing 4.16   Counting word frequency with maps

```
def textCorpus =
"""
Look for the bare necessities
The simple bare necessities
Forget about your worries and your strife
I mean the bare necessities
Old Mother Nature's recipes
That bring the bare necessities of life
"""

def words = textCorpus.tokenize()
def wordFrequency = [:]
words.each { word ->
    wordFrequency[word] = wordFrequency.get(word,0) + 1      ◁─❶
}
def wordList = wordFrequency.keySet().toList()
wordList.sort { wordFrequency[it] }      ◁─┐
                                          ❷

def statistic = "\n"
wordList[-1..-6].each { word ->
    statistic += word.padLeft(12)      + ': '
    statistic += wordFrequency[word] + "\n"
}
assert statistic ==
"""
        bare: 4
 necessities: 4
         the: 3
        your: 2
         for: 1
     recipes: 1
"""
```

❶ The example nicely combines our knowledge of Groovy's datatypes. Counting the word frequency is essentially a one-liner. It's even shorter than the pseudocode that we used to start this section.

❷ Having the sort method on the wordList accept a closure turns out to be very beneficial, because it is able to implement its comparing logic on the wordFrequency map—on an object totally different from the wordList. Just as an exercise, try to do that in Java, count the lines, and judge the expressiveness of either solution.

Lists and maps make a powerful duo. There are whole languages that build on just these two datatypes (such as Perl, with list and hash) and implement all other datatypes and even objects upon them.

Their power comes from the complete and mindfully engineered Java Collections Framework. Thanks to Groovy, this power is now right at our fingertips.

Until now, we carelessly switched back and forth between Groovy and Java collection datatypes. We will throw more light on this interplay in the next section.

4.4 *Notes on Groovy collections*

The Java Collections API is the basis for all the nice support that Groovy gives you through lists and maps. In fact, Groovy not only uses the same abstractions, it even works on the very same classes that make up the Java Collections API.

This is exceptionally convenient for those who come from Java and already have a good understanding of it. If you haven't, and you are interested in more background information, have a look at your Javadoc starting at `java.util.Collection`.

Your JDK also ships with a guide and a tutorial about Java collections. It is located in your JDK's doc folder under guide/collections.

One of the typical peculiarities of the Java collections is that you shouldn't try to *structurally* change one while iterating through it. A *structural* change is one that adds an entry, removes an entry, or changes the sequence of entries when the collection is sequence-aware. This applies even when iterating through a view onto the collection, such as using `list[range]`.

4.4.1 *Understanding concurrent modification*

If you fail to meet this constraint, you will see a `ConcurrentModificationException`. For example, you cannot remove all elements from a list by iterating through it and removing the first element at each step:

```
def list = [1, 2, 3, 4]
list.each{ list.remove(0) }
// throws ConcurrentModificationException !!
```

> **NOTE** *Concurrent* in this sense does not necessarily mean that a second thread changed the underlying collection. As shown in the example, even a single thread of control can break the "structural stability" constraint.

In this case, the correct solution is to use the `clear` method. The Collections API has lots of such specialized methods. When searching for alternatives, consider `collect`, `addAll`, `removeAll`, `findAll`, and `grep`.

This leads to a second issue: Some methods work on a copy of the collection and return it when finished; other methods work directly on the collection object they were called on (we call this the *receiver*[4] object).

4.4.2 *Distinguishing between copy and modify semantics*

Generally, there is no easy way to anticipate whether a method modifies the receiver or returns a copy. Some languages have naming conventions for this, but Groovy couldn't do so because all Java methods are directly visible in Groovy and Java's method names could not be made compliant to such a convention. But Groovy tries to adapt to Java and follow the heuristics that you can spot when looking through the Collections API:

- Methods that modify the receiver typically don't return a collection. Examples: `add`, `addAll`, `remove`, `removeAll`, and `retainAll`. Counter-example: `sort`.

- Methods that return a collection typically don't modify the receiver. Examples: `grep`, `findAll`, `collect`. Counter-example: `sort`. Yes, `sort` is a counter-example for both, because it returns a collection and modifies the receiver.

- Methods that modify the receiver have *imperative* names. They sound like there could be an exclamation mark behind them. (Indeed, this is Ruby's naming convention for such methods.) Examples: `add`, `addAll`, `remove`, `removeAll`, `retainAll`, `sort`. Counter-examples: `collect`, `grep`, `findAll`, which are imperative but do not modify the receiver and return a modified copy.

- The preceding rules can be mapped to operators, by applying them to the names of their method counterparts: `<<` `leftShift` is imperative and modifies the receiver (on lists, unfortunately not on strings—doing so would break Java's invariant of strings being immutable); `+` `plus` is not imperative and returns a copy.

These are not clear rules but only heuristics to give you some guidance. Whenever you're in doubt and object identity is important, have a look at the documentation or write a few assertions.

---

[4] From the Smalltalk notion of describing method calls on an object as sending a message to the receiver.

4.5 Summary

This has been a long trip through the valley of Groovy's datatypes. There were lots of different paths to explore that led to new interesting places.

We introduced ranges as objects that—as opposed to control structures—have their own time and place of creation, can be passed to methods as parameters, and can be returned from method calls. This makes them very flexible, and once the concept of a range is available, many uses beyond simple control structures suggest themselves. The most natural example you have seen is extracting a section of a list using a range as the operand to the list's subscript operator.

Lists and maps are more familiar to Java programmers than ranges but have suffered from a lack of language support in Java itself. Groovy recognizes just how often these datatypes are used, gives them special treatment in terms of literal declarations, and of course provides operators and extra methods to make life even easier. The lists and maps used in Groovy are the same ones encountered in Java and come with the same rules and restrictions, although these become less onerous due to some of the additional methods available on the collections.

Throughout our coverage of Groovy's datatypes, you have seen closures used ubiquitously for making functionality available in a simple and unobtrusive manner. In the next chapter, we will demystify the concept, explain the usual and the not-so-usual applications, and show how you can spice up your own code with closures.

Working with closures 5

I wouldn't like to build a tool that could only do what I had been able to imagine for it.

—Bjarne Stroustrup

Closures are important. Very important. They're arguably one of the most useful features of Groovy—but at the same time they can be a strange concept until you fully understand them. In order to get the best out of Groovy, or to understand anyone else's Groovy code, you're going to have to be comfortable with them. Not just "met them once at a wedding" comfortable, but "invite them over for a barbecue on the weekend" comfortable.

Now, we don't want to scare you away. Closures aren't *hard*—they're just different than anything you might be used to. In a way, this is strange, because one of the chief tenets of object-orientation is that objects have behavior as well as data. Closures are objects whose main purpose in life is their behavior—that's almost all there is to them.

In the past few chapters, you've seen a few uses of closures, so you might already have a good idea of what they're about. Please forgive us if we seem to be going over the same ground again—it's so important, we'd rather repeat ourselves than leave you without a good grasp of the basic principles.

In this chapter, we will introduce the fundamental concept of closures (again), explain their benefits, and then show how they can be declared and called. After this basic treatment, we will look in a bit more depth at other methods available on closures and the *scope* of a closure—that is, the data and members that can be accessed within it—as well as consider what it means to return from a closure. We end the chapter with a discussion of how closures can be used to implement many common design patterns and how they alleviate the need for some others by solving the problem in a different manner.

So, without further ado, let's take a look at what closures really are in the first place.

5.1 A gentle introduction to closures

Let's start with a simple definition of closures, and then we'll expand on it with an example. A *closure* is a piece of code wrapped up as an object. It acts like a method in that it can take parameters and it can return a value. It's a normal object in that you can pass a reference to it around just as you can a reference to any other object. Don't forget that the JVM has no idea you're running Groovy code, so there's nothing particularly odd that you *could* be doing with a closure object. It's just an object. Groovy provides a very easy way of creating closure objects and enables some very smart behavior.

If it helps you to think in terms of real-world analogies, consider an envelope with a piece of paper in it. For other objects, the paper might have the values of variables on it: "x=5, y=10" and so on. For a closure, the paper would have a list of instructions. You can give that envelope to someone, and that person might decide to follow the instructions on the piece of paper, or they might give the envelope to someone else. They might decide to follow the instructions lots of times, with a different context each time. For instance, the piece of paper might say, "Send a letter to the person you're thinking of," and the person might flip through the pages of their address book thinking of every person listed in it, following the instructions over and over again, once for each contact in that address book.

The Groovy equivalent of that example would be something like this:

```
Closure envelope = { person -> new Letter(person).send() }
addressBook.each (envelope)
```

That's a fairly long-winded way of going about it, and not idiomatic Groovy, but it shows the distinction between the closure itself (in this case, the value of the envelope variable) and its use (as a parameter to the each method). Part of what makes closures hard to understand when coming to them for the first time is that they're usually used in an abbreviated form. Groovy makes them very concise because they're so frequently used—but that brevity can be detrimental to the learning process. Just for the comparison, here's the previous code written using the shorthand Groovy provides. When you see this shorthand, it's often worth mentally separating it out into the longer form:

```
addressBook.each { new Letter(it).send() }
```

It's still a method call passing a closure as the single parameter, but that's all hidden—passing a closure to a method is sufficiently common in Groovy that there are special rules for it. Similarly, if the closure needs to take only a single parameter to work on, Groovy provides a default name—it—so that you don't need to declare it specifically. That's how our example ends up so short when we use all the Groovy shortcuts.

Now, we're in danger of getting ahead of ourselves here, so we'll pause and think about why we would want to have closures in the first place. Just keep remembering: They're objects that are associated with some code, and Groovy provides neat syntax for them.

5.2 *The case for closures*

Java as a *platform* is great: portable, stable, scalable, and reasonably well-performing. Java as a *language* has a lot of advantages but unfortunately also some shortcomings.

Some of those deficiencies can be addressed in Groovy through the use of closures. We'll look at two particular areas that benefit from closures: performing everyday tasks with collections, and using resources in a safe manner. In these two common situations, you need to be able to perform some logic that is the same for every case and execute arbitrary code to do the actual work. In the case of collections, that code is the body of the iterator; in the case of resource handling, it's the use of the resource after it's been acquired and before it's been released. In general terms, such a mechanism uses a *callback* to execute the work. Closures are Groovy's way of providing transparent callback targets as first-class citizens.

5.2.1 *Using iterators*

A typical construction in Java code is traversing a collection with an iterator:

```
// Java
for (Iterator iter = collection.iterator(); iter.hasNext();){
    ItemType item = (ItemType) iter.next();
    // do something with item
}
```

With a specific implementation of `Collection`, or an interface such as `List`, there may be options such as the following:

```
// Java
for (int i=0; i < list.size(); i++){
    ItemType item = (ItemType) list.get(i);
    // do something with item
}
```

Java 5 improves the situation with two new features: *generics* and the enhanced `for` statement. Generics allow both to be written without casts; indeed, straightforward iteration can be written in a form that is very similar to the Groovy `for` loop, using `:` instead of `in`:

```
// Java 5
for (ItemType item : list) {
    // do something with item
}
```

The syntax may not be ideal[1]—the Java 5 designers were constrained in terms of adding keywords—but it gets the job done, right? Well, nearly. For one thing, it's limited to Java 5—many developers still work with Java 1.4 or earlier and are forced to write a relatively large amount of code for what is such a common operation. It's relatively simple to get this code right—but familiarity breeds contempt, and it's all too easy to miss errors within loop constructs *because* you're so used to seeing them in method after method.

A second issue with the enhanced `for` statement brings us closer to closures, however. Clearly it's useful to have a `for` loop that iterates through every item in a collection—otherwise Groovy wouldn't have it, for starters. (Groovy's `for` statement is somewhat broader in scope than Java 5's—see chapter 6 for more details.) It's useful, but it's not everything we could wish for. There are common patterns for *why* we want to iterate through a collection, such as finding whether a particular condition is met by any element, finding *all* the elements met by a condition, or transforming each element into another, thereby creating a new collection.

It would be madness to have a specialized syntax for all of those patterns. Making a language too smart in a non-extensible way ends up like a road through the jungle—it's fine when you're doing something anticipated by the designers, but as soon as you stray off the path, life is tough. So, without direct language support for all those patterns, what's left? Each of the patterns relies on executing a particular piece of code again and again, once for each element of the collection. Java has no concept of "a particular piece of code" unless it's buried in a method. That method can be part of an interface implementation, but at that point each piece of code needs its own (possibly anonymous) class, and life gets very messy.

Groovy uses closures to specify the code to be executed each time and adds the extra methods (`each`, `find`, `findAll`, `collect`, and so forth) to the collection classes to make them readily available. Those methods aren't magic, though—they're simple Groovy, because closures allow the *controlling* logic (the iteration) to be separated from the code to execute for every element. If you find yourself wanting a similar construct that isn't already covered by Groovy, you can add it easily.

---

[1] The Groovy designers considered making the Groovy `for` loop appear exactly as it does in Java 5, but they found that the colon was an unfortunate choice because you cannot read the expression fluently without replacing the colon with an English word. Using the `in` keyword better reveals the meaning of the expression and the role of the operands in use.

Separating iteration logic from what to do on each iteration is not the only reason for introducing the closure concept. A second reason that may be even more important is the use of closures when handling resources.

5.2.2 *Handling resources*

How many times have you seen code that opens a stream but calls `close` at the end of the method, overlooking the fact that the `close` statement may never be reached when an exception occurs while processing? So, it needs to be protected with a `try-catch` block. No—wait—that should be `try-finally`, or should it? And inside the `finally` block, `close` can throw another exception that needs to be handled. There are too many details to remember, and so resource handling is often implemented incorrectly. With Groovy's closure support, you can put that logic in one place and use it like this:

```
new File('myfile.txt').eachLine { println it }
```

The `eachLine` method of `File` now takes care of opening and closing the file input stream properly. This guards you from accidentally producing a resource leak of file handles.

Streams are just the most obvious tip of the resource-handling iceberg. Database connections, native handles such as graphic resources, network connections—even your GUI is a resource that needs to be managed (that is, repainted correctly at the right time), and observers and event listeners need to be removed when the time comes, or you end up with a memory leak.

Forgetting to clean up correctly in all situations *ought* to be a problem that only affects neophyte Java programmers, but because the language provides little help beyond `try-catch-finally`, even experienced developers end up making mistakes. It is possible to code around this in an orderly manner, but Java leads inexperienced programmers away from centralized resource handling. Code structures are duplicated, and the probability of not-so-perfect implementations rises with the number of duplicates.

Resource-handling code is often tested poorly. Projects that measure their test coverage typically struggle to fully cover this area. That is because duplicated, widespread resource handling is difficult to test and eats up precious development time. Testing centralized handlers is easy and requires only a single test.

Let's see what resource handling solutions Java provides and why they are not used often, and then we'll show the corresponding Groovy solutions.

A common Java approach: use inner classes

In order to do centralized resource handling, you need to pass resource-using code to the handler. This should sound familiar by now—it's essentially the same problem we encountered when considering collections: The handler needs to know how to call that code, and therefore it must implement some known interface. In Java, this is frequently implemented by an inner class for two reasons: First, it allows the resource-using code to be close to the calling code (which is often useful for readability); and second, it allows the resource-using code to interact with the context of the calling code, using local variables, calling methods on the relevant object, and so on.

> **BY THE WAY** JUnit, one of the most prominent Java packages outside the JDK, follows this strategy by using the `Runnable` interface with its `runProtected` method.

Anonymous inner classes are almost solely used for this kind of pattern—if Java had closures, it's possible that anonymous inner classes might never have been invented. The rules and restrictions that come with them (and with plain inner classes) make it obvious what a wart the whole "feature" really is on the skin of what is otherwise an elegant and simple language. As soon as you have to start typing code like `MyClass.this.doSomething`, you know something is wrong—and that's aside from the amount of distracting clutter required around your code just to create it in the first place. The interaction with the context of the calling code is limited, with rules such as local variables having to be final in order to be used making life awkward.

In some ways, it's the right approach, but it looks ugly, especially when used often. Java's limitations get in the way too much to make it an elegant solution. The following example uses a `Resource` that it gets from a `ResourceHandler`, which is responsible for its proper construction and destruction. Only the boldface code is really needed for doing the job:

```java
// Java
interface ResourceUser {
  void use(Resource resource)
}

resourceHandler.handle(new ResourceUser(){
    public void use (Resource resource) {
        resource.doSomething()
    }
});
```

The Groovy equivalent of this code reveals all necessary information without any waste:

```
resourceHandler.handle { resource -> resource.doSomething() }
```

Groovy's scoping is also significantly more flexible and powerful, while removing the "code mess" that inner classes introduce.

An alternative Java approach: the Template Method pattern

Another strategy to centralize resource handling in Java is to do it in a superclass and let the resource-using code live in a subclass. This is the typical implementation of the Template Method [GOF] pattern.

The downside here is that you either end up with a proliferation of subclasses or use (maybe anonymous) inner subclasses, which brings us back to the drawbacks discussed earlier. It also introduces penalties in terms of code clarity and freedom of implementation, both of which tend to suffer when inheritance is involved. This leads us to take a close look at the dangers of abstraction proliferation.

If there were only *one* interface that could be used for the purpose of passing logic around, like our imaginary `ResourceUser` interface from the previous example, then things would not be too bad. But in Java there is no such beast—no single `ResourceUser` interface that serves all purposes. The signature of the callback method `use` needs to adapt to the purpose: the number and type of parameters, the number and type of declared exceptions, and the return type.

Therefore a variety of interfaces has evolved over time: Runnables, Observers, Listeners, Visitors, Comparators, Strategies, Commands, Controllers, and so on. This makes their use more complicated, because with every new interface, there also is a new abstraction or concept that needs to be understood.

In comparison, Groovy closures can handle any method signature, and the behavior of the controlling logic may even change depending on the signature of the closure provided to it, as you'll see later.

These two examples of pain-points in Java that can be addressed with closures are just that—examples. If they were the only problems made easier by closures, closures would still be worth having, but reality is much richer. It turns out that closures enable many patterns of programming that would be unthinkable without them.

Before you can live your dreams, however, you need to learn more about the basics of closures. Let's start with how we declare them in the first place.

5.3 *Declaring closures*

So far, we have used the simple abbreviated syntax of closures: After a method call, put your code in curly braces with parameters delimited from the closure body by an arrow.

Let's start by adding to your knowledge about the simple abbreviated syntax, and then we'll look at two more ways to declare a closure: by using them in assignments and by referring to a method.

5.3.1 *The simple declaration*

Listing 5.1 shows the simple closure syntax plus a new convenience feature. When there is only one parameter passed into the closure, its declaration is optional. The magic variable it can be used instead. See the two equivalent closure declarations in listing 5.1.

Listing 5.1 Simple abbreviated closure declaration

```
log = ''
(1..10).each{ counter -> log += counter }
assert log == '12345678910'

log = ''
(1..10).each{ log += it }
assert log == '12345678910'
```

Note that unlike counter, the magic variable it needs no declaration.

This syntax is an abbreviation because the closure object as declared by the curly braces is the last parameter of the method and would normally appear within the method's parentheses. As you will see, it is equally valid to put it inside parentheses like any other parameter, although it is hardly ever used this way:

```
log = ''
(1..10).each({ log += it })
assert log == '12345678910'
```

This syntax is simple because it uses only one parameter, the implicit parameter it. Multiple parameters can be declared in sequence, delimited by commas. A default value can optionally be assigned to parameters, in case no value is passed from the method to the closure. We will show examples in section 5.4.

TIP Think of the arrow as an indication that parameters are passed from the method on the left into the closure body on the right.

5.3.2 *Using assignments for declaration*

A second way of declaring a closure is to directly assign it to a variable:

```
def printer = { line -> println line }
```

The closure is declared inside the curly braces and assigned to the `printer` variable.

TIP Whenever you see the curly braces of a closure, think: `new Closure(){}`.

There is also a special kind of assignment, to the return value of a method:

```
def Closure getPrinter() {
    return { line -> println line }
}
```

Again, the curly braces denote the construction of a new closure object. This object is returned from the method call.

TIP Curly braces can denote the construction of a new closure object or a Groovy *block*. Blocks can be class, interface, static or object initializers, or method bodies; or can appear with the Groovy keywords `if`, `else`, `synchronized`, `for`, `while`, `switch`, `try`, `catch`, and `finally`. All other occurrences are closures.

As you see, closures are objects. They can be stored in variables, they can be passed around, and, as you probably guessed, you can call methods on them. Being objects, closures can also be returned from a method.

5.3.3 *Referring to methods as closures*

The third way of declaring a closure is to reuse something that is already declared: a method. Methods have a body, optionally return values, can take parameters, and can be called. The similarities with closures are obvious, so Groovy lets you reuse the code you already have in methods, but as a closure. Referencing a method as a closure is performed using the *reference.&* operator. The reference is used to specify which instance should be used when the closure is called, just like a normal method call to *reference.someMethod()*. Figure 5.1

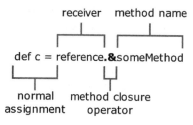

Figure 5.1
The anatomy of a simple method
closure assignment statement

shows an assignment using a method closure, breaking the statement up into its constituent parts.

Listing 5.2 demonstrates method closures in action, showing two different instances being used to give two different closures, even though the same method is invoked in both cases.

Listing 5.2 Simple method closures in action

```
class MethodClosureSample {
    int limit

    MethodClosureSample (int limit) {
        this.limit = limit
    }

    boolean validate (String value) {
        return value.length() <= limit
    }
}

MethodClosureSample first = new MethodClosureSample (6)      ① Normal
MethodClosureSample second = new MethodClosureSample (5)        constructor
                                                                calls

Closure firstClosure = first.&validate    ◁─② Method closure assignment

def words = ['long string', 'medium', 'short', 'tiny']      ④ Passing
                                          ③ Calling the       a method
                                             closure          closure
assert 'medium' == words.find (firstClosure)   ◁─            directly
assert 'short' == words.find (second.&validate)      ◁─
```

Each instance (created at ①) has a separate idea of how long a string it will deem to be valid in the `validate` method. We create a reference to that method with `first.&validate` at ② and `second.&validate`, showing that the reference can be assigned to a variable which is then passed (at ③) or passed as a parameter to the `find` method at ④. We use a sample list of words to check that the closures are doing what we expect them to.

Method closures are limited to instance methods, but they do have another interesting feature—runtime overload resolution, also known as *multimethods*. You will find out more about multimethods in chapter 7, but listing 5.3 gives a taste.

Listing 5.3 Multimethod closures—the same method name called with different parameters is used to call different implementations

```
class MultiMethodSample {

    int mysteryMethod (String value) {
        return value.length()
    }

    int mysteryMethod (List list) {
        return list.size()
    }

    int mysteryMethod (int x, int y) {
        return x+y
    }
}

MultiMethodSample instance = new MultiMethodSample()
Closure multi = instance.&mysteryMethod

assert 10 == multi ('string arg')
assert 3 == multi (['list', 'of', 'values'])
assert 14 == multi (6, 8)
```

❶ Only a single closure is created

❷ Different implementations are called based on argument types

Here a single instance is used, and indeed a single closure (at ❶)—but each time it's called, a different method implementation is invoked, at ❷. We don't want to rush ahead of ourselves, but you'll see a lot more of this kind of dynamic behavior in chapter 7.

Now that you've seen all the ways of declaring a closure, it's worth pausing for a moment and seeing them all together, performing the same function, just with different declaration styles.

5.3.4 *Comparing the available options*

Listing 5.4 shows all of these ways of creating and using closures: through simple declaration, assignment to variables, and method closures. In each case, we call the each method on a simple map, providing a closure that doubles a single value. By the time we've finished, we've doubled each value three times.

Listing 5.4 Full closure declaration examples

```
map = ['a':1, 'b':2]
map.each{ key, value -> map[key] = value * 2 }          ❶ Parameter sequence
assert map == ['a':2, 'b':4]                               with commas

doubler = {key, value -> map[key] = value * 2 }
map.each(doubler)                                       ❷ Assign and then call
assert map == ['a':4, 'b':8]                               a closure reference

def doubleMethod (entry){
    map[entry.key] = entry.value * 2                   ❸ A usual method
}                                                          declaration
doubler = this.&doubleMethod
map.each(doubler)                                       ❹ Reference and call a
assert map == ['a':8, 'b':16]                              method as a closure
```

In ❶, we pass the closure as the parameter directly. This is the form you've seen most commonly so far.

The declaration of the closure in ❷ is disconnected from its immediate use. The curly braces are Groovy's way to declare a closure, so we assign a closure object to the variable doubler. Some people incorrectly interpret this line as assigning the *result* of a closure call to a variable. Don't fall into that trap! The closure is not yet called, only declared, until we reach it. There you see that passing the closure as an argument to the each method via a reference is exactly the same as declaring the closure *in-place*, the style that we followed in all the previous examples.

The method declared in ❸ is a perfectly ordinary method. There is no trace of our intention to use it as a closure.

In ❹, the reference.& operator is used for referencing a method name as a closure. Again, the method is not immediately called; the execution of the method occurs as part of the next line. This is just like ❷. The closure is passed to the each method, which calls it back for each entry in the map.

Typing[2] is optional in Groovy, and consequently it is optional for closure parameters. A special thing about closure parameters with explicit types is that this type is not checked at compile-time but at runtime.

---

[2] The word *typing* has two meanings: declaring object types and typing keystrokes. Although Groovy provides optional typing, you still have to key in your program code.

In order to fully understand how closures work and how to use them within your code, you need to find out how to invoke them. That is the topic of the next section.

5.4 *Using closures*

So far, you have seen how to declare a closure for the purpose of passing it for execution, to the each method for example. But what happens inside the each method? How does it call your closure? If you knew this, you could come up with equally smart implementations. We'll first look at how simple calling a closure is and then move on to explore some advanced methods that the Closure type has to offer.

5.4.1 *Calling a closure*

Suppose we have a reference x pointing to a closure; we can call it with x.call() or simply x(). You have probably guessed that any arguments to the closure call go between the parentheses.

We start with a simple example. Listing 5.5 shows the same closure being called both ways.

Listing 5.5 Calling closures

```
def adder = { x, y -> return x+y }

assert adder(4, 3) == 7
assert adder.call(2, 6) == 8
```

We start off by declaring pretty much the simplest possible closure—a piece of code that returns the sum of the two parameters it is passed. Then we call the closure both directly and using the call method. Both ways of calling the closure achieve exactly the same effect.

Now let's try something more involved. In listing 5.6, we demonstrate calling a closure from within a method body and how the closure gets passed into that method in the first place. The example measures the execution time of the closure.

Listing 5.6 Calling closures

```
def benchmark(repeat, Closure worker){        ❶  Put closures last
    start = System.currentTimeMillis()        ❷  Some pre-work
```

```
    repeat.times{worker(it)}
    stop = System.currentTimeMillis()
    return stop - start
}
slow = benchmark(10000) { (int) it / 2 }
fast = benchmark(10000) { it.intdiv(2) }
assert fast * 15 < slow
```

❹ Some post-work

❸ Call closure the given number of times

❺ Pass different closures for analysis

Do you remember our performance investigation for regular expression patterns in listing 3.7? We needed to duplicate the benchmarking logic because we had no means to declare how to benchmark *something*. Now you know how. You can pass a closure into the benchmark method, where some pre- and post-work takes control of proper timing.

We put the closure parameter at the end of the parameter list in ❶ to allow the simple abbreviated syntax when calling the method. In the example, we declare the type of the closure. This is only to make things more obvious. The Closure type is optional.

We effectively start timing the benchmark at ❷. From a general point of view, this is arbitrary pre-work like opening a file or connecting to a database. It just so happens that our resource is time.

At ❸, we call the given closure as many times as our repeat parameter demands. We pass the current count to the closure to make things more interesting. From a general point of view, a resource is passed to the closure.

We stop timing at ❹ and calculate the time taken by the closure. Here is the place for the post-work: closing files, flushing buffers, returning connections to the pool, and so on.

The payoff comes at ❺. We can now pass *logic* to the benchmark method. Note that we use the simple abbreviated syntax and use the magic it to refer to the current count. As a side effect, we learn that the general number division takes more than 15 times longer than the optimized intdiv method.

BY THE WAY This kind of benchmarking should not be taken too seriously. There are all kinds of effects that can heavily influence such wall-clock based measurements: machine characteristics, operating system, current machine load, JDK version, Just-In-time compiler and Hotspot settings, and so on.

Figure 5.2 shows the UML sequence diagram for the general calling scheme of the declaring object that creates the closure, the method invocation on the caller, and the caller's callback to the given closure.

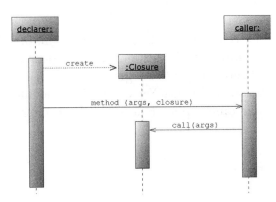

Figure 5.2
UML sequence diagram of the typical
sequence of method calls when a declarer
creates a closure and attaches it to a
method call on the caller, which in turn
calls that closure's `call` method

When calling a closure, you need to pass exactly as many arguments to the closure as it expects to receive, unless the closure defines default values for its parameters. This default value is used when you omit the corresponding argument. The following is a variant of the addition closure as used in listing 5.5, with a default value for the second parameter and two calls—one that passes two arguments, and one that relies on the default:

```
def adder = { x, y=5 -> return x+y }

assert adder(4, 3) == 7
assert adder.call(7) == 12
```

For the use of default parameters in closures, the same rules apply as for default parameters for methods. Also, closures can be used with a parameter list of variable length in the same way that methods can. We will cover this in section 7.1.2.

At this point, you should be comfortable with passing closures to methods and have a solid understanding of how the callback is executed—see also the UML diagram in figure 5.2. Whenever you pass a closure to a method, you can be sure that a callback will be executed one way or the other (maybe only conditionally), depending on that method's logic. Closures are capable of more than just being called, though. In the next section, you see what else they have to offer.

5.4.2 *More closure methods*

The class `groovy.lang.Closure` is an ordinary class, albeit one with extraordinary power and extra language support. It has various methods available beyond `call`. We will present the most the important ones—even though you will usually just declare and call closures, it's nice to know there's some extra power available when you need it.

Reacting on the parameter count

A simple example of how useful it is to react on the parameter count of a closure is map's each method, which we discussed in section 4.3.2. It passes either a Map.Entry object or key and value separately into the given closure, depending on whether the closure takes one or two arguments. You can retrieve the information about expected parameter count (and types, if declared) by calling closure's getParameterTypes method:

```
def caller (Closure closure){
    closure.getParameterTypes().size()
}

assert caller { one -> }       == 1
assert caller { one, two -> } == 2
```

As in the Map.each example, this allows for the luxury of supporting closures with different parameter styles, adapted to the caller's needs.

How to curry favor with a closure

Currying is a technique invented by Moses Schönfinkel and Gottlob Frege, and named after the logician Haskell Brooks Curry (1900..1982), a pioneer in *functional programming*. (Unsurprisingly, the functional language Haskell is also named after Curry.) The basic idea is to take a function with multiple parameters and transform it into a function with fewer parameters by fixing some of the values. A classic example is to choose some arbitrary value n and transform a function that sums two parameters into a function that takes a single parameter and adds n to it.

In Groovy, Closure's curry method returns a clone of the current closure, having bound one or more parameters to a given value. Parameters are bound to curry's arguments from left to right. Listing 5.7 gives an implementation.

Listing 5.7 A simple currying example

```
def adder = {x, y -> return x+y}
def addOne = adder.curry(1)
assert addOne(5) == 6
```

We reuse the same closure you've seen a couple of times now for general summation. We call the curry method on it to create a new closure, which acts like a simple adder, but with the value of the first parameter always fixed as 1. Finally, we check our results.

If you're new to closures or currying, now might be a good time to take a break—and pick the book up again back at the start of the currying discussion, to read it again. It's a deceptively simple concept to describe mechanically, but it can be quite difficult to internalize. Just take it slowly, and you'll be fine.

The real power of currying comes when the closure's parameters are themselves closures. This is a common construction in functional programming, but it does take a little getting used to.

For an example, suppose you are implementing a logging facility. It should support filtering of log lines, formatting them, and appending them to an output device. Each activity should be configurable. The idea is to provide a single closure for a customized version of each activity, while still allowing you to implement the overall pattern of when to apply a filter, do the formatting, and finally output the log line in one place. The following shows how currying is used to inject the customized activity into that pattern:

```
def configurator = { format, filter, line ->          ❶ Configuration
    filter(line) ? format(line) : null                     use
}
def appender = { config, append, line ->
    def out = config(line)                            ❷ Formatting
    if (out) append(out)                                   use
}

def dateFormatter    = { line -> "${new Date()}: $line" }      ❸ Filter,
def debugFilter      = { line -> line.contains('debug') }         format, and
def consoleAppender  = { line -> println line }                   output parts

def myConf = configurator.curry(dateFormatter, debugFilter)    ❹ Put it all
def myLog  = appender.curry(myConf, consoleAppender)              together

myLog('here is some debug message')
myLog('this will not be printed')
```

Closures ❶ and ❷ are like recipes: Given any filter, output format, destination, and a line to potentially log, they perform the work, delegating appropriately. The short closures in ❸ are the specific ingredients in the recipe. They could be specified every time, but we're always going to use the same ingredients. Currying (at ❹) allows us to remember just one object rather than each of the individual parts. To continue the recipe analogy, we've put all the ingredients together, and the result needs to be put in the oven whenever we want to do some logging.

Logging is often dismissed as a dry topic. But in fact, the few lines in the preceding code prove that conception wrong. As a mindful engineer, you know that log statements will be called often, and any logging facility must pay attention to performance. In particular, there should be the least possible performance hit when no log is written.

The time-consuming operations in this example are formatting and printing. Filtering is quick. With the help of closures, we laid out a code pattern which ensures that the expensive operations are not called for lines that don't need to be printed. The `configurator` and `appender` closures implement that pattern.

This pattern is extremely flexible, because the logic of how the filtering works, how the formatting is applied, and how the result is written is fully configurable (even at runtime).

With the help of closures and their `curry` method, we achieved a solution with the best possible coherence and lowest possible coupling. Note how each of the closures completely addresses exactly one concern.

This is the beginning of functional programming. See Andrew Glover's excellent online article on functional programming with Groovy closures at http://www-128.ibm.com/developerworks/library/j-pg08235/. It expands on how to use this approach for implementing your own expression language, capturing business rules, and checking your code for holding invariants.

Classification via the isCase method

Closures implement the `isCase` method to make closures work as classifiers in `grep` and `switch`. In that case, the respective argument is passed into the closure, and calling the closure needs to evaluate to a Groovy Boolean value (see section 6.1). As you see in

```
assert [1,2,3].grep{ it<3 } == [1,2]

switch(10){
    case {it%2 == 1} : assert false
}
```

this allows us to classify by arbitrary logic. Again, this is only possible because closures are objects.

Remaining methods

For the sake of completeness, it needs to be said that closures support the `clone` method in the usual Java sense.

The `asWriteable` method returns a clone of the current closure that has an additional `writeTo(Writer)` method to write the result of a closure call directly into the given `Writer`.

Finally, there are a setter and getter for the so-called *delegate*. We will cross the topic of what a delegate is and how it is used inside a closure when investigating a closure's scoping rules in the next section.

5.5 *Understanding scoping*

You have seen how to *create* closures when they are needed for a method call and how to *work* with closures when they are passed to your method. This is very powerful while still simple to use.

This section looks under the hood and deepens your understanding of what happens when you use this simple construction. We explore what data and methods you can access from a closure, what difference using the `this` reference makes, and how to put your knowledge to the test with a classic example designed to test any language's expressiveness.

This is a bit of a technical section, and you can safely skip it on first read. However, at some point you may want to read it and learn how Groovy can provide all those clever tricks. In fact, knowing the details will enable you to come up with particularly elegant solutions yourself.

What is available inside a closure is called its *scope*. The scope defines

- What local variables are accessible
- What `this` (the current object) refers to
- What fields and methods are accessible

We start with an explanation of the behavior that you have seen so far. For that purpose, we revisit a piece of code that does *something* 10 times:

```
def x = 0
10.times {
    x++
}
assert x == 10
```

It is evident that the closure that is passed into the `times` method can access variable x, which is locally accessible when the closure is *declared*. Remember: The curly braces show the *declaration* time of the closure, not the *execution* time. The closure can access x for both reading and writing at *declaration* time.

This leads to a second thought: The closure surely needs to also access x at execution time. How could it increment it otherwise? But the closure is passed to the `times` method, a method that is called on the `Integer` object with value 10. That method, in turn, calls back to our closure. But the `times` method has no chance of knowing about x. So it cannot pass it to the closure, and it surely has no means of finding out what the closure is doing with it.

The only way in which this can possibly work is if the closure somehow remembers the context of its birth and carries it along throughout its lifetime. That way, it can work on that original context whenever the situation calls for it.

This *birthday context* that the closure remembers needs to be a reference, not a copy. If that context were a copy of the original one, there would be no way of changing the original from inside the closure. But our example clearly does change the value of x—otherwise the assertion would fail. Therefore, the birthday context must be a reference.

5.5.1 *The simple variable scope*

Figure 5.3 depicts your current understanding of which objects are involved in the times example and how they reference each other.

The Script creates a Closure that has a back reference to x, which is in the local scope of its declarer. Script calls the times method on the Integer 10 object, passing the declared closure as a parameter. In other words, when times is executed, a reference to the closure object lies on the stack. The times method uses this reference to execute Closure's call method, passing its local variable count to it. In this specific example, the count is not used within Closure.call. Instead, Closure.call only works on the x reference that it holds to the local variable x in Script.

Through analysis, you see that local variables are bound as a reference to the closure at declaration time.

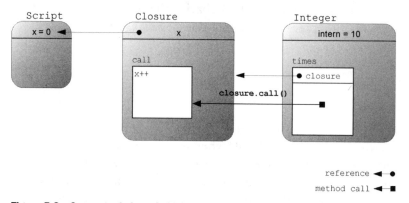

Figure 5.3   Conceptual view of object references and method calls between a calling script, an Integer object of value 10 that is used in the script, and the closure that is attached to the Integer's times method for defining something that has to be done 10 times

5.5.2 *The general closure scope*

It would not be surprising if other scope elements were treated the same as local variables: the value of `this`, fields, methods, and parameters.

This generalization is correct, but the `this` reference is a special case. Inside a closure, you could legitimately assume that `this` would refer to the current object, which is the closure object itself. On the other hand, it should make no difference whether you use `this.reference` or plain `reference` for locally accessible references. The first approach has long been used in Groovy but was changed in favor of the latter by the JSR expert group.[3]

A reference to the *declaring* object is held in a special variable called `owner`. Listing 5.8 extends the purpose of the initial example to reveal the remaining scope elements.

We implement a small class `Mother` that should give `birth` to a closure through a method with that name. The class has a field, another method, parameters, and local variables that we can study. The closure should return a list of all elements that are in the current context (aka scope). Behind the scenes, these elements will be bound at declaration time but not evaluated until the closure is called. Let's investigate the result of such a call.

> **Listing 5.8 Investigating the closure scope**

```
class Mother {
    int field = 1
    int foo(){
        return 2
    }
    Closure birth (param) {          ❶ This method creates and
        def local = 3                   returns the closure
        def closure = { caller ->
            [this, field, foo(), local, param, caller, this.owner]
        }
        return closure
    }
}

Mother julia = new Mother()
                                     ❷ Let a mother give
closure = julia.birth(4)                birth to a closure

context = closure.call(this)      ⬅❸ Call the closure
```

---

[3] The implementation of the new behavior was not yet available at the time of writing. Therefore the example contains no respective assertion but only a `println`.

```
println context[0].class.name        ◁─❹  Script
                                           ❺  No surprise?
assert context[1..4] == [1,2,3,4]    ◁┘
assert context[5] instanceof Script  ◁─❻  The calling object
assert context[6] instanceof Mother  ◁┐
                                       ❼  The declaring object
firstClosure  = julia.birth(4)
secondClosure = julia.birth(4)           ❽  Closure braces
assert false == firstClosure.is(secondClosure)  │    are like new
```

We added the optional return type to the method declaration in ❶ to point out that this method returns a closure object. A method that returns a closure is not the most common usage of closures, but every now and then it comes in handy. Note that we are at *declaration* time in this method. The list that the closure will return when called doesn't exist yet.

After having constructed a new Mother, we call its birth method at ❷ to retrieve a newly born closure object. Even now, the closure hasn't been called. The list of elements is not yet constructed.

Rubber meets road at ❸. Now we call the closure using the explicit call syntax to make it stand out. The closure constructs its list of elements from what it remembers about its birth. We store that list in a variable for further inspection. Notice that we pass ourselves as a parameter into the closure in order to make it available inside the closure as the caller.

At ❹ the example should print the script class name by the time you are reading this. Groovy versions before 1.0 printed the closure type.

The instance variable field, the result of calling foo(), the local variable local, and the parameter param all have the expected values, as demonstrated in ❺, although they were not known to the Script when it executed the closure. This is the birthday recall that we expected. Only foo() is a bit tricky. As always, it is a shortcut for this.foo(), and as we said, this refers to the closure, not to the declaring object. At this point, closures play a trick for us. They *delegate* all[4] method calls to a so-called delegate object, which by default happens to be the declaring object (that is, the *owner*). This makes the closure appear as if the enclosed code runs in the *birthday context*.

Passing the caller explicitly into the closure is the way to make it accessible inside. We demonstrate this at ❻. Throughout all previous closure examples in this book, the *calling* and the *declaring* object were identical. Therefore, we could

---

[4] Strictly speaking, not *all* method calls but only those that the closure cannot answer itself.

easily apply side effects on it. You may have thought we were side-effecting the *caller* while we were working on the *declarer*. If this sounds totally crazy to you, don't worry. The concept may be a bit too unfamiliar. Start over with the times example, if you want. Breathe deeply. It'll come in time.

Inside a closure, the magic variable owner refers to the declaring object, as shown at **❼**.

At **❽** you see that with every call to birth, a *new* closure is constructed. Think of the closures' curly braces as if the word *new* appeared before them. Behind this observation is a fundamental difference between closures and methods: Methods are constructed exactly once at class-generation time. Closures are objects and thus constructed at runtime, and there may be any number of them constructed from the same lines of code.

Figure 5.4 shows who refers to whom in listing 5.8.

Lectures about lexical scoping and closures from other languages such as Lisp, Smalltalk, Perl, Ruby, and Python typically end with some mind-boggling examples about variables with identical names, mutually overriding references, and mystic rebirth of supposed-to-be foregone contexts. These examples are like puzzles. They make for an entertaining pastime on a long winter evening, but they have no practical relevance. We will not provide any of those, because they can easily undermine your carefully built confidence in the scoping rules.

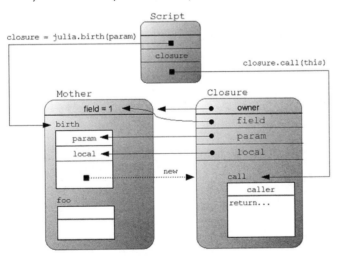

Figure 5.4
Conceptual view of object references and method calls for the general scoping example in listing 5.8, revealing the calls to the julia instance of Mother for creating a closure that is called in the trailing Script code to return all values in the current scope

Our intention is to provide a reasonable introduction to Groovy's closures. This should give you the basic understanding that you need when hunting for more complex examples in mailing lists and on the Web. Instead of giving a deliberately obscure example, however, we *will* provide one that shows how closure scopes can make an otherwise complex task straightforward.

5.5.3 *Scoping at work: the classic accumulator test*

There is a classic example to compare the power of languages by the way they support closures. One of the things it highlights is the power of the scoping rules for those languages as they apply to closures. Paul Graham first proposed this test in his excellent article "Revenge of the Nerds" (http://www.paulgraham.com/icad.html). Beside the test, his article is very interesting and informative to read. It talks about the difference a language can make. You will find good arguments in it for switching to Groovy.

In some languages, this test leads to a brain-teasing solution. Not so in Groovy. The Groovy solution is exceptionally obvious and straightforward to achieve.

Here is the original requirement statement:

"We want to write a function that generates accumulators—a function that takes a number n, and returns a function that takes another number i and returns n incremented by i."

The following are proposed solutions for other languages:

In Lisp:

```
(defun foo (n)
  (lambda (i) (incf n i)))
```

In Perl 5:

```
sub foo {
  my ($n) = @_;
  sub {$n += shift}
}
```

In Smalltalk:

```
foo: n
  |s|
  s := n.
  ^[:i| s := s+i. ]
```

The following steps lead to a Groovy solution, as shown in listing 5.9:

1 We need a function that returns a closure. In Groovy, we don't have functions, but methods. (Actually, we have not only methods, but also closures. But let's keep it simple.) We use `def` to declare such a method. It has only one line, which after `return` creates a new closure. We will call this method `foo` to make the solutions comparable in size. The name `createAccumulator` would better reflect the purpose.

2 Our method takes an initial value n as required.

3 Because n is a parameter to the method that *declares* the closure, it gets bound to the closure scope. We can use it inside the closure body to calculate the incremented value.

4 The incremented value is not only calculated but also assigned to n as the new value. That way we have a true accumulation.

We add a few assertions to verify our solution and reveal how the accumulator is supposed to be used. Listing 5.9 shows the full code.

> **Listing 5.9   The accumulator problem in Groovy**

```
def foo(n) {
    return {n += it}
}

def accumulator =  foo(1)
assert accumulator(2) == 3
assert accumulator(1) == 4
```

All the steps that led to the solution are straightforward applications of what you've learned about closures.

In comparison to the other languages, the Groovy solution is not only short but also surprisingly clear. Groovy has passed this language test exceptionally well.

Is this test of any practical relevance? Maybe not in the sense that we would ever need an accumulator generator, but it is in a different sense. Passing this test means that the language is able to dynamically put logic in an object and manage the context that this object lives in. This is an indication of how powerful abstractions in that language can be.

5.6 Returning from closures

So far, you have seen how to declare closures and how to call them. However, there is one crucial topic that we haven't touched yet: how to return from a closure.

In principle, there are two ways of returning:

- The last expression of the closure has been evaluated, and the result of this evaluation is returned. This is called *end return*. Using the return keyword in front of the last expression is optional.

- The return keyword can also be used to return from the closure *prematurely*.

This means the following ways of doubling the entries of a list have the very same effect:

```
[1, 2, 3].collect{ it * 2 }

[1, 2, 3].collect{ return it * 2 }
```

A premature return can be used to, for example, double only the even entries:

```
[1, 2, 3].collect{
    if (it%2 == 0) return it * 2
    return it
}
```

This behavior of the return keyword inside closures is simple and straightforward. You hardly expect any misconceptions, but there is something to be aware of.

WARNING There is a difference between using the return keyword inside and outside of a closure.

Outside a closure, any occurrence of return leaves the current method. When used inside a closure, it only ends the current evaluation of the closure, which is a much more localized effect. For example, when using List.each, returning early from the closure doesn't return early from the each method—the closure will still be called again with the next element in the list.

While progressing further through the book, we will hit this issue again and explore more ways of dealing with it. Section 13.1.8 summarizes the topic.

5.7 *Support for design patterns*

Design patterns are widely used by developers to enhance the quality of their designs. Each design pattern presents a typical problem that occurs in object-oriented programming along with a corresponding well-tested solution. Let's take a closer look at the way the availability of closures affects how, which, and when patterns are used.

If you've never seen design patterns before, we suggest you look at the classic book *Design Patterns: Elements of Reusable Object-Oriented Software* by Gamma et al, or one of the more recent ones such as *Head First Design Patterns* by Freeman et al or *Refactoring to Patterns* by Joshua Kerievsky, or search for "patterns repository" or "patterns catalog" using your favorite search engine.

Although many design patterns are broadly applicable and apply to any language, some of them are particularly well-suited to solving issues that occur when using programming languages such as C++ and Java. They most often involve implementing new abstractions and new classes to make the original programs more flexible or maintainable. With Groovy, some of the restrictions that face C++ and Java do not apply, and the design patterns are either of less value or more directly supported using language features rather than introducing new classes. We pick two examples to show the difference: the *Visitor* and *Builder* patterns. As you'll see, closures and dynamic typing are the key differentiators in Groovy that facilitate easier pattern usage.

5.7.1 *Relationship to the Visitor pattern*

The Visitor pattern is particularly useful when you wish to perform some complex business functionality on a composite collection (such as a tree or list) of existing simple classes. Rather than altering the existing simple classes to contain the desired business functionality, a `Visitor` object is introduced. The `Visitor` knows how to traverse the composite collection and knows how to perform the business functionality for different kinds of a simple class. If the composite changes or the business functionality changes over time, typically only the `Visitor` class is impacted.

Listing 5.10 shows how simple the Visitor pattern can look in Groovy; the composite traversal code is in the `accept` method of the `Drawing` class, whereas the business functionality (in our case to perform some calculations involving shape area) is contained in two closures, which are passed as parameters to the appropriate `accept` methods. There is no need for a separate `Visitor` class in this simple case.

Listing 5.10 The Visitor pattern in Groovy

```
class Drawing {
    List shapes
    def accept(Closure yield) { shapes.each{it.accept(yield)} }
}
class Shape {
    def accept(Closure yield) { yield(this) }
}
class Square extends Shape {
    def width
    def area() { width**2 }
}
class Circle extends Shape {
    def radius
    def area() { Math.PI * radius**2 }
}

def picture = new Drawing(shapes:
    [new Square(width:1), new Circle(radius:1)] )

def total = 0
picture.accept { total += it.area() }
println "The shapes in this drawing cover an area of $total units."
println 'The individual contributions are: '
picture.accept { println it.class.name + ":" + it.area() }
```

5.7.2 *Relationship to the Builder pattern*

The Builder pattern serves to encapsulate the logic associated with constructing a product from its constituent parts. When using the pattern, you normally create a `Builder` class, which contains logic determining what builder methods to call and in which sequence to call them to ensure proper assembly of the product. For each product, you must supply the appropriate logic for each relevant builder method used by the `Builder` class; each builder method typically returns one of the constituent parts.

Coding Java solutions based on the Builder pattern is not hard, but the Java code tends to be cumbersome and verbose and doesn't highlight the structure of the assembled product. For that reason, the Builder pattern is rarely used in Java; developers instead use unstructured or replicated builder-type logic mixed in with their other code. This is a shame, because the Builder pattern is so powerful.

Groovy's builders provide a solution using nested closures to conveniently specify even very complex products. Such a specification is easy to read, because the appearance of the code reflects the product structure. Groovy has built-in library classes based on the Builder pattern that allow you to easily build arbitrarily nested node structures, produce markup like HTML or XML, define GUIs in Swing or other widget toolkits, and even access the wide range of functionality in Ant. You will see lots of examples in chapter 8, and we explain how to write your own builders in section 8.6.

5.7.3 *Relationship to other patterns*

Almost all patterns are easier to implement in Groovy than in Java. This is often because Groovy supports more lightweight solutions that make the patterns less of a necessity—mostly because of closures and dynamic typing. In addition, when patterns are required, Groovy often makes expressing them more succinct and simpler to set up.

We discuss a number of patterns in other sections of this book, patterns such as Strategy (see 9.1.1 and 9.1.3), Observer (see 13.2.3), and Command (see 9.1.1) benefit from using closures instead of implementing new classes. Patterns such as Adapter and Decorator (see 7.5.3) benefit from dynamic typing and method lookup. We also briefly discuss patterns such as Template Method (see section 5.2.2), the Value Object pattern (see 3.3.2), the incomplete library class smell (see 7.5.3), MVC (see 8.5.6), and the DTO and DAO patterns (see chapter 10). Just by existing, closures can completely replace the Method Object pattern.

Groovy provides plenty of support for using patterns within your own programs. Its libraries embody pattern practices throughout. Higher-level frameworks such as Grails take it one step further. Grails provides you with a framework built on top of Groovy's libraries and patterns support. Because using such frameworks saves you from having to deal with many pattern issues directly—you just use the framework—you will automatically end up using patterns without needing to understand the details in most cases. Even then, it is useful to know about some of the patterns we have touched upon so that you can leverage the maximum benefit from whichever frameworks you use.

5.8 *Summary*

You have seen that closures follow our theme of *everything is an object*. They capture a piece of logic, making it possible to pass it around for execution, return it from a method call, or store it for later usage.

Closures encourage centralized resource handling, thus making your code more reliable. This doesn't come at any expense. In fact, the codebase is relieved from structural duplication, enhancing expressiveness and maintainability.

Defining and using closures is surprisingly simple because all the difficult tasks such as keeping track of references and relaying method calls back to the delegating owner are done transparently. If you don't care about the scoping rules, everything falls into place naturally. If you want to hook into the mechanics and perform tasks such as deviating the calls to the delegate, you can. Of course, such an advanced usage needs more care. You also need to be careful when returning from a delegate, particularly when using one in a situation where in other languages you might use a `for` loop or a similar construct. This has surprised more than one new Groovy developer, although the behavior is logical when examined closely. Re-read section 5.6 when in doubt.

Closures open the door to several ways of doing things that may be new to many developers. Some of these, such as currying, can appear daunting at first sight but allow a great deal of power to be wielded with remarkably little code. Additionally, closures can make familiar design patterns simpler to use or even unnecessary.

Although you now have a good understanding of Groovy's datatypes and closures, you still need a means to control the flow of execution through your program. This is achieved with control structures, which form the topic of the next chapter.

Groovy control structures 6

The pursuit of truth and beauty is a sphere of activity in which we are permitted to remain children all our lives.

—Albert Einstein

At the hardware level, computer systems use simple arithmetic and logical operations, such as jump to a new location if a memory value equals zero. Any complex flow of logic that a computer is executing can always be expressed in terms of these simple operations. Fortunately, languages such as Java raise the abstraction level available in programs we write so that we can express the flow of logic in terms of higher-level constructs—for example, looping through all of the elements in an array or processing characters until we reach the end of a file.

In this chapter, we explore the constructs Groovy gives us to describe logic flow in ways that are even simpler and more expressive than Java. Before we look at the constructs themselves, however, we have to examine Groovy's answer to that age-old philosophical question: What is truth?[1]

6.1 *The Groovy truth*

In order to understand how Groovy will handle control structures such as `if` and `while`, you need to know how it evaluates expressions, which need to have Boolean results. Many of the control structures we examine in this chapter rely on the result of a *Boolean test*—an expression that is first evaluated and then considered as being either true or false. The outcome of this affects which path is then followed in the code. In Java, the consideration involved is usually trivial, because Java requires the expression to be one resulting in the primitive `boolean` type to start with. Groovy is more relaxed about this, allowing simpler code at the slight expense of language simplicity. We'll examine Groovy's rules for Boolean tests and give some advice to avoid falling into an age-old trap.

6.1.1 *Evaluating Boolean tests*

The expression of a Boolean test can be of any (non-void) type. It can apply to any object. Groovy decides whether to consider the expression as being true or false by applying the rules shown in table 6.1, based on the result's runtime type. The rules are applied in the order given, and once a rule matches, it completely determines the result.[2]

---

[1] Groovy has no opinion as to what beauty is. We're sure that if it did, however, it would involve expressive minimalism. Closures too, probably.

[2] It would be rare to encounter a situation where more than one rule matched, but you never know when someone will subclass `java.lang.Number` and implement `java.util.Map` at the same time.

Table 6.1 Sequence of rules used to evaluate a Boolean test

Runtime type	Evaluation criterion required for truth
`Boolean`	Corresponding Boolean value is `true`
`Matcher`	The matcher has a match
`Collection`	The collection is non-empty
`Map`	The map is non-empty
`String, GString`	The string is non-empty
`Number, Character`	The value is nonzero
None of the above	The object reference is non-null

Listing 6.1 shows these rules in action, using the Boolean negation operator `!` to assert that expressions which ought to evaluate to `false` really do so.

Listing 6.1 Example Boolean test evaluations

```
assert true          Boolean values
assert !false        are trivial

assert ('a' =~ /./)    Matchers must
assert !('a' =~ /b/)   match

assert [1]     Collections must
assert ![]     be non-empty

assert ['a':1]   Maps must be
assert ![:]      non-empty

assert 'a'     Strings must be
assert !''     non-empty

assert 1
assert 1.1
assert 1.2f     Numbers
assert 1.3g     (any type)
assert 2L       must be
assert 3G       nonzero
assert !0

assert new Object()   Any other value
assert !null          must be non-null
```

These rules can make testing for "truth" simpler and easier to read. However, they come with a price, as you're about to find out.

6.1.2 Assignments within Boolean tests

Before we get into the meat of the chapter, we have a warning to point out. Just like Java, Groovy allows the expression used for a Boolean test to be an assignment—and the value of an assignment expression is the value assigned. Unlike Java, the type of a Boolean test is not restricted to `booleans`, which means that a problem you might have thought was ancient history reappears, albeit in an alleviated manner. Namely, an equality operator `==` incorrectly entered as an assignment operator `=` is valid code with a drastically different effect than the intended one. Groovy shields you from falling into this trap for the most common appearance of this error: when it's used as a top-level expression in an `if` statement. However, it can still arise in less usual cases.

Listing 6.2 leads you through some typical variations of this topic.

Listing 6.2   What happens when `==` is mistyped as `=`

```
def x = 1

if (x == 2) {            ❶ Normal
    assert false              comparison
}
/*******************
if (x =  2) {            ❷ Not allowed!
    println x               Compiler error!
}
*******************/
if ((x = 3)) {           ❸ Assign and test in
    println x               nested expression
}
assert x == 3

def store = []
while (x = x - 1) {      ❹ Deliberate assign
    store << x               and test in while
}
assert store == [2, 1]

while (x = 1) {          ❺ Ouch! This
    println x               will print 1!
    break
}
```

The equality comparison in ❶ is fine and would be allowable in Java. In ❷, an equality comparison was intended, but one of the equal signs was left out. This raises a Groovy compiler error, because an assignment is not allowed as a top-level expression in an if test.

However, Boolean tests can be nested inside expressions in arbitrary depth; the simplest one is shown at ❸, where extra parentheses around the assignment make it a subexpression, and therefore the assignment becomes compliant with the Groovy language. The value 3 will be assigned to x, and x will be tested for truth. Because 3 is considered true, the value 3 gets printed. This use of parentheses to please the compiler can even be used as a trick to spare an extra line of assignment. The unusual appearance of the extra parentheses then serves as a warning sign for the reader.

The restriction of assignments from being used in top-level Boolean expressions applies only to if and not to other control structures such as while. This is because doing assignment and testing in one expression are often used with while in the style shown at ❹. This style tends to appear with classical usages like processing tokens retrieved from a parser or reading data from a stream. Although this is convenient, it leaves us with the potential coding pitfall shown at ❺, where x is assigned the value 1 and the loop would never stop if there weren't a break statement.[3]

This potential cause of bugs has given rise to the idiom in other languages (such as C and C++, which suffer from the same problem to a worse degree) of putting constants on the left side of the equality operator when you wish to perform a comparison with one. This would lead to the last while statement in the previous listing (still with a typo) being

```
while (1 =  x) {        Should
    println x           be ==
}
```

This would raise an error, as you can't assign a value to a constant. We're back to safety—so long as constants are involved. Unfortunately, not only does this fail when both sides of the comparison are variables, it also reduces readability. Whether it is a natural occurrence, a quirk of human languages, or conditioning, most people find while (x==3) significantly simpler to read than while (3==x). Although neither is going to cause confusion, the latter tends to slow people

---

[3] Remember that the code in this book has been executed. If we didn't have the break statement, the book would have taken literally forever to produce.

down or interrupt their train of thought. In this book, we have favored readability over safety—but our situation is somewhat different than that of normal development. You will have to decide for yourself which convention suits you and your team better.

Now that we have examined which expressions Groovy will consider to be true and which are false, we can start looking at the control structures themselves.

6.2 Conditional execution structures

Our first set of control structures deals with conditional execution. They all evaluate a Boolean test and make a choice about what to do next based on whether the result was true or false. None of these structures should come as a completely new experience to any Java developer, but of course Groovy adds some twists of its own. We will cover `if` statements, the conditional operator, `switch` statements, and assertions.

6.2.1 The humble if statement

Our first two structures act *exactly* the same way in Groovy as they do in Java, apart from the evaluation of the Boolean test itself. We start with `if` and `if/else` statements.

Just as in Java, the Boolean test expression must be enclosed in parentheses. The conditional block is normally enclosed in curly braces. These braces are optional if the block consists of only one statement.[4]

A special application of the "no braces needed for single statements" rule is the sequential use of `else if`. In this case, the logical indentation of the code is often flattened; that is, all `else if` lines have the same indentation although their meaning is nested. The indentation makes no difference to Groovy and is only of aesthetic relevance.

Listing 6.3 gives some examples, using `assert true` to show the blocks of code that will be executed and `assert false` to show the blocks that won't be executed.

There should be no surprises in the listing, although it might still look slightly odd to you that non-Boolean expressions such as strings and lists can be used for Boolean tests. Don't worry—it becomes natural over time.

---

[4] Even though the braces are optional, many coding conventions insist on them in order to avoid errors that can occur through careless modification when they're not used.

Listing 6.3 The `if` statement in action

```
if (true)           assert true
else                assert false

if (1) {
    assert true
} else {
    assert false
}

if ('non-empty') assert true
else if (['x'])  assert false
else             assert false

if (0)              assert false
else if ([])        assert false
else                assert true
```

6.2.2 The conditional ?: operator

Groovy also supports the ternary conditional ?: operator for small inline tests, as shown in listing 6.4. This operator returns the object that results from evaluating the expression left or right of the colon, depending on the test before the question mark. If the first expression evaluates to `true`, the middle expression is evaluated. Otherwise, the last expression is evaluated. Just as in Java, whichever of the last two expressions isn't used as the result isn't evaluated at all.

Listing 6.4 The conditional operator

```
def result = (1==1) ? 'ok' : 'failed'
assert result == 'ok'

result = 'some string' ? 10 : ['x']
assert result == 10
```

Again, notice how the Boolean test (the first expression) can be of any type. Also note that because everything is an object in Groovy, the middle and last expressions can be of radically different types.

Opinions about the ternary conditional operator vary wildly. Some people find it extremely convenient and use it often. Others find it too Perl-ish. You may well find that you use it less often in Groovy because there are features that make its typical applications obsolete—for example, GStrings (covered in section 3.4.2) allow dynamic creation of strings that would be constructed in Java using the ternary operator.

So far, so Java-like. Things change significantly when we consider `switch` statements.

6.2.3 *The switch statement*

On a recent train ride, I (Dierk) spoke with a teammate about Groovy, mentioning the oh-so-cool `switch` capabilities. He wouldn't even let me get started, waving his hands and saying, "I never use `switch`!" I was put off at first, because I lost my momentum in the discussion; but after more thought, I agreed that I don't use it either—*in Java*.

The `switch` statement in Java is very restrictive. You can only switch on an `int` type, with `byte`, `char`, and `short` automatically being promoted to `int`.[5] With this restriction, its applicability is bound to either low-level tasks or to some kind of dispatching on a *type code*. In object-oriented languages, the use of type codes is considered smelly.[6]

The switch structure

The general appearance of the `switch` construct is just like in Java, and its logic is identical in the sense that the handling logic falls through to the next `case` unless it is exited explicitly. We will explore exiting options in section 6.4.

Listing 6.5 shows the general appearance.

Listing 6.5 General switch appearance is like Java or C

```
def a = 1
def log = ''
switch (a) {
    case 0  : log += '0'        Fall through
    case 1  : log += '1'
    case 2  : log += '2' ; break
    default : log += 'default'
}
assert log == '12'
```

Although the *fallthrough* is supported in Groovy, there are few cases where this feature really enhances the readability of the code. It usually does more harm than good (and this applies to Java, too). As a general rule, putting a break at the end of each case is good style.

---

[5] As of Java 5, enum types can also be switched on, due to some compiler trickery.

[6] See "Replace Conditional with Polymorphism" in *Refactoring* by Martin Fowler (Addison Wesley, 2000).

Switch with classifiers

You have seen the Groovy `switch` used for classification in section 3.5.5 and when working through the datatypes. A *classifier* is eligible as a `switch` case if it implements the `isCase` method. In other words, a Groovy `switch` like

```
switch (candidate) {
    case classifier1    : handle1()      ; break
    case classifier2    : handle2()      ; break
    default             : handleDefault()
}
```

is roughly equivalent (beside the fallthrough and exit handling) to

```
if      (classifier1.isCase(candidate)) handle1()
else if (classifier2.isCase(candidate)) handle2()
else    handleDefault()
```

This allows expressive classifications and even some unconventional usages with mixed classifiers. Unlike Java's constant cases, the candidate may match more than one classifier. This means that the order of cases is important in Groovy, whereas it does not affect behavior in Java. Listing 6.6 gives an example of multiple types of classifiers. After having checked that our number 10 is not zero, not in range 0..9, not in list [8,9,11], not of type `Float`, and not an integral multiple of 3, we finally find it to be made of two characters.

Listing 6.6 Advanced switch and mixed classifiers

```
switch (10) {
    case 0          : assert false ; break
    case 0..9       : assert false ; break
    case [8,9,11]   : assert false ; break
    case Float      : assert false ; break      ❶ Type case
    case {it%3 == 0}: assert false ; break      ❷ Closure case
    case ~/../      : assert true  ; break
    default         : assert false ; break      ❸ Regular expression case
}
```

The new feature in ❶ is that we can classify by type. `Float` is of type `java.lang.Class`, and the GDK enhances `Class` by adding an `isCase` method that tests the candidate with `isInstance`.

The `isCase` method on closures at ❷ passes the candidate into the closure and returns the result of the closure call coerced to a `Boolean`.

The final classification ❸ as a two-digit number works because `~/../` is a `Pattern` and the `isCase` method on patterns applies its test to the `toString` value of the argument.

In order to leverage the power of the switch construct, it is essential to know the available isCase implementations. It is not possible to provide an exhaustive list, because any custom type in your code or in a library can implement it. Table 6.2 has the list of known implementations in the GDK.

Table 6.2   Implementations of isCase for switch

Class	a.isCase(b) implemented as
Object	a.equals(b)
Class	a.isInstance(b)
Collection	a.contains(b)
Range	a.contains(b)
Pattern	a.matcher(b.toString()).matches()
String	(a==null && b==null) || a.equals(b)
Closure	a.call(b)

RECALL   The isCase method is also used with grep on collections such that collection.grep(*classifier*) returns a collection of all items that are a case of that classifier.

Using the Groovy switch in the sense of a classifier is a big step forward. It adds much to the readability of the code. The reader sees a simple classification instead of a tangled, nested construction of if statements. Again, you are able to reveal *what* the code does rather than *how* it does it.

As pointed out in section 4.1.2, the switch classification on ranges is particularly convenient for modeling business rules that tend to prefer discrete classification to continuous functions. The resulting code reads almost like a specification.

Look actively through your code for places to implement isCase. A characteristic sign of looming classifiers is lengthy else if constructions.

ADVANCED TOPIC   It is possible to overload the isCase method to support different kinds of classification logic depending on the type of the candidate. If you provide both methods, isCase(String candidate) and isCase(Integer candidate), then switch ('1') can behave differently than switch(1) with your object as classifier.

Our next topic, *assertions*, may not look particularly important at first glance. However, although assertions don't change the business capabilities of the code, they do make the code more robust in production. Moreover, they do something even better: enhance the development team's confidence in their code as well as their ability to remain agile during additional enhancements and ongoing maintenance.

6.2.4 *Sanity checking with assertions*

This book contains several hundred assertion statements—and indeed, you've already seen a number of them. Now it's time to go into some extra detail. We will look at producing meaningful error messages from failed assertions, reflect over reasonable uses of this keyword, and show how to use it for inline unit tests. We will also quickly compare the Groovy solution to Java's assert keyword and assertions as used in unit test cases.

Producing informative failure messages

When an assertion fails, it produces a stacktrace and a message. Put the code

```
a = 1
assert a==2
```

in a file called FailingAssert.groovy, and let it run via

```
> groovy Failing-Assert.groovy
```

It is expected to fail, and it does so with the message

```
Caught: java.lang.AssertionError: Expression: (a==2). Values: a = 1
    at FailingAssert.run(FailingAssert.groovy:2)
    at FailingAssert.main(FailingAssert.groovy)
```

You see that on failure, the assertion prints out the failed expression as it appears in the code plus the value of the variables in that expression. The trailing stacktrace reveals the location of the failed assertion and the sequence of method calls that led to the error. It is best read bottom to top:

- We are in the file FailingAssert.groovy.
- From that file, a class FailingAssert was constructed with a method main.
- Within main, we called FailingAssert.run, which is located in the file FailingAssert.groovy at line 2 of the file.[7]
- At that point, the assertion fails.

---

[7] The main and run methods are constructed for you behind the scenes when running a script.

This is a lot of information, and it is sufficient to locate and understand the error in most cases, but not always. Let's try another example that tries to protect a file reading code from being executed if the file doesn't exist or cannot be read.[8]

```
input = new File('no such file')
assert  input.exists()
assert  input.canRead()
println input.text
```

This produces the output

```
Caught: java.lang.AssertionError: Expression: input.exists()
  ...
```

which is not very informative. The missing information here is what the bad file name was. To this end, assertions can be instrumented with a trailing message:

```
input = new File('no such file')
assert input.exists()   , "cannot find '$input.name'"
assert input.canRead() , "cannot read '$input.canonicalPath'"
println input.text
```

This produces the following

```
... cannot find 'no such file'. Expression: input.exists()
```

which is the information we need. However, this special case also reveals the sometimes unnecessary use of assertions, because in this case we could easily leave the assertions out:

```
input = new File('no such file')
println input.text
```

The result is the following sufficient error message:

```
FileNotFoundException: no such file (The system cannot find the file
specified)
```

This leads to the following best practices with assertions:

- Before writing an assertion, let your code fail, and see whether any other thrown exception is good enough.
- When writing an assertion, let it fail the first time, and see whether the failure message is sufficient. If not, add a message. Let it fail again to verify that the message is now good enough.

---

[8] Perl programmers will see the analogy to or die.

- If you feel you need an assertion to clarify or protect your code, add it regardless of the previous rules.
- If you feel you need a message to clarify the meaning or purpose of your assertion, add it regardless of the previous rules.

Insure code with inline unit tests

Finally, there is a potentially controversial use of assertions as unit tests that live right inside production code and get executed with it. Listing 6.7 shows this strategy with a nontrivial regular expression that extracts a hostname from a URL. The pattern is first constructed and then applied to some assertions before being put to action. We also implement a simple method `assertHost` for easy asserting of a match grouping.[9]

Listing 6.7   Use assertions for inline unit tests

```
def host = /\/\/([a-zA-Z0-9-]+(\.[a-zA-Z0-9-])*?)(:|\/)/    ◁─┐ Regular
                                                                expression
assertHost 'http://a.b.c:8080/bla',     host, 'a.b.c'          matching
assertHost 'http://a.b.c/bla',          host, 'a.b.c'          hosts
assertHost 'http://127.0.0.1:8080/bla', host, '127.0.0.1'
assertHost 'http://t-online.de/bla',    host, 't-online.de'
assertHost 'http://T-online.de/bla',    host, 'T-online.de'

def assertHost (candidate, regex, expected){
    candidate.eachMatch(regex){assert it[1] == expected}
}
    ◁─  Code to use the regular expression for useful work goes here
```

Reading this code with and without assertions, their value becomes obvious. Seeing the example matches in the assertions reveals what the code is doing and verifies our assumptions at the same time. Traditionally, these examples would live inside a test harness or perhaps only within a comment. This is better than nothing, but experience shows that comments go out of date and the reader cannot *really* be sure that the code works as indicated. Tests in external test harnesses also often drift away from the code. Some tests break, they are commented out of a test suite under the pressures of meeting schedules, and eventually they are no longer run at all.

---

[9] Please note that we use regexes here only to show the value of assertions. If we really set out to find the hostname of a URL, we would use `candidate.toURL().host`.

Some may fear a bad impact on performance when doing this style of inline unit tests. The best answer is to use a profiler and investigate where performance is really relevant. Our assertions in listing 6.7 run in a few milliseconds and should not normally be an issue. When performance is important, one possibility would be to put inline unit tests where they are executed only once per loaded class: in a static initializer.

Relationships to other assertions

Java has had an `assert` keyword since JDK 1.4. It differs from Groovy assertions in that it has a slightly different syntax (colon instead of comma to separate the Boolean test from the message) and that it can be enabled and disabled. Java's assertion feature is not as powerful, because it works only on a Java Boolean test, whereas the Groovy assert takes a full Groovy conditional (see section 6.1).

The JDK documentation has a long chapter on assertions that talks about the disabling feature for assertions and its impact on compiling, starting the VM, and resulting design issues. Although this is fine and the design rationale behind Java assertions is clear, we feel the disabling feature is the biggest stumbling block for using assertions in Java. You can never be sure that your assertions are really executed.

Some people claim that for performance reasons, assertions should be disabled in production, after the code has been tested with assertions enabled. On this issue, Bertrand Meyer,[10] the father of *design by contract*, pointed out that it is like learning to swim with a swimming belt and taking it off when leaving the pool and heading for the ocean.

In Groovy, your assertions are always executed.

Assertions also play a central role in unit tests. Groovy comes with an included version of JUnit, the leading unit test framework for Java. JUnit makes a lot of specialized assertions available to its `TestCases`. Groovy adds even more of them. Full coverage of these assertions is given in chapter 14. The information that Groovy provides when assertions fail makes them very convenient when writing unit tests, because it relieves the tester from writing lots of messages.

Assertions can make a big difference to your personal programming style and even more to the culture of a development team, regardless of whether they are used inline or in separated unit tests. Asserting your assumptions not only

---

[10] See *Object Oriented Software Construction*, 2nd ed., by Bertrand Meyer (Prentice Hall, 1997).

makes your code more reliable, but it also makes it easier to understand and easier to work with.

That's it for conditional execution structures. They are the basis for any kind of logical branching and a prerequisite to allow looping—the language feature that makes your computer do all the repetitive work for you. The next two sections cover the looping structures `while` and `for`.

6.3 Looping

The structures you've seen so far have evaluated a Boolean test *once* and changed the path of execution once based on the result of the condition. Looping, on the other hand, repeats the execution of a block of code multiple times. The loops available in Groovy are `while` and `for`, both of which we cover here.

6.3.1 Looping with while

The `while` construct is like its Java counterpart. The only difference is the one you've seen already—the power of Groovy Boolean test expressions. To summarize very briefly, the Boolean test is evaluated, and if it's true, the body of the loop is then executed. The test is then re-evaluated, and so forth. Only when the test becomes false does control proceed past the `while` loop. Listing 6.8 shows an example that removes all entries from a list. We visited this problem in chapter 3, where you discovered that you can't use `each` for that purpose. The second example adds the values again in a one-liner body without the optional braces.

Listing 6.8   Example `while` loops

```
def list = [1,2,3]
while (list) {
    list.remove(0)
}
assert list == []

while (list.size() < 3) list << list.size()+1
assert list == [1,2,3]
```

Again, there should be no surprises in this code, with the exception of using just `list` as the Boolean test in the first loop.

Note that there are no do { } while(*condition*) or repeat { } until (*condition*) loops in Groovy.

6.3.2 Looping with for

Considering it is probably the most commonly used type of loop, the `for` loop in Java is relatively hard to use, when you examine it closely. Through familiarity, people who have used a language with a similar structure (and there are many such languages) grow to find it easy to use, but that is solely due to frequent use, not due to good design. Although the nature of the traditional `for` loop is powerful, it is rarely used in a way that can't be more simply expressed in terms of iterating through a collection-like data structure. Groovy embraces this simplicity, leading to probably the biggest difference in control structures between Java and Groovy.

Groovy `for` loops follow this structure:

```
for (variable in iterable) { body }
```

where *variable* may optionally have a declared type. The Groovy `for` loop iterates over the *iterable*. Frequently used iterables are ranges, collections, maps, arrays, iterators, and enumerations. In fact, any object can be an iterable. Groovy applies the same logic as for *object iteration*, described in chapter 8.

Curly braces around the body are optional if it consists of only one statement. Listing 6.9 shows some of the possible combinations.

Listing 6.9 Multiple `for` loop examples

```
def store = ''
for (String i in 'a'..'c') store += i          ❶ Typed, over string
assert store == 'abc'                              range, no braces

store = ''
for (i in [1, 2, 3]) {
    store += i               ❷ Untyped, over list as
}                               collection, braces
assert store == '123'

def myString = 'Equivalent to Java'
store = ''
for (i in 0 ..< myString.size()) {       ❸ Untyped, over half-exclusive
    store += myString[i]                     IntRange, braces
}
assert store == myString

store = ''
for (i in myString) {
    store += i              ❹ Untyped, over string
}                              as collection, braces
assert store == myString
```

Example ❶ uses explicit typing for i and no braces for a loop body of a single statement. The looping is done on a range of strings.

The usual for loop appearance when working on a collection is shown in ❷. Recall that thanks to the *autoboxing*, this also works for arrays.

Looping on a half-exclusive integer range as shown in ❸ is equivalent to the Java construction

```
for (int i=0; i < exclusiveUpperBound; i++) {      // Java !
```
⟵⌐ **Code using i would be here**
```
}
```

which is referred to as the classic for loop. It is currently not supported in Groovy but may be in future versions.

Example ❹ is provided to make it clear that ❸ is not the typical Groovy style when working on strings. It is more Groovy to treat a string as a collection of characters.

Using the for loop with *object iteration* as described in section 9.1.3 provides some very powerful combinations.

You can use it to print a file line-by-line via

```
def file = new File('myFileName.txt')
for (line in file) println line
```

or to print all one-digit matches of a regular expression:

```
def matcher = '12xy3'=~/\d/
for (match in matcher) println match
```

If the *container* object is null, no iteration will occur:

```
for (x in null) println 'This will not be printed!'
```

If Groovy cannot make the *container* object iterable by any means, the fallback solution is to do an iteration that contains only the *container* object itself:

```
for (x in new Object()) println "Printed once for object $x"
```

Object iteration makes the Groovy for loop a sophisticated control structure. It is a valid counterpart to using methods that iterate over an object with closures, such as using Collection's each method.

The main difference is that the body of a for loop is not a closure! That means this body is a block:

```
for (x in 0..9) { println x }
```

whereas this body is a closure:

```
(0..9).each { println it }
```

Even though they look similar, they are very different in construction.

A closure is an object of its own and has all the features that you saw in chapter 5. It can be constructed in a different place and passed to the `each` method.

The body of the `for` loop, in contrast, is directly generated as bytecode at its point of appearance. No special scoping rules apply.

This distinction is even more important when it comes to managing exit handling from the body. The next section shows why.

6.4 Exiting blocks and methods

Although it's nice to have code that reads as a simple list of instructions with no jumping around, it's often vital that control is passed from the current block or method to the enclosing block or the calling method—or sometimes even further up the call stack. Just like in Java, Groovy allows this to happen in an expected, orderly fashion with `return`, `break`, and `continue` statements, and in emergency situations with exceptions. Let's take a closer look.

6.4.1 Normal termination: return/break/continue

The general logic of `return`, `break`, and `continue` is similar to Java. One difference is that the `return` keyword is optional for the last expression in a method or closure. If it is omitted, the return value is that of the last expression. Methods with explicit return type `void` do not return a value, whereas closures always return a value.[11]

Listing 6.10 shows how the current loop is shortcut with `continue` and prematurely ended with `break`. Like Java, there is an optional `label`.

Listing 6.10 Simple `break` and `continue`

```
def a = 1
while (true) {          ⊲⎤  Do forever
    a++
    break               ⊲⎤  Forever is
}                          ⎦  over now
assert a == 2

for (i in 0..10) {
    if (i==0)  continue  ⊲⎤  Proceed
                           ⎦  with I
```

---

[11] But what if the last evaluated expression of a closure is a void method call? In this case, the closure returns `null`.

```
        a++
        if (i > 0) break        ◁─┐ Premature
    }                               │ loop end
    assert a==3
```

In classic programming style, the use of `break` and `continue` is sometimes considered smelly. However, it can be useful for controlling the workflow in services that run in an endless loop. Similarly, returning from multiple points in the method is frowned upon in some circles, but other people find it can greatly increase the readability of methods that might be able to return a result early. We encourage you to figure out what you find most readable and discuss it with whoever else is going to be reading your code—consistency is as important as anything else.

As a final note on return handling, remember that closures when used with iteration methods such as `each` have a different meaning of `return` than the control structures `while` and `for`, as explained in section 5.6.

6.4.2 *Exceptions: throw/try-catch-finally*

Exception handling is exactly the same as in Java and follows the same logic. Just as in Java, you can specify a complete `try-catch-finally` sequence of blocks, or just `try-catch`, or just `try-finally`. Note that unlike various other control structures, braces are required around the block bodies whether or not they contain more than one statement. The only difference between Java and Groovy in terms of exceptions is that declarations of exceptions in the method signature are optional, even for checked exceptions. Listing 6.11 shows the usual behavior.

Listing 6.11 Throw, `try`, `catch`, and `finally`

```
def myMethod() {
    throw new IllegalArgumentException()
}

def log = []
try {
    myMethod()
} catch (Exception e) {
    log << e.toString()
} finally {
    log << 'finally'
}
assert log.size() == 2
```

Despite the optional typing in the rest of Groovy, a type is mandatory in the catch expression.

There are no compile-time or runtime warnings from Groovy when checked exceptions are not declared. When a checked exception is not handled, it is propagated up the execution stack like a RuntimeException.

We cover integration between Java and Groovy in more detail in chapter 11; however, it is worthwhile noting an issue relating to exceptions here. When using a Groovy class from Java, you need to be careful—the Groovy methods will not declare that they throw any checked exceptions unless you've explicitly added the declaration, even though they might throw checked exceptions at runtime. Unfortunately, the Java compiler attempts to be clever and will complain if you try to catch a checked exception in Java when it believes there's no way that the exception can be thrown. If you run into this and need to explicitly catch a checked exception generated in Groovy code, you may need to add a throws declaration to the Groovy code, just to keep javac happy.

6.5 *Summary*

This was our tour through Groovy's control structures: conditionally executing code, looping, and exiting blocks and methods early. It wasn't too surprising because everything turned out to be like Java, enriched with a bit of Groovy flavor. The only structural difference was the for loop. Exception handling is very similar to Java, except without the requirement to declare checked exceptions.[12]

Groovy's handling of Boolean tests is consistently available both in conditional execution structures and in loops. We examined the differences between Java and Groovy in determining when a Boolean test is considered to be true. This is a crucial area to understand, because idiomatic Groovy will often use tests that are not simple Boolean expressions.

The switch keyword and its use as a general classifier bring a new object-oriented quality to conditionals. The interplay with the isCase method allows objects to control how they are treated inside that conditional. Although the use of switch is often discouraged in object-oriented languages, the new power given to it by Groovy gives it a new sense of purpose.

---

[12] Checked exceptions are regarded by many as an experiment that was worth performing but which proved not to be as useful as had been hoped.

In the overall picture, *assertions* find their place as the bread-and-butter tool for the mindful developer. They belong in the toolbox of every programmer who cares about their craft.

With what you learned in the tour, you have all the means to do any kind of procedural programming. But certainly, you have higher goals and want to master object-oriented programming. The next chapter will teach you how.

7
Dynamic object orientation, Groovy style

> *Any intelligent fool can make things bigger, more complex, and more violent. It takes a touch of genius—and a lot of courage—to move in the opposite direction.*
>
> —Albert Einstein

There is a common misconception about scripting languages. Because a scripting language might support loose typing and provide some initially surprising syntax shorthands, it may be perceived as a nice new toy for hackers rather than a language suitable for serious object-oriented (OO) programming. This reputation stems from the time when scripting was done in terms of shell scripts or early versions of Perl, where the lack of encapsulation and other OO features sometimes led to poor code management, frequent code duplication, and obscure hidden bugs. It wasn't helped by languages that combined notations from several existing sources as part of their heritage.

Over time, the scripting landscape has changed dramatically. Perl has added support for object orientation, Python has extended its object-oriented support, and more recently Ruby has made a name for itself as a full-fledged dynamic object-oriented scripting language with significant productivity benefits when compared to Java and C++.

Groovy follows the lead of Ruby by offering these dynamic object orientation features. Not only does it enhance Java by making it scriptable, but it also provides new OO features. You have already seen that Groovy provides reference types in cases where Java uses non-object primitive types, introduces ranges and closures as first-class objects, and has many shorthand notations for working with collections of objects. But these enhancements are just scratching the surface. If this were all that Groovy had to offer, it would be little more than syntactic sugar over normal Java. What makes Groovy stand apart is its set of *dynamic* features.

In this chapter, we will take you on a journey. We begin in familiar territory, with classes, objects, constructors, references, and so forth. Every so often, there's something a bit different, a little tweak of Grooviness. By the end of the chapter, we'll be in a whole new realm, changing the capabilities of objects and classes at runtime, intercepting method calls, and much, much more. Welcome to the Groovy world.

7.1 *Defining classes and scripts*

Class definition in Groovy is almost identical to Java; classes are declared using the `class` keyword and may contain *fields, constructors, initializers,* and *methods*.[1] Methods and constructors may themselves use *local variables* as part of their implementation code. Scripts are different—offering additional flexibility but

---

[1] *Interfaces* are also like their Java counterparts, but we will hold off discussing those further until section 7.3.2.

with some restrictions too. They may contain code, variable definitions, and method definitions as well as class definitions. We will describe how all of these members are declared and cover a previously unseen operator on the way.

7.1.1 Defining fields and local variables

In its simplest terms, a variable is a name associated with a slot of memory that can hold a value. Just as in Java, Groovy has *local variables*, which are scoped within the method they are part of, and *fields*, which are associated with classes or instances of those classes. Fields and local variables are declared in much the same way, so we cover them together.

Declaring variables

Fields and local variables must be declared before first use (except for a special case involving scripts, which we discuss later). This helps to enforce scoping rules and protects the programmer from accidental misspellings. The declaration always involves specifying a name, and may optionally include a type, modifiers, and assignment of an initial value. Once declared, variables are referenced by their name.

Scripts allow the use of undeclared variables, in which case these variables are assumed to come from the script's *binding* and are added to the binding if not yet there. The binding is a data store that enables transfer of variables to and from the caller of a script. Section 11.3.2 has more details about this mechanism.

Groovy uses Java's *modifiers*—the keywords `private`, `protected`, and `public` for modifying visibility;[2] `final` for disallowing reassignment; and `static` to denote *class variables*. A nonstatic field is also known as an *instance variable*. These modifiers all have the same meaning as in Java.

The default visibility for fields has a special meaning in Groovy. When no visibility modifier is attached to field declaration, a *property* is generated for the respective name. You will learn more about properties in section 7.4 when we present GroovyBeans.

Defining the type of a variable is optional. However, the identifier must not stand alone in the declaration. When no type and no modifier are given, the `def` keyword must be used as a replacement, effectively indicating that the field or variable is untyped (although under the covers it will be declared as type `Object`).

---

[2] Java's default *package-wide* visibility is not supported.

Listing 7.1 depicts the general appearance of field and variable declarations with optional assignment and using a comma-separated list of identifiers to declare multiple references at once.

Listing 7.1   Variable declaration examples

```
class SomeClass {

    public    fieldWithModifier
    String    typedField
    def       untypedField
    protected field1, field2, field3
    private   assignedField = new Date()

    static    classField

    public static final String CONSTA = 'a', CONSTB = 'b'

    def someMethod(){
        def localUntypedMethodVar = 1
        int localTypedMethodVar = 1
        def localVarWithoutAssignment, andAnotherOne
    }
}

def localvar = 1
boundvar1 = 1

def someMethod(){
    localMethodVar = 1
    boundvar2 = 1
}
```

Assignments to typed references must conform to the type—that is, you cannot assign a number to a reference of type `String` or vice versa. You saw in chapter 3 that Groovy provides autoboxing and coercion when it makes sense. All other cases are type-breaking assignments and lead to a `ClassCastException` at runtime, as can be seen in listing 7.2.[3]

---

[3] The `shouldFail` method as used in this example checks that a `ClassCastException` occurs. More details can be found in section 14.3.

Listing 7.2 Variable declaration examples

```
final static String PI = 3.14
assert PI.class.name == 'java.lang.String'
assert PI.length() == 4
new GroovyTestCase().shouldFail(ClassCastException.class){
    Float areaOfCircleRadiousOne = PI
}
```

As previously discussed, variables can be referred to by name in the same way as in Java—but Groovy provides a few more interesting possibilities.

Referencing and dereferencing fields

In addition to referring to fields by name with the $obj.fieldName$[4] syntax, they can also be referenced with the subscript operator, as shown in listing 7.3. This allows you to access fields using a dynamically determined name.

Listing 7.3 Referencing fields with the subscript operator

```
class Counter {
    public count = 0
}

def counter = new Counter()

counter.count = 1
assert counter.count == 1

def fieldName = 'count'
counter[fieldName] = 2
assert counter['count'] == 2
```

Accessing fields in such a dynamic way is part of the bigger picture of dynamic execution that we will analyze in the course of this chapter.

If you worked through the Groovy datatype descriptions, your next question will probably be, "can I override the subscript operator?" Sure you can, and you will *extend* but not *override* the general field-access mechanism that way. But you can do even better and extend the *field access* operator!

Listing 7.4 shows how to do that. To extend both set and get access, provide the methods

---

[4] This notation can also appear in the form of $obj.@fieldname$, as you will see in section 7.4.2.

```
Object get (String name)
void   set (String name, Object value)
```

There is no restriction on what you do inside these methods; get can return arti-ficial values, effectively *pretending* that your class has the requested field. In list-ing 7.4, the same value is always returned, regardless of which field value is requested. The set method is used for counting the write attempts.

Listing 7.4   Extending the general field-access mechanism

```
class PretendFieldCounter {
    public count = 0

    Object get (String name) {
        return 'pretend value'
    }
    void set (String name, Object value) {
        count++
    }
}

def pretender = new PretendFieldCounter()

assert pretender.isNoField == 'pretend value'
assert pretender.count     == 0

pretender.isNoFieldEither  = 'just to increase counter'

assert pretender.count     == 1
```

With the count field, you can see that it looks like the get/set methods are not used if the requested field is present. This is true for our special case. Later, in section 7.4, you will see the full set of rules that produces this effect.

Generally speaking, overriding the get method means to override the *dot-fieldname* operator. Overriding the set method overrides the *field assignment* operator.

FOR THE GEEKS   What about a statement of the form x.y.z=*something?* This is equivalent to getX().getY().setZ(*something*).

Referencing fields is also connected to the topic of *properties*, which we will explore in section 7.4, where we will discuss the need for the additional obj.@fieldName syntax.

7.1.2 Methods and parameters

Method declarations follow the same concepts you have seen for variables: The usual Java modifiers can be used; declaring a return type is optional; and, if no modifiers or return type are supplied, the def keyword fills the hole. When the def keyword is used, the return type is deemed to be untyped (although it can still have no return type, the equivalent of a void method). In this case, under the covers, the return type will be java.lang.Object. The default visibility of methods is public.

Listing 7.5 shows the typical cases in a self-describing manner.

Listing 7.5 Declaring methods

```
class SomeClass {                          ❶ Implicit
                                             public
    static void main(args) {      <──┘
        def some = new SomeClass()
        some.publicVoidMethod()
        assert 'hi' == some.publicUntypedMethod()
        assert 'ho' == some.publicTypedMethod()
        combinedMethod()          <──┐ Call static method
    }                                  of current class

    void publicVoidMethod(){
    }

    def publicUntypedMethod(){
        return 'hi'
    }
    String publicTypedMethod(){
        return 'ho'
    }

    protected static final void combinedMethod(){
    }
}
```

The main method ❶ has some interesting twists. First, the public modifier can be omitted because it is the default. Second, args usually has to be of type String[] in order to make the main method the one to start the class execution. Thanks to Groovy's method dispatch, it works anyway, although args is now implicitly of static type java.lang.Object. Third, because return types are not used for the dispatch, we can further omit the void declaration.

So, this Java declaration

```
public static void main (String[] args)
```

boils down to this in Groovy:

```
static main (args)
```

NOTE   The Java compiler fails on missing return statements when a return type is declared for the method. In Groovy, return statements are optional, and therefore it's impossible for the compiler to detect "accidentally" missing returns.

The `main(args)` example illustrates that declaring explicit parameter types is optional. When type declarations are omitted, `Object` is used. Multiple parameters can be used in sequence, delimited by commas. Listing 7.6 shows that explicit and omitted parameter types can also be mixed.

Listing 7.6   Declaring parameter lists

```
class SomeClass {
    static void main (args){
        assert 'untyped' == method(1)
        assert 'typed'   == method('whatever')
        assert 'two args'== method(1,2)
    }
    static method(arg) {
        return 'untyped'
    }
    static method(String arg){
        return 'typed'
    }
    static method(arg1, Number arg2){
        return 'two args'
    }
}
```

In the examples so far, all method calls have involved *positional* parameters, where the meaning of each argument is determined from its position in the parameter list. This is easy to understand and convenient for the simple cases you have seen, but suffers from a number of drawbacks for more complex scenarios:

- You must remember the exact sequence of the parameters, which gets increasingly difficult with the length of the parameter list.[5]

---

[5] We recommend a coding style that encourages small numbers of parameters, but this is not always possible.

■ If it makes sense to call the method with different information for alternative usage scenarios, different methods must be constructed to handle these alternatives. This can quickly become cumbersome and lead to a proliferation of methods, especially where some parameters are optional. It is especially difficult if many of the optional parameters have the same type. Fortunately, Groovy comes to the rescue with using maps as *named* parameters.

NOTE Whenever we talk about *named* parameters, we mean keys of a map that is used as an argument in method or constructor calls. From a programmer's perspective, this looks pretty much like native support for named parameters, but it isn't. This trick is needed because the JVM does not support storing parameter names in the bytecode.

Listing 7.7 illustrates Groovy method definitions and calls supporting positional and named parameters, parameter lists of variable length, and optional parameters with default values. The example provides four alternative summing mechanisms, each highlighting different approaches for defining the method call parameters.

Listing 7.7 Advanced parameter usages

```
class Summer {                                  ❶ Explicit arguments
    def sumWithDefaults(a, b, c=0){                and a default value
        return a + b + c
    }                                           ❷ Define arguments
    def sumWithList(List args){                    as a list
        return args.inject(0){sum,i -> sum += i}
    }                                           ❸ Optional arguments
    def sumWithOptionals(a, b, Object[] optionals){  as an array
        return a + b + sumWithList(optionals.toList())
    }
    def sumNamed(Map args){                     ❹ Define arguments
        ['a','b','c'].each{args.get(it,0)}         as a map
        return args.a + args.b + args.c
    }
}

def summer = new Summer()

assert 2 == summer.sumWithDefaults(1,1)
assert 3 == summer.sumWithDefaults(1,1,1)

assert 2 == summer.sumWithList([1,1])
assert 3 == summer.sumWithList([1,1,1])
```

```
assert 2 == summer.sumWithOptionals(1,1)
assert 3 == summer.sumWithOptionals(1,1,1)

assert 2 == summer.sumNamed(a:1, b:1)
assert 3 == summer.sumNamed(a:1, b:1, c:1)
assert 1 == summer.sumNamed(c:1)
```

All four alternatives have their pros and cons. In ❶, sumWithDefaults, we have the most obvious declaration of the arguments expected for the method call. It meets the needs of the sample script—being able to add two or three numbers together—but we are limited to as many arguments as we have declared parameters.

Using lists as shown in ❷ is easy in Groovy, because in the method call, the arguments only have to be placed in brackets. We can also support argument lists of arbitrary length. However, it is not as obvious what the individual list entries should mean. Therefore, this alternative is best suited when all arguments have the same meaning, as they do here where they are used for adding. Refer to section 4.2.3 for details about the List.inject method.

The sumWithOptionals method at ❸ can be called with two or more parameters. To declare such a method, define the last argument as an array. Groovy's dynamic method dispatch bundles excessive arguments into that array.

Named arguments can be supported by using a map as in ❹. It is good practice to reset any missing values to a default before working with them. This also better reveals what keys will be used in the method body, because this is not obvious from the method declaration.

When designing your methods, you have to choose one of the alternatives. You may wish to formalize your choice within a project or incorporate the Groovy coding style.

NOTE There is a second way of implementing parameter lists of variable length. You can hook into Groovy's method dispatch by overriding the invokeMethod(*name*, *params*[]) that every GroovyObject provides. You will learn more about these hooks in section 7.6.2.

Advanced naming

When calling a method on an object reference, we usually follow this format:

```
objectReference.methodName()
```

This format imposes the Java restrictions for method names; for example, they may not contain special characters such as minus (-) or dot (.). However, Groovy

allows you to use these characters in method names if you put quotes around
the name:

```
objectReference.'my.method-Name'()
```

The purpose of this feature is to support usages where the method name of a call
becomes part of the functionality. You won't normally use this feature directly, but
it will be used under the covers by other parts of Groovy. You will see this in action
in chapter 8 and chapter 10.

> **FOR THE GEEKS** Where there's a string, you can generally also use a GString. So how about
> `obj."${var}"()`? Yes, this is also possible, and the GString will be
> resolved to determine the name of the method that is called on the object!

That's it for the basics of class members. Before we leave this topic, though, there
is one convenient operator we should introduce while we're thinking about referring to members via references.

7.1.3 *Safe dereferencing with the ?. operator*

When a reference doesn't point to any specific object, its value is `null`. When calling a method or accessing a field on a `null` reference, a `NullPointerException`
(NPE) is thrown. This is useful to protect code from working on undefined pre-
conditions, but it can easily get in the way of "best effort" code that should be executed for valid references and just be silent otherwise.

Listing 7.8 shows several alternative approaches to protect code from NPEs. As
an example, we wish to access a deeply nested entry within a hierarchy of maps,
which results in a *path expression*—a dotted concatenation of references that is typically cumbersome to protect from NPEs. We can use explicit `if` checks or use the
`try-catch` mechanism. Groovy provides the additional `?.` operator for safe dereferencing. When the reference before that operator is a `null` reference, the evaluation of the current expression stops, and `null` is returned.

Listing 7.8 Protecting from `NullPointerExceptions` using the `?.` operator

```
def map = [a:[b:[c:1]]]

assert map.a.b.c == 1                          ❶ Protect with if: short-
                                                 circuit evaluation
if (map && map.a && map.a.x){
    assert map.a.x.c == null
}
```

```
try {
    assert map.a.x.c == null                ❷  Protect with
} catch (NullPointerException npe){  ◁⌐        try/catch
}
                                       ❸  Safe
assert map?.a?.x?.c == null   ◁⌐          dereferencing
```

In comparison, using the safe dereferencing operator in ❸ is the most elegant and expressive solution.

Note that ❶ is more compact than its Java equivalent, which would need three additional nullity checks. It works because the expression is evaluated from left to right, and the && operator stops evaluation with the first operand that evaluates to false. This is known as *shortcut evaluation.*

Alternative ❷ is a bit verbose and doesn't allow fine-grained control to protect only selective parts of the path expression. It also abuses the exception-handling mechanism. Exceptions weren't designed for this kind of situation, which is easily avoided by verifying that the references are non-null before dereferencing them. Causing an exception and then catching it is the equivalent of steering a car by installing big bumpers and bouncing off buildings.

Some software engineers like to think about code in terms of *cyclomatic complexity*, which in short describes code complexity by analyzing alternative pathways through the code. The safe dereferencing operator merges alternative pathways together and hence reduces complexity when compared to its alternatives; essentially, the metric indicates that the code will be easier to understand and simpler to verify as correct.

7.1.4 Constructors

Objects are instantiated from their classes via *constructors*. If no constructor is given, an implicit constructor without arguments is supplied by the compiler. This appears to be exactly like in Java, but because this is Groovy, it should not be surprising that some additional features are available.

In section 7.1.2, we examined the merits of *named* parameters versus *positional* ones, as well as the need for *optional* parameters. The same arguments applicable to method calls are relevant for constructors, too, so Groovy provides the same convenience mechanisms. We'll first look at constructors with positional parameters, and then we'll examine named parameters.

Positional parameters

Until now, we have only used implicit constructors. Listing 7.9 introduces the first explicit one. Notice that just like all other methods, the constructor is public by default. We can call the constructor in three different ways: the usual Java way, with enforced type coercion by using the as keyword, and with implicit type coercion.

Listing 7.9 Calling constructors with positional parameters

```
class VendorWithCtor {
    String name, product

    VendorWithCtor(name, product) {          Constructor
        this.name    = name                  definition
        this.product = product
    }
}

def first = new VendorWithCtor('Canoo','ULC')      Normal
                                                   constructor use

def second = ['Canoo','ULC'] as VendorWithCtor     ❶ Coercion with as

VendorWithCtor third = ['Canoo','ULC']    ❷ Coercion in assignment
```

The coercion in ❶ and ❷ may be surprising. When Groovy sees the need to coerce a list to some other type, it tries to call the type's constructor with all arguments supplied by the list, in list order. This need for coercion can be enforced with the as keyword or can arise from assignments to statically typed references. The latter of these is called *implicit construction*, which we cover shortly.

Named parameters

Named parameters in constructors are handy. One use case that crops up frequently is creating *immutable* classes that have some parameters that are optional. Using positional parameters would quickly become cumbersome because you would need to have constructors allowing for all combinations of the optional parameters.

As an example, suppose in listing 7.9 that VendorWithCtor should be immutable and name and product can be optional. We would need four[6] constructors: an empty one, one to set name, one to set product, and one to set both attributes. To make things worse, we couldn't have a constructor with only one argument,

---

[6] In general, 2^n constructors are needed, where n is the number of optional attributes.

because we couldn't distinguish whether to set the `name` or the `product` attribute (they are both strings). We would need an artificial extra argument for distinction, or we would need to strongly type the parameters.

But don't panic: Groovy's special way of supporting named parameters comes to the rescue again.

Listing 7.10 shows how to use named parameters with a simplified version of the `Vendor` class. It relies on the implicit default constructor. Could that be any easier?

> **Listing 7.10 Calling constructors with named parameters**

```
class Vendor {
    String name, product
}

new Vendor()
new Vendor(name:    'Canoo')
new Vendor(product:'ULC')
new Vendor(name:    'Canoo', product:'ULC')

def vendor = new Vendor(name: 'Canoo')
assert 'Canoo' == vendor.name
```

The example in listing 7.10 illustrates how flexible named parameters are for your constructors. In cases where you don't want this flexibility and want to lock down all of your parameters, just define your desired constructor explicitly; the implicit constructor with named parameters will no longer be available.

Coming back to how we started this section, the *empty* default constructor call `new Vendor` appears in a new light. Although it looks exactly like its Java equivalent, it is a special case of the default constructor with *named* parameters that happens to be called without any being supplied.

Implicit constructors

Finally, there is a way to call a constructor implicitly by simply providing the constructor arguments as a list. That means that instead of calling the `Dimension(width, height)` constructor explicitly, for example, you can use

```
java.awt.Dimension area

area = [200, 100]

assert area.width  == 200
assert area.height == 100
```

Of course, Groovy must know what constructor to call, and therefore implicit constructors are solely available for assignment to statically typed references where the type provides the respective constructor. They do not work for abstract classes or even interfaces.

Implicit constructors are often used with builders, as you'll see in the Swing-Builder example in section 8.5.7.

That's it for the usual class members. This is a solid basis we can build upon. But we are not yet in the penthouse; we have four more levels to go. We walk through the topic of how to organize classes and scripts to reach the level of advanced object-oriented features. The next floor is named GroovyBeans and deals with simple object-oriented information *about* objects. At this level, we can play with Groovy's *power features*. Finally, we will visit the highest level, which is *meta* programming in Groovy—making the environment fully dynamic, and responding to ordinary-looking method calls and field references in an extraordinary way.

7.2 *Organizing classes and scripts*

In section 2.4.1, you saw that Groovy classes are Java classes at the bytecode level, and consequently, Groovy objects are Java objects in memory. At the source-code level, Groovy class and object handling is almost a superset of the Java syntax, with the exception of nested classes that are currently not supported by the Groovy syntax and some slight changes to the way arrays are defined. We will examine the organization of classes and source files, and the relationships between the two. We will also consider Groovy's use of packages and type aliasing, as well as demystify where Groovy can load classes from in its classpath.

7.2.1 *File to class relationship*

The relationship between files and class declarations is not as fixed as in Java. Groovy files can contain any number of public class declarations according to the following rules:

- If a Groovy file contains *no* class declaration, it is handled as a script; that is, it is transparently wrapped into a class of type `Script`. This automatically generated class has the same name as the source script filename[7] (without the extension). The content of the file is wrapped into a `run` method, and an additional `main` method is constructed for easily starting the script.

---

[7] Because the class has no package name, it is implicitly placed in the default package.

- If a Groovy file contains exactly *one* class declaration with the same name as the file (without the extension), then there is the same one-to-one relationship as in Java.

- A Groovy file may contain *multiple* class declarations of any visibility, and there is no enforced rule that any of them must match the filename. The `groovyc` compiler happily creates *.class files for all declared classes in such a file. If you wish to invoke your script directly, for example using `groovy` on the command line or within an IDE, then the first class within your file should have a `main` method.[8]

- A Groovy file may *mix* class declarations and scripting code. In this case, the scripting code will become the main class to be executed, so don't declare a class yourself having the same name as the source filename.

When not compiling explicitly, Groovy finds a class by matching its name to a corresponding *.groovy source file. At this point, naming becomes important. Groovy only finds classes where the class name matches the source filename. When such a file is found, all declared classes in that file are parsed and become known to Groovy.

Listing 7.11 shows a sample script with two simple classes, `Vendor` and `Address`. For the moment, they have no methods, only public fields.

Listing 7.11 Multiple class declarations in one file

```
class Vendor {
    public String      name
    public String      product
    public Address      address = new Address()
}
class Address  {
    public String      street, town, state
    public int         zip
}

def canoo = new Vendor()
canoo.name               = 'Canoo Engineering AG'
canoo.product            = 'UltraLightClient (ULC)'
canoo.address.street     = 'Kirschgartenst. 7'
canoo.address.zip        =  4051
```

---

[8] Strictly speaking, you can alternatively extend `GroovyTestCase` or implement the `Runnable` interface.

```
canoo.address.town    = 'Basel'
canoo.address.state   = 'Switzerland'

assert canoo.dump()            =~ /ULC/
assert canoo.address.dump() =~ /Basel/
```

`Vendor` and `Address` are simple data storage classes. They are roughly equivalent to `structs` in C or Pascal `records`. We will soon explore more elegant ways of defining such classes.

Listing 7.11 illustrates a convenient convention supported by Groovy's source file to class mapping rules, which we discussed earlier. This convention allows small helper classes that are used only with the current main class or current script to be declared within the same source file. Compare this with Java, which allows you to use nested classes to introduce locally used classes without cluttering up your public class namespace or making navigation of the codebase more difficult by requiring a proliferation of source code files. Although it isn't exactly the same, this convention has similar benefits for Groovy developers.

7.2.2 *Organizing classes in packages*

Groovy follows Java's approach of organizing files in packages of hierarchical structure. The package structure is used to find the corresponding class files in the filesystem's directories.

Because *.groovy source files are not necessarily compiled to *.class files, there is also a need to look up *.groovy files. When doing so, the same strategy is used: The compiler looks for a Groovy class `Vendor` in the `business` package in the file business/Vendor.groovy.

In listing 7.12, we separate the `Vendor` and `Address` classes from the script code, as shown in listing 7.11, and move them to the `business` package.

Classpath

The lookup has to start somewhere, and Java uses its *classpath* for this purpose. The classpath is a list of possible starting points for the lookup of *.class files. Groovy reuses the classpath for looking up *.groovy files.

When looking for a given class, if Groovy finds both a *.class and a *.groovy file, it uses whichever is newer; that is, it will recompile source files into *.class files if they have changed since the previous class file was compiled.[9]

---

[9] Whether classes are checked for runtime updates can be controlled by the `CompilerConfiguration`, which obeys the system property `groovy.recompile` by default. See the API documentation for details.

Packages

Exactly like in Java, Groovy classes must specify their package before the class definition. When no package declaration is given, the default package is assumed.

Listing 7.12 shows the file business/Vendor.groovy, which has a package statement as its first line.

Listing 7.12 `Vendor` **and** `Address` **classes moved to the** `business` **package**

```
package business

class Vendor {
    public String   name
    public String   product
    public Address  address = new Address()
}

class Address  {
    public String   street, town, state
    public int      zip
}
```

To reference `Vendor` in the `business` package, you can either use `business.Vendor` within the code or use *imports* for abbreviation.

Imports

Groovy follows Java's notion of allowing `import` statements before any class declaration to abbreviate class references.

> **NOTE** Please keep in mind that unlike in some other scripting languages, `import` has nothing to do with literal inclusion of the imported class or file. It merely informs the compiler how to resolve references.

Listing 7.13 shows the use of the `import` statement, with the `.*` notation advising the compiler to try resolving all unknown class references against all classes in the `business` package.

Listing 7.13 Using `import` **to access** `Vendor` **in the** `business` **package**

```
import business.*

def canoo = new Vendor()
canoo.name          = 'Canoo Engineering AG'
```

```
canoo.product        = 'UltraLightClient (ULC)'

assert canoo.dump() =~ /ULC/
```

NOTE   By default, Groovy imports six packages and two classes, making it seem
like every groovy code program contains the following initial statements:

```
import java.lang.*
import java.util.*
import java.io.*
import java.net.*
import groovy.lang.*
import groovy.util.*
import java.math.BigInteger
import java.math.BigDecimal
```

Type aliasing

The `import` statement has another nice twist: together with the `as` keyword, it can
be used for *type aliasing*. Whereas a normal `import` allows a fully qualified class to
be referred to by its base name, a type alias allows a fully qualified class to be
referred to by a name of your choosing. This feature resolves naming conflicts
and supports local changes or bug fixes to a third-party library.

Consider the following library class:

```
package thirdparty

class MathLib {
    Integer twice(Integer value) {
        return value * 3        // intentionally wrong!
    }
    Integer half(Integer value) {
        return value / 2
    }
}
```

Note its obvious error[10] (although in general it might not be an error but just a
locally desired modification). Suppose now that we have some existing code that
uses that library:

```
assert 10 == new MathLib().twice(5)
```

----

[10] Where are the library author's unit tests?

We can use a type alias to rename the old library and then use inheritance to make a fix. No change is required to the original code that was using the library, as you can see in listing 7.14.

Listing 7.14 Using `import as` for local library modifications

```
import thirdparty.MathLib as OrigMathLib

class MathLib extends OrigMathLib {
    Integer twice(Integer value) {
        return value * 2
    }
}

// nothing changes below here          Usage code for library
def mathlib = new MathLib()            remains unchanged

assert 10 == mathlib.twice(5)      Invoke fixed method
assert 2 == mathlib.half(5)     Invoke original method
```

Now, suppose that we have the following additional math library that we need to use:

```
package thirdparty2

class MathLib {
    Integer increment(Integer value) {
        return value + 1
    }
}
```

Although it has a different package, it has the same name as the previous library. Without aliasing, we have to fully qualify one or both of the libraries within our code. With aliasing, we can avoid this in an elegant way and also improve communication by better indicating intent within our program about the role of the third-party library's code, as shown in listing 7.15.

Listing 7.15 Using `import as` for avoiding name clashes

```
import thirdparty.MathLib as TwiceHalfMathLib
import thirdparty2.MathLib as IncMathLib

def math1 = new TwiceHalfMathLib()
def math2 = new IncMathLib()

assert 3 == math1.half(math2.increment(5))
```

For example, if we later find a math package with both increment and twice/half functionality, we can refer to that new library twice and keep our more meaningful names.

You should consider using aliases within your own program, even when using simple built-in types. For example, if you are developing an adventure game, you might alias Map[11] to SatchelContents. This doesn't provide the strong typing that defining a separate SatchelContents class would give, but it does greatly improve the human understandability of the code.

7.2.3 *Further classpath considerations*

Finding classes in *.class and *.groovy files is an important part of working with Groovy, and unfortunately a likely source of problems.

If you installed the J2SDK including the documentation, you will find the classpath explanation under %JAVA_HOME%/docs/tooldocs/windows/classpath.html under Windows, or under a similar directory for Linux and Solaris. Everything the documentation says equally applies to Groovy.

A number of contributors can influence the effective classpath in use. The overview in table 7.1 may serve as a reference when you're looking for a possible *bad guy* that's messing up your classpath.

Table 7.1   Forming the classpath

Origin	Definition	Purpose and use
JDK/JRE	%JAVA_HOME%/lib %JAVA_HOME%/lib/ext	Bootclasspath for the Java Runtime Environment and its extensions
OS setting	CLASSPATH variable	Provides general default settings
Command shell	CLASSPATH variable	Provides more specialized settings
Java	-cp --classpath option	Settings per runtime invocation
Groovy	%GROOVY_HOME%/lib	The Groovy Runtime Environment
Groovy	-cp	Settings per groovy execution call
Groovy	.	Groovy classpath defaults to the current directory

---

[11] Here we mean java.util.Map and not TreasureMap, which our adventure game might allow us to place within the satchel!

Groovy defines its classpath in a special configuration file under %GROOVY_
HOME%/conf. Looking at the file groovy-starter.conf reveals the following lines
(beside others):

```
# Load required libraries
load ${groovy.home}/lib/*.jar

# load user specific libraries
# load ${user.home}/.groovy/lib/*
```

Uncommenting the last line by removing the leading hash sign enables a cool
feature. In your personal home directory user.home, you can use a subdirectory
.groovy/lib (note the leading dot!), where you can store any *.class or *.jar files
that you want to have accessible whenever you work with Groovy.

If you have problems finding your user.home, open a command shell and execute

```
groovy -e "println System.properties.'user.home'"
```

Chances are, you are in this directory by default anyway.

Chapter 11 goes through more advanced classpath issues that need to be
respected when embedding Groovy in environments that manage their own classloading infrastructure—for example an *application server.*

You are now able to use constructors in a number of different ways to make
new instances of a class. Classes may reside in packages, and you have seen how to
make them known via imports. This wraps up our exploration of object basics.
The next step is to explore more advanced OO features, which we discuss in the
following section.

7.3 *Advanced OO features*

Before beginning to embrace further parts of the Groovy libraries that make fundamental use of the OO features we have been discussing, we first stop to briefly
explore other OO concepts that change once you enter the Groovy world. We will
cover inheritance and interfaces, which will be familiar from Java, and *multimethods*, which will give you a taste of the dynamic object orientation coming later.

7.3.1 *Using inheritance*

You have seen how to explicitly add your own fields, methods, and constructors
into your class definitions. Inheritance allows you to implicitly add fields and
methods from a base class. The mechanism is useful in a range of use cases. We
leave it up to others[12] to describe its benefits and warn you about the potential

---

[12] *Designing Object-Oriented Software*, Rebecca Wirfs-Brock et al (Prentice-Hall, 1990).

overuse of this feature. We simply let you know that all the inheritance features of Java (including abstract classes) are available in Groovy and also work (almost seamlessly[13]) between Groovy and Java.

Groovy classes can extend Groovy and Java classes and interfaces alike. Java classes can also extend Groovy classes and interfaces. You need to compile your Java and Groovy classes in a particular order for this to work. See section 11.4.2 for more details. The only other thing you need to be aware of is that Groovy is more dynamic than Java when it selects which methods to invoke for you. This feature is known as *multimethods* and is discussed further in section 7.3.3.

7.3.2 Using interfaces

A frequently advocated style of Java programming involves using Java's interface mechanism. Code written using this style refers to the dependent classes that it uses solely by interface. The dependent classes can be safely changed later without requiring changes to the original program. If a developer accidentally tries to change one of the classes for another that doesn't comply with the interface, this discrepancy is detected at compile time. Groovy fully supports the Java interface mechanism.

Some[14] argue that interfaces alone are not strong enough, and design-by-contract is more important for achieving safe object substitution and allowing nonbreaking changes to your libraries. Judicious use of abstract methods and inheritance becomes just as important as using interfaces. Groovy's support for Java's abstract methods, its automatically enabled `assert` statement, and its built-in ready access to test methods mean that it is ideally suited to also support this stricter approach.

Still others[15] argue that dynamic typing is the best approach, leading to much less typing and less scaffolding code without much reduced safety—which should be covered by tests in any case. The good news is that Groovy supports this style as well. To give you a flavor of how this would impact you in everyday coding, consider how you would build a plug-in mechanism in Java and Groovy.

---

[13] The only limitation that we are aware of has to do with `Map`-based constructors, which Groovy provides by default. These are not available directly in Java if you extend a Groovy class. They are provided by Groovy as a runtime trick.

[14] See *Object-oriented Software Construction*, 2nd ed., by Bertrand Meyer (Prentice-Hall, 1997) and http://cafe.elharo.com/java/the-three-reasons-for-data-encapsulation/.

[15] See http://en.wikipedia.org/wiki/Duck_typing.

In Java, you would normally write an interface for the plug-in mechanism and then an implementation class for each plug-in that implements that interface. In Groovy, dynamic typing allows you to more easily create and use implementations that meet a certain need. You are likely to be able to create just two classes as part of developing two plug-in implementations. In general, you have a lot less scaffolding code and a lot less typing.

FOR THE GEEKS If you decide to make heavy use of interfaces, Groovy provides ways to make them more dynamic. If you have an interface `MyInterface` with a single method and a closure `myClosure`, you can use the as keyword to coerce the closure to be of type `MyInterface`. Similarly, if you have an interface with several methods, you can create a map of closures keyed on the method names and coerce the map to your interface type. See the Groovy wiki for more details.

In summary, if you've come from the Java world, you may be used to following a strict style of coding that strongly encourages interfaces. When using Groovy, you are not compelled to stick with any one style. In many situations, you can minimize the amount of typing by making use of dynamic typing; and if you really need it, the full use of interfaces is available.

7.3.3 *Multimethods*

Remember that Groovy's mechanics of method lookup take the dynamic type of method arguments into account, whereas Java relies on the static type. This Groovy feature is called *multimethods*.

Listing 7.16 shows two methods, both called `oracle`, that are distinguishable only by their argument types. They are called two times with arguments of the same static type but different dynamic types.

Listing 7.16   Multimethods: method lookup relies on dynamic types

```
def oracle(Object o) { return 'object' }
def oracle(String o) { return 'string' }

Object x = 1
Object y = 'foo'

assert 'object' == oracle(x)
assert 'string' == oracle(y)    ◁─┐  This would return
                                     object in Java
```

The x argument is of static type `Object` and of dynamic type `Integer`. The y argument is of static type `Object` but of dynamic type `String`.

Both arguments are of the same *static* type, which would make the equivalent Java program dispatch both to `oracle(Object)`. Because Groovy dispatches by the *dynamic* type, the specialized implementation of `oracle(String)` is used in the second case.

With this capability in place, you can better avoid duplicated code by being able to override behavior more selectively. Consider the `equals` implementation in listing 7.17 that overrides `Object`'s default `equals` method only for the argument type `Equalizer`.

Listing 7.17   Multimethods to selectively override `equals`

```
class Equalizer {
    boolean equals(Equalizer e){
        return true
    }
}

Object same  = new Equalizer()
Object other = new Object()

assert   new Equalizer().equals( same  )
assert ! new Equalizer().equals( other )
```

When an object of type `Equalizer` is passed to the `equals` method, the specialized implementation is chosen. When an arbitrary object is passed, the default implementation of its superclass `Object.equals` is called, which implements the equality check as a reference identity check.

The net effect is that the caller of the `equals` method can be fully unaware of the difference. From a caller's perspective, it looks like `equals(Equalizer)` would override `equals(Object)`, which would be impossible to do in Java. Instead, a Java programmer has to write it like this:

```
public class Equalizer {              // Java
    public boolean equals(Object obj)
    {
        if (obj == null)                 return false;
        if (!(obj instanceof Equalizer)) return false;
        Equalizer w = (Equalizer) obj;
        return true;                     // custom logic here
    }
}
```

This is unfortunate, because the logic of how to correctly override `equals` needs to be duplicated for every custom type in Java. This is another example where Java uses the static type `Object` and leaves the work of dynamic type resolution to the programmer.

> **NOTE**   Wherever there's a Java API that uses the static type `Object`, this code effectively loses the strength of static typing. You will inevitably find it used with typecasts, compromising compile-time type safety. This is why the Java type concept is called *weak* static typing: You lose the merits of static typing without getting the benefits of a dynamically typed language such as multimethods.

Groovy, in contrast, comes with a single and consistent implementation of dispatching methods by the dynamic types of their arguments.

7.4 *Working with GroovyBeans*

The JavaBeans specification[16] was introduced with Java 1.1 to define a lightweight and generic software component model for Java. The component model builds on naming conventions and APIs that allow Java classes to expose their properties to other classes and tools. This greatly enhanced the ability to define and use reusable components and opened up the possibility of developing component-aware tools.

The first tools were mainly visually oriented, such as visual builders that retrieved and manipulated properties of visual components. Over time, the Java-Beans concept has been widely used and extended to a range of use cases including server-side components (in Java Server Pages [JSP]), transactional behavior and persistence (Enterprise JavaBeans [EJB]), object-relational mapping (ORM) frameworks, and countless other frameworks and tools.

Groovy makes using JavaBeans (and hence most of these other JavaBean-related frameworks) easier with special language support. This support covers three aspects: special Groovy syntax for creating JavaBean classes; mechanisms for easily accessing beans, regardless of whether they were declared in Groovy or Java; and support for JavaBean event handling. This section will examine each part of this language-level support as well as cover the library support provided by the `Expando` class.

---

[16] See http://java.sun.com/products/javabeans/docs/spec.html.

7.4.1 Declaring beans

JavaBeans are normal classes that follow certain naming conventions. For example, to make a `String` property `myProp` available in a JavaBean, the bean's class must have public methods declared as `String getMyProp` and `void setMyProp` (`String value`). The JavaBean specification also strongly recommends that beans should be *serializable* so they can be persistent and provide a parameterless constructor to allow easy construction of objects from within tools. A typical Java implementation is as follows:

```java
// Java
public class MyBean implements java.io.Serializable {
  private String myprop;
  public String getMyprop(){
    return myprop;
  }
  public void setMyprop(String value){
    myprop = value;
  }
}
```

The Groovy equivalent is

```groovy
class MyBean implements Serializable {
  String myprop
}
```

The most obvious difference is size. One line of Groovy replaces seven lines of Java. But it's not only about less typing, it is also about self-documentation. In Groovy, it is easier to assess what fields are considered exposed properties: all fields that are declared with default visibility. The three related pieces of information—the field and the two accessor methods—are kept together in one declaration. Changing the type or the name of the property requires changing the code in only a single place.

> **NOTE** Older versions of Groovy used an `@Property` syntax for denoting properties. This was considered ugly and was removed in favor of handling properties as a "default visibility."

Underneath the covers, Groovy provides public accessor methods similar to this Java code equivalent, but you don't have to type them. Moreover, they are generated only if they don't already exist in the class. This allows you to *override* the standard accessors with either customized logic or constrained visibility. Groovy also provides a private backing field (again similar to the Java equivalent code).

Note that the JavaBean specification cares only about the available accessor methods and doesn't even require a backing field; but having one is an intuitive and simple way to implement the methods—so that is what Groovy does.

NOTE It is important that Groovy constructs the accessor methods and adds them to the bytecode. This ensures that when using a `MyBean` in the Java world, the Groovy `MyBean` class is recognized as a proper JavaBean.

Listing 7.18 shows the declaration options for properties with optional typing and assignment. The rules are equivalent to those for fields (see section 7.2.1).

Listing 7.18 Declaring properties in GroovyBeans

```
class MyBean implements Serializable {
    def untyped
    String typed
    def item1, item2
    def assigned = 'default value'
}

def bean = new MyBean()
assert 'default value' == bean.getAssigned()
bean.setUntyped('some value')
assert 'some value' == bean.getUntyped()
bean = new MyBean(typed:'another value')
assert 'another value' == bean.getTyped()
```

Properties are sometimes called *readable* or *writeable* depending on whether the corresponding getter or setter method is available. Groovy properties are both readable and writeable, but you can always roll your own if you have special requirements. When the `final` keyword is used with a property declaration, the property will only be readable (no setter method is created and the backing field is final).

Writing GroovyBeans is a simple and elegant solution for fully compliant Java-Bean support, with the option of specifying types as required.

7.4.2 *Working with beans*

The wide adoption of the JavaBeans concept in the world of Java has led to a common programming style where bean-style accessor methods are limited to simple access (costly operations are strictly avoided in these methods). These are the types of accessors generated for you by Groovy. If you have complex additional logic related to a property, you can always override the relevant getter or setter, but you are usually better off writing a separate business method for your advanced logic.

Accessor methods

Even for classes that do not fully comply with the JavaBeans standard, you can usually assume that such an accessor method can be called without a big performance penalty or other harmful side-effects. The characteristics of an accessor method are much like those of a direct field access (without breaking the *uniform access principle*[17]).

Groovy supports this style at the language level according to the mapping of method calls shown in table 7.2.

Table 7.2 Groovy accessor method to property mappings

Java	Groovy
`getPropertyname()`	`propertyname`
`setPropertyname(value)`	`propertyname = value`

This mapping works regardless of whether it's applied to a Groovy or *plain old Java object (POJO)*, and it works for beans as well as for all other classes. Listing 7.19 shows this in a combination of bean-style and derived properties.

Listing 7.19 Calling accessors the Groovy way

```
class MrBean {
    String firstname, lastname        ⟵┘ Groovy style
                                          properties
                          ❶ Getter for derived property
    String getName(){     ⟵
        return "$firstname $lastname"
    }
}
                                          Generic
                                          constructor
def bean = new MrBean(firstname: 'Rowan')   ⟵┘
bean.lastname = 'Atkinson'                    ❷ Call setter
                                            ⟵
assert 'Rowan Atkinson' == bean.name   ⟵❸ Call getter
```

Note how much the Groovy-style property access in ❷ and ❸ looks like direct field access, whereas ❶ makes clear that there is no field but only some derived value. From a caller's point of view, the access is truly *uniform*.

---

[17] See http://en.wikipedia.org/wiki/Uniform_access_principle.

Because field access and the accessor method shortcut have an identical syntax, it takes rules to choose one or the other.

RULES   When both a field and the corresponding accessor method are accessible to the caller, the property reference is resolved as an accessor method call. If only one is accessible, that option is chosen.

That looks straightforward, and it is in the majority of cases. However, there are some points to consider, as you will see next.

Field access with .@

Before we leave the topic of properties, we have one more example to explore: listing 7.20. The listing illustrates how you can provide your own accessor methods and also how to bypass the accessor mechanism. You can get directly to the field using the .@ *dot-at* operator when the need arises.

Listing 7.20   Advanced accessors with Groovy

```
class DoublerBean {
    public value      <--  Visible field

    void setValue(value){            ❶   Inner field access
        this.value = value    <--┘
    }

    def getValue(){        ❷   Inner field access
        value * 2     <--┘
    }
}

def bean = new DoublerBean(value: 100)
                      ❸  Property access
assert 200 == bean.value   <--┘
assert 100 == bean.@value   <--  Outer field access
```

Let's start with what's familiar: `bean.value` at ❸ calls `getValue` and thus returns the doubled value. But wait—`getValue` calculates the result at ❷ as `value * 2`. If `value` was at this point interpreted as a bean shortcut for `getValue`, we would have an endless recursion.

A similar situation arises at ❶, where the assignment `this.value =` would in bean terms be interpreted as `this.setValue`, which would also let us fall into endless looping. Therefore the following rules have been set up.

RULES Inside the lexical scope of a field, references to `fieldname` or `this.fieldname` are resolved as field access, not as property access. The same effect can be achieved from outside the scope using the `reference.@fieldname` syntax.

It needs to be mentioned that these rules can produce pathological corner cases with logical but surprising behavior, such as when using @ from a static context or with `def x=this; x.@fieldname`, and so on. We will not go into more details here, because such a design is discouraged. Decide whether to expose state as a field, as a property, or via explicit accessor methods, but do not mix these approaches. Keep the access uniform.

Bean-style event handling

Besides properties, JavaBeans can also be *event sources* that feed *event listeners*.[18] An event listener is an object with a *callback method* that gets called to notify the listener that an event was *fired*. An *event object* that further qualifies the event is passed as a parameter to the callback method.

The JDK is full of different types of event listeners. A simple event listener is the `ActionListener` on a button, which calls an `actionPerformed(ActionEvent)` method whenever the button is clicked. A more complex example is the `VetoableChangeListener` that allows listeners to throw a `PropertyVetoException` inside their `vetoableChange(PropertyChangeEvent)` method to roll back a change to a bean's property. Other usages are multifold, and it's impossible to provide an exhaustive list.

Groovy supports event listeners in a simple but powerful way. Suppose you need to create a Swing JButton with the label "Push me!" that prints the label to the console when it is clicked. A Java implementation can use an anonymous inner class in the following way:

```java
// Java
final JButton button = new JButton("Push me!");
button.addActionListener(new IActionListener(){
    public void actionPerformed(ActionEvent event){
        System.out.println(button.getText());
    }
});
```

The developer needs to know about the respective listener and event types (or interfaces) as well as about the registration and callback methods.

---

[18] See the JavaBeans Specification.

A Groovy programmer only has to attach a closure to the button as if it were a field named by the respective callback method:

```
button = new JButton('Push me!')
button.actionPerformed = { event ->
    println button.text
}
```

The event parameter is added only to show how we could get it when needed. In this example, it could have been omitted, because it is not used inside the closure.

> **NOTE** Groovy uses *bean introspection* to determine whether a field setter refers to a callback method of a listener that is supported by the bean. If so, a *ClosureListener* is transparently added that calls the closure when notified. A ClosureListener is a proxy implementation of the required listener interface.

Event handling is conceived as a JavaBeans standard. However, you don't need to somehow declare your object to be a bean before you can do any event handling. The dependency is the other way around: As soon as your object supports this style of event handling, it is called a bean.

Although Groovy adds the ability to register event listeners easily as closures, the Java style of bean event handling remains fully intact. That means you can still use all available Java methods to get a list of all registered listeners, adding more of them, or removing them when they are no longer needed.

7.4.3 Using bean methods for any object

Groovy doesn't distinguish between beans and other kinds of object. It solely relies on the accessibility of the respective getter and setter methods.

Listing 7.21 shows how to use the getProperties method and thus the properties property (sorry for the tricky wording) to get a map of a bean's properties. You can do so with any object you fancy.

Listing 7.21 GDK methods for bean properties

```
class SomeClass {
    def       someProperty
    public    someField
    private   somePrivateField
}

def obj = new SomeClass()
```

```
def store = []
obj.properties.each { property ->
    store += property.key
    store += property.value
}
assert store.contains('someProperty')
assert store.contains('someField')         == false
assert store.contains('somePrivateField') == false
assert store.contains('class')
assert store.contains('metaClass')

assert obj.properties.size() == 3
```

In addition to the property that is explicitly declared, you also see *class* and *meta-Class* references. These are artifacts of the Groovy class generation.[19]

This was a taste of what will be explained in more detail in section 9.1.

7.4.4 *Fields, accessors, maps, and Expando*

In Groovy code, you will often find expressions such as `object.name`. Here is what happens when Groovy resolves this reference:

- If `object` refers to a map, `object.name` refers to the value corresponding to the `name` key that is stored in the map.

- Otherwise, if `name` is a is a property of `object`, the property is referenced (with precedence of accessor methods over fields, as you saw in section 7.4.2).

- Every Groovy object has the opportunity to implement its own `getProperty(name)` and `setProperty(name, value)` methods. When it does, these implementations are used to control the property access. Maps, for example, use this mechanism to expose keys as properties.

- As shown in section 7.1.1, field access can be intercepted by providing the `object.get(name)` method. This is a last resort as far as the Groovy runtime is concerned: It's used only when there is no appropriate JavaBeans property available and when `getProperty` isn't implemented.

It is worth noting that when *name* contains special characters that would not be valid for an identifier, it can be supplied in string delimiters: for example, `object.'my-name'`. You can also use a GString: `def name = 'my-name'; object.`

---

[19] The `class` property stems from Java. However, tools that use Java's bean introspection often hide this property.

"$name". As you saw in section 7.1.1 and we will further explore in section 9.1.1, there is also a getAt implementation on Object that delegates to the property access such that you can access a property via object[name].

The rationale behind the admittedly nontrivial reference resolution is to allow dynamic state and behavior for Groovy objects. Groovy comes with an example of how useful this feature is: *Expando*. An Expando can be thought of as an *expandable* alternative to a bean, albeit one that can be used only within Groovy and not directly in Java. It supports the Groovy style of property access with a few extensions. Listing 7.22 shows how an Expando object can be expanded with properties by assignment, analogous to maps. The difference comes with assigning closures to a property. Those are executed when accessing the property, optionally taking parameters. In the example, the boxer fights back by returning multiple times what he has taken before.

Listing 7.22   Expando

```
def boxer = new Expando()

assert null == boxer.takeThis

boxer.takeThis = 'ouch!'

assert 'ouch!' == boxer.takeThis

boxer.fightBack = {times -> return this.takeThis * times  }

assert 'ouch!ouch!ouch!' == boxer.fightBack(3)
```

In a way, Expando's ability to assign closures to properties and have property access calling the stored closures is like dynamically attaching methods to an object.

Maps and Expandos are extreme solutions when it comes to avoiding writing dump data structures as classes, because they do not require *any* extra class to be written. In Groovy, accessing the keys of a map or the properties of an Expando doesn't look different from accessing the properties of a full-blown JavaBean. This comes at at a price: Expandos cannot be used as beans in the Java world and do not support any kind of typing.

7.5 *Using power features*

This section presents three power features that Groovy supports at the language level: *GPath*, the *Spread* operator, and the use keyword.

We start by looking at GPaths. A GPath is a construction in Groovy code that powers object navigation. The name is chosen as an analogy to XPath, which is a standard for describing traversal of XML (and equivalent) documents. Just like XPath, a GPath is aimed at expressiveness: realizing short, compact expressions that are still easy to read.

GPaths are almost entirely built on concepts that you have already seen: field access, shortened method calls, and the GDK methods added to `Collection`. They introduce only one new operator: the `*.` *spread-dot* operator. Let's start working with it right away.

7.5.1 Querying objects with GPaths

We'll explore Groovy by paving a path through the Reflection API. The goal is to get a sorted list of all getter methods for the current object. We will do so step-by-step, so please open a `groovyConsole` and follow along. You will try to get information about your current object, so type

```
this
```

and run the script (by pressing Ctrl-Enter). In the output pane, you will see something like

```
Script1@e7e8eb
```

which is the string representation of the current object. To get information about the class of this object, you could use `this.getClass`, but in Groovy you can type

```
this.class
```

which displays (after you run the script again)

```
class Script2
```

The class object reveals available methods with `getMethods`, so type

```
this.class.methods
```

which prints a long list of method object descriptions. This is too much information for the moment. You are only interested in the method names. Each method object has a `getName` method, so call

```
this.class.methods.name
```

and get a list of method names, returned as a list of string objects. You can easily work on it applying what you learned about strings, regular expressions, and lists. Because you are only interested in getter methods and want to have them sorted, type

```
this.class.methods.name.grep(~/get.*/).sort()
```

and voilà, you will get the result

```
["getBinding", "getClass", "getMetaClass", "getProperty"]
```

Such an expression is called a GPath. One special thing about it is that you can call the `name` property on a list of method objects and receive a list of string objects—that is, the *names*.

The rule behind this is that

```
list.property
```

is equal to

```
list.collect{ item -> item?.property }
```

This is an abbreviation of the special case when properties are accessed on lists. The general case reads like

```
list*.member
```

where `*.` is called the *spread-dot* operator and `member` can be a field access, a property access, or a method call. The *spread-dot* operator is needed whenever a method should be applied to all elements of the list rather than to the list itself. It is equivalent to

```
list.collect{ item -> item?.member }
```

To see GPath in action, we step into an example that is reasonably close to reality. Suppose you are processing invoices that consist of line items, where each line refers to the sold product and a multiplicity. A product has a price in dollars and a name.

An invoice could look like table 7.3.

Table 7.3 Sample invoice

Name	Price in $	Count	Total
ULC	1499	5	7495
Visual Editor	499	1	499

Figure 7.1 depicts the corresponding software model in a UML class diagram. The `Invoice` class aggregates multiple `LineItems` that in turn refer to a `Product`.

Listing 7.23 is the Groovy implementation of this design. It defines the classes as GroovyBeans, constructs sample invoices with this structure, and finally uses GPath expressions to query the object graph in multiple ways.

Figure 7.1 UML class diagram of an Invoice class that aggregates multiple instances of a LineItem class, which in turn aggregates exactly one instance of a Product class

---

Listing 7.23   Invoice example for GPath

```
class Invoice {
    List    items
    Date    date
}
class LineItem {
    Product product
    int     count                        Set up data
    int total() {                        structures
        return product.dollar * count
    }
}
class Product {
    String  name
    def     dollar
}

def ulcDate = new Date(107,0,1)
def ulc = new Product(dollar:1499, name:'ULC')
def ve  = new Product(dollar:499,  name:'Visual Editor')

def invoices = [
    new Invoice(date:ulcDate, items: [
        new LineItem(count:5, product:ulc),       Fill with
        new LineItem(count:1, product:ve)         sample data
    ]),
    new Invoice(date:[107,1,2], items: [
        new LineItem(count:4, product:ve)
    ])
]
assert [5*1499, 499, 4*499] == invoices.items*.total()     ⟵  Total for each
                                                          ❶ line item
assert ['ULC'] ==
    invoices.items.grep{it.total() > 7000}.product.name    ⟵  Query of
                                                          ❷ product names
def searchDates = invoices.grep{
    it.items.any{it.product == ulc}     ❸ Query of
}.date*.toString()                         invoice date
assert [ulcDate.toString()] == searchDates
```

The queries in listing 7.23 are fairly involved. The first, at ❶, finds the total for each invoice, adding up all the line items. We then run a query, at ❷, which finds all the names of products that have a line item with a total of over 7,000 dollars. Finally, query ❸ finds the date of each invoice containing a purchase of the ULC product and turns it into a string.

Printing the full Java equivalent here would cover four pages and would be boring to read. If you want to read it, you can find it in the book's online resources.

The interesting part is the comparison of GPath and the corresponding Java code. The GPath

```
invoices.items.grep{ it.total() > 7000 }.product.name
```

leads to the Java equivalent

```
// Java
private static List getProductNamesWithItemTotal(Invoice[] invoices) {
    List result = new LinkedList();
    for (int i = 0; i < invoices.length; i++) {
        List items = invoices[i].getItems();
        for (Iterator iter = items.iterator(); iter.hasNext();) {
            LineItem lineItem = (LineItem) iter.next();
            if (lineItem.total() > 7000){
                result.add(lineItem.getProduct().getName());
            }
        }
    }
    return result;
}
```

Table 7.4 gives you some metrics about both full versions, comparing lines of code (LOC), number of statements, and complexity in the sense of nesting depth

There may be ways to slim down the Java version, but the order of magnitude remains: Groovy needs less than 25% of the Java code lines and fewer than 10% of the statements!

Writing less code is not just an exercise for its own sake. It also means lower chances of making errors and thus less testing effort. Whereas some new developers think of a good day as one in which they've *added* lots of lines to the codebase, we consider a really good day as one in which we've added functionality but *removed* lines from the codebase.

In a lot of languages, less code comes at the expense of clarity. Not so in Groovy. The GPath example is the best proof. It is much easier to read and understand than its Java counterpart. Even the complexity metrics are superior.

Table 7.4   GPath example: Groovy and Java metrics compared

	LOC[a]		Statements[b]		Complexity	
	Groovy	**Java**	**Groovy**	**Java**	**Groovy**	**Java**
CallingScript	16	84	7	72	1	4
Invoice	4	16	0	4	0	1
LineItem	7	19	1	5	1	1
Product	4	16	0	4	0	1
Total	31	135	7	85		

a. Lines of code without comments and newlines
b. Assignments, method calls, and returns

As a final observation, consider maintainability. Suppose your customer refines their requirements, and you need to change the lookup logic. How much effort does that take in Groovy as opposed to Java?

7.5.2 *Injecting the spread operator*

Groovy provides a * *spread* operator that is connected to the spread-dot operator in that it deals with tearing a list apart. It can be seen as the reverse counterpart of the subscript operator that creates a list from a sequence of comma-separated objects. The spread operator distributes all items of a list to a receiver that can take this sequence. Such a receiver can be a method that takes a sequence of arguments or a list constructor.

What is this good for? Suppose you have a method that returns multiple results in a list, and your code needs to pass these results to a second method. The spread operator distributes the result values over the second method's parameters:

```
def getList(){
    return [1,2,3]
}
def sum(a,b,c){
    return a + b + c
}
assert 6 == sum(*list)
```

This allows clever meshing of methods that return and receive multiple values while allowing the receiving method to declare each parameter separately.

The distribution with the spread operator also works on ranges and when distributing all items of a list into a second list:

```
def range = (1..3)
assert [0,1,2,3] == [0,*range]
```

The same trick can be applied to maps:

```
def map = [a:1,b:2]
assert [a:1, b:2, c:3] == [c:3, *:map]
```

The spread operator eliminates the need for boilerplate code that would otherwise be necessary to merge lists, ranges, and maps into the expected format. You will see this in action in section 10.3, where this operator helps implement a user command language for database access.

As shown in the previous assertions, the spread operator is conveniently used inside expressions, supporting a functional style of programming as opposed to a procedural style. In a procedural style, you would introduce statements like `list.addAll(otherlist)`.

Now comes Groovy's ultimate power feature, which you can use to assign new methods to any Groovy or Java class.

7.5.3 *Mix-in categories with the use keyword*

Consider a program that reads two integer values from an external device, adds them together, and writes the result back. Reading and writing are in terms of strings; adding is in terms of integer math. You can't write

```
write( read() + read() )
```

because this would result in calling the `plus` method on strings and would concatenate the arguments rather than adding them.

Groovy provides the `use` method,[20] which allows you to augment a class's available instance methods using a so-called *category*. In our example, we can augment the `plus` method on strings to get the required Perl-like behavior:

```
use(StringCalculationCategory) {
    write( read() + read() )
}
```

---

[20] Like most Groovy programmers, we prefer to call `use` a keyword, but strictly speaking it is a method that Groovy adds to `java.lang.Object`.

A category is a class that contains a set of static methods (called *category methods*). The use keyword makes each of these methods available on the class of that method's first argument, as an instance method:

```
class StringCalculationCategory {

    static String plus(String self, String operand) {
        // implementation
    }
}
```

Because self is the first argument, the plus(operand) method is now available (or overridden) on the String class.

Listing 7.24 shows the full example. It implements these requirements with a fallback in case the strings aren't really integers and a usual concatenation should apply.

Listing 7.24   The use keyword for calculation on strings

```
class StringCalculationCategory {
    static def plus(String self, String operand) {
        try {
            return self.toInteger() + operand.toInteger()
        }
        catch (NumberFormatException fallback){
            return (self << operand).toString()
        }
    }
}

use (StringCalculationCategory) {
    assert 1    == '1' + '0'
    assert 2    == '1' + '1'
    assert 'x1' == 'x' + '1'
}
```

The use of a category is limited to the duration of the attached closure and the current thread. The rationale is that such a change should not be globally visible to protect from unintended side effects.

Throughout the language basics part of this book, you have seen that Groovy adds new methods to existing classes. The whole GDK is implemented by adding new methods to existing JDK classes. The use method allows any Groovy programmer to use the same strategy in their own code.

A category can be used for multiple purposes:

- To provide special-purpose methods, as you have seen with `StringCalculationCategory`, where the calculation methods have the same receiver class and may override existing behavior. Overriding operator methods is special.

- To provide additional methods on library classes, effectively solving the *incomplete library class* smell.[21]

- To provide a collection of methods on different receivers that work in combination—for example, a new `encryptedWrite` method on `java.io.OutputStream` and `decryptedRead` on `java.io.InputStream`.

- Where Java uses the *Decorator*[22] pattern, but without the hassle of writing lots of relay methods.

- To split an overly large class into a core class and multiple aspect categories that are used with the core class as needed. Note that `use` can take any number of category classes.

When a category method is assigned to `Object`, it is available in all objects—that is, everywhere. This makes for nice all-purpose methods like logging, printing, persistence, and so on. For example, you already know everything to make that happen for persistence:

```
class PersistenceCategory {
    static void save(Object self) {
        // whatever you do to store 'self' goes here
    }
}
use (PersistenceCategory) {
    save()
}
```

Instead of `Object`, a smaller area of applicability may be of interest, such as all `Collection` classes or all your business objects if they share a common interface.

Note that you can supply as many category classes as you wish as arguments to the `use` method by comma-separating the classes or supplying them as a list.

```
use (ACategory, BCategory, CCategory) {}
```

---

[21] See chapter 3 (written by Kent Beck and Martin Fowler) of *Refactoring* (Addison-Wesley, 2000).

[22] See page 195 of *Design Patterns: Elements of Reusable Object-Oriented Software* by Gamma et al (Addison Wesley, 1994).

By now, you should have some idea of Groovy's power features. They are impressive even at first read, but the real appreciation will come when you apply them in your own code. It is worth consciously bearing them in mind early on in your travels with Groovy so that you don't miss out on some elegant code just because the features and patterns are unfamiliar. Before long, they will become so familiar that you will miss them a lot when you are forced to go back to Java. The good news is that Groovy can easily be used from Java, as we will explore in chapter 11.

The use of category classes in closures is a feature that Groovy can provide because of its *Meta* concept, which is presented in the next section.

7.6 *Meta programming in Groovy*

In order to fully leverage the power of Groovy, it's beneficial to have a general understanding of how it works inside. It is not necessary to know all the details, but familiarity with the overall concepts will allow you to work more confidently in Groovy and find more elegant solutions.

This section provides you with a peek inside how Groovy performs its magic. The intent is to explain some of the general concepts used under the covers, so that you can write solutions that integrate more closely with Groovy's inner runtime workings. Groovy has numerous interception points, and choosing between them lets you leverage or override different amounts of the built-in Groovy capabilities. This gives you many options to write powerful yet elegant solutions outside the bounds of what Groovy can give you out of the box. We will describe these interception points and then provide an example of how they work in action.

The capabilities described in this section collectively form Groovy's implementation of the *Meta-Object Protocol* (MOP). This is a term used for a system's ability to change the behavior of objects and classes at runtime—to mess around with the guts of the system, to put it crudely.

At the time of writing, a redesign of the MOP is ongoing and is called the *new MOP*. It is mainly concerned with improving the internals with respect to consistency of the implementation and runtime performance. We highlight where changes are expected for the programmer.

7.6.1 *Understanding the MetaClass concept*

In Groovy, everything starts with the `GroovyObject` interface, which, like all the other classes we've mentioned, is declared in the package `groovy.lang`. It looks like this:

```
public interface GroovyObject {
    public Object     invokeMethod(String name, Object args);
    public Object     getProperty(String property);
    public void²³     setProperty(String property, Object newValue);
    public MetaClass getMetaClass();
    public void       setMetaClass(MetaClass metaClass);
}
```

All classes you program in Groovy are constructed by the *GroovyClassGenerator* such that they implement this interface and have a default implementation for each of these methods—unless you choose to implement it yourself.

NOTE If you want a usual Java class to be recognized as a Groovy class, you only have to implement the GroovyObject interface. For convenience, you can also subclass the abstract class GroovyObjectSupport, which provides default implementations.

GroovyObject has an association with MetaClass, which is the navel of the Groovy meta concept. It provides all the meta-information about a Groovy class, such as the list of available methods, fields, and properties. It also implements the following methods:

```
Object invokeMethod(Object obj, String methodName, Object args)
Object invokeMethod(Object obj, String methodName, Object[] args)
Object invokeStaticMethod(Object obj, String methodName, Object[] args)
Object invokeConstructor(Object[] args)
```

These methods do the real work of method invocation,²⁴ either through the Java Reflection API or (by default and with better performance) through a transparently created *reflector* class. The default implementation of GroovyObject. invokeMethod relays any calls to its MetaClass.

The MetaClass is stored in and retrieved from a central store, the MetaClassRegistry.

Figure 7.2 shows the overall picture (keep this picture in mind when thinking through Groovy's process of invoking a method).

---

²³ New MOP: return boolean to indicate success of the operation. No more exceptions are thrown.

²⁴ New MOP: These methods no longer throw an exception in case of errors but return an error token. The same is true for getProperty. The internals of the implementation may also change; for example, more specialized methods may be used for faster dispatch.

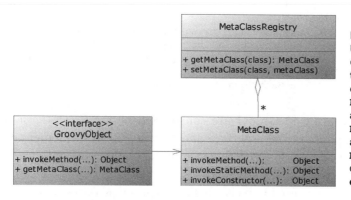

Figure 7.2
UML class diagram of the
`GroovyObject` interface
that refers to an instance
of class `MetaClass`, where
`MetaClass` objects are
also aggregated by the
`MetaClassRegistry` to
allow class-based retrieval of
`MetaClasses` in addition to
`GroovyObject`'s potentially
object-based retrieval

NOTE The `MetaClassRegistry` class is intended to be a `Singleton` but it is not used as such, yet. Anyway, throughout the code, a factory method on `InvokerHelper` is used to refer to a single instance of this registry.

The structure as depicted in figure 7.2 is able to deal with having one `MetaClass` *per object*, but this capability is not used in the default implementations. Current default implementations use one `MetaClass` *per class* in the `MetaClassRegistry`. This difference becomes important when you're trying to define methods that are accessible only on certain instances of a class (like *singleton methods* in Ruby).

NOTE The `MetaClass` that a `GroovyObject` refers to and the `MetaClass` that is registered for the type of this `GroovyObject` in the `MetaClassRegistry` do not need to be identical. For instance, a certain object can have a special `MetaClass` assigned that differs from the `MetaClass` of all other objects of this class.

7.6.2 *Method invocation and interception*

Groovy generates its Java bytecode such that each method call (after some redirections) is handled by one of the following mechanisms:

1 The class's own `invokeMethod` implementation (which may further choose to relay it to some `MetaClass`)

2 Its own `MetaClass`, by calling `getMetaClass().invokeMethod(…)`

3 The `MetaClass` that is registered for its type in the `MetaClassRegistry`

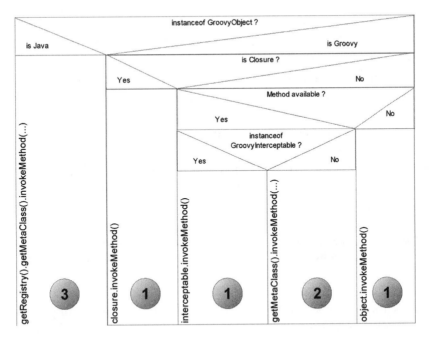

Figure 7.3 **Nassi-Shneidermann diagram of Groovy's decision logic for three distinct kinds of method invocation based on the method's receiver type and method availability. Follow the conditions like a flow diagram to discover which course of action is taken.**

The decision is taken by an *Invoker* singleton that applies the logic as shown in figure 7.3.[25] Each number in the diagram refers to the corresponding mechanism in the previous numbered list.

This is a relatively complex decision to make for every method call, and of course most of the time you don't need to think about it. You certainly shouldn't be mentally tracing your way through the diagram for every method call you make—after all, Groovy is meant to make things easier, not harder! However, it's worth having the details available so that you can always work out exactly what will happen in a complicated situation. It also opens your mind to a wide range of possibilities for adding dynamic behavior to your own classes. The possibilities include the following:

---

[25] New MOP: Closures will no longer be handled as a special case in the default `MetaClass`. Instead, a custom `MetaClass` for closures will produce the same effect.

- You can *intercept* method calls with cross-cutting concerns (aspects) such as logging/tracing all invocations, applying security restrictions, enforcing transaction control, and so on.

- You can *relay* method calls to other objects. For example, a *wrapper* can relay to a *wrapped* object all method calls that it cannot handle itself.

BY THE WAY This is what closures do. They relay method calls to their *delegate*.

- You can *pretend* to execute a method while some other logic is applied. For example, an `Html` class could pretend to have a method `body`, while the call was executed as `print('body')`.

BY THE WAY This is what *builders* do. They pretend to have methods that are used to define nested product structures. This will be explained in detail in chapter 8.

The invocation logic suggests that there are multiple ways to implement *intercepted*, *relayed*, or *pretended* methods:

- Implementing/overriding `invokeMethod` in a `GroovyObject` to *pretend* or *relay* method calls (all your defined methods are still called as usual).

- Implementing/overriding `invokeMethod` in a `GroovyObject`, and also implementing the `GroovyInterceptable` interface to additionally *intercept* calls to your defined methods.

- Providing an implementation of `MetaClass`, and calling `setMetaClass` on the target `GroovyObjects`.

- Providing an implementation of `MetaClass`, and registering it in the `MetaClassRegistry` for all target classes (Groovy and Java classes). This scenario is supported by the `ProxyMetaClass`.

Generally speaking, overriding/implementing `invokeMethod` means to override the *dot-methodname* operator.

The next section will teach you how to leverage this knowledge.

7.6.3 *Method interception in action*

Suppose we have a Groovy class `Whatever` with methods `outer` and `inner` that call each other, and we have lost track of the intended calling sequence. We would like to get a runtime trace of method calls like

```
before method 'outer'
  before method 'inner'
  after  method 'inner'
after  method 'outer'
```

to confirm that the `outer` method calls the `inner` method.

Because this is a `GroovyObject`, we can override `invokeMethod`. To make sure we can intercept calls to our defined methods, we need to implement the `GroovyInterceptable` interface, which is only a *marker* interface and has no methods.

Inside `invokeMethod`, we write into a trace log before and after executing the method call. We keep an indentation level for tidy output. Trace output should go to `System.out` by default or to a given `Writer`, which allows easy testing. We achieve this by providing a writer property.

To make our code more coherent, we put all the tracing functionality in a superclass `Traceable`. Listing 7.25 shows the final solution.

Listing 7.25 Trace implementation by overriding `invokeMethod`

```
import org.codehaus.groovy.runtime.StringBufferWriter
import org.codehaus.groovy.runtime.InvokerHelper

class Traceable implements GroovyInterceptable {        ⊲┘ Tagged
                                                            superclass

    Writer writer = new PrintWriter(System.out)    ⊲┘ Default : stdout
    private int indent = 0
                                                       Override
    Object invokeMethod(String name, Object args){  ⊲┘ default
        writer.write("\n" + '  '*indent + "before method '$name'")
        writer.flush()
        indent++
        def metaClass = InvokerHelper.getMetaClass(this)    ❶ Execute
        def result = metaClass.invokeMethod(this, name, args)  call
        indent--
        writer.write("\n" + '  '*indent + "after  method '$name'")
        writer.flush()
        return result
    }                              Production
}                               ┌┘ class
class Whatever extends Traceable {  ⊲┘
    int outer(){
        return inner()
    }
    int inner(){
        return 1
    }
}
```

```
def log = new StringBuffer()
def traceMe = new Whatever(writer: new StringBufferWriter(log))    ◁⌐  Test
                                                                         settings
assert 1 == traceMe.outer()    ◁❷  Start

assert log.toString() == """
before method 'outer'
  before method 'inner'
  after  method 'inner'
after  method 'outer'"""
```

It's crucial not to step into an endless loop when relaying the method call, which would be unavoidable when calling the method in the same way the interception method was called (thus falling into the same column in figure 7.3). Instead, we enforce falling into the leftmost column with the invokeMethod call at ❶.

We use Groovy's convenient StringBufferWriter to access the output at ❷. To see the output on System.out, use new Whatever without parameters.

The whole execution starts at ❷. We also assert that we still get the proper result.

Unfortunately, this solution is limited. First, it works only on GroovyObjects, not on arbitrary Java classes. Second, it doesn't work if the class under inspection already extends some other superclass.

Recalling figure 7.3, we need a solution that replaces our MetaClass in the MetaClassRegistry with an implementation that allows tracing. There is such a class in the Groovy codebase: ProxyMetaClass.

This class serves as a decorator over an existing MetaClass and adds interceptability to it by using an Interceptor (see groovy.lang.Interceptor in the Groovy Javadocs). Luckily, there is a TracingInterceptor that serves our purposes. Listing 7.26 shows how we can use it with the Whatever class.

> **Listing 7.26 Intercepting method calls with ProxyMetaClass
>   and TracingInterceptor**

```
import org.codehaus.groovy.runtime.StringBufferWriter

class Whatever {
    int outer(){
        return inner()
    }
    int inner(){
        return 1
    }
}
```

```
def log = new StringBuffer("\n")
def tracer = new TracingInterceptor()          ◁─┘ Construct the
                                                    Interceptor         Retrieve a
tracer.writer = new StringBufferWriter(log)                             suitable
def proxy = ProxyMetaClass.getInstance(Whatever.class)    ◁─┘           ProxyMetaClass
proxy.interceptor = tracer
proxy.use {                    ◁─┘ Determine scope for using it
    assert 1 == new Whatever().outer()    ◁─┐ Start
}                                             execution

assert log.toString() == """
before Whatever.ctor()
after  Whatever.ctor()
before Whatever.outer()
  before Whatever.inner()
  after  Whatever.inner()
after  Whatever.outer()
"""
```

Note that this solution also works with all Java classes when called from Groovy.

For `GroovyObjects` that are not invoked via the `MetaClassRegistry`, you can pass the object under analysis to the `use` method to make it work:

```
proxy.use(traceMe){
    // call methods on traceMe
}
```

`Interceptor` and `ProxyMetaClass` can be useful for debugging purposes but also for simple profiling tasks. They open the door for all the cross-cutting concerns that we mentioned earlier.

> **NOTE**   Take care when applying wide-ranging changes to the `MetaClassReg-istry`. This can potentially have unintended effects on parts of the code-base that seem unrelated. Be careful with your cross-cutting concerns, and avoid cutting too much or too deeply!

That's it for our tour through Groovy's Meta capabilities. The magician has revealed all his tricks (well, at least most of them), and you can now be a magician yourself.

MOP makes Groovy a *dynamic* language. It is the basis for numerous inventions that Groovy brings to the Java platform. The remainder of this book will show the most important ones: builders, markup, persistency, distributed programming, transparent mocks and stubs for testing purposes, and all kinds of dynamic APIs over existing frameworks, such as for Windows scripting with Scriptom or object-relational mapping through Hibernate.

This dynamic nature makes a framework such as Grails (see chapter 16) possible on the Java platform.

Groovy is often perceived as a scripting language for the JVM, and it is. But making Java scriptable is not the most distinctive feature. The Meta-Object Protocol and the resulting dynamic nature elevate Groovy over other languages.

7.7 Summary

Congratulations on making it to the end of this chapter and the end of part 1 of this book. If you are new to dynamic languages, your head may be spinning right now—it's been quite a journey!

The chapter started without too many surprises, showing the similarities between Java and Groovy in terms of defining and organizing classes. As we introduced named parameters for constructors and methods, optional parameters for methods, and dynamic field lookup with the subscript operator, as well as Groovy's "load at runtime" abilities, it became obvious that Groovy has more spring in its step than Java.

Groovy's handling of the JavaBeans conventions reinforced this, as we showed Groovy classes with JavaBean-style properties that were simpler and more expressive to both create and use than their Java equivalents. By the time you saw Groovy's power features such as GPath and categories, the level of departure was becoming more apparent, and Groovy's dynamic nature was beginning to show at the seams.

Finally, with a discussion of Groovy's implementation of the Meta-Object Protocol, this dynamic nature came out in the open. What began as a "drip, drip, drip" of features with a mixture of dynamic aspects and syntactic sugar ended as a torrent of options for changing almost every aspect of Groovy's behavior dynamically at runtime.

In retrospect, the dependencies and mutual support between these different aspects of the language become obvious: using the map datatype with default constructors, using the range datatype with the subscript operator, using operator overriding with the switch control structure, using closures for grepping through a list, using the list datatype in generic constructors, using bean properties with a field-like syntax, and so on. This seamless interplay not only gives Groovy its power but also makes it fun to use.

What is perhaps most striking is the compactness of the Groovy code while the readability is preserved if not enhanced. It has been reported[26] that developer productivity hasn't improved much since the '70s in terms of lines of code written per day. The boost in productivity comes from the fact that a single line of code nowadays expresses much more than in previous eras. Now, if a single line of Groovy can replace multiple lines of Java, we could start to see the next major boost in developer productivity.

---

[26] The Journal of Defense Software Engineering, 08/2000, http://www.stsc.hill.af.mil/crosstalk/2000/08/jensen.html, based on the work of Gerald M. Weinberg.

Part 2

Around the Groovy library

Part 1 has lifted you to the level where you can confidently work with the Groovy *language*. You have also seen a glimpse of some of the fundamental parts of Groovy *library*. Part 2 builds upon this knowledge, diving into other parts of the Groovy library and exploring how Groovy extends the Java Runtime Environment. You have already seen how Groovy tries to make commonly performed tasks as easy as possible in the language—this part of the book shows how the same principle is applied in Groovy's libraries, using many of the advanced language features available to let you do more work with less code.

Chapter 8 introduces the builder concept, which is one of Groovy's distinctive capabilities, because it can only be implemented in a general library class with a truly dynamic language. We will examine the builders that come as part of the Groovy distribution and show you how to implement your own builders.

Chapter 9 covers at the object/method level pure GDK library capabilities that were not presented in part 1, because they are not directly related to language features.

Chapter 10 goes through Groovy's library support for dealing with relational database systems, providing total flexibility where necessary and significant shortcuts where simple solutions suffice.

Chapter 11 presents various ways of making Java applications more dynamic by integrating them with Groovy, allowing for rich runtime customization and interaction.

Chapter 12 dives into the special topic of XML support in Groovy: reading and writing XML documents, transforming them into other representations, and using XML for interoperation of heterogeneous systems.

Part 3 will finally show how to put all the Groovy language and library capabilities into action for your everyday tasks.

Working with builders 8

As software developers, everything we do day in and day out is building: We build graphical applications, command-line tools, data stores, and a lot of other, often invisible products. To this end, we make use of components and frameworks as building blocks assembled on a fundamental base. We build by following the rules of the architecture and the best practices of our trade.

Not surprisingly, the general task of building faces us with recurring activities and structures. Over time, developer experience has led to proven standard solutions for repetitive building tasks captured in terms of patterns. One such pattern is the *Builder* pattern. In this pattern, a *builder* object is used to help build a complex object, called the *product*. It encapsulates the logic of how to assemble the product from given pieces.[1]

Products can be complex because they maintain a tricky internal state (think of a parser object) or because they are built out of numerous objects with interdependencies. The latter case is frequently seen when there are tree-like structures that you find everywhere in the world of software:

- Most obviously, a filesystem is a tree of directories and files.
- This book is a tree of parts, chapters, sections, subsections, and paragraphs.
- HTML and XML documents have a tree-like document object model.
- Test cases are bundled into suites, and suites are bundled into higher-level suites such that a tree of tests is constructed.
- Graphical user interfaces are built from components that are assembled into containers. A Swing `JFrame` may include multiple `JPanels` that include multiple `JPanels`, and so forth.
- Less obviously, business objects often form a tree at runtime: `Invoice` objects that refer to multiple *LineItems* that refer to *Products*, and so on.

Surprisingly, most programming languages have a hard time modeling this oh-so-common structure, especially *building* a tree-like structure in program code. Most of the time, the programmer is left with the task of calling several `addChild` and `setParent` methods.

This has two major drawbacks:

- The logic of how to properly build the tree structure is often subject to massive duplication.
- When reading the code, it is hard to get an overall picture of the nesting structure.

---

[1] Erich Gamma et al, *Design Patterns: Elements of Reusable Object-Oriented Software* (Addison-Wesley, 1995).

To overcome the latter drawback, many approaches store the nesting structure in some external format, typically XML, and construct runtime objects from there. This, of course, has other limitations: You lose all the merits of your programming language when defining the structure. This leads to a lack of flexibility and is likely to produce a lot of duplication in the XML.

Groovy offers an alternative approach. Its builder support allows you to define nested, tree-like structures in the code, being descriptive and flexible at the same time. When you view the code, at least in *reasonably* simple situations, the resulting hierarchy is easily visible on the screen. Groovy enables this as a *language* through the use of closures, the Meta-Object Protocol (MOP), and simple map declarations. The *library* support comes from `BuilderSupport` and its subclasses including `NodeBuilder`, `MarkupBuilder`, `AntBuilder`, and `SwingBuilder`.

Understanding the sample code doesn't require a deep understanding of the MOP; but if you feel uncertain about closures and map literals, you might want to look back at chapters 4 (for maps) and 5 (for closures), or at least have them earmarked for quick reference.

In this chapter, we visit each of these subclasses in turn to see specific uses of builders, and then we give more details of how you can implement your own builder using `BuilderSupport`.

8.1 Learning by example—using a builder

Builders are easier to understand with concrete examples, so we'll take a brief look at some sample code and compare it with how we'd achieve the same result without builders. At this point, we're not going to present the *details* of builders, just the *feeling* of using them. We happen to use `MarkupBuilder`, but the general principle is the same for all of the builders.

Builders provide a convenient way to build hierarchical data models. They don't allow you to create anything you couldn't have created before, but the convenience they add is enormous, giving a direct correlation between hierarchy in the code and the hierarchy of the generated data. We demonstrate this by building the short XML[2] document shown in listing 8.1. The XML contains information about the numbers 10 through 15, their square values, and their factors—for every number x the factors y such that x % y == 0. Obviously, this isn't a terribly useful document in real-world terms, but it means we can focus on the code for generating the XML instead of code required to gather more interesting data.

---

[2] For more information about XML processing in Groovy, see chapter 12.

There is nothing in the example that wouldn't apply just as much in a more complex case.

Listing 8.1 XML example data: squares and factors of 10 through 15

```
<?xml version="1.0"?>
<numbers>
  <description>Squares and factors of 10..15</description>
  <number value="10" square="100">
    <factor value="2" />
    <factor value="5" />
  </number>
  <number value="11" square="121" />
  <number value="12" square="144">
    <factor value="2" />
    <factor value="3" />
    <factor value="4" />
    <factor value="6" />
  </number>
  <number value="13" square="169" />
  <number value="14" square="196">
    <factor value="2" />
    <factor value="7" />
  </number>
  <number value="15" square="225">
    <factor value="3" />
    <factor value="5" />
  </number>
</numbers>
```

Before we show the Groovy way of generating this, let's look at how we'd do it in Java using the W3C DOM API. Don't worry if you haven't used DOM before—the idea isn't to understand the details of the code, but to get an idea of the shape and complexity of the code required. To keep the example in listing 8.2 short, we'll assume we've already constructed an empty Document, and we won't do anything with it when we've finished. All we're interested in is creating the data.

Listing 8.2 Java snippet for producing the example XML

```
// Java!
// … doc made available here …
Element numbers     = doc.createElement("numbers");
Element description = doc.createElement("description");
doc.appendChild(numbers);
numbers.appendChild(description);
description.setTextContent("Squares and factors of 10..15");
```

```
for (int i=10; i <= 15; i++)
{
    Element number = doc.createElement("number");
    numbers.appendChild(number);
    number.setAttribute("value",  String.valueOf(i));
    number.setAttribute("square", String.valueOf(i*i));
    for (int j=2; j < i; j++)
    {
        if (i % j  == 0)
        {
            Element factor = doc.createElement("factor");
            factor.setAttribute("value", String.valueOf(j));
            number.appendChild(factor);
        }
    }
}
```

Note how there's a lot of text in listing 8.2 that isn't directly related to the data itself—all the calls to methods, and explicitly stating the hierarchy using variables. This is remarkably error-prone—just in creating this simple example, we accidentally appended two elements to the wrong place. The hierarchy isn't evident, either—the numbers element appears at the same indentation level as the description element, despite one being a parent of the other. The loops create a feeling of hierarchy, but it's only incidental—in a different example, they could be setting attributes on another element, without adding to the depth of the tree.

Now let's look at the Groovy equivalent in listing 8.3. This is a complete script that writes the XML out to the console when it's run. You'll see later how simple it is to write the content elsewhere, but for the moment the default behavior makes testing the example easy.

This time, there's little to the program *apart* from the data. There's no need for variables to hold elements while we build up the data for them—the data is constructed inline, with method parameters specifying attributes and closures specifying nested elements. The hierarchy is much clearer, too—every child element is indented further than the parent element. The exact amount of indentation depends on other control structures such as the if and for statements, but there is no danger of accidentally having, say, factor elements show up as siblings of number elements.

Listing 8.3 Using `MarkupBuilder` to produce the sample XML

```
def builder = new groovy.xml.MarkupBuilder()
builder.numbers {

    description 'Squares and factors of 10..15'

    for (i in 10..15) {                          ◁─── Emit number elements
        number (value: i, square: i*i) {              10 through 15
            for (j in 2..<i) {
                if (i % j == 0) {
                    factor (value: j)        ◁─── Emit each factor
                }                                 element
            }
        }
    }
}
```

The example may feel slightly like magic at the moment. That's a natural first reaction to builders, because we appear to be getting something almost for nothing. We generally view anything magical as somewhat suspicious—if it appears too good to be true, it usually is. As you'll see, however, builders are clever but not miraculous. They use the language features provided by Groovy—particularly closures and meta-programming—and combine them to form an elegant coding pattern.

Now that you have a first impression of what using a builder looks like and what builders are good for, let's go into more detail and see how they work, as you learn how to create hierarchies of straightforward objects instead of XML elements.

8.2 Building object trees with NodeBuilder

We start the more detailed explanation of builders with the same example we used in section 7.5.1 to demonstrate GPath: modeling `Invoices` with `LineItems` and `Products`. We will build a runtime structure of *nodes* rather than specialized business objects and watch the building process closely. You will learn not only about how `NodeBuilder` works, but also how the general principle of builders is applied in Groovy. We will then consider how the declarative style of builder use can be freely mixed with normal logic.

Builders can be *used* without any special knowledge, but in order to *understand* how they work, it is a prerequisite to know about *pretended* and *relayed* methods (section 7.6) and closure scoping (section 5.5).

Based on our invoice example from section 7.5.1, we set out to build a runtime object structure as depicted in figure 8.1.

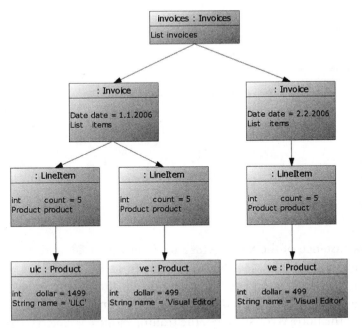

Figure 8.1
Runtime structure of objects and references in the invoice example where an invoices node refers to multiple instances of the `Invoice` class that in turn holds one or more `LineItem` objects that further refer to a single `Product` object each

In listing 7.23, we built this runtime structure with three defined classes `Invoice`, `LineItem`, and `Product` and through calling their default constructors in a nested manner.

8.2.1 *NodeBuilder in action—a closer look at builder code*

Listing 8.4 shows how to implement the invoice example using a `NodeBuilder`. The `NodeBuilder` can replace all three of our classes, assuming that we're just treating them as data storage types (that is, we don't need to add methods for business logic or other behavior). Also added is a final GPath expression to prove that we can still walk conveniently through the object graph. This is the same query we used in section 7.5.1. Note how the tree structure from figure 8.1 is reflected in the code!

Listing 8.4 Invoice example with `NodeBuilder`

```
def builder = new NodeBuilder()      ← ❶  Builder creation
def ulcDate = new Date(107,0,1)
def invoices = builder.invoices{     ← ❷  Root node creation
    invoice(date: ulcDate){                    ←┐
        item(count:5){                         ❸  Invoice creation
            product(name:'ULC', dollar:1499)
        }
```

```
            item(count:1){
                product(name:'Visual Editor', dollar:499)
            }
        }
        invoice(date: new Date(106,1,2)){
            item(count:4) {
                product(name:'Visual Editor', dollar:499)
            }
        }
    }

    soldAt = invoices.grep {                                    ❹  GPath
            it.item.product.any{ it.'@name' == 'ULC' }              query
        }.'@date'
    assert soldAt == [ulcDate]
```

We make a new instance of the `NodeBuilder` for later use at ❶, and then we call the `invoices` method on the `NodeBuilder` instance at ❷. This is a *pretended* method: The `NodeBuilder` intercepts the method call. It constructs a *node* based on the name of the intercepted method name and returns it into the `invoices` variable.[3] Before the node is constructed, the trailing closure is called to construct its nested nodes. To make this possible, the `BuilderSupport` that `NodeBuilder` inherits from sets the closure's *delegate* to the `NodeBuilder` instance.

The `invoice` method call is *relayed* to the `NodeBuilder` instance in ❸, because it is the current closure's *delegate*. This method also takes a map as a parameter. The content of this map describes the attributes of the constructed node.

Finally, we need to adapt the GPath a little to use it in ❹. First, we've broken it into multiple lines to allow proper typesetting in the book. Second, node attributes are no longer accessible as properties but as map entries. Therefore, `product.name` now becomes `product['@name']` or, even shorter, `product.'@name'`. The additional at-sign is used for denoting attributes in analogy to *XPath* attribute conventions. A third change is that through the general handling mechanism of nodes, `item.product` is now a list of products, not a single one.

---

[3] Because `invoices` is the root node, the method name makes no difference in how we use the node in the example. Listing 8.4 also works if you replace `builder.invoice` with `builder.whatever`.

8.2.2 *Understanding the builder concept*

From the previous example, we extract the following general rules:

- Nodes are constructed from *pretended* method calls on the builder.

- Method names determine node names.

- When a map is passed as a method argument, it determines the node's attributes. Generally speaking, each *key/value* pair in the map is used to call the field's setter method named by the *key* with the *value*. This refinement will later be used with `SwingBuilder` to register event listeners.

- Nesting of nodes is done with closures. Closures *relay* method calls to the builder.

This concept is an implementation of the Builder pattern [GOF]. Instead of programming *how* some tree-like structure is built, only the result, the *what*, is specified. The *how* is left to the builder.

Note that only simple attribute names can be declared in the attribute map without enclosing them in single or double quotes. Similarly, node names are constructed from method names, so if you need names that aren't valid Groovy identifiers—such as x.y or x-y—you will again need to use quotes.

So far, we have done pretty much the same as we did with hand-made classes, but without writing the extra code. This is already a useful advantage, but there is more to come.

8.2.3 *Smart building with logic*

With builders, you can mix declarative style and Groovy logic, as listing 8.5 shows. We create nested invoices in a loop for three consecutive days, with sales of the product growing each day. To assess the result, we use a pretty-printing facility available for nodes.

Listing 8.5 Using logic inside the `NodeBuilder`

```
System.setProperty("user.timezone","CET")
def builder = new NodeBuilder()
def invoices = builder.invoices {          ❶ Loop in
    for(day in 1..3) {                         declaration
        invoice(date: new Date(107,0,day)){
            item(count:day){
                product(name:'ULC', dollar:1499)
            }
        }
    }
```

```
        }
    }

    def writer = new StringWriter()                        Print to a StringWriter
    invoices.print(new PrintWriter(writer))                for testing
    def result = writer.toString().replaceAll("\r","")     Reduce CR/LF
    assert "\n"+result == """                              to LF to allow
    invoices() {                                           comparison
      invoice(date:Mon Jan 01 00:00:00 CET 2007) {
        item(count:1) {
          product(name:'ULC', dollar:1499)
        }
      }
      invoice(date:Tue Jan 02 00:00:00 CET 2007) {
        item(count:2) {
          product(name:'ULC', dollar:1499)
        }
      }
      invoice(date:Wed Jan 03 00:00:00 CET 2007) {
        item(count:3) {
          product(name:'ULC', dollar:1499)
        }
      }
    }
    """
```

The code in ❶ calls the NodeBuilder methods directly. This is fine for loops like for and while; but when looping with closures as in an [1..3].each{} loop, you have to call the NodeBuilder like builder.invoice, because it wouldn't be known otherwise. The closure passed to each will have a *delegate* of the calling context (the script), whereas the rest of the method calls appear within closures that have had their delegates set to the instance of NodeBuilder. It is important to understand what the delegate of each closure is. Just remember that the first thing a method call to NodeBuilder does is set the closure of the delegate parameter to the builder.

Of course, more options are available than for/while. The closure is normal code—you can use other control structures such as if and switch as well.

Nodes as constructed with the NodeBuilder have some interesting methods, as listed in table 8.1. Note that these methods being present on the *nodes* doesn't prevent you from having nodes of the same name (such as a node called iterator)—you build child nodes by calling methods on the NodeBuilder, not on the nodes themselves. For a complete and up-to-date description, look at Node's API documentation at http://groovy.codehaus.org/apidocs/groovy/util/Node.html.

Nodes are used throughout the Groovy library for transparently storing tree-like structures. You will see further usages with `XmlParser` in section 12.1.2.

Table 8.1 Public node methods (excerpt)

Return type	Method name	Purpose
Object	name()	The name of the node, such as `invoice`
Object	value()	The node itself
Map	attributes()	All attributes in a map
Node	parent()	The backreference to the parent
List	children()	The list of all children
Iterator	iterator()	The iterator over all children
List	depthFirst()	A collection of all the nodes in the tree, using a depth-first traversal
List	breadthFirst()	A collection of all the nodes in the tree, using a breadth-first traversal
void	print(PrintWriter out)	Pretty-printing as a nested structure

With this in mind, you may want to have some fun by typing

```
println invoices.depthFirst()*.name()
```

That's all there is to `NodeBuilder`. It makes a representative example for all builders in the sense that whenever you use a builder, you create a builder instance and call methods on it with attached nested closures that result in an object tree.

8.3 *Working with MarkupBuilder*

In listing 8.5, you saw the structured, pretty-printed output from the tree of nodes. This can be useful when debugging object structures, but we frequently want to exchange that information with non-Groovy programs or store it in a standard format for later retrieval. XML is the most obvious candidate format, so of course Groovy makes it easy to generate. You've already encountered `Markup-Builder` in our quick introduction, and now we'll look more closely at its capabilities with both XML and HTML.

8.3.1 *Building XML*

Listing 8.6 shows how simple that is: Replace the NodeBuilder with a Markup-Builder, and voilà—you're done. The only other difference is the way you obtain the results. Because markup is usually generated for formatted output, the printing is done implicitly as soon as the construction is finished. To make this possible, a Writer is passed into the MarkupBuilder's constructor.

Listing 8.6 Invoice example with MarkupBuilder

```
writer = new StringWriter()
builder = new groovy.xml.MarkupBuilder(writer)    ⟵┐ New: MarkupBuilder
invoices = builder.invoices {                         │ replaces NodeBuilder
    for(day in 1..3) {
        invoice(date: new Date(106,0,day)){
            item(count:day){
                product(name:'ULC', dollar:1499)
            }
        }
    }
}

result = writer.toString().replaceAll("\r","")

assert "\n"+result == """
<invoices>
  <invoice date='Sun Jan 01 00:00:00 CET 2006'>
    <item count='1'>
      <product name='ULC' dollar='1499' />
    </item>
  </invoice>
  <invoice date='Mon Jan 02 00:00:00 CET 2006'>
    <item count='2'>
      <product name='ULC' dollar='1499' />
    </item>
  </invoice>
  <invoice date='Tue Jan 03 00:00:00 CET 2006'>
    <item count='3'>
      <product name='ULC' dollar='1499' />
    </item>
  </invoice>
</invoices>"""
```

There is no change whatsoever in the two listings as far as the nested builder calls are concerned. That means you can extract that code in a method and pass it different builders for different purposes. This is an inherent benefit of the Builder pattern.

Just as with `NodeBuilder`, you need to be careful about node and attribute names containing special characters. This frequently occurs when using `Markup-Builder`, because multiword names often appear with hyphens in XML. Suppose you want to generate a J2EE web.xml descriptor with a `MarkupBuilder`. You need to construct markup like `<web-app>`, but you cannot have a minus sign in a method name, so you need quotes, like this:

```
def writer = new StringWriter()
def builder = new groovy.xml.MarkupBuilder(writer)

def web = builder.'web-app' {
    builder.'display-name'('Groovy WebApp')
}

def result = writer.toString().replaceAll("\r","")

assert "\n"+result == """
<web-app>
  <display-name>Groovy WebApp</display-name>
</web-app>"""
```

Note that a method name in quotes also needs an object reference to be called on, like `this` or `builder`.

8.3.2 Building HTML

XML and HTML follow the common strategy of bringing structure to a text using markup with *tags*. Rules for HTML are more special, but for the sole purpose of building a *well-formed* serialized format, the same rules apply.

It should come as no surprise that `MarkupBuilder` can also produce HTML to realize web pages, as shown in figure 8.2.

This web page is created from the following HTML source code:

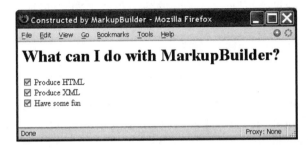

Figure 8.2
Screenshot of a web page that is rendered by the browser from HTML source code that was built from `MarkupBuilder` to show a level-one heading and three check boxes with labels

```
<html>
 <head>
  <title>Constructed by MarkupBuilder</title>
 </head>
 <body>
  <h1>What can I do with MarkupBuilder?</h1>
  <form action='whatever'>
   <input checked='checked' type='checkbox' id='Produce HTML'/>
   <label for='Produce HTML'>Produce HTML</label>
   <br/>
   <input checked='checked' type='checkbox' id='Produce XML'/>
   <label for='Produce XML'>Produce XML</label>
   <br/>
   <input checked='checked' type='checkbox' id='Have some fun'/>
   <label for='Have some fun'>Have some fun</label>
   <br/>
  </form>
 </body>
</html>
```

Listing 8.7 shows how this HTML source code is built with a `MarkupBuilder`. It's all straightforward. To build the check boxes, we use a list of labels and do the iterations with the `for` loop.

Listing 8.7   HTML GUI with `MarkupBuilder`

```
def writer = new FileWriter('markup.html')
def html   = new groovy.xml.MarkupBuilder(writer)
html.html {
  head {
    title 'Constructed by MarkupBuilder'
  }
  body {
    h1 'What can I do with MarkupBuilder?'
    form (action:'whatever') {
      for (line in ['Produce HTML','Produce XML','Have some fun']){
        input(type:'checkbox',checked:'checked', id:line, '')
        label(for:line, line)
        br('')
} } } }
```

HTML source code as produced by the `MarkupBuilder` is always properly built with respect to balancing and nesting tags. It also deals with a number of character encoding issues such as replacing the `<` character with the `&lt;` entity. See the Groovy API Javadocs for details.

`MarkupBuilder` expects that the last argument to each method call will be either a closure for further nesting or a string that forms the text content.

> **NOTE** `MarkupBuilder` does not support elements with intermingled text and child elements, such as `<parent>Some text<child>Child text</child> More text</parent>`. Every element has either a list of child elements or just text. Use an HTML division tag like `div(text)` if all else fails.

That's it for `MarkupBuilder`. It is often used whenever some XML processing is to be done and when developing web applications. `MarkupBuilder` works nicely in combination with Groovy's templating engines, which are the topic of section 9.4.

8.4 Task automation with AntBuilder

Ant (http://ant.apache.org/) is a *build* automation tool. If you've never worked with Ant, you should give it a try. It's a great tool for any kind of automation task and works nicely in combination with Groovy. For the remainder of this section, it is assumed that you have some basic understanding of Ant.

`AntBuilder` is a Groovy builder that is used to build and execute Ant datatypes and tasks. This allows you to harness the power of Ant directly within Groovy scripts and classes. Often, representing interactions with the outside world—manipulating the filesystem, compiling code, running unit tests, fetching the contents of web sites—is more easily expressed in Ant than with the standard Java libraries. Using Ant within normal Java programs is clumsy in various ways, but Groovy makes it straightforward with `AntBuilder`. This section shows how Ant scripts can be represented in Groovy, examines how `AntBuilder` works, and demonstrates what a powerful combination the two technologies can form.

> **NOTE** During the final stages of preparation for this book, a new module called Gant was being developed. It builds on `AntBuilder`, allowing additional build logic and dependency resolution to be captured in Groovy syntax. Check out the Groovy web site for further details.

Ant uses the notion of a *build* for describing its work. Unfortunately, this naming sometimes clashes with what we do in a builder. For distinction in the text, *build* is always set in italics when referring to the Ant meaning of the word.

8.4.1 From Ant scripts to Groovy scripts

Ant *build* scripts are typically used for automating tasks that need to be done as part of the process of transforming source files and other resources into project deliverables (executables and other artifacts). *Build* scripts often involve a range of tasks: cleaning directories, compiling code, running unit tests, producing documentation, moving and copying files, bundling archive files, deploying the application, and much more.

A first example of an Ant *build* script was shown in the introductory sections of this book in listing 1.2. Listing 8.8 provides another tiny example to show the XML-based syntax of Ant *build* scripts. It achieves one of the tasks that *build* this book: cleaning the target directory and copying the raw documents to it, excluding any temporary Word documents.

Listing 8.8 Tiny Ant script for file manipulation

```
<project name="prepareBookDirs" default="copy">

  <property name="target.dir"   value="target"/>
  <property name="chapters.dir" value="chapters"/>

  <target name="copy">
    <delete dir="${target.dir}" />
    <copy todir="${target.dir}">
      <fileset dir="${chapters.dir}"
        includes="*.doc"
        excludes="~*"    />
    </copy>
  </target>
</project>
```

After saving such a script to build.xml, you can start it from the command line via the ant command, which produces output like

```
C:\safe\subversion\groovy-book>ant
Buildfile: build.xml

copy:
  [delete] Deleting directory C:\safe\subversion\groovy-book\target
    [copy] Copying 10 files to C:\safe\subversion\groovy-book\target

BUILD SUCCESSFUL
Total time: 0 seconds
```

The real production process doesn't use this build.xml file but an AntBuilder in a Groovy script:

```
TARGET_DIR    = 'target'
CHAPTERS_DIR  = 'chapters'
ant           = new AntBuilder()

ant.delete(dir:TARGET_DIR)
ant.copy(todir:TARGET_DIR){
```

```
        fileset(dir:CHAPTERS_DIR, includes:'*.doc', excludes:'~*')
    }
```

When transferring Ant *build* scripts to Groovy scripts by using the `AntBuilder`, the following rules apply:

- Ant *task* names map to `AntBuilder` method names.
- Ant *attributes* are passed as a map to `AntBuilder` methods.
- In places where traditional Ant uses strings for other datatypes (such as `boolean` and `int`), Groovy code can directly pass data of the correct type: for example, `ant.copy(…, overwrite:`**`true`**`)`.
- Nested Ant tasks or elements map to method calls in the attached closure.

Ant comes with a cornucopia of useful tasks, far more than we could possibly describe here. Please refer to the Ant documentation: http://ant.apache.org/manual.

Groovy comes with a bundled version of Ant that is used automatically (without any further setup) whenever you use `AntBuilder`.

8.4.2 *How AntBuilder works*

Looking at the similarity between build.xml and the corresponding Groovy script, you could easily assume that `AntBuilder` builds this XML like a `MarkupBuilder` and passes it to Ant for execution. This is not the case.

The Groovy `AntBuilder` works directly on the Java classes that Ant uses for doing its work. We need to take a quick detour into the internals of Ant to build a better picture of `AntBuilder`'s approach.

When Ant has parsed build.xml, it iterates through the XML nodes and builds Java objects. For example, when it sees the `copy` element, it looks into a `taskdef` and finds that it must construct an `org.apache.tools.ant.taskdefs.Copy` object. Similarly, the nested `fileset` element results in a `FileSet` object that is *added* to the `Copy` object. When all the task objects are created, their `perform` method is called and finally executes the task logic. Figure 8.3 shows the resulting object dependencies in a UML class diagram.

`AntBuilder` follows the same approach, but without the need to work on the XML structure. When the `copy` method is called on `AntBuilder`, it uses Ant's helper methods to construct an instance of Ant's `Copy` object. The nested `fileset` call is handled equivalently. As a result, the same object structure as depicted in figure 8.3 is created.

When the construction of a *top-level* element is finished, `AntBuilder` automatically calls its `perform` method to start task execution.

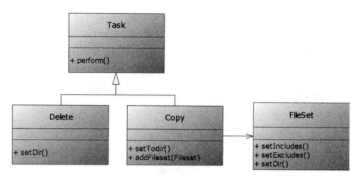

Figure 8.3
UML class diagram of Ant's Delete and Copy tasks, which both inherit from the Task class, where Copy also refers to a FileSet object that was added at build time via Copy's addFileset method

8.4.3 *Smart automation scripts with logic*

AntBuilder shines when it comes to using Ant functionality mixed with logic. In Ant, even the simplest conditional logic is cumbersome to use.

Suppose your *build* fails with an error message when you try to run it on an unsupported version of Java. Look at a possible build.xml that implements this feature,[4] to get an impression of the complexity, not to go through all the details:

```
<project name="AntIf" default="main" >

    <target name="check.java.version">
        <condition property="java.version.ok">
            <contains string="${java.version}" substring="1.4"/>
        </condition>
        <fail unless="java.version.ok">
            This build script requires JDK 1.4.x.
        </fail>
    </target>

    <target name="main"
        depends="check.java.version"
        if="java.version.ok">

        <!-- further action -->

    </target>

</project>
```

The same can be achieved with the following Groovy script:

```
ant = new AntBuilder()
if ( ! System.properties.'java.version'.contains('1.4')) {
```

---

[4] It may seem odd to think of failure as a feature—but if you've ever fought against a build that didn't quite work, you'll understand that a failure with an explanation can save hours of frustration!

```
        ant.fail 'This build script requires JDK 1.4.x'
    }
// further action
```

We think the advantage is obvious.

When it comes to putting looping logic inside an Ant *build*, plain Ant cannot offer much. Additional packages such as *Jelly* and *AntContrib* enhance Ant with logic, but then you end up programming in XML syntax, which is not for everybody. Using AntBuilder, in contrast, allows you to smoothly integrate any kind of Groovy looping logic with Ant's declarative style of task definitions.

For all the usual automation tasks that you encounter in software development projects, the combination of Groovy and AntBuilder is a one-two punch. Ant-Builder gives you simple access to a huge amount of Ant's functionality while Groovy lets you set this functionality into action in flexible ways. Whenever you find yourself struggling with Ant's XML approach, check whether you can use Groovy to make things easier. If you're struggling with an automation task in Groovy, look at the Ant documentation and search for a task that does the trick. One powerful technique is to use Ant-in-Groovy-in-Ant: The <groovy> task allows you to run Groovy code within an Ant script and sets up an AntBuilder attached to the project containing the script. You can express sophisticated logic within your build and reference the results elsewhere in the Ant script. We will look at this functionality further in chapter 13.

AntBuilder is a prominent example of providing an intuitive API to a Java framework by using Groovy builders, but it's not the only one. The next section presents SwingBuilder, which simplifies implementing graphical user interfaces (GUIs) with the Java Swing framework.

8.5 *Easy GUIs with SwingBuilder*

Even in the era of web applications, it's beneficial to know how to build interactive desktop applications with a user-friendly GUI in terms of presentation and responsiveness. For this purpose, Java provides two frameworks: the Abstract Window Toolkit (AWT) and Swing, where Swing is the recommended option.

Groovy's SwingBuilder is a simplified API to the Swing framework that enables quicker development and easier maintenance through a lot of shortcut expressions and by revealing the GUI's containment structure in the structure of the code.

We will start our presentation of SwingBuilder with a simple initial example that reads a password from user input for further processing in a script. With this example in mind, we'll explain the main concept: the range of features and the rationale of the implementation. Finally, we will apply this knowledge in a complete Swing application.

For the remainder of this section, it is assumed that you have some basic understanding of how to program with Swing. If you are new to Swing, you may want to first work through the Swing tutorial at http://java.sun.com/docs/books/tutorial/uiswing.

8.5.1 Reading a password with SwingBuilder

In a recent project, we used a Groovy automation script to connect to a secure web site. We needed to give it a password, but we didn't want to hard-wire the password in the code. The script was used for a corporate client, so we couldn't read the password from a file, the command line, or the standard input stream, because it would then possibly be visible to others.

Luckily, we remembered that Swing provides a
JPasswordField that shields user input from accidental
over-the-shoulder readers with an echo character (* by
default). Placed inside a JFrame, the simplest solution
looks like figure 8.4.

Figure 8.4 Screenshot of a JPasswordField to read a password from user input

Using SwingBuilder, it was easy to integrate that dialog
in the script. Listing 8.9 contains the snippet that achieves
this. It follows the same strategy that you have already seen for other builders: It creates a builder instance, and calls methods on it with attached closures that make up the nesting structure and argument maps that further define properties of the product.

For the case of the password dialog, the nesting structure is simple: There is only one container—the outermost JFrame—containing one simple component—the JPasswordField.

Because we are working with Swing widgets, we need to add an ActionListener to the password field, whose actionPerformed method is called as soon as the user finishes their input. In Groovy, we can do that with a simple closure.

Finally, we need to call JFrame's layout manager via the pack method, make it visible, and start the main loop via show.

Listing 8.9 A simple password dialog with SwingBuilder

```
import groovy.swing.SwingBuilder

swing = new SwingBuilder()
frame = swing.frame(title:'Password') {
```

```
    passwordField(columns:10, actionPerformed: { event ->
        println event.source.text
        // any further processing is called here
        System.exit(0)
        }
    )
}
frame.pack()
frame.show()
```

The example shows some idiosyncrasies of `SwingBuilder`:

- For constructing a `JFrame`, the apppropriate method name is `frame`, not *jFrame* as you may expect. This allows us to reuse code with builders for other widget sets such as `AWTBuilder` (not yet available), `SWTBuilder`, or `ULCBuilder`[5] (under development).

- Adding the `ActionListener` to the password field follows the style you saw in section 7.4.2; we define a closure that is executed when the field notifies its listener's `actionPerformed` method. In this closure, we print the current content of the field and exit the application. It's important to spot that the closure is specified as a value in the map, *not* as a closure one level down from the password field.

The flow of execution is different from normal console-based scripts but similar to normal Swing applications. The flow doesn't wait for the user input, but runs right until the end, where Swing's main loop is started implicitly. When the user has committed their input with the Enter key, the flow proceeds in the `actionPerformed` closure. This is where any trailing activities must reside.

The initial example was basic. For more elaborate usages, you need more information about `SwingBuilder`'s access to Swing's views and models, as well as guidance on how to use layout managers and Swing's *action* concept. The next sections are about those features.

If you would rather look at some advanced examples at this point, you can do so within your Groovy distribution and online. Table 8.2 gives directions; GROOVY_SOURCES refers to the Groovy Subversion source tree.

---

[5] ULC is a server-side widget set you can use to write web applications on the server in a Swing-equivalent manner. The user interface is presented on the client through an application-independent UI engine. `ULCBuilder` will enable you to write Groovy ULC applications analogous to writing Swing applications with `SwingBuilder`. See http://www.canoo.com/ulc .

Table 8.2 `SwingBuilder` usages within the Groovy distribution and online source repository

Example	Location	Purpose/Features
groovyConsole	GROOVY_HOME /lib/groovy-*.jar groovy/ui/Console.groovy	Interactive Groovy shell; using MenuBar, Menu, MenuItem, Accelerator, CaretListener, Action, TextArea, TextPane, StyledDocument, Look&Feel, FileChooser, and Dialog
ObjectBrowser	GROOVY_HOME /lib/groovy-*.jar groovy/inspect/swingui/ ObjectBrowser.groovy	Inspecting objects; using Label, TabbedPane, Table, TableModel, ClosureColumn, MouseListener, BorderLayout, FlowLayout, Look&Feel, ScrollPane, and Dialog
paintingByNumbers	GROOVY_SOURCES /examples/groovy2d/ paintingByNumbers.groovy	Random patchwork graphics; using simple Java2D API graphics
BloglinesClient	GROOVY_SOURCES /examples/swing/ BloglinesClient.groovy	RSS Reader; using Lists, ListModels, ScrollPanes, ValueChangedListeners, and a define-before-layout approach
Widgets	GROOVY_SOURCES /examples/swing/ Widgets.groovy	Swing Widget demonstrator; using various Dialogs, MenuBar, Menu, MenuItem, Action, TabbedPane, Panel, GridLayout, GridBagLayout, Constraints, BorderLayout, FormattedTextField, Slider, and Spinner (with model)
SwingDemo	GROOVY_TEST_SOURCES /groovy/swing/ SwingDemo.groovy	SwingBuilder demonstrator, giving access to groovy.model.MvcDemo, TableDemo and TableLayoutDemo; additionally featuring VBox, ComboBox, Table, TableModel, TableLayout (td, tr), PropertyColumn, and ClosureColumn

8.5.2 *Creating Swing widgets*

`SwingBuilder` is simple in appearance but elaborate inside. Its methods not only create and connect the plain Swing widgets that represent *views* but also give access to the objects Swing uses to glue together the final GUI, such as *actions*, *models*, *layout managers*, and *constraints*.

This section lists the factory method calls for building views. The following sections go into detail about building supporting objects.

`SwingBuilder` knows about the Swing widgets that are listed in table 8.3. If no other indication is given, the factory methods in the table return the product object, optionally setting properties from a supplied map.

`SwingBuilder` cares about proper containment of widgets by following the closure's nesting structure. Only *standalone* containers can be used without a parent.

See the Swing API documentation for full coverage of the product classes and their properties.

Table 8.3 `SwingBuilder`'s widget factory methods

`SwingBuilder` method	Product
button	JButton
buttonGroup	ButtonGroup Invisible; used to group radio buttons and check boxes
checkBox	JCheckBox
checkBoxMenuItem	JCheckBoxMenuItem
colorChooser	JColorChooser
comboBox	JComboBox Obeys an optional argument *items*
desktopPane	JDesktopPane
dialog	JDialog Can be used inside a parent container as well as *standalone*
editorPane	JEditorPane
fileChooser	JFileChooser
formattedTextField	JFormattedTextField Obeys either the `format` or `value` property (in that order)
frame	JFrame Standalone container
internalFrame	JInternalFrame
label	JLabel
layeredPane	JLayeredPane
list	JList
menu	JMenu
menuBar	JMenuBar
menuItem	JMenuItem
optionPane	JOptionPane
panel	JPanel
passwordField	JPasswordField
popupMenu	JPopupMenu

continued on next page

Table 8.3 `SwingBuilder`'s widget factory methods *(continued)*

SwingBuilder method	Product
progressBar	JProgressBar
radioButton	JRadioButton
radioButtonMenuItem	JRadioButtonMenuItem
scrollBar	JScrollBar
scrollPane	JScrollPane
separator	JSeparator
slider	JSlider
spinner	JSpinner
splitPane	JSplitPane Initializes its subcomponents
tabbedPane	JTabbedPane
table	JTable
textArea	JTextArea
textField	JTextField
textPane	JTextPane
toggleButton	JToggleButton
toolBar	JToolBar
tree	JTree
viewport	JViewport

window	JWindow
	  Can be used inside a parent container as well as *standalone*;
	  obeys the `owner` argument to override containment

What is missing in `SwingBuilder` is `JToolTip`, which cannot be set as a nested element but only via the `toolTipText` attribute. Also missing is `JApplet`, which is not implemented at the time of writing.

With the information from table 8.3, you can construct a GUI that looks like figure 8.5. The outermost container is a `JFrame` that contains two top-level elements: a `JMenuBar` and a `JPanel`. The `JMenuBar` in turn contains a `JMenu` with `JMenuItems`. The `JPanel` contains three `JComponents`: a `JLabel`, a `JSlider`, and a `JComboBox` with a simple list.

We were tempted to show this simple containment structure in a diagram, and we would have done so if we were programming in Java. But because we're using Groovy's `SwingBuilder`, the containment structure is nicely reflected in the code, as you can see in listing 8.10. The code is its own documentation.

Figure 8.5 Screenshot of a Swing GUI with multiple contained widgets

Listing 8.10 Simple widget containment demo with `SwingBuilder`

```
import groovy.swing.SwingBuilder

swing = new SwingBuilder()
frame = swing.frame(title:'Demo') {
    menuBar {
        menu('File') {
            menuItem 'New'
            menuItem 'Open'
        }
    }
    panel {
        label 'Label 1'
        slider()
        comboBox(items:['one','two','three'])
    }
}
frame.pack()
frame.show()
```

The Java equivalent is not only three to four times longer (and thus too long to print here), but, perhaps more important, it also fails to reveal the widget containment in the code layout. If you have ever written Swing GUIs in Java, the code in listing 8.10 will probably feel like a big improvement.

NOTE We made use of `SwingBuilder`'s default text key in the attribute map; `menu(text:'File')` can be abbreviated as `menu('File')`. Where parentheses are optional, even `menuItem 'New'` is possible, as demonstrated in the listing.

The label, slider, and combo box need to be contained in a panel, because a frame's root pane can contain at most one element. The panel serves as this single element.

> **NOTE** SwingBuilder is an ideal place to use the *implicit constructor,* as introduced in section 7.1.4. Say you want to set a frame's `size` attribute. In Java, you need to create a `Dimension` object for that purpose. With Groovy's general constructor, you write `frame(size:[100,100])`.

The panel in listing 8.10 needs to visually arrange its contained widget. For that purpose, it uses its default layout manager, which is `FlowLayout` for `JPanels`. `SwingBuilder` also gives access to Swing's other layout managers, as shown in the next section.

8.5.3 *Arranging your widgets*

For visual arrangement of widgets, the builder's nesting structure doesn't provide enough information. Suppose a panel contains two buttons. Are they to be arranged horizontally or vertically? Swing's layout management provides this information.

Layout management with `SwingBuilder` can be achieved in two ways: by setting the appropriate properties on the widgets or by using nested method calls.

We start with the first option, which works without any layout-specific treatment in `SwingBuilder`. This is shown with an example that uses Swing's `BorderLayout` with `JButtons` in figure 8.6.

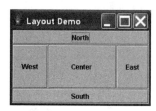

Listing 8.11 produces the layout in figure 8.6 and shows that no special methods need to be called. It is sufficient to set the appropriate properties on the Swing widgets: `layout` and `constraints`. We use Groovy's `import as` feature (see section 7.2.2) for convenience, to ease access to `BorderLayout` with the `BL` abbreviation.

Figure 8.6 Screenshot of a Swing `BorderLayout` defined through `SwingBuilder`

Listing 8.11 Laying out widgets the common Swing way

```
import groovy.swing.SwingBuilder
import java.awt.BorderLayout as BL

swing = new SwingBuilder()
frame = swing.frame(title:'Layout Demo') {
    panel(layout: new BL()) {
        button(constraints: BL.NORTH,  'North' )
        button(constraints: BL.CENTER, 'Center')
        button(constraints: BL.SOUTH,  'South' )
        button(constraints: BL.EAST,   'East'  )
        button(constraints: BL.WEST,   'West'  )
```

```
    }
}
frame.pack()
frame.show()
```

The second option for laying out widgets is to use method calls that work inside the nesting structure, as listed in table 8.4. In addition to Swing's standard layout options, `SwingBuilder` also provides simplified access to supporting objects such as constraints, glues, and struts. See the Swing API documentation for full coverage of the layout managers, descriptions of their layout strategies, their properties together with predefined constant values, and the constraints they rely on.

Table 8.4 `SwingBuilder`'s methods for laying out components within a user interface

SwingBuilder method	Swing class/method	Notes
borderLayout	BorderLayout	Layout manager
boxLayout	BoxLayout	Layout manager; obeys `axis`, default: X_AXIS
cardLayout	CardLayout	Layout manager
flowLayout	FlowLayout	Layout manager
gridBagLayout	GridBagLayout	Layout manager
gridBagConstraints	GridBagConstraints	Constraints to be used with GridBagLayout
gbc	GridBagConstraints	Abbreviation for gridBagConstraints
gridLayout	GridLayout	Layout manager
overlayLayout	OverlayLayout	Layout manager
springLayout	SpringLayout	Layout manager
tableLayout	n/a	Container; needs nested tr() / td() calls
hbox	Box.createHorizontalBox	Container
hglue	Box.createHorizontalGlue	Widget

continued on next page

Table 8.4 `SwingBuilder`'s methods for laying out components within a user interface *(continued)*

SwingBuilder method	Swing class/method	Notes
`hstrut`	`Box.createHorizontalStrut`	Widget; obeys `width`, default: 6
`vbox`	`Box.createVerticalBox`	Container
`vglue`	`Box.createVerticalGlue`	Widget
`vstrut`	`Box.createVerticalStrut`	Widget; obeys `height`, default: 6
`glue`	`Box.createGlue`	Widget
`rigidArea`	`Box.createRigidArea`	Widget; obeys `size` or (`width`, `height`), default: 6

All layout management methods in table 8.4 can be used as nested elements of the laid-out container, which arranges two buttons horizontally:

```
panel {
    boxLayout()
    button 'one'
    button 'two'
}
```

In contrast, container methods as marked in table 8.4 start their own nesting structure to lay out their nested widgets. Here we arrange two buttons vertically:

```
vbox {
    button 'one'
    button 'two'
}
```

In HTML-based web applications, tables are often used to control the page layout. `SwingBuilder` lets you to follow this approach with a genuine `TableLayout` that almost looks like HTML made by `MarkupBuilder`:

```
tableLayout{
    tr {
        td { button 'one' }
        td { button 'two' }
    }
    tr {
        td(colspan:2) { button 'three' }
    }
}
```

Note `td`'s `colspan` attribute. The table layout can be adjusted with such cell attributes. The list of available cell attributes is in table 8.5, or it can be derived from the API documentation of `groovy.swing.impl.TableLayoutCell`.

Table 8.5   Cell attributes in table layouts

Attribute	Type	Range/Default
align	String	'LEFT', 'CENTER', 'RIGHT'
valign	String	'TOP', 'MIDDLE', 'BOTTOM'
colspan	int	Default: 1
rowspan	int	Default: 1
colfill	boolean	Default: false
rowfill	boolean	Default: false

What's still left to explain from table 8.4 are the invisible horizontal and vertical glues and struts, and the rigid area. Within SwingBuilder, they are used like any other widget in the containment structure. They fill excessive space in the layout. Struts are of fixed size, whereas glues grow and shrink with the available space. A rigid area is a two-dimensional strut.

The following is a simple example of a vertical glue between two buttons. It fills vertical space, effectively forcing button "one" to flow to the left and button "two" to flow to the right of the surrounding panel:

```
panel {
    button 'one'
    glue()
    button 'two'
}
```

More precisely, a glue is an invisible widget that has an indefinite maximum size and a minimum size of [0,0]. The effect of adding a glue to a container depends on that container's layout management and the (preferred, minimum, maximum) size of other contained widgets.

So far, you have seen how to create and compose widgets and how to arrange them. To be set into action, widgets and their according event listeners need a way to refer to each other. The next sections show how to do that.

8.5.4   Referring to widgets

Suppose we have an application with a text field and a button. When the button is clicked, the current content of the text field is to be printed to the console. This simplistic application could look like figure 8.7.

The corresponding code would contain a snippet like the following (which is incomplete):

```
textField(columns:10)
button(text:'Print', actionPerformed: { event ->
    println 'the entered text is ... ???'
})
```

Figure 8.7 Screenshot of a simple application that prints the content of the text field to the console

To print the content of the text field, the `actionPerformed` closure would need a reference to it. This section is about various ways of obtaining such a reference:

- By traversing the containment structure
- By *id*
- By *variables*

The first option makes use of the `event` object that gets passed to the closure. It has a `source` property that refers to the source of the event: the button. So, at least, we have a reference to the button.

Button and text fields are nested in the same parent container, available via the button's `parent` property. That parent in turn reveals its nested *components*, and the text field happens to be the first one of those. The final traversal looks like the following:

```
panel {
    textField(columns:10)
    button(text:'Print', actionPerformed: { event ->
        println event.source.parent.components[0].text
    })
}
```

This works, but it's ugly for a number of reasons. First, the path expression doesn't nicely reveal that we are referring to the text field. Second, when rearranging the containment structure, the code will break. Third, the purpose of the text field remains unexplained.

The second option of referencing addresses these concerns. An `id` attribute can be attached to the text field. It is subsequently available as a property on the `SwingBuilder`:

```
swing = new SwingBuilder()
frame = swing.frame(title:'Printer') {
    panel {
        textField(id:'message', columns:10)
        button(text:'Print', actionPerformed: {
            println swing.message.text
```

```
        })
    }
}
```

This is much better, but it raises the question why this special handling is needed. Why not use variables to reference an object? We can do so, and the following snippet works as well:

```
message = textField(columns:10)
button(text:'Print', actionPerformed: {
    println message.text
})
```

This looks appealing at first, but you need to be careful when things are not as simple as in this example. Variables need to be known in the scope of the referrer, and they must have been properly assigned before use. SwingBuilder's appearance can easily lead to overlooking this requirement. Remember that we are in a closure and thus in a closed block. We cannot introduce a variable to the enclosing scope.

Suppose we set out to print not the text field content, but the frame title. We already have a variable called frame. A first—unsuccessful—try could be

```
button(text:'Print', actionPerformed: {
    println frame.title                   // fails !!!
})
```

This fails because we are still in the process of frame construction when we try to reference the frame. It isn't even declared yet!

Obviously, when going the "reference by variable" route, it makes sense to first fully construct your widgets and take care of nesting, layout, and referencing afterward.

This can look like the following code, where we first construct the frame and hold a reference to it. When defining the containment structure, we can use this reference at two places: where the frame widget is needed for containment, and in the actionPerformed closure. SwingBuilder's widget method lets us place a predefined widget in the containment structure:

```
swing = new SwingBuilder()
frame = swing.frame(title:'Printer')

swing.widget(frame) {
    panel {
        textField(columns:10)
        button(text:'Print', actionPerformed: {
```

```
            println frame.title
        })
    }
}
```

Or we can do the same with the button and attach the listener after the frame construction is finished:

```
swing = new SwingBuilder()
button = swing.button('Print')

frame = swing.frame(title:'Printer') {
    panel {
        textField(columns:10)
        widget(button)
    }
}

button.actionPerformed = {
    println frame.title
}
```

The latter is particularly handy when constructing views or attaching listeners gets more complex, such that it would hamper understanding the containment structure if done inline.

A further Swing abstraction that helps code readability is the *action* concept. The next section shows how it is supported in SwingBuilder.

8.5.5 *Using Swing actions*

The full description of Swing's action concept is in the API documentation of javax.swing.Action; but in short, an action is an ActionListener that can be used from multiple widgets. In addition to a shared actionPerformed method, it stores common properties and broadcasts property changes to its widgets.

This is particularly helpful when a menu item and a toolbar button should do the same thing, for example. With a shared action, they share, for instance, the enabled state such that disabling the action instantly disables both the menu item and the toolbar button.

Table 8.6 lists the predefined action properties with a short description.

The accelerator and keyStroke properties both take string representations of a keystroke as described with javax.swing.KeyStroke.getKeyStroke(String); you don't have to bother with the keystroke abstractions but can use 'ctrl ENTER' and the like.

Table 8.6 Predefined action properties

Property	Type	Note
closure	Closure	Introduced by `SwingBuilder`; the closure to be called for `actionPerformed`
accelerator	String	Keystroke to invoke a `JMenuItem`, even if not visible
mnemonic	Single-char `String`	Character in the `name` used for quick navigation to the widget
name	String	Default text for widgets
shortDescription	String	Used for tooltip text
longDescription	String	Can be used for context help
enabled	Boolean	Shared enabled state
smallIcon	javax.swing.Icon	Shared icon for widgets (toolbar buttons), typically `javax.swing.ImageIcon`
keyStroke	String	General keystroke to invoke the action

As expected, `SwingBuilder` uses the `action` method to create an action object:

```
swing = new SwingBuilder()

printAction = swing.action(name:'Print', closure: {
    println swing.message.text
})
```

Such a reference can be used with the `action` property of its widgets:

```
frame = swing.frame(title:'Printer') {
    panel {
        textField(action: printAction, id:'message',columns:10)
        button   (action: printAction)
    }
}
```

We added the action to both widgets. Therefore, the action closure also gets called when we press the Enter key in the text field.

The button no longer needs a `text` property. Instead, the button retrieves its label from the action name.

There is a second option for referring to an action that is equally valid but less intuitive: An action can be nested. For this purpose, a second flavor of the `action` method makes the given action known to the parent (similar to the `widget` method).

```
frame = swing.frame(title:'Printer') {
    panel {
        textField(id:'message',columns:10) { action(printAction) }
        button                             { action(printAction) }
    }
}
```

PERSONAL NOTE This second option seems questionable to us. We can't see any benefit, only the drawback of making things more complicated. We wouldn't be surprised if it was discontinued by the time you are reading this.

Using SwingBuilder's action support is usually a good choice. It helps in terms of structuring the code, achieving consistent action behavior, and providing user-friendly GUIs that can be controlled by the keyboard or mouse.

8.5.6 *Using models*

Swing follows the Model-View-Controller (MVC) pattern, and thus models are used to provide widgets with data. All the usual Swing models can be used with SwingBuilder. In addition, SwingBuilder provides factory methods for models, as listed in table 8.7.

Table 8.7   Factory methods for models

Method	Model	Note
boundedRangeModel	DefaultBoundedRangeModel	For JSlider and JProgressBar
spinnerDateModel	SpinnerDateModel	For JSpinner
spinnerListModel	SpinnerListModel	For JSpinner
spinnerNumberModel	SpinnerNumberModel	For JSpinner
tableModel	groovy.model. DefaultTableModel	For JTable; obeys the model and list properties for ValueModel (in that order); supports nested TableColumns
propertyColumn	TableColumn	Supports header, propertyName, and type(Class)
closureColumn	TableColumn	Supports header, read(Closure), write(Closure), and type(Class)

NOTE At the time of this writing, there is no special SwingBuilder support for TreeModel to be used with JTree or ListModel to be used with JList and JComboBox.

In table 8.7, the tableModel is most special. We start its presentation with a small example table that lists the nicknames and full names of some Groovy committers.[6] It produces the GUI shown in figure 8.8.

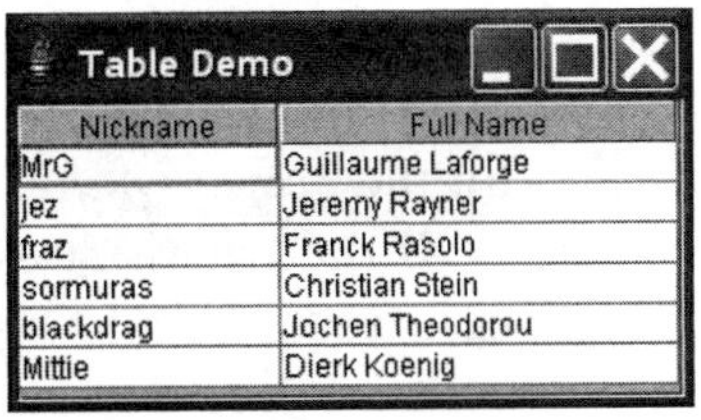

Listing 8.12 contains the code that makes up the GUI in figure 8.8. The tableModel method uses nested TableColumn objects, propertyColumn in this example. Note the containment of scroll-Pane—table—tableModel—propertyColumn that is reflected in the code layout.

Figure 8.8 Screenshot of a table backed by tableModel and propertyColumns

---

Listing 8.12   Example of a table backed by tableModel and propertyColumns

```
import groovy.swing.SwingBuilder

data = [
    [nick:'MrG',      full:'Guillaume Laforge' ],
    [nick:'jez',      full:'Jeremy Rayner'     ],
    [nick:'fraz',     full:'Franck Rasolo'     ],
    [nick:'sormuras', full:'Christian Stein'   ],
    [nick:'blackdrag', full:'Jochen Theodorou' ],
    [nick:'Mittie',   full:'Dierk Koenig'      ]
]

swing = new SwingBuilder()
frame = swing.frame(title:'Table Demo') {
  scrollPane {
    table() {
      tableModel(list:data) {
        propertyColumn(header:'Nickname', propertyName:'nick')
        propertyColumn(header:'Full Name',propertyName:'full')
      }
    }
  }
```

---

6 Please forgive us for not listing all the committers here. It's a question of space. We concentrated on unusual nicknames for this example. The list of all committers is available at http://groovy.codehaus.org/team-list.html.

```
    }
  }
  frame.pack()
  frame.show()
```

When you use `propertyColumn`, the data must be a list of objects that can be asked for the `propertyName`.

If the data isn't exactly in the format that should be displayed in the table, `closureColumn` allows you to funnel all read and write access to the data through a `read` or `write` closure.

Suppose you have to work on the preceding data but you want to display only the first name, not the full name. Replace the previous `propertyColumn` lines with

```
closureColumn(header:'Nickname',  read:{it.nick})
closureColumn(header:'First Name',read:{it.full.tokenize()[0]})
```

When your table is editable by the user or you change the table content programmatically, consider providing an additional `write` closure. It is used to convert the external format of a value back to the table's internal format. Think about it as the *reverse* operation of the `read` closure.

`SwingBuilder`'s special support for `TableColumn` makes using `TableModel` much easier. Normally there is no more need to implement extra `TableModel` classes on your own, but you can still do so when the need arises and use them with `JTable`'s `model` property. Nested `tableModel` methods can also take a custom `model` argument to allow this.

So far, you have seen only small examples and snippets that discuss possible variations. We still owe you a comprehensive example of a Swing application built with `SwingBuilder`. We will keep that promise in the next section.

8.5.7 *Putting it all together*

Finally, we implement a complete application using `SwingBuilder`. The idea is to create something that shows how all the pieces fit together and that also reveals the benefit that Groovy's dynamic nature brings to application development.

Gathering requirements

The application plots arbitrary mathematical functions with one free variable, *f(x)* in mathematical terms. The user enters the function in the format of a Groovy expression on x.

The application is shown in figure 8.9.

GUI features include the following:

- The user defines the function.

- To plot the graph, the user can press Enter in any input field, click the Paint button, choose from a menu, or press Ctrl-P.

- The user can define the domain and range upper and lower bounds either by typing in a new value or by increasing/decreasing the current value with the mouse or arrow keys. A repaint is triggered immediately when any of these values changes.

- Resizing the window shell resizes the plotting canvas.

- All menus and buttons support quick navigation.

- A Help/About box as shown in figure 8.10 is provided via menu and via the F1 function key.

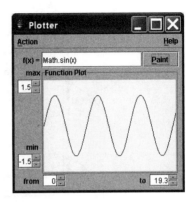

Figure 8.9   Screenshot of a general function plotter built with `SwingBuilder`

Getting prepared

`SwingBuilder` makes it possible to start with a minimal design and refine and extend the containment structure and

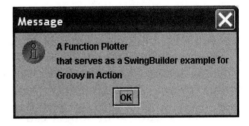

Figure 8.10   Screenshot of a Help/About message made by `SwingBuilder`

layout management as the application grows. This is a big improvement over ordinary Swing programming in Java and competitive to using visual builders.[7]

However, sketching the design in advance prevents us from getting lost. Figure 8.11 splits the expected GUI in pieces, gives hints about the general layout management, and notes some ideas about the components.

The requirements suggest a `BorderLayout`. All function-specific controls can float to NORTH, and dimension controls can be placed WEST and SOUTH. Most important, the plotting canvas can be CENTERed and will thus expand when resized.

All subcontainers can be arranged as horizontal or vertical boxes.

The dimension controls max/min/from/to that are placed at the corners share some commonalities: They are built from a label, a small space, a spinner, and a

---

[7] Because many visual builders create source code that is effectively usable only within the builder and is virtually unreadable on its own, `SwingBuilder` can be said to have the edge over them.

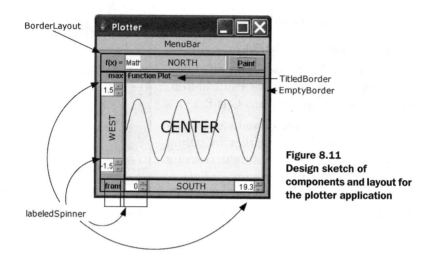

**Figure 8.11
Design sketch of
components and layout for
the plotter application**

spinner model. It would be nice to avoid code duplication and have something like a `labeledSpinner` concept.

Two questions are still open: how to plot a graph using Swing and how to dynamically evaluate the function text. This is not explained in much detail, because our current focus is on `SwingBuilder`. In brief, however:

- Any Swing widget can be asked for its `Graphics` object (and thus, we can use a simple panel). This object in turn has a number of painting methods. See the API documentation of `java.awt.Graphics`. The main point to consider is the system of coordinates. It starts at the upper-left corner with [0,0] and expands *right* and *down*. We need some transformation of coordinates to handle that.

- Dynamic code evaluation will be handled in depth in chapter 11. For our purpose we can ask a `GroovyShell` to *parse* the text into a `script`. We pass it the current value of x; calling `script.run` returns *f(x)*.

This should be enough preparation to start implementing.

Implementation

The code in listing 8.13 resides in a single file. It is made up of four steps:

- Defining actions
- Building widgets, containment structure, and layout in one place; *id*s are used for referencing widgets

- Starting the main loop
- Defining additional helper methods and classes

Event listener closures are implemented as methods and referred to as method closures (the .& operator; see chapter 5). They are used in two places: in actions and the spinner's ChangeListener (stateChanged method).

The Dynamo class encapsulates the dynamic expression evaluation. It caches the current script to avoid excessive reparsing.

Listing 8.13 The mathematical function plotter application

```groovy
import groovy.swing.SwingBuilder
import java.awt.Color
import java.awt.BorderLayout         as BL      Type aliases
import javax.swing.WindowConstants   as WC      as shortcuts
import javax.swing.BorderFactory     as BF
import javax.swing.JOptionPane

swing = new SwingBuilder()

paint = swing.action(
    name:        'Paint',
    closure:     this.&paintGraph,     ◁——  Refer to method
    mnemonic:    'P',                         closure
    accelerator: 'ctrl P'
)
about = swing.action(
    name:        'About',
    closure:     this.&showAbout,
    mnemonic:    'A',
    accelerator: 'F1'
)

frame = swing.frame(title:'Plotter',           General
    location:[100,100], size:[300,300],  ◁—   constructor
    defaultCloseOperation:WC.EXIT_ON_CLOSE) {
    menuBar () {
        menu(mnemonic:'A','Action'){
            menuItem(action:paint)
        }
        glue()                             Separate
        menu(mnemonic:'H','Help'){    ◁——  help menu
            menuItem(action:about)
        }
    }
    panel (border:BF.createEmptyBorder(6,6,6,6)) {
        borderLayout()
        vbox (constraints: BL.NORTH){
```

```
            hbox {
                hstrut(width:10)
                label 'f(x) = '
                textField(id:'function',action:paint,'Math.sin(x)')
                button(action:paint)
            }
        }
        vbox (constraints: BL.WEST){          ⎤  Use factory
            labeledSpinner('max',1d)      ⟵─┘  method
            20.times { swing.vglue() }         // todo: check 'swing'
            labeledSpinner('min',-1d)
        }
        vbox(constraints: BL.CENTER,
            border:BF.createTitledBorder('Function Plot')) {
            panel(id:'canvas')
        }
        hbox (constraints: BL.SOUTH){
            hstrut(width:10)
            labeledSpinner('from',0d)     ❶  Build
            10.times { swing.hglue() }  ⟵─┘  with logic
// todo: check 'swing'
            labeledSpinner('to',6.3d)
        }
    }
  }
}
frame.show()

// implementation methods                ❷  Factory
                                             method
def labeledSpinner(label, value){  ⟵─┘
    swing.label(label)
    swing.hstrut()
    swing.spinner(id:label, stateChanged:this.&paintGraph,
        model:swing.spinnerNumberModel(value:value)
    )
}                              ❸  Method used
def paintGraph(event) {  ⟵─┘      as closure
    calc = new Dynamo(swing.function.text)
    gfx  = swing.canvas.graphics
    int width  = swing.canvas.size.width
    int height = swing.canvas.size.height
    gfx.color  = new Color(255, 255, 150)
    gfx.fillRect(0, 0, width, height)
    gfx.color  = Color.blue
    xFactor    = (swing.to.value - swing.from.value) / width
    yFactor    = height / (swing.max.value - swing.min.value)
    int ceiling = height + swing.min.value * yFactor
    int lastY  = calc.f(swing.from.value) * yFactor     ⎤  Main plotting
    for (x in (1..width)) {                          ⟵─┘  loop
        int y = calc.f(swing.from.value + x * xFactor) * yFactor
        gfx.drawLine(x-1, ceiling-lastY, x, ceiling-y)
```

```
            lastY = y
        }
    }
}                                    Show message
void showAbout(event) {      ←┘  dialog
    JOptionPane.showMessageDialog(frame,
'''A Function Plotter
that serves as a SwingBuilder example for
Groovy in Action''')
}
// Keep all dynamic invocation handling in one place.
class Dynamo {
    static final GroovyShell SHELL = new GroovyShell()
    Script functionScript
    Dynamo(String function){                      Once per
        functionScript = SHELL.parse(function)  ←┘ paint
    }
    Object f(x) {
        functionScript.x = x                  For
        return functionScript.run()     ←┘  each x
    }
}
```

It doesn't happen often, but sometimes *building with logic* that you have seen with other builders is also useful with `SwingBuilder`, as it is in ❶. At this point, the rationale is that adding a single glue isn't enough to push the labeled spinners into their corners, because a box layout tries to distribute component sizes evenly. The same effect could have been achieved by using a more complex layout manager.

The `labeledSpinner` method at ❷ is perfect for putting your builder and closure knowledge to the test: Why is the extra `swing.` prefix needed? Because `labeledSpinner` is a callback from the closure's delegate (`swing`) to the enclosing scope (our main script). But this raises a second question: How can `swing` then ever add the label to the parent box, for example? Builders keep track of the current parent in their internal state. So, `swing` still knows that we're adding something to that box.

There's no point in going into too much detail about the actual plotting performed in ❸. We figure out the current dimension because the user may have resized the panel, fill it with the background color to erase any old function plot, calculate scaling factors, and finally draw in an upside-down manner to cope for Swing's way of handling coordinates.

Assessment

Even though we set out to produce a complete application example, and we achieved a lot within a hundred lines of code, the application isn't production ready. We should have included exception handling for invalid scripts and those that do not return a number, together with warnings and failure indications, in a dialog or a status bar, for example.

Allowing users to provide executable code can also be a security issue. This topic will be examined in chapter 11.

Performance could be improved by a number of means, such as:

- Double buffering (plotting on an invisible canvas and toggling canvases afterward)
- Sweeping through the domain with a step size > 1 when plotting
- Reparsing function text only when changed

If you liked this example and aim to improve your SwingBuilder skills, why not extend the example with new features? Some useful additions could include:

- Coordinate lines, tickmarks, and labels
- History of plotted functions
- Table of x/y values
- Immediate repaint on focusGained, resize, and so forth.

There is much more about Swing that we haven't mentioned: *drag and drop, look and feel,* all kinds of *ModelListeners, renderers, editors* and so on. Even so, we hope we've piqued your curiosity about Swing and shown how Groovy's SwingBuilder provides a smooth introduction into the world of desktop applications.

One thing that we particularly like about SwingBuilder is that it is instantly available wherever there's Groovy. Other scripting languages often require you to additionally install a special GUI toolkit (tk, Gtk, Fox, and others), and you can bet that when downloading a program, it requires the one toolkit you haven't installed on your current machine. SwingBuilder only relies on Swing, and that comes with your Java installation.

Having seen the merits of NodeBuilder, MarkupBuilder, AntBuilder, and now SwingBuilder, it's reasonable to ask whether you can use that concept for your own kind of builder. You know the answer already, right? Of course you can—and of course Groovy makes it easy. The next section gives the details.

8.6 *Creating your own builder*

The built-in builders are useful, but they aren't tailored for your specific needs. Given how frequently hierarchies are used within software development, it wouldn't be surprising to find that you had a domain-specific use for builders that isn't *quite* covered with NodeBuilder and its colleagues. Fortunately, Groovy makes it easy to build your own builder (which isn't as recursive as it sounds). We'll give you a few examples of why you might want to write your own builder and go through the support Groovy gives you.

Suppose you are creating an application that serves different user groups and supplies each with a customized *portal*. You may want do specify the portal for your business user group. Imagine a builder like

```
businessPortal = new PortalBuilder()
businessPortal.entry {
    corporateMessages (TOP)
    navigationBar      (LEFT)
    content            (CENTER) {
        keyAccounts()
    }
    advertisements     (RIGHT)
    stockTicker        (BOTTOM)
    meetingReminder    (POPUP)
}
```

Such a builder would give you the opportunity to use your specification regardless of the underlying technology. It could be used for plain HTML, portlets, Rich Internet Applications, and even for a Swing client. It's only a matter of how to implement the builder.

Note that such a specification is more flexible than one that resides in a fixed data-structure or in an XML file: You can use variables, constants, method calls, and any other Groovy feature.

A second idea: Suppose you have a technical application such as a persistence framework with the feature to shield your users from SQL. Imagine building a hypothetical query for customers named like Bill with invoices greater than $1000, like this:

```
query = new QueryBuilder()
query.table(customer:'c',    invoice:'i') {
    join   (c:'invoice_id', i:'id')
    and {
        greater('i.total': 1000)
        like   ('c.name' : '%Bill%')
    }
}
```

The builder could map this specification to the SQL dialect you are using or to special types of your persistence framework[8] (such as selection *criteria*).

Implementing these examples is beyond the scope of this book, but we hope to give you all the builder knowledge you require in order to create them for yourself. This section shows how well Groovy supports implementing builders, taking you through an instructive example.

8.6.1 Subclassing BuilderSupport

All builders in the Groovy library are subclasses of `groovy.util.BuilderSupport`. This class implements the general builder strategy: allowing you to *pretend* your builder methods, to recursively process any attached closures, to *relay* method calls in closures back to your builder, and to call your builder's *template* methods.

To implement your own builder, you subclass `BuilderSupport` and implement the template methods as listed in table 8.8.

Table 8.8 List of template methods for builders

Info	Returns	Name	Parameters	Call triggered by
Abstract	Object	createNode	Object name	foo()
Abstract	Object	createNode	Object name, Object value	foo('x')
Abstract	Object	createNode	Object name, Map attributes	foo(a:1)
Abstract	Object	createNode	Object name, Map attributes, Object value	foo(a:1, 'x')
Abstract	void	setParent	Object parent, Object child	createNode finished
Empty	void	nodeCompleted	Object parent, Object node	Recursive closure call finished

`BuilderSupport` follows this construction algorithm:

- When hitting a builder method, call the appropriate `createNode` method.
- Call `setParent` with the current parent and the node you've just created (unless it's a root node, which has no parent).

---

[8] When this paragraph was first written, such builders were purely hypothetical. Now, Grails has such builders for defining Hibernate criteria.

- Process any attached closure (this is where recursion happens).
- Call `nodeCompleted` with the current parent and the created node (even if parent is `null`).

That means a code fragment like

```
builder = new MyBuilder()
builder.foo() {
    bar(a:1)
}
```

will result in method calls like (pseudocode; indentation indicates recursion depth)

```
builder = new MyBuilder()
foo = builder.createNode('foo')
// no setParent() call since we are a root node
    bar = builder.createNode('bar',[a:1])
    builder.setParent(foo, bar)
        // no closure to process for bar
    builder.nodeCompleted(foo, bar)
builder.nodeCompleted(null, foo)
```

Note that the *foo* and *bar* variables are not used inside the *real* builder. They are used in this pseudocode only for illustrating identities.

In terms of the implementation, `nodeCompleted` isn't a template method in the strict meaning of the word, because it is not declared `abstract` in `BuilderSupport` but has an empty default implementation. However, it is added to table 8.8 because most builders need to override it anyway.

Further methods of `BuilderSupport` are listed in table 8.9. See their API documentation for more details.

Table 8.9 More `BuilderSupport` methods

Returns	Name	Parameters	Use
Object	getCurrent		The node under construction, i.e. the *parent* when processing a closure
Object	getName	String methodName	Override to allow builder-specific name conversions; default obeys `nameMappingClosure`
Void	setClosureDelegate	Closure closure, Object node	Override to allow a mix of builders

The next section puts all this together in a complete example.

8.6.2 *The DebugBuilder example*

Our example of how to implement a self-made builder is aimed at being as close to the point as possible. It does little more than reveal how your builder methods were called and is therefore named DebugBuilder.

Despite looking like a textbook example, it is of practical relevance. Let's assume you write an automation script with AntBuilder that behaves unexpectedly. You can then use DebugBuilder in place of AntBuilder to find out whether your Ant tasks were called in the expected sequence with the expected values.

Listing 8.14 contains the implementation of DebugBuilder as a subclass of BuilderSupport with a trailing script that shows how to use it and asserts its behavior.

In the process of building, all relevant information about node creation is appended to a result property whenever setParent is called. Because this never happens for the root node, a check method recognizes the creation of the root node.

The nesting depth of recursive closure calls is reflected by indenting the according lines when appending to the result. This depth is increased on any call to createNode and decreased on nodeCompleted.

Listing 8.14 Using `BuilderSupport` for `DebugBuilder`

```
class DebugBuilder extends BuilderSupport {
    def result = ''<<''          ⟵┐ Empty
    def indent = ' ' * 4           │ StringBuffer
    int indentCount = -1

    def createNode(name) {        ⟵┐ Builder calls goes
        indentCount++               │ through this method
        return check(name)
    }
    def createNode(name, value) {
        return check(createNode(name) << format(value))
    }
    def createNode(name, Map attributes) {
        return check(createNode(name) << format(attributes))
    }
    def createNode(name, Map attributes, value) {
        return check(createNode(name, attributes) << format(value))
    }
    void setParent(parent, child) {
        result << "\n" << indent*indentCount << child.toString()
    }
    void nodeCompleted(parent, node) {
```

```
            indentCount--
    }

    private check(descr){                    Special root
        if (!current) result << descr    ◁┘  handling
        return descr
    }
    private format(value) {
        return '(' << value.toString() << ')'
    }
    private format(Map attributes) {
        StringBuffer formatted = '' << '['
        attributes.each { key, value ->
            formatted << key << ':' << value << ', '
        }
        formatted.length = formatted.size() - 2
        formatted << ']'
        return formatted
    }
}

def builder = new DebugBuilder()
builder.foo(){
    bar()
    baz('x') { map(a:1) }
}
assert "\n" + builder.result == '''
foo
    bar
    baz(x)
        map[a:1]'''
```

The final assertion in listing 8.14 suggests that DebugBuilder can generally be used to support unit-testing with builders. For example, by injecting a Debug-Builder into code that expects a SwingBuilder, you can use such an assertion to unit-test that code.

DebugBuilder also supports *duck typing* with the result property. Because the only operator that is ever applied to result is the << *leftshift* operator, the result property can be set to an object of any type that supports that operator. The default is a StringBuffer, but it can be set to an array, any collection, or even a Writer. For example, to print the results to the console, use the following:

```
builder = new DebugBuilder(result: new PrintWriter(System.out))
...
builder.result.flush()
```

That's all there is to implementing your own builder. We hope we've convinced you of the simplicity of that task. At least the core steps of making your code work as a builder are simple. It goes without saying that any specific builder can still be as complex as any piece of code.

8.7 Summary

The way Groovy works with builders and the simplicity that it brings to defining your own is one of Groovy's genuine contributions to the open-source community. In fact, it is so appealing that other well-established languages copied the concept. This is fair enough, because Groovy has adopted many great features from other languages.

What makes builders special is their *descriptive* nature while still being ordinary executable code. Together with Groovy's feature of executing code dynamically, this combination comes close to the ambition of Lisp: working as an *executable specification*.

Builders can be seen as a way of implementing *domain specific languages (DSLs)*. You have seen many domains in this chapter, from runtime structures (Node-Builder) through text structures (MarkupBuilder), task automation (AntBuilder), and desktop UIs (SwingBuilder), to ones we just dreamed up—business portals and query abstraction. These are distinct domains, and making them easy to work with is the job of a DSL. This notion is rapidly attracting mindshare at the moment.[9]

With DSLs, it should be possible to express domain facts in a way that is more flexible, more powerful, and easier to read than XML, but not as demanding as full-blown programming languages. Groovy builders are an ideal vehicle to achieve this. We look forward to seeing which domains will have Groovy builders created for them. How about a workflow engine, for example? Animation? A new way of considering threading, built from parallel pieces of logic? Who knows—perhaps you will be the one to bring the Next Big Thing to Groovy. Whatever domain you may choose to tackle, Groovy's support for builders is likely to be able to help you.

Now that we have examined builders, it is time to revisit a topic we've frequently mentioned in passing: the GDK, or Groovy's way of extending the JDK.

---

[9] http://www.martinfowler.com/bliki/DomainSpecificLanguage.html

Working with the GDK

9

> *Einstein argued that there must be simplified explanations of nature, because God is not capricious or arbitrary. No such faith comforts the software engineer.*
>
> —Fred Brooks

Learning a new programming language is a twofold task: learning the syntax and learning the standard library. Whereas learning the syntax is a matter of days and getting proficient with new language idioms may require a matter of a few weeks, working through a new library can easily take several months.

Luckily, no Java programmer needs to go through this time-consuming activity when learning Groovy. They already know most of the Groovy Standard Library, because that is the set of APIs that the Java Runtime provides. You can work with Groovy by solely using objects and methods as provided by the Java platform, although this approach doesn't fully leverage the power of Groovy.

Groovy extends (and in a few places modifies) the JRE to make it more convenient to work with, provide new dynamic features, and adapt the APIs to Groovy language idioms. The total of these extensions and modifications is called the GDK. Figure 9.1 gives the architectural overview.

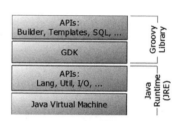

A big part of the GDK concerns the datatypes that Groovy supports at the language level, such as strings, numbers, lists, and maps. That part of the GDK was covered in part 1 of this book.

Figure 9.1 GDK's place in the Groovy architecture

This chapter focuses on GDK capabilities that come from extending prominent JDK concepts such as `Object`, `File`, `Stream`, `Thread`, `Process`, and text processing with templates.

Let's start with `Object`, the most general and most important concept in the JDK, and see how Groovy further extends the concept with features for exploration and control.

9.1 Working with Objects

Java comes with a narrow API of 11 methods for its central abstraction `java.lang.Object`. These methods deal with the object lifecycle (`clone`, `finalize`), object equality (`equals`, `hashCode`), information (`toString`), self-reflection (`get-Class`), and multithreading support (`notify`, `notifyAll`, three versions of `wait`).

Groovy adds much to the self-reflective and informational aspects of the API to better support live exploration of objects. It handles identity/equality differently and therefore needs to extend the respective API. It adds convenience methods to `Object` for the purpose of making these methods available anywhere in the code. Finally, it adds collection-aware methods to `Object` that are useful when the object can be seen as some kind of collection even though it is not necessarily of static type `java.util.Collection`. This last category also includes the handling of object arrays.

We will go through these categories one by one, starting with self-reflective and informational methods.

9.1.1 Interactive objects

When working on a program, you often need to inspect your objects, whether for debugging, logging, or tracing purposes. In dynamic languages such as Groovy, this need is even greater, because you may work with your programming language in an interactive fashion, asking your objects about their state and capabilities to subsequently send them messages.

Object information in strings

Often, the first task is to ask an object for some general information about itself: `toString()` in Java parlance. Groovy adds two more methods of this kind:

- `dump` returns a description of the object's state, namely its fields and their values.
- `inspect` makes a best effort to return the object as it could appear in Groovy source code, with lists and maps in the format of their literal declaration. If it cannot do better, it falls back to `toString`.

Listing 9.1 shows these methods called on a string that contains a single newline character.

Listing 9.1 Usage of `dump` and `inspect`

```
def newline = "\n"

assert newline.toString() == "\n"

assert newline.dump() ==
'''<java.lang.String@a value=[
] offset=0 count=1 hash=10>'''

assert newline.inspect() == /"\n"/
```

Note how `inspect` returns a string that is equivalent to `newline`'s literal declaration: the characters backslash and n enclosed in double quotes (four characters total), whereas `toString` returns only the newline character (one character). The `dump` of a string object may yield different results in other JVMs.

If these methods are not sufficient when working with Groovy interactively, remember that you can fire up the graphical `ObjectBrowser` via

```
groovy.inspect.swingui.ObjectBrowser.inspect(obj)
```

You have seen the `dump` method reveal the object's fields and their values. The same and more can be done with the object's properties.

Accessing properties

Remember that any Groovy object can be seen as a JavaBean, as you saw in section 7.4. You have already seen that its properties can be inspected with the `get-Properties` method or the `properties` property. The method returns a read-only map of property names and their current values. During inspection, printing the whole map of properties is as easy as

```
println properties
```

or

```
println someObj.properties
```

When doing so, you may see more properties than you expected, because Groovy's class-generation mechanism introduces accessors for that object's *class* and `MetaClass` properties behind the scenes.[1]

Listing 9.2 shows property reflection in use. The example uses a class with a `first` property and a `second` read-only property that returns a derived value and is not backed by a field. A `third` property is only a field without accessor methods. The listing shows how to list all keys of that object's properties.

Of course, you can ask the map of properties for the value of a property either with the subscript operator or with the dot-propertyname syntax. This last option looks exactly the same as directly asking the object for the value of a property if its name is known at coding time. This raises the question of whether you can ask an object directly for a property value if its name is only known at runtime and resides in a variable. Listing 9.2 shows that you can do so by using the subscript operator directly on the object without the need for redirection over the `properties` map.

---

[1] It is planned to remove the appearance of `MetaClass` at this point, which may have happened by the time you read this. Listing 9.2 is also affected by this removal.

Because we know that the subscript operator is implemented via the `getAt` method, it would be surprising if the `putAt` method for subscript-assignment weren't implemented in the same manner. Again, listing 9.2 shows that this works and allows us to assign a value to a property whose name is derived dynamically.

Listing 9.2   Reflecting on properties

```
class MyClass {
    def first = 1                    // read-write property
    def getSecond() { first * 2 }    // read-only  property
    public third = 3                 // public field property
}

obj = new MyClass()

keys = ['first','second','third',
        'class','metaClass']
assert obj.properties.keySet() == new HashSet(keys)

assert 1 == obj.properties['first']      Properties
assert 1 == obj.properties.first         map

assert 1 == obj.first                 ❶ Direct
assert 1 == obj['first']   // getAt('first')   access

one = 'first'
two = 'second'                        ❷ Dynamic
obj[one] = obj[two]        // putAt(one)   assignment
assert obj.dump() =~ 'first=2'        ❸ Field introspection
```

At ❶ and ❷, you see that objects implement the `getAt` and `putAt` methods by default, such that the code appears to be accessing a map of properties as far as the subscript operator is concerned.

❸ shows a simple way of introspecting an object via the `dump` method. Because the `first` property is backed by a field of the same name, this field and its current value appear in the dump. Note that this field is private and wouldn't be visible otherwise. This trick is useful, especially in test cases.

> **NOTE**   When working with Groovy code, you may also come across `Object`'s method `getMetaPropertyValues`. It is used internally with an object's meta information and returns a list of `PropertyValue` objects that encapsulate the *name*, *type*, and *value* of a property.

Working with properties means working on a higher level of abstraction than working with methods or even fields directly. We will now take one step down and look at dynamic method invocation.

Invoking methods dynamically

In the Java world, methods (and fields) belong to `Class` rather than to `Object`. This is appropriate for most applications of reflection, and Groovy generally follows this approach. When you need information about an object's methods and fields, you can use the following GPath expressions:

```
obj.class.methods.name
obj.class.fields.name
```

This covers methods and fields as they appear in the bytecode. For dynamically added methods like those of the GDK, Groovy's `MetaClass` provides the information:

```
obj.metaClass.metaMethods.name
```

> **NOTE**   You can add a `.unique` or `.sort` to the preceding GPaths to narrow down the list.

Groovy follows a slightly different approach than Java when it comes to invoking these methods dynamically. You saw the `invokeMethod` functionality for `Groovy-Objects` in section 7.1.2. The GDK makes this functionality ubiquitously available on any (Java) object. In other words, a Groovy programmer can call

```
object.invokeMethod(name, params)
```

on any arbitrary object.

> **NOTE**   This simple call is much easier than JDK reflection, where you need to go through the `Class` object to fetch a `Method` object from a list, invoke it by passing it your object, and take care of handling numerous exceptions.

Dynamic method invocation is useful when the names of the method or its parameters are not known before runtime.

Consider this scenario: You implement a persistence layer with *Data Access Objects* (DAOs), or objects that care for accessing persistent data. A `Person` DAO may have methods like `findAll`, `findByLastName`, `findByMaximum`, and so on. This DAO may be used in a web application setting as depicted in figure 9.2. It may respond to HTTP requests with request parameters for the type of *find* action and

Figure 9.2
Dispatching from HTTP request values to method calls in a Data Access Object

additional parameters. This calls for a way to dispatch from the request parameters to the method call.

Such a dispatch can be achieved with `if-else` or `switch` constructions. Listing 9.3 shows how dynamic method invocation[2] makes this dispatching logic a one-liner. Because this is only an illustrative example, we return the SQL statement strings from the DAO methods, not the `Person` objects as we would probably do in real DAOs.

Listing 9.3 Dynamic method invocation in DAOs

```
class PersonDAO {
    String findAll() {
        'SELECT * FROM Person'
    }
    String findByLastname(name) {
        findAll() + " WHERE p.lastname = '$name'"
    }
    String findByMaximum(attribute) {
        findAll() + " WHERE $attribute = " +
        "SELECT maximum($attribute) FROM Person"
    }
}
dao = new PersonDAO()
```

---

[2] In real-life applications, you need to consider certain security constraints. This kind of dispatch should be used only when the user is allowed to safely use all available methods.

```
action = 'findAll'  // some external input
params = [] as Object[]
assert dao.invokeMethod(action, params) == 'SELECT * FROM Person'
```

The `action` and `params` variables refer to external input, such as from an HTTP request. Note that this example is characteristic for a variety of applications. Almost every reasonably sophisticated client-server application has to deal with this kind of dispatching and can thus benefit from dynamic method invocation.

As a second example, an external configuration in plain-text files, tables, or XML may specify what action to take under certain circumstances. Think about *domain specific languages* (DSLs), the specification of a finite state machine, a workflow description, a rule engine, or a Struts configuration. Dynamic method invocation can be used to trigger such actions.

These scenarios are classically addressed with the Command pattern. In this pattern, dynamic invocation can fully replace simple commands that only encapsulate actions (that is, they don't encapsulate state or support additional functionality like *undo*).

While we are on this topic, dynamic invocation can be applied not only to methods but also to closures. In order to select a closure *by name*, you can store such closures in properties. An idiomatic variant of listing 9.3 could thus be

```
class PersonDAO {
    public findAll = {
        'SELECT * FROM Person'
    }
    // more finder methods as Closure fields ...
}
dao = new PersonDAO()

action = 'findAll'  // some external input
params = []
assert dao[action](*params) == 'SELECT * FROM Person'
```

Note that `findAll` is now a public field with a closure assigned to it, dynamically accessed via `dao[action]`. This dynamically accessed closure can be called in various ways. We choose the shortest variant of putting parentheses after the reference, including any arguments. The `*` spread operator distributes the arguments over the closure parameters (if—unlike `findAll`—the closure has any parameters).

These variants differ slightly in size where the closure variant is a bit shorter but may be less readable for the casual Groovy user. The closure variant additionally offers the possibility of changing the closure at runtime by assigning a new closure to the respective field. This can be handy in combination with the State or Strategy pattern.[3]

To further make programming Groovy a satisfying experience, the GDK adds numerous convenience methods to `Object`.

9.1.2 Convenient Object methods

How often have you typed `System.out.println` when programming Java? In Groovy, you can achieve the same result with `println`, which is an abbreviation for `this.println`; and because the GDK makes `println` available on `Object`, you can use this anywhere in the code. This is what we call a convenience method.

This section walks through the available convenience methods and their usage, as listed in table 9.1.

Table 9.1 `Object` **convenience methods**

Introduced `Object` method	Meaning
`is(other)`	Compare `Object` identities (references)
`isCase(caseValue, switchValue)`	Default implementation: equality
`obj.identity {closure}`	Call closure with object identity (delegate)
`print()`, `print(value)`, `println()`, `println(value)`	`System.out.print…`
`printf(formatStr, value)` `printf(formatStr, value[])`	Java 5 `printf…`
`sleep(millis)` `sleep(millis) {onInterrupt}`	`static Thread.currentThread().` `sleep(millis)`
`use(categoryClass)     {closure}` `use(categoryClassList) {closure}`	Use meta-methods as defined in `categoryClass` for the scope of the closure

Let's go through the methods.

Because Groovy uses the `==` operator for equality instead of identity checking, you need a replacement for the Java meaning of `==`. That is what the `is` method provides.

In Java:

```
if ( a == b ) { /* more code here */}
```

---

[3] Erich Gamma et al, *Design Patterns: Elements of Reusable Object-Oriented Software*, (Addison-Wesley, 1995).

In Groovy:

```
if ( a.is(b)) { /* more code here */}
```

The is method saves you the work of comparing the System.identityHash-Code(obj) of a and b manually.

The isCase method occurred often in the Groovy language description in part 1. For Object, the GDK provides a default implementation that checks for object equality. Note that this means you can use any (Java) object in a Groovy grep or switch:

```
switch(new Date(0)){
    case new Date(0) : println 'dates are equal'
}
```

The identity method calls the attached closure with the receiver object as the closure's delegate. This has an effect similar to that of the WITH keyword in Visual Basic. Use it when a piece of code deals primarily with only one object, like the following:

```
new Date().identity {
    println "$date.$month.$year"
}
```

The properties date, month, and year will now be resolved against the current date. Such a piece of code has by definition the smell of *inappropriate intimacy*.[4] This calls for making this closure a method on the receiver object (Date), which you can do in Groovy with the use method as covered in section 7.5.3.

The versions of print and println print to System.out by default, whereas println emits an additional line feed. Of course, you can still call these methods on any kind of PrintStream or PrintWriter to send your output in other directions.

The same is true for the printf method. It is based on Java's formatted print support, which has been available since Java 5 and (currently) works only if you run Groovy under Java 5 or higher. A RuntimeException is thrown otherwise. In terms of supported formatting features, we cannot present the full list here. Have a look at the Javadoc for class java.util.Formatter. The full description covers about 1,800 lines.

In Groovy, printf isn't as crucial as in other languages, because GStrings already provide excellent support at the language level and the string datatype provides the most common features of left and right padding and centering text.

---

[4] Fowler et al, *Refactoring: Improving the Design of Existing Code* (Addison-Wesley, 1999).

However, there are times when formatted output is more convenient to achieve with a *format* string, especially when the user should be able to configure the output format to their preferences. The following line

```
printf('PI=%2.5f and E=%2.5f', Math.PI, Math.E) // with Java 5 only !
```

prints

```
PI=3.14159 and E=2.71828
```

Note that we have used `printf` with three arguments, but because a format string may contain an arbitrary number of placeholders, `printf` supports an argument list of arbitrary length. It goes without saying that the number of additional arguments must match the number of placeholders in the format string, unless you explicitly specify the argument number to use in the format string. You can also provide a single argument of type `list`—for example, `[Math.PI, Math.E]`.

When working through the Formatter API documentation, you will notice some advanced topics around `printf`:

- *Conversions* apply when a placeholder and the corresponding argument are of different types.
- Placeholders can be prefixed with $n\$$ to map the placeholder to the nth argument in the list. This may get you in conflict with the GString meaning of $\$$. Therefore, it's wise to use only single-quoted string literals as `printf` format strings.

The last convenience method in our list is `sleep`, which suspends the current thread for a given number of milliseconds. It enhances the JDK method `Thread.sleep` by automatically handling interruptions such that sleep is re-called until the given time has elapsed (as closely as the machine timer can tell). This makes the effective sleep time more predictable.

If you want to handle interruptions differently, you can attach a closure that is called when `sleep` encounters an `InterruptedException`.

With the `sleep` method, you can have some fun, as with the following example. Run it from the Groovy shell or console after predicting its output. Did you guess correctly what it does?

```
text = """
This text appears
slowly on the screen
as if someone would
tpye \b\b \b\b \b\b \bype it.
"""
for (c in text) {
```

```
        sleep 100
        print c
}
```

These are all methods that the GDK adds to every object for convenience. However, objects frequently come in a crowd. For such cases, the GDK provides methods to select them one-by-one, as shown in the next section.

9.1.3 Iterative Object methods

In the Java world, any *collection* (in the general meaning of the word) of objects can support inspection of its contained items by providing an Iterator, a separate object that knows how to walk through that collection. Oh—wait, sometimes an Enumeration is used instead. As a further inconsistency, Iterators are not directly available on arrays and a lot of other common types.

Even if you are lucky and found how to get an Iterator object in the API documentation, you cannot do much more with it than use it in a procedural way like this:[5]

```
// Java !
for (Iterator collection.iterator(); iterator.hasNext(); ){
    MyClass obj = (MyClass) iterator.next();
    // do something with obj
}
```

Groovy instead provides a simple and consistent way of doing this:

```
collection.each { /* do something with it */}
```

Besides the simple each method, you can use any of the methods that are listed in table 9.2.

Table 9.2   Iterative Object methods

Return value	Method
Boolean	any {closure}
List	collect {closure}
Collection	collect(Collection collection) {closure}
(void)	each {closure}

continued on next page

---

[5] Java 5 allows a simpler syntax, but it has chosen to use a symbol instead of introducing a keyword. We end up with for (MyClass obj : collection). Better, but not ideal.

Table 9.2 Iterative `Object` methods *(continued)*

Return value	Method
`(void)`	`eachWithIndex {closure}`
`Boolean`	`every {closure}`
`Object`	`find {closure}`
`List`	`findAll {closure}`
`Integer`	`findIndexOf {closure}`
`List`	`grep(Object filter)`

What's so useful about the methods in table 9.2 is that you can use them on *any* object you fancy. The GDK makes these methods available on `Object` and yields the respective items. As we described in section 6.3.2, this iteration strategy is also used in Groovy's `for` loop.

Getting the items is done with a best-effort strategy for the candidate types listed in table 9.3, where the first matching possibility is chosen.

Table 9.3 Priority of `Object`'s iteration strategy

No.	Candidate	Use with
1	`java.util.Iterator`	Itself
2	`org.w3c.dom.NodeList`	Iterator over `Nodes`
3	`java.util.Enumeration`	Convert to iterator
4	`java.util.regex.Matcher`	Iterator over matches
5	Responds to `iterator` method	Call it
6	Collectable	`Collection.iterator()`
7	`java.util.Map`	Iterator over `Map.Entry` objects
8	Array	Iterator over array items
9	`MethodClosure`	Iterator over calls
10	`java.lang.String`	Iterator over characters
11	`java.io.File`	Iterator over lines
12	`null`	Empty iterator
13	Otherwise	Iterator that only contains the candidate

This allows for flexible usages of Groovy's iteration-aware methods. There is no more need to care whether you work with an iterator, an enumeration, a collection, or whatever, for example within a GPath expression.

The possible candidates in table 9.3 are fairly straightforward, but some background information certainly helps:

Candidate 2: A `NodeList` is used with a *Document Object Model (DOM)*. Such a DOM can be constructed from, for example, XML or HTML documents. We will revisit this topic in chapter 12.

Candidate 5: A candidate object may provide its `Iterator` with the `iterator` method. Instead of a single static interface, the availability of the `iterator` method is used in the sense of duck-typing. An example of such an object is `groovy.util.Node`.

Candidate 6: A candidate object is *collectable* if it can be coerced into an object of type `java.util.Collection`.

Candidate 9: This is an unconventional way of providing an `Iterator`, but it's interesting because it puts our Groovy knowledge to the test.

Suppose you have a method that takes a closure as a parameter and calls the closure back with a single argument, multiple times, using a different argument each time. This could be seen as successively passing arguments to a closure. *Successively passing arguments* is exactly what an `Iterator` does. To make this method work as an iterator, refer to it as a `MethodClosure`, as described in section 5.3.3.

As an example, imagine calculating *sin(x)* for sample domain values of *x* between zero and 2π. A `domain` method can feed an arbitrary `yield` closure with these *x* samples:

```
samples = 4

def domain(yield) {
    step = Math.PI * 2 / samples
    (0..samples).each { yield it*step }
}
```

Printing the *x* values would be as simple as invoking

```
domain { println it}
```

As the `domain` method successively passes objects to the given closure, it can be used with the object-iteration methods—for example, with `collect` to get a list of sine values for all samples from the domain. Use a reference to the `domain` method: `this.&domain`, which makes it a `MethodClosure`.

```
this.&domain.collect { Math.sin(it) }
```

Using a `MethodClosure` as an `Iterator` doesn't seem to provide much advantage other than reusing a method that possibly already exists. Our `domain` method could have returned a list of *x* values. Things would have been easier to understand that way. There also isn't a performance or memory consumption gain, because this list is constructed behind the scenes anyway when converting the closure.

However, it may be handy when the method does more than our simple example. It could produce side-effects—for example, for statistical purposes. It could get data from a live datafeed or some expensive resource with an elaborate caching strategy. Because references to `MethodClosures` can be held in variables, you could change this strategy at runtime (Strategy pattern).[6]

Those were the GDK methods for `Object`. There are more methods in the GDK for arrays of objects. They make arrays usable as lists such that Groovy programmers can use them interchangeably. These methods were described in section 4.2.

Not surprisingly, GDK's object methods are about all-purpose functionality such as revealing information about an object's state and dynamically accessing properties and invoking methods. Iterating over objects can be done regardless of each object's behavior.

The next sections will cover GDK methods for more specialized but frequently used JDK classes used for I/O, such as `File`.

9.2 *Working with files and I/O*

Hardly any script (let alone whole applications) can do without file access and other input/output-related issues. The JDK addresses this need with its `java.io` and `java.net` packages. It provides elaborate support with the `File` and `URL` classes and numerous versions of *streams, readers,* and *writers*.

However, the programmer is left with the repetitive, tedious, and error-prone task of managing I/O resources, such as properly closing an opened file even if exceptions occur while processing.

This is where the GDK steps in and provides numerous methods that let you focus on the task at hand rather than thinking about I/O boilerplate code. This results in faster development, better readability of your code, and more stable solutions, because resource leaks are less likely with centralized error-handling. Having read chapter 5, you may correctly surmise that this is a job for closures.

---

[6] Gamma et al.

In table 9.3, you saw that File objects work with Object's iteration methods. Listing 9.4 uses this approach to print itself to the console: The output is exactly what you see as listing 9.4. Assertions are used to show the use of any, findAll, and grep. Note that file.grep{it} returns only non-empty lines, because empty strings evaluate to false.

Listing 9.4   File's object iteration method examples

```
file = new File('Listing_9_4_File_Iteration.groovy')
file.each{println it}
assert file.any {it =~ /File/}
assert 3 == file.findAll{it =~ /File/}.size()

assert 5 ==  file.grep{it}.size()
```

Additionally, the GDK defines numerous methods with overloaded variants on File, URL, Reader, Writer, InputStream, and OutputStream. Table 9.4 gives an overview where the numbers reflect the number of available variants for each method. Use this table by row or by column to find either all supported receiver classes for a given method name or all GDK methods for a given I/O class.

The full list of all methods is in appendix C. We will present detailed explanations and examples for at least one variant of every important or commonly used method. The usage of the remaining methods/variants is analogous.

Table 9.4   GDK file and I/O methods overview

Method	File	Input stream	Reader	URL	Output stream	Buffered reader	Buffered writer	Object input stream	Writer
append	2								
asWriteable	2								
eachByte	1	1		1					
eachDir	1								
eachFile	1								
eachFileMatch	1								
eachFileRecurse	1								
eachLine	1	1	1	1					

continued on next page

Table 9.4 GDK file and I/0 methods overview *(continued)*

Method	File	Input stream	Reader	URL	Output stream	Buffered reader	Buffered writer	Object input stream	Writer
eachObject	1							1	
filterLine	2	2	2						
getText	2	2	1	2		1			
leftShift <<	1				3				1
newInputStream	1								
newObjectInput-Stream	1								
newOutputStream	1								
newPrintWriter	2								
newReader	2	1							
newWriter	4								
readBytes	1								
readLine		1	1						
readLines	1	1	1						
splitEachLine	1		1						
transformChar			1						
transformLine			1						
withInputStream	1								
withOutputStream	1								
withPrintWriter	1								
withReader	1	1	1	1					
withStream		1			1				
withWriter	2				2				1
withWriterAppend	1								
write	2								
writeLine							1		

Obviously, some of the methods in table 9.4 are concerned with reading, others with writing; we will explain them separately. There are also methods that are specifically concerned with conversions. Their method names start with `transform` or `new`. We will illustrate their use in a separate section. Finally, we will cover the serialization support provided.

The `eachDir` and `eachFile` methods stand out as dealing with aspects of the filesystem rather than I/O operations. We will cover them first.

9.2.1 *Traversing the filesystem*

Groovy follows the Java approach of using the `File` class for both files and directories, where a `File` object represents a location (not *content*, contrary to a common misconception).

Using a `File` object from Groovy often includes calling its JDK methods in a property-style manner. For example, to display information about the current directory, you can use

```
file = new File('.')
println file.name
println file.absolutePath
println file.canonicalPath
println file.directory
```

Listing 9.5 shows this in conjunction with the GDK methods `eachDir`, `eachFile`, `eachFileMatch`, and `eachFileRecurse`. They all work with a closure that gets a `File` object passed into it, disregarding the filesystem entries that represent the current and parent dir (".” and “..”). Whereas `eachFile` yields `File` objects that may represent files or directories, `eachDir` yields only the latter.

Filtering can be achieved with `eachFileMatch`, which applies the `isCase` method of its filter argument on each filename. Like the name suggests, `eachFileRecurse` runs recursively through all subdirectories.

In listing 9.5, we investigate directories in a GROOY_HOME installation on the top level and recursively in the documentation folder to find the number of descendant directories. Groovy's source tree is analyzed for files in its root and groovy* directories.

Listing 9.5　File methods for traversing the filesystem

```
homedir = new File('/java/groovy')
dirs = []
homedir.eachDir{dirs << it.name }          Closure recording
                                           directory names
assert ['bin','conf','docs','embeddable','lib'] == dirs
```

```
cvsdir = new File('/cygwin/home/dierk/groovy')
files = []
cvsdir.eachFile{files << it.name}          ◁┐  Closure recording
assert files.contains('.cvsignore')          │  filenames
assert files.contains('CVS')
                                                    Closure recording
files = []                                          filenames matching
cvsdir.eachFileMatch(~/groovy.*/){files << it.name}  ◁┘  a pattern
assert ['groovy-core', 'groovy-native'] == files

docsdir = new File('/java/groovy/docs')             Closure counting
count = 0                                        ◁─  directories recursively
docsdir.eachFileRecurse{if (it.directory) count++}
assert 104 == count
```

Inside the preceding closures, we get access to a reference of type `File`. We will further explore what we can do with such a reference.

9.2.2 *Reading from input sources*

Suppose we have a file example.txt in the data directory below our current one. It contains

```
line one
line two
line three
```

One of the most common operations with such small text files is to read them at once into a single string. Doing so and printing the contents to the console is as easy as calling the file's `text` property (similar to the `getText` method):

```
println new File('data/example.txt').text
```

What's particularly nice about the `text` property is that it is available not only on `File`, but also on `Reader`, `InputStream`, and even `URL`. Where applicable, you can pass a `Charset` to the `getText` method. See the API documentation of `java.nio.charset.Charset` for details of how to obtain a reference to a `Charset`.

> **BY THE WAY** Groovy comes with a class `groovy.util.CharsetToolkit` that can be used to guess the encoding. See its API documentation for details.

Listing 9.6 goes through some examples of file reading with more fine-grained control. The `readLines` method returns a list of strings, each representing one line in the input source with newline characters chopped.

Listing 9.6 File-reading examples

```
example = new File('data/example.txt')

lines = ['line one','line two','line three']
assert lines == example.readLines()

example.eachLine {
    assert it.startsWith('line')
}

hex = []
example.eachByte { hex << it }
assert hex.size() == example.length()

example.splitEachLine(/\s/){
    assert 'line' == it[0]
}

example.withReader { reader ->
    assert 'line one' == reader.readLine()
}

example.withInputStream { is ->
    assert 'line one' == is.readLine()
}
```

The eachLine method works on files exactly like the iteration method each does. The method is also available on Reader, InputStream, and URL. Input sources can be read a byte at a time with eachByte, where an object of type java.lang.Byte gets passed into the closure.

When the input source is made of formatted lines, splitEachLine can be handy. For every line, it yields a list of items to its closure determined by splitting the line with the given regular expression.

Generally, the with<Resource> methods pass the <Resource> into the closure, handling resource management appropriately. So do the methods withReader and withInputStream. The readLine method can then be used on such a given Reader or InputStream.

This file-reading code reads nicely because Groovy relieves us of all the resource handling. You'd be disappointed if writing wasn't equally straightforward…

9.2.3 *Writing to output destinations*

Listing 9.7 uses the corresponding methods for writing to an output destination. Writing a whole file at once can be achieved with `File`'s `write` method; appending is done with `append`. The `with<Resource>` methods work exactly as you would expect. The use of `withWriter` and `withWriterAppend` is shown in the listing; `withPrintWriter` and `withOutputStream` are analogous. The leftshift operator on `File` has the meaning of *append*.

Listing 9.7 File-writing examples

```
def outFile = new File('data/out.txt')

def lines = ['line one','line two','line three']

outFile.write(lines[0..1].join("\n"))        Writing/appending with
outFile.append("\n"+lines[2])                simple method calls

assert lines == outFile.readLines()

outFile.withWriter { writer ->
    writer.writeLine(lines[0])
}                                            Writing/appending
outFile.withWriterAppend('ISO8859-1') { writer ->   with closures
    writer << lines[1] << "\n"
}                                  Appending with the
outFile << lines[2]                leftshift operator

assert lines == outFile.readLines()
```

The example file in listing 9.7 has been opened and closed seven times: five times for writing, two times for reading. You see no error-handling code for properly closing the file in case of exceptions. `File`'s GDK methods handle that on our behalf.

Note the use of the `writeLine` and `<<` leftshift methods. Other classes that are enhanced by the GDK with the leftshift operator with the exact same meaning are `Process` and `Socket`.

The leftshift operator on `Writer` objects is a clever beast. It relays to `Writer`'s `write` method, which in the GDK makes a best effort to write the argument. The idea is to write a string representation with special support for arrays, maps, and collections. For general objects, `toString` is used.

If the argument is of type `InputStream` or `Reader`, its content is pumped into the writer. Listing 9.8 shows this in action.

Listing 9.8   Using `Writer`'s smart leftshift operator

```
reader = new StringReader('abc')
writer = new StringWriter()

writer << "\nsome String"    << "\n"
writer << [a:1, b:2]         << "\n"
writer << [3,4]              << "\n"
writer << new Date(0)        << "\n"
writer << reader             << "\n"

assert writer.toString() == '''
some String
["a":1, "b":2]
[3, 4]
Thu Jan 01 01:00:00 CET 1970
abc
'''
```

Note that connecting a *reader* with a *writer* is as simple as

```
writer << reader
```

It may seem like magic, but it is a straightforward application of operator over-riding done by the GDK.

Finally, the leftshift operator on `Writer` objects has special support for arguments of type `Writable`. In general, a `Writable` is an object with a `write` method: It knows how to write something. This makes a `Writable` applicable to

```
writer << writable
```

The `Writable` interface is newly introduced by the GDK and used with Groovy's template engines, as you will see in section 9.4. It is also used with filtering, as shown in the next section.

9.2.4 *Filters and conversions*

There are times when ready-made resource handling as implemented by the `with<Resource>` methods is not what you want. This is when you can use the methods `newReader`, `newInputStream`, `newOutputStream`, `newWriter`, and `newPrintWriter` to convert from a `File` object to the type of resource you need.

Two other conversions of this kind are from `String` and `StringBuffer` to their respective `Writers` via

```
StringWriter writer = myString.createStringWriter()
StringBufferWriter sbw = myStringBuffer.createStringBufferWriter()
```

A second kind of conversion is transformation of the content, either character by character or line by line. Listing 9.9 shows how you can use `transformChar` and `transformLine` for this task. They both take a closure argument that determines the transformation result. Whatever that closure returns gets written to the `writer` argument.

Also shown is filtering with the `filterLine` method. Here, each line is relayed to the writer if the closure returns true (see section 6.1).

Listing 9.9 Transforming and filtering examples

```
reader = new StringReader('abc')
writer = new StringWriter()

reader.transformChar(writer) { it.next() }        ⟵  Transform
assert 'bcd' == writer.toString()                     'abc' to 'bcd'

reader = new File('data/example.txt').newReader()
writer = new StringWriter()
                                                      Chop 'line' from each
reader.transformLine(writer) { it - 'line' }      ⟵  line of the example file
assert " one\r\n two\r\n three\r\n" == writer.toString()

input  = new File('data/example.txt')
writer = new StringWriter()
                                                      Read only lines
input.filterLine(writer) { it =~ /one/ }          ⟵  containing "one"
assert "line one\r\n" == writer.toString()

writer = new StringWriter()                        ❶  Read only
writer << input.filterLine { it.size() > 8 }      ⟵     long lines
assert "line three\r\n"  == writer.toString()
```

Note that the last example of `filterLine` at ❶ doesn't take a `writer` argument but returns a `Writable` that is then written to the `writer` with the leftshift operator.

> **NOTE**   The *Line methods use the `newLine` method of the according writer, thus producing system-dependent line feeds. They also produce a line feed after the last line, even if a source stream did not end with it.

Finally, a frequently used conversion is from binary data to strings with base-64 encoding, where binary data is represented only in printable characters, as specified in RFC 2045. This can be useful for sending binary coded data in an email, for example. The name of this codec comes from it having 64 symbols in its "alphabet",[7] just as the decimal system is base 10 (10 symbols: 0–9) and binary is base 2 (2 symbols: 0 and 1):

```
byte[] data = new byte[256]
for (i in 0..255) { data[i] = i }

store = data.encodeBase64().toString()

assert store.startsWith('AAECAwQFBg')
assert store.endsWith  ('r7/P3+/w==')

restored = store.decodeBase64()

assert data.toList() == restored.toList()
```

An interesting feature of the `encodeBase64` method is that it returns a `Writable` and can thus be used with writers, whereas the returned object also implements `toString` conveniently. This has saved us the work of pushing the `Writable` into a `StringWriter`.

Base-64 encoding works with arbitrary binary data with no meaning attached to it. In order to encode *objects* instead, we need to venture into the world of serialization, which is the topic of the next section.

9.2.5 *Streaming serialized objects*

Java comes with a serialization protocol that allows objects of type `Serializable` to be stored in a format so that they can be restored in VM instances that are disconnected in either space or time (see http://java.sun.com/j2se/1.5.0/docs/api/java/io/Serializable.html). Serialized objects can be written to `ObjectOutputStreams` and read from `ObjectInputStreams`. These streams allow making deep copies of objects (with `ByteArrayIn/OutputStream`), sending objects across networks, and storing objects in files or databases.

Listing 9.10 shows the special GDK support for reading serialized objects from a file. First, an `Integer`, a `String`, and a `Date` are written to a file. They are then restored with `File`'s new `eachObject` method. A final assertion checks whether the restored objects are equal to the original.

---

[7] One extra character is used for padding at the end of a block of data, but that isn't relevant when considering the effective base of the codec.

Listing 9.10   Reading serialized objects from files

```
file = new File('data/objects.dta')
out  = file.newOutputStream()
oos  = new ObjectOutputStream(out)

objects = [1, "Hello Groovy!", new Date()]
objects.each {
    oos.writeObject(it)          Serialize each object
}                                in the list in turn
oos.close()

retrieved = []                              Deserialize each
file.eachObject { retrieved << it }    ◁─┘  object in turn

assert retrieved == objects
```

As a variant,

```
file.eachObject
```

can be written as

```
file.newObjectInputStream().eachObject
```

That's it for file access and I/O as far as the GDK is concerned. Daily work with files and streams is a combination of using JDK, GDK, and often `AntBuilder` functionality. Thanks to Groovy's seamless integration, it still looks like a single library, as you will see in the code examples in part 3.

9.3 *Working with threads and processes*

The only reason for time is so that everything doesn't happen at once.

— Albert Einstein

One of Java's merits is its great support for multithreading. The Java platform provides various means for scheduling and executing threads of control efficiently, whereas the Java language allows easy definition of `Runnable` objects for multithreaded execution and control by `wait`/`notify` schemes and the `synchronized` keyword.

Threads are useful for organizing execution flow inside an application. Processes, in contrast, deal with functionality outside your Java or Groovy application. They cannot share objects but need to communicate via streams or other external means. They often appear in Groovy automation scripts, because by nature such scripts trigger machine-dependent functionality.

The GDK supports working with threads and processes by introducing new Groovy-friendly methods for these classes, as you will see in the following subsections. For the remainder of this section, it is assumed that you have some basic understanding of Java's multithreading. It is useful to look at the API documentation of `java.lang.Thread` and `java.lang.Process`.

9.3.1 Groovy multithreading

The first and foremost Groovy feature for multithreading support is that `Closure` implements `Runnable`. This allows simple thread definitions like

```
t = new Thread() { /* Closure body */ }
t.start()
```

This can even be simplified with two new static methods on the `Thread` class:

```
Thread.start { /* Closure body */ }
```

Java has the concept of a *daemon thread*, and therefore so does Groovy. The runtime system handles such a thread differently than a non-daemon thread. Usually, a Java or Groovy application doesn't exit as long as one of its threads is still alive. This does not apply to daemon threads—they do not prevent the application from exiting. A daemon thread can be started via

```
Thread.startDaemon { /* Closure body */ }
```

For a deferred start of a closure in its own thread, there is a new method `runAfter(milliseconds)` on `java.util.Timer`. To start after a one-second delay, use it like

```
new Timer().runAfter(1000){ /* Closure body */}
```

Let's look at a listing showing the Groovy solution for the classical producer/consumer problem. The producer pushes integer values on a stack, and the consumer pops them when available. The push/pop actions are reported; the report might look like the leftmost column of the listing. Additional columns (not generated by the code) show how over time the producer refills the storage that the consumer has emptied:

```
           Producer    Storage    Consumer
push: 0      0 ->       0
push: 1      1 ->       01
push: 2      2 ->       012
pop : 2                 01         -> 2
push: 3      3 ->       013
push: 4      4 ->       0134
```

```
pop : 4                    013          -> 4
push: 5         5 ->       0135
push: 6         6 ->       01356
pop : 6                    0135         -> 6
push: 7         7 ->       01357
push: 8         8 ->       013578
pop : 8                    01357        -> 8
push: 9         9 ->       013579
pop : 9                    01357        -> 9
pop : 7                    0135         -> 7
pop : 5                    013          -> 5
pop : 3                    01           -> 3
pop : 1                    0            -> 1
pop : 0                                 -> 0
```

The actual sequence is not predictable (that's part of the fun). We use closures for running *something* (producing and consuming) in a separate thread and `sleep` to slow down the consumer. We introduce a `Storage` class that holds our stack and synchronizes access to it. If we try to `pop` from an empty stack, we will `wait` until the producer has caught up.

Listing 9.11 shows the code.

Listing 9.11 Using threads with synchronization for the producer/consumer problem

```
class Storage {
    List stack = []
    synchronized void leftShift(value){      ◁── Override the
        stack << value                           leftShift operator
        println "push: $value"              ┐ Wake up any
        notifyAll()                         ◁── listeners
    }
    synchronized Object pop() {
        while (stack.isEmpty()) {            ┐ Wait until a value
            try{ wait() }                    │ is available
            catch(InterruptedException e){}
        }
        def value = stack.pop()
        println "pop : $value"
        return value
    }
}
storage = new Storage()

Thread.start {
    for (i in 0..9) {
        storage << i            Start a thread
        sleep 100               producing 10 items
    }
}
```

```
Thread.start {
    10.times {
        sleep 200
        value = storage.pop()
    }
}
```
Start a thread consuming 10 items

Try to run this code multiple times, and you will see varying output depending on your system's scheduler. It's also fun to play with different `sleep` values.

Note that Groovy obeys the `synchronized` method modifier just like Java does.

Groovy makes concurrent programming *syntactically* easy, although the issue is inherently tricky and can lead to subtle errors. If you set out to deeply dive into the topic, get one the excellent books[8] on the topic.

9.3.2 *Integrating external processes*

A *process* is an abstraction for concurrent execution that happens outside your JVM. Control is relayed from the VM to the system's runtime, the operating system that also runs your VM. Such functionality provides access to your machine, which can be both a blessing and a source of problems. It's a blessing because you can leverage the power of your machine, for example reformatting a hard disk programmatically or doing something less intrusive such as calling shell scripts. Problems occur when you try to use processes across platforms or when the need for synchronization arises.

In order to create a process, you need to work with a string whose value is the command to execute. The GDK allows this with the `execute` method on strings that returns the corresponding `Process` object:

```
Process proc = myCommandString.execute()
```

Instead of a string, the command can also be a list (or array) of strings. This is useful when the command is made up of multiple entries that would require putting arguments in quotes, which may also require character escaping (when the argument contains quotes).

Suppose you create a method that creates a process from Windows's `dir` command. You may get passed a directory name that contains backslashes or whitespace characters. The simplest way to deal with this is something like

---

[8] For example, Doug Lea, *Concurrent Programming in Java: Design Principles and Patterns*, 2nd ed (Addison Wesley, 1999).

```
def dircmd = ['cmd','/c','dir']
def dir    = /\Program Files/
def proc   = (dircmd + dir).execute()
```

NOTE   Depending on your system, you need a command processor to execute console commands. On Windows, that's cmd.exe (command.com on Win98). The /c option closes the console shell when the command has finished.

When creating a process, you can further define environment settings: Use the so-called environment variables as a list (or array) of *key=value* strings and a File object to specify the directory where the process is executed (null stays in the current directory).

For example, you can list the Windows settings for your process with the set command:

```
def env = ['USERNAME=mittie']
def proc = 'cmd /c set'.execute(env, new File('/'))
```

You'll notice that providing your own environment parameters also suppresses the inheritance of current environment parameters to your *child* process (with the possible exception of default parameters).

Now that we have obtained a Process object, we would like to see the produced output. The GDK adds the getText method to achieve this. In other words, the text property gives you the output as a String:

```
println proc.text
```

More fine-grained control can be achieved by using the input, output, and error streams of the process as available in the respective properties:

```
InputStream  in  = proc.in
InputStream  err = proc.err
OutputStream out = proc.out
```

Note that the naming is from the Groovy/Java point of view as opposed to the point of view of the external process. What's the *stdin* for the external process is proc.out on the Groovy/Java side. Figure 9.3 depicts the mapping.

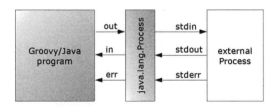

**Figure 9.3
How java.lang.Process streams map
to the streams from an external process**

Instead of appending to `proc.out`, you can also append to the process itself with the same effect:

```
proc.out  << "one\n"
proc      << "two\n"
```

Finally, you never know whether your process might possibly hang forever. The common way of dealing with this problem is to start a watchdog thread that waits for a maximum time and destroys the process if it hasn't finished by then. The GDK provides the method `waitForOrKill(millis)` on `Process`:

```
proc.waitForOrKill(1000)
```

This gives us enough to start a little experiment.

We wrote this book mostly in our spare time, on weekends and in the evening, sometimes well after midnight. This is reflected in the creation dates of the example listing files, for example. Let's suppose we need to find out the earliest time of day when such a listing was created and what file that was.

Listing 9.12 shows how we can use a combination of command-line capabilities and Groovy streams to achieve this. The `dir` command[9] lists all Listing* files with their creation date (`/T:C`), the `find` filter ensures that we only consider lines containing a colon, and `sort` is performed starting at column 10 where the time of day is located. These commands are chained together with the pipe sign (vertical bar).

We are interested in only the first line of the output, so we read only the first line of the stream. The file we search for happens to be about `MarkupBuilder` and was created six minutes after midnight.

Listing 9.12 Finding the earliest listing via command-line processing

```
command    = 'cmd /c dir /T:C Listing* | find ":" | sort /+10'
line       = command.execute().in.readLine()

assert line =~ /00:06 .* Listing_7_3_MarkupBuilderLogic/
println 'earliest file: '
println line
```

The observant reader (yes, that's all of you!) will have recognized that although the code is a slick solution, there also is a pure Groovy solution that is platform

---

[9] This applies only to Windows shells. Shells on other systems have different commands, such as `ls`.

independent. Coming up with a pure Groovy solution is left as an exercise to you. This chapter should have given you all necessary means to do so.

Of course, communicating with external processes can be much more elaborate. Consider the following session at your command line (Windows).

You ask the system for the current date

```
date /t
```

and it answers with, let's say

```
The current date is: 12.10.06
Enter the new date: (dd-mm-yy)
```

You enter some bad input like

```
no-such-date
```

which causes the system to complain at you:

```
The system cannot accept the date entered.
Enter the new date: (dd-mm-yy)
```

You finally satisfy it by entering

```
12-10-06
```

End.

That's a small but representative transcript of working with an external process. Listing 9.13 shows the same thing (including the initial failed attempt at setting the date) where the human user is replaced by some Groovy logic. The purpose of listing 9.13 is to show how to interact with the console programmatically (not to show how the date can be set in the most efficient way).

We additionally make sure that we enter today's date to prevent screwing up the date on our machine when we run all the listings.

Listing 9.13 Talking with a process programmatically

```
today = 'cmd /c date /t'.execute().text.split(/\D/)

proc = 'cmd /c date'.execute()

Thread.start { System.out  << proc.in  }
Thread.start { System.err  << proc.err }

proc << 'no-such-date'  + "\n"
proc << today.join('-') + "\n"

proc.out.close()
proc.waitForOrKill(0)
```

Listing 9.13 nicely combines our knowledge about processes, threads, and streams. Relaying the process streams to `System.out/err` needs to be done in two extra threads. They get blocked when there is nothing to write, and thus the main thread can proceed.

The code reads almost absurdly simply. If you're feeling masochistic, you may want to try writing the equivalent code in Java. We don't recommend it, though.

> **NOTE** The code in listing 9.13 works on Windows only. For other environments (such as cygwin, Solaris, Linux, or Mac OS), you can play with other commands such as `cat` or `echo`. Leave out the leading `cmd /c` in this case.

Working with external processes is inherently platform-dependent. The difference is not only in what capabilities each platform provides, but also in how to call such processes correctly from Java. For cross-platform scripting, things can get really hairy.

Luckily, we can follow the footsteps of pioneers. The Ant developers did all the grunt work and captured it in the `exec` task. For example, to call the *cvs*[10] executable and capture the command output for later analysis, we can use `AntBuilder`:

```
ant = new AntBuilder()

ant.exec(
    dir            : '.'       ,
    executable     : 'cvs.exe' ,
    outputproperty : 'cvsout'  ,
    errorproperty  : 'cvserror',
    resultproperty : 'cvsresult')
    {
        arg(line   : ' checkout MyModule')
    }

println ant.project.properties.cvsresult
```

In trailing code, just refer to `ant.project.properties.cvsout` as a simple string.

Traditionally, scripts have often been associated with running other processes to perform the bulk of their work. Although Groovy brings the full power of the Java platform (and then some!) to scripting, it doesn't shy away from this situation.

---

[10] There is also a specialized CVS task for Ant that we would use if the example was about connecting to CVS rather than showing different means of talking to external processes.

Another common use of scripting languages is for processing text. Again, Groovy is up to the task, as we show in the next section.

9.4 *Working with templates*

Groovy is a pragmatic language. Rather than following any dogma in language and library design, it focuses on getting recurring tasks done. Working with templates is such a task.

A template is essentially some text. Unlike fixed literal text, a template allows predefined modifications. These modifications follow some structure; they do not occur wildly.

If you think about a web application, literal text would be a static HTML page. The other end of the continuum are web application frameworks that create such HTML solely by programming logic, such as *Java Server Faces (JSF)*. In between are approaches like *Java Server Pages (JSP)* and others that create the final HTML from a template.

The use of templating is not limited to web applications. It is equally useful for

- Organizing database queries
- Helping to connect to web services
- Generating code
- Transforming XML
- Predefining PostScript documents
- Standard emails

and much more, as you will see in the remainder of the book.

We briefly describe what templates look like before launching into a full example. We also examine some of the more advanced uses of templates. Understanding the content of this section is also important when we come to the next topic, Groovlets.

9.4.1 *Understanding the template format*

The *format* of templates is inspired by the JSP syntax, the JSP *Expression Language (EL)*, the Velocity framework, and GStrings. The idea is to use placeholders inside the running text. Table 9.5 lists the supported placeholders and their purpose. If you have ever worked with JSP or a similar technology, it will feel familiar.

Table 9.5   Template placeholders

Marker	Purpose
`$variable`	Insert the value of the `variable` into the text
`${groovycode}`	Evaluate single-line *groovycode*, and insert the result into the text
`<%=groovycode%>`	Evaluate the *groovycode*, and insert the result into the text
`<%groovycode%>`	Evaluate the *groovycode*

The `groovy.text` package defines multiple *template engines*. These engines (the name *factory* would better reveal their purpose) have `createTemplate` methods that read the template's raw text from an input source (`String`, `Reader`, `File`, or `URL`) and return a `Template` object.

Template objects can make a final text by replacing all the placeholders with their respective values. A map of variable names and their respective values (the *binding*) is therefore passed to template's `make` method, which returns the final text in terms of a `Writable`. Figure 9.4 shows how all this fits together.

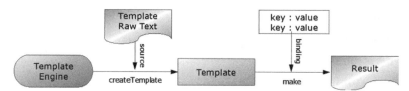

Figure 9.4   Templates are created from a template engine and called with a binding to make the final result.

Different `Template` classes provide different runtime characteristics. One implementation might fully read the raw text and cache it for the later *make* step; other implementations might only store a reference to the source and merge it with the binding at *make* time. The latter *streaming* scenario can use source `Readers` and result `Writers` for optimized performance and scalability.

9.4.2   *Templates in action*

Suppose you have been asked to write a tool that sends out monthly email reminders, and your boss wants it to support *mail merge* functionality (in other words, personalized content). A sample mail may look like this with variable items in bold:

```
Dear Mrs. Davis,
another month has passed and it's time for these
2 tasks:
- visit the Groovy in Action (GinA) page
- chat with GinA readers

your collaboration is very much appreciated.
```

First, we need to think about placeholders.

Davis seems to be a last name, so we need a variable for that; we refer to it as $lastname.

Mrs. should get some extra handling, because not all people have a salutation and we don't want to have that extra space character when there is none. This leads to a simple Groovy expression that we enclose in curly braces. The placeholder becomes `${salutation?salutation+' ':''}`

For the tasks, we use a simple list of strings and ask for the list's `<%=tasks. size()%>`. Iteration is trickier, but listing 9.14 shows how to use `<% %>` to solve that. Note that we can open the each closure in one placeholder and close it in a second one. The text that is between these two is processed for each task. We can even use the closure's it reference.

In listing 9.14, we use the `SimpleTemplateEngine`, which is the standard choice when no specialized behavior is required.

Listing 9.14 Using a simple template engine for email text

```
mailReminder = '''
Dear ${salutation?salutation+' ':''}$lastname,          Text of
another month has passed and it's time for these        template
<%=tasks.size()%> tasks:                                containing
<% tasks.each { %>- $it                                  placeholders
<% } %>
your collaboration is very much appreciated
'''

def engine   = new groovy.text.SimpleTemplateEngine()
def template = engine.createTemplate(mailReminder)
def binding  = [
    salutation: 'Mrs.',                                  Variables to
    lastname  : 'Davis',                                 substitute in
    tasks     : ['visit the Groovy in Action (GinA) page', the template
                 'chat with GinA readers']
]

assert template.make(binding).toString() == '''         Evaluate the template
Dear Mrs. Davis,                                         against the binding
another month has passed and it's time for these
```

```
2 tasks:
- visit the Groovy in Action (GinA) page
- chat with GinA readers

your collaboration is very much appreciated
'''
```

△ **Evaluate the template
against the binding**

∎

If you'd prefer, you can construct the engine via `SimpleTemplateEngine(true)` to make it print out additional information on how it works inside. You'll see the following output:

```
-- script source --
/* Generated by SimpleTemplateEngine */
out.print("\n");
out.print("Dear ${salutation?salutation+' ':''}$lastname,\n");
out.print("another month has passed and it's time for these\n");
out.print("");out.print("${tasks.size()}");
out.print(" tasks:\n");
out.print(""); tasks.each { ;
out.print("- $it \n");
out.print(""); } ;
out.print(" \n");
out.print("your collaboration is very much appreciated\n");
out.print("");

-- script end --
```

That means the template is a Groovy script, generated from the template source and invoked dynamically. All the `$` and `${}` placeholders work because they are placed inside double quotes. The iteration logic (in bold) is literally inserted in the script as it appears between `<% %>`.

The log output is also useful in case of errors in the script. Error messages with line and column indications relate to that generated script.

9.4.3 *Advanced template issues*

Also interesting is the `out` variable in the preceding output. It refers to a `Writer` that is placed into the binding by default and is thus also available in template placeholders. You can use it like

```
<%
    tasks.each { out.println('- '+it) }
%>
```

When working with templates, here are two points to consider.

- If you choose to declare the template's raw text in a string (as in listing 9.14), you should use single-quoted string literals, rather than double-quoted ones, which may be transformed into GStrings. Using GStrings would result in resolving $ and ${} placeholders at the time you call `createTemplate`,[11] not at *make* time. Sometimes this may be what you want, but most of the time probably not.

- Templates have no defined escaping: For the rare case when you need to include %> in your template literally, you need a trick to make the engine accept it. One way is to put the offending text in a variable, pass that into the binding, and refer to it in the text via $*variable*.

The `groovy.text` package currently provides three template engines that all obey the same format of placeholders but have different characteristics:

- `SimpleTemplateEngine` produces the template in terms of a script as discussed previously. At *make* time, that script writes line-by-line to the output destination. The script is cached.

- `GStringTemplateEngine` holds the template in terms of a writable closure, possibly providing better performance and scalability for large templates and for stateless streaming scenarios. See section 12.2.2.

- `XmlTemplateEngine` is optimized when the template's raw text and the resulting text are both valid XML. It operates on nodes in the DOM and can thus provide a pretty-printed result. Unlike other engines, it produces system-dependent line feeds.

For more details on these engines, see the respective API documentation pages.

So far you have seen four ways to generate text dynamically: GStrings, `Formatter` (with `printf` calls, for example), `MarkupBuilder`, and templates. Each has its own sweet spot of applicability. GStrings and `Formatter` work best for simple in-code purposes, `MarkupBuilder` for producing structured text with mostly dynamic content, and templates for mostly static text with few dynamic parts injected. Of course, combinations are not only possible but normal in real-world applications.

One obvious application where templates and markup go together is for web applications. Our next section introduces Groovlets, Groovy's built-in support for simple yet powerful web applications.

---

[11] Maybe even earlier; see section 13.2.5.

9.5 *Working with Groovlets*

The Java platform is available in a standard edition (J2SE/JSE) and an enterprise edition (J2EE/JEE). So far, we have only worked with features of the standard edition; we will now look at a special capability that Groovy adds to the enterprise edition.

J2EE contains the Servlet API (see http://java.sun.com/products/servlet/) for implementing web applications. For the remainder of this chapter, it is assumed that you have some basic understanding of servlets.

Groovlets are to Groovy what servlets are to Java: a basic, standardized way of writing web applications. The pure usage of Groovlets is good for small and simple applications, whereas more demanding applications benefit from frameworks such as Grails (see chapter 16).

We're going to start with a simple "hello world" program, which we use to demonstrate installation. We will then move on to a guessing game that lets us examine how data flows in Groovlets, before rewriting the same game using the templating technology you saw in section 9.4.

9.5.1 *Starting with "hello world"*

What's the bare minimum that we have to do to see the greeting message shown in figure 9.5?

First, we have to get a J2EE-compliant web server. There are lots of open-source pure Java servers available for free, ranging from Jetty (lightweight, in-process capabilities) to Tomcat (feature rich) to JBoss (application server). If you have no other preference, Tomcat is a good default choice.

Figure 9.5 "Hello world" as done with Groovlets

After installing the server, you will notice that it has a webapps directory. We will go for the simplest possible configuration and develop our code right there.[12]

---

[12] All server experts: Please forgive me. This section is about Groovlets and not about the best possible server setup. An alternative is to configure your server such that it picks up your development directory: for example, for Tomcat, adding `<Context path="/myGroovlets" docBase="`*path-to-myGroovlet-dir*`"/>` to the `<Host>` element of your config/server.xml.

Below the webapps dir, create the directory structure shown in figure 9.6. It shows the structure for a web application named *myGroovlets* and a sample Groovlet residing in Start.groovy. The web.xml file is needed for configuration purposes and the groovy-all-1.0.jar file for making the web server groovy.

Before we can create any Groovlets, we must make the web server aware of this capability. In the usual J2EE manner, we achieve this via the standard web.xml file. Listing 9.15 contains a sample. The symbolic name `Groovy` is mapped to the class `GroovyServlet`. This class is able to load *.groovy scripts to handle them as Groovlets.

Figure 9.6   Directory structure for a sample Groovlet web application below the webapps dir

---

Listing 9.15   Sample web.xml file for configuring a web application for Groovlet use

```xml
<!DOCTYPE web-app
    PUBLIC "-//Sun Microsystems, Inc.//DTD Web Application 2.2//EN"
    "http://java.sun.com/j2ee/dtds/web-app_2_2.dtd" >

<web-app>
    <display-name>Groovlet Demonstrator</display-name>
    <description>
        Showing the use of Groovlets for Groovy in Action
    </description>

    <servlet>
        <servlet-name>Groovy</servlet-name>
        <servlet-class>groovy.servlet.GroovyServlet</servlet-class>
    </servlet>

    <servlet-mapping>
        <servlet-name>Groovy</servlet-name>
        <url-pattern>*</url-pattern>
    </servlet-mapping>

</web-app>
```

All requests (the URL pattern *) are dispatched to `Groovy`. All other entries, such as `display-name` and `description`, are for documentation purposes only.

With this configuration in place, we can start writing our first actual Groovlet. Listing 9.16 implements it by using the default builder that is available under the name `html` in the Groovlets binding. You should save it as Start.groovy under the webapps/myGroovlets directory, as shown in figure 9.6.

Listing 9.16   The "hello world" Groovlet using the HTML builder

```
html.html{
    head {
        title 'Groovlet Demonstrator'
    }
    body { h1 'Welcome to the World of Groovlets' }
}
```

Pretty slick, eh? You can see its output by starting your web server and pointing your browser to http://localhost:8080/myGroovlets/Start.groovy.[13]

At this point, it is fun to play around with changing the Groovlet, saving the file and reloading the page in the browser.

NOTE   No server restart or application reload is needed to see changed output. This makes for rapid application development!

A Groovlet is essentially an ordinary Groovy script that sends its output to your browser. To understand what is achievable with Groovlets, you need to know what information they can work on.

9.5.2 *The Groovlet binding*

Like all other Groovy scripts, Groovlets have a binding that contains information, which can be accessed with the `binding` property. For Groovlets, this information is provided by the `GroovyServlet` that handles the request. Listing 9.17 asks the binding what is inside and puts it on your browser screen if you request http://localhost:8080/myGroovlets/Inspect.groovy. Save the code in a file named Inspect. groovy, and place it in your myGroovlets web application directory, right beside the Start.groovy file.

Listing 9.17   Inspect.groovy Groovlet reveals what's in the Groovlet binding

```
html.html{
    head {
        title 'Groovlet Demonstrator'
    }
```

---

[13] This assumes the default values are used. If your server starts on a different port, you will have to adapt the URL accordingly.

```
body {
    h1 'Variables in the Binding:'
    table(summary:'binding') {
        tbody {
            binding.variables.each { key, value ->
                tr {
                    td key.toString()
                    td(value ? value.toString() : 'null')
} } } } } }
```

This little Groovlet gives us a valid HTML table. Note the summary attribute of the table element and the nested tbody element. They are often forgotten because browsers do not complain if they are missing. However, without them, the HTML will not be fully compliant with recent HTML standards.

Table 9.6 lists the output as produced by listing 9.17 and some additional usage information.

Table 9.6 Information available to Groovlets

Name	Note	Example usage
headers	Map of HTTP request headers	headers.host
params	Map of HTTP request parameters	params.myParam
session	ServletSession, can be null	session?.myParam
request	HttpServletRequest	request.remoteHost
response	HttpServletResponse	response.contentType='text/xml'
context	ServletContext	context.myParam
application	ServletContext (same as context)	application.myParam
out	response.writer	Lazy init, not in binding
sout	response.outputStream	Lazy init, not in binding
html	Builder initialized as new MarkupBuilder(out)	Lazy init, not in binding

The variables out, sout, and html are initialized lazily; they are null until the Groovlet uses them the first time. This allows us to work on the response object before the output stream is opened. For example, this can be necessary to set response properties such as the contentType.

The `session` variable is `null` unless there is session information for the current conversation. This allows optimization for stateless Groovlets that do not need session information. To use session information in Groovlets, you typically start like so:

```
if (!session) // error handling here if needed
session = request.session
```

BY THE WAY Session-related error handling may be needed if the Groovlet is to be used only after some prework has been done that should have initialized the session already. Think about an online shop where the user has put a product in their shopping cart. This information is stored in the session. When the user tries to check out but the session has expired, there will be no item to pay for because the session is null.

A Groovlet is also evaluated with the use of the `ServletCategory` that adds the methods `get/set` and `getAt/putAt` to the classes `ServletContext`, `HttpSession`, `ServletRequest`, and `PageContext`.

A small example will show how all this works together. Figure 9.7 shows the user interface of a little web game. It takes a random number between 0 and 100 and lets the user guess it, giving indications whether the guess was too high or too low.

Listing 9.18 shows the Groovlet code that implements the game. Save it to a file Number-Guesser.groovy in your myGroovlets directory, and point your browser to http://localhost:8080/myGroovlets/NumberGuesser.groovy.

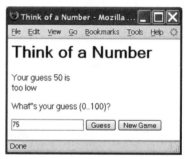

Figure 9.7   HTML user interface of the HighLow game

The game needs to handle session data and request parameters. The target number is stored as an `Integer` value in the session under the symbolic name `goal`. It is initialized to a random number on first use as well as when a new game is requested.

The request parameter `guess` carries the last input value; `restart` is submitted if the user clicks the New Game button. When dealing with request parameters, you need to be aware that they can be `null` (if not submitted) or an empty string (when submitted without value).

Listing 9.18 Groovlet code of the HighLow game

```
def session = request.session
def guess   = params.guess
guess = guess ? guess.toInteger() : null
if (params.restart) guess = null

if (!session.goal || params.restart) {            Generate a number to
    session.goal = (Math.random()*100).toInteger()   guess, if necessary
}
def goal = session.goal
                                                  Start a builder to
html.html{ head { title 'Think of a Number'  }  ←  generate the HTML
    body {
        h1 'Think of a Number'
        if (goal && guess) {                       Use a GString as a simple
            div "Your guess $guess is "  ←          template for text
            switch (guess) {
                case goal         : div 'correct!'; break    Classify the guess
                case {it < goal} : div 'too low' ; break    appropriately
                case {it > goal} : div 'too high'; break
            }
        }
        p "What's your guess (0..100)?"            Display a form posting
        form(action:'NumberGuesser.groovy'){  ←    to the same page again
            input(type:'text', name:'guess', '')
            button(type:'submit', 'Guess')
            button(type:'submit', name:'restart', value:'true',
                   'New Game')
}   }   }
```

The code is divided into two pieces. It starts with a *controller* part that cares about the current state (the session) and requested actions (the parameters). The second part is the HTML builder, which plays the role of the *view*, visualizing the current state.

So far, our Groovlets have built the view only through the HTML builder, but there are more options.

9.5.3 *Templating Groovlets*

With the out writer available in the Groovlet binding, you can write directly to the response object. That means you can do things like

```
out << '<HTML>'
                // more output here …
out << '</HTML>'
```

or output the current date and time as GStrings like

```
out << "<HTML><BODY>${new Date().toGMTString()}</BODY></HTML>"
```

In section 9.4, you found that Groovy templates almost read like JSPs, so using them in this scenario is an obvious choice. Listing 9.19 stores a HTML template for the HighLow game that works with the goal and guess parameters.

> **Listing 9.19 Number.template.html as a view for the HighLow game**

```
<html>
  <head>
    <title>Think of a Number</title>
  </head>
  <body>
    <h1>Think of a Number</h1>
    Your guess $guess is <%
        switch (guess) {
            case goal       : out << 'correct!'; break
            case {it < goal} : out << 'too low' ; break
            case {it > goal} : out << 'too high'; break
        }
    %>
    <p>What&quot;s your guess (0..100)?</p>
    <form action='Templater.groovy'>
      <input type='text' name='guess'>
      <button type='submit'>Guess</button>
      <button type='submit' name='restart' value='true'>New Game
      </button>
    </form>
  </body>
</html>
```

Notice how the template contains a GString (the guess) and Groovy code inside <%...%>. This template can be used from a controlling Groovlet like so:

```
def engine   = new groovy.text.SimpleTemplateEngine()
def source   = getClass().classLoader.
                        getResource('/Number.template.html')
def template = engine.createTemplate(source)

out << template.make(goal:50, guess:49)
```

The template is evaluated appropriately, with the GString placeholder being replaced and the embedded code being executed.

A specialty of this approach is that the controlling Groovlet needs to read the template source as a resource from the classpath, because it cannot know where the respective file would be located. To make this possible, the template file must be stored in the `classes` directory of your web application.

The organizational style of having a controller Groovlet and a view template allows a practical division of labor. While the programmer can concentrate on implementing the control flow, the business logic, and database access, the designer can use their usual tools to work on the HTML templates.

When the emphasis of the web application is on the templates rather than on the controlling logic, Groovy also supports a full JSP-like approach sometimes dubbed *Groovy Server Pages (GSP)*. It works exactly like the preceding templates with the same binding as for Groovlets.

A special `TemplateServlet` acts in the role of the controlling Groovlet. Configure it in your web.xml by adding this snippet:

```
<servlet>
    <servlet-name>template</servlet-name>
    <servlet-class>groovy.servlet.TemplateServlet</servlet-class>
</servlet>

<servlet-mapping>
    <servlet-name>template</servlet-name>
    <url-pattern>*.html</url-pattern>
</servlet-mapping>
```

All *.html requests will then be relayed to the appropriate template. `Template-Servlet` will also care for properly caching each template. This gives better performance than reconstructing the template for every request.

Of course, there is more to implementing web applications than mastering the basic technology. However, our focus here is only on the Groovy aspects, leaving much room for more books to be written about how to implement full web applications with Groovy. We will give a more tutorial-style introduction into developing web applications with Groovy in chapter 16.

For further pointers to Groovy-related web technologies, see http://freshmeat.net/projects/gvtags, http://groovestry.sourceforge.net, and http://biscuit.javanicus.com/biscuit/.

9.6 *Summary*

The GDK—the way that Groovy augments and enhances the JDK—provides key devices for a wide range of programming tasks.

The GDK makes I/O handling a breeze. It takes away low-level considerations in common situations, dealing with resource management automatically. The difference is not only in terms of development speed when writing the program code initially. You may even be a little slower in the beginning, because you need some time to adapt, and typing time is rarely the bottleneck of programming. The real benefit comes from working on a slightly higher level of abstraction.

Similarly, instead of teasing the programmer with *how* to properly walk through an enumeration/iteration/collection/array, the GDK lets you focus on *what* to achieve—for example, to find something using `col.find{}` regardless of what `col` is.

Working with threads and processes is equally easy in Groovy. Multithreading is a tricky topic at the best of times, and again Groovy reduces the amount of scaffolding code required, making it easier to see what's going on. Process handling can be vital in a scripting language, and Groovy not only makes working with the plain Java `Process` class straightforward, but also facilitates the executable handling semantics from Ant using `AntBuilder`.

Dynamically filling in templates can be important in a variety of applications, and Groovy comes with an easy-to-grasp templating technology, using a syntax that is familiar to most Java programmers.

Although the standard JDK is important, the importance of J2EE cannot be overstated. Groovy participates in this arena, too, providing Groovlets as yet another web application framework. You will learn more about web applications when we consider Grails in chapter 16.

It may look like the Groovy *language* made much of this possible, but this is only one side of the story. The Groovy language—and its Meta-Object Protocol in particular—provides the means that the GDK employs. What the GDK does with the JDK can be done with any library or API. That's what some people call *language-oriented programming*: lifting your code up to a level where it directly expresses your concerns.

Database programming with Groovy

10

As far as the laws of mathematics refer to reality, they are not certain, and as far as they are certain, they do not refer to reality.

—Albert Einstein

Relational[1] databases are data stores that are based on a *relational model*. It is this model that makes them so powerful. Its mathematical foundation allows us to reason about the results of operations and lets database engines perform appropriate optimizations.

Database access is also highly standardized, allowing multiple applications to coordinate by sharing their data even if these applications are built with different technologies. The standard that incorporates the relational algebra is the *Structured Query Language (SQL)*.

Because using SQL and connecting to relational databases is such an important task, any programming language worth talking about provides a way of doing it. Scripting languages—notably PHP, Python, and Ruby—provide simple and immediate access, whereas Java comes with the *Java Database Connectivity (JDBC)* API, which is not as simple.

Now comes Groovy. The Groovy database connectivity support (Groovy SQL for short) is plain JDBC with sugar from Groovy's `groovy.sql` library package. It takes only four classes of sugar (`Sql`, `DataSet`, `GroovyResultSet`, and `GroovyRowResult`) to make database work short and sweet. Figure 10.1 shows where Groovy SQL fits into the API stack.

Groovy SQL lifts JDBC to a level of user-friendliness that is comparable to, and in some respects better than, that offered by other scripting languages.

But it also plays nicely at the object level. JDBC is often used with database-related design patterns that evolved around it. In this chapter, you will see some of them in the form of *Data Transfer Objects (DTOs)* and *Data Access Objects (DAOs)*. You will witness how Groovy SQL reduces the need for creating such extra classes, sometimes eliminating the extra work.

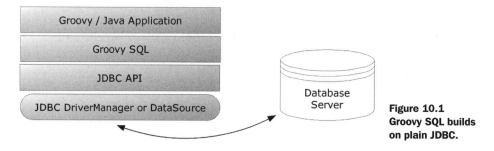

Figure 10.1 Groovy SQL builds on plain JDBC.

---

[1] For the purpose of this chapter, we use the term *database* for relational databases only, recognizing that there are other valid databases as well, such as object databases, hierarchical databases, and even XML databases.

Database systems and SQL make a topic of their own, and many books have been written about them. You need this knowledge for our examples, but explaining it here would exceed the scope of this book.[2] In return for your understanding, we keep the SQL examples reasonably basic.

For the remainder of this chapter, it is assumed that you have some basic knowledge about SQL and how to work with relational databases in Java.

When you have finished this chapter, you will be able to work on your databases through Groovy for any kind of administration task, automated or ad-hoc reporting, persisting your business objects, and leveraging the power of the relational data model—all in a simple yet organized manner.

10.1 Basic database operations

Groovy follows the design guideline that simple tasks should be easy and advanced tasks should be possible. This section is solely about simple tasks. That means you can expect an easy introduction into the topic. We will go through:

- Connecting to the database
- Creating the database schema
- Working with sample data

Working with data is done through four operations: *create*, *read*, *update*, and *delete*, together called CRUD operations.

Relational database systems also reveal information about themselves in so-called *metadata*. This is "data about the data"—in its simplest terms, information like the types and names of columns, tables, and so forth.

At the end of this section, you will be able to do standard database work with Groovy. The knowledge in this section will be sufficient to write whole applications that utilize databases. The remainder of the chapter will expand your design choices to more elaborate solutions.

10.1.1 Setting up for database access

It's fairly obvious that you cannot do anything before you have a database system that you can use. Groovy has no database in its distribution. If you already have a database system that comes with a JDBC driver, you can go with it. Everybody else

---

[2] See *An Introduction to Database Systems* by C. J. Date (Addison Wesley, 2003) for a good introduction.

has to install one, where *install* can mean totally different things for different database products.

Installing a database

All the examples in this chapter work with the popular open-source *Hypersonic* database system (HSQLDB), which you can download from http://hsqldb.org/ (use version 1.7 or higher). Installing it means putting the hsqldb.jar file on your classpath when executing this chapter's examples. See section 7.2.3 for details of how to do that. Remember that you can drop a jar file into your <user.home>/.groovy/lib directory to have it on your classpath whenever you start the groovy interpreter.

If you decide to use a different database system, follow its installation instructions. Typically, you will also have a jar file that needs to be added to the classpath, because at least the product-specific driver class needs to be found there.

SIDE NOTE The JdbcOdbcDriver is on the classpath by default because it ships with the JDK. It allows connections to database systems that implement the Open DataBase Connectivity (ODBC) standard over the so-called JDBC-ODBC bridge. Popular ODBC data sources are Microsoft Excel and Microsoft Access. This driver is not intended for production use, however. It's an easy way to explore a database exposed by ODBC, but a dedicated JDBC driver is usually a more stable and better-performing long-term solution.

Database products also differ in the SQL they accept. Every system has its own *dialect*.[3] Because our examples use HSQLDB, the SQL that you'll see in the examples is in HSQLDB dialect. See the manual of your database product for possible deviations.

First contact

Regardless of your technology, you must provide four pieces of information to access a database:

- The database *uniform resource locator* (URL)
- Username
- Password
- Driver class name (which can sometimes be derived automatically)

---

[3] "The wonderful thing about standards is: there are so many to choose from."—Prof. Andrew Tennenbaum.

The database URL needs a short explanation. A database URL (a JDBC URL in our context) is a platform-independent way of addressing a database. It always starts with `jdbc:` followed by a vendor-specific subprotocol. You need to refer to your database system's documentation for possible subprotocols.

Because we use HSQLDB, we have the choice of subprotocols listed in table 10.1.

Table 10.1   HSQLDB subprotocols

URL pattern	Purpose
`jdbc:hsqldb:hsql://` `server/`*dbname*	Connects to a HSQLDB server process; use when multiple clients or processes need to share the database
`jdbc:hsqldb:file:/`*dir/* *dbname*	Connects to a single-client HSQLDB instance with file-based persistence; multiple files starting with *dbname* will be created if the database doesn't yet exist
`jdbc:hsqldb:mem:`*dbname*	Connects to a nonpersistent in-memory database

When using the HSQLDB in-memory database, for example, our database URL will be `jdbc:hsqldb:mem:GinA`. Changing to the server or file-based version is as easy as changing the URL accordingly.

We will use standard username/password settings: `sa` for sysadmin and an empty password string. It goes without saying that this is acceptable only for experimental purposes.

The driver class name will be `org.hsqldb.jdbcDriver`. If you use a different vendor, this name will also be different.

Where do you put this information? In Groovy, you access the database through an object of type `groovy.sql.Sql`.[4] You get such an object through `Sql`'s `newInstance` factory method, passing the preceding information as parameters:

```
import groovy.sql.Sql
db = Sql.newInstance(
    'jdbc:hsqldb:mem:GinA',
    'sa',
    '',
    'org.hsqldb.jdbcDriver')
```

Congratulations; you have successfully connected to the database!

When you look into `Sql`'s API documentation, you will find more versions of the `newInstance` factory method, but we will always use this one.

---

[4] If you think this naming is questionable, we fully agree.

DriverManager versus DataSource

If you look back to figure 10.1, you will notice two concepts below the JDBC API: *DriverManager* and *DataSource*. The Sql.newInstance methods always go through the DriverManager facility, which can be seen as the classical low-level way of connecting. Since JDK 1.4, there has been a second way that uses the DataSource concept.

Although the DriverManager facility is still supported for backward compatibility, using DataSource is generally preferable. In addition to providing a connection to the database, it may optionally manage a *connection pool* and support *distributed transactions* (not explained here). Because obtaining connections to a database is a time-consuming operation, it's common to reuse them. The pool is the storage facility that provides you with a connection. You have to pass the connection back after use so that others can reuse it. If you forget to return it, the pool becomes pointless. In order to avoid that, Groovy SQL transparently returns the connection for you.

DataSources become even more important when running in a managed environment such as within an application server. A managed environment provides its applications with DataSource objects to make its special features (such as connection pooling) available. In this scenario, DataSource objects are often retrieved through the *Java Naming and Directory Interface (JNDI)*.

Now that you have heard about the merits of DataSources, how do you use them in Groovy? Your database vendor provides its own implementation of the javax.sql.DataSource interface. HSQLDB, for example, provides the class org.hsqldb.jdbc.jdbcDataSource for that purpose. To obtain a Sql instance for a DataSource, create it, optionally set its properties, and pass it to the Sql constructor:

```
source = new org.hsqldb.jdbc.jdbcDataSource()
source.database = 'jdbc:hsqldb:mem:GinA'
source.user     = 'sa'
source.password = ''
db = new groovy.sql.Sql(source)
```

> **NOTE**   If you are using an application server, you might retrieve the DataSource using JNDI as previously mentioned. The advantage of this approach is that it allows administration of the database to be more independent from your program. Your program doesn't need to mention specific database drivers or DataSource classes, and you could migrate from one database to another with reduced effort. But we did mention the dialect differences, didn't we?

No matter whether you use a DataSource in the `Sql` constructor or the Driver-Manager facility through `Sql.newInstance`, in the end you have a reference to a `Sql` instance (as the value of the `db` variable). You can work with this reference regardless of how it was constructed.

These are the recommended ways of connecting to the database in Groovy. In situations when you already have a database connection and you would like to work on it through Groovy, you can use `new Sql(connection)`. But beware that in this case, Groovy SQL cannot manage that connection and you have to take care of properly closing it yourself.

Finally, if you have a `Sql` instance and you need a second one with the same characteristics (a clone), you can use `new Sql(db)`.

Now that you have a `Sql` instance that represents your connection to the database, you will use it to execute some SQL statements.

10.1.2 Executing SQL

Once you have a `Sql` instance in the `db` reference, executing a SQL statement on the database is as easy as

```
db.execute(statement)
```

Groovy SQL carries out all the management work around that call: getting a connection (possibly from the DataSource connection pool), constructing and configuring the statement, sending it, logging encountered exceptions, and closing resources (statement and connection) properly even if exceptions have been thrown. It even does a bit more, as you will see in the course of this chapter.

Creating the database schema

The first thing you can use the `execute` method for is creating the database schema. Let's assume we are going to store data about athletes and their performances. In order to identify an athlete, we need the first name, last name, and date of birth. A first attempt might be

```
db.execute '''
    CREATE TABLE Athlete (
        firstname    VARCHAR(64),
        lastname     VARCHAR(64),
        dateOfBirth  DATE
    );
'''
```

This does the job but isn't very realistic because we will need a primary key to look up athletes and we didn't define one. It's obvious that none of these fields listed is unique in itself. A combination of all three is unlikely to have duplicates, but such a compound key is always tricky to deal with and is still not guaranteed to be unique.

It's conventional to use an artificial key (also known as a *surrogate key*) in such cases, so we will introduce one. Because we are all lazy, we will let the database figure out how to create one. For efficient lookup, we also put an index on the artificial key:[5]

```
db.execute '''
    CREATE TABLE Athlete (
        athleteId    INTEGER GENERATED BY DEFAULT AS IDENTITY,
        firstname    VARCHAR(64),
        lastname     VARCHAR(64),
        dateOfBirth DATE
    );
    CREATE INDEX athleteIdx ON Athlete (athleteId);
'''
```

That's the minimal schema we will start with. We will work with it in an agile way; the schema will grow over time. Reconstructing the schema programmatically every time we need it makes this agile database programming possible. But wait. If we issue the preceding statement to a database instance that already has an Athlete table (maybe from our last run), it will throw a SqlException. We need to drop the old one, but only if an old one exists, and do the same with the index:

```
db.execute '''
    DROP    INDEX athleteIdx IF EXISTS;
    DROP    TABLE Athlete    IF EXISTS;
    CREATE TABLE Athlete (
        athleteId    INTEGER GENERATED BY DEFAULT AS IDENTITY,
        firstname    VARCHAR(64),
        lastname     VARCHAR(64),
        dateOfBirth DATE
    );
    CREATE INDEX athleteIdx ON Athlete (athleteId);
'''
```

As the SQL boilerplate code grows, it starts to bury the interesting information. We take note that this should be refactored into a template as soon as we find ourselves writing it a second time.

---

[5] Many databases, including HSQLDB, automatically create indexes for their primary keys. We have included the index creation explicitly here for the sake of clarity.

Inserting data

With the schema defined, we can start putting data in. We can use the `execute` method for this purpose. Let's add the world's top marathon runners:[6]

```
db.execute '''
    INSERT INTO Athlete (firstname, lastname,    dateOfBirth)
                VALUES ('Paul',    'Tergat',     '1969-06-17');
    INSERT INTO Athlete (firstname, lastname,    dateOfBirth)
                VALUES ('Khalid',  'Khannouchi', '1971-12-22');
    INSERT INTO Athlete (firstname, lastname,    dateOfBirth)
                VALUES ('Ronaldo', 'da Costa',   '1970-06-07');
'''
```

We were once in a project where we used this approach to insert a thousand records of carefully hand-managed test data. However, this approach is difficult to read and manage, because it contains a lot of duplication. Therefore, you can make the `execute` method produce what is called a *prepared statement*.

A prepared statement is a SQL statement with occurrences of values replaced by placeholders (question marks). You can reuse the same statement for a possibly large sequence of calls with different values per call. The JDBC driver therefore has to do its per-statement work only once instead of numerous times. The work per statement includes parsing the SQL, validating, optimizing access paths, and constructing an execution plan. The more complex the statement, the more time-consuming this work becomes. In other words, using a prepared statement is always a good move. In Java, prepared statements are represented using the `java.sql.PreparedStatement` interface.

The following example separates the SQL from the data used:

```
String athleteInsert = '''
    INSERT INTO Athlete (firstname, lastname, dateOfBirth)
                VALUES  (?, ?, ?);
'''
db.execute athleteInsert, ['Paul',    'Tergat',     '1969-06-17']
db.execute athleteInsert, ['Khalid',  'Khannouchi', '1971-12-22']
db.execute athleteInsert, ['Ronaldo', 'da Costa',   '1970-06-07']
```

The execute method is smart enough to know when it needs to work with a prepared statement. The preceding construction also better supports reading the list of fields from an external source such as a file and populating the database with it.

---

[6] It is possible that this distinguished list of runners may have changed by the time you read this.

> **NOTE** In SQL, string values are placed in single quotes like `'Paul'`. But with a prepared statement, these single quotes must not be used. They are not present in the prepared statement, nor are they part of the string data passed in the list of values. (In other words, the single quotes in those values are for Groovy, not for SQL.) Similarly, even though dates have been represented here as strings, they really are dates in the database. We could have passed an instance of `java.util.Date` to our `execute` method, and in production code this would be more likely, but the sample code in this chapter is clearer using simple string representations.

When the statement gets more complicated, the mapping between each question mark and the corresponding list entry can become difficult to follow. In the course of development, the statement or the list may change, and the task of keeping both in sync is a likely source of errors.

It would be nicer if we could use a placeholder that better reveals its purpose and goes around the strong sequence constraint. Toward that end, `execute` can also produce a prepared statement from a GString. We show this with a list that holds each athlete's data as a map (you could just as easily use a full-blown `Athlete` object instead—with the additional work of creating an `Athlete` class to start with, of course):

```
def athletes = [
    [first: 'Paul',    last: 'Tergat',     birth: '1969-06-17'],
    [first: 'Khalid',  last: 'Khannouchi', birth: '1971-12-22'],
    [first: 'Ronaldo', last: 'da Costa',   birth: '1970-06-07']
]
athletes.each { athlete ->
  db.execute """
    INSERT INTO Athlete (firstname, lastname, dateOfBirth)
      VALUES (${athlete.first}, ${athlete.last}, ${athlete.birth});
  """
}
```

Pay attention to the tripled double quotes around the statement, and remember that this construction produces a prepared statement and will therefore be just as efficient on the database as the question-mark version.

This might sound like magic to you and might leave some doubts, because after all you cannot *see* whether we are telling the truth. But we can enable logging and assess our claim. Use the following lines to see what happens behind the curtain:

```
import java.util.logging.*

Logger.getLogger('groovy.sql').level = Level.FINE
// your db.execute(GString)
```

This produces

```
30.10.2005 19:08:27 groovy.sql.Sql execute
FINE:
    INSERT INTO Athlete (firstname, lastname, dateOfBirth)
                VALUES (?, ?, ?);
```

It goes without saying that logging the SQL that is eventually executed is always a good practice during development. Also note that because we have a real prepared statement, the SQL expression uses no single quotes around the placeholder. The special use of GStrings as SQL statements limits the use of placeholders to places where a question mark would otherwise be allowed in a prepared statement.

Updating and deleting data

The first important steps have been done: We connected to the database, created the schema, and inserted some data. In other words, we have covered the C in CRUD. Still missing are *read*, *update*, and *delete*.

We will cover *read* separately in the next section because it is a topic of its own. The *update* and *delete* operations work with the execute method in the same way you have seen so far. The following is an example of a *insert-update-delete* cycle. We insert a middle-of-the-pack marathon runner, update his first name because the original spelling was incorrect, and finally delete him from the database because he doesn't belong to this fine circle. Just for the fun of it, we demonstrate all three execute versions—a plain statement, the prepared statement with question marks, and the same with GStrings:

```
db.execute '''
    DELETE FROM Athlete WHERE firstname = 'Dierk';
'''

db.execute '''
    INSERT INTO Athlete (firstname, lastname, dateOfBirth)
                VALUES (?, ?, ?);
''', ['Dirk', 'Koenig', '1968-04-19']

String wrong = 'Dirk'
String right = 'Dierk'
db.execute """
    UPDATE Athlete SET firstname = $right WHERE firstname = $wrong;
"""
```

The execute method comes with a second version, executeUpdate, which works the same way but provides a different return value. Whereas execute returns a Boolean indicating whether the statement returned a ResultSet, executeUpdate returns the

number of rows that were changed by the update. See the API documentation of
`java.sql.PreparedStatement` for details. Table 10.2 shows the summary.

Table 10.2   Versions of the `execute` method

Returns	Method name	Parameters
boolean	execute	String statement
boolean	execute	String prepStmt, List values
boolean	execute	GString prepStmt
int	executeUpdate	String statement
int	executeUpdate	String prepStmt, List values
int	executeUpdate	GString prepStmt

Until now, we have created tables and inserted, updated, and deleted rows. These
are important basic operations, but the most frequently used operation is *reading*
data.[7] Reading has different aspects, depending on whether you look for a single
row or multiple rows, what query information is available, and how you intend to
process the retrieved data.

The next section leads you through the various ways of fetching data from
a database.

10.1.3 Fetching data

Reading from the database is done through `Sql`'s methods, as listed in table 10.3,
where the handling of prepared statements is the same as for `execute`.

Table 10.3   Methods for reading data from the database

Returns	Method	Parameters	
void	eachRow	String statement	{ row -> code }
void	eachRow	String prepStmt, List values	{ row -> code }
void	eachRow	GString prepStmt	{ row -> code }

continued on next page

---

[7] This is not necessarily true in all databases—when a database is used essentially for audit logging, for
instance, it may be read very rarely. However, *most* databases are more frequently read than changed.

Table 10.3   Methods for reading data from the database *(continued)*

Returns	Method	Parameters
void	query	`String statement            { resultSet -> code }`
void	query	`String prepStmt, List values { resultSet -> code }`
void	query	`GString prepStmt             { resultSet -> code }`
List	rows	`String statement`
List	rows	`String prepStmt, List values`
Object	firstRow	`String statement`
Object	firstRow	`String prepStmt, List values`

The methods `eachRow` and `query` use a closure for processing the result. Whereas `query` calls the given closure once and passes the full `java.sql.ResultSet` into it, `eachRow` calls the closure for each row of the result, thus relieving the programmer from the usual iteration work.

Fetching a row at a time with eachRow

Suppose we would like to print a report about all known athletes that should look like this:

```
----- Athlete Info ------
Paul Tergat
born on 17. Jun 1969 (Tue)
------------------------
Khalid Khannouchi
born on 22. Dec 1971 (Wed)
------------------------
Ronaldo da Costa
born on 07. Jun 1970 (Sun)
------------------------
```

We can achieve this by using `eachRow` and a simple selection statement. The *row* that is passed into the closure is an interesting object. We can use the column names as if they were property names of that object:

```
println ' Athlete Info '.center(25,'-')
def fmt = new java.text.SimpleDateFormat('dd. MMM yyyy (E)',
                                         Locale.US)
db.eachRow('SELECT * FROM Athlete'){ athlete ->
    println athlete.firstname + ' ' + athlete.lastname
    println 'born on '+ fmt.format(athlete.dateOfBirth)
    println '-' * 25
}
```

Note how we are using the row as if it were an `Athlete` object, which it isn't. But we can also use the row as if it were a list (which it isn't either) and call the subscript operator on it. In order to print

```
Paul Tergat
Khalid Khannouchi
Ronaldo da Costa
```

we could call

```
db.eachRow('SELECT firstname, lastname FROM Athlete'){ row ->
    println row[0] + ' ' + row[1]
}
```

> **NOTE**   When working with column indexes, it's always safer to explicitly specify the sequence of column names in the select statement. `'SELECT *'` may sometimes return the columns in the expected order (the order they were defined in `CREATE TABLE`), but this is not guaranteed for all database management systems.

So what is that row object, after all? It's of type `groovy.sql.GroovyResultSet`, which is a decorator around the underlying `java.sql.ResultSet`. Being a Groovy object, it can pretend to have properties and provide Groovy-friendly indexing (starting from zero, allowing negative indexes that count from the end).

Fetching a ResultSet with query

The `query` method allows you to customize the iteration over the query results at the expense of convenience, because you can only work with the good old `java.sql.ResultSet`. Suppose we are only interested in the first athlete, and we don't want to go through all results for that purpose. We can use `query` like this:

```
db.query('SELECT firstname, lastname FROM Athlete'){ resultSet ->
    if(resultSet.next()){
        print    resultSet.getString(1)
        print    ' '
        println resultSet.getString('lastname')
    }
}
```

Just like the `eachRow` method, the `query` method manages your resources (the connection and the statement). The downside is that the `ResultSet` that gets passed into the closure is less convenient to work with. You need to call `next` to move the cursor forward, you need to call type-specific getters (`getString`, `getDate`, and so on), and—most annoyingly—indexes start at *one* instead of *zero*.

Fetching all rows at once

As shown in table 10.3, it's also possible to fetch all rows at once into a (possibly long) list with the `rows` method. Each list item can be used with an index or a property name (just like in `eachRow`). Suppose we need a simple usage, like printing the following:

```
There are 3 Athletes:
Paul Tergat, Khalid Khannouchi, Ronaldo da Costa
```

We can use a simple database call like

```
List athletes = db.rows('SELECT firstname, lastname FROM Athlete')
println "There are ${athletes.size()} Athletes:"
println athletes.collect{"${it[0]} ${it.lastname}"}.join(", ")
```

Having the selection results in a list makes them eligible to be put in GPath expressions. The example shows this with the `collect` method, but you can imagine `find`, `findAll`, `grep`, `any`, `every`, and so forth in its place.

NOTE The list items are implemented as `GroovyRowResult` objects, the equivalent of `GroovyResultSet` as used with `eachRow`.

Finally, the `firstRow(stmt)` method returns `rows(stmt)[0]`.

So far, you have seen methods to fetch data from the database when we had a good idea what the statement will return. But there are times when you don't know. In this case, the metadata comes into play.

Fetching metadata

Consider writing a helper method that should dump the content of a given table. The table name is provided as a method parameter. If we call the method as `dump('Athlete')`, it should print

```
------- CONTENT OF TABLE Athlete -------
0: ATHLETEID        0
1: FIRSTNAME        Paul
2: LASTNAME         Tergat
3: DATEOFBIRTH      1969-06-17
----------------------------------------
0: ATHLETEID        1
1: FIRSTNAME        Khalid
2: LASTNAME         Khannouchi
3: DATEOFBIRTH      1971-12-22
----------------------------------------
0: ATHLETEID        2
1: FIRSTNAME        Ronaldo
```

```
2: LASTNAME        da Costa
3: DATEOFBIRTH     1970-06-07
----------------------------------------
```

For proper display, we need some information about

- How many columns we should display
- What the column names are

Luckily, `ResultSet` (and thus also the `GroovyResultSet`) provides a method called `getMetaData` that returns a `ResultSetMetaData` object. This contains all the necessary information. See its API documentation for details.

```
def dump (tablename){
    println " CONTENT OF TABLE ${tablename} ".center(40,'-')
    db.query('SELECT * FROM '+tablename){ rs ->
        def meta = rs.metaData
        if (meta.columnCount <= 0) return
        for (i in 0..<meta.columnCount) {
            print "${i}: ${meta.getColumnLabel(i+1)}".padRight(20)
            print rs[i]?.toString()
            print "\n"
        }
        println '-' * 40
    }
}
dump('Athlete')
```

Like all the classes from the `java.sql` package, `ResultSetMetaData` works with indexes starting at *one*. Therefore, we need to call `getColumnLabel` with `(i+1)`. We also use the safe dereferencing operator (see section 7.1.3) in case the value at the given index is `null`.

You have now seen all the CRUD operations in Groovy, some of them in various versions. However, because database code tends to be verbose, you have only seen snippets. The next section puts these snippets together.

10.1.4 *Putting it all together*

It's time to assemble the presented operations into a full self-contained example of database programming with Groovy. It starts with connecting to the database; creating a schema; performing insert, update, and deletion of data; and reading data in between all operations to assert the desired effect.

Listing 10.1 shows how everything works in combination. Every type of operation is handled in its own method, and method parameters are used inside GStrings to allow the use of prepared statements in a self-describing manner.

Listing 10.1   CRUD operations with Groovy

```
// requires hsqldb.jar in classpath
import groovy.sql.Sql

dbHandle = null
def getDb() {                    Lazily init the
    if (dbHandle) return dbHandle    DataSource
    def source = new org.hsqldb.jdbc.jdbcDataSource()
    source.database = 'jdbc:hsqldb:mem:GIA'
    source.user = 'sa'
    source.password = ''
    dbHandle = new Sql(source)
    return dbHandle
}                                Define the schema
def reset() {                    programmatically
    db.execute '''
        DROP   INDEX athleteIdx IF EXISTS;
        DROP   TABLE Athlete IF EXISTS;
        CREATE TABLE Athlete (
            athleteId   INTEGER GENERATED BY DEFAULT AS IDENTITY,
            firstname   VARCHAR(64),
            lastname    VARCHAR(64),
            dateOfBirth DATE
        );
        CREATE INDEX athleteIdx ON Athlete (athleteId);
    '''
}                                            ❶ Create
def create(firstname, lastname, dateOfBirth) {    operation
    db.execute """
        INSERT INTO Athlete ( firstname, lastname, dateOfBirth)
                    VALUES ($firstname,$lastname,$dateOfBirth);
    """
}              ❷ Read
def findAll() {    operation
    db.rows 'SELECT * FROM Athlete'
}                                      ❸ Update
def updateFirstName(wrong, right) {       operation
    db.execute """
        UPDATE Athlete
            SET firstname = $right WHERE firstname = $wrong;
    """
}                              ❹ Delete
def delete(firstname) {           operation
    db.execute "DELETE FROM Athlete WHERE firstname = $firstname;"
}

reset()
assert ! findAll(), 'we are initially empty'
create 'Dirk', 'Koenig', '1968-04-19'
```

```
assert 'Dirk'   == findAll()[0].firstname      ◁┐    GroovyRowResult
updateFirstName  'Dirk', 'Dierk'               ❺    as DTO
assert 'Dierk' == findAll()[0].firstname
delete 'Dierk'
assert ! findAll(), 'after delete, we are empty again'
```

The code in listing 10.1 seems at first glance like a mere collection of snippets that were presented before, but sometimes "the whole is more than the sum of its parts" (Aristotle, in *Metaphysics*). Two patterns loom from behind: DTOs and DAOs.

Data Transfer Objects encapsulate state without behavior. They transfer a set of named values between the database and the client code. In listing 10.1, this is the transfer from ❷ to ❺ as done transparently by the GroovyRowResult. In other words, you can work as if you have a DTO without writing one!

Data Access Objects encapsulate the knowledge of how a given type works with the database. They implement the CRUD operations for this type. We haven't explicitly defined any specific type in listing 10.1, but ❶, ❷, ❸, and ❹ make our script almost work like a DAO for an Athlete type.

You've seen how easy it is to execute SQL with Groovy. Wouldn't it be nice not to have to worry about the SQL at all? Unlikely as that concept sounds, it's the topic of our next section.

10.2 DataSets for SQL without SQL

We demanded that simple tasks should be easy. So far, you have seen simple SQL and easy ways for sending it to the database. It's hard to believe that database programming can be any simpler, but it can.

Groovy provides a basic way of working with the database that doesn't even work with SQL. This approach is based on the concept of a DataSet, and we will look at each of the operations it supports:

- Adding a row to a table
- Working through all rows of a table or a view
- Selecting rows of a table or a view by simple expressions

You cannot define a schema that way or use *delete* or *update* operations. However, you can mix the use of DataSets with other Groovy SQL operations and use whatever seems most appropriate for the task at hand.

A `groovy.sql.DataSet` is a subclass of and a decorator around `groovy.sql.Sql`. Figure 10.2 shows the UML class diagram.

The conventional way of retrieving a `DataSet` instance is to call `Sql`'s factory method `dataSet`. You pass it the name of the table that this `DataSet` should work with. For more alternatives, see the API documentation of `Sql` and `DataSet`:

```
// if db refers to an instance of Sql
athleteSet = db.dataSet('Athlete')
```

Let's explore what you can do with such an instance.

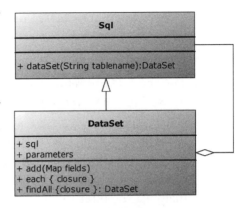

Figure 10.2 UML class diagram of `groovy.sql.DataSet` **decorating** `groovy.sql.Sql`

10.2.1 *Using DataSet operations*

With an instance of a `DataSet`, you can call its methods, as listed in figure 10.2. We can add a new row to the `Athlete` table with

```
athleteSet.add(
    firstname:    'Paula',
    lastname:     'Radcliffe',
    dateOfBirth:  '1973-12-17')
```

That's all we need to do. A SQL insert statement will be created behind the scenes and executed immediately. If we omit any of the fields, a `null` value will be inserted instead.

We can also use the `athleteSet` to work with what's currently in the table. The following lines

```
athleteSet.each {
    println it.firstname
}
```

print

```
Paul
Khalid
Ronaldo
Paula
```

This works analogously to the `GroovyResultSet` you saw before: You can use fieldnames as if they were properties and use positive or negative indexes with `it`.

Now comes the `findAll` method, which looks simple at first but turns out to be *very* sophisticated. Let's start with trying

```
athleteSet.findAll{ it.dateOfBirth > '1970-1-1' }
```

This method call returns a new `DataSet`, which can in turn be used with the `each` method to work over the filtered result:

```
youngsters = athleteSet.findAll{ it.dateOfBirth > '1970-1-1' }
youngsters.each { println it.firstname }
```

What is behind this construction? At first sight, you might guess that the `findAll` method fetches all the rows from the table, applying the closure and adding rows that pass the filter to a list internally. This would be far too time consuming for large tables. Instead, `findAll` produces a SQL statement that reflects the expression within the closure. This generated statement is encapsulated in the returned youngsters `DataSet`.

It's hard to believe that Groovy can do that,[8] but proof is available. Any `DataSet` encapsulates a statement in its `sql` property, and because that is the SQL of a prepared statement, it also needs parameters, which are stored in the parameters property. Let's find out what these properties are for our sample code:

```
youngsters = athleteSet.findAll{ it.dateOfBirth > '1970-1-1' }
println youngsters.sql
println youngsters.parameters
youngsters.each { println it.firstname }
```

These lines print

```
select * from Athlete where dateOfBirth > ?
["1970-1-1"]
Khalid
Ronaldo
Paula
```

So take note:

- `findAll` only creates a new `DataSet` (with the enclosed prepared statement).
- `findAll` does not even access the database.
- Only the trailing `each` triggers the database call.

---

[8] It may be slightly easier to believe if you've looked at Microsoft's LINQ project. Of course, Groovy has been released, whereas LINQ certainly hasn't at the time of writing.

To prove this to yourself, you can add logging to the program in the same way we did in section 10.1.2. Logging is useful during development to see *when* the database is accessed, as well as *how* it is accessed.

But the buck doesn't stop here. Because the findAll method returns a DataSet that can be interpreted as a filtered selection of the original DataSet (which was the whole Athlete table in our example), it would be surprising if it weren't possible to combine filters. And yes, you can. The following lines

```
youngsters = athleteSet.findAll{ it.dateOfBirth > '1970-1-1' }
paula      = youngsters.findAll{ it.firstname == 'Paula' }
println paula.sql
println paula.parameters
```

print

```
select * from Athlete where dateOfBirth > ? and firstname = ?
[1970-1-1, Paula]
```

Interestingly enough, we can achieve the same effect by providing a combined filter expression in the findAll closure:

```
youngsters = athleteSet.findAll{
    it.dateOfBirth > '1970-1-1' && it.firstname == 'Paula'
}
```

You can legitimately ask how this could possibly work. Here is the answer: The expression in the findAll closure *is never executed!* Instead, the DataSet implementation fetches Groovy's internal representation of the closure's code. This internal representation is called the Abstract Syntax Tree (AST) and was generated by the Groovy parser. By walking over the AST (with a Visitor pattern), the DataSet implementation emits the SQL equivalent of each AST node. The mapping is listed in table 10.4.

Table 10.4 Mapping of Groovy AST nodes to their SQL equivalents

AST node	SQL equivalent
&&	and
||	or
==	=
Other operators	Themselves, literally
it.*propertyname*	propertyname
Constant expression	? (Expression is added to the parameters list)

This also means that the following restrictions apply for expressions inside the findAll closure:

- They must be legal Groovy code (otherwise, the Groovy parser fails).
- They must contain only expressions as listed in table 10.4, excluding variables and method calls.

These restrictions limit the possibilities of filtering DataSets. On the other hand, this approach brings a new quality to database programming: using the parser of your programming language for checking your selection expression at *compile* time.

If you put syntactically invalid SQL into a string and pass it to Sql's execute method, you will not notice the error until the database is accessed and throws an SqlException.

If you put a syntactically invalid expression into a findAll closure and choose to compile your code, the compiler fails without accessing the database. You also get better error messages that way, because the compiler can point you to the offending code. With good IDE support, your IDE can open the editor on such failing code or even highlight the error while editing.

Now might be a good time to have a cup of coffee. Let the last couple of pages sink in. Read them again. Try a few example queries for yourself. This ability to view the code within the closure as *data* and transform it into another type of code (SQL) rather than a block to be executed may be one of the most important concepts in ushering in a new era of database application development.

So far, you have seen DataSets working on a single table only. We will next explore how to use this concept more generally.

10.2.2 *DataSets on database views*

DataSets are a convenient way to work on a single table. However, working on a single table is usually not of much value in a relational model.

Suppose our athletes have running performances that we would like to keep track of. This calls for another table, which we will call Run. Each row in this table captures the distance the athlete went (in meters), how many seconds it took, and when and where this happened. For relating such a row with the according athlete, we refer to the athlete's unique id, the athleteId, by the foreign key fkAthlete. Figure 10.3 shows the relationship.

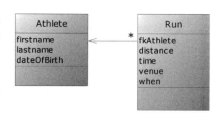

Figure 10.3   Entity-relationship diagram of athletes and multiple runs

This results in the following SQL code for creating the `Run` table. Note that we also introduce a `runId`[9] to give this performance a unique handle, and we let the database know that `fkAthlete` is a foreign key in the `Athlete` table by adding the according *constraint*. We use `ON DELETE CASCADE` such that when deleting an athlete from the `Athlete` table, all the athlete's runs also get deleted automatically:

```
DROP    TABLE Run IF EXISTS;
CREATE TABLE Run (
    runId       INTEGER GENERATED BY DEFAULT AS IDENTITY,
    distance    INTEGER,    // in meters
    time        INTEGER,    // in seconds
    venue       VARCHAR(64),
    when        TIMESTAMP,
    fkAthlete   INTEGER,
    CONSTRAINT fk FOREIGN KEY (fkAthlete)
        REFERENCES Athlete (athleteId) ON DELETE CASCADE
);
```

For filling the `Run` table with example data, we unfortunately cannot easily use a `DataSet`; we would need to know the corresponding `athleteId`, which we cannot foresee because it is dynamically generated by the database. The next best solution is to use a helper method that executes an insert statement to retrieve the `athleteId` from a subselect. Here's some sample code, which uses parameters for most values but has a hard-coded distance for demonstration purposes. Likewise, it assumes there will be only one athlete with a given last name—something we would not do in real life code:

```
def insertRun(h, m, s, venue, date, lastname){
    def time = h*60*60 + m*60 + s
    db.execute """
        INSERT INTO Run (distance, time, venue, when, fkAthlete)
            SELECT 42195, $time, $venue, $date,
                athleteId FROM Athlete WHERE lastname=$lastname;
    """
}
```

We can now call the `insertRun` method with some example data:

```
insertRun(2,4,55, 'Berlin',  '2003-09-28', 'Tergat')
insertRun(2,5,38, 'London',  '2002-04-14', 'Khannouchi')
insertRun(2,5,42, 'Chicago', '1999-10-24', 'Khannouchi')
insertRun(2,6,05, 'Berlin',  '1998-09-20', 'da Costa')
```

---

[9] There is no pressing need for the `runId`. We introduce it because that is our usual working pattern when creating tables.

After this preparation, how can we use `DataSets` to list runs for an athlete name? We need to join the information from that `Run` table with the information from the `Athlete` table to retrieve the names.

Of course, we could read both tables and do the join programmatically, but that wouldn't leverage the power of the relational model and wouldn't perform well because of the overhead of each database call.

The trick is to create a database *view* that behaves like a read-only table made up from an arbitrary selection.

Here is how to create a view named `AthleteRun` that combines athletes with their runs as if we has a combined table that contains both tables but only for athletes for whom we have run information:

```
DROP   VIEW AthleteRun IF EXISTS;
CREATE VIEW AthleteRun AS
    SELECT * FROM Athlete INNER JOIN Run
        ON fkAthlete=athleteId;
```

With this view, we can create a `DataSet` and work with it as if it were one big table. To find where Khalid Knannouchi performed his runs, we can use

```
record = db.dataSet('AthleteRun').findAll{ it.firstname=='Khalid' }
record.each{ println it.lastname + ' ' + it.venue }
```

which prints

```
Khannouchi London
Khannouchi Chicago
```

What we have done here is remove SQL-specific knowledge, such as how to join two tables, from the application. This makes the code more portable across database vendors, as well as making it readable to developers who may not be particularly skilled in SQL. This comes at the expense of putting it into the infrastructure (the database setup code). This requires the database structure to be under our control. In large organizations, where the database is maintained by an entirely different set of people, the challenge is to get these administrators on board for efficient collaboration and for leveraging their database knowledge in your project.

You now have the tools you need to access a database. Giving someone a chisel doesn't make them a carpenter, though—how the tools are used is as important as the tools themselves.

10.3 *Organizing database work*

Knowing the technical details of database programming is one thing, but organizing a whole application for database usage takes more than that. You have to take care of design considerations such as separation of concerns, assigning responsibility, and keeping the codebase manageable and maintainable—free from duplication.

This section will give you some insight into how Groovy SQL fits into the overall architecture of a database application. We will plan the architecture, define what the application has to be capable of, and then implement the application in a layered fashion, examining how Groovy makes things easier at every level. No single and authoritative solution fits all needs. Instead, you need to use your imagination and creativity to find out how to relate the presented rules, structures, and patterns to the situation at hand.

10.3.1 *Architectural overview*

Today's architectural patterns usually call for a layered architecture, as depicted in figure 10.4. The lowest layer is the *infrastructure* that shields all upper layers from SQL specifics. It presents DAOs to the *domain model* layer above it. There often is a one-to-one relationship between *business objects* in the domain model layer and DAOs. Classically, DAOs and business objects pass DTOs back and forth for communication.

Above the domain model layer is the *application* layer, which makes use of the business objects in its workflow and presents them within the user interface.

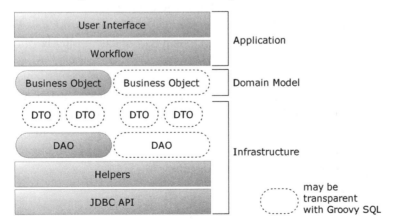

Figure 10.4   Layered architecture for database programming

Layering also means that any layer may call the layer below it, but never the one above. *Strict* layering also forbids calling layers deeper than the one directly below; for example, calls from the application layer to the infrastructure would be forbidden.

With the advent of Groovy SQL, things can be done more easily. First, custom-built DTOs become obsolete, due to the dynamic nature of Groovy's classes. There is no more need to create special classes for each DTO type. A DAO can exchange information with *transparent* types—types that are independent of any DAO or business object specifics. Good candidates for transparent DTOs are `GroovyRowResult`, `Map`, `List`, and `Expando`. For DTOs that should encapsulate a collection of business objects, a list of these DTOs or a `DataSet` may be used.

> **NOTE**   With layering as in figure 10.4, DAOs are not allowed to directly return business objects, because calling their constructor would mean calling into the upper domain model layer. As a trick, they can pass back a map of properties and let the caller object do the construction, such as `new MyBusinessObject(map)`.

For simple read-only data, business objects can also be replaced by transparently using a `GroovyRowResult`, a `Map`, or an `Expando`. Suppose the following line exists in the application code:

```
out << athlete.firstname
```

To a reader of this code, everything looks like `athlete` is a business object. However, you cannot tell whether it is really of type `Athlete`. It could just as well be a `GroovyRowResult`, a `Map`, or an `Expando`. From the code, it all looks the same.

Of course, this works only in simple scenarios. If you go for *domain driven design*,[10] you will want to implement your business objects explicitly (most often with the help of GroovyBeans).

DAOs can sometimes be replaced by transparently using a `DataSet`, as you saw in the previous section. There is a crucial point about `DataSet`s that makes this possible: the way they handle `findAll`. DAOs should not expose SQL specifics to their caller, because that makes the infrastructure layer *leaky*. Conventional DAOs often break this constraint by allowing the caller to pass parts of the `WHERE` clause; or they end up with a plethora of methods like

```
findByFirstName(firstname)
findByLastName(lastname)
```

---

[10] Eric Evans, *Domain-Driven Design: Tackling Complexity in the Heart of Software* (Addison Wesley, 2003)

```
findByFirstAndLastName(firstname, lastname)
findByBirthdateBefore(date)
...
```

You have also seen that `DataSets` can replace DAOs, which represent sophisticated relations by providing the appropriate view in the database schema.

All this is interesting in theory, but it's what it looks like in practice that counts. In the next section, we'll examine some real code.

10.3.2 *Specifying the application behavior*

Thinking through the architecture is nice, but only the code tells the truth. So let's go for a full example of managing our athletes.

We will use a layered architecture similar to figure 10.4, albeit not a strict version. Our general approach is bottom-up. We begin at the infrastructure layer, starting with helpers and deciding what DAOs we are going to provide. DTOs will all be transparent. From our decisions about DAOs, the business objects will fall into place almost automatically. Finally, we have to implement the application. Because our current focus is on database programming, we will keep the user interface and workflow basic and provide a small command-line interface.

Here is how the application should work. The application should start by creating the database schema. With logging enabled, we should see the following output when the application starts:

```
DROP    INDEX athleteIdx IF EXISTS;
DROP    TABLE Athlete    IF EXISTS;
CREATE TABLE Athlete (
    athleteId     INTEGER GENERATED BY DEFAULT AS IDENTITY,
    dateOfBirth   DATE,
    firstname     VARCHAR(64),
    lastname      VARCHAR(64)
);
CREATE INDEX athleteIdx ON Athlete (athleteId);
```

Entering athletes should be like in this transcript (input in bold):

```
create Paul Tergat 1969-06-17
1 Athlete(s) in DB:
id firstname  lastname     dateOfBirth
0: Paul       Tergat       1969-06-17
create Khalid Khannouchi
2 Athlete(s) in DB:
id firstname  lastname     dateOfBirth
0: Paul       Tergat       1969-06-17
1: Khalid     Khannouchi   null
```

Note that we use the *create* operation and pass parameters in a well-known sequence. Missing parameters result in `null` values. The current list of athletes is displayed after the operation, sorted by the automatically generated id.

The *update* operation should work for a given id, field name, and new value:

```
update 1 dateOfBirth 1971-12-22
1 row(s) updated
2 Athlete(s) in DB:
id firstname  lastname    dateOfBirth
0: Paul       Tergat      1969-06-17
1: Khalid     Khannouchi  1971-12-22
```

The list of athletes should be sortable, where the sort is performed by the database, not in the application code. It needs to support multiple-column sorts:

```
sort firstname
2 Athlete(s) in DB:
id firstname  lastname    dateOfBirth
1: Khalid     Khannouchi  1971-12-22
0: Paul       Tergat      1969-06-17
```

The *delete* operation should accept an id and delete the corresponding row:

```
delete 1
1 row(s) deleted
1 Athlete(s) in DB:
id firstname  lastname    dateOfBirth
0: Paul       Tergat      1969-06-17
```

The application is to be terminated with the *exit* operation.

No validation of user input needs to be implemented; we also don't need to gracefully handle database errors resulting from bad user input.

Let's see how to design and implement the infrastructure, domain model, and application layer to make this functionality work.

10.3.3 *Implementing the infrastructure*

The infrastructure contains helpers and DAOs. For our example, we have a single helper class `DbHelper`, an `AthleteDAO`, and a general abstract `DataAccessObject` as depicted in figure 10.5.

The `DbHelper` is responsible for providing access to an instance of `groovy.sql.Sql` through its `db` property and setting it to a default value. The second responsibility is to support automatic schema creation by executing the Data Definition Language (DDL) for a given `DataAccessObject`.

The `DataAccessObject` is a general implementation of the basic CRUD operations. The `AthleteDAO` is a specialization of a `DataAccessObject` providing the

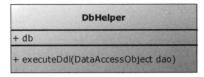

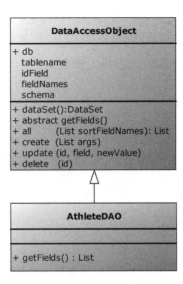

Figure 10.5 UML class diagram of the athlete example's infrastructure layer

least possible information for accessing an `Athlete` table: the fieldnames and their types.

We will next go through the classes to see how they implement their responsibilities.

Implementing DbHelper

The implementation of `DbHelper` as in listing 10.2 yields no surprises. It contains the code for a database connection via the `Sql` class and the SQL template for creating a table. Unlike in previously presented variants, we now use a `SimpleTemplateEngine` for separation of concerns.

The template contains the *structure* of a simple table definition in SQL, whereas the `DataAccessObject` as passed into `executeDdl` is used for getting *details* about the table name and other schema details, such as field names and their SQL types.

Listing 10.2 Athlete example infrastructure: `DbHelper`

```
import groovy.sql.Sql
import groovy.text.SimpleTemplateEngine as STE

class DbHelper {
    Sql db

    DbHelper() {
        def source = new org.hsqldb.jdbc.jdbcDataSource()
```

```
            source.database = 'jdbc:hsqldb:mem:GIA'
            source.user = 'sa'
            source.password = ''
            db = new Sql(source)
    }

    def simpleTemplate = new STE().createTemplate('''
DROP    INDEX ${lowname}Idx IF EXISTS;
DROP    TABLE $name     IF EXISTS;
CREATE TABLE $name (
    ${lowname}Id    INTEGER GENERATED BY DEFAULT AS IDENTITY,
$fields
);
CREATE INDEX ${lowname}Idx ON $name (${lowname}Id);''')

    def executeDdl(DataAccessObject dao) {
        def template = simpleTemplate
        def binding = [
            name:     dao.tablename,
            lowname:  dao.tablename.toLowerCase(),
            fields:   dao.schema.collect{ key, val ->
                "    ${key.padRight(12)} $val" }.join(",\n")
        ]
        def stmt = template.make(binding).toString()
        db.execute stmt
    }
}
```

At first glance, this may look like an oversimplification of SQL table definitions, because we don't have to deal with foreign keys or other constraints, views, joins, and so forth. However, it would be easy to expand DbHelper to also cover those scenarios by providing correspondingly amended templates.

Because this class works in collaboration with a DataAccessObject, that's the next class to implement.

Implementing DataAccessObject

DAOs encapsulate the knowledge of how to do basic CRUD operations with the database, and DataAccessObject is the general superclass that collects common functionality for DAOs. With Groovy SQL, so many operations can be done generally that this superclass grows large in comparison to its subclasses.

In addition to the CRUD operations, DataAccessObject uses the structural information that its subclasses provide through their class names and the getFields method to build the DAOs' meta information in a general way.

Subclasses are expected to follow the naming convention of `MyTableDAO` for a table of name `MyTable`. Their `getFields` method is expected to return a list of strings, alternating between the field names and their SQL type descriptions.

Listing 10.3 shows how `DataAccessObject` uses this information to expose the table name, field names, schema, and so forth.

Listing 10.3   Athlete example infrastructure: `DataAccessObject`

```
abstract class DataAccessObject {
    Sql db
                                          ❶ Subclass implements
    abstract List getFields()    ←┘        this to provide field list

    def dataSet()     { db.dataSet(tablename) }          ❷
    def getIdField() { tablename.toLowerCase() + 'Id' }  Properties for use
    def getWhereId() { "WHERE $idField = ?"}             in SQL statements

    String getTablename() {
        def name = this.getClass().name
        return name[name.lastIndexOf('.')+1..-4]
    }
    def create(List args) {   ←❸ Create operation
        Map argMap = [:]
        args.eachWithIndex { arg, i -> argMap[fieldNames[i]] = arg }
        dataSet().add argMap
    }
    Map getSchema() {
        Map result = [:]
        fieldNames.each {result[it] = fields[fields.indexOf(it)+1]}
        return result
    }
    List getFieldNames() {
        List result = []
        0.step(fields.size(),2) { result << fields[it] }
        return result
    }
    def update(field, newValue, id) {
        def stmt = "UPDATE $tablename SET $field = ? $whereId"
        db.executeUpdate stmt, [newValue, id]
    }
    def delete(id) {
        def stmt = "DELETE FROM $tablename $whereId"
        db.executeUpdate stmt, [id]
    }                                  ❹ Sample read
    def all(sortField) {      ←┘         operation
        def selects = fieldNames + idField
        def result = []
        def stmt = "SELECT " + selects.join(',') +
            " FROM $tablename ORDER BY $sortField"
```

```
        db.eachRow(stmt.toString()){ rs ->
            Map businessObject = [:]
            selects.each { businessObject[it] = rs[it] }
            result << businessObject
        }
        return result
    }
}
```

Note that the CRUD operations work with prepared statements. The *update* and *delete* statements both use the id column to identify a row, obtaining the appropriate *where* clause using properties ❷. The creation operation at ❸ takes a list of values, which it converts into a map by assuming they are in the same order as the field list provided by the subclass via the getFields method at ❶. A single *read* operation ❹ is provided, but because db is available as a property, callers can provide their own queries easily enough. For this particular application, we don't need any other *read* operations anyway.

The all method returns business objects transparently as maps.

Implementing AthleteDAO

With all the hard work already done in DataAccessObject, implementing the AthleteDAO is a breeze. It's hardly worth an object.

Listing 10.4 shows how AthleteDAO needs to do nothing else but subclass DataAccessObject and provide the field information.

Listing 10.4 Athlete example infrastructure: AthleteDAO

```
class AthleteDAO extends DataAccessObject {

    List getFields() {
        return [
            'firstname',   'VARCHAR(64)',
            'lastname',    'VARCHAR(64)',
            'dateOfBirth', 'DATE'
        ]
    }
}
```

If you ever need specialized versions of CRUD operations or elaborate finder methods, such a DAO provides the place to put it in.

10.3.4 *Using a transparent domain model*

Our application uses transparent business objects, implemented as maps. There is no `Athlete` class as you might expect.

Of course, if we ever needed one, we *could* easily create it like this:

```
class Athlete {
    def firstname
    def lastname
    def dateOfBirth
}
```

Inside the application, we *could* create these objects, for example from an `AthleteDAO` call like

```
athletes = athleteDAO.all('firstname').collect{ new Athlete(it) }
```

The reason for not introducing such business objects is that they currently add no value. All their information (the field names) is already available in the DAO.

The point at which to start using such business objects is when they begin to depend on other objects in the domain layer or when they provide additional behavior, such as specialized methods.

In the next section, you will see that simple applications are even easier when using transparent business objects.

10.3.5 *Implementing the application layer*

The application layer consists of only one class: `AthleteApplication`. Listing 10.4 reveals that it does little more than call the infrastructure and display the transparent business objects.

The `mainLoop` method reads the user input from the console, interpreting the first word as the operation and any additional input as parameters. It passes this information to `invokeMethod`, which automatically dispatches to the according method call. Each keyword is implemented by a method of the same name.

Listing 10.5 Athlete example application layer: AthleteApplication

```
class AthleteApplication {
    def helper    = new DbHelper()
    def athleteDAO = new AthleteDAO(db: helper.db)
    def sortBy    = 'athleteId'                          ❶ Initialization

    def init() {
        helper.executeDdl(athleteDAO)
    }
    def exit() { System.exit(0) }
```

```
def sort(field) {
    sortBy = field.join(',')
    list()
}
def create(List args) {
    athleteDAO.create(args)
    list()
}
def list() {
    def athletes = athleteDAO.all(sortBy)
    println athletes.size() + ' Athlete(s) in DB: '
    println 'id firstname  lastname     dateOfBirth'
    athletes.each { athlete ->
        println athlete.athleteId +': ' +
            athlete.firstname.padRight(10) + ' ' +
            athlete.lastname.padRight(12)   + ' ' +
            athlete.dateOfBirth
    }
}
def update(id, field, newValue){
    def count = athleteDAO.update(field, newValue, id)
    println count +' row(s) updated'
    list()
}
def delete(id) {
    def count = athleteDAO.delete(*id)
    println count +' row(s) deleted'
    list()
}
def mainLoop() {
    while(true) {
        println 'commands: create list update delete sort exit'
        def input = System.in.readLine().tokenize()
        def method = input.remove(0)
        invokeMethod(method, input)
    }
}
}

app = new AthleteApplication()
app.init()
app.mainLoop()
```

❷ **Entry point after initialization**

Commands are provided as methods, then arguments

❸ **Real entry point**

The script begins running with the code at the bottom of the listing, at ❸. This initializes the application ❶ and database before calling the main loop of the class ❷—in some ways, the entry point of the main application logic. Because the commands are provided as the method name followed by the arguments, we can tokenize each line and treat it as a method call. Of course, we would have lots of validation in a real system, but it's amazing how a *functional* console interface can be implemented with so little code.

It wasn't intended originally, but this little application effectively implements a *domain specific language*: a simple line-oriented command language for manipulating the `Athlete` table. This example provides a good way to learn Groovy SQL. It's worth playing with the given code and expanding it in multiple dimensions: more DAOs, relationships between DAOs (one-to-one, one-to-many), views, more operations, and a more sophisticated user interface.

By now, you should have a good idea of how to possibly organize your code around Groovy SQL. Before we close the door on database access, however, there is one topic we wish to discuss further: Object-Relational Mapping.

10.4 *Groovy and ORM*

For some time now, language and library providers have been trying to make databases easier to use. There have been many approaches, including several along the lines of *Object-Relational Mapping (ORM)*. In the most general terms, ORM frameworks allow developers to describe their data models, including the relationships, for use in an object-oriented language. The idea is to retrieve data from the database as objects using an object-oriented search facility, manipulate the objects, and then persist any changes back to the database. The ORM system takes care of adding/deleting records in the right order to satisfy constraints, datatype conversions, and similar concerns.

This sounds wonderful, but reality is more complicated than theory, as always. In particular, new databases can often be designed to be "ORM-friendly," but existing databases are sometimes significantly harder to work with. The situation can become sufficiently complex that the author Ted Neward has referred to ORM as "the Vietnam of computer science."[11]

There are many different approaches and libraries, both free and commercial, for many different platforms. In the Java world, two of the best-known players in the field are the *Java Data Objects (JDO)* specification and *Hibernate*. The latest *Enterprise Java Beans (EJB)* specification includes ORM to allow implementation-independent expression of relationships. It has yet to be seen how well this independence will work in practice.

As you've seen, Groovy provides more object-oriented database access than good-old JDBC, but it does not implement a full-blown ORM solution. Of course,

---

[11] http://blogs.tedneward.com/2006/06/26/The+Vietnam+Of+Computer+Science.aspx.

because it integrates seamlessly with Java, any of the solutions available in Java can be used in Groovy too.

Even within the Groovy library, more can be done without crossing the line into full ORM. We expect future versions of Groovy to ship with `DataSets` that support all CRUD operations, a general DAO implementation, and possibly ready-made ActiveRecord support.

Beyond the Groovy library are activities to come up with a special *Groovy ORM (GORM)*. This is an approach that builds on Hibernate but relieves the programmer of all the configuration work by relying on code and naming conventions. GORM is developed as a part of the *Grails* project.

Finally, we'd like to emphasize that it would be a misconception to see ORM as *the* final solution to database programming and to dismiss all other approaches. ORM is targeted at providing object persistence and transaction support. It tries to shield you from the relational model (to some extent). When selecting an ORM solution, make sure it allows you to exploit the relational model. Otherwise, you are losing most of the power that you paid your database vendor for.

We find the Groovy SQL approach appealing: It provides good means for working with the relational model with an almost ORM-like feeling for the simple cases while keeping all statements under programmatic control.

10.5 *Summary*

In this chapter, we have shown that Groovy has considerable support for database programming within its standard library. Groovy SQL is available wherever Groovy is. You don't need to install any additional modules.

Groovy SQL is made up from a small set of classes that build on JDBC and make it Groovy-friendly. Important features are as follows:

- Minimal setup for database access
- Simple execution of SQL statements
- Improved reliability through automatic, transparent resource handling (`DataSource`, `Connection`, `Statement`, `ResultSet`)
- Easy transparent usage of prepared statements with GStrings
- Convenience with `DataSets` (adding, nested filtering with expressions)
- Transparent DTOs
- Optionally transparent DAOs and business objects

The filtering available in the DataSet class is particularly important in terms of closures being understood not only as a block of code but also as an abstract syntax tree. This can allow logic to be expressed in a manner familiar to the developer without the potentially huge inefficiency of retrieving all the data from the database and filtering it within the application.

You have seen how an example application can be written with the help of Groovy SQL such that the code organization fits into architectural layers and database programming patterns with little work.

Although Groovy does not provide any true Object-Relational Mapping facilities, it integrates well with existing solutions; and where the full complexities of ORM are not required, the facilities provided above and beyond straight JDBC can help tremendously.

11

Integrating Groovy

One of the biggest advantages of Groovy (even one of the reasons for its inception) is the fact it integrates natively with Java because both languages run on the same platform. It is important to understand what makes Groovy such an attractive option when you need to embed a scripting language in your application.

First of all, from a corporate perspective, it makes sense to build on the same platform that most of your projects are already running on. This protects the investment in skills, experience, and technology, mitigating risk and thus costs.

Where Java isn't a perfect fit as a language, Groovy's expressiveness, brevity, and power features may be more appropriate. Conversely, when Groovy falls short because of the inevitable trade-off between agility and speed, performance-critical code can be replaced with raw Java. These balancing decisions can be made early or late with few repercussions due to the close links between the two languages. Groovy provides you with a transparent integration mechanism that permits a one-to-one mix-and-match of Java and Groovy classes. This is not always the case with other scripting solutions, some of which just provide wrappers or proxies that break the object hierarchy contract.

This chapter will show you how to integrate Groovy with Java in various ways. First we'll examine three facilities provided by Groovy: `GroovyShell`, `Groovy-ScriptEngine`, and `GroovyClassLoader`. We will then consider the scripting support provided by the Spring framework and Java 6, code-named Mustang.

You will see that by integrating Groovy and Java, you can leverage the vast libraries of available Java classes and also enjoy the benefits of the extremely agile dynamic capabilities Groovy provides. All this can be done with seamless integration of the two languages.

11.1 *Getting ready to integrate*

The interplay between Groovy and Java means that it is easy to make them cooperate in various ways. The most obvious way is to make Groovy code call into Java code, either using one of the command-line tools to load and run Groovy scripts directly, or using `groovyc` to compile Groovy into normal Java class files. This assumes that all the code is known before the application needs to be compiled. It doesn't allow for any just-in-time provision of code, whether that's through users entering expressions as they might into a graphing calculator or developers providing replacement scripts for just the bits of code that require frequent changes within a live system.

As an idea of how widely used this kind of facility can be, consider *Visual Basic (VB)*. We're not in the business of judging its pros and cons, but it would be hard to deny that VB is popular and has been for a long time. Although many developers write whole applications in VB from scratch, far more use the capability of various products to *embed* pieces of VB code in order to customize behavior in ways the original developers may never have even considered.

Now consider allowing that kind of flexibility in your application. Instead of hearing people talking about writing VB in Microsoft Office, imagine those same people talking about writing Groovy in *your* application. Imagine them using your product in ways you never contemplated—making it more and more valuable for them.

Before seeing how this can be done, we should step back and think about why we would need to integrate Groovy in a Java application, the situations in which it's useful to do so, and the dependencies we need to set up before we get started.

11.1.1 *Integrating appropriately*

No-one can tell you what your application needs are or what is going to be suitable for your particular situation. You must look carefully at your requirements and consider whether you will benefit from integrating Groovy at all. We can't make that decision for you—but we hope we can give a few ideas to guide you.

First, it's worth explicitly acknowledging that not all applications benefit from integrating a scripting language such as Groovy. We can go as far as saying that most don't need that. If you're writing an e-Commerce web site, a multimedia player, or an FTP client, chances are that you won't need a scripting language. But now, suppose you were building an advanced word processor, a spreadsheet application, or a complex risk-calculation module for an even more complicated bank software suite that had to evolve quickly to follow the rapid changes of the market, legislation, or new business rules. These applications might need an extension point where end users can customize them to suit their needs. Figure 11.1 shows one example of where you could integrate Groovy.

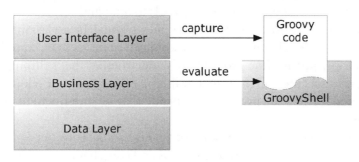

Figure 11.1
One example of an integration solution. Groovy code is entered by the user in the user interface layer and then executed in the business layer.

For instance, the banking application might require the definition of business rules in a script that could be defined at runtime without requiring a new and tedious development/test/qualification phase, reducing the time to market and increasing the responsiveness to changes in financial practices. Another example could be an office suite of applications offering a macro system to create reusable functions that could be invoked with a keystroke. It becomes obvious that a dichotomy of the software world differentiates monolithic applications, which don't need to evolve over time and have a fixed functional scope, from more fluid applications whose logic can be extended or modified during their lifespan to accommodate context changes.

Before considering using Groovy in your application, you need to analyze whether you need to customize it, and see whether you want to customize, extend, or amend the logic, and not just simple parameters. If parameterization will fulfill your needs, you may be better off with classic configuration mechanisms such as an administration web interface through a set of web services; or, for more advanced monitoring and action management, you may also consider exposing JMX[1] MBeans. Sometimes, even if the logic has to change, if the choice is between a small and well-defined set of business rules that are known to begin with, you can also embed all those rules within the application and decide through parameterization which one is to be used. Once you have examined your needs and come to the conclusion that a scripting environment is what your application requires, this chapter should provide you with all the information you need to make your application extendable at runtime with logic written in Groovy.[2]

In the following sections, you'll learn how to use the `GroovyShell` class to evaluate simple expressions and scripts, as well as the `GroovyClassLoader` for further loading of Groovy classes. In addition to the techniques provided by Groovy for integrating your scripts in Java, you'll discover alternatives for leveraging the Spring framework and the scripting API within the upcoming Java 6 release.

11.1.2 Setting up dependencies

In order to use Groovy within your project, you will need to set it up to use the Groovy libraries. This section covers the dependencies required for Groovy integration. The fact that it's so short should be a source of comfort—there's little

---

[1] Find more information at http://java.sun.com/products/JavaManagement/.

[2] Of course, we don't wish to discourage you from reading the chapter even if you don't have any integration needs right now. Gaining knowledge is a worthy pursuit in and of itself.

work to do to get up and running. However, problems can sometimes crop up during integration that you wouldn't see if you were using Groovy by itself. We will discuss these potential issues and how to resolve them.

The Groovy distribution comes with a directory containing all the core libraries that form the Groovy runtime. The minimum for embedding Groovy consists of the three jar files listed in table 11.1.

Table 11.1   The minimal jar files required for integrating Groovy

File	Purpose
groovy-1.0.jar	Groovy core library
antlr-2.7.5.jar	Grammar parser and generator
asm-2.2.jar	Bytecode toolkit used to generate classes

But these three dependencies may sometimes conflict with the other libraries your project uses. In particular, if you are using Hibernate and/or Spring, which both use ASM for generating proxies, you will not be able to use Groovy unless the version of Hibernate or Spring you are using requires the same version of ASM. However, there is a solution to this problem. The Groovy distribution also comes with a specific Groovy jar file that embeds the dependencies in their own packages. This library is often called the *embeddable jar file*, because you can embed it beside any other library without any conflict. You will find this jar file in the directory named embeddable of your Groovy installation: groovy-all-1.0.jar.

Remember that if your project depends on ASM or Antlr, you can use this "magic" jar file to solve your versioning issues between Groovy and your other dependencies. Also, keep in mind that your project will have to run under a JRE 1.4 or above, which is a requirement for Groovy.

It's not just Java applications that can benefit from the availability of a scripting engine: You can even integrate custom Groovy scripts and expressions from an application written in Groovy! While explaining the various embedding mechanisms, we will show how the Groovy interpreters and classloaders can be exploited from both sides of the language fence. Now that we have set up our environment, we can look at the first of our three ways of directly integrating with Groovy: `GroovyShell`.

11.2 Evaluating expressions and scripts with GroovyShell

The first Groovy API we'll examine is `GroovyShell`. This is in many ways the simplest of the integration techniques, and if it covers your situation, it may well be all you need. With all the libraries in place, we will start dynamically evaluating expressions in a few simple lines of code. We will then move gradually into more complex scenarios, passing data between the calling code and the dynamically executing script, and then creating classes in the script for use outside. We examine different ways of executing scripts—precompiling them or executing them just once—and the different types of scripts that can be run. Finally, we look at ways you can tweak `GroovyShell` for more advanced uses. Don't worry if it seems there's a lot to learn—in simple situations, simple solutions often suffice. Also, much of the information presented here is relevant when looking at the other APIs Groovy provides.

11.2.1 Starting simply

The simplest imaginable integration requirement evaluates an expression. For example, some math applications may require users to input arbitrary expressions in a form input field that can't be hardwired at development time in a function or a closure—for instance, a spreadsheet application where formulas are Groovy expressions. Those applications then ask the runtime to calculate the entered formula. In such situations, the tool of choice for evaluating expressions and scripts is the `GroovyShell` class. The usage of this class is straightforward and is similar if you are using it from Java or from Groovy. A simple expression evaluator can look like listing 11.1.[3]

> **Listing 11.1   A trivial example of expression evaluation in Groovy**

```
def shell = new GroovyShell()
def result = shell.evaluate("12 + 23")
assert result == 35
```

---

[3] You might wonder why we choose to integrate from Groovy to Groovy. Well, we would be more likely to do it from Java, but using Groovy simplifies our examples. Doing so can be handy even from Groovy, so that you can organize utility code in external scripts, run scripts with certain security policies in place, or execute user-provided input at runtime.

The equivalent full Java program is naturally somewhat longer due to the scaffolding code and imports required, but the core logic is exactly the same. Listing 11.2 gives the complete Java code required to perform the evaluation, albeit it with no error handling. Java examples later in the chapter have been cut down to just the code involved in integration. Imports are usually shown only when they are not clear from the context.

> **Listing 11.2 The same trivial example from listing 11.1, in Java this time**

```
// Java
import groovy.lang.GroovyShell;

public class HelloIntegrationWorld {
    public static void main(String[] args) {
        GroovyShell shell = new GroovyShell();
        Object result = shell.evaluate("12+23");
        assert new Integer(35).equals(result);
    }
}
```

In both cases, we first instantiate an instance of `groovy.lang.GroovyShell`. On this instance, we call the `evaluate` method, which takes a string as a parameter containing the expression to evaluate. This `evaluate` method returns an object holding the value of the expression. We won't show the Java equivalent for all the examples in this chapter, but we sometimes provide one, as much as anything to remind you of how easy it is.[4]

Among the `evaluate` overloaded methods present in `GroovyShell`, here are the most interesting ones:

```
Object evaluate(File file)
Object evaluate(InputStream in)
Object evaluate(InputStream in, String fileName)
Object evaluate(String scriptText)
Object evaluate(String scriptText, String fileName)
```

You can evaluate expressions coming from a string, an input stream, or a file. The additional filename parameter is used to specify the name of the class to be created upon evaluation of the script—because Groovy always generates classes for scripts, too.

---

[4] It's rarely *quite* as easy as the Groovy equivalent, but by now you should realize that this has nothing to do with the features being shown and everything to do with Groovy making life easier in general.

From Groovy scripts, a shortcut can be used: Scripts are classes extending the `Script` class, which already has an `evaluate` method, too. In the context of a script, our previous example can be shortened to the following:

```
assert evaluate("12 + 23") == 35
```

The string parameter passed to `evaluate` can be a full script with several lines of code, not just a simple expression, as you see in listing 11.3.

Listing 11.3 Evaluating a multiline script with GroovyShell

```
def shell = new GroovyShell()
def kineticEnergy = shell.evaluate('''
    def mass = 22.3
    def velocity = 10.6
    mass * velocity**2 / 2
''')
assert kineticEnergy == 1252.814
```

Building on `GroovyShell`, the `groovy.util.Eval` class can save you the boilerplate code of instantiating `GroovyShell` to evaluate simple expressions with zero to three parameters. Listing 11.4 shows how to use `Eval` for each case from Groovy (the same applies for Java, of course).

Listing 11.4 `Eval` saves explicitly creating a `GroovyShell` for simple cases

```
assert "Hello" == Eval.me("'Hello'")
assert 1 == Eval.x  (1, "x")
assert 3 == Eval.xy (1, 2, "x+y")
assert 6 == Eval.xyz(1, 2, 3, "x+y+z")
```

The `me` method is used when no parameters are required. The other methods are used for one, two, and three parameters, where the first, second, and third parameters are made available as `x`, `y`, and `z`, respectively. This is handy when your sole need is to evaluate some simple expressions or even mathematical functions. Next, you will see how you can go further with parameterization of script evaluation with `GroovyShell`.

11.2.2 *Passing parameters within a binding*

In listing 11.3, we used a multiline script defining two variables of mass and velocity to compute the kinetic energy of an object of mass 22.3 kilograms with a speed of 10.6 km/h. However, notice that this is of limited interest if we can't reuse the expression evaluator. Fortunately, it is possible to pass variables to the evaluator with a `groovy.lang.Binding` object, as shown in listing 11.5.

Listing 11.5 Making data available to a `GroovyShell` **using a** `Binding`

```
def binding = new Binding()
binding.mass = 22.3                    ❶ Create and populate
binding.velocity = 10.6                   the binding

def shell = new GroovyShell(binding)
def expression = "mass * velocity ** 2 / 2"   ❷ Evaluate the expression
assert shell.evaluate(expression) == 1252.814    using the binding

binding.setVariable("mass", 25.4)          ❸ Change the binding
assert shell.evaluate(expression) == 1426.972    data and re-evaluate
```

To begin with, a `Binding` object is instantiated. Because `Binding` extends `GroovyObjectSupport`, we can directly set variables on it as if we were manipulating properties: The `mass` and `velocity` variables have been defined in the binding ❶. The `GroovyShell` constructor takes the binding as a parameter, and further on, all evaluations use variables from that binding as if they were global variables of the script ❷. When we change the value of the `mass` variable, we see that the result of the equation is different ❸. This line is particularly interesting because we have redefined the `mass` variable thanks to the `setVariable` method on `Binding`. That is how we could set or modify variables from Java; Java would not recognize `binding.mass`, because this is a shortcut introduced in Groovy by `Binding` extending `GroovyObjectSupport`.

You may have already guessed that if there is a `setVariable` method available, then `getVariable` also exists. Whereas the former allows you to create or redefine variables from the binding, the latter is used to retrieve the value of a variable from the binding. The `evaluate` method can return only one value: the value of the last expression of the evaluated script. When multiple values are needed in the result, the script can use the binding to make them available to the calling context. Listing 11.6 shows how a script can modify values of existing variables, or it can create new variables in the binding that can be retrieved later.

Listing 11.6 Data can flow out of the binding as well as into it

```
def binding = new Binding(x: 6, y: 4)      ❶ Prepopulating the
def shell = new GroovyShell(binding)          binding data
shell.evaluate('''
    xSquare = x * x          ❷ Setting binding data within
    yCube   = y * y * y         the evaluated script
''')
                                           ❸ Method access
assert binding.getVariable("xSquare") == 36   to binding data
assert binding.yCube == 64   ◁❹ Groovy property access to binding data
```

In this example, we create a binding instance to which we add two parameters x and y by passing a map to the `Binding` constructor ❶. Our evaluated script creates two new variables in the binding by assigning a value to nondefined variables: xSquare and yCube ❷. We can retrieve the values of these variables with `getVariable` from both Java and Groovy ❸, or we can use the property-like access from Groovy ❹.

Not all variables can be accessed with `getVariable` because Groovy makes a distinction in scripts between defined variables and undefined variables: If a variable is defined with the `def` keyword or with a type, it will be a local variable, but if you are not defining it and are assigning it a value without prior definition, a variable will be created or assigned in the binding. Here, `"localVariable"` is not in the binding, and the call to `getVariable` would throw a `MissingPropertyException`:

```
def binding = new Binding()
def shell = new GroovyShell(binding)
shell.evaluate('''
    def localVariable = "local variable"
    bindingVariable   = "binding variable"
''')

assert binding.getVariable("bindingVariable") == "binding variable"
```

Anything can be put into or retrieved from the binding, and only one return value can be returned as the evaluation of the last statement of the script. The binding is the best way to pass your domain objects or instances of predefined or prepopulated sessions or transactions to your scripts. Let's examine a more creative way of returning a value from your script evaluation.

11.2.3 *Generating dynamic classes at runtime*

Using `evaluate` can also be handy for generating new dynamic classes on the fly. For instance, you may need to generate classes for a web service at runtime, based on XML elements from the WSDL for the service. A contrived example for evaluating and returning a dummy class is shown in listing 11.7.

Listing 11.7   Defining a class in an evaluated script

```
def shell = new GroovyShell()
def clazz = shell.evaluate('''
    class MyClass {                        Define a
        def method() { "value" }           new class
    }
    return MyClass
```

```
''')
assert clazz.name == "MyClass"                    Create an instance
def instance = clazz.newInstance()        ⊲┘      of the class
assert instance.method() == "value"       ⊲─  Use the object as normal
```

In all the examples you've seen so far, we have used the `evaluate` method, which compiles and runs a script in one go. That's fine for one-shot evaluations, but other situations benefit from separating the compilation (parsing) from the execution, as you will see next.

11.2.4 Parsing scripts

The `parse` methods of `GroovyShell` return instances of `Script` so that you can reuse scripts at will without re-evaluating them each time—hence without compiling them all over again. (Remember our `SwingBuilder` plotter from chapter 8.) This method is similar to `evaluate`, taking the same set of arguments; but rather than executing the code, it generates an instance of the `Script` class. All scripts you can write are always instances of `Script`.

Let's take a concrete example. Suppose we're running a bank, and we have customers asking for a loan to buy a house. We need to compute the monthly amount they will have to pay back, knowing the total amount of the loan, the interest rate, and the number of months to repay the loan. But of course, we want to reuse this formula, and we are storing it in a database or elsewhere on the filesystem in case the formula evolves in the future.

Let's assume the variables of the algorithm are as follows:

- `amount`: The total amount of the loan (the principle)
- `rate`: The annual interest rate
- `numberOfMonths`: The number of months to reimburse the loan

With these variables, we want to compute the monthly payment. The script in listing 11.8 shows how we can reuse the formula to calculate this important figure.

Listing 11.8   Multiple uses of a monthly payment calculator

```
def monthly = "amount*(rate/12) / (1-(1+rate/12)**-numberOfMonths)"

def shell = new GroovyShell()                   Parse formula into
def script = shell.parse(monthly)     ⊲┘        reusable script

script.binding.amount = 154000     ⊲─  Access binding variable
```

```
script.rate = 3.75/100                      Access binding variable
script.numberOfMonths = 240                  using shorthand

assert script.run() == 913.0480050387338

script.binding = new Binding(amount: 185000,     Create new
                             rate: 3.50/100,      binding
                             numberOfMonths: 300)

assert script.run() == 926.1536089487843
```

After defining our formula, we parse it with `GroovyShell.parse` to retrieve an instance of `Script`. We then set the variables of the script binding for our three variables. Note how we can shorten `script.binding.someVariable` to `script.someVariable` because `Script` implements `GroovyObject` and overrides its `setProperty` method. Once the variables are set, we call the `run` method, which executes the script and returns the value of the last statement: the monthly payment we wanted to calculate in the first place.

To reuse this formula without having to recompile it, we can reuse the script instance and call it with another set of values by defining a new binding, rather than by modifying the original binding as in the first run.

11.2.5 *Running scripts or classes*

The `run` methods of `GroovyShell` can execute both scripts and classes. When a class is parsed and recognized as extending `GroovyTestCase`, a text test runner will run the test case.

The three main `run` method signatures can take a `String`, a `File`, or an `InputStream` to read and execute the script or class, a name for the script, and an array of `String`s for the arguments:

```
run(String script, String[] args)
run(File scriptFile, String scriptName, String[] args)
run(InputStream scriptStream, String scriptName, String[] args)
```

The execution of `run` is a bit different than that of `evaluate`. Whereas `evaluate` evaluates only scripts, `run` can also execute classes with a `main` method as well as unit tests. The following rules are applied:

- If the class to be run has a `main(Object[] args)` or `main(String[] args)` method, it will be run. Note that a script is a normal Java class that implements `Runnable` and whose `run` method is called by a `main` method.

- If the class extends GroovyTestCase, a JUnit test runner executes it.
- Otherwise, if the class implements Runnable, it is instantiated with a constructor taking a String array, or a default constructor, and the class is run with its run method.

11.2.6 *Further parameterization of GroovyShell*

We used the Binding class to pass variables to scripts and to retrieve modified or new variables defined during the evaluation of the script. We can further configure our GroovyShell instance by passing two other objects in the constructor: a parent ClassLoader and/or a CompilerConfiguration.

For reference, here are the constructor signatures available in GroovyShell:

```
public GroovyShell()
public GroovyShell(Binding binding)
public GroovyShell(Binding binding,
                   CompilerConfiguration config)
public GroovyShell(CompilerConfiguration config)
public GroovyShell(ClassLoader parent)
public GroovyShell(ClassLoader parent,
                   Binding binding)
public GroovyShell(ClassLoader parent,
                   Binding binding,
                   CompilerConfiguration config)
```

Choosing a parent classloader

Groovy uses classloaders to load Groovy classes. The consequence is that you must have a minimal understanding of how classloaders work when integrating Groovy. Alas, mastering classloaders is not the most trivial task on a Java developer's journey. When you're working with libraries generating classes or dynamic proxies at runtime with bytecode instrumentation, or with a complex hierarchy of classloaders to make critical code run in isolation in a secured sandbox, the task becomes even trickier. It is important to understand how the hierarchy of classloaders is structured.

A common use case is represented in figure 11.2.

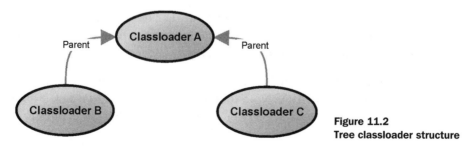

Figure 11.2
Tree classloader structure

A class loaded by classloader B can't be seen by classloader C. The standard way classloaders load classes is by first asking the parent classloader if it knows the class, before trying to load the class. Classes are looked up by navigating up the classloader hierarchy; however, a class loaded by C won't be able to see a class loaded by B, because B is not a parent of C. Fortunately, by cleverly setting the parent classloader of C to be B, the problem is solved, as shown in figure 11.3. This can be done by using `GroovyShell`'s constructors, which permits you to define a parent classloader for the scripts being evaluated.

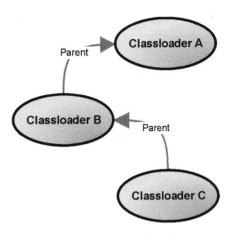

Figure 11.3 Linear classloader structure

To specify `GroovyShell`'s classloader, specify the parent classloader to flatten your hierarchy:

```
def parentClassLoader = objectFromB.classloader
def shellForC = new GroovyShell(parentClassLoader)
```

If you have classloader issues, you will get a `ClassNotFoundException` or, worse still, a `NoClassDefFoundError`. To debug these issues, the best thing to do is to print the classloader for all affected classes and also print each classloader's parent classloader, and so on up to the root of all classloaders. You'll then have a good picture of the whole classloader hierarchy in your application, and the final step will be to set parent classloaders accordingly to flatten the hierarchy—even better, try to make classes be loaded by the same classloaders if possible.

Configuring the compilation

In the list of constructors of the `GroovyShell` class, you will have noticed the `CompilerConfiguration` parameter. An instance of this class can be passed to `GroovyShell` to customize various options of the compilation process. You will also see how to take advantage of this class with the `GroovyClassLoader` in a following section.

Without studying all the options available, let's review the most useful ones, as shown in table 11.2.

Of these methods, `setScriptBaseClass` is particularly worthy of note. If you want all of your scripts to share a common set of methods, you can specify a base class extending `groovy.lang.Script` that will host these methods and then be

Table 11.2 The most useful methods in `CompilerConfiguration`

Method signature	Description
setClasspath (String path)	Define your own classpath used to look for classes, allowing you to restrict the application classpath and/or enhance it with other libraries
setDebug (boolean debug)	Set to true to get full, unfiltered stacktraces when exceptions are written on the error stream
setOutput (PrintWriter writer)	Set the writer compilation errors will be printed to
setScriptBaseClass (String clazz)	Define a subclass of `Script` as the base class for script instances
setSourceEncoding (String enc)	Set the encoding of the scripts to evaluate, which is important when parsing scripts from files or input streams that use a different encoding than the platform default
setRecompileGroovySource (boolean b)	Set to true to reload Groovy sources that have changed after they have been compiled—by default, this flag is set to false
setMinimumRecompilationInterval (int millis)	Set the minimum amount of time to wait before checking if the sources are more recent than the compiled classes

available inside the scripts. Sharing methods among scripts is a good technique to inject hooks to your own framework services. Let's consider a base script class that extends `Script` and whose role will be to inject a global multiplication function[5] into all scripts evaluated by `GroovyShell`:

```
abstract class BaseScript extends Script {
    def multiply(a, b) { a * b }
}
```

`BaseScript` extends `Script`, which is an abstract class, so the class must be declared abstract, because the `run` method is abstract. When compiling or interpreting scripts, Groovy will extend this base script and will inject the script's statements in the `run` method.

To make this class the base class of your scripts, you now need to pass a `org.codehaus.groovy.control.CompilerConfiguration` instance to `GroovyShell`'s constructor, as explained by the following Groovy example:

---

[5] Multiplication is easy to demonstrate in a book, but real-world examples might include handling transactional resources, configuration, and logging.

```
def conf = new CompilerConfiguration()
conf.setScriptBaseClass("BaseScript")
def shell = new GroovyShell(conf)
def value = shell.evaluate('''
    multiply(5, 6)
''')
assert value == 30
```

This is not the only way to inject functions in all your scripts. Another trick to share functions between scripts is to store closures in the binding of `GroovyShell` without needing to use `CompilerConfiguration`. This can be seen in listing 11.9.

Listing 11.9   Using the `Binding` to share functions between scripts

```
def binding = new Binding(multiply: { a, b -> a * b })   ◁──┐ Create closure
def shell = new GroovyShell(binding)                        │ within the
def value = shell.evaluate('''                              │ binding
    multiply(5, 6)   ◁──┐ Call the closure like
''')                    │ a normal method
assert value == 30
```

However, you also need to be able to write the same code in Java, so we must be able to create closures and put them in the binding. From Java, creating a closure is not as neat as in Groovy. You must create a class that derives from `groovy.lang.Closure` and implement an `Object doCall(Object arguments)` method. An alternative technique is to create an instance of `org.codehaus.groovy.runtime.MethodClosure`, which delegates the call to a multiplication method on a custom `multiplicator` class instance:

```
// Java
MethodClosure mclos = new MethodClosure(multiplicator, "multiply");
Binding binding = new Binding();
binding.setVariable("multiply", mclos);
GroovyShell shell = new GroovyShell(binding);
shell.evaluate("multiply(5, 6)");
```

We have now fully covered how `GroovyShell` can be operated both from Java and from Groovy to extend your application. `GroovyShell` is a nice utility class to create extension points in your own code and to execute logic that can be externalized in scripts stored as strings, on the filesystem, or in a database. This class is great for evaluating, parsing, or running scripts that represent a single and self-contained unit of work, but it is less easy to use when your logic is spread across dependent scripts. This is where the `GroovyScriptEngine` and `GroovyClassLoader` can help. These are the topics of the next two sections.

11.3 *Using the Groovy script engine*

The `GroovyShell` class is ideal for standalone and isolated scripts, but it can be less easy to use when your scripts are dependent on each other. The simplest solution at that point is to use `GroovyScriptEngine`. This class also provides the capability to reload scripts as they change, which enables your application to support live modifications of your business logic. We will cover the basic uses of the script engine and show you how to tell the engine where to find scripts.

11.3.1 *Setting up the engine*

The scripting engine has several constructors to choose from when you instantiate it. You can pass different arguments to these constructors, such as an array of paths or URLs where the engine will try to find the Groovy scripts, a classloader to be used as the parent classloader, or a special `ResourceConnector` that provides `URLConnections`. In our examples, we will assume that we are loading and running scripts from the filesystem:

```
def engine = new GroovyScriptEngine(".")
```

or with an array of URLs or of strings representing URLs:

```
def engine = new GroovyScriptEngine([".", "../folder "])
```

The engine assumes that strings represent filesystem locations. If your scripts are to be loaded from somewhere other than the filesystem, you should use URLs instead:

```
def engine = new GroovyScriptEngine(
    ["file://.", "http://someUrl"]*.toURL() as URL[])
```

The engine will search the resource following each URL sequentially until it finds the script.

The various constructors can also take a classloader, which will then be used by the engine for the parent classloader of the compiled classes:

```
def engine = new GroovyScriptEngine(".", parentCL)
```

The parent classloader can also be defined with the `setParentClassLoader` method.

Once you have instantiated the engine, you can eventually run your scripts.

11.3.2 *Running scripts*

To run a script, the primary mechanism is the `run` method of `GroovyScript-Engine`. This method takes two arguments: the name of the script to run as the relative path of the file and the binding to store the variables that the script will need to operate. The method also returns the value of the last expression evaluated by the script, as `GroovyShell` does.

For instance, if you intend to run a file named MyScript.groovy situated in the `test` folder relative to the current directory, you might run it as shown here:

```
def engine = new GroovyScriptEngine(".")
def value  = engine.run("test/MyScript.groovy", new Binding())
```

Loaded scripts are automatically cached by the engine, and they are updated whenever the resource is updated. The engine can also load script classes directly with the `loadScriptByName` method; it returns a `Class` object representing the class of the script, which is a derived class of `groovy.lang.Script`. There is a pitfall to watch out for with this method, however: It takes a script with a fully qualified class name notation rather than the relative path of the file:

```
def engine = new GroovyScriptEngine(".")
def clazz  = engine.loadScriptByName("test.MyScript")
```

This example returns the class of the myScript.groovy script situated in the test folder. If you are not using the filesystem, you will be using URLs instead of files, and in that case it is mandatory to use a special resource connector that is responsible for loading the resources.

11.3.3 *Defining a different resource connector*

If you wish to load scripts from a particular location, you may want to provide your own resource connector. This is done by passing it as an argument to the constructor of `GroovyScriptEngine`, either with or without the specification of a parent classloader. The following example shows both overloaded methods:

```
def myResourceConnector = getResourceConnector()
def engine  = new GroovyScriptEngine(myResourceConnector)
def engine2 = new GroovyScriptEngine(myResourceConnector, parent)
```

To implement your own connector, you have to create a class implementing the `groovy.util.ResourceConnector` interface, which contains only one method:

```
public URLConnection getResourceConnection(String name)
    throws ResourceException;
```

The `getResourceConnection` method takes a string parameter representing the name of the resource to load, and it returns an instance of `URLConnection`. If you are also creating your own `URLConnection`, at least three methods need to be implemented properly (you could potentially leave the others aside and throw `UnsupportedOperationException` or `UnknownServiceException`, like some JDK classes from the `java.net` package do):

```
public long       getLastModified()
public URL        getURL()
public InputStream getInputStream() throws IOException
```

Although usually you'll store your script on the filesystem or inside a database, implementing your own `ResourceConnector` and `URLConnection` allows you to provide a handle on scripts coming from any location: from a database, a remote file system, an XML document, or an object data store.

GroovyScriptEngine is perfect for dealing with scripts, but it falls short for more complex manipulation of classes. In fact, both `GroovyShell` and `Groovy-ScriptEngine` rely on a single mechanism for loading scripts or classes: the `GroovyClassLoader`. This special classloader is what we will discuss in the following section.

11.4 Working with the GroovyClassLoader

The `GroovyClassLoader` is the Swiss-army knife with all possible tools for integrating Groovy into an application, whether explicitly or via classes such as `GroovyShell`. This class is a custom classloader, which is able to define and parse Groovy classes and scripts as normal classes that can be used either from Groovy or from Java. It is also able to compile all the required and dependent classes. Let's see how you can compile a Groovy class.

This section will take you through how to use the `GroovyClassLoader`, from the simplest uses to more involved situations. We examine how to get around circular dependency issues, how to load scripts that are stored outside the local filesystem, and finally how to make your integration environment safe and sandboxed, permitting the scripts to perform only the operations you wish to allow.

11.4.1 Parsing and loading Groovy classes

Say we have a simple Groovy class `Hello` like the following:

```
class Hello {
    def greeting() { "Hello!" }
}
```

We want to parse and load this class with the GroovyClassLoader. In Groovy, we can do it like so:

```
def    gcl = new GroovyClassLoader()
Class greetingClass = gcl.parseClass(new File("Hello.groovy"))
assert "Hello!" == greetingClass.newInstance().greeting()
```

NOTE   *Instantiating GroovyClassLoader*—In our example, we use the default constructor. But this class offers more constructors. GroovyClassLoader (ClassLoader loader) lets you define a parent classloader to avoid problems with a complex hierarchy, as we explained in the section about GroovyShell. The constructor GroovyClassLoader(ClassLoader loader, CompilerConfiguration config) gives you more control over the behavior of the classloader, as explained in the section about Groovy-Shell, thanks to the parameterization of CompilerConfiguration.

An instance of GroovyClassLoader is created, and its parseClass method is called and passed our Hello.groovy file. The method returns a Class object that can then be instantiated by using Class's newInstance method, which invokes the default constructor of Hello. Once Hello is instantiated, because Groovy supports duck typing, we can directly call the greeting method defined in Hello. However, in a strongly typed language, you could not directly call the method. So, from Java, to invoke a method, you have to either use reflection explicitly—which is usually pretty ugly—or rely on the fact that all Groovy classes automatically implement the groovy.lang.GroovyObject interface, exposing the invokeMethod, getProperty, and setProperty methods.

DUCK TYPING   As coined by the dynamic language community, "If it walks like a duck and quacks like a duck, it must be a duck." Weakly typed languages usually let you call any method or access any property on an object, even if you don't know at compile-time or even at runtime that the object is of a known type that contains that method or property. This means you know the kind of objects you expect will have the relevant signature or property. It's an assumption. If you can call the method or access the property, it must be the type you were expecting—hence, it's a duck because it walks and quacks like a duck!

Duck typing implies that as long as an object has a certain set of method signatures, it is interchangeable with any other object that has the same set of methods, regardless of whether the two have a related inheritance hierarchy.

Whereas `getProperty` and `setProperty` are responsible for accessing properties of your Groovy class from Java, `invokeMethod` allows you to call any method on Groovy classes easily from Java:

```
// Java
GroovyClassLoader gcl = new GroovyClassLoader();
Class greetingClass = gcl.parseClass(new File("Hello.groovy"));
GroovyObject hello  = (GroovyObject) greetingClass.newInstance();
Object[] args        = {};
assert "Hello!".equals(hello.invokeMethod("greeting", args));
```

The `invokeMethod` method takes two parameters: The first one is the name of the method to call, and the second corresponds to the parameters to pass to the method we're trying to call. If the method takes only one parameter, pass it directly as an argument; otherwise, if several parameters are expected, they have to be wrapped inside an array of `Objects`, which becomes the argument. For instance, if you wish to call a method that adds two objects together with a signature like `add(a,b)`, you call it like this:

```
a.invokeMethod("add", new Object[] {obj1, obj2}); // Java
```

However, if a method you want to call requires an array as its single parameter, you also have to wrap it inside an array:

```
a.invokeMethod("takesAnArray", new Object[] {anArray}); // Java
```

Despite the fact that it is possible to call any method in a Groovy class from Java with `invokeMethod`, doing so is not Java-friendly because the Java compiler will not know these classes exist and will not let you use the `greeting` method directly—unless you precompiled your Groovy classes and packed them up inside a jar file. Fortunately, there is a workaround to circumvent this shortcoming of `javac`. To make Java understand your Groovy classes, both Groovy and Java have to find a common ground of agreement. This is what we call the *chicken and egg problem*.

11.4.2 *The chicken and egg dependency problem*

Groovy and Java both have no problem accessing, extending, or implementing compiled classes or interfaces from the other language. But at the source code level, neither compiler is really aware of the other language's source files. If you want to work seamlessly between the two languages, the trick is to always compile dependent classes using the appropriate compiler prior to compiling a class that uses a dependent class.

This sounds simple, but in practice, there are many tricky scenarios, such as compiling a Java file that depends on a Groovy file that depends on a Java file. Before you know it, you can quickly end up with intricate dependencies crossing the boundaries of each language. In the best scenario, you may have to alternate back and forth between the two language compilers until all the relevant classes are compiled. A more likely scenario is that it will become difficult to determine which compiler to call when. The worst case scenario—and it's not uncommon—occurs when you have circular dependencies. You will reach a deadlock where neither language will compile because it needs the other language to be compiled first.

Example problem

This is the chicken and egg problem: Java classes depending on Groovy classes in turn depending on Java classes! To solve this puzzle, you can rely on a simple remedy: depending on Java base classes or interfaces.

To illustrate the problem, consider the following Java application:

```
// Java
public class ShapeInfoMain {
    public static void main(String[] args) {
        Square s = new Square(7);
        Circle c = new Circle(4);
        new MaxAreaInfo().displayInfo(s, c);
        new MaxPerimeterInfo().displayInfo(s, c);
    }
}
```

Suppose that the `Square` and `MaxPerimeterInfo` classes are written in Java and the `Circle` and `MaxAreaInfo` classes are written in Groovy. We might be tempted to try using `javac` on all the *.java source files followed by `groovyc` on all the *.groovy files. However, this won't work because the `displayInfo` method in `MaxPerimeterInfo` requires `Circle` to be compiled first. We can't swap the order around, either, because we will have the reverse problem with `MaxAreaInfo` if `Square` is not compiled first.

The dependencies between the files are shown in figure 11.4.

Removing the dependency cycle

The trick is to first compile `Square` and `Circle` using their respective compilers. Next, compile `MaxAreaInfo` and `MaxPerimeterInfo`. Finally, compile `ShapeInfoMain`. Usually, using an interface written in Java is the easiest way to make these dependencies less cumbersome. In our example, `Circle` and `Square` should both

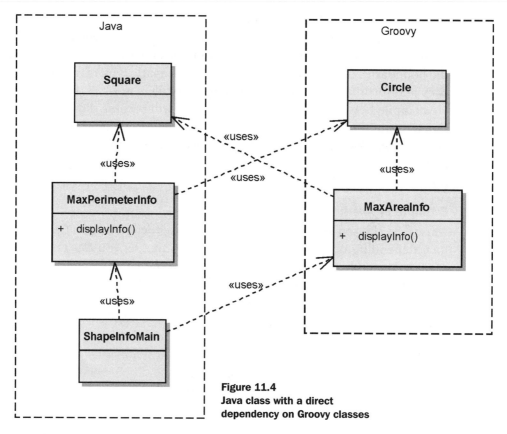

**Figure 11.4
Java class with a direct
dependency on Groovy classes**

implement Shape, whereas MaxPerimeterInfo and MaxAreaInfo should implement ShapeInfo. Adding these interfaces results in the dependencies illustrated in figure 11.5.

Listing 11.10 shows what the Circle class might look like, implementing the Shape interface.

Listing 11.10   Groovy class implementing a Java interface

```
import common.Shape

class Circle implements Shape {          Java interface
    double radius                        implemented in Groovy
    Circle(double radius) { this.radius = radius }
    double area() { return Math.PI * radius ** 2 }      Implement the
    double perimeter() { return 2 * Math.PI * radius }  methods of the
}                                                        interface
```

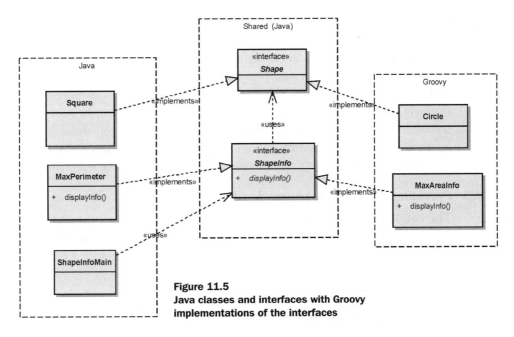

Figure 11.5
Java classes and interfaces with Groovy
implementations of the interfaces

The following is what `MaxAreaInfo` might look like. This time, we're implementing the `ShapeInfo` interface:

```
import common.Shape
import common.ShapeInfo

class MaxAreaInfo implements ShapeInfo {
    void displayInfo(Shape s1, Shape s2) {
        print "The shape with the biggest area is: "
        println s1.area() > s2.area() ? s1.class.name :
                                        s2.class.name
    }
}
```

Building the solution in phases

Once the work of decoupling the concrete types from their interfaces is done, the Java compiler will be able to compile the Java classes first, and then groovyc will be able to compile the Groovy classes. It is a good practice to divide such a codebase into three modules: the Java code, the Groovy code, and the shared Java interfaces. The shared interfaces need to be compiled first. After that, you can javac the Java code and groovyc the Groovy code in either order.

Until the Java compiler is aware of classes not yet compiled in other languages, you have to use intermediary interfaces or abstract classes in Java to make the interaction between Java and Groovy smoother during the compilation process. Let's hope some day the Java compilers will provide hooks for interacting with foreign compilers of alternative languages for the JVM.

In the meantime, we usually compile scripts and classes found on the filesystem of our computer; your sources may lie on a different medium—that's particularly true when you are embedding Groovy in your application. A common scenario is when your sources are stored inside a database. In that case, you will have to provide your own resource loader to the GroovyClassLoader in the form of an instance of GroovyResourceLoader, as explained in the following section.

11.4.3 *Providing a custom resource loader*

The GroovyClassLoader has various methods to let you parse and load Groovy classes from different origins: from a file, from an input stream, or from a string. Here are a few of the methods to explicitly ask the classloader to load a given class:

```
public Class parseClass(File file)
    throws CompilationFailedException
public Class parseClass(String text, String fileName)
    throws CompilationFailedException
public Class parseClass(InputStream in, String fileName)
    throws CompilationFailedException
```

If you are storing your sources in a database, a possible solution is to retrieve them as a String or as an InputStream. Then, you can use the classloader's parseClass methods to parse and load your classes. But rather than explicitly implementing the plumbing and the lookup and parsing yourself, Groovy provides a better solution, in the form of a groovy.lang.GroovyResourceLoader. The resource loader is an interface that you have to implement to specify where your sources are to be found: Give it a name of a resource, and a URL is returned that points at the location of the resource. This is done by a single method from that interface:

```
URL loadGroovySource(String filename) throws MalformedURLException
```

An implementation of the resource loader in Java will look something like the following class:

```
public class MyResourceLoader extends GroovyResourceLoader {
    public URL loadGroovySource(final String filename)
        throws MalformedURLException {
        URL url = ... // create the URL pointing at the resource
        return url;
    }
}
```

NOTE *Extending* URL *and* URLConnection—As was the case with GroovyScript-Engine, if you are creating your own URL and URLConnection derived classes, make sure your URL overrides its openConnection method, which returns an instance of URLConnection; and make sure you also override the getLastModified, getURL, and getInputStream methods of the returned URLConnection.

Once you have defined this class, you have to register it in your classloader before use:

```
GroovyClassLoader gcl = new GroovyClassLoader();
gcl.setResourceLoader(new MyResourceLoader());
```

Your classloader will now use your resource loader to find the resources it needs from wherever you want! At this point, you may find that you have less control than you like over what code is executed. You may need to lock down how much access the code has to the rest of the system, depending on how much you know about the code's origins. This is where the Java and Groovy security model come into play, as you'll see in the next section.

11.4.4 *Playing it safe in a secured sandbox*

When packaging an application, you know all your source code is trusted. When you open the doors for some dynamic code that might evolve over time, such as changing business rules due to a legislation change, you have to be sure that this code can be trusted too. Only trusted users should be able to change the dynamic code by logging in and providing the relevant credentials. But even with authentication and authorization in place, you're never sheltered against human mistakes. That is why Groovy provides a second level of confidence in dynamic code in the form of a secured sandbox that you can set up to load this foreign code.

Modifying, loading, and executing dynamic code at runtime is a nice way to extend your application in an agile way, lessening the time required to adapt it as necessary. Long and tedious repackaging, requalifying, and redeployment scenarios can vanish in no time. This is not a subject to take lightly, and of course, you will always have to hand over your application to the acceptance team and pass the relevant integration tests; but embedding code from a scripting language in your application can help you to be more versatile when the requirements are changing.

The Java security model

However cool embedding a scripting or dynamic language can be, and however well designed your system is in terms of security, you can potentially add another layer of trust by letting this code run in a secured sandbox. Java provides the infrastructure for securing source code through its security model with the help of a *security manager* and the associated *policy* that dictates what permissions are granted to the code. For a simple example of what harm can happen to your application, imagine a user uploads a script containing System.exit(1): Your whole system could go down in a second if it's not secured correctly! Fortunately, with some setup, it is possible to protect yourself from such malicious code.

> **JAVA SECURITY** Covering the whole Java security model with its security managers, permissions, and policy files is beyond the scope of this chapter. We assume that you are already familiar with these concepts. If this is not the case, we recommend that you look at the online resources provided on Sun's web site to get an in-depth view of how security works on the Java platform.

In the Java security model, code sources are granted permissions according to their *code source*. A code source is composed of a *codebase* in the form of a URL from which the source code was loaded by the classloader, and potentially a certificate used to verify the code when it is obtained from a signed jar file.

There are two cases you have to consider. If all your Groovy sources are compiled first into .class files and eventually bundled in a jar file, the standard security mechanisms apply. Those classes are like normal Java compiled sources, so you can always use the same security managers as normal. But when you are compiling Groovy sources on the fly, through the various integration means we have studied so far, extra steps need to be followed.

GroovyCodeSource and the security manager

When scripts and classes are loaded from the filesystem, they are loaded by a GroovyClassLoader, which searches the classpath for Groovy files and gives them a code source constructed from a codebase built from the URL of the source file. When Groovy sources are loaded from an input stream or from a string, no particular URL is associated with them. However, it is possible to associate a codebase with Groovy sources to be compiled by specifying a GroovyCodeSource—as long as the caller loading sources has the permission to specify the codebase. The codebase you associate with the sources need not refer to a real physical location. Its importance is to the security manager and policy, which allocate permissions based on URLs.

A concrete example is always better than long explanations. Say we are running an application on a server, and this application loads Groovy scripts that need to be sandboxed and should only be allowed to access the `file.encoding` system property. The server application should have all possible permissions; however, we have to restrict the loaded Groovy script reading the property. We write a policy file explicitly indicating those rules:

```
grant codeBase "file:${server.home}/classes/-" {
    permission java.security.AllPermission;
};

grant codeBase "file:/restricted" {
    permission java.util.PropertyPermission "file.encoding", "read";
};
```

The first part grants all permissions to our server application, whereas the second part only allows the scripts from the `file:/restricted` codebase to access the `file.encoding` property in read-only mode. This policy file should be available in the classpath of the application, and the system property `java.security.policy` defining the policy file to use should be specified either on the command line that launches the JVM or in code.

A script requesting to read the system property would include code such as:

```
def encoding = System.getProperty("file.encoding")
```

Your server application will load and evaluate the script using `GroovyShell`, using the methods that take a `GroovyCodeSource` to wrap the script and define its code source:

```
def script = '''
    System.getProperty("file.encoding")
'''
def gcs = new GroovyCodeSource(script, "ScriptName", "/restricted")
def shell = new GroovyShell()
println shell.evaluate(gcs)
```

A `GroovyCodeSource` can be built in various ways depending on how you retrieve the source code: from a string, a file, an input stream, or a URL. Here are the four constructors that allow you to build a `GroovyCodeSource`:

```
public GroovyCodeSource(String script, String name, String codeBase)
public GroovyCodeSource(InputStream inputStream, String name,
                        String codeBase)
public GroovyCodeSource(File file) throws FileNotFoundException
public GroovyCodeSource(URL url) throws IOException
```

In order for the calling application to be able to create a `GroovyCodeSource` with a specific codebase, it must be granted permission by the policy. The specific permission required is a `groovy.security.GroovyCodeSourcePermission`, which the calling application implicitly has because the policy file granted it the `java.security.AllPermission`, which grants all possible rights.

GroovyShell and GroovyClassLoader with GroovyCodeSource

Both `GroovyShell` and `GroovyClassLoader` allow you to specify `GroovyCodeSources` to wrap scripts or classes that must be secured—but `GroovyScriptEngine` doesn't at the time of writing. If the Groovy source code is not wrapped inside a `GroovyCodeSource`, the policy will not be enforced, thus letting untrusted code run within the application.

In the sections related to `GroovyShell` and `GroovyClassLoader`, we enumerated several methods that allow you to evaluate, parse, or run Groovy scripts and classes. Let us mention now the methods that take a `GroovyCodeSource`, which you can use to make integrating dynamic code safer.

`GroovyShell` has two methods that take a `GroovyCodeSource`, one for evaluating scripts, and the other for parsing scripts:

```
public Object evaluate(GroovyCodeSource codeSource)
    throws CompilationFailedException
public Script parse(GroovyCodeSource codeSource)
    throws CompilationFailedException
```

`GroovyClassLoader` also has two methods; both parse classes, but the latter also provides an option to control whether the parsed class should be put in the classloader cache:

```
public Class parseClass(GroovyCodeSource codeSource)
    throws CompilationFailedException
public Class parseClass(GroovyCodeSource codeSource,
                        boolean shouldCache)
    throws CompilationFailedException
```

Armed with different means of integrating Groovy securely in your application, you can build extremely flexible applications. Of course, those mechanisms are specific to Groovy. These aren't the only means available, however. If you are using the Spring framework as a common base for your application, or if you are living on the edge and already using the pre-release builds of the next generation Java platform (JDK 6.0—Mustang), you can use the mechanisms provided in these platforms to load your dynamic code in a way that would make it easy to move away from Groovy, should you ever wish to.[6]

---

[6] Not that we can think of any reason why you'd want to, but we like the principle of avoiding vendor lock-in where possible.

11.5 *Spring integration*

As it says on the tin, Spring is an innovative layered Java/J2EE application framework and lightweight container invented by Rod Johnson, which matured while Rod was writing the book *Expert One-on-One J2EE Design and Development*. Spring generalized the concepts and patterns of *Inversion of Control (IoC)* and *Dependency Injection (DI)* and is built from two main building blocks: its IoC container and its *Aspect Oriented Programming (AOP)* system. The framework brings an additional abstraction layer that wraps common APIs such as transactions, JDBC, or Hibernate to help the developer focus on the core business tasks; gives access to AOP; and even provides its own *Model View Controller (MVC)* technology. The Spring framework can be used as a whole or piece by piece as needs arise.

Spring lets you wire your application components through dependency injection by instantiating, configuring, and defining the relationships between your objects in a central XML configuration file. Your objects are usually Plain Old Java Objects (POJOs), but they can also be Plain Old Groovy Objects (POGOs) because Groovy objects are also standard JavaBeans! This section explores how you can inject Groovy dependencies in your application object model, with options for letting beans refresh themselves automatically and specifying the bodies of scripts directly in the configuration file.

Spring 2.0 introduces support for integrating beans written in various scripting languages. Spring supports Groovy, BeanShell, and JRuby—some of the best known and proven scripting languages for the JVM. With this support, any number of classes written in these languages can be wired and injected in your application as transparently as if they were normal Java objects.

> **NOTE** *Spring Framework documentation*—It is beyond the scope of this section to explain how Spring can be installed, used, or configured. We are assuming that the interested reader is already familiar with the framework. If this is not the case, the creators of Spring have comprehensive and detailed online documentation at http://www.springframework.org/documentation that should be ideal for discovering what it is all about.

We will explain how you can wire up POGOs in Spring, discuss reloading Groovy source code on the fly, and finally cover how Groovy source can be specified directly in the configuration file, where appropriate. Let's start with the simplest situation before working our way toward more complicated scenarios.

11.5.1 *Wiring GroovyBeans*

Let's take the shape information classes from section 11.4 as an example.

We are going to use Spring's bean factory to create the Groovy objects that our main program needs. All the definitions for our class are captured declaratively in a Spring configuration file, sometimes referred to as a *wiring XML file*. This is illustrated in figure 11.6.

We would normally wire both Java and Groovy classes in the wiring file and also indicate the dependencies between the different parts of our system in this file. In this case, though, we are going to keep it simple. We are going to specify simple definitions in the file to illustrate integration between Spring and Groovy. For now, we assume that all of our Groovy files are precompiled.

Here is what the Spring definition file, called beans.xml in our case, looks like:

```xml
<?xml version="1.0" encoding="UTF-8"?>
<beans>
  <bean id="circle" class="spring.groovy.Circle">
    <constructor-arg value="4"/>
    <property name="color" value="Black"/>
  </bean>
  <bean id="maxareainfo" class="spring.groovy.MaxAreaInfo"/>
</beans>
```

In our Groovy source file, we have the same constructor that we had previously, and we have also added a `color` property to our `Circle` class. In the Spring definition file, the nested `constructor` element indicates the value to pass to the constructor during creation of our `Circle`. The `property` element indicates that the `color` property should also be set as part of initialization. To make use of these definitions, we need to change our `main` method in `ShapeInfoMain` to become

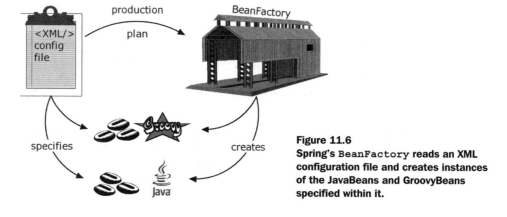

Figure 11.6
Spring's BeanFactory reads an XML configuration file and creates instances of the JavaBeans and GroovyBeans specified within it.

```
try {
    ApplicationContext ctx =
        new ClassPathXmlApplicationContext("beans.xml");
    Shape s = new Square(7);
    Shape c = (Shape) ctx.getBean("circle");
    ShapeInfo info = (ShapeInfo) ctx.getBean("maxareainfo");
    info.displayInfo(s, c);
    new MaxPerimeterInfo().displayInfo(s, c);
} catch (Exception e) {
    e.printStackTrace();
}
```

Spring provides a number of mechanisms to create beans for you. In this instance, we use what is called the *application context*. It has a getBean method that allows us to ask for a bean by name.

As we mentioned earlier, we are assuming here that all of our Groovy classes are precompiled. So, what have we gained? We have begun the process of removing explicit dependencies from our codebase. Over time, we could start moving more dependency information into the wiring file and allow our system to be configured more readily. As a consequence, our design also becomes more flexible, because we can swap our concrete implementations readily. This is particularly important for unit testing, where we might replace concrete implementations with mock implementations.

There is more we can do, though: Spring supports dynamic compilation of our Groovy scripts through a special Groovy factory class. Here is how we would use it. We would extend our bean configuration file as follows:

```
...
<lang:groovy id="maxareainfo2"
        script-source="classpath:MaxAreaInfo.groovy">
    <lang:property name="prefix" value="Live Groovy says" />
</lang:groovy>
...
```

Spring 2.0 supports a number of dynamic scripting languages through special language-specific factories. The namespace lang:groovy accesses the special Groovy factory automatically. Now we can use maxareainfo2 as the name we pass to the bean factory when creating our bean, and Spring will automatically compile the necessary Groovy source files.

Note that unlike the previous wiring file, which could mix setter and constructor-based injection, at the time of writing, only setter-based injection is supported when using the lang:groovy mechanisms.

11.5.2 *Refreshable beans*

Another feature that Spring provides is the ability to dynamically detect when Groovy source files change and automatically compile and load the latest version of any Groovy file during runtime. The concept is known as *refreshable beans* and is enabled in our definition file using the `refresh-check-delay` attribute as follows (in this case, setting the delay to five seconds):

```
...
<lang:groovy id="maxareainfo2"
        refresh-check-delay="5000"
        script-source="classpath:MaxAreaInfo.groovy">
    <lang:property name="prefix" value="Live Groovy says" />
</lang:groovy>
...
```

Refreshing beans on the fly can make development faster, but you should consider disabling it again for production systems—restarting the system after a change has been made tends to avoid confusing situations where for some period of time (however brief) only *part* of the system has seen the refresh.

11.5.3 *Inline scripts*

Although it's arguably a bad idea to put code inside Spring's configuration file, Spring offers another way to define scripted beans by *inlining* them—including the source directly in the configuration file. The Spring documentation mentions some scenarios for such a case, such as sketching and defining validators for Spring MVC controllers or scripting controllers for quick prototyping or defining logic flow.

In listing 11.11, we inline a variation of `MaxAreaInfo` (we need to change our factory `getBean` call to use `maxareainfo3`).

Listing 11.11 Spring configuration with inline Groovy class

```
<lang:groovy id="maxareainfo3">        <──  Tell Spring we're using Groovy
    <lang:inline-script>                <─┐  Define the class we
    import spring.common.Shape            │  want an instance of
    import spring.common.ShapeInfo

    class SuffixMaxAreaInfo implements ShapeInfo {
        String suffix
        void displayInfo(Shape s1, Shape s2) {
            print "The shape with the biggest area is: "
            if (s1.area() > s2.area()) println s1 + ":" + suffix
            else println s2 + ":" + suffix
        }
```

```
    }
    </lang:inline-script>
    <lang:property name="suffix"
                   value="Did you guess correctly?"/>
</lang:groovy>
```

Specify a bean property

In this case, because the content is hard-coded, setting the refreshable attribute of the script factory doesn't apply for those inline scripted beans. One last remark: If your script contains a less-than sign (<), the XML Spring configuration will be invalid, because the XML parser will think it is the start of a new tag. To circumvent this problem, you should wrap the whole scripted bean in a CDATA section.

This has been a brief introduction to the scripting bean capabilities of Spring 2.0. For further details and more in-depth explanations, we suggest you refer to the project documentation available at http://www.springframework.org.

Spring isn't the only recent technology to embrace scripting, however. The following section looks forward to the next release of the Java platform and explores what support will be provided for Groovy integration.

11.6 Riding Mustang and JSR-223

Scripting and dynamic languages are in fashion again thanks to Groovy, Asynchronous JavaScript And XML (AJAX) as popularized by Google, and the Ruby on Rails web framework. This frenzy led Sun to recognize that for certain tasks, scripting languages can help to simplify the development of applications. New Java Specification Requests have been accepted by the Java Community Process to standardize languages such as Groovy and BeanShell, and to create a common API allowing access to various scripting engines from your Java applications.

This section guides you through running Groovy scripts in the new "Java standard" way, highlighting the features of the new API as well as some ways in which it is unavoidably clunky.

11.6.1 Introducing JSR-223

JSR-223, titled "Scripting for the Java Platform," provides a set of classes and interfaces used to hold and register scripting engines and to represent scripts, namespaces of *key/value* pairs available to scripts, or execution contexts. Like all JSRs, JSR-223 provides three key deliverables: a specification document, a *reference implementation (RI)* implementing the specification, and a test compatibility kit that can be used to check that the specification is accurately and fully implemented. The RI is already usable and can be downloaded from the dedicated web site as long as you are using at least Java 5. It offers an elegant and simple API that supports a few scripting languages—Groovy being one of them. Out of the box, the RI doesn't provide the runtime environments of those engines except for Rhino's JavaScript, so in order to use the Groovy engine, you will have to download Groovy and its JSR-223 engine from http://scripting.dev.java.net. A disadvantage of the RI is that it might not always be in sync with Mustang's scripting APIs, so you will have to check the potential differences in the APIs. Here, we'll focus on the ones delivered by Mustang, rather than the RI. But if you need to use the latest `javax.script.*` classes from Mustang, it will also mean you must develop and deploy your applications with JDK 6, whereas the RI allows you to use JDK 5.

Before studying what JSR-223 brings to the table, we should mention that this API is particularly important because it is included by default in Mustang, the next version of the Java Platform—Java SE 6. This means that scripting finds its way in the JDK and will certainly become the preferred way for integrating scripting languages in your applications. This is also why we haven't covered the use of Apache Bean Scripting Framework (BSF), because although it provides a similar API in terms of functionality, it will progressively be abandoned in favor of JSR-223.

Mustang already provides support for the new `javax.script.*` interfaces and classes. It also distributes a new command-line tool called `jrunscript` to run scripts, which is a bit like Groovy's own `groovy` and `groovysh` commands. Here is the usage of this new tool:

```
Usage: jrunscript [options] [arguments...]
where [options] include:
-classpath, -cp <path>     Specify where to find user class files
-D<name>=<value>           Set a system property
-J<flag>                   Pass <flag> directly to the runtime system
-l <language>              Use specified scripting language
-e <script>                Evaluate given script
-encoding <encoding>       Specify character encoding used by script files
-f <script file>           Evaluate given script file
-f -                       Interactive mode, read script from
                           standard input
-q                         List all scripting engines available and exit
```

Although the command line enables you to execute Groovy through the new API without writing any code to do so, if your application is going to embed Groovy, you'll be using the API directly rather than relying on the tool. Let's meet the core classes involved in running scripts through JSR-223.

11.6.2 *The script engine manager and its script engines*

The main entry point of the JSR-223 API is `javax.script.ScriptEngineManager`. To get started, create an instance of this class from your Java application:

```
ScriptEngineManager manager = new ScriptEngineManager();
```

The manager is able to retrieve script engines through different lookup mechanisms: by file extension, by mime type, or by name, with three dedicated methods:

```
ScriptEngine getEngineByExtension(java.lang.String extension)
ScriptEngine getEngineByMimeType (java.lang.String mimeType)
ScriptEngine getEngineByName     (java.lang.String shortName)
```

So, if you want to retrieve the Groovy script engine supplied with the reference implementation, you can look it up by name:

```
ScriptEngine gEngine = manager.getEngineByName("groovy");
```

With a `ScriptEngine`, you can evaluate Groovy expressions and scripts provided through an instance of `Reader` or of a `String` with the set of `eval` methods, which return an `Object` as the result of the evaluation. You can evaluate a simple expression as follows:

```
ScriptEngineManager manager = new ScriptEngineManager();
ScriptEngine gEngine = manager.getEngineByName("groovy");
String result = (String)gEngine.eval("'+-----' * 3 + '+'");
```

Here are the other `eval` methods available:

```
Object eval(java.io.Reader    reader)
Object eval(java.io.Reader    reader, Bindings b)
Object eval(java.io.Reader    reader, ScriptContext context)
Object eval(java.lang.String script)
Object eval(java.lang.String script, Bindings b)
Object eval(java.lang.String script, ScriptContext context)
```

They can throw a `ScriptException`, which can contain a root exception cause, a message, a filename, and even a line number and column number where an error occurred, particularly when the error is a compilation error. The optional `ScriptContext` parameters correspond to the environment within which a script is evaluated, and a `Bindings` is a special map containing an association between a key and an object you want to pass to your scripts. These affect what information is available to your scripts and how different scripts can pass each other data. See the detailed JSR-223 documentation for more information on this topic.

11.6.3 *Compilable and invocable script engines*

Beyond the basic script-evaluation capabilities, the Groovy engine also implements two other interfaces: `javax.script.Compilable` and `javax.script.Invocable`. The first lets you precompile and reuse scripts, and the latter lets you execute a method, a unit of execution, rather than executing a whole script as you do with the `eval` method. Implementing these interfaces is not mandatory, but the Groovy engine provides this feature:

```java
// Java
ScriptEngineManager manager = new ScriptEngineManager();
ScriptEngine gEngine  = manager.getEngineByName("groovy");
Compilable compilable = (Compilable)gEngine;
compilable.put("name", "Dierk");
CompiledScript script = compilable.compile("return name");
String dierksName      = script.eval();
compilable.put("name", "Guillaume");
String guillaumesName = script.eval();
```

Once you've got a handle on the `Compilable` engine (by casting the engine to the `Compilable` interface), you can call two `compile` methods that either take a reader or a string containing the script to precompile. These methods return an instance of `CompiledScript`, which holds a precompiled script that you can execute several times at will without the need to reparse or recompile it. Then, the `Compiled-Script` can be evaluated with three `eval` methods: one without any parameters, one taking a `Namespace`, and the last taking a `ScriptContext`.

Even after precompiling a script, you still can't directly call methods declared in that script. The `javax.script.Invocable` interface makes this possible in a manner reminiscent of calling normal Java methods with reflection.

Imagine we have a script whose role is to change a string parameter into its uppercase representation:

```java
// Java
ScriptEngineManager manager = new ScriptEngineManager();
ScriptEngine gEngine = manager.getEngineByName("groovy");

Invocable invocable  = (Invocable)gEngine;
invocable.eval("def upper(s) { s.toUpperCase() }");
Object s = invocable.invokeFunction("upper", "Groovy");

invocable.eval("def add(a, b) { a + b }");
invocable.invokeFunction("add", new Integer(1), new Integer(2));

assertTrue(invocable.invokeMethod(s, "endsWith", "Y"));
```

The script is evaluated and retained in the script-execution context; then, the defined function can be called with the invokeFunction method, which takes the name of the function to call and a vararg list of objects to pass to the underlying scripted function as parameters. Be careful, though, because you can only invoke functions defined in the last evaluated script. An invokeMethod method goes further and lets you call arbitrary methods on objects resulting from the execution of scripts. This is how we call the endsWith method on the string returned by the first function invoked and pass it the letter *Y* as an argument.

Of course, in the last case, we could have cast the return value of upper to String directly. Although this may seem obvious, it's possible because Groovy plays nicely with Java, returning real and normal classes. Some other scripting languages would return some kind of proxy or wrapper, making the integration with Java trickier.

Despite the convenience of being able to call any function defined in a script, it is not yet as Java friendly as we might hope. Nevertheless, the Invocable interface gives you another handy method for your toolbox: the getInterface method. With this method, you can create a proxy of a given interface that will delegate all method invocations to methods defined in the script.

Say we have a Java interface representing a business service like the following one:

```
// Java
interface BusinessService {
    void    init();
    Object  execute(Object[] parameters);
    void    release();
}
```

We create a script that contains functions mapping the same signatures as the ones provided in the BusinessService interface:

```
// Groovy
void init() { println "init" }
Object execute(Object[] objs) { println "execute" }
void release() { println "release" }
```

We can make such a script appear to implement the BusinessService interface by calling the getInterface method of the invocable script engine:

```
// Java
ScriptEngineManager manager = new ScriptEngineManager();
ScriptEngine gEngine = manager.getEngineByName("groovy");
Invocable invocable = (Invocable)gEngine;
invocable.eval(scriptAsAString);
```

```
BusinessService service =
        invocable.getInterface(BusinessService.class);

service.init();
Object result = service.execute(new Object[] {});
service.release();
```

First, we evaluate the script shown earlier, then we call the `getInterface` method with the class of the implementation we want our script to implement, and then we retrieve an instance implementing that interface. Our script doesn't even have to explicitly implement the `BusinessService` interface, but through the proxy mechanism, it appears as if it were the case. With such a mechanism, you can manipulate scripts as if they were normal Java beans, without having to call some kind of `invoke` method.

You now know about the native Groovy techniques to integrate Groovy in your Java application and the more language-neutral solutions using Spring or JSR-223. The great thing about this is that it presents you with a choice. The downside is that you need to make a decision, so we provide some guidance in the last section of this chapter.

11.7 *Choosing an integration mechanism*

This section is similar to the first one in the chapter, in that we can't make any decisions for you. Good guidance *tends* to be right more than it's wrong, but there will always be cases that appear to fit one pattern but that benefit more from another after close examination. We don't know what your needs are, so we can't make that close examination. All we can do is give suggestions and reasons for them.

To give a good rule of thumb, if your application is built on Spring, you should prefer using the Spring integration. If you are able to use Java 6 and want to be able to change or mix various scripting languages at the same time, or you have the freedom to change at will, using the scripting integration of JSR-223 makes perfect sense. But if you want to do more advanced things or if you are concerned about the potential security hole opened by dynamic code, you should probably choose some of the standard Groovy mechanisms for embedding and executing Groovy code with `GroovyShell`, `GroovyScriptEngine`, or the almighty `GroovyClassLoader`. Table 11.3 shows a summary of the pros and cons of each integration mechanism.

The basis of Groovy's integration is its excellent compatibility with Java. We've listed the most common ways of integrating Groovy with Java, but anywhere that

Table 11.3 The sweet spots and limitations of the different integration mechanisms

Mechanism	Sweet spot	Limitations
GroovyShell	Perfect for single-line user input and small expressions Supports reloading Robust security available	Will not scale to dependent scripts
GroovyScriptEngine	Nice for dependent scripts Supports reloading	Does not support classes Does not support security
GroovyClassLoader	Most powerful integration mechanism Supports reloading Robust security available	Trickier to handle in the case of a complex classloader hierarchy
Spring scripting support	Integrates well with Spring Lets you switch languages easily Supports reloading	Requires Spring
JSR-223	Lets you switch languages easily	Requires Java 6 Does not support security Does not support reloading
Bean Scripting Framework	Lets you switch languages easily Doesn't require Java 6	Does not support security Does not support reloading More limited capabilities than JSR-223

Java can be integrated, Groovy can work too. Some databases allow stored procedures to be written in Java, for instance—so Groovy can be used in the same way. Additional integration mechanisms may well appear over time in various guises—don't assume that the options given here are exhaustive!

11.8 *Summary*

This chapter has given you glimpses into how you might allow your applications to become more flexible, giving appropriate users the ability to customize behavior in a way that may enable them to solve the *exact* problem they are facing, rather than the one that was as close as you could imagine when designing the application.

The means of integrating Groovy into your application broadly fall into two camps: those provided directly by the Groovy libraries and those provided in a language-neutral fashion by Spring and Java 6 through JSR-223. As is often the case, the more specific solutions prove to be the most powerful ones, at the cost of language neutrality.

As bookends to the chapter, we discussed the kinds of applications that benefit from this sort of integration and gave some guidance as to which integration mechanism might be best for your situation.

Scripting languages in one form or another have always been common on various systems, from DOS's command shell to the widespread Perl on many Unix and Linux systems. They give a good return on investment because of their ease of use and because they do what you need them to do with less deployment overhead and reduced boilerplate code. But they have often failed to become general-purpose languages for building enterprise applications. With scripting languages coming to a JVM near you, you can benefit from the advantages of both worlds: You can build big and scalable enterprise applications while still using scripting languages for the customization logic, allowing you to profit from their agility through their expressiveness and advanced power features.

Working with XML

12

Perfection is achieved not when you have nothing more to add, but when you have nothing left to take away.

—Antoine de Saint-Exupery

XML, the eXtensible Markup Language, is a reasonably young innovation. It's just becoming a teenager, but we use it so commonly these days that it's hard to believe there were times without it. The World Wide Web Consortium (W3C) standardized the first version of XML in 1996.

The widespread use of XML and worldwide adoption of Java took place at about the same time. This may be one of the reasons why the Java platform developed such excellent support for working with XML. Not only are there the built-in SAX and DOM APIs, but many other libraries have appeared over time for parsing and creating XML and for working with it using standards such as XPath.

The topic of XML has the unusual property of being simple and complex at the same time. XML is straightforward until you bring in namespaces, entities, and the like. Similarly, although it's feasible to demonstrate *one* way of working with XML fairly simply, giving a good overview of *all* (or even most) of the ways of working with XML would require more space than we have in this book. We will concentrate on the new capabilities that Groovy brings, as well as mention the enhanced support for the DOM API. Even limiting ourselves to these topics doesn't let us explore every nook and cranny.

This chapter is broadly divided into three parts. First, you'll see the different techniques available for parsing XML in Groovy. Second, you will learn some tricks about processing and transforming XML. Finally, we will examine the Groovy support for web services—one of the most common uses of XML in business today.

We assume you already have a reasonable understanding of XML. If you find yourself struggling with any of the XML concepts we use in this chapter, please refer to one of the many available XML books.[1]

XML processing typically starts with reading an XML document, which is our first topic.

12.1 Reading XML documents

When working with XML, we have to somehow *read* it to begin with. This section will lead you through the many options available in Groovy for parsing XML: the normal DOM route, enhanced by Groovy; Groovy's own `XmlParser` and `XmlSlurper` classes; SAX event-based parsing; and the recently introduced StAX pull-parsers.

---

[1] We recommend *XML Made Simple* by Deane and Henderson (Made Simple, 2003) as an introductory text and *XML 1.1 Bible* by Elliotte Rusty Harold (Wiley, 2004) for more comprehensive coverage.

Let's suppose we have a little datastore in XML format for planning our Groovy self-education activities. In this datastore, we capture how many hours per week we can invest in this training, what tasks need to be done, and how many hours each task will eat up in total. To keep track of our progress, we will also store how many hours are "done" for each task.

Listing 12.1 shows our XML datastore as it resides in a file named data/plan.xml.

Listing 12.1 The example datastore data/plan.xml

```
<plan>
    <week capacity="8">
        <task done="2" total="2" title="read XML chapter"/>
        <task done="3" total="3" title="try some reporting"/>
        <task done="1" total="2" title="use in current project"/>
    </week>
    <week capacity="8">
        <task done="0" total="1" title="re-read DB chapter"/>
        <task done="0" total="3" title="use DB/XML combination"/>
    </week>
</plan>
```

We plan for two weeks, with eight hours for education each week. Three tasks are scheduled for the current week: reading this chapter (two hours for a quick reader), playing with the newly acquired knowledge (three hours of real fun), and using it in the real world (one hour done and one still left).

This will be our running example for most of the chapter.

For reading such a datastore, we will present several different approaches: first using technologies built into the JRE, and then using the Groovy parsers. We'll start with the more familiar DOM parser.

12.1.1 *Working with a DOM parser*

Why do we bother with Java's classic DOM parsers? Shouldn't we restrict ourselves to show only Groovy specifics here?

Well, first of all, even in Groovy code, we sometimes need DOM objects for further processing, for example when applying XPath expressions to an object as we will explain in section 12.2.3. For that reason, we show the Groovy way of retrieving the DOM representation of our datastore with the help of Java's DOM parsers. Second, there is basic Groovy support for dealing with DOM `NodeLists`, and Groovy also provides extra helper classes to simplify common tasks within DOM.

Finally, it's much easier to appreciate how slick the Groovy parsers are after having seen the "old" way of reading XML.

We start by loading a DOM tree into memory.

Getting the document

Not surprisingly, the Document Object Model is based around the central abstraction of a *document*, realized as the Java interface org.w3c.dom.Document. An object of this type will hold our datastore.

The Java way of retrieving a document is through the parse method of a DocumentBuilder (= parser). This method takes an InputStream to read the XML from. So a first attempt of reading is

```
def doc = builder.parse(new FileInputStream('data/plan.xml'))
```

Now, where does builder come from? We are working slowly backward to find a solution. The builder must be of type DocumentBuilder. Instances of this type are delivered from a DocumentBuilderFactory, which has a factory method called newDocumentBuilder:

```
def builder = fac.newDocumentBuilder()
def doc     = builder.parse(new FileInputStream('data/plan.xml'))
```

Now, where does this factory come from? Here it is:

```
import javax.xml.parsers.DocumentBuilderFactory

def fac     = DocumentBuilderFactory.newInstance()
def builder = fac.newDocumentBuilder()
def doc     = builder.parse(new FileInputStream('data/plan.xml'))
```

Java's XML handling API is designed with flexibility in mind.[2] A downside of this flexibility is that for our simple example, we have a few hoops to jump through in order to retrieve our file. It's not too bad, though, and now that we have it we can dive into the document.

Walking the DOM

The document object is not yet the root of our datastore. In order to get the top-level element, which is plan in our case, we have to ask the document for its documentElement property:

```
def plan = doc.documentElement
```

---

[2] The DocumentBuilderFactory can be augmented in several ways to deliver various DocumentBuilder implementations. See its API documentation for details.

We can now work with the `plan` variable. It's of type `org.w3c.dom.Node` and so it can be asked for its `nodeType` and `nodeName`. The `nodeType` is `Node.ELEMENT_NODE`, and `nodeName` is `plan`.

The design of such DOM nodes is a bit strange (to put it mildly). Every node has the same properties, such as `nodeType`, `nodeName`, `nodeValue`, `childNodes`, and `attributes` (to name only a few; see the API documentation for the full list). However, what is stored in these properties and how they behave depends on the value of the `nodeType` property.

We will deal with types `ELEMENT_NODE`, `ATTRIBUTE_NODE`, and `TEXT_NODE` (see the API documentation for the exhaustive list).

It is not surprising that XML elements are stored in nodes of type `ELEMENT_NODE`, but it is surprising that attributes are also stored in node objects (of `nodeType` `ATTRIBUTE_NODE`). To make things even more complex, each value of an attribute is stored in an extra node object (with `nodeType` `TEXT_NODE`). This complexity is a large part of the reason why simpler APIs such as JDOM, dom4j, and XOM have become popular.

As an example, the nodes and their names, types, and values are depicted in figure 12.1 for the first `week` element in the datastore.

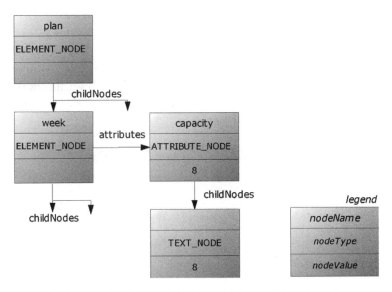

Figure 12.1   Example of a DOM object model (excerpt) for element, attribute, and text nodes

The fact that node objects behave differently with respect to their `nodeType` leads to code that needs to work with this distinction. For example, when reading information from a node, we need a method such as this:

```
import org.w3c.dom.Node

String info(node) {
    switch (node.nodeType) {
        case Node.ELEMENT_NODE:
            return 'element: '+ node.nodeName
        case Node.ATTRIBUTE_NODE:
            return "attribute: ${node.nodeName}=${node.nodeValue}"
        case Node.TEXT_NODE:
            return 'text: '+ node.nodeValue
    }
    return 'some other type: '+ node.nodeType
}
```

With this helper method, we have almost everything we need to read information from our datastore. Two pieces of information are not yet explained: the types of the `childNodes` and `attributes` properties.

The `childNodes` property is of type `org.w3c.dom.NodeList`. Unfortunately, it doesn't extend the `java.util.List` interface but provides its own methods, `getLength` and `item(index)`. This makes it inconvenient to work with. However, as you saw in section 9.1.3, Groovy makes its object iteration methods (`each`, `find`, `findAll`, and so on) available on that type.

The `attributes` property is of type `org.w3c.dom.NamedNodeMap`, which doesn't extend `java.util.Map` either. We will use its `getNamedItem(name)` method.

Listing 12.2 puts all this together and reads our plan from the XML datastore, walking into the first task of the first week.

Listing 12.2   Reading plan.xml with the classic DOM parser

```
import javax.xml.parsers.DocumentBuilderFactory
import org.w3c.dom.Node

def fac     = DocumentBuilderFactory.newInstance()
def builder = fac.newDocumentBuilder()
def doc     = builder.parse(new FileInputStream('data/plan.xml'))
def plan    = doc.documentElement

String info(node) {
    switch (node.nodeType) {
        case Node.ELEMENT_NODE:
            return 'element: '+ node.nodeName
        case Node.ATTRIBUTE_NODE:
            return "attribute: ${node.nodeName}=${node.nodeValue}"
```

```
        case Node.TEXT_NODE:
            return 'text: '+ node.nodeValue
    }
    return 'some other type: '+ node.nodeType
}

assert 'element: plan' == info(plan)                              ❶ Object
                                                                     iteration
def week =  plan.childNodes.find{'week' == it.nodeName}  ⊲┘         method
assert 'element: week' == info(week)
                                          ❷  Indexed
                                              access
def task =  week.childNodes.item(1)    ⊲┘
assert 'element: task' == info(task)

def title = task.attributes.getNamedItem('title')
assert 'attribute: title=read XML chapter' == info(title)
```

Note how we use the object iteration method `find` ❶ to access the first `week` element under `plan`. We use indexed access to the first `task` child node at ❷. But why is the index *one* and not *zero*? Because in our XML document, there is a line break between `week` and `task`. The DOM parser generates a text node containing this line break (and surrounding whitespace) and adds it as the first child node of `week` (at index zero). The `task` node floats to the second position with index one.

Making DOM groovier

Groovy wouldn't be groovy without a convenience method for the lengthy parsing prework:

```
def doc  = groovy.xml.DOMBuilder.parse
                (new FileReader('data/plan.xml'))
def plan = doc.documentElement
```

> **NOTE**   The DOMBuilder is not only for convenient parsing. As the name suggests, it is a builder and can be used like any other builder (see chapter 8). It returns a tree of `org.w3c.dom.Node` objects just as if they'd been parsed from an XML document. You can add it to another tree, write it to XML, or query it using XPath (see section 12.2.3).

Dealing with child nodes and attributes as in listing 12.2 doesn't feel groovy either. Therefore, Groovy provides a `DOMCategory` that you can use for simplified access. With this, you can index child nodes via the subscript operator or via their node name. You can refer to attributes by getting the `@attributeName` property:

```
use(groovy.xml.dom.DOMCategory) {
    assert 'plan' == plan.nodeName
    assert 'week' == plan[1].nodeName
    assert 'week' == plan.week.nodeName
    assert '8'    == plan[1].'@capacity'
}
```

Although not shown in the example, DOMCategory has recently been improved to provide additional syntax shortcuts such as name, text, children, iterator, parent, and attributes. We explain these shortcuts later in this chapter, because they originated in Groovy's purpose-built XML parsing classes. Consult the online Groovy documentation for more details.

This was a lot of work to get the DOM parser to read our data, and we had to face some surprises along the way. We will now do the same task using the Groovy parser with less effort and fewer surprises.

12.1.2 *Reading with a Groovy parser*

The Groovy way of reading the plan datastore is so simple, we'll dive headfirst into the solution as presented in listing 12.3.

Listing 12.3 Reading plan.xml with Groovy's XmlParser

```
def plan = new XmlParser().parse(new File('data/plan.xml'))

assert 'plan' == plan.name()
assert 'week' == plan.week[0].name()
assert 'task' == plan.week[0].task[0].name()
assert 'read XML chapter' == plan.week[0].task[0].'@title'
```

No fluff, just stuff. The parsing is only a one-liner. Because Groovy's XmlParser resides in package groovy.util, we don't even need an import statement for that class. The parser can work directly on File objects and other input sources, as you will see in table 12.2. The parser returns a groovy.util.Node. You already came across this type in section 8.2. That means we can easily use GPath expressions to walk through the tree, as shown with the assert statements.

Up to this point, you have seen that Groovy's XmlParser provides all the functionality you first saw with the DOM parser. But there is more to come. In addition to the XmlParser, Groovy comes with the XmlSlurper. Let's explore the commonalities and differences between those two before considering more advanced usages of each.

Commonalities between XmlParser and XmlSlurper

Let's start with the commonalities of XmlParser and XmlSlurper: They both reside in package groovy.util and provide the constructors listed in table 12.1.

Table 12.1   Common constructors of XmlParser and XmlSlurper

Parameter list	Note
()	Parameterless constructor.
(boolean validating, boolean namespaceAware)	After parsing, the document can be validated against a declared DTD, and namespace declarations shall be taken into account.
(XMLReader reader)	If you already have a org.xml.sax.XMLReader available, it can be reused.
(SAXParser parser)	If you already have a javax.xml.parsers.SAXParser available, it can be reused.

Besides sharing constructors with the same parameter lists, the types share parsing methods with the same signatures. The only difference is that the parsing methods of XmlParser return objects of type groovy.util.Node whereas XmlSlurper returns GPathResult objects. Table 12.2 lists the uniform parse methods.

Table 12.2   Parse methods common to XmlParser and XmlSlurper

Signature	Note
parse(InputSource input)	Reads from an org.xml.sax.InputSource
parse(File file)	Reads from an java.io.File
parse(InputStream input)	Reads from an java.io.InputStream
parse(Reader in)	Reads from an java.io.Reader
parse(String uri)	Reads the resource that the uri points to after connecting to it
parseText(String text)	Uses the text as input

These are the most commonly used methods on XmlParser and XmlSlurper. The description of additional methods (such as for using specialized DTD handlers and entity resolvers) is in the API documentation.

The result of the parse method is either a Node (for XmlParser) or a GPathResult (for XmlSlurper). Table 12.3 lists the common available methods for both result types. Note that because both types understand the `iterator` method, all object iteration methods are also instantly available.

GPathResult and `groovy.util.Node` provide additional shortcuts for method calls to the parent object and all descendent objects. Such shortcuts make reading a GPath expression more like other declarative path expressions such as XPath or Ant paths.[3]

Table 12.3 Common methods of `groovy.util.Node` and `GPathResult`

Node method		GPathResult method		Shortcut
Object	name()	String	name()	
String	text()	String	text()	
String	toString()	String	toString()	
Node	parent()	GPathResult	parent()	`'..'`
List	children()	GPathResult	children()	`'*'`
Map	attributes()[a]	Map	attributes()	
Iterator	iterator()	Iterator	iterator()	
List	depthFirst()	Iterator	depthFirst()	`'**'`
List	breadthFirst()	Iterator	breadthFirst()	

a. Strictly speaking, `attributes()` is a method of `NodeChild`, not `GPathResult`, but this is transparent in most usages.

Objects of type `Node` and `GPathResult` can access both child elements and attributes as if they were properties of the current object. Table 12.4 shows the syntax and how the leading @ sign distinguishes attribute names from nested element names.

Table 12.4 Element and attribute access in `groovy.util.Node` and `GPathResult`

Node (XmlParser)	GPathResult (XmlSlurper)	Meaning
`['elementName']`	`['elementName']`	All child elements of that name
`.elementName`	`.elementName`	

continued on next page

---

[3] See http://ant.apache.org/manual/using.html#path.

Table 12.4   Element and attribute access in `groovy.util.Node` **and** `GPathResult` *(continued)*

Node (XmlParser)	GPathResult (XmlSlurper)	Meaning
`[index]`	`[index]`	Child element by index

`['@attributeName']`
 	
`.'@attributeName'`
	`['@attributeName']`
	
	`.'@attributeName'`
	
	`.@attributeName`
		The attribute value stored under that name

Listing 12.4 plays with various method calls and uses GPath expressions to work on objects of type `Node` and `GPathResult` alike. It uses `XmlParser` to return `Node` objects and `XmlSlurper` to return a `GPathResult`. To make the similarities stand out, listing 12.4 shows doubled lines, one using `Node`, one using `GPathResult`.

Listing 12.4   Using common methods of `groovy.util.Node` **and** `GPathResult`

```
def node = new XmlParser().parse(new File('data/plan.xml'))
def path = new XmlSlurper().parse(new File('data/plan.xml'))

assert 'plan' == node.name()
assert 'plan' == path.name()

assert 2 == node.children().size()
assert 2 == path.children().size()

assert 5 == node.week.task.size()          ❶ All tasks
assert 5 == path.week.task.size()

                                                    ❷ All hours
                                                       done
assert 6 == node.week.task.'@done'*.toInteger().sum()   ◁

assert path.week[1].task.every{ it.'@done' == '0' }   ◁─❸ Second week
```

Note that the GPath expression `node.week.task` ❶ first collects all child elements named `week`, and then, for each of those, collects all their child elements named `task` (compare the second row in table 12.4). In the case of `node.week.task`, we have a `list` of `task` nodes that we can ask for its `size`. In the case of `path.week.task`, we have a `GPathResult` that we can ask for its `size`. The interesting thing here is that the `GPathResult` can determine the size without collecting intermediate results (such as `week` and `task` nodes) in a temporary datastructure such as a list. Instead, it stores whatever *iteration logic* is needed to determine the result and then executes that logic and returns the result (the `size` in this example).

At ❷, you see that in GPath, attribute access has the same effect as access to child elements; `node.week.task.'@done'` results in a list of all values of the `done` attribute of all `tasks` of all `weeks`. We use the spread-dot operator (see section 7.5.1) to apply the `toInteger` method to all strings in that list, returning a list of integers. We finally use the GDK method `sum` on that list.

The line at ❸ can be read as: "Assert that the `done` attribute in *every* task of `week[1]` is `'0'`." What's new here is using indexed access and the object iteration method `every`. Because indexing starts at zero, `week[1]` means the second week.

This example should serve as an appetizer for your own experiences with applying GPath expressions to XML documents.

In addition to the convenient GPath notation, you might also wish to make use of traversal methods; for example, we could add the following lines to listing 12.4:

```
assert 'plan->week->week->task->task->task->task->task' ==
        node.breadthFirst()*.name().join('->')

assert 'plan->week->task->task->task->week->task->task' ==
        node.depthFirst()*.name().join('->')
```

So far, you have seen that `XmlParser` and `XmlSlurper` can be used in a similar fashion to produce similar results. But there would be no need for two separate classes if there wasn't a difference. That's what we cover next.

Differences between XmlParser and XmlSlurper

Despite the similarities between `XmlParser` and `XmlSlurper` when used for simple reading purposes, there are differences when it comes to more advanced reading tasks and when processing XML documents into other formats.

`XmlParser` uses the `groovy.util.Node` type and its GPath expressions result in lists of nodes. That makes working with `XmlParser` feel like there always is a *tangible* object representation of elements—something that we can inspect via `toString`, print, or change in-place. Because GPath expressions return lists of such elements, we can apply all our knowledge of the `list` datatype (see section 4.2).

This convenience comes at the expense of additional up-front processing and extra memory consumption. The GPath expression `node.week.task.'@done'` generates three lists: a temporary list of weeks[4] (two entries), a temporary list of tasks (five entries), and a list of `done` attribute values (five strings) that is finally

---

[4] This is short for: a list of references to objects of type `groovy.util.Node` with `name()=='week'`.

returned. This is reasonable for our small example but hampers processing large or deeply nested XML documents.

XmlSlurper in contrast does not store intermediate results when processing information after a document has been parsed. It avoids the extra memory hit when processing. Internally, XmlSlurper uses iterators instead of extra collections to reflect every step in the GPath. With this construction, it is possible to defer processing until the last possible moment.

> **NOTE** This does not mean that XmlSlurper would work without storing the parsed information in memory. It still does, and the memory consumption rises with the size of the XML document. However, for *processing* that stored information via GPath, XmlSlurper does not need *extra* memory.

Table 12.5 lists the methods unique to Node. When using XmlParser, you can use these methods in your processing.

Table 12.5 XmlParser: methods of groovy.util.Node not available in GPathResult

Method	Note
Object value()	Retrieves the payload of the node, either the children() or the text()
void setValue(Object value)	Changes the payload
Object attribute(Object key)	Shortcut to attributes().get(key)
NodeList getAt(QName name)	Provides namespace support for selecting child elements by their groovy.xml.QName
void print(PrintWriter out)	Pretty-printing with NodePrinter

Table 12.6 lists the methods that are unique to or are optimized in GPathResult. As an example, we could add the following line to listing 12.4 to use the optimized findAll in GPathResult:

```
assert 2 == path.week.task.findAll{ it.'@title' =~ 'XML' }.size()
```

Additionally, some classes may only work on one type or the other; for example, there is groovy.util.XmlNodePrinter with method print(Node) but no support for GPathResult. Like the name suggests, XmlNodePrinter pretty-prints a Node tree to a PrintStream in XML format.

Table 12.6 `XmlSlurper:` **methods of** `GPathResult` **not available in** `groovy.util.Node`

Method	Note
`GPathResult parents()`	Represents all parent elements on the path from the current element up to the root
`GPathResult declareNamespace` `(Map newNamespaceMapping)`	Registers namespace prefixes and their URIs
`List       list()`	Converts a `GPathResult` into a list of `groovy.util.slurpersupport.Node` objects for list-friendly processing
`int        size()`	The number of result elements (memory optimized implementation)
`GPathResult find(Closure closure)`	Overrides the object iteration method `find`
`GPathResult findAll(Closure closure)`	Overrides the object iteration method `findAll`

You have seen that there are a lot of similarities and some slight differences when reading XML via `XmlParser` or `XmlSlurper`. The real, fundamental differences become apparent when processing the parsed information. Coming up in section 12.2, we will look at these differences in more detail by exploring two examples: processing with direct in-place data manipulation and processing in a *streaming* scenario. However, first we are going to look at event style parsing and how it can be used with Groovy. This will help us better position some of Groovy's powerful XML features in our forthcoming more-detailed examples.

12.1.3 *Reading with a SAX parser*

In addition to the original Java DOM parsing you saw earlier, Java also supports what is known as *event-based parsing*. The original and most common form of event-based parsing is called *SAX*. SAX is a push-style event-based parser because the parser pushes events to your code.

When using this style of processing, no memory structure is constructed to store the parsed information; instead, the parser notifies a *handler* about parsing events. We implement such a handler interface in our program to perform processing relevant to our application's needs whenever the parser notifies us.

Let's explore this for our simple plan example. Suppose we wish to display a quick summary of the tasks that are underway and those that are upcoming; we aren't interested in completed activities for the moment. Listing 12.5 shows how to *receive* start element events using SAX and perform our business logic of printing out the tasks of interest.

Listing 12.5 Using a SAX parser with Groovy

```
import javax.xml.parsers.SAXParserFactory
import org.xml.sax.*
import org.xml.sax.helpers.DefaultHandler

class PlanHandler extends DefaultHandler {        ◁──┘  Declare our
                                                         handler
    def underway = []
    def upcoming = []                                          Interested in
    void startElement(String namespace, String localName,     element start
            String qName, Attributes atts) {        ◁──┘       events
        if (qName != 'task') return         ◁─┐   Interested only
        def title = atts.getValue('title')       in task elements
        def total = atts.getValue('total')
        switch (atts.getValue('done')) {
            case '0'             : upcoming << title ; break
            case { it != total } : underway << title ; break
        }
    }
}

def handler = new PlanHandler()
def reader = SAXParserFactory.newInstance()
        .newSAXParser().xMLReader       ◁─┐  Declare our SAX reader
reader.contentHandler = handler
def inputStream = new FileInputStream('data/plan.xml')
reader.parse(new InputSource(inputStream))
inputStream.close()

assert handler.underway == [
    'use in current project'
]
assert handler.upcoming == [
    're-read DB chapter',
    'use DB/XML combination'
]
```

Note that with this style of processing, we have more work to do. When our
`startElement` method is called, we are provided with SAX event information
including the name of the element (along with a namespace, if provided) and all
the attributes. It's up to us to work out whether we need this information and process or store it as required during this method call. The parser won't do any further storage for us. This minimizes memory overhead of the parser, but the
implication is that we won't be able to do GPath-style processing and we aren't in a
position to manipulate a tree-like data structure. We'll have more to say about SAX
event information when we explore `XmlSlurper` in more detail in section 12.2.

12.1.4 *Reading with a StAX parser*

In addition to the push-style SAX parsers supported by Java, a recent trend in processing XML with Java is to use pull-style event-based parsers. The most common of these are called *StAX-based parsers*.[5] With such a parser, you are still interested in events, but you ask the parser for events (you pull events as needed) during processing[6], instead of waiting to be informed by methods being called.

Listing 12.6 shows how you can use StAX with Groovy. You will need a StAX parser in your classpath to run this example. If you have already set up Groovy-SOAP, which we explore further in section 12.3, you may already have everything you need.

Listing 12.6   Using a StAX parser with Groovy

```
// requires stax.jar and stax-api.jar
import javax.xml.stream.*

def input = 'file:data/plan.xml'.toURL()
def underway = []
def upcoming = []

def eachStartElement(inputStream, Closure yield) {
    def token = XMLInputFactory.newInstance()
        .createXMLStreamReader(inputStream)        ◁┘ Declare parser
    try {
        while (token.hasNext()) {        ◁┘ Loop through events of interest
            if (token.startElement) yield token
            token.next()
        }
    } finally {
        token?.close()
        inputStream?.close()
    }
}

class XMLStreamCategory {
    static Object get(XMLStreamReader self, String key) {    Category
        return self.getAttributeValue(null, key)            for simple
    }                                                        attribute
}                                                            access
```

---

[5] See http://www.xml.com/pub/a/2003/09/17/stax.html for a tutorial introduction.

[6] This is the main event-based style supported by .NET and will also be included with Java 6.

```
use (XMLStreamCategory) {
    eachStartElement(input.openStream()) { element ->
        if (element.name.toString() != 'task') return
        switch (element.done) {
            case '0' :
                upcoming << element.title
                break
            case { it != element.total } :
                underway << element.title
        }
    }
}

assert underway == [
    'use in current project'
]
assert upcoming == [
    're-read DB chapter',
    'use DB/XML combination'
]
```

Note that this style of parsing is similar to SAX-style parsing except that we are running the main control loop ourselves rather than having the parser do it. This style has advantages for certain kinds of processing where the code becomes simpler to write and understand.

Suppose you have to respond to many parts of the document differently. With push models, your code has to maintain extra state to know where you are and how to react. With a pull model, you can decide what parts of the document to process at any point within your business logic. The flow through the document is easier to follow, and the code feels more natural.

We have now explored the breadth of parsing options available in Groovy. Next we explore the advantages of the Groovy-specific parsing options in more detail.

12.2 *Processing XML*

Many situations involving XML call for more than just reading the data and then navigating to a specific element or node. XML documents often require transformation, modification, or complex querying. When we look at the characteristics of XmlParser and XmlSlurper when *processing* XML data in these ways, we see the biggest differences between the two. Let's start with a simple but perhaps surprising analogy: heating water.

There are essentially two ways of boiling water, as illustrated in figure 12.2. You can pour water into a tank (called a *boiler*), heat it up, and get the hot water from

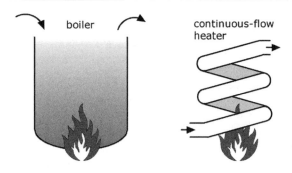

Figure 12.2
Comparing the strategies of boiling
vs. continuous-flow heating

the outlet. The second way of boiling is with the help of a continuous-flow heater, which heats up the water while it streams from the cold-water inlet through the heating coil until it reaches the outlet. The heating happens only when requested, as indicated by opening the outlet tap.

How does XML processing relate to boiling water? Well, processing XML means you are not just using bits of the stored information, but retrieving it, adding some new quality to it (making it *hot* in our analogy), and outputting the whole thing. Just like boiling water, this can be done in two ways: by storing the information in memory and processing it in-place, or by retrieving information from an input stream, processing it on the fly, and streaming it to an output device.

In general, processing XML with `XmlParser` (and `groovy.util.Node`) is more like using a boiler, whereas `XmlSlurper` can serve as a source in a streaming scenario analogous to continuous-flow heating.

We're going to start by looking at the "boiling" strategy of in-place modification and processing and then proceed to explore streamed processing and combinations with XPath.

12.2.1 *In-place processing*

In-place processing is the conventional means of XML processing. It uses the `XmlParser` to retrieve a tree of nodes. These nodes reside in memory and can be rearranged, copied, or deleted, and their attributes can be changed. We will use this approach to generate an HTML report for keeping track of our Groovy learning activities.

Suppose the report should look like figure 12.3. You can see that new information is derived from existing data: tasks and weeks have a new property that we will call `status` with the possible values of `scheduled`, `in progress`, and `finished`.

For tasks, the value of the status property is determined by looking at the done and total attributes. If done is zero, the status is considered scheduled; if done is equal to or exceeds total, the status is finished; otherwise, the status is in progress.

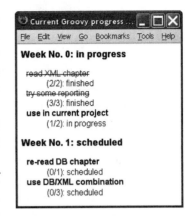

Figure 12.3 An HTML progress report of Groovy learning activities

Weeks are finished when all contained tasks are finished. They are in progress when at least one contained task is in progress.

This sounds like we are going to do lots of number comparisons with the done and total attributes. Unfortunately these attributes are stored as strings, not numbers. These considerations lead to a three-step "heating" process:

1 Convert all string attribute values to numbers where suitable.

2 Add a new attribute called status to all tasks, and determine the value.

3 Add a new attribute called status to all weeks, and determine the value.

With such an improved data representation, it is finally straightforward to use MarkupBuilder to produce the HTML report.

We have to produce HTML source like

```
<html>
  <head>
    <title>Current Groovy progress</title>
    <link href='style.css' type='text/css' rel='stylesheet' />
  </head>
  <body>
    <h1>Week No. 0: in progress</h1>
    <dl>
      <dt class='finished'>read XML chapter</dt>
      <dd>(2/2): finished</dd>
...
    </dl>
  </body>
</html>
```

where the stylesheet style.css contains the decision of how a task is finally displayed according to its status. It can for example use the following lines for that purpose:

```
dt             { font-weight:bold }
dt.finished { font-weight:normal; text-decoration:line-through }
```

Listing 12.7 contains the full solution. The `numberfy` method implements the string-to-number conversion for those attributes that we expect to be of integer content. It also shows how to work recursively through the node tree.

The methods `weekStatus` and `taskStatus` make the new `status` attribute available on the corresponding node, where `weekStatus` calls `taskStatus` for all its contained tasks to make sure it can work on their status inside GPath expressions.

The final `htmlReport` method is the conventional way of building HTML. Thanks to the "heating" prework, there is no logic needed in the report. The report uses the `status` attribute to assign a stylesheet *class* of the same value.

Listing 12.7   Generating an HTML report with in-memory data preparation

```
void numberfy(node) {
    def atts = node.attributes()
    atts.keySet().grep(['capacity', 'total', 'done']).each {
        atts[it] = atts[it].toInteger()          ⟵┐ Convert strings
    }                                                │  to numbers
    node.each { numberfy(it) }
}                                   ┌ Calculate and
void taskStatus(task){      ⟵──┘ assign task status
    def atts = task.attributes()
    switch (atts.done) {
        case 0 :                atts.status = 'scheduled';   break
        case 1..<atts.total : atts.status = 'in progress'; break
        default:                atts.status = 'finished';
    }
}                                   ┌ Calculate and assign
void weekStatus(week) {     ⟵──┘ week status
    week.task.each{ taskStatus(it) }
    def atts = week.attributes()
    atts.status = 'scheduled'
    if (week.task.every{ it.'@status' == 'finished'})
        atts.status = 'finished'
    if (week.task.any{ it.'@status' == 'in progress'})
        atts.status = 'in progress'
}                                   ┌ Report
void htmlReport(builder, plan) {  ⟵──┘ building logic
    builder.html {
        head {
            title('Current Groovy progress')
            link(rel:'stylesheet',
                type:'text/css',
                href:'style.css')
        }
        body {
            plan.week.eachWithIndex { week, i ->
                h1("Week No. $i: ${week.'@status'}")
                dl{
```

```
                     week.task.each { task ->
                         dt(class:task.'@status', task.'@title')
                         dd(
        "(${task.'@done'}/${task.'@total'}): ${task.'@status'}")
}   }   }   }   }   }

def node = new XmlParser().parse(new File('data/plan.xml'))
numberfy(node)                          Prepare data
node.week.each{ weekStatus(it) }        for reporting

new File('data/GroovyPlans.html').withWriter { writer ->
    def builder = new groovy.xml.MarkupBuilder(writer)
    htmlReport(builder, node)
}
```

After the careful prework, the code in listing 12.7 is not surprising. What's a bit unconventional is having a lot of closing braces on one line at the end of `htmlReport`. This is not only for compact typesetting in the book. We also sometimes use this style in our everyday code. We find it nicely reveals what levels of indentation are to be closed and still allows us to check brace-matching by column. It would be great to have IDE support for toggling between this and conventional code layout.

Now that you have seen how to use the in-memory "boiler," let's investigate the streaming scenario.

12.2.2 *Streaming processing*

In order to demonstrate the use of streaming, let's start with the simplest kind of processing that we can think of: pumping out what comes in without any modification. Even this simple example is hard to understand when you first encounter it. We recommend that if you find it confusing, keep reading, but don't worry too much about the details. It's definitely worth coming back later for a second try, though—in many situations, the benefits of stream-based processing are well worth the harder conceptual model.

Unmodified piping

You use `XmlSlurper` to parse the original XML. Because the final output format is XML again, you need some device that can generate XML in a streaming fashion. The `groovy.xml.StreamingMarkupBuilder` class is specialized for outputting markup on demand—in other words, when an *information sink* requests it. Such a sink is an operation that requests a `Writable`—for example, the leftshift operator call on streams or the evaluation of GStrings. The trick that `StreamingMarkup-Builder` uses to achieve this effect is similar to the approach of template engines. `StreamingMarkupBuilder` provides a `bind` method that returns a `WritableClosure`. This object is a `Writable` and a closure at the same time. Because it is a `Writable`, you can use it wherever the final markup is requested. Because it is a closure, the generation of this markup can be done lazily on-the-fly, without storing intermediate results.

Listing 12.8 shows this in action. The `bind` method also needs the information about what logic is to be applied to produce the final markup. Wherever logic is needed, closures are the first candidate, and so it is with `bind`. We pass a closure to the `bind` method that describes the markup logic.

For our initial example of pumping the `path` through, we use a special feature of `StreamingMarkupBuilder` that allows us to yield the markup generation logic to a `Buildable`, an object that knows how to build itself. It happens that a `GPathResult` (and thus `path`) is buildable. In order to yield the building logic to it, we use the `yield` method. However, we cannot use it unqualified because we would produce a `<yield/>` markup if we did. The special symbol `mkp` marks our method call as belonging to the namespace of markup keywords.

Listing 12.8 Pumping an XML stream without modification

```
import groovy.xml.StreamingMarkupBuilder

def path = new XmlSlurper().parse(new File('data/plan.xml'))

def builder = new StreamingMarkupBuilder()
def copier = builder.bind{ mkp.yield(path) }
def result = "$copier"

assert result.startsWith('<plan><week ')
assert result.endsWith('</week></plan>')
```

There is a lot going on in only a few lines of code. The `result` variable for example refers to a GString with one value: a reference to `copier`. Note that we didn't call it "copy" because it is not a thing but an actor.

When we call the `startsWith` method on `result`, the string representation of the GString is requested, and because the one GString value `copier` is a `Writable`, its `writeTo` method is called. The `copier` was constructed by the `builder` such that `writeTo` relays to `path.build()`.

Figure 12.4 summarizes this streaming behavior.

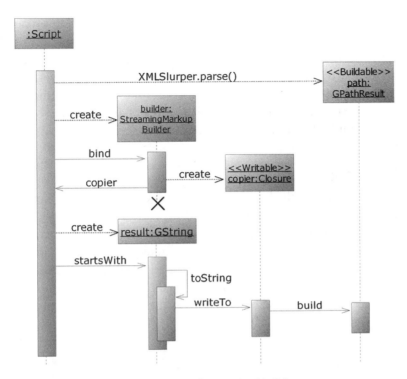

Figure 12.4 UML sequence diagram for streamed building

Note how in figure 12.4, the processing doesn't start before the values are requested. Only after the GString's toString method is called does the copier start running and is the path iterated upon. Until then, the path isn't touched! No memory representation has been created for the purpose of markup or iteration. This is a simplification of what is going on. XmlSlurper does have memory requirements. It stores the SAX event information you saw in section 12.1.3 but doesn't process or store it in the processing-friendly Node objects.

Calling startsWith is like opening the outlet tap to draw the markup from the copier, which in turn draws its source information from the path inlet. Any code before that point is only the plumbing.

As a variant of listing 12.8, you can also directly write the markup onto the console. Use the following:

```
System.out << copier
```

Remember that System.out is an OutputStream that understands the leftshift operator with a Writable argument.

For this simple example, we could have used the SAX or StAX approaches you saw earlier. They would be even more streamlined solutions. Not only would they not need to process and store the tree-like data structures that XmlParser creates for you, but they also wouldn't need to store the SAX event information. The same isn't true for the more complicated scenarios that follow. As is common in many XML processing scenarios, the remaining examples have processing requirements that span multiple elements. Such scenarios benefit greatly from the ability to use GPath-style expressions.

Heating up to HTML

Until now, we copied only the "cold" input. It's time to light our heater. The goal is to produce the same GUI as in figure 12.3.

We start with the basis of listing 12.8 but enhance the markup closure that gets bound to the builder. In listing 12.9, building looks almost the same as in the "boiling" example of listing 12.7; only the evaluation of the week and task status needs to be adapted. We do not calculate the status in advance and store it for later reference, but do the classification on-the-fly when the builder lazily requests it.

Listing 12.9 Streamed heating from XML to HTML

```
def taskStatus(task){          ⟵┘ Calculate task status
    switch (task.'@done'.toInteger()) {
        case 0 :                                  return 'scheduled'
        case 1..<task.'@total'.toInteger() : return 'in progress'
        default:                                  return 'finished'
    }
}                              │ Calculate
def weekStatus(week) {     ⟵┘ week status
    if (week.task.every{ taskStatus(it) == 'finished'})
      return 'finished'
    if (week.task.any{ taskStatus(it) == 'in progress'})
      return 'in progress'
    return 'scheduled'
}
                                                          │ "Slurp" in
def plan = new XmlSlurper().parse(new File('data/plan.xml'))   ⟵┘ the XML

Closure markup = {    ⟵┐ Express the processing
    html {                │ as a closure
        head {
            title('Current Groovy progress')
            link(rel:'stylesheet',
                type:'text/css',
```

```
                href:'style.css')
        }
        body {
            plan.week.eachWithIndex { week, i ->
                h1("Week No. $i: ${owner.weekStatus(week)}")
                dl{
                week.task.each { task ->
                    def status = owner.taskStatus(task)
                    dt(class:status, task.'@title')
                    dd(
      "(${task.'@done'}/${task.'@total'}): $status")
}   }   }   }   }   }
```
Bind the parsed XML to the processing logic

```
def heater = new groovy.xml.StreamingMarkupBuilder().bind(markup)
```

```
new File('data/StreamedGroovyPlans.html').
    withWriter{ it << heater }
```
Write out the result to a file

The cool thing here is that at first glance it looks similar to listing 12.7, but it works very differently:

- All evaluation is done lazily.
- Memory consumption for GPath operations is minimized.
- No in-memory assembly of HTML representation is built before outputting.

This allows us to produce lots of output, because it is not assembled in memory but directly streamed to the output as the building logic demands. However, because of the storage of SAX event information on the input, this approach will not allow input documents as large as would be possible with SAX or StAX.

Figure 12.5 sketches the differences between both processing approaches with respect to processing requirements and memory usage. The process goes from left to right either in the top row (for "boiling") or in the bottom row (for "streaming"). Either process encompasses *parsing, evaluating, building,* and *serializing* to HTML, where *evaluating* and *building* are not necessarily in strict sequence. This is also where the differences are: working on intermediate data structures (trees of lists and nodes) or on lightweight objects that encapsulate logic (iterators and closures).

That's it for the basics of processing XML with the structures provided by the Groovy XML parsers.

In section 12.1.1, you saw that classic Java DOM parsers return objects of type org.w3c.dom.Node, which differs from what the Groovy parsers return. The Java way of processing such nodes is with the help of XPath. The next section shows how Java XPath and Groovy XML processing can be used in combination.

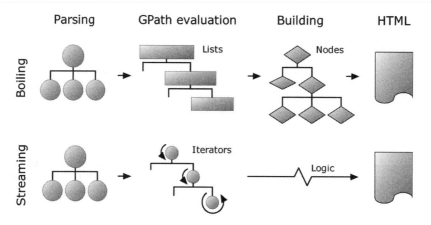

Figure 12.5 Memory usage characteristics for the "boiling" vs. "streaming" strategies

12.2.3 *Combining with XPath*

XPath is for XML what SQL `select` statements are for relational databases or what regular expressions are for plain text. It's a means to select parts of the whole document and to do so in a descriptive manner.

Understanding XPath

An XPath is an expression that appears in Java or Groovy as a string (exactly like regex patterns or SQL statements do). A full introduction to XPath is beyond the scope of this book, but here is a short introduction from a Groovy programmer's point of view.[7]

Just like a GPath, an XPath selects nodes. Where GPath uses dots, XPath uses slashes. For example

```
/plan/week/task
```

selects all `task` nodes of all `week`s below `plan`. The leading slash indicates that the selection starts at the root element. In this expression, `plan`, `week`, and `task` are each called a *node test*. Each node test may be preceded with an *axis specifier* from table 12.7 and a double colon.

---

[7] For a full description of the standard, see http://www.w3.org/TR/xpath; and for a tutorial, see http://www.w3schools.com/xpath/.

Table 12.7 XPath axis specifiers

Axis	Selects nodes	Shortcut
`child`	Directly below	nothing or *
`parent`	Directly above	..
`self`	The node itself (use for further references)	.
`ancestor`	All above	
`ancestor-or-self`	All above including self	
`descendant`	All below	
`descendant-or-self`	All below including self	//
`following`	All on the same level trailing in the XML document	
`following-sibling`	All with the same parent trailing in the XML document	
`preceding`	All on the same level preceding in the XML document	
`preceding-sibling`	All with the same parent preceding in the XML document	
`attribute`	The attribute node	@
`namespace`	The namespace node	

With these specifiers, you can select all `task` elements via

```
/descendant-or-self::task
```

With the shortcut syntax, you can select all `total` attribute nodes of all `tasks` via

```
//task/@total
```

A node test can have a trailing *predicate* in square brackets to constrain the result. A predicate is an expression made up from path expressions, functions, and operators for the datatypes `node-set`, `string`, `number`, and `boolean`. Table 12.8 lists what's possible.[8]

Table 12.9 shows some examples.

The next obvious question is how to use such XPath expressions in Groovy code.

---

[8] This covers only XPath 1.0 because XPath 2.0 is not yet finalized at the time of writing.

Table 12.8 XPath predicate expression cheat sheet

Category	Appearance	Note
Path operators	`/, //, @, [], *, .., .`	As above
Union operator	`|`	Union of two node-sets
Boolean operators	`and, or, not()`	`not()` is a function
Arithmetic operators	`+, -, *, div, mod`	
Comparison operators	`=, !=, <, >, <=, >=`	
String functions	`concat(), substring(), contains(), substring-before(), substring-after(), translate(), normalize-space(), string-length()`	See the docs for exact meanings and parameters
Number functions	`sum(), round(), floor(), ceiling()`	
Node functions	`name(), local-name(), namespace-uri()`	
Context functions	`position(), last()`	`[n]` is short for `[position()=n]`
Conversion functions	`string(), number(), boolean()`	

Table 12.9 XPath examples

XPath	Meaning and notes	Note
`/plan/week[1]`	First[a] week node	Indexing starts at *one*
`//task[@done<@total]`	All unfinished tasks	Auto-conversion to a number
`//task[@done<@total][@done>0]`	All tasks in progress	Implicit and between brackets
`sum(//week[1]/task/@total)`	Total hours in the first week	Returns a number

a. More specifically: the `week` node at position 1 below `plan`.

Using the XPath API

Groovy comes with all the support you need for using XPath expressions in your code. This is because of the xml-apis*.jar and xerces*.jar files in your GROOVY_HOME/lib dir. In case you are running Groovy in an embedded scenario, make sure these jars are on your classpath.

We will use XPath through the convenience methods in `org.apache.xpath.XPathAPI`. This class provides lot of static helper methods that are easy to use even though the implementation is not always efficient.[9] We will use

```
Node       selectSingleNode(Node contextNode, String xpath)
NodeList selectNodeList  (Node contextNode, String xpath)
XObject   eval           (Node contextNode, String xpath)
```

where `XObject` wraps the XPath datatype that `eval` returns. For converting it into a Groovy datatype, we can use the methods `num`, `bool`, `str`, and `nodelist`.

In practice, we may want to do something with all weeks. We select the appropriate list of nodes via `XPathAPI.selectNodeList(plan, 'week')`. Because this returns a `NodeList`, we can use the object iteration methods on it to get hold of each week:

```
XPathAPI.selectNodeList(plan, 'week').eachWithIndex{ week, i ->
    // do something with week
}
```

For each week, we want to print the sum of the `total` and `done` attributes with the help of XPath. Each week node becomes the new context node for the XPath evaluation:

```
XPathAPI.selectNodeList(plan, 'week').eachWithIndex{ week, i ->
    println "\nWeek No. $i\n"
    println XPathAPI.eval(week, 'sum(task/@total)').num()
    println XPathAPI.eval(week, 'sum(task/@done)').num()
}
```

Listing 12.10 puts all this together with a little reporting functionality that produces a text report for each week, stating the capacity, the total hours planned, and the progress in hours done.

Listing 12.10   XPath to text reporting

```
// requires xalan.jar, xml-apis.jar
import org.apache.xpath.XPathAPI
import groovy.xml.DOMBuilder
import groovy.xml.dom.DOMCategory

def doc  = DOMBuilder.parse(new FileReader('data/plan.xml'))
def plan = doc.documentElement

def out = new StringBuffer()        Use DOMCategory for        Selection via ❶
use(DOMCategory) {                  simple attribute access    XPath, retrieving
    XPathAPI.selectNodeList(plan, 'week').eachWithIndex{ week, i ->   index and value
```

---

[9] When performance is crucial, consider using the Jaxen XPath library which is used by *JDOM*, *dom4j,* and *XOM* for their processing needs as well as being useful on its own.

```
        out << "\nWeek No. $i\n"
        int total = XPathAPI.eval(week, 'sum(task/@total)').num()
        int done  = XPathAPI.eval(week, 'sum(task/@done)').num()
        out << " planned $total of ${week.'@capacity'}\n"
        out << " done    $done of $total"
    }
}
assert out.toString() == '''
Week No. 0
 planned 7 of 8
 done    6 of 7
Week No. 1
 planned 4 of 8
 done    0 of 4'''
```

❷ Evaluation using XPath

Evaluation using DOM attributes directly ❸

XPath is used in two ways here—the querying capability is used to select all the week elements ❶, and then attributes `total` and `done` are extracted with the `eval` method ❷. We mix and match ways of accessing attributes, using `DOMCategory` to access the `capacity` attribute with the `node.@attributeName` syntax ❸.

Such a text report is fine to start with, but it would certainly be nicer to show the progress in a chart. Figure 12.6 suggests an HTML solution. In a normal situation, we would use colors in such a report, but they would not be visible in the print of this book. Therefore, we use only a simple box representation of the numbers.

Each box is made from the border of a styled `div` element. The style also determines the width of each box.

This kind of HTML production task calls for a templating approach, because there are multiple recurring patterns for HTML fragments: for the boxes, for each attribute row, and for

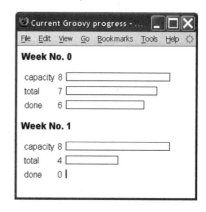

Figure 12.6 Screenshot of an HTML based reporting

each week. We will use template engines, GPath, and XPath in combination to make this happen.

Listing 12.11 presents the template that we are going to use. It is a simple template as introduced in section 9.4. It assumes the presence of two variables in the binding: a `scale`, which is needed to make visible box sizes from the attribute values, and `weeks`, which is a list of week maps. Each week map contains the keys `'capacity'`, `'total'`, and `'done'` with integer values.

The template resides in a separate file. We like to name such files with the word *template* in the name and ending in the usual file extension for the format they produce. For example, the name GroovyPlans.template.html reveals the nature of the file, and we can still use it with an HTML editor.

Listing 12.11 HTML reporting layout in data/GroovyPlans.template.html

```
<html>
  <head>
    <title>Current Groovy progress</title>
  </head>
  <body>
    <% weeks.eachWithIndex{ week, i -> %>
    <h1>Week No. $i</h1>
    <table cellspacing="5" >
        <tbody>
            <% ['capacity','total','done'].each{ attr -> %>
            <tr>
              <td>$attr</td>
              <td>${week[attr]}</td>
                <td>
                    <div style=
"border: thin solid #000000; width: ${week[attr]*scale}px">
                         </div>
                </td>
            </tr>
            <% } // end of attribute %>
        </tbody>
    </table>
    <% } // end of week %>
  </body>
</html>
```

This template looks like a JSP file, but it isn't. The contained logic is expressed in Groovy, not plain Java. Instead of being processed by a JSP engine, it will be evaluated by Groovy's SimpleTemplateEngine as shown in listing 12.12. We use XPath expressions to prepare the values for binding. A special application of GPath comes into play when calculating the scaling factor.

Scaling is required so that the longest capacity bar is of length 200, so we have to find the maximum capacity for the calculation. Because we have already put these values in the binding, we can use a GPath to get a list of those and play our GDK tricks with it (calling max).

Listing 12.12 Using XPath, GPath, and templating in combination for HTML reporting

```
// requires xalan.jar, xml-apis.jar
import org.apache.xpath.XPathAPI
import groovy.xml.DOMBuilder
import groovy.xml.dom.DOMCategory
import groovy.text.SimpleTemplateEngine as STE

def doc  = DOMBuilder.parse(new FileReader('data/plan.xml'))
def plan = doc.documentElement

def binding = [scale:1, weeks:[] ]
use(DOMCategory) {
  XPathAPI.selectNodeList(plan, 'week').each{ week ->          XPath on
    binding.weeks << [                                          DOM nodes
      total:    (int) XPathAPI.eval(week, 'sum(task/@total)').num(),
      done:     (int) XPathAPI.eval(week, 'sum(task/@done)').num(),
      capacity: week.'@capacity'.toInteger()
    ]
  }
}
def max = binding.weeks.capacity.max()          GPath on
if (max > 0) binding.scale = 200.intdiv(max)     binding

def templateFile = new File('data/GroovyPlans.template.html')
def template     = new STE().createTemplate(templateFile)     Templating

new File('data/XPathGroovyPlans.html').withWriter {
    it << template.make(binding)
}
```

The code did not change dramatically between the text reporting in listing 12.10 and the HTML reporting in listing 12.12. However, listing 12.12 provides a more general solution, because we can also get a text report from it solely by changing the template.

The kind of transformation from XML to HTML that we achieve with listing 12.12 is classically addressed with *XML Stylesheet Transformation (XSLT)*, which is a powerful technology. It uses stylesheets in XML format to describe a transformation mapping, also using XPath and templates. Its logical means are equivalent to those of a functional programming language.

Although XSLT is suitable for mapping tree structures, we often find it easier to use the Groovy approach when the logic is the least bit complex. XPath, templates, builders, and the Groovy language make a unique combination that allows for elegant and concise solutions. There may be people who are able to look at significant amounts of XSLT for more than a few minutes at a time without risking their mental stability, but they are few and far between. Using the technologies you've encountered, you can play to your strengths of understanding Groovy instead of using a different language with a fundamentally different paradigm.

Leveraging additional Java XML processing technologies

Before wrapping up our introduction of processing XML with Groovy, we should mention that although we think that you will find Groovy's built-in XML features are suitable for many of your processing needs, you are not locked into using just those APIs. Because of Groovy's Java heritage, many libraries and technologies are available for you to consider. We have already mentioned StAX and Jaxen. Here are a few more of our favorites:[10]

- Although XmlParser, XmlSlurper, and of course the Java DOM and SAX should meet most of your needs, you can always consider JDOM, dom4j, or XOM.
- If you need to compare two XML fragments for differences, consider XMLUnit.
- If you wish to process XML using XQuery, consider Saxon.
- If you need to persist your XML, consider JAXB or XmlBeans.
- If you need to do high-performance streaming, consider Nux.

Our introduction to Groovy XML could finish at this point, because you have seen all the basics of XML manipulation. You should now be able to write Groovy programs that read, process, and write XML in a basic way. You will need more detailed documentation when the need arises to deal with more advanced issues such as namespaces, resolving entities, and handling DTDs in a customized way.

The final section of this chapter deals not with the details of XML but with one of its most important modern applications: exchanging data between systems, and talking to web services in particular.

---

[10] More information is available at: http://xmlbeans.apache.org/, http://saxon.sourceforge.net/, http://dsd.lbl.gov/nux/, http://xmlunit.sourceforge.net/, and http://java.sun.com/webservices/jaxb/.

12.3 *Distributed processing with XML*

XML describes data in a system-independent way. This makes it an obvious candidate for exchanging data across a network. Interconnected systems can be heterogeneous. They may be written in different languages, run on different platforms (think .NET vs. Java), use different operating systems, and run on different hardware architectures. But no matter how different these systems are, they can exchange data through XML, so long as both sides have some idea of how to interpret the XML they are given.

At a simple level, sharing data happens every time you surf the Web. With the help of your browser, you *request* a URL. The server *responds* with an HTML document that your browser knows how to display. The server and the browser are interconnected through the *Hypertext Transfer Protocol (HTTP)* that implements the request-response model, and they use HTML as the data-exchange format.

Now imagine a program that surfs the Web on your behalf. Such a program could visit a list of URLs to check for updates, browse a list of news providers for new information about your favorite topics (we suggest "Groovy"), access a stock ticker to see whether your shares have exceeded the target price, and check the local weather service to warn you about upcoming thunderstorms.

Such a program would have significant difficulties to overcome if it had to find the requested information in the HTML of each web site. The HTML describes not only what the data is, but also how it should broadly be presented. A change to the presentation aspect of the HTML could easily break the program that was trying to understand the data. Instead of dealing with the two aspects together, it would be more reliable if there were an XML description of the pure content. This is what web services are about.

A full description of all web service formats and protocols is beyond the scope of this book, but we will show how you can use some of them with Groovy. We cover reading XML resources via RSS and ATOM, followed by using REST and Groovy's special XML-RPC support on the client and server side, and finally request SOAP services from Groovy as well as writing a simple web service using Groovy.

In case REST and SOAP make it sound like we're talking about having a bath instead of accessing web services, you'll be pleased to hear we're starting with a brief description of some of these protocols and conventions.

12.3.1 *An overview of web services*

Web service solutions cover a spectrum of approaches from the simple to what some regard as extremely complex. Perhaps the simplest approach is to use the stateless HTTP protocol to request a resource via a URL. This is the basis of the *Representational State Transfer (REST)* architecture. The term REST has also been used more widely as a synonym for any mechanism for exposing content on the Web via simple XML.

The REST architecture is popular for making content of weblogs available. Two of the most commonly used formats in this area are *Really Simple Syndication*[11] *(RSS)* and *ATOM (RFC-4287)*. The next logical extension from using a URL to request a resource is to use simple XML embodied within a normal HTTP POST request. This also can be regarded as a REST solution. We will examine an XML API of this nature as part of our REST tour.

When the focus is not on the remote resource but on triggering an operation on the remote system, the XML Remote Procedure Call (XML-RPC) can be used. XML-RPC uses HTTP but adds context, which makes it a stateful protocol (as opposed to REST).

The SOAP[12] protocol extends the concept of XML-RPC to support not only remote operations but even remote *objects*. Web service enterprise features that build upon SOAP provide other functionality such as security, transactions, and reliable messaging, to name a few of the many advanced features available.

Now that you have your bearings, let's look at how Groovy can access two of the most popular web service formats in use today.

12.3.2 *Reading RSS and ATOM*

Let's start our day by reading the news. The BBC broadcasts its latest news on an RSS channel. Because we are busy programmers, we are interested only in the top three headlines. A little Groovy program fetches them and prints them to the console. What we would like to see is the headline, a short description, and a URL pointing to the full article in case a headline catches our interest.

Here is some sample output:

```
The top three news items today:
Three Britons kidnapped in Gaza
```

---

[11] Also called *Rich Site Summary (RSS 0.9x)* or *Resource Description Framework (RDF) Site Summary (RSS 1.0)*.

[12] SOAP used to stand for *Simple Object Access Protocol*, but this meaning has been dropped since version 1.2 because SOAP does more than access objects and the word *simple* was questionable from the start.

```
http://news.bbc.co.uk/go/rss/-/1/hi/world/middle_east/4564586.stm
Three British citizens have been kidnapped by unidentified gunmen in southern
    Gaza, police say.
----
Geldof defends Tory adviser role
http://news.bbc.co.uk/go/rss/-/1/hi/uk_politics/4564130.stm
Bob Geldof promises to stay politically "non-partisan" after agreeing to
    advise the Tories on global poverty.
----
Glitter 'pays money to accusers'
http://news.bbc.co.uk/go/rss/-/1/hi/world/asia-pacific/4563542.stm
Former singer Gary Glitter paid his alleged victims' families "for co-
    operation", his Vietnamese lawyer says.
----
```

Listing 12.13 implements this newsreader. It requests the web resource that contains the news as XML. It finds the resource by its URL. Passing the URL to the parse method implicitly fetches it from the Web. The remainder of the code can directly work on the node tree using GPath expressions.

Listing 12.13   A simple RSS newsreader

```
def base = 'http://news.bbc.co.uk/rss/newsonline_uk_edition/'
def url  = base +'front_page/rss091.xml'

println 'The top three news items today:'
def items = new XmlParser().parse(url).channel[0].item
for (item in items[0..2]) {
    println item.title.text()
    println item.link.text()
    println item.description.text()
    println '----'
}
```

Of course, for writing such code, we need to know what elements and attributes are available in the RSS format. In listing 12.13, we assumed that at least the following structure is available:

```
<rss ...>
  <channel>
    ...
    <item>
      <title>...      </title>
      <description>...</description>
      <link>...      </link>
      ...
```

This is only a small subset of the full information. You can find a full description of the RSS and ATOM formats and their various versions in *RSS and ATOM in Action*.[13] Reading an ATOM feed is equally easy, as shown in listing 12.14. It reads the weblog of David M. Johnson, one of the fathers of the weblog movement. At the time of writing this chapter, it prints

```
Sun portal 7 to include JSPWiki, hey what about LGPL?
ApacheCon Tuesday
ApacheCon Tuesday: Tim Bray's keynote
...
```

One thing that's new in listing 12.14 is the use of XML namespaces. The ATOM format makes use of namespaces like so:

```
<feed xmlns="http://www.w3.org/2005/Atom">
    ...
    <entry>
        <title>Sun portal ...</title>
        ...
```

In order to traverse nodes that are bound to namespaces with GPath expressions, qualified names (QName objects) are used. A QName object can be retrieved from a Namespace object by requesting the property of the corresponding element name.

Listing 12.14   Reading an ATOM feed

```
import groovy.xml.Namespace

def url = 'http://rollerweblogger.org/atom/roller?catname=/Java'

def atom   = new Namespace('http://www.w3.org/2005/Atom')
def titles = new XmlParser().parse(url)[atom.entry][atom.title]

println titles*.text().join("\n")
```

That was all fairly easy, right? The next topic, REST, will be more elaborate but covers a wider area of applicability, because it is a more general approach.

12.3.3 *Using a REST-based API*

Although most web services are bound to a standard, REST is an open concept rather than a standard. The common denominator of REST services is that

---

[13] Dave Johnson, *RSS and ATOM in Action* (Manning, 2006).

- XML is used for exchanging data between client and server.
- Communication is done on a stateless request/response model over HTTP(S).
- Resources or services are addressed by a URL.

No binding standard describes the structure of the XML that is sent around. You need to look into the documentation of each REST service to find out what information is requested and provided.

For an example, we will look into the REST services of the BackPack web application. BackPack is an online authoring system based on the Wiki[14] concept: It publishes web pages that the author can edit through the browser. You can find it at http://www.backpackit.com. If you want to run the examples from this section, you need to create a free account. You will receive a user-id and a 40-character token for identification. In the following examples, we will use the user-id `user` and `***` as the token. When trying the examples, you need to replace these placeholders with your personal values.

Occasionally, it's helpful to update the published information programmatically through the REST API. Suppose you have published information about your favorite books' selling rank, your corporate web site's Alexa[15] rating, or your current project's tracking status. With the REST API, you can update such information automatically.

BackPack describes its REST API under http://www.backpackit.com/api. You will find 32 operations together with the XML structure they expect in the request and the XML they respond with.

For example, the *create new page* operation is available under the URL

```
http://user.backpackit.com/ws/pages/new
```

It expects this XML in the request:

```
<request>
  <token>***</token>
  <page>
    <title>new page title</title>
    <description>initial page body</description>
  </page>
</request>
```

---

[14] Bo Leuf and Ward Cunningham, *The Wiki Way: Quick Collaboration on the Web* (Addision-Wesley Professional, 2001).

[15] www.alexa.com is a rating service for the popularity of web sites.

If the operation is successful, it returns

```
<response success='true'>
  <page title='new page title' id='1234' />
</response>
```

Now, how do you get this running from Groovy? You need some way to connect to the URL and send the request XML. You can do this with a UrlConnection and the POST method. The API additionally demands that you set the request header 'X-POST_DATA_FORMAT' to 'xml'. It would be nice to put all the infrastructure code in one place and provide your own little Groovy-friendly API.

To use this API to create a new page, update the content, and finally delete it, the code should be as simple as in Listing 12.15.

Listing 12.15 BackPack page manipulation through the Groovy REST API

```
def bp = new BackPack(account:"user", key:"***")

def response = bp.newPage("Page Title", "Page Description")
def pageId = response.page.@id
println  "created page $pageId"

response    = bp.updateBody(pageId, "new Body")
println  "updating body ok: ${response.@success}"

response    = bp.destroyPage(pageId)
println  "destroying page ok: ${response.@success}"
```

When every operation succeeds (and when you have the appropriate API in place), listing 12.15 prints

```
created page 383655
updating body ok: true
destroying page ok: true
```

The infrastructure class BackPack that implements the Groovy API to the Back-Pack REST API was written by John Wilson, the grandmaster of Groovy XML, and the full version is available at http://www.wilson.co.uk/Groovy/BackpackAPI.txt.

Listing 12.16 shows a stripped-down version of the original, not covering all operations and without proper error handling. This implementation makes the code in listing 12.15 run, shows the infrastructure code needed for using the HTTP POST method, uses the typical Groovy trick of overriding invokeMethod to make a nice API, and is another compelling example of using builders and parsers with streams.

Listing 12.16 BackPack infrastructure class that implements the Groovy REST API

```groovy
import groovy.xml.StreamingMarkupBuilder

class BackPack {
  def account
  def key
  def slurper = new XmlSlurper()
  def builder = new StreamingMarkupBuilder()      ❶ Map method names
  def methods = [                                     to closures
      newPage: { title, description ->
          makeRemoteCall("pages/new",
              { it.page {
                  it.title(title); it.description(description)
      } } )   },
      destroyPage: { pageNumber ->
          makeRemoteCall("page/${pageNumber}/destroy", "")   ❷ Empty
      },                                                         body
      updateBody: { pageNumber, description ->
          makeRemoteCall("page/${pageNumber}/update_body",
              { it.page { it.description(description) } })
      },
  ]

  def makeRemoteCall(typeOfRequest, body) {
      def url="http://${account}.backpackit.com/ws/$typeOfRequest"
      def httpConnection = new URL(url).openConnection()
      httpConnection.addRequestProperty("X-POST_DATA_FORMAT","xml")
      httpConnection.requestMethod = "POST"
      httpConnection.doOutput = true
      httpConnection.outputStream.withWriter("ASCII") {    ❸
          it << builder.bind {                            Build and
              request { token key; delegate.mkp.yield body }   send XML
          }                                               request
      }
      if (httpConnection.responseCode == httpConnection.HTTP_OK) {
          return slurper.parse(httpConnection.inputStream)
      }
      def msg = "Operation failed: ${httpConnection.responseCode}"
      throw new GroovyRuntimeException(msg)
  }                                              Parse the XML response
                                                 into a GPathResult

  public invokeMethod(String name, params) {     When a method is
      def method = methods[name]                  invoked, use the
      return method(*params.toList())             closure map
  }
}
```

A call to `bp.newPage` will be handled by `invokeMethod`, which looks up the name *newPage* in the `methods` map declared at ❶. The `methods` map stores a closure under that name, which `invokeMethod` immediately calls ❸, relaying all parameters (`title` and `description`) to it.

The closure calls the `makeRemoteCall` method, providing the distinctive part of the URL that locates the service and a markup closure that is used at ❷ to build the request XML.

When using a REST API, it is often beneficial to create an infrastructure class like `BackPack` in listing 12.16. It is hardly possible to provide a more general solution that can be used with every REST service, because there is no standard that you can build upon.

You will see how useful such a standard is when we look into XML-RPC in the next section.

12.3.4 *Using XML-RPC*

The XML-RPC specification is almost as old as XML. It is extremely simple and concise. See http://www.xmlrpc.com for all details.

Thanks to this specification, Groovy can provide a general implementation for many of the infrastructure details that you have to write for REST. This general implementation comes with the Groovy distribution.[16] There is nothing extra you have to do or install to make this easy distributed processing environment work.

Perhaps the best way to convince you of its merits is by example. Suppose you have a simple XML-RPC server running on your local machine on port 8080 that exposes an `echo` operation that returns whatever it receives. Using this service from a Groovy client is as simple as

```
import groovy.net.xmlrpc.XMLRPCServerProxy as Proxy

def remote = new Proxy('http://localhost:8080/')

assert 'Hello world!' == remote.echo('Hello world!')
```

Installing a server that implements the `echo` operation is equally easy. Create a server instance, and assign a closure to its `echo` property:

```
import groovy.net.xmlrpc.XMLRPCServer as Server

def server = new Server()

server.echo = { return it }
```

---

[16] It's not in groovy-all-*.jar but in the GROOVY_HOME/lib directory.

Finally, the server must be started on a `ServerSocket` before the client can call it, and it must be stopped afterward. Listing 12.17 installs the echo server, starts it, requests the `echo` operation, and stops it at the end.

Listing 12.17   Self-contained XML-RPC server and client for the `echo` operation

```
// requires groovy-xmlrpc-0.3.jar in classpath
import groovy.net.xmlrpc.XMLRPCServerProxy as Proxy
import groovy.net.xmlrpc.XMLRPCServer as Server
import java.net.ServerSocket

def server = new Server()
server.echo = { return it }

def socket = new ServerSocket(8080)
server.startServer(socket)

remote = new Proxy("http://localhost:8080/")          Client
assert 'Hello world!' == remote.echo('Hello world!')  code

server.stopServer()
```

Having client and server together as shown in listing 12.17 is useful for testing purposes, but in production these two parts usually run on different systems.

XML-RPC also defines fault handling, which in Groovy XML-RPC is available through the `XMLRPCCallFailureException` with the properties `faultString` and `faultCode`.

The areas of applicability for XML-RPC are so wide that any list we could come up with would be necessarily incomplete. It is used for reading and posting to blogs, connecting to instant messaging systems (over the Jabber protocol for systems such as GoogleTalk[17]), news feeds, search engines, continuous integration servers, bug-tracking systems, and so on.

It's appealing because it is powerful and simple at the same time. Let's for example find out information about the projects managed at Codehaus.[18] Codehaus provides the *JIRA*[19] bug-tracking system for its hosted projects.

---

[17] See Guillaume's excellent article on how to use GoogleTalk through Groovy at http://glaforge.free.fr/weblog/index.php?itemid=142.

[18] www.codehaus.org is the open source platform that hosts popular open source projects such as Groovy and Maven.

[19] Find information about the JIRA XML-RPC methods at http://confluence.atlassian.com/display/JIRA/JIRA+XML-RPC+Overview.

Printing all project names can be done easily with the following code:

```
import groovy.net.xmlrpc.XMLRPCServerProxy as Proxy

def remote = new Proxy('http://jira.codehaus.org/rpc/xmlrpc')

def loginToken = remote.jira1.login('user','***')
def projects   = remote.jira1.getProjects(loginToken)
projects.each { println it.name }
```

It's conventional for operations exposed via XML-RPC to have a dot-notation like `jira1.login`. Groovy's XML-RPC support can deal with that.

However, if you call a lot of methods, using `remote.jira1.` gets in the way of readability. It would be nicer to avoid that. Listing 12.18 has a solution. Calls to proxy methods can always optionally take a closure. Inside that closure, method names are resolved against the proxy. We extend this behavior with a specialized `JiraProxy` that prefixes method calls with `jira1.`.

To make things a bit more interesting this time, we print some information about the Groovy project in the Codehaus JIRA.

Listing 12.18 Using the JIRA XML-RPC API on the Groovy project

```
import groovy.net.xmlrpc.XMLRPCServerProxy as Proxy

class JiraProxy extends Proxy {
    JiraProxy (url) { super ( url ) }
    Object invokeMethod(String methodname, args) {
        super.invokeMethod('jira1.'+methodname, args)
    }
}

def jira = new JiraProxy('http://jira.codehaus.org/rpc/xmlrpc')

jira.login('user','***') { loginToken ->
    def projects = getProjects(loginToken)
    def groovy   = projects.find { it.name == 'groovy' }
    println groovy.key
    println groovy.description
    println groovy.lead
}
```

This prints

```
GROOVY
Groovy JVM language.
guillaume
```

Note the simplicity of the code. Unlike with REST, you don't need to work on XML nodes, either in the request or in the response. You can just use Groovy datatypes such as strings (*user*), lists (*projects*), and maps (*groovy*). Who can ask for more?

There would be a book's worth more to say about XML-RPC and its Groovy module, especially about implementing the server side. But this book has only so many pages, and you need to refer to the online documentation for more details and usage scenarios.

You now have the basic information to start your work with XML-RPC. Try it! Of all the distributed processing approaches, this is the one that feels the most groovy to us.

We will close our tour through the various options for distributed processing with the all-embracing solution: SOAP.

12.3.5 *Applying SOAP*

SOAP is the successor of XML-RPC and follows the approach of providing a binding standard. This standard is maintained by the W3C; see http://www.w3.org/TR/soap/.

The SOAP standard extends the XML-RPC standard in multiple dimensions. One extension is datatypes. Where XML-RPC allows only a small fixed set of datatypes, SOAP provides means to define new service-specific datatypes. Other frameworks, including CORBA, DCOM, and Java RMI, provide functionality similar to that of SOAP, but SOAP messages are written entirely in XML and are therefore platform and language independent. The general approach of SOAP is to allow a web service to describe its public API: where it is located, what operations are available, and the request and response formats (called *messages*). A SOAP service makes this information available via the *Web Services Definition Language (WSDL)*.

SOAP has been widely adopted by the industry, and numerous free services are available, ranging from online shops through financial data, maps, music, payment systems, online auctions, order tracking, blogs, news, picture galleries, weather services, credit card validation—the list is endless.

Numerous programming languages and platforms provide excellent support for SOAP. Popular SOAP stack implementations on the Java platform include Jakarta Axis (http://ws.apache.org/axis/) and XFire (http://xfire.codehaus.org/). Built-in SOAP support for Groovy is still in its infancy, but it's already in use for production projects. First, we will explore how you can use SOAP with pure Groovy in an effective yet concise manner.

Doing SOAP with plain Groovy

Our example uses a web service at http://www.webservicex.net, which provides a lot of interesting public web services. First, we fetch the service description for its currency converter like so:

```
import groovy.xml.Namespace

def url = 'http://www.webservicex.net/CurrencyConvertor.asmx?WSDL'

def wsdl = new Namespace('http://schemas.xmlsoap.org/wsdl/','wsdl')
def doc  = new XmlParser().parse(url)

println doc[wsdl.portType][wsdl.operation].'@name'
```

This prints the available operations:

```
["ConversionRate", "ConversionRate", "ConversionRate"]
```

The service exposes three operations named `ConversionRate` with different characteristics.[20] We are interested in one that takes `FromCurrency` and `ToCurrency` as input parameters and returns the current conversion rate. Currencies can be expressed using a format like `'USD'` or `'EUR'`.

SOAP uses something called an *envelope format* for the request. The details are beyond the scope of this chapter—see the specifications for details. Our envelope looks like this:

```
<?xml version="1.0" encoding="utf-8"?>
<soap:Envelope
  xmlns:xsi="http://www.w3.org/2001/XMLSchema-instance"
  xmlns:xsd="http://www.w3.org/2001/XMLSchema"
  xmlns:soap="http://schemas.xmlsoap.org/soap/envelope/">
  <soap:Body>
    <ConversionRate xmlns="http://www.webserviceX.NET/">
      <FromCurrency>${from}</FromCurrency>
      <ToCurrency>${to}</ToCurrency>
    </ConversionRate>
  </soap:Body>
</soap:Envelope>
```

As you see from the ${} notation, this envelope is a template that we can use with a Groovy template engine.

Listing 12.19 reads this template, fills it with parameters for US dollar to euro conversion, and adds it to a POST request to the service URL. The request needs some additional request headers—for example, the `SOAPAction` to make the

---

[20] For advice on how to read a WSDL service description, refer to http://www.w3.org/TR/wsdl.

server understand it. We explicitly use UTF-8 character encoding to avoid any cross-platform encoding problems.

The service responds with a SOAP result envelope. We know it contains a node named ConversionRateResult belonging to the service's namespace. We locate the first such node in the response and get the conversion rate as its text value.

Listing 12.19 Using the ConversionRate SOAP service

```
import groovy.text.SimpleTemplateEngine as TEMPLATE
import groovy.xml.Namespace

def file     = new File('data/conv.templ.xml')        Templated envelope
def template = new TEMPLATE().createTemplate(file)     of SOAP request

def params   = [from:'USD', tofil:'EUR']
def request  = template.make(params).toString().getBytes('UTF-8')

def url  = 'http://www.webservicex.net/CurrencyConvertor.asmx'
def conn = new URL(url).openConnection()
def reqProps = [                                    Request headers to
    'Content-Type': 'text/xml; charset=UTF-8',       use every time
    'SOAPAction'  : 'http://www.webserviceX.NET/ConversionRate',
    'Accept'      : 'application/soap+xml, text/*'
]
reqProps.each { key,value -> conn.addRequestProperty(key,value) }

conn.requestMethod = 'POST'
conn.doOutput      = true                            Send the
conn.outputStream << new ByteArrayInputStream(request)   request
if (conn.responseCode != conn.HTTP_OK) {
    println "Error - HTTP:${conn.responseCode}"
    return
}
                                                     Parse the
def resp   = new XmlParser().parse(conn.inputStream)   response

def serv   = new Namespace('http://www.webserviceX.NET/')
def result = serv.ConversionRateResult      Extract the result

print   "Current USD to EUR conversion rate: "
println resp.depthFirst().find{result == it.name()}.text()
```

At the time of writing, it prints

```
Current USD to EUR conversion rate: 0.8449
```

This is straightforward in terms of each individual step, but taken as a whole, the code is fairly cumbersome. One point to note about the implementation is hidden in locating the result in the response envelope. We use the `serv` namespace and ask it for its `ConversionRateResult` property, which returns a `QName`. We assign it to the `result` variable and make use of the fact that `QName` implements the `equals` method with strings such that we find the proper node.

SOAP is verbose compared to other approaches. It is verbose in the code it demands for execution and—more important—it is verbose in its message format. It is not unusual for SOAP messages to have 10 times more XML markup then the payload size.

However, the SOAP standard makes it possible to provide general tools for dealing with its complexity.

Simplifying SOAP access with the GroovySOAP module

One of these tools is the GroovySOAP module, which eases the process of using web services. Download the required jar files as outlined at http://groovy. codehaus.org/Groovy+SOAP, and drop them into your GROOVY_HOME/lib directory. As an example of what you get from the GroovySOAP, listing 12.20 implements the SOAP client for the conversion rate service with a minimum of effort.

Listing 12.20 Using the `SoapClient` from the GroovySOAP module

```
import groovy.net.soap.SoapClient

def url = 'http://www.webservicex.net/CurrencyConvertor.asmx?WSDL'
def remote = new SoapClient(url)

println 'USD to EUR rate: '+remote.ConversionRate('USD', 'EUR')
```

Now, that's a lot groovier! Should your server be using a complex datatype in its response, GroovySOAP will unmarshall it and define a variable in your script. This can be demonstrated using the weather forecast located at webservicex.net. Using a place name located in the USA as an input, the web service replies with a one-week weather forecast in a complex document. Listing 12.21 nicely presents the data with the help of GroovySOAP.

Listing 12.21 Using complex data types with the `SoapClient`

```
import groovy.net.soap.SoapClient

def url = 'http://www.webservicex.net/WeatherForecast.asmx?WSDL'
def proxy = new SoapClient(url)
def result=proxy.GetWeatherByPlaceName("Seattle")

println result.latitude
println result.details.weatherData[0].weatherImage
```

Here's the output:

```
47.6114349
http://www.nws.noaa.gov/weather/images/fcicons/sct.jpg
```

Publishing a SOAP service with GroovySOAP

Suppose now that you want to develop your own server. GroovySOAP allows the construction of such a service from a simple Plain Old Groovy Object (POGO) representing your business logic. If you wanted to set up a small math server,[21] you could have a script that looks like listing 12.22.

Listing 12.22 The Groovy SOAP service script `MathService.groovy`

```
double add(double op1, double op2) {
  return (op1 + op2)
}

double square(double op1) {
  return (op1 * op1)
}
```

Note that there is nothing about the script that suggests it has anything to do with a web service. Listing 12.23 exposes this POGO as a web service.

Listing 12.23 Using the `SoapServer` from the GroovySOAP module

```
import groovy.net.soap.SoapServer

def server = new SoapServer("localhost", 6990)
server.setNode("MathService")
System.out.println("start Math Server")
server.start()
```

---

[21] Simple calculations and currency conversions have become the "hello world" of web service examples.

This little bit of magic is possible thanks to the delegation pattern and introspection that enables GroovySOAP to generate automatically the web service interface by filtering the methods inherited from the `GroovyObject` interface.

It's worth paying attention to this area of ongoing Groovy development. We anticipate that before long, new SOAP tools will arise and provide more functionality for using web services with Groovy.

12.4 Summary

XML is such a big topic that we cannot possibly touch all bases in an introductory book on Groovy. We have covered the most important aspects in enough detail to provide a good basis for experimentation and further reading. When pushing the limits with Groovy XML, you will probably encounter topics that are not covered in this chapter. Don't hesitate to consult the online resources.

At this point, you have a solid basis for understanding the different ways of working with XML in Groovy.

Using the familiar Java DOM parsers in Groovy enables you to work on the standard `org.w3c.com.Node` objects whenever the situations calls for it. Such nodes can be retrieved from the `DOMBuilder`, conveniently accessed with the help of `DOMCategory`, and investigated with XPath expressions. Groovy makes life with the DOM easier, but it can't rectify some of the design decisions that give surprises or involve extra work for no benefit.

Groovy's internal `XmlParser` and `XmlSlurper` provide access to XML documents in a Groovy-friendly way that supports GPath expressions for working on the document. `XmlParser` provides an in-memory representation for in-place manipulation of nodes, whereas `XmlSlurper` is able to work in a more stream-like fashion. For even further memory reductions, you can also use SAX and StAX.

Finally, it's easy to send XML around the world to make networked computers work together, sharing information and computing power. XML-RPC and SOAP have support in the Groovy libraries, although that support is likely to change significantly over time. REST can't benefit from such support as easily (not even in the dynamic world of Groovy) due to a lack of standardization, but you have seen how the use of builders can make the development of an API for a specific REST service straightforward.

Whatever your XML-based activity, Groovy is likely to have *something* that will ease your work. By now, that shouldn't come as a surprise.

Part 3

Everyday Groovy

In the course of this book, you have seen a large portion of Groovyland. Part 1 introduced you to the Groovy language, datatypes, operators, control structures, and even the Meta-Object Protocol. Part 2 led you through the Groovy library, showing builders, templates, numerous JDK enhancements, working with databases, and XML support. Your backpack is filled with lots of valuable knowledge that waits to be brought to new horizons.

Part 3 will give you guidance on how to best apply your knowledge in your day-to-day work, where the happy paths of Groovy lead though uncharted terrain, and how to employ your tools wisely.

It starts with chapter 13, which reveals tips and tricks of the experts: how to avoid common pitfalls; making use of a snippet collection; command-line and automation support; and finally laying out the workspace such that coding, debugging, profiling, and the like work well together.

Chapter 14 elaborates on unit testing, an activity that no self-respecting professional developer can work without. With a clever mix of the Groovy wisdom you've already acquired and a bit of guidance through Groovy's excellent testing support, you will be able to appreciate unit testing as another strength of Groovy.

Chapter 15 bridges the world of Java and Groovy to the Windows platform, where lots of developers do their daily work. It presents how to put Groovy's expressiveness into action for automation of Windows controls and applications.

Finally, chapter 16 comes as a bonus for all the diligent readers who held out until the very end. You will be reimbursed with a sneak peek into Grails, the (web) application framework that leverages J2EE, Hibernate, Spring, and Groovy to allow rapid application development at industrial strength.

13 Tips and tricks

> *The competent programmer is fully aware of the limited size of his own skull. He therefore approaches his task with full humility, and avoids clever tricks like the plague.*
>
> —Edsger Dijkstra

Learning language features and library APIs is one thing; using a language for your everyday programming tasks has its own challenges. As the saying goes, "In theory, practice and theory are one and the same. In practice, they're not." This chapter attempts to bridge the gap, giving some insight into what it's like to use Groovy *for real*, and (we hope) steering you clear of some of the potholes others (including us) have run into.

Closures are a good example of the gulf between practice and theory. They may appear unfamiliar and difficult in the language description, but they turn out to be simple and straightforward in everyday use. Other concepts may appear simple but have certain consequences that the programmer needs to be aware of to avoid typical pitfalls. This is covered in section 13.1.

Furthermore, the features of Groovy often suggest a certain way of approaching a task that is different from Java or other languages. In such cases, although there is a certain comfort level in staying with what you know, you will generally become more productive if you follow the Groovy idioms. This isn't because "Groovy knows best" (although of course we believe that the Groovy way is usually the best way), but because it's generally easier to go with the flow of a language than to fight against it. We show a few pieces of Groovy idiom in sections 13.2, 13.3, and 13.4.

Software development consists of more than just the programming; it also includes debugging, profiling, and setting up the working environment to make programming easier. Section 13.5 gives hints for organizing your work.

13.1 Things to remember

The following sections should remind you about some Groovy idiosyncrasies that result from its language design and dynamic nature. Take this as a checklist of topics that have been presented earlier in this book and that you should not forget. It's also handy as a list of potential "gotchas" to run down if your code isn't behaving as you expect it to.

13.1.1 Equality versus identity

The distinction between equality and identity is one of the first things you learn about Groovy. There are some consequences you should be aware of. Table 13.1 has the comparison between Java and Groovy idioms of equality and identity.

Groovy equality isn't necessarily commutative; it isn't guaranteed that a==b is the same as b==a. A programmer may choose to override equals and break this behavior, even though you shouldn't do so.

Table 13.1 Equality and identity in Groovy compared to Java

	Groovy	Java
Equality	`a == b`	`a.equals(b)`
Identity	`a.is(b)`	`a == b`

Furthermore, Groovy allows `null` in equality checks:

```
null == null // is true
null == 1    // is false
```

You cannot do that in Java, because `null.equals(b)` would throw a `NullPointer-Exception`.

13.1.2 *Using parentheses wisely*

When in doubt, you can use the Java style of using parentheses: always putting parentheses around method arguments. On the other hand, leaving out parentheses can often enhance readability by focusing the eye of the reader on the guts of the code. You have the choice between the following:

```
println 'hi'
println('hi')
```

However, if no arguments are given, the parentheses are mandatory to distinguish method calls from property access:

```
println()  // ok
println    // <- fails with MissingPropertyException
```

The `MissingPropertyException` is thrown because with no arguments and no parentheses given, Groovy assumes you are looking for the `println` property and would call `getPrintln` if there were such a method.

Note that this is different from other languages with optional elements of syntax, such as Ruby. Another difference is that parentheses can be omitted only for method calls that are top-level statements. In other words, parentheses are mandatory for method calls that are used in expressions:

```
'abc'.substring 1,3        // ok
x = 'abc'.substring 1,3    // assignment expression -> parser error
println 'abc'.substring 1,3 // argument expression -> parser error
```

Finally, putting symbols in parentheses forces the Groovy parser to resolve the symbol as an expression. This can be helpful when specifying keys in maps. Consider a map like

```
map = [x:1]
```

which is equivalent to

```
map = ['x':1]
```

Now, what if you have a variable x in scope, and you would like to use its content as a key in the map? You can enforce that with parentheses around x:

```
def x = 'a'
assert ['a':1] == [(x):1]
```

This trick is also described in section 14.3.

13.1.3 *Returning from methods and closures*

Remember that inside a closure, return returns from the closure, not from the method the closure was passed to as an argument, nor from any method surrounding the closure definition. Suppose you run a line like

```
[1,2,3].each { print it; return }
```

This prints 123, not 1 as some might expect, because return returns from the closure, not from the each method. The closure is called three times, and each time it is left via return. Compare this to

```
for (it in [1,2,3]) { print it; return }
```

which prints 1 because return now leaves the current block. With this difference in mind, you can guess what this snippet does:

```
def myMethod() {
    [1,2,3].each { print it; return }
}
myMethod()
```

Right, it prints 123. Again, the return keyword only leaves the closure, not the surrounding myMethod.

So, how can you write closure code that leaves a method prematurely? There currently is only one way—by throwing an exception:

```
def myMethod() {
    [1,2,3].each { print it; throw new RuntimeException() }
}
try {myMethod()} catch (Exception e){}
```

This prints 1. However, this code is really ugly. Alternatives are in the works but not yet available at the time of writing. See also section 5.6.

The groovier way to leave an iteration prematurely is different. If possible, you should attempt to iterate over the right set of elements to start with, rather than aborting the iteration early. The methods `find`, `findAll`, and `grep` and the subscript operator with indexes or ranges are your friends here. The following lines show some alternatives:

```
list[0..1]                .each { processing(it) }
list.find{ it == 2 }      .each { processing(it) }
list.findAll{ it % 2 == 0}.each { processing(it) }
list.grep(~/\d/)          .each { processing(it) }
```

In essence, you're using a GPath to restrict the work items declaratively rather than using control structures in a procedural way. This course of action isn't always available, but it should be used where it is both possible and elegant. When you follow this style, you have the additional benefit of separating the concerns of selecting items and processing them.

13.1.4 *Calling methods in builder code*

Suppose you are going to build nodes with `NodeBuilder` such that you get an outer node containing a nested middle node with an inner node like this:

```
outer() {
  middle() {
    inner()
  }
}
```

The usual code for producing this structure with `NodeBuilder` is straightforward:

```
new NodeBuilder().outer {
    middle {
        inner()
    }
}
```

Now, suppose you would like to extract the production of the `middle` and `inner` nodes to a method. You might want to do this because the production is complicated or you use that production logic in multiple places. Let's call the new method `produce`.

You cannot implement it as

```
def produce(){
    middle {      // fails - no such method!
        inner()
    }
}
```

and call it like this:

```
new NodeBuilder().outer {
    produce()
}
```

Groovy will complain because it can't find the `middle` method. Within the scope of
the `produce` method, you have to make the builder known to the first method call
on the builder:

```
def builder = new NodeBuilder()

builder.outer {
    produce()
}
def produce(){
    builder.middle(){ // needs the builder reference
        inner()        // now it's known
    }
}
```

Alternatively, you can use the following to avoid using a shared variable—if
your production code is in a different class to the declaration of the builder,
for example:

```
def builder = new NodeBuilder()

builder.outer {
    produce(builder)
}
def produce(builderContext){
    builderContext.middle(){
        inner()
    }
}
```

In both cases, you make the reference to the `NodeBuilder` available in the `produce`
method in order to get back into the context of the builder. Once the first method
call has been made, the builder will set the delegate of the closure to the builder,
which is why the call to `inner` doesn't need to be made explicitly on the builder.

Apart the builder reference, there is another issue to keep in mind when using
methods from within builder code: how the `produce` method is looked up. Why
does the preceding code call the `produce` method we've defined rather than creating a new node called `produce`?

Before doing any builder-specific handling of a method call, the builder first
tries calling the method on the *owner*. The builder handles the method call (by
building nodes, for example) only if the owner doesn't handle the method.

Consequently, in the preceding code, there would be a conflict if there were
another method called `inner` within the script.

All builders that come with the Groovy distribution obey this rule. All builders that subclass `BuilderSupport` also have this behavior by default. However, the priority of local method lookup in builders cannot be guaranteed for all possible builders, because a pathological builder implementation may choose to override it, even though this is not advised.

13.1.5 *Qualifying access to "this"*

When referring to fields or methods from within the same class, most of the time it's optional to prefix the name of the field or method with the `this.` qualifier. This behavior is equivalent to that of Java.

Disambiguation in Java

Even in Java, this prefix is sometimes used for disambiguation. The typical use is to distinguish between a local variable and an instance variable, either in a constructor or in a property setter, for example:

```
MyClass (Object myField) {          // Java constructor example
    this.myField = myField;
}

void setField (Object myField) { // Java property setter example
    this.myField = myField;
}
```

Disambiguation in Groovy

In Groovy, the need for distinction goes beyond that. Listing 13.1 combines examples for using the `this` prefix to differentiate between local variables, fields, and properties.

> **Listing 13.1   Using `this` to distinguish between property and field access**

```
class ExplicitThisTest extends GroovyTestCase {
    def zero = 0

    def getZero() { return 1 }

    def callMePlain(zero) {
        return zero
    }
    def callMeQualified(zero) {
        return this.zero
    }

    void testZero() {
```

```
assert 0 == zero
assert 0 == this.zero          Field is used
assert 0 == this.@zero         if available
assert 1 == getZero()
assert 2 == callMePlain(2)      ◁──┘ Parameter is used by method
assert 0 == callMeQualified(2)  ◁── Field is used by method
assert 1 == new ExplicitThisTest().zero   ◁── Property is used
assert 0 == new ExplicitThisTest().@zero  ◁─┐ Field is
    }                                        │ used
}
```

It goes without saying that it is always good practice to avoid such name clashes. But they sometimes occur accidentally, such as when performing a renaming refactoring.

If you ever find yourself unsure about what's going on but *do* want to make a lookup against this, it's worth qualifying it, even if you decide that would be the default behavior anyway. There's no need to make a maintenance engineer go through the same hoops as you to work out behavior.

A reference prefix like this is always needed when denoting method closures. A reference like &myMethod will never work; only using a reference like this.&myMethod works. The same is true for field access with the @ sign, as in this.@zero, which cannot be used without a preceding reference.

13.1.6 *Considering number types*

Groovy shines at capturing business logic in a declarative style. In the financial business and in scientific research, this often means lots of formulas and calculations.

In this scenario, you need to remember that Groovy returns BigDecimal objects from the division operator, and any BigDecimal math is slow compared to other number types.

When calculations are used extensively, it is profitable to avoid full floating-point division operations where possible. For example, you may want to calculate monetary values with cents instead of dollars and use intdiv for division. This proved to be useful in the first big commercial project that was fully implemented in Groovy.

Although Groovy relieves the programmer of tinkering with number types in a lot of places, there are remaining areas that need attention. Suppose we need to print the *sine* values from zero to 2π at every increment of $\pi/2$. Expected values would be close to 0, 1, 0, -1. The following solution would be straightforward, but wrong:

```
0.step(Math.PI*2, Math.PI/2){          // wrong!
  println "$it : ${Math.sin(it)}"
}
```

The `Integer.step` method takes an `Integer` argument for the upper bound. The preceding code is like using `0.step(6,PI/2)`. The correct version needs to call the `step` method on a non-integer, such as the `BigDecimal 0.0` :

```
0.0G.step(Math.PI*2, Math.PI/2){ println "$it : ${Math.sin(it)}" }
```

Note that the `G` suffix is optional, but helps to make it obvious which dot is part of the number and which dot is involved in the method call. Whenever you encounter unexpected values with your calculations, check the number types being used and the method signatures.

13.1.7 *Leveraging Ant*

Groovy and Ant make a power duo. From within a Groovy script, all Ant capabilities are easily accessible via `AntBuilder`. From within an Ant script, all Groovy capabilities are easily accessible via the `<groovy>` task. You can take the best of both worlds, mixing and matching as needed.

Using Ant from Groovy

In section 8.4, you saw how to use AntBuilder. This is a valuable possibility to keep in mind. There are so many well-engineered Ant tasks that you will often find a good solution there.

But there are more reusable components in the Ant distribution than just the tasks. For example, the Ant `fileScanner` allows you to get all the `File` objects of one or multiple filesets, as shown in listing 13.2. The example scans all the listings in the current directory and—in our usual self-checking manner—asserts that the result contains our example script.

Listing 13.2 Ant `fileScanner` example

```
def files = new AntBuilder().fileScanner {
    fileset(dir: '.') {
        include(name: 'Listing*.groovy')
    }
}
def scriptName = getClass().name + '.groovy'
assert files.collect{ it.name }.contains(scriptName)
```

The `files` variable refers to a `FileScanner` object. Because it has an `iterator` method, it supports all Groovy object iteration methods such as `collect`, which we use here.

A special task that is useful for calling a full Ant script file from Groovy is Ant's ant task. It is straightforward to use. To call the build.xml Ant script, use it like

```
new AntBuilder().ant(antfile:'build.xml')
```

You can see this as a way to *include* an Ant build script into a Groovy script. This is also possible in the opposite direction: You can use Groovy scripts from Ant.

Using Groovy from Ant

Although Ant is extremely powerful, it can't cater to every eventuality. It uses a declarative paradigm that is great for many tasks but can get in the way on occasion. As an example, you may have a classpath that is specified as a property in a compressed form—for instance, as a list of library names (dom4j, hibernate, spring) instead of as a full list of jar files. The code required (even with the AntContrib library) to build a classpath from such a list is horrendous, whereas in Groovy it can be specified very cleanly.

The <groovy> Ant task allows you to run Groovy code directly from an Ant file, either using a script file that is specified as a parameter to the task, or inline as the text content of the task. Listing 13.3 shows a simple Ant build file that calls a Groovy script included in the body of the build file.

Listing 13.3   A simple Ant script running some Groovy code

```xml
<?xml version="1.0" ?>
<project name="groovy-test" default="test" >

  <taskdef name="groovy"
    classname="org.codehaus.groovy.ant.Groovy"
    classpath="groovy-all-1.0.jar"/>

  <target name="test">
    <groovy>
      println "Running in Groovy"
    </groovy>
  </target>

</project>
```

The easiest way to make Groovy available to Ant is with a <taskdef> that refers to the embeddable Groovy jar file. The Groovy script is run within a binding which knows about various Ant-specific properties, as shown in table 13.2.

Table 13.2 The properties available in the binding when running a Groovy script from Ant with the `<groovy>` task

Name in binding	Description
`ant`	An AntBuilder with knowledge of the current project
`project`	The project currently being built
`properties`	The current properties (can be modified)
`target`	The currently executing target
`task`	The task wrapping Groovy

Using the `ant` variable from the binding allows you to use an AntBuilder that is transparently aware of the enclosing Ant project and shares its properties, such as the `basedir`. Therefore it's easy to use tasks such as copy, move, and delete, and to use filesets in general:

```
<groovy>
    def dirMap = ['old1': 'new1', 'old2': 'new2']
    dirMap.each {old, new -> ant.copy(dir: old, toDir: new) }
</groovy>
```

The `project` variable from the binding can also be useful, because `project` provides access to a number of interesting features, such as properties, references,[1] build listeners,[2] and task definitions. Suppose we want to implement a `RulePrinter` task in Groovy and add it to the project:

```
<groovy>
    class RulePrinter extends Task {
        def size = 40
        def symbol = '*'
        public void execute() { println symbol * size }
    }
    project.addTaskDefinition('ruler', RulePrinter)
</groovy>

<ruler/>
<ruler symbol="--8<--" size="10"/>
```

---

[1] Projects can store arbitrary objects in references.

[2] You can register Groovy listener objects that get notified whenever a task is started and ended; see http://ant.apache.org/manual/listeners.html.

The usual way of implementing such an Ant custom task would have been with Ant's `<scriptdef>` task. However, our solution is more elegant and demonstrates again Groovy's seamless integration with any Java-based technology.

The `properties` property is particularly useful, because it allows you to use the same means of parameterization within your script as in the rest of your build file. Note that it lets you set the value of properties, which can be useful when setting the value involves applying some logic:

```
properties.'out' = properties.'user.dir'+System.currentTimeMillis()
```

Ant usually doesn't modify the value of properties during the run of a build. Although doing so is technically possible, it is better to avoid this, in order to comply with the Ant property contract.

When writing code inline, you need to be careful about characters that have special meaning within XML—particularly angle brackets. It's often easiest to use CDATA sections to avoid even having to worry about it. For example:

```
<groovy><![CDATA[
  println (Math.random() < 0.5 ? "Lower" : "Higher")
]]></groovy>
```

An alternative to using the `<groovy>` task directly is to use Ant's own `<script>` task. Consult the Ant documentation for the options available. The language should be specified as `"groovy"`.

Using Groovy in your Ant scripts gives you a way to execute arbitrary logic without resorting to compiling extra Ant tasks from Java. Although a build tool would otherwise need to build other tools before it can complete its build, it's nice to have an ace up your sleeve such as Groovy.

13.1.8 Scripts are classes but different

One of the biggest misconceptions about Groovy is that a Groovy script will be interpreted line-by-line. This is not the case.

When a Groovy script gets executed, it is transformed into a class, and then the class is executed. This transformation happens transparently to the developer. However, the process has some consequences that are helpful to be aware of.

Script naming

First and foremost, a class must have a name. Groovy chooses to name your class by the filename (without the .groovy extension of course). So if you create a script with content

```
println x
```

and save it to a file named x.groovy, executing the script via `groovy x` gives you

```
class x
```

This can be surprising. You can lower the risk of such surprises by naming your script files like classes, with Pascal-cased names such as FileNameFinder.groovy rather than findFileNames.groovy.

As soon as you have the file x.groovy on the classpath, using the undeclared variable x in any of your scripts can produce some odd behavior, because x will then refer to the class x.

Script inclusion

Only in the simplest possible cases does all script code reside in one file. What is the Groovy way of including dependent files into a script? There are no *include* or *require* directives, unlike in some other scripting languages.

The compilation process from scripts to classes would make it difficult to allow a directive that does a *literal* inclusion of code that is stored in a dependent script file. The concept doesn't fit into the Java world.

Instead, Groovy offers two alternatives:

- Make your dependent script a declared class.
- Evaluate the dependent script via `evaluate(file)`.

We've used the first alternative many times throughout the book, even in the earliest examples. Do you remember the Book example that we started the whole Groovy adventure with? The `Book` class was declared in a file called Book.groovy. We then called it from a script using code such as

```
Book gina = new Book('Groovy in Action')
```

and called methods on the reference stored in the `gina` variable. No special directive is needed for finding the Book.groovy file. The only prerequisite is that Groovy must be able to find the file on the classpath and must be able to compile its content. If the lookup or the compilation fails, you'll encounter a `ClassNotFoundException`.[3]

The second alternative is using the `evaluate` method that all scripts inherit from `GroovyShell`. The overloads for this method include passing it a `File` object

---

[3] When a `ClassNotFoundException` is encountered, it helps to explicitly compile the dependent .groovy file with `groovyc` to get a more detailed error message from the compiler. This advice is sometimes misconstrued as "dependent scripts need to be compiled," which is of course not true.

to evaluate (see chapter 11). The evaluation of the file will work on the current binding: It can use variables from the binding, read and change their values, and add new variables to the binding. The `evaluate` method returns the value of the script's last evaluated expression.

Let's assume we have a *smart* configuration as in listing 13.4 to store a person's preferences in nodes, dynamically constructed with `NodeBuilder` and mixed with iteration logic to assemble the hours when this person is supposed to appear at work. We save that script to a file named Preferences.groovy.

Listing 13.4   Preferences.groovy as a smart configuration

```
def builder = new NodeBuilder()
builder.prefs(name:'Dierk') {
    language('Groovy')
    conference('http://www.waterfall2006.com')
    for (i in 9..17) {
        workingHour(i)
    }
}
```

The script does not have an explicit return statement, because that would be atypical for a script. The last evaluated expression serves this purpose, which is the `prefs` node. Of course, it is also valid to use an explicit return statement.

We have a second script in listing 13.5 that makes use of this smart configuration. It does so by using the `evaluate` method. Some assertions show how to access information from the smart configuration.

Listing 13.5   Including the configuration as a dependent script

```
def prefs = evaluate(new File('Preferences.groovy'))

assert prefs.'@name' == 'Dierk'
assert prefs.workingHour*.value().contains(16)
```

For successful execution of listing 13.5, Preferences.groovy must be saved to the working directory. Because the filename is used to find the dependent script, this solution gets brittle in more complex scenarios. As soon as you have multiple scripts depending on each other, scripts being stored in subdirectories and so on, you are better off relying on declared classes and the classpath.

> **FOR THE GEEKS** If you are keen to work with dependent files but seek more flexibility, look at the JDK `File` API to set the parent of a file or use `ClassLoader.getResourceAsStream` to read the dependent file as a stream from the classpath and pass it to the `evaluate` method.

Now you know a few problems to avoid—but more positive examples are called for as well. In the next section, we will provide some pieces of code that are self-contained and can give you ideas during your own product development. They also give you opportunities for experimentation and enhancement.

13.2 Useful snippets

Here are some code snippets that you may find useful when programming in Groovy. They are aimed at being idiomatic. We will show you a novel use of closures, a neat way to modify text with regular expressions, a useful way of indicating progress in command-line applications, a useful tool to display execution results line by line, and some advanced uses of GStrings.

13.2.1 Shuffling a collection

Suppose you have a collection—a list, for example—and you would like to shuffle the content. For instance, you may have track numbers for your Groovy MP3 player and wish to create a random playlist. The Groovy variant of a solution that is often suggested for scripting languages is

```
[1, 2, 3, 4, 5].sort { Math.random() } // very questionable solution
```

This works the following way: when a closure that is passed to the `sort` method does *not* take two parameters (in which case it would have been used as a *Comparator*) then `sort` applies the closure to each element before comparing. Because we return random numbers each comparison has a random outcome.

Although this works, it is neither *efficient* nor guaranteed to be stable with all sort algorithms, nor does it deliver good results.

Programming in Groovy means you have the wealth of Java at your disposal, and thus you can use the `shuffle` method of `java.util.Collections`:

```
def list = [1,2,3,4,5]
Collections.shuffle(list)
println list
```

This solution is efficient and stable, and it leads leads to an even distribution of the shuffled object; each item has an equal probability of being shuffled to a given index.

We will reuse this functionality in the next example.

13.2.2 *Scrambling text with regular expressions*

You may have heard about the experiment where text remains readable even though the words in the text are scrambled, as long as the first and last character don't change. Look at the following scrambled text. Can you read what it means?

```
Sarbmlce the inner crharatces of words
laenvig the text sltil reabldae for poeple but
not for cutoermps.
```

Listing 13.6 implements this scrambling process in Groovy.

Listing 13.6   Scrambling the inner character of words

```
def text = '''
Scramble the inner characters of words          Text to be
leaving the text still readable for people but  scrambled
not for computers.
'''
println text.replaceAll(/\B\w+\B/) { inner ->
    def list = inner.toList()
    Collections.shuffle(list)
    list.join ''
}
```

We use a regular expression to find all inner word characters. Then, `replaceAll` replaces all occurrences with the result of a closure that is fed the corresponding match. The match is converted to a list, shuffled, converted to a string, and returned. The regular expression for finding the inner characters of a word models the first and last character as a non-word-boundary (\B) with one or more word characters (\w+) in between.

The ability to use a closure to build the replacement value for a regular expression match is often very useful.

We proceed with other helpful examples of closures.

13.2.3 *Console progress bar*

Suppose you have a time-consuming task that you need to apply to every file in a directory. It would be helpful to get some information about the progress: how much has already been processed, how much is still left to do, and which file is currently being processed.

The output should not be longer than a single line on the console, showing updated information on-the-fly.

When started on the directory containing this book's listings, this line may for example read

```
:::::::::  AthleteDAO.groovy
```

in between be refreshed to

```
####:::::  Mailman.groovy
```

and finally be

```
#########  x.groovy
```

Note: This is all one single displayed line that is updated over time, like a normal progress bar. If you have used the wget command-line tool for fetching web content, you have seen the same kind of display there.

The processFiles method in listing 13.7 takes a closure argument called notify. This closure is notified whenever a new files starts being processed. This is equivalent to the Observer pattern.[4]

The processFiles method is called with a closure that updates the progress bar whenever it receives a notification. For simplicity, our processing only consists of sleeping a little, and processing is done for files in the current directory only.

Listing 13.7   Printing a progress bar on the console

```
def processFiles(notify) {
    def names = new File('.').list()
    names.eachWithIndex { name, i ->
        notify(i * 10 / names.size(), name)
        sleep 50        ◁─┐ The real file operation
    }                       │ would go here
}
processFiles { filled, info ->
    print '\b' * 61
    print '#'*filled + ':'*(10-filled) +' '+ info.padRight(50)
}
```

Of course, this snippet could be extended in a number of ways. However, even running this simple version on the console is fun and worthwhile.

We will look into more cool things you can do with the console in the next example.

---

[4] See Erich Gamma et al, *Design Patterns: Elements of Reusable Object-Oriented Software* (Addison-Wesley, 1995) for an explanation.

13.2.4 Self-commenting single-steps

How about a snippet that reads a codebase and prints it to the console with an indication what each line evaluates to? Example output could look like this:

```
data = [0,1,2,3]          //-> [0, 1, 2, 3]
data[1..2]                //-> [1, 2]
data.collect { it / 2 }   //-> [0, 0.5, 1, 1.5]
```

Saving this output back to the original file would mean we have written a piece of code that is able to write comments about itself.

Listing 13.8 reveals how to achieve this. We split the code by line, ignore empty lines, print each line, and finally evaluate the line and print the result.

Listing 13.8 Evaluating and printing line-by-line

```
def show(code) {
    for (line in code.split("\n")){
        if (!line) continue
        print line.padRight(25) + '//-> '
        println evaluate(line).inspect()     ◁──┐ Evaluate each non-empty
    }                                            │ line in its own GroovyShell
}
show '''
data = [0,1,2,3]
data[1..2]
data.collect { it / 2 }
'''
```

But wait—didn't we say that you cannot evaluate Groovy code line-by-line? Yes, and the example works only because data has no declaration, which Groovy takes as a hint to put it into the current binding. Each line is evaluated separately, but the binding is passed onto the GroovyShell that conducts the evaluation. The first line adds data to the binding; the second line reads data from the binding when getting the 1..2 range from it.

What would happen if the first line read List data = [0,1,2,3]? At that point, data would be a local variable in the script and so would not be added to the binding. The first line would still evaluate correctly, but the second line will fail because data would not be known in the scope of the GroovyShell that evaluates the second line.

That means that the applicability of our single-step printer is very restricted. However, it makes a good example to sharpen your understanding of scripts being classes rather than sequences of evaluated lines.

13.2.5 *Advanced GString usage*

In the majority of cases, GStrings are used for simple formatting with the placeholders resolved immediately, as in

```
println "Now is ${new Date()}"
```

GStrings have a special way in which they resolve any contained placeholders. At the time of the GString creation, they evaluate each placeholder and store a reference to the result of that evaluation within the GString object. At the time of transformation into a `java.lang.String`, each reference is asked for its string representation in order to construct the fully concatenated result.

In other words: Although the placeholder resolution is *eager*, writing the references is *lazy*. The interesting point comes when a placeholder reference refers to an object that changes its string representation over time, especially after the GString was constructed. There are a number of objects that behave like this, such as lists and maps that base their string representation on their current content. Listing 13.9 uses a list to demonstrate this behavior and a typical Groovy object that writes itself lazily: a writable closure.

Listing 13.9   Writing GString content lazily

```
def count = 0
def data  = []

def counter = { it << count }.asWritable()

def stanza = "content $counter is $data"    ←❶ GString works
                                                as template
assert 'content 0 is []'  == stanza

count++
data << 1

assert 'content 1 is [1]'  == stanza
```

Note how the stanza GString ❶ first works on the current values of count and data but changes its string representation when count and data change.

This behavior enables GStrings to be used as a lightweight alternative to Groovy's template engines (see section 9.4).

One word of caution: You need to be extremely careful when using such dynamic GStrings as elements of a HashSet or as keys in a HashMap. In general, you should avoid doing so, because the hash code of the GString will change if its string representation changes. If the hash code changes after the GString has been inserted into a map, the map cannot find the entry again, even if you present it with the exact same GString reference.

Writing idiomatic Groovy is one side of working *with* the language instead of fighting *against* it. Another side is using the tools provided as effectively as possible. In the next section, we will give more information on the groovy tool used to run scripts and classes.

13.3 *Using groovy on the command line*

While working through the book, you have used the groovy command to execute Groovy programs and scripts. It has some additional options to use it on the command line or as a client-server program. We will explore the evaluation of short scripts specified on the command line, processing text files line-by-line, setting up very simple servers, and performing in-place file modifications.

Table 13.3 lists the command-line options for the groovy command.

Table 13.3   Command-line options for the groovy tool

Option	Argument	Meaning
-c, --encoding	Character encoding	Specify the encoding of the files
-d, --debug		Debug mode will print out full stack traces
-e	Text to execute	Specify an in-line command-line script
-h, --help		Usage information
-i	Extension	Modify files in place
-l	Port	Listen on a port, and process inbound lines
-n		Process files line by line
-p		Process files line by line, and print the result
-v, --version		Display the Groovy and JVM versions

The -c/--encoding, -d/--debug, and -v/--version options are self-explanatory. The other options will be demonstrated by example. But first, let's try running a short script.

13.3.1 *Evaluating a command-line script*

The -e option (*e* stands for *evaluate*) lets you pass one-line scripts to groovy on the command line as well as pipe output from one command or script as input to the groovy command. It is similar to the -e option in Perl, Ruby, and other languages.

A simple one-liner using -e follows. This script prints the vendor of the JVM in which Groovy is running, using the java.lang.System class to retrieve the java.vendor System property value:

```
> groovy -e "println System.properties.'java.vendor'"

Sun Microsystems Inc.
```

Note the enclosing quotes around the script: When using -e to pass scripts to groovy on the command line, make sure you enclose the script in single or double quotes so that the command or shell interpreter in which you are running (cmd on Windows or bash on UNIX, for example) does not interpret the contents of your Groovy script as commands or wildcards for itself.

Here is an example demonstrating piping the output of one Groovy script to another Groovy script that takes it as input and transforms the characters to uppercase. Enter the whole input in one line:

```
> groovy -e "println System.properties.'java.vendor'" |
  groovy -e "println System.in.text.toUpperCase()"

SUN MICROSYSTEMS INC.
```

You can also do this with native operating system commands, of course.

If you pass additional arguments on the command line, they are available to the script in the args variable. That means you can, for example, count lines in a file like so:

```
> groovy -e "println new File(args[0]).readLines().size()" jokes.txt

1024
```

Alternatively, you could print a random joke:

```
> groovy -e "lines = new File(args[0]).readLines();
  println lines[(int)(lines.size()*Math.random())]" jokes.txt

A horse goes into a bar … "Hey buddy, why the long face?"
```

So far, so good—but we're not making particularly extensive use of the *piping* feature of most shells, where the result of one operation can be the input to the next. That's just one of the uses for the options we deal with next.

13.3.2 *Using print and line options*

The -e option becomes more interesting when combined with other options. The -p (*print*) and -n (*line*) options tell groovy to create an implicit variable named line from each line of input the groovy command receives from standard input. Standard input may be sourced from a pipe or from files given as trailing command-line arguments.

The line variable is useful when you want to do something for each line of input rather than for the text of the input stream as a whole.

Assume there is a file example.txt in the subdirectory data containing

```
line one
line two
line three
```

You can cut off the line prefix with

```
> groovy -pe "line-'line '" data\example.txt
one
two
three
```

The -p option is essentially the same as -n, except it ensures that the result of processing each line is printed to the console (it is an implicit println for each line processed), whereas with -n you need to explicitly specify print or println for anything you want to output.

This can be helpful when filtering, for example, the directory entries for a given date:

```
> dir | groovy -ne "if (line.contains('05.02.06')) println line"
05.02.06  17:48    <DIR>             .
05.02.06  17:48    <DIR>             ..
05.02.06  14:16                272 BraceCounter.groovy
```

Here's a second example for system administrators, which uses the input redirection capabilities of your command shell with the < sign. In a cygwin shell, you might do something like this:

```
> groovy -ne 'if (line =~ /dierk/) println line' < /etc/passwd
dierk:unused_by_nt/2000/xp:…:/home/dierk:/bin/bash
```

Note how the examples read from different input sources: from a file given on the command line, from the piped output stream of the dir command, and from streams redirected by the shell. On the command line, you always have a close interaction with your command shell.

13.3.3 *Using the listen mode*

The -1 (*listen*) option lets you run a Groovy script in client-server mode. You execute a script (using -e or specifying a file to execute), and Groovy starts a simple server on port 1960 (by default; you may override the port setting if you choose). You can then connect to that server via a telnet application, for example, and run the script or pass arguments to the script for it to process and return results to your client.

> **NOTE** Case in point: Jeremy Rayner, one of the core Groovy developers, wrote a simple HTTP server[5] in less than 75 lines of Groovy code!

Here is an example of a tiny script that looks up and returns the IP address of any hostname it receives. You will need two console windows for this example, one for the server and one for the client. First start the server. By default, the server will start on port 1960, but you can specify any unused port on the command line after the -1 option. We're using port 5000 here:

```
> groovy -l 5000 -e "println 'ip address: ' +
  InetAddress.getByName(line).hostAddress"

groovy is listening on port 5000
```

Now the server is running, has opened a socket, and is listening for input on port 5000. Run a telnet client to connect to the server, and send it some hostnames to look up:

```
> telnet localhost 5000
Trying ::1...
Connected to localhost.
Escape character is '^]'.
localhost
ip address: 127.0.0.1
java.sun.com
ip address: 209.249.116.141
manning.com
ip address: 64.49.223.143
```

Line-oriented client-server programming could hardly be simpler.

---

[5] See http://svn.codehaus.org/groovy/trunk/groovy/groovy-core/src/examples/commandLineTools/
SimpleWebServer.groovy.

13.3.4 In-place editing from the command line

Finally, the -i (*in-place edit*) option is used when you want your Groovy script to iterate over a file or list of files, modifying them in place and, optionally, saving backups of the original files. Here is an example that goes through all *.java files in the current directory and replaces author tags in the Javadoc such that Dierk's full name appears instead of his nickname. For every file, a backup is generated with a .bak extension:

```
> groovy -p -i .bak -e
  "line.replaceAll('@author Mittie','@author Dierk Koenig')" *.java
```

If you do not provide a backup extension, no visible backup file will be generated. The "visible" part is necessary for accuracy's sake because behind the scenes, Groovy creates a backup anyway in your personal temporary folder and deletes it when finished normally. So, in the worst case, such as when your power supply is interrupted in the middle of such an operation and your working file is corrupted, you can still recover it from the temporary folder. However, providing a backup extension is the safer choice.

> **NOTE** You can collapse option sequences such as collapsing -p -e to -pe as long as, at most, the last one of these options takes an additional parameter. So groovy -pie will not work as expected because this is interpreted as using e for an extension (because it's trailing after i). Additional parameters can be appended with or without whitespace, so -i.bak and -i .bak are both valid.

That's it for the numerous options that groovy can be started with. If you come from Ruby or Perl, they probably look familiar.

Now that you can write useful scripts, you can use them to handle minor chores you have to perform time and time again. Our next section helps to smooth the process of automating away annoyance.

13.4 Writing automation scripts

A software developer's range of responsibilities includes many activities that require monitoring either constantly or on a repetitive schedule. Is the web server still running? Is the latest state on the build server OK? Is there so much data in the spam folder that it needs to be cleaned up? Did some prospect download an evaluation copy of our product?

You can easily feel like a juggler who spins as many plates as possible and merely keeps them from falling down. Figure 13.1 suggests that life would be easier if there were some device that would take care of keeping the plates spinning without our constant attention.

Groovy is well suited to writing those little "house-elf" scripts that automate our daily work. We will go through some issues that are special to command-line scripts, explore the

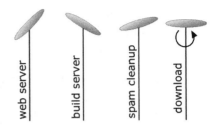

Figure 13.1 Keeping the plates spinning with lots of scheduled scripts

support provided by Groovy, and visit a series of examples. In particular, we examine the simple processing of command-line options, starting Java programs with the minimum of fuss, and scheduling tasks for delayed or repeated execution.

13.4.1 Supporting command-line options consistently

Helper scripts are often started automatically from a scheduler such as *cron* or *at*, or as a *service*. Therefore, they have no graphical user interface but receive all necessary configuration on the command line. Starting a script generally looks like this:

```
> groovy MyScript -o value
```

where -o value stands for assigning value to the o option. This is a standard way of dealing with command-line options that users expect nowadays, and Groovy supports it in its libraries.

The standard option handling

An option can have a short name and a long name, where the short name consists of only one character. Short options are tagged on the command line with a single dash, such as -h; long names use two dashes, such as --help. Most options are *optional*, but certain options may be required.

Options may have zero, one, or multiple trailing arguments such as *filename* in -f filename. Multiple arguments may be separated by a character. When the separation character is a comma, this looks like --lines 1,2,3.

When the user enters an invalid command, it is good practice to give an error indication and print a *usage* statement. Options may be given in any sequence, but when multiple arguments are supplied with an option, they are sequence dependent.

If you had to re-implement the option-parsing logic for every script, you would probably shy away from the work. Luckily, there's an easy way to achieve the standard behavior.

Declaring command-line options

Groovy provides special support for dealing with command-line options. The Groovy distribution comes with the Jakarta Commons *command-line interface (CLI)*.[6] Groovy provides a specialized wrapper around it.

The strategy is to specify what options should be supported by the current script and let the CLI do the work of parsing, validating, error handling, and capturing the option values for later access in the script.

The specification is done with `CliBuilder`. With this builder, you specify an option by calling its short name as a method on the builder, provide a map of additional properties, and provide a help message. You specify a help option, for example, via

```
def cli = new CliBuilder()
cli.h(longOpt: 'help', 'usage information')
```

Table 13.4 contains the properties that you can use to specify an option with `CliBuilder`.

Table 13.4 `CliBuilder` option properties

Property name	Type	Meaning
argName	String	Alias for being more descriptive when looking up values
longOpt	String	The long name for the option as used with doubled dashes
required	boolean	Whether the option is required; default: false
args	int	Number of arguments for this option; default: 0
optionalArg	boolean	Whether there is an optional argument; default: false
type	Object	Type of the argument
valueSeparator	char	The character to use for separating multiple arguments

---

[6] See http://jakarta.apache.org/commons/cli/.

When the options are specified to the builder, the Groovy command-line support has all the information it needs to achieve the standard behavior. `CliBuilder` exposes two special methods:

- `parse(args)` to parse the command line
- `usage()` to print the usage statement

We will explain each of these before embarking on a full example.

Working with options

Letting `CliBuilder` parse the command-line arguments is easy. Just use its `parse` method, and pass it the arguments the script was called with. Groovy puts the list of command-line arguments in the binding of the script under the name `args`. Therefore, the call reads

```
def options = cli.parse(args)
```

with `options` being an `OptionAccessor` that encapsulates what options the user requested on the command line. When parsing fails, it prints the usage statement and returns `null`. If parsing succeeds, you can ask `options` whether a certain option was given on the command line—for example, whether -h was requested—and print the usage statement if requested:

```
if (options.h) cli.usage()
```

The `options` object is a clever beast. For any option x, the property `options.x` returns the argument that was given with -x `somearg`. If no argument was supplied with -x, it returns `true`. If -x was not on the command line at all, it returns `false`.

If an `argName` such as `myArgName` was specified for the x option, then `options.x` and `options.myArgName` return the same value.

If the x option is specified to have multiple arguments, the list of values can be obtained by appending an s character to the property name—for example, `options.xs` or `options.myArgNames`.

Finally, `options` has a method `arguments` to return a list of all arguments that were trailing after all options on the command line.

Let's go through an example to see how all this fits together.

The Mailman example

Assume we set out to provide a Groovy command-line script that sends a message via email on our behalf. Our *Mailman* script should be reusable, and therefore it cannot hard-wire all the details. On the command line, it expects to get information about the mail server, the mail addresses it should use, the text to send, and optionally the mail subject.

Here is how a casual user can request the information about the script and its options:

```
> groovy Mailman -h
error: sft
usage: groovy Mailman -sft[mh] "text"
 -f,--from <address>       from mail address (like me@home.com)
 -h,--help                 usage information
 -m,--subject <matter>     subject matter (default: no subject)
 -s,--smtp <host>          smtp host name
 -t,--to <address>         to address (like you@home.com)
```

The user will also see this output whenever they pass options and arguments that are incomplete or otherwise insufficient.

Listing 13.10 implements the script starting with a specification of its command-line options. It proceeds with parsing the given arguments and using them for instrumenting the Ant task that finally delivers the mail.

Listing 13.10   Mailman.groovy script using `CliBuilder`

```
def cli = new CliBuilder( usage: 'groovy Mailman -sft[mh] "text"' )

cli.h(longOpt: 'help', 'usage information')
cli.s(argName:'host',     longOpt:'smtp',    args: 1, required: true,
    'smtp host name')
cli.f(argName:'address', longOpt:'from',    args: 1, required: true,
    'from mail address (like me@home.com)')
cli.t(argName:'address', longOpt:'to',      args: 1, required: true,
    'to address (like you@home.com)')
cli.m(argName:'matter', longOpt:'subject', args: 1,
    'subject matter (default: no subject)')

def opt = cli.parse(args)
if (!opt)  return            ◁┐  Stop processing
if (opt.h) cli.usage()        │  on parse error

def ant = new AntBuilder()
def subj = (opt.matter) ? opt.matter : 'no subject'
ant.mail(mailhost: opt.host, subject: subj) {
    from(address: opt.f)
    to  (address: opt.t)
    message( opt.arguments().join(' '))
}
```

There are multiple aspects to consider about listing 13.10. It shows how the compact declarative style of `CliBuilder` not only simplifies the code, but also improves the documentation as well: better for the user because of the instant availability of the usage statement, and better for the programmer because of the inherent self-documentation.

The multiple uses for documentation, parsing, and validation pay off after the initial investment in the specification. With this support in place, you are likely to produce professional command-line interfaces more often.

Providing command-line options is one part of starting a program, but you won't get very far if the program can't find all the classes it requires. Next, you will see how Groovy helps you with that perennial Java bugbear, the classpath.

13.4.2 *Expanding the classpath with RootLoader*

Suppose you'd like to start a script using `groovy MyScript` but your script code depends on libraries that are not on the default classpath (<GROOVY_HOME>/lib/*.jar and <USER_HOME>/.groovy/lib/*.jar).

In this case, you'd need to set the classpath before calling the script, just like you need to do for any Java program.

Starting Java is considered tricky

When starting a Java program, you have to either make sure your CLASSPATH environment variable is set up correctly for specifically this program or you have to pass the `classpath` command-line option to the `java` executable.

Either way is cumbersome, requires a lot of typing, and is hard to remember how to do correctly. The common solution to this problem is to write a shell script for the startup. This works but requires knowledge about yet another language: your shell script language (Windows command script or `bash`).

Java is platform independent, but this value is lost if you cannot *start* your program on all platforms. When trying to provide startup scripts for all popular systems (Windows in its various versions, Cygwin, Linux, Solaris), things get complex. For examples, look at Ant's various starter scripts in <ANT_HOME>/bin.

All the work is required only because a Java program cannot easily expand the classpath programmatically to locate the classes it needs. But Groovy can.

Groovy starters

Groovy comes with a so-called `RootLoader`, which is available as a property on the current classloader whenever the Groovy program was started by the `groovy` starter. It is not guaranteed to be available for Groovy code that is evaluated from Java code.

That means the `RootLoader` can be accessed as

```
def loader = this.class.classLoader.rootLoader
```

The trick with this is that it has an `addURL(url)` method that allows you to add a URL at runtime that points to the classpath entry to add, for example, the URL of a jar file:

```
loader.addURL(new File('lib/mylib.jar').toURL())
```

Sometimes it is also useful to know what URLs are currently contained in the `RootLoader`, such as for debugging classloading problems:

```
loader.URLs.each{ println it }
```

With this, you can easily write a platform-independent starter script in Groovy. Let's go through a small example.

We need a Groovy script that depends on an external library. For the fun of it, we shall use `JFugue`, an open-source Java library that allows us to play music as defined in strings. Download jfugue.jar from http://www.jfugue.org, and copy it into a subdirectory named lib.

Listing 13.11 contains an example that uses the `JFugue` library to play a theme from *Star Wars*. Save it to file StarWars.groovy.

Listing 13.11   StarWars.groovy uses the `JFugue` external library

```
import org.jfugue.*

def darthVaderTheme = new Pattern('T160 I[Cello] '+
    'G3q G3q G3q Eb3q Bb3i G3qi Eb3q Bb3i G3hi')

new Player().play(darthVaderTheme)
```

To start this script, we would normally need to set the classpath from the outside to contain lib/jfugue.jar. Listing 13.12 calls the `StarWars` script by making up the classpath. It adds all jar files from the lib subdirectory to the `RootLoader` before evaluating StarWars.groovy.

Listing 13.12   Starting JFugue by adding all *.jar files from lib to `RootLoader`

```
def loader = this.class.classLoader.rootLoader

def dir = new File('lib')
dir.eachFileMatch(~/.*\.jar$/) {
    loader.addURL(it.toURL())
}
evaluate(new File('StarWars.groovy'))
```

With this functionality in place, you can easily distribute your automated player together with the libraries it depends on. There is no need for the user to install libraries in their <USER_HOME>/.groovy/lib directory or change any environment variables.

Also, everything is self-contained, and the user is less likely to run into version conflicts with the external libraries.

If you use dependency resolution packages such as *Maven*[7] or *Ivy*,[8] you can directly refer to their downloaded artifacts. Groovy may provide even more sophisticated support for this scenario in the future.

We've been trying to lower the difficulty level of starting Groovy programs, and we've made it simple to start them from the command line. The next obvious step is to make programs so simple to run that the user doesn't even need to use the command line.

13.4.3 *Scheduling scripts for execution*

Automation scripts really shine when running unattended on a background schedule. As the saying goes, "They claim it's automatic, but actually you have to press this button."

There are numerous ways to schedule your automation scripts:

- Your operating system may provide tools for scheduled execution. The standard mechanisms are the *cron* scheduler for UNIX/Linux/Solaris systems and the *at* service on Windows platforms. The downsides with these solutions are that you might not be authorized to use the system tools and that you cannot ship a system-independent scheduling mechanism with your application.

- The Java platform supports scheduling with the Timer class. It uses an implementation based on Java threads and their synchronization features. Although this cannot give any real-time guarantees, it is good enough for many scenarios and scales well.

- There also several third-party scheduler libraries for Java, both open-source and commercial. The Quartz scheduler is a well-known example, and one that is supported in Spring. It's available from http://www.

---

[7] Maven is a project build tool including dependency resolution: http://maven.apache.org.
[8] Ivy is a dependency resolution tool: http://jayasoft.org/ivy. Note: This is *not* JavaSoft!

opensymphony.com/quartz/. Of course, the cost of using advanced features tends to be higher complexity.

■ Roll your own scheduler with the simplest possible means.

In a lot of scenarios, it is sufficient to schedule an execution like so:

```
while(true) {
    println "execution called at ${new Date().toGMTString()}"
    // call execution here
    sleep 1000
}
```

Remember that unlike in Java, the Groovy `sleep` method really sleeps at least a second, even if interrupted (see section 9.1.2).

Listing 13.13 extends this simple scheduling to a real-life[9] scenario. A task should be scheduled to run all working days (Monday through Friday) at office hours (08:00 a.m. to 06:00 p.m.). Within this timeframe, the task is to be started every 10 minutes.

Listing 13.13 Scheduling a task for every 10 minutes during office hours

```
def workDays    = Calendar.MONDAY..Calendar.FRIDAY
def officeHours = 8..18

while(true) {
    def now = new Date()
    if (
        workDays.contains(now.day)         &&
        officeHours.contains(now.hours) &&
        0 == now.minutes % 10
    ) {
        println "execution called at ${now.toGMTString()}"
        // call execution here
        sleep 31 * 1000
    }
    sleep 31 * 1000
}
```

The purpose of sleeping 31 seconds is to make sure the check is performed at least once per minute. The extra sleep after execution is needed to avoid a second execution within the same minute.

---

[9] Canoo has a corporate client that has run such a schedule for over two years now.

The solution in listing 13.13 is certainly not suited for scheduling at the granularity of milliseconds. It is also not perfect, because it uses deprecated `Date` methods.[10] However, it is sufficient for the majority of scheduling tasks, such as checking the source code repository for changes every 10 minutes, generating a revenue report every night, or cleaning the database every Sunday at 4:00 a.m.

We've examined how to make scripts easy to run and easy to schedule, but we've said little about the kinds of things you might want such a script to *do*. Our next section gives a few examples to whet your appetite.

13.5 Example automation tasks

We couldn't possibly tell you what your automation needs are. However, many tasks have similar flavors. By giving you a few examples, we hope we'll set some sparks going in your imagination. You may have a moment where you spot that a repetitive task that has been getting under your skin could easily be automated in Groovy. If that's the case, feel free to rush straight to your nearest computer before you lose inspiration. We'll wait until you've finished.

Still here? Let's roll up our sleeves and get groovy.

13.5.1 Scraping HTML pages

The web is not only full of endless information, but it is also full of interesting new and updated information. Regularly visiting your favorite pages for updated content is one of the plates you need to keep spinning. It's easy to delegate this task to a Groovy script.

The script needs to

1 Connect to a URL.

2 Read the HTML content.

3 Find the interesting information in the HTML.

Finding the information of interest is the tricky part, because HTML source code can be complex. Also, our script should be forgiving in terms of whitespaces, attribute sequences, quoting of attribute values, and so on. In other words, we cannot use regular expressions to cut the information out of the source code.

---

[10] Using the day/hours/minutes properties of `Date` has been deprecated since JDK 1.1. However, correctly using `Calendar` methods here would distract from the focus of the example.

If we could work in XML rather than HTML, we could use an XML parser and GPath or XPath expression to scrape off the interesting parts reliably.

BY THE WAY The term *scraping* stems from olden times when users were faced with a 25x80 character terminal screen. New automation features could be added by reading characters off this screen. This technique was called *screen scraping*.

The good news is that there are free open-source parsers that read HTML and expose the content as SAX events such that Groovy's XML parsers can work with it. The popular NekoHTML parser can be found at http://people.apache.org/~andyc/neko/doc/index.html. Download it, and copy its jar file to the classpath.

As an example, consider analyzing the HTML page of http://java.sun.com as captured in figure 13.2. Let's assume we're interested in the news items, or everything that appears as links in bold type. For the screen shown in figure 13.2, our script should print

```
Developing Web Services Using JAX-WS
More Enhancements in Java SE 6 (Mustang)
"Get Java" Software Button Now Available
Gosling T-Shirt Hurling Contest
```

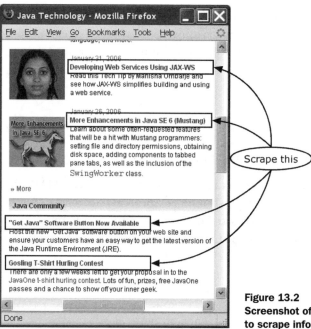

Figure 13.2
Screenshot of http://java.sun.com
to scrape information off

The links in bold appear in the page's HTML source like this (pretty-printed):

```
<B>
  <A href="http://logos.sun.com/spreadtheword/">
    "Get Java" Software Button Now Available
  </A>
</B>
```

Listing 13.14 shows the surprisingly compact solution to extract this data.

Listing 13.14 Scraping news off the Java homepage

```
import org.cyberneko.html.parsers.SAXParser

def url = 'http://java.sun.com'

def html = new XmlSlurper(new SAXParser()).parse(url)

def bolded = html.'**'.findAll{ it.name() == 'B' }
def out = bolded.A*.text().collect{ it.trim() }
out.removeAll([''])
out[2..5].each{ println it }
```

We only need to wrap the NekoHTML `SAXParser` with the Groovy `XmlSlurper`. With the help of the slurper, we find all `B` nodes and their nested `A` nodes. Finally, we trim surrounding whitespace and remove empty links for nicer output.

Of course, if the web site offers XML datafeeds such as RSS or ATOM, or even as web services, then it's more reliable to use those. See chapter 12 for more details. But think about all those web pages that have no such luxury, but still convey important information: webmail clients, web server administration pages, web-based planning tools, calendaring systems, conference pages, project build information, and so forth. The list is literally endless.

In combination with a task scheduler, you can use this approach to regularly check whether your server is alive and kicking. If it doesn't respond in a timely manner or contains an error indication in the page, you can send a notification to the admin.

Reading HTML is nice, but how about clicking links and submitting forms? We'll show that next.

13.5.2 *Automating web actions*

HTML-based web applications are perfect candidates for automating all the actions that you would do manually otherwise. Think about the steps you repeatedly take in web applications: filling in your daily timesheet, updating the project plan, synchronizing with the address database, posting your current location to the corporate intranet, and so on.

To automate these steps, you can download HtmlUnit[11] from http://htmlunit. sourceforge.net/ and put its jars on the classpath. HtmlUnit was originally designed for testing web applications and thus developed all the means to operate them. We will only use the operation controls here.

Our example of an interactive web interface is the ubiquitous Google search form, as shown in figure 13.3, with search results for "Groovy" in figure 13.4.

Our example is a basic interaction, but nevertheless it contains all the steps for automated web actions:

Figure 13.3 The Google search form when searching for "Groovy"

- Starting at an initial page
- Filling an input field in a web form
- Submitting the form
- Working on the results

From the results, we filter the top three hits and report them as follows:

```
http://groovy.codehaus.org/   : Groovy - Home
http://www.groovy.de/         : Groovy.de - Headshop Growshop...
http://www.jeronimogroovy.com/ : JERONIMO GROOVY RADIO
```

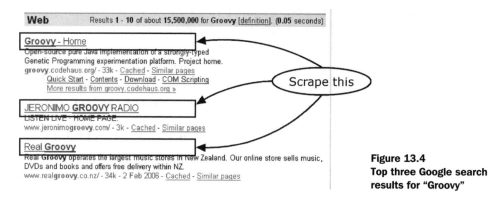

**Figure 13.4
Top three Google search results for "Groovy"**

---

[11] The examples use HtmlUnit version 1.9.

Listing 13.15 uses HtmlUnit to achieve this. With a newly constructed `WebClient`, it gets the starting page with the Google URL. From the page, it reads the form and input field by the names they are tagged with. The input field is filled and the form submitted. The form submission returns the result page with the main result anchors having the class attribute `'l'`.

Listing 13.15 Finding the top three hits in Google

```
import com.gargoylesoftware.htmlunit.WebClient

def client = new WebClient()
def page   = client.getPage('http://www.google.com')
def input  = page.forms[0].getInputByName('q')
input.valueAttribute = 'Groovy'
page       = page.forms[0].submit()

def hits   = page.anchors.grep { it.classAttribute == 'l' } [0..2]
hits.each  { println it.hrefAttribute.padRight(30) + ' : ' +
             it.asText() }
```

HtmlUnit offers a lot of sophisticated features. It also includes NekoHTML and can deliver the current pages `asXml`, allowing Groovy to fully leverage its XML support. It can also deal with a wide range of JavaScript content and present the DOM for XPath processing. See its API documentation for details.

All this makes it an ideal companion to Groovy when implementing a *remote control* for web applications.

13.5.3 *Inspecting version control*

One nice feature of version-control systems such as *Concurrent Versioning System (CVS)* or *Subversion (SVN)* is that they come with command-line clients. This makes them ideal candidates for inspection by Groovy scripts.

Let's go through a CVS example. CVS comes with a command-line client that supports a variety of options. You can achieve *almost* everything with these options, but sometimes you need a little more. For example, when trying to find out who accessed the repository since a certain date, you can use the history command:

```
cvs history -a -e -D 2006-02-04
```

But that prints too much and in a rather cryptic way, with countless lines such as

```
M 2006-02-03 23:52 +0000 denis 1.8 website_base.css …
```

It would be nice if a Groovy script could consolidate the output into something that displays the information as a summary:

```
2006-02-04    cruise   update: delete
2006-02-04    denis    commit: modified
2006-02-04    marc     update: delete
2006-02-04    paul     commit: add
2006-02-04    paul     commit: modified
```

This summary tells you that the user named *cruise*[12] updated from the repository, deleting a local file as a result. You can see who accessed the repository and the resulting operations.

The output is the result of running listing 13.16 against the CVS repository of the open-source *Canoo WebTest* project. It issues the cvs command and processes the output line by line. Each line is split on whitespace, and the fields of interest are extracted and joined to a string. Each string is put into a HashSet, which has the effect of removing duplicates. The result set is finally printed in a sorted order.

Listing 13.16 Summarizing cvs command output for access surveillance

```
def cvscommand = 'cvs history -a -e -D 2006-02-04'
def codes = [
    F: 'release',
    O: 'checkout',
    E: 'export',
    T: 'rtag ',
    C: 'update: conflict',
    G: 'update: merge',
    U: 'update: copy',
    W: 'update: delete',
    A: 'commit: add',
    M: 'commit: modified',
    R: 'commit: removed'
]
def result = new HashSet()                           ❶ Run cvs and process one
cvscommand.execute().in.eachLine { line ->             output line at a time
    def fields = line.split(/\s/)
    fields[0]  = codes[fields[0]]                     ❷ Collate and format
    result << [1,4,0].collect{ fields[it] }.join("\t")   the results
}
result.sort().each { println it }   ⟵ Sort and print the formatted results
```

[12] This is not the famous actor but the technical user for the cruisecontrol continuous integration service.

Some aspects in listing 13.16 are particularly Groovy in style. The command is first executed in an extremely simple and readable fashion. The output of the resulting process is processed line by line ❶. Using list and string operations, including a literal list, we transform the raw output into the more readable format ❷.

Note that we could have replaced the last two data extraction lines with a single line of code:

```
result << "${fields[1]}\t${fields[4]}\t${codes[fields[0]]}"
```

This would have been even shorter, because it saves one line. However, it doesn't read as declaratively, because it mixes the concerns of field selection and presentation. Changing *either* the fields to be displayed *or* the formatting of those fields is a simple task in the original code, requiring no duplication.

13.5.4 *Pragmatic code analysis*

In our consulting work, we're asked to do code reviews every now and then. We even review and analyze code of our own projects regularly. In the course of this activity, we've learned to value pragmatic tools that work on any codebase.

When reviewing, you need a starting point. A good move is to assemble some statistical data such as the number of files per directory, files sizes, line count per file, and so on for that purpose. It's amazing how much you can tell about a project from this data. Put it in a spreadsheet, and generate charts for the various dimensions. You will soon spot the hot candidates for review.

There are some helpful measures (we wouldn't dare to call them *metrics*) that you can assemble with the help of Groovy. For example, it helps to know the revision number of each file in the version-control system. Unusually high revision numbers can indicate a problematic area, just like files with the most conflicts (see the previous section).

Listing 13.17 points to another interesting measure: maximum nesting depth of braces. It's a pragmatic approach, because it doesn't use a real parser for the language and may thus be slightly off when braces occur in comments or strings. However, the solution can be applied to a wide range of languages and gives a good indication of complexity.

Listing 13.17   Finding the maximum brace nesting depth

```
def source = new File(args[0]).text

def nesting = 0
def maxnest = 0
```

```
for (c in source) {
    switch (c) {
        case '{' : nesting++
                   if (nesting > maxnest) maxnest++
                   break
        case '}' : nesting--
                   break
    }
}
println maxnest
```

When applying this measure to Groovy code, you can expect higher numbers than for Java, due to the usage of braces in builders, closures, and GPath expressions. On the other hand, the line count is likely to be significantly lower!

13.5.5 *More points of interest*

There is a huge list of external libraries that are specifically helpful when used together with Groovy scripts.

First, automation often sends notifications. There are Ant tasks for this purpose, but for fine-grained control, you can use the JavaMail[13] API that comes as an external package of the JRE (`javax.mail`). Via mail gateways, you can also send text messages to a cell phone.

When automation is used for periodic reporting, libraries for producing graphs and charts are useful. You will find many of these on the Web, such as *Snip-Graph*, *JCCKit*, and *JFreeChart*. They all work from a textual representation of data, and using them with Groovy is therefore easy. Groovy templates can make the production of such text input files much simpler.

Reporting can also mean producing Microsoft Office documents. When running on a Windows platform, you can relay such tasks to Groovy's Scriptom module, which we will describe in chapter 15. There also are platform-independent solutions with restricted functionality that may nonetheless be sufficient for your needs: POI (http://jakarta.apache.org/poi) for Office documents, and for spreadsheets in particular, JExcelApi (http://jexcelapi.sourceforge.net).

A variety of projects implement customized Groovy support. You can find the list at http://groovy.codehaus.org/Related+Projects. There is, for example, special

---

[13] A good introduction is available at http://java.sun.com/developer/onlineTraining/JavaMail/contents.html.

support for the *Lucene* search engine. Running its indexer repeatedly would be a typical automation task.

When reports are to be published on the Web, using a Groovy-enabled Wiki can be handy, because the pages can contain Groovy code to update themselves. Currently, the known implementations[14] are *Biscuit*, *SnipSnap*, and *XWiki*.

The Groovy developers provide specialized modules for making particularly interesting libraries more groovy. Have a look at the modules section at http://groovy.codehaus.org. For example, you will find Groovy support for Google's calendaring package, allowing constructions such as

```
import org.codehaus.groovy.runtime.TimeCategory

use(TimeCategory) {
    Date reminder = 1.week.from.now
}
```

and expressions such as `2.days + 10.hours`, basically allowing convenient definitions of dates, timestamps, and durations as usual Java objects. Over time, such a module may be promoted to the Groovy distribution.

Because you can use any Java library, there is an endless list of possibilities. The goal was to trigger your curiosity and make you think about the wide range of applicability.

Next, we will go through various aspects of making your life as a Groovy programmer easier.

13.6 *Laying out the workspace*

When your work with Groovy only encompasses writing a few little scripts, it is sufficient to use an all-purpose text editor. Groovy doesn't force you to use big programs for small tasks.

However, as soon as you start developing more elaborate programs in Groovy, you will benefit from using one of the IDEs mentioned in section 1.5. The benefit comes not only from the available Groovy plug-ins but also from the general Java programming support: integration of version-control clients, local versioning, browsing dependent Java libraries, search and replace, classpath management, and so on.

This section collects some hints for how to make your daily programming life with Groovy easier using the features of any Java IDE. It explains how to create a

---

[14] See http://groovy.codehaus.org/Related+Projects.

comfortable environment for working with Groovy, describes how to use Java debuggers and profilers with Groovy code, and discusses the current state of the Groovy refactoring landscape.

13.6.1 IDE setup

As soon as you step into serious Groovy programming, you should look at the available IDE plug-ins and select the one of your choice.

Make sure you have your JDK configured to also include the JDK source and its API documentation. Unlike Java, Groovy plug-ins cannot always provide you with instant code completion. Therefore, you will look up JDK classes and methods more often than you are used to when programming Java. With a proper setup, such a lookup by name can still be efficient.

Most IDEs support the notion of a *library* that assembles jar files, classes, resources, source code, and API documentation of a common purpose. Create such a library for Groovy, including the Groovy source tree. This enables you to quickly look up important information such as GDK methods. For example, you could run a search for method definitions of the name eachFile*.

Note that Groovy comes with a comprehensive suite of unit tests. Most of these are written in Groovy. This is also a good source of information to have around when programming.

What is true for the JDK and the Groovy distribution is also true for any other external library. The better your setup and the more complete your local information, the less time you will spend scanning through external documentation.

If your IDE can include a Java decompiler such as *JAD*, get it. It helps a lot when decompiling class files that were generated by groovyc. Make sure the decompilation writes into a directory that will not be used to pick up source files for your next run or compile operation.

IDEs often support a mechanism to break the whole source tree into *modules* or *projects* with an option to define their dependencies. In case of a mixed Groovy/Java project, you can use this feature to avoid compile problems with mutual dependencies. For example, you can have three modules: a Groovy-only module, a Java-only module, and a module of shared Java interfaces.

Figure 13.5 illustrates the dependencies of the Groovy and Java modules to the shared interface module.

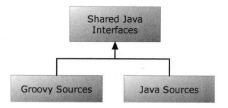

Figure 13.5   Groovy and Java source modules depending on a shared interface module

This setup ensures that you can compile either module and the whole project easily. Once you have your code compiling, you'll want to run it sooner or later—and sometimes that will mean running it in a debugger.

13.6.2 *Debugging*

Debugging is the act of removing bugs from the code. Some people claim that this implies that programming is the act of putting them in.

The best advice we can possibly give about debugging is advice on how to avoid it. The need for debugging is drastically reduced when solid unit testing is in place and when code is created in a test-first manner.

The next best approach is to make wise use of assertions throughout your code, making it fail early for obvious reasons.

The debugging tool that everybody uses every day is putting `println` statements in the code under development. This is certainly helpful, and Groovy makes it a workable way of debugging, because transparent compiling and instant class-reloading lead to quick coding cycles.

However, don't fall into the trap of leaving `println` statements in the code after debugging is done. Don't even put them in comments. Depending on the purpose of the line, you can change it into an assertion or into a log statement.

> **BY THE WAY** Consistent use of logging makes debugging much easier. In Groovy, you can use the same mechanics for logging as for any other Java code running on JDK 1.4. See the JDK documentation for details.

Generally, debugging offers a chance to learn something new about your code and improve it. After finding the bug, you can ask yourself how you could have found it earlier or could have avoided it altogether: what log statement would have helped, what assertion, what unit test, and how could the wrong behavior have been more visible in the code?

Until then, you first have to locate the bug.

Exploiting groovyc

When you get errors from Groovy scripts, precompilation with `groovyc` can provide more detailed error messages, especially when you're working with multiple dependent scripts. In this case, use `groovyc` on all scripts.

When things get really tricky and you suspect Groovy is parsing your code incorrectly or producing bad constructions from it, you can use the properties listed in table 13.5 to make `groovyc` produce more artifacts. Set the environment variable `JAVA_OPTS` to the appropriate value before calling `groovyc`.

Table 13.5 System properties that `groovyc` is sensitive to

JAVA_OPTS	Purpose	Destination
`-Dantlr.ast=groovy`	Pretty printing	Foo.groovy.pretty.groovy
`-Dantlr.ast=html`	Writing a colored version of source, with each AST node as a rollover tooltip	Foo.groovy.html
`-Dantlr.ast=mindmap`	Writing the AST as a mind map (view with http://freemind.sf.net)	Foo.groovy.mm

The pretty-printer gives a first indication of possible misconceptions about the nesting structure in the code. This can easily occur when you're using single-statement control statements without braces, such as

```
if (true)
    println "that's really true"
```

If you later add more lines to the if-block but forget to add the braces that are then needed, you end up with an error that you can spot by looking at the pretty-print.

The pretty-printer is an obvious candidate to integrate in the Groovy IDE plug-ins.

The HTML and *mindmap* options in table 13.5 are two other interesting views on the Abstract Syntax Tree (AST) that the Groovy parser creates from your source code. The HTML view is rather conventional, but the mindmap allows you to navigate and expand/collapse the AST nodes. Figure 13.6 shows the AST mindmap for the brace-matching analyzer in listing 13.17.

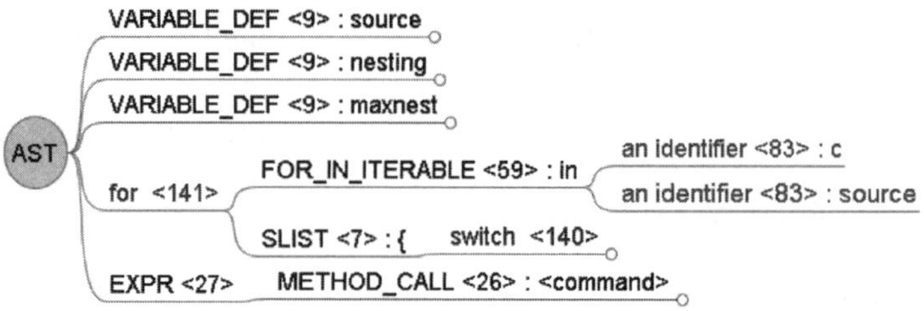

Figure 13.6 Mindmap AST of listing 13.17 expanded on a `for` loop

So far, we have assessed only the static aspects of the code. We will now look into the live execution of the code.

Groovy runtime inspection

Groovy's `MetaClass` concepts allow a full new range of options when inspecting code for debugging purposes. Because all method calls, the method dispatch, dynamic name resolution, and the property access are funneled through this device, it makes an ideal point of interception.

You came across the usage of `MetaClasses` and the `TracingInterceptor` in section 7.6.3. The `TracingInterceptor` can be engaged by attaching it to a `ProxyMetaClass` that acts as a decorator over the original one. This results in a non-intrusive tracing facility—one that doesn't change the code under inspection.

Revisit the code in chapter 7 for more examples.

Another groovy way to do live-system debugging is integration of an inspection capability. Examples of this are Grash, a shell-like inspection utility,[15] and the ULC Admin Console.[16] Although there are security implications in providing these capabilities in your applications, the potential for diagnosing problems that may occur in the field is immense.

Using debugging tools

Groovy runs inside the Java Virtual Machine as ordinary Java bytecode. The bytecode is constructed such that it contains all information required by the *Java Platform Debugger Architecture (JPDA)*. In other words, you can use any JPDA-compliant Java debugger with Groovy and get Groovy source-level debugging!

The debugger that ships with your preferred Java IDE is most likely JPDA compliant. For graphical standalone debuggers, good experiences have been reported with JSwat,[17] which shines when it comes to Groovy source-level debugging.

One debugging tool that ships with every JDK is the *jdb* Java command-line debugger. The JDK documentation describes it in detail: the various ways of starting it, the commands it understands, and how to use it for in-process and remote debugging.

Let's go through a sample usage with the script in listing 13.18. It prints the numbers from 1 to 100, stating whether each number is a prime number. An integral number x is a prime number if no integral number y between 2 and x-1 divides into x without a remainder. Note how the `isPrime` method implements this specification in a declarative way.

---

[15] http://biscuit.javanicus.com/grash.

[16] http://ulc-community.canoo.com/snipsnap/space/Contributions/Utilities/Admin+Console.

[17] http://www.bluemarsh.com/java/jswat/.

Listing 13.18   Primer.groovy for printing prime number information

```
boolean isPrime(int x) {
    ! (2..<x).any { y ->  x % y == 0 }
}

for (i in 1..100) {
    println "$i : ${isPrime(i)}"
}
```

To work with this script in the jdb, you need to set the CLASSPATH environment variable to include the current dir (.) and all jars in the GROOVY_HOME/lib dir.

For ease of use, place a file named jdb.ini in your USER_HOME or current directory to set up defaults when using jdb. When working with Groovy, it is convenient to make it contain the line

```
exclude groovy.*,java.*,org.codehaus.*,sun.*
```

to go avoid stepping through the Java and Groovy internals.

Jdb session transcript

With this preparation in place, you can start as follows:

```
> %JAVA_HOME%\bin\jdb groovy.lang.GroovyShell Primer
Initializing jdb ...
*** Reading commands from …\jdb.ini
```

Let's set a breakpoint at the second line for inspecting the call. You do this before running the program. Otherwise, it would complete so quickly that you couldn't see anything.

There are various ways to set breakpoints. Type help to see them. We use a simple one with a classname and a line number. Note that scripts compile to classes, with the name of the script file becoming the classname:

```
> > stop at Primer:2
Deferring breakpoint Primer:2.
It will be set after the class is loaded.
```

Now, start the program:

```
> run
run groovy.lang.GroovyShell Primer
Set uncaught java.lang.Throwable
Set deferred uncaught java.lang.Throwable
>
VM Started: Set deferred breakpoint Primer:2
```

```
Breakpoint hit: "thread=main", Primer.isPrime(), line=2 bci=13
2        ! (2..<x).any { y ->  x % y == 0 }
```

Jdb has started the program, told you that it will not catch any `Throwables` on your behalf, and reported the breakpoint where it stopped.

It's good to see the line of the breakpoint, but you can hardly understand it without seeing the surrounding lines. The `list` command shows the neighborhood:

```
main[1] list
1      boolean isPrime(int x) {
2 =>       ! (2..<x).any { y ->  x % y == 0 }
3      }
4
5      for (i in 1..9) {
6          println "$i : ${isPrime(i)}"
7      }
```

Let's see what local variables you have at this point:

```
main[1] locals
Method arguments:
Local variables:
x = instance of groovy.lang.Reference(id=726)
```

The `x` variable is not a simple `int`, but a `Reference` object, because we're looking at Groovy code through Java glasses. `Reference` objects have a `get` method that returns their value. You can `eval` this method call:

```
main[1] eval x.get()
 x.get() = "1"
```

That's what you expected. You are done with the `isPrime` method. Let's ask jdb to bring you back to the caller of this method:

```
main[1] step out
>
Step completed: "thread=main", Primer.run(), line=6 bci=76
6          println "$i : ${isPrime(i)}"
```

Time to end the jdb session:

```
main[1] exit
```

Dear passengers, thank you very much for flying with jdb airlines.

Debugging gives you control over the execution so you can make the code run as slowly as you need it to in order to understand it. Profiling helps you do the reverse—with the aid of a profiler, you can usually make your code run faster and more efficiently. Although Groovy code is rarely used when absolute performance is important, it can nevertheless be instructive to see where your code is spending the most time or what the most memory is being used for.

13.6.3 *Profiling*

Profiling is the task of analyzing a run of your program for memory and CPU time consumption. Groovy code can be profiled with any ordinary Java profiling tool. Profiling our `Primer` script as shown in listing 13.18 can easily be done with the profiling support that comes with the Java Runtime Environment. The JDK documentation comes with extensive documentation of this topic. In short, you can a run a compact command-line profiler with

```
java -Xprof groovy.lang.GroovyShell Primer
```

A more sophisticated solution is available with

```
java -agentlib:hprof groovy.lang.GroovyShell Primer
```

This second way of starting the JRE profiler writes extensive data to a file named java.hprof.txt. There are a lot of options that you can set when profiling this way. For a list of options, type

```
java -agentlib:hprof=help
```

That extensive output of the JRE profiler requires some time to understand. Therefore, commercial profiling solutions are used more often. Figure 13.7 shows profiling data from a `Primer` run as presented by the commercial YourKit profiler, which grants a free license to the Groovy committers.

From looking at the profiling analysis in figure 13.7, you can tell (line 2) that we started the profiling run from within the Intellij IDE. A special YourKit plug-in for that IDE allows easy profiling setup.

Because scripts are created with `main` and `run` methods, you see these method calls in lines 4 and 6. Line 8 shows that calls to the `isPrime` method took almost no time. Almost all the time was used for writing the resulting GString to the

Call tree (by thread)

Name	Time (ms)	
⊟ 🌐 main group: 'main'	2'443	100 %
⊟ 🢆 com.intellij.rt.execution.application.**AppMain.main**(String[])	2'373	97 %
⊟ 🢆 java.lang.reflect.**Method.invoke**(Object, Object[])	2'373	97 %
⊟ 🢆 **Primer.main**(String[])	1'742	71 %
⊟ 🢆 org.codehaus.groovy.runtime.**ScriptBytecodeAdapter.invokeMethod**	1'742	71 %
⊟ 🢆 **Primer.run**()	1'742	71 %
⊟ 🢆 org.codehaus.groovy.runtime.**ScriptBytecodeAdapter.invokeMethod**	30	1 %
⊞ 🢆 **Primer.isPrime**(int)	10	0 %

Figure 13.7 Profiling data from YourKit for the `Primer` script

console. This is not surprising, because I/O operations are always expensive compared to mere calculations.

In between the calls to `Primer`, you see calls to the Groovy runtime system. The icon indicates that these lines are filtered; in other words, they represent a series of hidden calls. Setting such filters is important to make the interesting parts of the stack stand out.

Profiling and debugging are expert activities, and it takes some time to get proficient with the tools and their usage. But this is not particular to Groovy. It is also true for Java.

What *is* particular to Groovy is that you will be faced with lots of the internals of the Groovy runtime system: how classes are constructed, what objects get created, how the method dispatch works, and so on.

13.6.4 *Refactoring*

Refactoring is the activity of improving the design of existing code. The internal structure of the code changes, but the external behavior remains unchanged.

The classic book on refactoring is *Refactoring: Improving the Design of Existing Code* by Martin Fowler. All the listed *refactorings* and *mechanics* can be applied to Groovy exactly as shown for Java code in the book. Where the mechanics suggest compiling the changed code, such a compilation check should be accompanied with running the unit tests for Groovy code.

For the Java world, lots of the standard refactorings such as *Extract Method, Introduce Explaining Variable*, *Pull Members Up*, and so on have been automated for use from inside the IDE.

For Groovy, refactoring support is currently not as complete. The future will show which IDE vendor or open source project will be able to provide a compelling solution.

13.7 *Summary*

Groovy is a unique language. It has a lot of similarities with Java and is fully integrated into the Java runtime architecture. This can sometimes lead us to forget about the differences. On the other hand, if you have a background in scripting languages such as Perl, Ruby, or Python, the biggest difference that you need to be aware of is—again—the Java runtime. Having gone through section 13.1, you are less likely to fall for the most common traps.

The uniqueness of Groovy leads to its own style of tackling programming tasks. Groovy still lets you write code in a procedural or Java-like way, but the idiomatic solutions as shown in section 13.2 have their own appeal.

Groovy is a good friend for all kinds of ad-hoc command-line scripting and serious automation solutions. This ranges from the `groovy` command and its various options for one-liners to scheduled execution of complex automation actions. Whether you want to surf the Web automatically or play some music, Groovy can do it for you. The important point is that Groovy can use any Java library to fulfill these tasks.

Finally, everyday programming work needs good organization to make it an efficient and satisfying experience. With the information provided in section 13.6, you are now able to make the best possible use of the existing Groovy and Java tools.

Although we have largely avoided making assumptions about your development process, one practice that is becoming more and more widely used is *unit testing*. The developers of Groovy believe strongly in the merits of unit testing (as do we), so it would be strange if Groovy didn't have good support for it. The next chapter shows that our expectations are met once again.

Unit testing with Groovy

> *The major difference between a thing that might go wrong and a thing that cannot possibly go wrong is that when a thing that cannot possibly go wrong goes wrong, it usually turns out to be impossible to get at or repair.*
>
> —Douglas Adams

Developer unit testing has become a de facto standard in the Java community.[1] The confidence and structure that JUnit[2] and other testing frameworks bring to the development process are almost revolutionary, if you think about it. To those of us who were actively developing Java applications in the latter years of the 20th century, automated unit testing was almost unheard of. Sure, we wrote tests, but they were hardly automated or even a part of a standard build!

Fast-forward to the present, and many people wouldn't think of writing, let alone *releasing*, code without corresponding unit tests! We write tests all the time, and we expect everyone else on our teams to do the same. Moreover, there is growing momentum behind the idea of writing code by always writing tests first. Although this is not universal, it is another indicator that the recent growth in the importance of tests will continue.

We test at all levels, from unit testing to integration testing to system testing. It is sometimes more fun to write the tests than the code under test, because doing so improves not only the code itself, but also the design of the code. When tests are written often and continually, code has the benefit of being highly extensible, in addition to being obviously freer of defects and easier to repair when needed.

Combine this increased awareness of developer testing with Groovy, and you have a match made in heaven. With Groovy, tests can be written more quickly and easily. It gets even better when you combine the simplicity of unit testing in Groovy with normal Java. You can write Groovy tests for your Groovy-based systems and leverage the many Java libraries and test-extension packages. You can write Groovy tests for your Java-based systems and leverage Groovy's enhanced syntax benefits and extended test functionality.

Groovy makes unit testing a breeze, whichever way you use it, mainly due to four key aspects. First, Groovy embeds JUnit, so there is no need to set up a new dependency. Second, Groovy has an enhanced test-case class, which adds a plethora of new assertion methods. Third, Groovy has built-in mock, stub, and other dynamic class-creation facilities that simplify isolating a test class from its collaborators. Finally, tests written in Groovy can be easily run from Ant, Maven, or your favorite IDE.

---

[1] See Kevin Tate, *Sustainable Software Development: An Agile Perspective* (Addison Wesley Professional, 2005) for a good discussion of recent trends.

[2] See Vincent Massol with Ted Husted, *JUnit in Action* (Manning, 2003); J. B. Rainsberger, *JUnit Recipes* (Manning, 2004), and www.junit.org for more information.

Our focus in this chapter is unit testing; however, many of the ideas can be extended to other kinds of testing as well. We'll mention specific examples throughout the chapter.

14.1 *Getting started*

The section header implies that you have to do some preparation work before you can start your testing activities. But you don't. There is no external support to download or install. Groovy treats unit testing as a first-class developer duty and ships with everything you need for that purpose.

Even more important, it simplifies testing by making assertions part of the language,[3] automatically executing test cases by transparently invoking its TestRunner when needed, and providing the means to run suites of test cases easily, both from the command line and through integration with your IDE or build environment. This section will show you how simple it can be and introduce you to GroovyTestCase, the base class used for most unit testing in Groovy.

14.1.1 *Writing tests is easy*

Assume you have a simple Groovy script that converts temperatures measured in Fahrenheit (F) to Celsius (C). To that end, you define a celsius method like so:

```
def celsius(fahrenheit) { (fahrenheit - 32) * 5 / 9 }
```

Is this implementation correct? Probably, but you can't be sure. You need to gain additional confidence in this method before the next non-US traveler uses your method to understand the US weather forecast.

A common approach with unit testing is to call the code under test with static sample data that produces well-known results. That way, you can compare the calculated results against your expectations.

Choosing a good set of samples is key. As a rule of thumb, having a few typical cases and all the corner cases you can think of is a good choice.[4] Typical cases would be 68° F = 20° C for having a garden party or 95° F = 35° C for going to the beach. Corner cases would be 0° F, which is between -17° C and -18° C, the

---

[3] Java also supports assertions at the language level but disables them by default.

[4] Finding good test data is a science of its own and involves activities such as structural analysis of the parameter domain. For our purposes, we keep it simple. Refer to the background literature for more information.

coldest temperature that Gabriel Daniel Fahrenheit could create with a mixture of ice and ordinary salt in 1714. Another corner case is when water freezes at 32° F = 0° C.

Sound complicated? It isn't. Listing 14.1 contains the method together with inline unit tests made with the simple assertions that are built into the language itself.

Listing 14.1   Inline unit tests for the Fahrenheit to Celsius conversion method.

```
def celsius (fahrenheit) { (fahrenheit - 32) * 5 / 9 }

assert 20  == celsius(68)
assert 35  == celsius(95)
assert -17 == celsius(0).toInteger()
assert 0   == celsius(32)
```

Inline tests of this kind are very useful. Just look at this book: Most listings contain such self-checking asserts to ensure the code works and to help reveal your expectations from the code at the same time.

Whenever the environment of self-testing code changes, the inline tests assert that it is still working. Environmental changes can happen for a number of reasons: evaluating the script on a different machine, using an updated JDK or Groovy version, or running with different versions of packages that the script depends upon.

There are circumstances when tests cannot be inlined, such as due to performance requirements. In such cases, it is conventional to pack all the tests of a given script or class into a separate class residing in a separate file. This is where GroovyTestCase appears on stage.

14.1.2 *GroovyTestCase: an introduction*

Groovy bundles an extended JUnit class dubbed GroovyTestCase, which facilitates unit testing in a number of ways. It includes a host of new assert methods, and it also facilitates running Groovy scripts masquerading as test cases.

The added assertions are listed in table 14.1. We won't go into the details of each method, mostly because they are descriptively named—where it's not absolutely obvious what the meaning is, the description provided in the table should be sufficient. Even though we won't discuss them explicitly, we will use them in the assertions elsewhere in this chapter, so you'll see how useful they are.

Table 14.1 Enhanced assertions available in `GroovyTestCase`

Method	Description
`void assertArrayEquals(Object[] expected, Object[] value)`	Compares the contents and length of each array
`void assertLength(int length, char[] array)`	Convenience method for asserting the length of an array
`void assertLength(int length, int[] array)`	Convenience method for asserting the length of an array
`void assertLength(int length, Object[] array)`	Convenience method for asserting the length of an array
`void assertContains(char expected, char[] array)`	Verifies that a given array of `chars` contains an expected value
`void assertContains(int expected, int[] array)`	Verifies that a given array of `ints` contains an expected value
`void assertToString(Object value, String expected)`	Invokes the `toString` method on the provided object and compares the result with the expected string
`void assertInspect(Object value, String expected)`	Similar to the assertToString method, except that it calls the inspect method
`void assertScript(final String script)`	Attempts to run the provided script
`void shouldFail(Closure code)`	Verifies that the closure provided fails
`void shouldFail(Class clazz, Closure code)`	Verifies that the closure provided throws an exception of type `clazz`

However, Groovy doesn't force you to extend `GroovyTestCase`, and you are free to continue to extend the traditional `TestCase` class provided by JUnit.[5] Having said that, unless you need the functionality of a different subclass of `TestCase`, there are plenty of reasons to use `GroovyTestCase` and no reasons to specifically avoid it. Along with the assertions listed in table 14.1, it's easier to work with `GroovyTestCase` than `TestCase`, as you'll see in the next section.

---

[5] These methods extend the 3.8.2 version of JUnit, which is bundled with Groovy. JUnit 4 has some built-in support for arrays.

14.1.3 *Working with GroovyTestCase*

To utilize Groovy's enhanced `TestCase` class, extend it as follows:[6]

```
class SimpleUnitTest extends GroovyTestCase {
    void testSimple() {
        assertEquals("Groovy should add correctly", 2, 1 + 1)
    }
}
```

Remember, you are free to extend *any* TestCase class you choose, so long as it is in your classpath. For example, you can easily extend JUnit's `TestCase` as follows:

```
import junit.framework.TestCase

class AnotherSimpleUnitTest extends TestCase{
    void testSimpleAgain() {
        assertEquals("Should subtract correctly too", 2, 3 - 1)
    }
}
```

`GroovyTestCase` has the added benefit that it also allows test cases to be run via the groovy command, which is not possible for test cases that extend the normal JUnit `TestCase` class. For example, the `SimpleUnitTest` script seen earlier, which extends `GroovyTestCase`, can be run by typing the command groovy `SimpleUnitTest`:

```
> groovy SimpleUnitTest
.
Time: 0

OK (1 test)
```

If the output looks familiar to you, that's probably because it is the standard JUnit output you'd expect to see if you ran a normal Java JUnit test using JUnit's text-based test runner.

Now that you've got your feet wet, let's go back and start again from scratch, this time testing a little more methodically.

14.2 *Unit-testing Groovy code*

We have introduced you to Groovy's testing capabilities, but we skipped over some of the details. We'll now explore more of those details by exploring a slightly larger Groovy application in need of testing. We will start with a new example and build up our test class, refactoring tests as we go, validating boundary data, testing

---

[6] There is no need to import it—it resides in one of the packages imported by default.

that inputs aren't inadvertently changed, and even checking that the tests themselves haven't been adversely changed!

Let's imagine we've built a small calculator class that determines how many numbers in a list are larger than a target threshold number. The Groovy code is fairly trivial but useful as our example class under test:

```
class Calculator {
    def countHowManyBiggerThan(items, target) {
        return items.grep{ it > target }.size()
    }
}
```

Testing this class is easy. First, we define our test case class, CalulatorTest, which extends GroovyTestCase:

```
class CalculatorTest extends GroovyTestCase {
    ...
}
```

Next, we follow the common unit-testing practice of writing a method to set up the variables we'll need in the tests that follow:

```
class CalculatorTest extends GroovyTestCase {
    private calc
    void setUp() {
        calc = new Calculator()
    }
    ...
}
```

We are now in a position to write a test:

```
void testCalculatorWorks() {
    assertEquals(2, calc.countHowManyBiggerThan([5, 10, 15], 7))
}
```

We could continue adding tests in this way, but first let's introduce some constants that capture useful boundary case data and refactor out a helper method:

```
static final NEG_NUMBERS   = [-2, -3, -4]
static final POS_NUMBERS   = [ 4,  5,  6]
static final MIXED_NUMBERS = [ 4, -6,  0]

private check(expectedCount, items, target) {
    assertEquals(expectedCount,
                 calc.countHowManyBiggerThan(items, target))
}
```

This lets us specify more tests in a compact form:

```
void testCalcHowManyFromSampleNumbers () {
    check(2, NEG_NUMBERS, -4)
```

```
check(2, POS_NUMBERS, 4)
check(1, MIXED_NUMBERS, 0)
...
}
```

Once you have written sufficient tests to cover all the boundary cases you think are important (or to meet your project's coverage requirements[7]), you may think you are finished, but there is more that you can do. First, you might want to ensure that your method doesn't change the input items. You might provide the correct answer but accidentally modify the input data and cause errors to occur elsewhere. Here one example of such a test:

```
void testInputDataUnchanged() {
    def numbers = NEG_NUMBERS.clone()
    def origLength = numbers.size()
    calc.countHowManyBiggerThan(numbers, 0 /* don't care */)
    assertLength(origLength, numbers.toArray())
    assertArrayEquals(NEG_NUMBERS.toArray(), numbers.toArray())
}
```

You can add items[0] = 0 as the first line of the countHowManyBiggerThan method to show how this test would pick up an accidental bug in the code.

We now have some sound tests in place, but we can be more paranoid about our test data and introduce a final test. Over time, we expect further developers to work on the code, and they will likely change the test constants. To ensure that our key cases remain covered, we can create a test that validates our assumptions about the data:

```
void testInputDataAssumptions() {
    assertTrue(NEG_NUMBERS.every{ it < 0 })
    assertTrue(POS_NUMBERS.every{ it > 0 })
    assertContains(0, MIXED_NUMBERS as int[])
    def negCount = MIXED_NUMBERS.grep{it < 0}.size()
    assert negCount, 'at least one negative number expected'
    def posCount = MIXED_NUMBERS.grep{it > 0}.size()
    assert posCount, 'at least one positive number expected'
}
```

This will ensure that our positive, negative, and mixed numbers retain the properties we intend.[8]

---

[7] See the discussion later in this chapter in section 14.7.1.

[8] You could argue that we are being too paranoid here. Maybe, but it gives us a chance to show off a few more example test assertions.

Now for a neat bit of Groovy magic. It turns out that even though we set out to create a calculator for numbers, there was nothing in our original method that was specific to numbers. We add another test to illustrate this using strings with their natural order:

```
void testCalcHowManyFromSampleStrings() {
    check(2, ['Dog','Cat','Antelope'], 'Bird')
}
```

Putting this altogether results in the code in Listing 14.2.

Listing 14.2   A complete test example, including implementation at the end

```
class CalculatorTest extends GroovyTestCase {
    static final NEG_NUMBERS   = [-2, -3, -4]
    static final POS_NUMBERS   = [ 4,  5,  6]
    static final MIXED_NUMBERS = [ 4, -6,  0]
    private calc

    void setUp() {
        calc = new Calculator()
    }

    void testCalcHowManyFromSampleNumbers() {
        check(0, NEG_NUMBERS, -1)
        check(0, NEG_NUMBERS, -2)
        check(2, NEG_NUMBERS, -4)
        check(3, NEG_NUMBERS, -5)
        check(0, POS_NUMBERS,  7)
        check(0, POS_NUMBERS,  6)
        check(2, POS_NUMBERS,  4)
        check(3, POS_NUMBERS,  3)
        check(0, MIXED_NUMBERS,  5)
        check(1, MIXED_NUMBERS,  2)
        check(1, MIXED_NUMBERS,  1)
        check(1, MIXED_NUMBERS,  0)
        check(2, MIXED_NUMBERS, -1)
        check(3, MIXED_NUMBERS, -7)
    }
    void testInputDataUnchanged() {
        def numbers = NEG_NUMBERS.clone()
        def origLength = numbers.size()
        calc.countHowManyBiggerThan(numbers, 0 /* don't care */)
        assertLength(origLength, numbers.toArray())
        assertArrayEquals(NEG_NUMBERS.toArray(), numbers.toArray())
    }
    void testCalcHowManyFromSampleStrings() {
        check(2, ['Dog', 'Cat', 'Antelope'], 'Bird')
```

Annotations:
- **Constants repeated in the test**
- **Use a helper method to make code simpler**
- **Tests proving we don't change the array**
- **Calculator doesn't only work with numbers**

```
        }

        void testInputDataAssumptions() {
            assertTrue(NEG_NUMBERS.every{ it < 0 })
            assertTrue(POS_NUMBERS.every{ it > 0 })
            assertContains(0, MIXED_NUMBERS as int[])
            def negCount = 0
            def posCount = 0
            MIXED_NUMBERS.each {
                if (it < 0) negCount++ else if (it > 0) posCount++
            }
            assert negCount > 0 && posCount > 0
        }

        private check(expectedCount, items, target) {
            assertEquals(
                expectedCount,
                calc.countHowManyBiggerThan(items, target)
            )
        }
    }

    class Calculator {
        def countHowManyBiggerThan(items, target) {
            return items.grep{ it > target }.size()
        }
    }
```

Test constants sanity check

Implementation of calculator

Looks familiar, doesn't it? It's darn close to normal JUnit test code, but with some slight improvements thanks to Groovy's extra assert methods, proper closure support, and more compact syntax. Groovy hasn't made the code much shorter here, just a bit more convenient. As is often true, there's more test code than production code (although in this case, the difference is more pronounced than usual).

Although it's immediately obvious that Groovy code should be able to test Groovy code, it may not be as clear to you that you can test your existing Java using the benefits of GroovyTestCase, too. You'll see this in action in the next section.

14.3 Unit-testing Java code

At this point in your career, you've probably coded more Java applications than Groovy ones. It stands to reason that one of the quickest ways to experience the pleasures of Groovy is to use this nifty language to test normal Java applications. As it turns out, this process is amazingly simple.

Using Groovy to test normal Java code involves three steps:

1 Write your tests in Groovy.

2 Ensure that the Java .class files you wish to test are on the classpath.

3 Run your Groovy tests in the normal way (on the command line or via your IDE or favorite build environment).

That's it most of the time. Of course, there are more complicated scenarios. For example, if you are running a complicated integration test and want to run your Groovy test code on a server, you can always run groovyc on your test code and then follow the same steps that you'd go through for a Java application.

Let's explore this further by looking at an example. Rather than spending a lot of time describing a Java application that you may not have seen before, we will consider how you might write some tests for two old Java favorites: Hashtable and HashMap.

One of the first things you would do if you were writing some Java tests for Hashtable and HashMap is set up test fixtures. You do the same thing in Groovy, but you have Groovy's convenient syntax to make your tests shorter and easier to understand. For example, this is how we set up our test fixtures for an arbitrary key object and a sample map:

```
static final KEY = new Object()
static final MAP = [key1: new Object(), key2: new Object()]
```

One of the complicated things to test with Java-based tests is proper exception handling. Groovy's built-in shouldFail assert method can be of great assistance for such tests. For example, it is part of Hashtable's expected behavior to disallow null values. Trying to store a null value as in new Hashtable()[KEY] = null should lead to a NullPointerException. The shouldFail method asserts that this exception is thrown from within its closure:

```
void testHashtableRejectsNull() {
    shouldFail(NullPointerException) {
        new Hashtable()[KEY] = null
    }
}
```

If the attached closure fails to throw any exception, the test fails with a message like the following:[9]

```
junit.framework.AssertionFailedError: testHashtableRejectsNull() should
have failed with an exception of type java.lang.NullPointerException
```

---

[9] Edited slightly for easier reading.

If the closure fails but with an incorrect exception, the test fails with a message similar to

```
junit.framework.AssertionFailedError: testHashtableRejectsNull() should
have failed with an exception of type java.lang.NullPointerException,
instead got Exception java.lang.IllegalArgumentException:
Illegal Capacity: -1
```

The `shouldFail` method additionally returns the exception message so that you can test that the correct message is being generated by the exception, as in the following example:

```
void testBadInitialSize() {
    def msg = shouldFail(IllegalArgumentException) {
        new Hashtable(-1)
    }
    assertEquals "Illegal Capacity: -1", msg
}
```

If the incorrect exception message was returned, your test would fail with a message similar to the following:

```
junit.framework.ComparisonFailure:
Expected :Illegal Capacity: -1
Actual   :Illegal Capacity: -2
```

Groovy's object-inspection methods (see section 9.1.1 for further details) also prove useful for writing our Groovy tests. Here is how you might use `dump`:

```
assert MAP.dump().contains('java.lang.Object')
```

Putting all this together results in the code in listing 14.3.

Listing 14.3   Testing `Hashtable` and `HashMap` from Groovy

```
class HashMapAndTableTest extends GroovyTestCase {
    static final KEY = new Object()
    static final MAP = [key1: new Object(), key2: new Object()]

    void testHashtableRejectsNull() {
        shouldFail(NullPointerException) {
            new Hashtable()[KEY] = null
        }
    }

    void testBadInitialSize() {
        def msg = shouldFail(IllegalArgumentException) {      ◁┘ Check that
            new Hashtable(-1)                                        the right kind
        }                                                           of exception
        assertEquals "Illegal Capacity: -1", msg    ◁┘ Check the     is thrown
    }                                                       message
```

Check that
the right kind
of exception
is thrown

Check the
message

```
void testHashMapAcceptsNull() {
    def myMap = new HashMap()
    myMap[KEY] = null
    assert myMap.keySet().contains(KEY)
}

void testHashMapReturnsOriginalObjects() {
    def myMap = new HashMap()
    MAP.entrySet().each {
        myMap[it] = MAP[it]
        assertSame  MAP[it], myMap[it]
    }
    assert MAP.dump().contains('java.lang.Object')   ◁┘
    assert myMap.size() == MAP.size()
}
```

Use Groovy inspection to examine the map

None of the behavior here is unexpected—after all, the classes we're testing are familiar ones. Using `shouldFail` is more compact and readable than the equivalent in Java with a `try`/`catch`, which fails if it reaches the end of the `try` block. It's also safer than the new JUnit4 annotation for exception testing, which will only check whether *anything* in the method throws the desired exception, rather than just the line of code we want to check.

The use of `dump` in this test isn't as elegant as it tends to be in real testing. When you know the internal structure of the class, you can perform more useful tests against the introspected representation.

The final point we'll mention about using Groovy to test your Java code is related to the agile software development practice of *test-driven development* (TDD).[10] Using this practice, code is developed by first writing a failing test and then writing production code to make that test pass, followed by refactoring and then repeating the process. Modern IDEs provide strong support for this practice; for example, they will offer to automatically create a nonexistent class mentioned in a test.

You can still adopt TDD using a hybrid Groovy/Java environment, but current IDEs provide minimal support to assist making this as streamlined as pure Java environments. We expect this to change over time as IDE support for Groovy steadily improves.

Having considered individual test classes, you will now see how to run sets of tests together.

---

[10] See *Test-Driven Development: By Example* by Kent Beck (Addison Wesley, 2002).

14.4 *Organizing your tests*

So far, we have been running our Groovy tests individually. For large systems, tests typically aren't run individually but are grouped into test suites that are run together. JUnit has built-in facilities for working with suites. These facilities allow you to add individual test cases (and other nested suites) to test suites. JUnit's test runners know about suites and run all the tests they contain. Unfortunately, these facilities require you to manually add all of your tests to a suite and assume you are using Java classes for your tests. We'll look at ways of making life easier with Groovy.

Because grouping tests into suites is so important, numerous solutions have popped up in the Java world for automatically creating suites, but these too typically assume you are using Java classes. The good news is that because Groovy classes compile to Java classes, you don't have to abandon any of your current practices for grouping tests—as long as you are willing to compile your Groovy files using groovyc first. The even better news is that there are solutions that allow you to work more naturally directly with your Groovy files.

First, we should mention GroovyTestSuite, which is a Java class. It allows you to invoke Groovy test scripts from the command line as follows:

```
> java groovy.util.GroovyTestSuite src/test/Foo.groovy
```

Being a Java class, GroovyTestSuite can be used with any conventional Java IDE or Java build environment for running JUnit tests. It allows you to add Groovy files into your test suites, as shown in listing 14.4. This creates a suite containing the two previous tests. You could also add Java tests to the same suite.

Listing 14.4 Adding Groovy scripts to a JUnit suite with GroovyTestSuite

```
import junit.framework.*

static Test suite() {
    def suite = new TestSuite()
    def gsuite = new GroovyTestSuite()
    suite.addTestSuite(gsuite.compile
                    ("Listing_14_2_Calculator_Test.groovy"))
    suite.addTestSuite(gsuite.compile
                    ("Listing_14_3_Hash_Test.groovy"))
    return suite
}

junit.textui.TestRunner.run(suite())
```

We create a normal JUnit `TestSuite` and call `GroovyTestSuite`'s `compile` method to compile the Groovy source code so that `TestSuite` knows how to run it. We then use the normal JUnit console UI to run the tests. It isn't aware that it's running anything other than normal Java.

Next, we look at `AllTestSuite`, which can be thought of as an improved version of `GroovyTestSuite`. It allows you to specify a base directory and a filename pattern, and then it adds all the matching Groovy files to a suite. Listing 14.5 shows how you would use it to run the same tests as we did in listing 14.4.

> **Listing 14.5 Adding Groovy scripts to a JUnit suite with `AllTestSuite`**

```
def suite = AllTestSuite.suite(".", "Listing_14_*_Test.groovy")
junit.textui.TestRunner.run(suite)
```

This time, we use the return value of the `suite` method directly, but if we wanted to add multiple directories or patterns, we could have called `suite` multiple times, adding the tests to a suite before running them all together.

We will have more to say about grouping tests into suites and running test suites when we look at IDE, Ant, and Maven integration later in this chapter.

Unit testing can be difficult in some situations, particularly if you are adding tests for code that was originally developed without any thought of testing. Groovy's dynamic nature eases the pain with a number of advanced ways of testing, which we shall examine next.

14.5 *Advanced testing techniques*

Automated testing is easy if you develop your automated tests in close interplay with your production code, because you immediately design your system for testability. Unfortunately, this level of test awareness is not yet mainstream, and you'll sometimes find yourself in the position where you have to write tests for code that already exists. This is when you need advanced testing techniques, just as you'd need a more specialized tool than a normal fork to efficiently extract a single strand of spaghetti from a bowl of pasta.

A number of bad programming habits make testing difficult. One is writing incoherent classes and methods that do more than they should, resulting in overly long classes and methods.

Even worse is code with lots of dependencies to other classes that we will call *collaborators*. Unit-testing your *class under test (CUT)* in its purist form means that you test it in isolation without the collaborators so that you are just focused on finding bugs in your code.[11]

The advanced testing techniques we are about to explore are mainly concerned with replacing such collaborators for the purpose of unit-testing the CUT in isolation. To that end, we will first show how you can employ Groovy's core language features to provide "fake" collaborators. We then explore Groovy's special support for so-called stubs and mocks, which allow flexible simulation of collaborator behavior, as well as let you specify exactly *how* the collaborators must be used. We finish with a technique that can be used when all else fails: using logs to test that your classes are behaving as you expect them to.

14.5.1 *Testing made groovy*

Once, I (Dierk) gave a lecture on unit testing where I asked the audience to challenge me with the most difficult testing problem they could think of, something they believed would be impossible to unit test. Their proposal was to test the load-balancer of a server farm. How could we test this in Groovy?

The core logic of a load balancer is to relay a received request to the machine in the server farm that currently has the lowest load. Suppose we already have collaborator classes that describe *requests*, *machines*, and the *farm*; a Groovy load balancer could have the following method:

```
def relay(request, farm) {
    farm.machines.sort { it.load }[0].send(request)
}
```

The method finds the machine with the lowest load by sorting all machines in the farm by the `load` property, taking the first one, and calling the `send` method on that machine object.

In order to unit-test this logic, we need to somehow call the `relay` method to verify its behavior. We can do this only if we have `request` and `farm` objects, but we don't want our test to depend on any of the production collaborator classes. Luckily, our Groovy solution doesn't demand any specific types, and we can use any type we fancy.

What would be a good object to use for the `farm` parameter? Thanks to Groovy's duck typing of the relay parameters, any object that we can ask for a `machines` property would do—a map for example. The `machines` property in turn

---

[11] Other kinds of integration tests should pick up bugs that come from integrating your code with the collaborators.

needs to be something that can be *sorted* by a `load` property and understands the `send(request)` method. Listing 14.6 follows this route by testing the load balancer logic with a map-based farm of fake machines that are made using a `FakeMachine` class. Fake machines return a self-reference from their `send` method to allow subsequent asserts to verify that the `send` method was called on the expected machine.

Listing 14.6   Unit-testing a load balancer with Groovy collaborator replacements

```
import junit.framework.Assert;

def relay(request, farm) {                              Code
    farm.machines.sort { it.load }[0].send(request)     under test
}
                                      Replacement
class FakeMachine {        ⊲──┘       class
    def load
    def send(request) { return this }
}

final LOW_LOAD = 5, HIGH_LOAD = 10
def farm = [machines: [                   Map replaces
    new FakeMachine(load:HIGH_LOAD),      farm
    new FakeMachine(load:LOW_LOAD)]]

Assert.assertSame(LOW_LOAD, relay(null, farm).load)
```

Note that we don't need to create a special stub for the `request` parameter. Since it is relayed and no methods are ever called on it, `null` is fine.

The important point about listing 14.6 is that the load-balancing logic is tested in full isolation. No accidental change to any of the collaborator classes can possibly affect this test. When this test fails, we can be sure that the load-balancing logic and nothing else is in trouble.

Up to this point, the Groovy support for dynamic typing, property-style access to maps, and the ease of declaring small helper classes has saved us lot of work, but Groovy has even more useful features in stock.

Listing 14.7 tests the same logic, but using Expandos (see section 7.4 for an introduction). Expando objects are great for replacing duck-typed collaborator objects, because they can mimic method calls by having a closure assigned to the property that is named after the method. You can easily create two instances of Expando, which respond to method calls in different ways, just by specifying different closures as their property values for that method:

Listing 14.7   Using Expando objects for replacing collaborators in unit tests

```
def relay(request, farm) {
    farm.machines.sort { it.load }[0].send(request)
}

def fakeOne = new Expando( load:10, send: { false } )
def fakeTwo = new Expando( load:5,  send: { true } )

def farm = [machines: [ fakeOne, fakeTwo ]]

assert relay(null, farm)
```

Both listings achieve the same effect, but the latter feels more Groovy. They are pushing demanded behavior into the faked collaborators, which is an often-used advanced testing technique. You will see this approach reapplied and extended when we look at Groovy's built-in support for *stubs* and *mocks*.

14.5.2   Stubbing and mocking

So far, our load balancer was fairly easy to test in isolation because we could feed all collaborator objects into the relay method. That wasn't a real challenge. Things get more interesting when we need to replace objects that cannot be set from the outside.[12]

Example problem: collaborator construction

Suppose our load balancer directly creates its collaborator farm object:

```
def relay(request) {
    new Farm().getMachines().sort { it.load }[0].send(request)
}
```

The Farm class looks like this:

```
class Farm {
    def getMachines() {
        /* some expensive code here */
    }
}
```

From an implementer's perspective, such a solution could be justifiable for a number of reasons. Perhaps the Farm's getMachines method provides support for finding all machines via a network scan and then caches that information. Any-

---

[12] In UML terms: when the collaborator is *composed*, not *aggregated*.

way, we would not want to perform an expensive operation if we didn't need it, so placing the `new Farm().getMachines()` statement within `relay` seems like the way to go. From a tester's perspective, however, even allowing for potential caching, calling the real code is going to be too expensive an operation for a unit-test environment, where tests should execute in the blink of an eye if developers are to be expected to run them often. Also, we need to run our tests even when there are no real machines available.

The implementation is not easily testable. We can't use the Expando or fake implementation techniques in the way you saw earlier, because there is no way to sneak such a subclass into our code under test. One common trick when testing would be to subclass `Farm`. That won't help us here either, for the same reasons. Should we give up? No!

Stubbing out the collaborator

Groovy's Meta-Object capabilities come to the rescue in the form of Groovy stubs. The trick provided by Groovy stubs is to intercept all method calls to instances of a given class (`Farm` in this case) and return a predefined result. Here is how it works.

We first construct a *stub* object for calls to the `Farm` class:

```
import groovy.mock.interceptor.StubFor

def farmStub = new StubFor(Farm)
```

Next, we create two fake machines that we will use to help define our expectations from the stub:

```
def fakeOne = new Expando( load:10, send: { false } )
def fakeTwo = new Expando( load:5,  send: { true }  )
```

Then, we demand that when the `getMachines` method is called on our stub, our fake machines are returned. Registering this behavior is done by calling the respective method on the stub's `demand` property and passing a closure argument to define the behavior:

```
farmStub.demand.getMachines { [fakeOne, fakeTwo] }
```

Finally, we pass our test code as a closure to the stub's `use` method. This ensures that the stub is in charge when the test is executed: Any call to any `Farm` object will be intercepted and handled by our stub. The full test scenario reads like listing 14.8.

Listing 14.8 Using Groovy stubs to test an otherwise untestable load balancer

```
import groovy.mock.interceptor.StubFor

def relay(request) {
    new Farm().getMachines().sort { it.load }[0].send(request)
}

def fakeOne = new Expando(load:10, send: { false } )
def fakeTwo = new Expando(load:5,  send: { true } )

def farmStub = new StubFor(Farm)              ◁┘ Create stub                      Specify demanded
farmStub.demand.getMachines { [fakeOne, fakeTwo ] }    ◁┘ behavior

farmStub.use {
    assert relay(null)        Call the class under
}                             test using stub
```

Note that for the use of Groovy stubs, it makes no difference whether the collaborator class is written in Java or Groovy. The class under test, however, must be a Groovy class.

Stub expectations

Groovy stubs support a flexible specification of the demanded behavior. To demand calls to different methods, demand them in sequence:

```
someStub.demand.methodOne { 1 }
someStub.demand.methodTwo { 2 }
```

When calls to the stubbed method should yield different results per call, add the respective demands in sequence:

```
someStub.demand.methodOne { 1 }
someStub.demand.methodOne { 2 }
```

You can additionally provide a range to specify how often the demanded closure should apply; the default is (1..1):

```
someStub.demand.methodOne(0..35) { 1 }
```

Finally, it is also possible to react to the method argument that the CUT passes to the collaborator's method. Each argument of the method call is passed into the demand closure and can thus be evaluated inside it. Suppose you expect that the stubbed method is called only with even numbers, and you would like to assert that *invariant* while testing. You can achieve this with

```
someStub.demand.methodOne {
    number -> assert 0 == number % 2
    return 1
}
```

Of course, you can also combine all these kinds of demand declarations, producing an elaborate specification of call sequences on the collaborator and returned values. The more elaborate that specification is, the more likely it is that you will want to additionally assert that all demanded method calls happened. For stubs, this is not asserted by default, but you can enforce this check by calling

```
someStub.expect.verify()
```

after the use closure.

Stubs use a `LooseExpectation` for verifying the demanded method calls. It is called *loose* because it only verifies that all demanded methods were called, not whether they were called in the sequence of the specification.

Comparing stubs and mocks

Strict expectations are used with *mocks*. A mock object has all the behavior of a stub plus more. The strict expectation of a mock verifies that all the demanded method calls happen in exactly the sequence of the specification. The first method call that breaks this sequence causes the test to fail immediately. Also, with mocks there is no need to explicitly call the `verify` method, because that happens by default when the use closure ends.

At first glance, it appears that mocks and stubs are almost the same thing, with mocks being a bit more rigorous. But there is a deep fundamental difference in the purpose behind their use:[13] Stubs enable your CUT to run in isolation and allow you to make assertions about state changes of the CUT. With mocks, the test focus moves to the interplay of the CUT and its collaborators. What gets asserted is whether the CUT follows a specified *protocol* when talking with the outside world. A protocol defines the rules that the CUT has to obey when calling the collaborator. Typical rules would be: the first method call must be `init`, the last method call must be `close`, and so on.

Consider a new variant of our load balancer that uses a `SortableFarm` class, which provides a `sort` method to change its internal representation of machines such that any subsequent call to `getMachines` returns them sorted by load:

```
class SortableFarm extends Farm {
    def sort() {
```

---

[13] See http://www.martinfowler.com/articles/mocksArentStubs.html for more details.

```
              /* here the Farm would sort its machines by load */
        }
    }
```

Our CUT now has to follow a certain protocol when using `SortableFarm`: first `sort` must be called, and then `getMachines`:

```
def relay(request) {
    def farm = new SortableFarm()
    farm.sort()
    farm.getMachines()[0].send(request)
}
```

Listing 14.9 uses a mock as constructed with the `MockFor` class to verify that our CUT exactly follows this protocol. Only the compliance to the protocol is tested and nothing else; for this special test, we don't even verify that the call is relayed to the machine with the lowest load.

Listing 14.9 Using Groovy mock support to verify protocol compliance

```
import groovy.mock.interceptor.MockFor

class SortableFarm extends Farm {
    void sort() {
        /* here the Farm would sort its machines by load */
    }
}

def relay(request) {
    def farm = new SortableFarm()
    farm.sort()
    farm.getMachines()[0].send(request)
}

def farmMock = new MockFor(SortableFarm)          ◁──┘ Create
                                                        mock

farmMock.demand.sort(){}                               Specify demanded
farmMock.demand.getMachines { [new Expando(send: {} )] }   behavior

farmMock.use {
    relay(null)
}
```

If you are unfamiliar with mock objects, protocol-based testing[14] will probably appear strange to you. In traditional testing, we tend to focus on state changes

---

[14] Also called *interaction-based testing*.

and return values rather than on the effects caused to collaborating objects. In some cases, interactions with collaborators are implementation details and shouldn't be tested. If, however, they are part of the object's guaranteed behavior, mock testing is appropriate.

Groovy's clever way of providing stubs and mocks even for objects that cannot be passed to the CUT is a two-edged sword. Testing should lead you into a design of high coherence and low coupling. Without resorting to clever Java tricks, Java mocks only work if you can pass them to the CUT, forcing you to expose the collaborator, which usually leads to a more flexible design. In Groovy, there is no such restriction, because you can more easily test even a rotten design. The implication is that Groovy won't stop you from building a less-flexible design even when using the latest development practices.

On the other hand, Java projects often suffer from the deadlock that appears when developers find large sections of untestable code. They cannot easily refactor such a section of code because it has no tests. They cannot easily write tests without refactoring the code to make it more testable. With Groovy's built-in mocking facilities, you have a better chance of escaping this deadlock.

14.5.3 *Using GroovyLogTestCase*

Sometimes, even with stubs and mocks, testing a particular object can be difficult. The amount of work involved in setting up all the mocked interactions in a tricky scenario may outweigh the benefits of your testing efforts. To be realistic, if your system (and resulting tests) is that complex, perhaps you will have a bug in your tests. In such cases, another useful feature provided by Groovy is GroovyLogTestCase. You have already seen in listing 14.2 that it was relatively easy to test the fictitious countHowManyBiggerThan calculator. Suppose, though, that is was much harder to test. We could resort to writing some information to a log file, and then we could manually check the log file to see if it appears to contain the correct information. In these scenarios, GroovyLogTestCase can be extremely useful. Consider the following modified LoggingCalculator:

```
import java.util.logging.*

class LoggingCalculator {
    static final LOG = Logger.getLogger('LoggingCalculator')
    def countHowManyBiggerThan(items, target) {
        def count = 0
        items.each{
            if (it > target) {
                count++
                LOG.finer "item was bigger - count this one"
```

```
            } else if (it == target) {
                LOG.finer "item was equal - don't count this one"
            } else {
                LOG.finer "item was smaller - don't count this one"
            }
        }
        return count
    }
}
```

Note that the calculator outputs log messages for each of three scenarios: the item being tested was smaller than, equal to, or bigger than the target value. We can now test this class with the assistance of `GroovyLogTestCase`, as shown in listing 14.10.

Listing 14.10 Using `GroovyLogTestCase` for tricky cases

```
import java.util.logging.*

class LoggingCalculatorTest extends GroovyLogTestCase {          Test
    static final MIXED_NUMBERS = [99, 2, 1, 0, -1, -2, -99]  ◁┘ data
    private calc

    void setUp() {
        calc = new LoggingCalculator()
    }
                                                          Set up
                                                          stringLog
    void testCalculatorAndLog(){
        def log = stringLog(Level.FINER, 'LoggingCalculator') {  ◁┘
            def count = calc.countHowManyBiggerThan
                            (MIXED_NUMBERS, -1)   ◁─ Invoke CUT
            assertEquals(4, count)          ◁─ Traditional JUnit
        }                                      style assert
        checkLogCount(1, "was equal", log)
        checkLogCount(4, "was bigger", log)
        checkLogCount(2, "was smaller", log)
        checkLogCount(4, /[^d][^o][^n][^'][^t] count this one/, log)
        checkLogCount(3, "don't count this one", log)
    }                                            Helper method
                                                 asserting patterns
    private checkLogCount(expectedCount, regex, log) {  ◁─ within the log
        def matcher = (log =~ regex)
        assertTrue log, expectedCount == matcher.count
    }
}
```

If you look at the test data in the MIXED_NUMBERS list, you would expect four entries to be bigger than -1, two to be smaller, and one to be the same. Log messages corresponding to these cases will be stored in the log variable thanks to the stringLog statement. Our test then uses regular expressions to ensure that the log contains the correct number of each kind of log message.

GroovyLogTestCase makes use of the *Log String* testing pattern[15] in a test scenario that would otherwise be cumbersome and error-prone to implement. It relieves you of the work of setting the appropriate log levels and registering string appenders for the CUT logger. After the test, it cleans up properly and restores the old logging configuration.

You have seen that Groovy makes even advanced testing techniques easily available through core language features. The running theme of improving developer convenience with Groovy finds its logical continuation in the next section, where we integrate Groovy unit testing in Java IDEs.

14.6 IDE integration

In section 1.6, you saw that some major Java IDEs (with the addition of plug-ins) have useful support for editing and running Groovy code. The same mechanisms are suitable for editing and running your Groovy tests. But the story doesn't end there.

Java IDEs often have additional features to better support Java unit testing, such as enhanced test runners. Fortunately, you'll see that many of these enhanced features can be leveraged for your Groovy unit testing. We explore how to use the two test suite classes you saw earlier within an IDE, before taking a brief look at how Groovy's close relationship with Java allows it to be used with cutting-edge IDE testing features.

14.6.1 Using GroovyTestSuite

While editing a Groovy test file within your IDE, you can run it like any other Groovy file. Eclipse users with the Groovy plug-in installed might *right-click*, select Run As, and then select Groovy. IntelliJ IDEA users with the GroovyJ plug-in installed might press Ctrl-Shift-F10. In both cases, the corresponding tests within the current file would run. If your Groovy file was several assert statements in a script file, like listing 14.1, then you wouldn't see any output—this is as expected because assert statements make noise only when something goes wrong. If you don't want to run your tests individually or want some additional feedback when running your tests, GroovyTestSuite may be what you are after.

---

[15] See chapter 27 of *Test-Driven Development: By Example*.

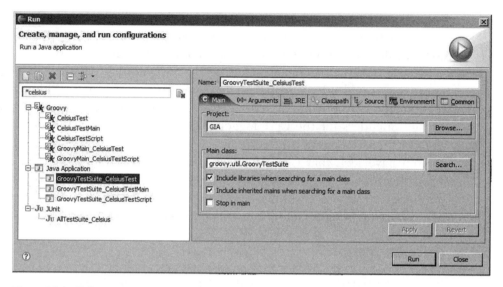

Figure 14.1 Eclipse run configuration for Main tab using GroovyTestSuite

In section 14.4, you saw that GroovyTestSuite could be used to invoke a Groovy test from the command line. You also saw how it could be used to add Groovy files into a standard JUnit suite.[16] We are now going to look at another way of using GroovyTestSuite: as part of an IDE run configuration. Figure 14.1 shows how to configure Eclipse to use GroovyTestSuite as part of a run configuration. Select Run -> Run, and create a new Java Application configuration. Set the Project to be your current project, and select groovy.util.GroovyTestSuite as the Main class.

Next, click the Arguments tab; in the Program Arguments box, include the path to your Groovy script, as shown in figure 14.2.

When you run this configuration, you should see output similar to that shown in figure 14.3.

Users of JUnit's text-based runner will now feel quite at home and will be seeing a bit more feedback than the previously empty output.

---

[16] Test suites remain an important concept you typically use in conjunction with other IDE integration.

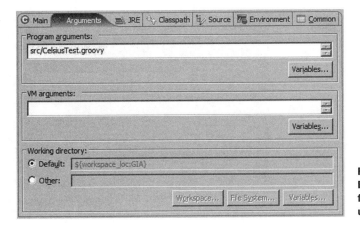

**Figure 14.2
Eclipse run configuration
for the Arguments tab
using `GroovyTestSuite`**

14.6.2 *Using AllTestSuite*

JUnit's green/red bar reporting mechanism found in graphical test runners can be addictive when you are "in the groove." The default behavior of Groovy's `GroovyTestSuite`, however, doesn't easily fit into the graphical runner model, because those runners usually prefer to run normal Java classes, rather than Groovy files.

One strategy is to rely on `groovyc` to compile all test cases and then run them via a Java-aware GUI runner; however, that takes an extra step. It's more fun to see the green bar *immediately* after coding! This is where `AllTestSuite`, which we discussed earlier in section 14.4, really shines. In addition to its uses for organizing your tests into suites, `AllTestSuite` can also be used as part of configuring your test runs.

Figure 14.3   Eclipse `GroovyTestSuite` example run output

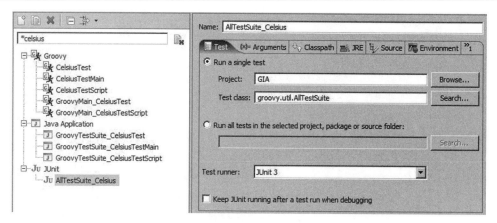

Figure 14.4   Eclipse `AllTestSuite` run configuration Test tab

To configure Eclipse to use `AllTestSuite`, create a new JUnit run configuration, select your project, and set the Test class to `groovy.util.AllTestSuite`, as shown in figure 14.4.

Then, in the Arguments tab, define two properties that tell `AllTestSuite` which Groovy tests to run. These properties need to be supplied as two VM Arguments. The properties will need to be adjusted for your system but will look something like `-Dgroovy.test.dir=src` for the directory and `-Dgroovy.test.pattern=CelsiusTest*.groovy` for the filename pattern. Your configuration will be similar to that shown in figure 14.5.

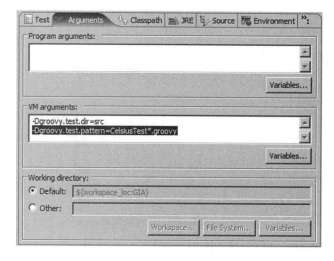

**Figure 14.5
Eclipse `AllTestSuite` run
configuration Arguments tab**

Figure 14.6 Eclipse and IntelliJ IDEA `AllTestSuite` example test run output

When you run this configuration, you should see the familiar green and red bar, as shown in figure 14.6. We don't have time to illustrate how to set up other IDEs, but we included the output from running the same configuration in IntelliJ in figure 14.6 so that you would know what to expect.

14.6.3 *Advanced IDE integration*

Groovy's close relationship with Java opens up a whole world of additional integration possibilities. Most technologies as new as Groovy suffer from immature tools. Although Groovy doesn't totally escape this condition, it can frequently leverage the mature Java tool set. We will give you one brief example based on the Eclipse TPTP platform to give you the idea.

The Eclipse open source *Test & Performance Tools Platform (TPTP)* project provides a framework that supports test editing and execution, monitoring, tracing and profiling, and log analysis capabilities.[17] The platform is multifaceted and would probably require its own book to fully describe all of its features. For our purposes, you only need know that one feature it provides is a mechanism to support creation of test suites by non-Java programmers. A typical scenario is a Java programmer creating a set of base Java test classes. A tester can then combine tests into suites, create loops involving tests, run performance tests based on these tests, and supply data from spreadsheets and other sources to be used in the tests.

---

[17] See http://www.eclipse.org/tptp for more details.

It is beyond the scope of this book to describe all the details, but we wanted to show you the results of an initial attempt to leverage TPTP's great features in the Groovy world. First, we followed an introductory tutorial included in the TPTP documentation called *Creating a datapool driven JUnit test application.*[18] Toward the end of the tutorial, it generated some Java JUnit tests for us. We replaced the Java tests it created with our own Groovy tests using `GroovyTestSuite`.

TPTP then allowed us to combine our Groovy tests in a graphical manner within the tool without having to see the code again, and it let us create data for the tests using a built-in datapool mechanism that TPTP provides. Figure 14.7 shows how we entered the data required for our test. We could have imported it from a spreadsheet or a number of other sources. For those who have

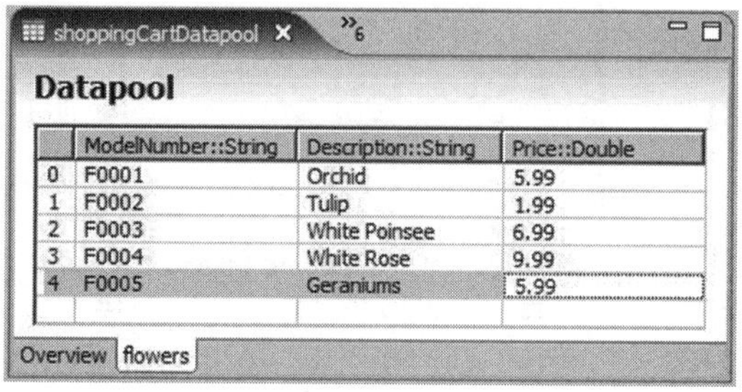

Figure 14.7   Eclipse TPTP sample data

looked up the tutorial, you will note that we changed the last data value from 4.99 to 5.99 so that we can show you what a failed test looks like.

When we ran the test, a test log was created and stored away for us. If you examine the events in the log, you can observe the graphical representation of the steps in the left pane of figure 14.8. Because we intentionally modified one of the data values, you observe a JUnit failure message in the description of the failure, along with a stacktrace showing that our Groovy test was running.

We ask you to excuse us for skipping many of the details in this example. It wasn't meant to be a TPTP tutorial or even to suggest that the integration we have shown you is the best way to use TPTP with Groovy. It was just meant to provide you with a glimpse of the possibilities available to Groovy because of its Java heritage.

Of course, Java has more to offer than just IDEs, and many tools have been written to make testing simpler and more effective. Again, these tools can be used with Groovy code, as you'll see in our next section.

---

[18] See http://help.eclipse.org/help31/topic/org.eclipse.hyades.test.doc.user/samples/saccessdp.htm.

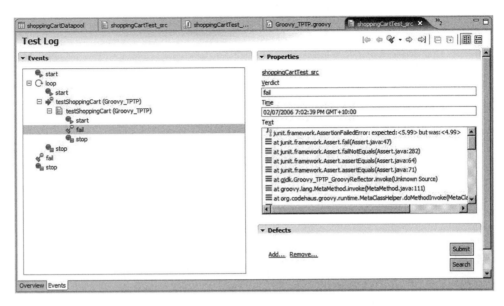

Figure 14.8 Eclipse TPTP sample output

14.7 *Tools for Groovy testing*

In the previous section, you saw some value-added IDE support from the Java world for testing. It turns out there are also quite a few value-added non-IDE tools with Java heritage that you can leverage for your Groovy tests. We don't have the space to cover all of them, but we will talk about Cobertura and JUnitPerf to show that whatever library you want to use can be used from Groovy.

14.7.1 *Code coverage with Groovy*

Code-coverage tools are now a mainstream part of any serious agile Java developer's toolkit. They provide useful feedback on how well your testing efforts are going. To leverage any existing Java code coverage tool for Groovy, you need to compile your Groovy into bytecode and then run the tool as before.

However, if you are interested in the coverage of your Groovy code and you try this technique with an older coverage tool, you will probably not have the ability to see reports indicating which lines of code were executed, because the tool or its reporting infrastructure doesn't know about Groovy source files.

The good news is that efforts are being made to provide native Groovy support in code-coverage tools. One open source tool that has gained Groovy support is

Cobertura, available from http://cobertura.sourceforge.net. For example, consider the following Groovy class:[19]

```
class BiggestPairCalc
{
    int sumBiggestPair(int a, int b, int c) {
        def op1 = a
        def op2 = b
        if (c > a) {
            op1 = c
        } else if (c > b) {
            op2 = c
        }
        return op1 + op2
    }
}
```

Here's a test for this code:

```
class BiggestPairCalcTest extends GroovyTestCase
{
    void testSumBiggestPair() {
        def calc = new BiggestPairCalc()
        assertEquals(9, calc.sumBiggestPair(5, 4, 1))
    }
}
```

At this stage, we could run our test and make sure it passes. To get coverage, however, requires a few extra steps. We used an Ant build file to capture these steps. The first part of the build file looks like the following:

```
<!-- set up definitions and properties ... -->
<!-- compile java code, if any ... -->
<javac .../>
<!-- compile groovy code ... -->
<groovyc .../>
```

Here, we are compiling our source files into class files so that Cobertura can *instrument* them, as shown in the next lines:

```
<cobertura-instrument todir="target/instrumented-classes">
  <fileset dir="${dir.build}">
      <include name="**/*.class"/>
  </fileset>
</cobertura-instrument>
```

---

[19] If we were trying to be really Groovy, we could have written `[a,b,c].sort()[-2..-1].sum()`, but that would have made it harder to show some lines covered and some not!

By this stage in the build process, Cobertura has modified our bytecode so that while it is executing, it will write out information about which code paths have been executed. This information will be stored away in a form suitable for later processing by the coverage tool. We can now use our classes in the normal way, which in this case means running them using Ant's `junit` task as follows:

```
<!-- run tests with the junit task as normal,
  - making sure we use the instrumented classes -->
<junit …/>
```

We follow our test run with the `cobertura-report` task to generate a coverage report similar to the one shown in figure 14.9:

```
<cobertura-report srcdir="${dir.src}"
       destdir="${dir.report}/cobertura"/>
<!-- cleanup … -->
```

Note that nothing special was required to get the Groovy coverage. All Java classes (if any) and Groovy classes in our project will be part of the coverage analysis.

If we drill down into the report by clicking an appropriate link for one of our source files, we can see which lines are covered by tests. Figure 14.10 shows that lines 7 and 9 are not covered yet by tests.

Now that we can see where we're missing coverage, we can add more tests to our test method:

```
assertEquals(15, calc.sumBiggestPair( 5, 9, 6))
assertEquals(16, calc.sumBiggestPair(10, 2, 6))
```

We can run the tests to make sure they all still work and then check the coverage again to see how our coverage is going. The result is shown in figure 14.11.

So, is the code correct? The tests all pass, and we have 100 percent coverage—that means we don't have any bugs, right? Just for fun, let's add one more test:

```
assertEquals(11, calc.sumBiggestPair(5, 2, 6))
```

Coverage Report - All Packages

Package	# Classes	Line Coverage		Branch Coverage		Complexity
(default)	2	78%	7/9	100%	3/3	0
All Packages	2	78%	7/9	100%	3/3	0

Classes in this Package	Line Coverage		Branch Coverage		Complexity
BiggestPairCalc	71%	5/7	100%	2/2	0
BiggestPairCalcTest	100%	2/2	100%	1/1	0

Report generated by Cobertura 1.8 on 2/07/06 22:17.

Figure 14.9 Cobertura code-coverage summary report

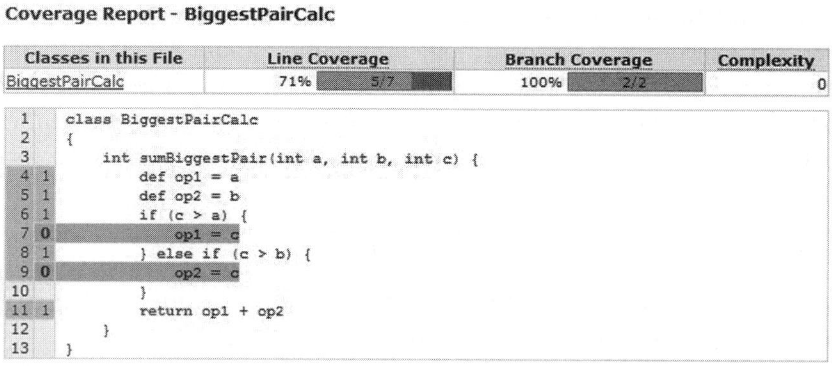

Coverage Report - BiggestPairCalc

Classes in this File	Line Coverage		Branch Coverage		Complexity
BiggestPairCalc	71%	5/7	100%	2/2	0

```
 1    class BiggestPairCalc
 2    {
 3        int sumBiggestPair(int a, int b, int c) {
 4  1        def op1 = a
 5  1        def op2 = b
 6  1        if (c > a) {
 7  0            op1 = c
 8  1        } else if (c > b) {
 9  0            op2 = c
10             }
11  1        return op1 + op2
12        }
13    }
```

Figure 14.10   Cobertura code-coverage file report showing partial coverage

If we run our tests again, they now fail. There was a bug in our original algorithm. That was nothing to do with Groovy, but just a reminder that coverage is a necessary but not sufficient condition to show that you have all the tests that you need. We can fix up the calculator as follows:

```
int sumBiggestPair(int a, int b, int c) {
    int op1 = a
    int op2 = b
    if (c > [a,b].min()) {
        op1 = c
        op2 = [a,b].max()
    }
    return op1 + op2
}
```

Now we can run all our tests. They should all pass, and Cobertura should report 100 percent coverage.

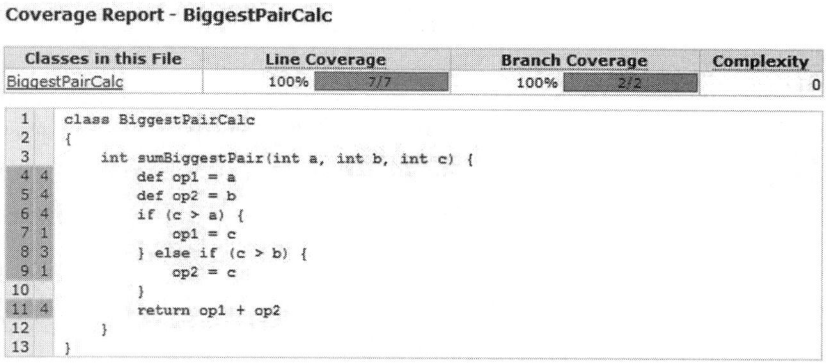

Coverage Report - BiggestPairCalc

Classes in this File	Line Coverage		Branch Coverage		Complexity
BiggestPairCalc	100%	7/7	100%	2/2	0

```
 1    class BiggestPairCalc
 2    {
 3        int sumBiggestPair(int a, int b, int c) {
 4  4        def op1 = a
 5  4        def op2 = b
 6  4        if (c > a) {
 7  1            op1 = c
 8  3        } else if (c > b) {
 9  1            op2 = c
10             }
11  4        return op1 + op2
12        }
13    }
```

Figure 14.11   Cobertura code-coverage file report showing full coverage

14.7.2 *JUnit extensions*

Most JUnit extension frameworks integrate easily with Groovy. For example, you can easily employ XMLUnit, DbUnit, and jWebUnit via JUnit tests written in Groovy, because these frameworks expose an API that facilitates delegation. Decorator-based frameworks, however, are slightly more challenging to utilize within Groovy using the techniques we have shown you so far.

JUnitPerf is an extension framework for JUnit that offers the ability to ascertain fine-grained performance and scalability (at a method level). For instance, JUnitPerf enables scenarios such as "the `findTrades` method must return a `collection` of `Trade` objects within one second, or the test fails (even if the test did return a valid `collection` of `Trade` objects)." The framework also adds scalability via threading. Using this scenario, you can add the requirement that under a load of 100 invocations, the `findTrades` method must return a `collection` of `Trade` objects within one second.

Understandably, there are scenarios within Groovy where this type of framework could come in handy:

- Testing the performance and scalability of Groovy applications
- Testing the performance and scalability of normal Java code in tests *written in Groovy*

Using JUnitPerf with Groovy can be tricky. JUnitPerf is a decorator-based framework. It decorates test cases by individually wrapping them with a decorator. This is typically done within a `suite` method. Groovy's `GroovyTestSuite` and `AllTestSuite` test runners, however, ignore `suite` definitions and provide alternative mechanisms for determining which tests to run.

To allow JUnitPerf to work with Groovy involves following a few simple steps. First, you need a way to select a single JUnit test that you want to decorate. If you look at JUnit's `TestCase` class, you will notice that it provides a constructor which takes the name of a test method and allows a single test case to be selected. We can make use of this for JUnitPerf by declaring a constructor that takes a method name and have it call `super(methodName)`:

```
RegexFilterPerfGTest(test){
    super(test)
}
```

Then we create a `suite` method that defines a test case using this constructor:

```
static Test suite() {
    def testCase = new RegexFilterPerfGTest("testOr")
```

```
      ...
}
```

Now we can apply the appropriate decorators on the test case according to JUnit-Perf's documentation for load and stress testing scenarios:

```
def loadTest = new LoadTest(testCase, 20, new ConstantTimer(100))
...
```

It sounds complicated, but really it is the same steps you would follow to use JUnitPerf in Java.

As an example, listing 14.11 utilizes JUnitPerf to verify that invoking testOr 20 times (each thread staggered by 100 milliseconds) returns within 2100 milliseconds.

Listing 14.11 Using JUnitPerf decorators to perform load and time tests

```
//...imports removed

class RegexFilterPerfGTest extends TestCase {

  RegexFilterPerfGTest(test){
    super(test)             ◁─┐  Call super
  }
                          ┌── Traditional nontimed JUnit test
  void testOr() {     ◁──┘
    def filter = new RegexPackageFilter("java|org")       ◁──┐  Class under test,
    assertTrue("value should be true",                        │  code not shown
      filter.applyFilter("org.sf.String"))
  }

  static main(args) {
    TestRunner.run(RegexFilterPerfGTest.suite())
  }
                                                        ┌─  Define
  static Test suite() {                                 │   test case
    def testCase = new RegexFilterPerfGTest("testOr")  ◁──┘
    //20 users for load staggered at 100 ms
    def loadTest = new LoadTest(testCase, 20,       ◁──┐  Decorator to
      new ConstantTimer(100))                           │  simulate load
    //each thread must return within 2100 ms
    return new TimedTest(loadTest, 2100)   ◁──┐  Decorator to assert
  }                                             │  time contraint
}
```

When you run this program, you should see output indicating that the program is running your tests, followed by the time it took to complete the tests. Because there are 20 users, starting 100ms apart, we expect the test to run for at least 2 seconds. If the time is less than 2.1 seconds, then the test will be successful:

```
...................TimedTest (WAITING): LoadTest (NON-ATOMIC):
    ThreadedTest: testOr(RegexFilterPerfGTest): 2016 ms
Time: 2.016
OK (20 tests)
```

If the test takes too long to run (suppose we expect it to complete in 2.01 seconds), then the test will fail:

```
There was 1 failure:
1) LoadTest (NON-ATOMIC): ThreadedTest: testOr(RegexFilterPerfGTest)
    junit.framework.AssertionFailedError: Maximum elapsed time exceeded!
    Expected 2010ms, but was 2015ms.
```

The next time you need figure out the performance of some Groovy code or you want to test the performance and scalability of your Java application with Groovy, give JUnitPerf a try!

We have shown you a couple of technologies that originated in the Java world but that Groovy can now benefit from. There are many more. Why not have some fun now and explore how to use your favorite Java technology with Groovy? Alternatively, read on, and find out how to integrate your build automation technology with Groovy.

14.8 Build automation

We have looked at how to run tests individually or in suites from the command line and using IDEs. For a team environment, however, the automated build environment should also run all the tests.[20] Two of the more popular build automation technologies in the Java world are Ant and Maven. We'll briefly look at how to integrate Groovy with each of these technologies.

14.8.1 Build integration with Ant

Ant is a commonly used build environment for running unit, system, integration, and acceptance testing in an automated fashion. For the moment, we are mainly focusing on unit tests. If you want to see some additional example related to acceptance testing, see chapter 16 for coverage of how Grails automatically generates WebTest acceptance tests in Groovy for your Grails web-based CRUD applications.

---

[20] See *Pragmatic Project Automation: How to Build, Deploy, and Monitor Java Apps* by Mike Clark (The Pragmatic Programmers, 2004) for more details on why this is important.

As an example of unit testing, we are going to examine the build file we used for generating the Cobertura report in the previous section. Here are the lines that compiled the Java and Groovy production and test classes:

```
<javac srcdir="${dir.src}" destdir="${dir.build}" debug="true">
    <classpath refid="project.classpath"/>
</javac>
<groovyc srcdir="${dir.src}" destdir="${dir.build}"
        stacktrace="true">
    <classpath refid="project.classpath"/>
</groovyc>
```

Here is the relevant part, which ran the unit tests:

```
<junit printsummary="yes" haltonerror="no" haltonfailure="no"
        fork="yes">
    <formatter type="plain" usefile="false"/>
    <batchtest>
        <fileset dir="target/instrumented-classes"
                includes="**/*Test.class" />
    </batchtest>
    <classpath refid="cover-test.classpath"/>
</junit>
```

These examples show how easy it is to make Groovy work in your Ant build files. We would be remiss if we didn't show you some more power that Groovy can bring to your Ant build files. You can access the power of Groovy in your build files in one of two ways:

- You can use Groovy from normal Ant build files using the `<script>` or external `<groovy>` task, as you saw in section 13.1.7.

- You can start from Groovy and use the Ant builder syntax to have full programming capabilities, as shown in section 8.3.

Listing 14.12 shows an example that combines both techniques.

Listing 14.12 Using Groovy with Ant for testing

```
<groovy>                                         File scanner for
def scanner = ant.fileScanner {        ◁┘       all XML files
    fileset(dir: properties['src.dir']) {
        include(name: '**/*.xml')
    }
}
def nameCheck = scanner.every{                   Check that all filenames
    file -> file.name.contains('build')   ◁┘    contain 'build'
}
def totalSize = 0
```

```
def fileCount = 0
def maxSize   = 0                      Iterate through
for(file in scanner){   ⊲──           selected files
    fileCount++
    if (file.size() > maxSize) maxSize = file.size()
    totalSize += file.size()
}
if (nameCheck || totalSize / fileCount > 50 ||
        maxSize > 100 || fileCount > 10)
    properties.shouldCompress = true  ⊲──  Set property based on
</groovy>                                  results of iteration
```

In listing 14.12, we set up a property for subsequent use in an `if` or `unless` attribute. The property is called `shouldCompress` and is set based on the properties of selected XML files in the directory in which the script is run. The property will be set if every file in the selected fileset has the characters "build" in its name, if there are more than 10 files, if the average file size is greater than 50, or if the maximum file size is more than 100.

You can use fancy checks like this within your build file. Based on such a check, you might decide to run a totally different set of tests or include some optional tests. The sky is the limit.

14.8.2 *Build integration with Maven*

Maven is a software project-management framework that can help you manage the many activities associated with producing a project's deliverable artifacts. This may include acquiring your project's dependent software, compiling your software, testing it, packaging it, and generating test and metrics reports. Two main versions of Maven are in use today: the original Maven (versions up to 1.x) and Maven 2 (versions 2.0 and above).

Maven supports the concept of plug-ins to perform many of the project lifecycle activities that it manages for you. For example, there are plug-ins to compile Java files, test them, package them up as jar files, and so forth. Because Groovy tests are easily compiled to normal Java bytecode, it should come as no surprise that you can leverage many of the existing Maven Java tasks to assist you. In addition, there are purpose-built Maven 2 tasks for Groovy that you can utilize.

If you are already a Maven 2 user, consider using the generic Maven 2 plug-in: `groovy-maven-plugin`.[21] This allows you to run a Groovy script in your build but

---

[21] See http://mojo.codehaus.org/groovy-maven-plugin/examples.html for more details.

has no knowledge per se about test features of your project. Alternatively, consider using the Maven 2 plug-in for running Ant files: `maven-antrun-plugin`.[22] With this plug-in, you can make use of the Ant `groovyc` task you saw in the previous section. If you are a Maven 1 user, or you want to find out about a plug-in specifically aimed at testing, read on.

In the approach we are going to use to ensure that our Groovy tests automatically run as part of our Maven build, we first need to compile the Groovy files down to bytecode. By defining a new goal and a few `attainGoal` elements in your maven.xml file, you can create a process by which Groovy scripts are compiled and then run via a passed in command, such as test.

First, the `groovyc` command must be defined in your maven.xml file:

```
<goal name="groovyc-tests" prereqs="java:compile,test:compile">
  <path id="groovy.classpath">
    <pathelement path="${maven.build.dest}"/>
    <pathelement path="target/classes"/>
    <pathelement path="target/test-classes"/>
  <path refid="maven.dependency.classpath"/>
  </path>
  <taskdef name="groovyc"
           classname="org.codehaus.groovy.ant.Groovyc">
    <classpath refid="groovy.classpath"/>
  </taskdef>
  <groovyc destdir="${basedir}/target/test-classes"
           srcdir="${basedir}/test/src"
           listfiles="true">
    <classpath refid="groovy.classpath"/>
  </groovyc>
</goal>
```

In order for the `groovyc` task to work, we need Groovy to be in our Java classpath. In Maven terms, we've introduced Groovy as a dependency, so we'll also have to update Maven's project.xml file and add groovy-all-<version>.jar as an additional compile time dependency.

Next, we'll create a new goal named test that will force the `groovyc-tests` goal to run followed by the standard `test:test` goal:

```
<goal name="test">
  <attainGoal name="groovyc-tests"/>
  <attainGoal name="test:test"/>
</goal>
```

---

[22] See http://codeforfun.wordpress.com/2006/05/19/groovy-and-maven2-in-action/ for an example.

Last, because the default Maven configuration looks for Java files to find matching unit tests (such as `**/*Test.*`), we need to configure Maven to look at class files. This is easily done by setting the `maven.test.search.classdir` to true in your build.properties or project.properties file.

We are now ready to run our tests. This can be done from a DOS or UNIX command shell:

```
$> maven test
```

The output should look something like this:

```
build:start:

test:
test:prepare-filesystem:

java:prepare-filesystem:

groovyc-tests:
Overriding previous definition of reference to groovy.classpath
    [taskdef] Trying to override old definition of task groovyc

java:prepare-filesystem:

java:compile:
    [echo] Compiling to c:\dev\projects\gd/target/classes

java:jar-resources:
Copying 2 files to c:\dev\projects\gd\target\classes
Copying 4 files to c:\dev\projects\gd\target\classes

test:prepare-filesystem:

test:test-resources:

test:compile:

test:test:
    [junit] Running test.com.vanward.adana.hierarchy.
  GroovyHierarchyBuilderTest
    [junit] Tests run: 3, Failures: 0, Errors: 0, Time elapsed: 1.382 sec
BUILD SUCCESSFUL
Total time: 7 seconds
Finished at: Fri Aug 12 19:34:31 EDT 2005
```

Configuring Maven to run test cases in Groovy is fairly straightforward, and the beauty of Maven is its ability to easily encapsulate common operations into a plug-in. You can, for example, take the `groovyc-tests` part of your maven.xml file as is and make it available as a plug-in for other Maven users to use. The advantage of this plug-in over a standard plug-in that just runs Groovy scripts is that this one is intended for developers coding on the Java platform who wish to utilize Groovy in a noninvasive manner. The plug-in handles all associated Groovy dependencies, compiles each Groovy test into normal Java bytecode, and invokes JUnit to run the tests. If you wanted to integrate additional non-Groovy-aware plug-ins that worked on the resulting compiled Java classes (for example, to perform dependency analysis on the classes), your plug-in would have everything in the correct place.

As you can see, plugging Groovy into your normal Java build processes is a cinch, whether they are Ant or Maven based.

14.9 *Summary*

That wraps up our exploration of how Groovy adds immense value to your unit-testing activities.

We believe that unit testing is not only a worthwhile activity but also sometimes even more demanding and full of variations and engineering challenges than writing production code. Our experiences with Groovy are that it assists with meeting those demands and challenges. We hope you felt this too when we examined the benefits that Groovy brings to unit testing: the automatic availability of JUnit, the enhanced test case class with its additional assert methods, and the in-built support for mocks, stubs, and other dynamic classes.

Groovy's integrated unit-test support lets you test Groovy and Java code alike. Our more detailed examination of how to unit-test Groovy code with Groovy tests, how to test Java code with Groovy tests, and how to organize your tests into meaningful suites gave you the grounding to begin testing your own systems using Groovy.

Our investigation of advanced testing techniques led us to explore how to use stubs, mocks, and other dynamic classes such as `Expando` and `Groovy-LogTestCase`. With the help of these advanced features, it is possible to test complex scenarios with minimal to moderate effort. Previously tricky scenarios can sometimes be tackled with much less work. This can often be the difference between being able to justify unit testing and it being too expensive.

For sustainable software development with a high level of test coverage, unit testing must be both pleasant and efficient. What makes it pleasant is seamless integration into the developer's IDE of choice to provide immediate feedback in develop, test, refactor cycles. What makes it efficient is the frequent unsupervised self-running execution of the test suite in an automated build process. In the Groovy world, both of these have excellent support.

Groovy gains much from its Java heritage. This was clearly shown when we looked at additional Java-level tool integration: in particular, one technology that enabled us to do code coverage and another that enabled us to do stress and performance testing. We examined only two tools, but there are hundreds of tools available for Java and many yet-unexplored possibilities for leveraging them in Groovy.

To advocates of unit testing, Groovy can only be seen as a powerful and positive addition to the Java and Groovy developer's toolkit. With Groovy, you can write your tests more quickly and easily. Just think, with all the time you'll save by writing tests in Groovy, you can now go back to your customer and ask for more feature requests!

15

Groovy on Windows

You might wonder why this book contains a specific chapter about Groovy on Microsoft's famous and ubiquitous operating system. After all, Groovy is a language that lives on the Java platform and its Java Virtual Machine, so it is a language that also obeys the mantra "write once, run everywhere"—on all operating systems with a JVM. So why is it worth talking about Windows specifically? Because of *Scriptom*.

Scriptom's name stems from a mix of the word *scripting* and the acronym COM, Microsoft's *component object model*. Groovy's meta-programming capabilities allow manipulating COM and ActiveX objects with Scriptom to be as simple as it is in Visual Basic or JavaScript. Combining Scriptom and Groovy means that you can leverage the wealth of the Java world and its multitude of outstanding libraries at the same time as controlling applications such as Microsoft Word or Excel from Groovy. This gives you the best of both worlds, bridging the gap between them.

Scriptom is not part of the Groovy distribution; it is an external module that can be easily installed on a standard Groovy installation. In this chapter, you'll see where to download and install Scriptom and discover what scripting native applications looks like. We'll then start hacking away by controlling some applications such as Internet Explorer, Word, and Excel. We'll then show more advanced integration with the native applications by providing our own event support to react to user actions or application state changes. Finally, we will show a real-world use of Scriptom and various other automation tasks.

15.1 Downloading and installing Scriptom

Before getting started with the Windows native integration that Groovy offers, you first need to download and install Scriptom. It is an add-on that you can choose to use if you are running Windows on your machine. Downloading and installing Scriptom is as easy as unzipping an archive. First, point your web browser to the Scriptom documentation page on the Groovy web site: http://groovy.codehaus.org/COM+Scripting. Click the link for the zip bundle, download it, and unpack it in your Groovy installation directory. That's all there is to do!

The archive contains only three files:

- A jar called scriptom-*.jar (the star denoting the latest version number), which is the meat of the animal
- A DLL named jacob.dll
- A jar called jacob.jar

The last two do the heavy lifting of providing an API using the Java Native Interface (JNI) to access the native functions of COM and ActiveX objects in a groovy way.

To test the installation, let's write our first Groovy script to use ActiveX:

```
import org.codehaus.groovy.scriptom.ActiveXProxy

def wshell = new ActiveXProxy('WScript.Shell')
wshell.popup('Scriptom is Groovy!')
```

Run it like any other Groovy script—there's no need for any classpath changes or anything else. If everything has worked, you should see a dialog box like the one shown in figure 15.1.

It's hard to imagine how integration with COM/ActiveX could be much easier than that. Now that we've shown you a little of what can be done, let's look at how Groovy, Scriptom, and Jacob fit together to let you script native applications.

Figure 15.1   A pop-up dialog showing a customized message

15.2 Inside Scriptom

Magic tricks like rabbits coming out of hats are usually best left unexplained. Similarly, you *can* use Scriptom without knowing how it works. Unlike stage magic, however, understanding how Scriptom makes integration so easy takes nothing away from the effect—indeed, seeing the elegance of the solution enhances the appreciation of it. Toward this end, you'll learn a bit of the mechanics behind Scriptom while exploring how to use it. First we will look at the library Scriptom relies on for the native code interaction. After that, you'll be ready to create component instances and learn how to call their methods, interrogate their properties, and subscribe to their events.

15.2.1 Introducing Jacob

The Scriptom module uses *Jacob* (Java COM Bridge), a project hosted on Source-Forge,[1] which is a Java/COM bridge that allows you to call COM automation components from Java. It uses JNI to make native calls into the COM and Win32 libraries. Figure 15.2 shows the interaction between those different elements.

---

[1] http://jacob-project.sourceforge.net.

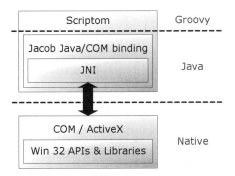

Figure 15.2
Layered view of the interactions between
Scriptom, Jacob, JNI, and the native platform

Jacob offers a generic API that can be used to access any native object. For instance, you can manipulate Internet Explorer with this sample Java code—imports, exception handling, classes, and methods are omitted for brevity:

```
// Java
ActiveXComponent ie =
    new ActiveXComponent("InternetExplorer.Application");
Dispatch.put(ie, "Visible", new Variant(true));
Dispatch.put(ie, "AddressBar", new Variant(true));
Dispatch.call(ie, "Navigate",
    new Variant("http://groovy.codehaus.org"));
ie.invoke("Quit", new Variant[] {});
```

Scriptom builds on top of Jacob API to provide a more intuitive syntax similar to what VB programmers are used to. This example becomes

```
import org.codehaus.groovy.scriptom.ActiveXProxy

def explorer = new ActiveXProxy('InternetExplorer.Application')
explorer.Visible = true
explorer.AddressBar = true
explorer.Navigate 'http://groovy.codehaus.org'
explorer.Quit()
```

We create a proxy that wraps the native application, set one property to make the application visible, set another one to show the address bar, and call a method to make the browser visit the Groovy web site.

Jacob does a good job of being concise, but the code to deal with native objects is harder to read in the Java form. Scriptom leverages the underlying Jacob API to make it look like standard object handling. As we hinted before, Scriptom performs its magic using Groovy's Meta-Object Protocol, and in particular the facilities of the `GroovyObject` class. Scriptom consists of only three classes:

- `ActiveXProxy` wraps the COM or ActiveX component, which is the class you use to instantiate native applications.

- `VariantProxy` wraps all properties and return values of the wrapped application.

- `EventSupport` deals with event support; but you should not have to deal with this class, as you'll see when we review how to subscribe to events the Windows applications generate.

As shown in figure 15.3, `ActiveXProxy`, `VariantProxy`, and `EventSupport` extend `GroovyObjectSupport` (which in turn implements `GroovyObject`). They intercept method calls by overriding `invokeMethod` and intercept properties with `getProperty` and `setProperty`. They then delegate to Jacob for the work.

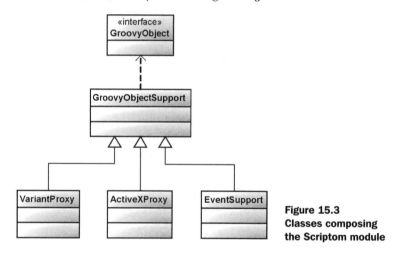

**Figure 15.3
Classes composing
the Scriptom module**

What do you need to do to manipulate a Windows application or component? First, you have to instantiate an `ActiveXProxy` that will wrap the Jacob component, and then you can access its properties and call its methods. Let's see how you can do that.

15.2.2 *Instantiating an ActiveX component*

To make direct use of native code on the Java platform, you have to use JNI. Although this is powerful, it is difficult to use, and the resulting code tends to be hard to read. Thanks to the Groovy meta-programming capabilities, Scriptom provides a simplified syntax for interacting with native COM/ActiveX components as easily as possible. The result can often appear as simple as Visual Basic component interactions—but with the full power of Groovy behind it, of course.

The first step to instantiate a native component is to import `ActiveXProxy` with the following directive:

```
import org.codehaus.groovy.scriptom.ActiveXProxy
```

Once the class is imported, you can instantiate it through its only constructor, which takes a string parameter. You can pass the constructor either the application name or *Program ID* of the application, or its *class identifier (CLSID)*, which is a globally unique identifier that identifies a COM class object.

For instance, you can use Excel by using its application name

```
def xls = new ActiveXProxy('Excel.Application')
```

or by referring to its related class identifier:

```
def clsid = 'clsid:{00024500-0000-0000-C000-000000000046}'
def xls = new ActiveXProxy(clsid)
```

Jacob utilizes the `clsid:` prefix to differentiate application names from class identifiers.

Usually, for the sake of clarity and readability, it is preferable to use the application name. However, it can sometimes be handy to reference a component by its class identifier, particularly if you need to use a specific version of an application and multiple versions might be installed on a single machine. If you want to discover the class identifier associated with a given application, you should search in the Windows registry under the following key:

```
HKEY_LOCAL_MACHINE\Software\Classes\
```

Figure 15.4 shows what you would see in the Registry Editor if you searched for Excel. In this case, you can see that Excel's class identifier can be found under

```
HKEY_LOCAL_MACHINE\Software\Classes\Excel.Application\CLSID
```

and its value is `{00024500-0000-0000-C000-000000000046}`.

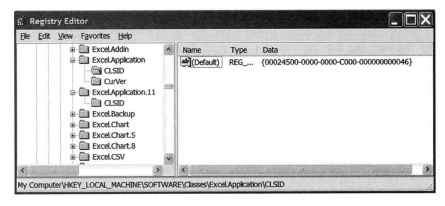

Figure 15.4 View of the Windows Registry, showing where Excel-related keys can be found

Just to get you started automating a few Microsoft applications with Scriptom, table 15.1 provides a list of some common applications and their Program IDs.

Table 15.1   A few Windows applications and their Program IDs

Application	Program ID
Access	`Access.Application`
Excel	`Excel.Application`
Explorer	`Shell.Application`
FrontPage	`FrontPage.Application`
Internet Explorer	`InternetExplorer.Application`
Notepad	`Notepad.Application`
Outlook	`Outlook.Application`
PowerPoint	`Powerpoint.Application`
Windows Media Player	`WMPlayer.OCX`
Word	`Word.Application`

For Microsoft Office applications, there are different program names for the various Office releases. If you want to address a given version (in case several are installed at the same time, or because your script targets a specific version), you can append the version number to the Program ID with the suffixes given in table 15.2.

Table 15.2   Association of Office versions and Program ID suffixes

Office version	Program ID suffix
Office 95	`${PRGID}.7`
Office 97	`${PRGID}.8`
Office 2000	`${PRGID}.9`
Office XP	`${PRGID}.10`
Office XP 2003	`${PRGID}.11`

With this table in mind, you'll be able to use a specific version of an Office application. If you refer to `Word.Application.9`, you use Word 2000; but if you want to stay more general and use the latest version installed on the computer, you can use `Word.Application` without any version suffix.

In addition to applications, several utilities available on the Windows platform let you interact with the operating system in a simple fashion. This is handy when your automation tasks include activities such as reading and writing keys in the registry, popping up file dialogs, or sending keystrokes to running applications. Table 15.3 has a few of these utilities and their uses.

Table 15.3 Utility components and their purpose

Utility	Purpose
ScriptControl	Evaluate Visual Basic or JavaScript expressions
Scripting.FileSystemObject	Deal with the filesystem
Shell.Application	File explorer; manipulate running application windows
WScript.Network	Access network information
WScript.Shell	Interact with the registry and the Windows shell; show pop-ups

We will be using those utilities to explain how you can invoke methods as well as set and retrieve properties on those native objects.

15.2.3 Invoking methods

You've already seen an example of method invocation when we manipulated Internet Explorer. Invoking a method on a COM component is no different than invoking a method on a standard Java or Groovy object. Using the file explorer, which has a Program ID of `Shell.Application`, you can call a method to minimize all the windows opened on your desktop:

```
import org.codehaus.groovy.scriptom.ActiveXProxy

def sh = new ActiveXProxy('Shell.Application')
sh.MinimizeAll()
```

Contrary to the Java naming conventions, in the Microsoft universe, method names and properties are often capitalized. This looks a bit strange when you see it in the midst of a Groovy script, but Scriptom keeps the same convention: The case is unchanged. In our example, on the Shell object, we call the `MinimizeAll` method; true to its name, all windows will be minimized.

Obviously, we can also use methods with parameters. Let's go back to our first example using `WScript.Shell`, the Windows Scripting Host shell, to show a pop-up message window. The code is reproduced here for reference. (It's so short, there's no reason not to!)

```
import org.codehaus.groovy.scriptom.ActiveXProxy

def wshell = new ActiveXProxy('WScript.Shell')
wshell.Popup('Scriptom is Groovy!')
```

The `Popup` method takes a string parameter representing the message that will be shown inside the pop-up dialog. The Jacob API wraps all values or parameters inside `Variant` instances. Scriptom wraps these values inside instances of `VariantProxy`. Through that wrapper implementing `GroovyObject`, other methods can be called without resorting to using the raw Jacob API. Let's see an example of chained methods. We're going to show a file-chooser dialog like the one shown in figure 15.5.

Here is the script that displays the file chooser:

Figure 15.5 A file chooser is shown thanks to a `WScript.Shell` component.

```
import
  org.codehaus.groovy.scriptom.ActiveXProxy

def sh     = new ActiveXProxy('Shell.Application')
def PARENT = 0
def OPTS   = 0
def folder = sh.BrowseForFolder(PARENT, 'Choose a folder', OPTS)
println "Chosen folder: ${folder.Items().Item().Path.value}"
```

With the shell, you can use `BrowseForFolder`, a utility method, which shows a file-chooser widget to allow you to select a file or directory. The `PARENT` and `OPTS` values are the parent window (where 0 means there is no parent) and the option flags to use, respectively. On the last line, you can see that the method returns an object representing a file selection. On this object, you can call the `Items` method to retrieve the selected files and `Item` to select the chosen one. This item has a property called `Path` to retrieve the path of the chosen file. Finally, `value` is a Groovy property that lets you unmarshal the value of the `Path`, as you shall see further. This is a bit of black magic; but you can find the documentation of this

ActiveX component by looking at its API on the Microsoft Developer Network library, which is always of great help when you need to script those components.

Native components have more than methods, though—they also expose properties that can be accessed and modified. The next section explains how to access these properties and also how to deal with the return values of the methods you invoke.

15.2.4 *Accessing properties and return values*

You already saw a few examples showing how to access properties and method return values. Again, doing so is not very different from standard property access in the Java or Groovy world. The following example will print the name of the computer:

```
import org.codehaus.groovy.scriptom.ActiveXProxy

net = new ActiveXProxy('WScript.Network')
println "Name of this computer: ${net.ComputerName.value}"
assert net.ComputerName.value == net.ComputerName.getValue()
```

This time, we're using the WScript.Network component, which is used for network-related needs. In our example, we retrieve the name of the computer, which is represented through the ComputerName property. However, you will have noticed that we append another property called value. Because all methods that return values and properties are wrapped in VariantProxy objects, we need to use a trick to retrieve the real value. VariantProxy has a special value property that will give you a value usable from Groovy. The name of the computer is contained in a VariantProxy, and value returns the string representing that name. In case a property named value already exists in the wrapped object, you can also retrieve the real value with the getValue method as shown by the last line of the script. This has the same effect as the value property.

Now that you know how to call methods and access properties of the objects of the native Windows component, it is time to also be able to respond to events happening in the application by subscribing to them.

15.2.5 *Event support*

Being able to script running applications is one side of the story, but there's also the other side: the person in front of the computer being able to use the application and click buttons, type in text, or execute shortcuts. It would be beneficial if our script control could recognize and react on these user-triggered events. Additionally, the application could receive other notifications, such as reaching the end of a media stream.

This is where event support comes into play, and your Groovy scripts need to know what is happening and how to react to changes or actions. Most applications that expose a part of their internals through ActiveX or COM objects also expose a set of events that a caller can subscribe to.

`ActiveXProxy` has a special property called `events`, which can be retrieved either with the `myProxy.events` property access notation, or through a method call with `proxy.getEvents()`. It's through this special object that you can interact with a component's events.

Subscribing to events and registering your own event listener isn't rocket science, even though the effect can be impressive when you consider the layering of Groovy on top of native code. It can be achieved with two easy steps:

1   Define a closure taking an array of `VariantProxy` that will be called whenever the associated event is triggered, and specify it using the `events` property. The property within `events` to which you assign the closure should be named after the event you're subscribing to. For a given event, you can define a single handling routine by assigning a new closure to the property `events.myEventName`.

2   Once all event handling closures are defined, call the `events.listen` method to make the event subscriptions active.

Again, a code sample will make things crystal clear, as shown in listing 15.1, where we are evaluating VBScript expressions in Groovy! Evaluating VBScript expressions can produce errors. When this happens, all error listeners are notified. We register a Groovy error listener to demonstrate the mechanics.

Who would have thought it would be so simple to invoke Visual Basic code from Groovy? Windows offers a COM component called `ScriptControl`, which allows you to evaluate JavaScript or Visual Basic expressions. We subscribe to an event called `Error`, and when this event is triggered, the associated closure is executed in a separate thread to the main thread of control.

Listing 15.1   Evaluating VBScript expressions from Groovy

```
import org.codehaus.groovy.scriptom.ActiveXProxy

def sc = new ActiveXProxy("ScriptControl")          ❶ Create a VBScript
sc.Language = "VBScript"                                ScriptControl

sc.events.Error = { println "Evaluation error!" }    ❷ Register error
sc.events.listen()                                      listener
```

```
try {
    assert 3 == sc.Eval("1 + 2").value
    println sc.Eval("+").value          Force
                                        error
} catch (Exception e) {
    println "An exception was thrown due to a failing evaluation"
}
```

Let's take a close look at this code. At ❶, a ScriptControl is instantiated with the VBScript language. We subscribe to the Error event and assign a closure event handler at ❷. In the try/catch block ❸, we evaluate 1+2, which will print 3. We then try to evaluate +, which will throw an exception and call the event handler. Finally, we catch the exception thrown in case an expression wasn't parsed successfully—which is the case in the last evaluation.

Now, let's see a more complex example. Let's play the DJ, and illustrate the use of events subscription by scripting Windows Media Player. In listing 15.2, we play all the songs in the directory from which the script is launched.

Listing 15.2 Playing all the media files in the current directory

```
import org.codehaus.groovy.scriptom.ActiveXProxy

def player = new ActiveXProxy('WMPlayer.OCX')
player.events.PlayStateChange = { variants ->          Register event
    if (variants[0].value == 1)                        handler
        synchronized(player) { player.notify() }
}
player.events.listen()          Subscribe
                                to events
def folder = new File('.')
println "Playing files from: ${folder}"
folder.eachFileMatch(~/.*\.(wav|au|wma|mp3)/) { song ->    Play each
    println "Listening to: $song"                          media file
    player.URL = song.absolutePath                         in turn
    player.controls.play()
    synchronized(player) { player.wait() }          Wait until the
}                                                   song finishes
player.close()
```

The Windows Media Player is instantiated at ❶ from its Program ID name.

We register an event handler at ❷ for the PlayStateChange event by defining a new property on the events special property of the ActiveX proxy, whose value is a closure corresponding to the code that will be executed once the event is triggered.

The closures used as event handlers have only one argument, which is an array of `VariantProxy` instances that wrap the values passed to the native event handler routine. Here, for this `PlayStateChange` event, the array of `VariantProxy` contains only an `int` corresponding to the state of the player: In our case, we're interested in the state `1`, which means a media playback just finished.

When the end of the playback happens, we notify the player at ❸ in the main loop that it can process the next media file. We take advantage of the fact that Groovy fully complies with Java's thread and object model. Therefore, we can use the same wait/notify handling for coordination. For the use of `synchronized` blocks, the same rules apply as in Java.

The special method `listen` on events is the method at ❹ that registers all the closure event handlers and starts the subscription to events we're interested in.

On the local directory, we call `eachFileMatch` at ❺ to iterate over all files matching the regular expression pattern: files ending with some common media extensions.

We call the `play` method ❻ on the `controls` object to play the song.

Once the playback is started, we're waiting at ❼ for the event handler to give us back control and continue looping over the media files to play, when the currently playing song is finished.

We finally close the player when the song has finished playing.

It is high time we take the bull by the horns and start developing an even bigger example, integrating different native applications and leveraging some Groovy or Java APIs. In the next section, we're going to introduce a real-world scenario right from the battlefield and show how you can provide an elegant and useful solution to the problem at hand.

15.3 *Real-world scenario: automating localization*

For an example of how Scriptom can help in the real world, we'll consider an example from a leading European car manufacturer. They had created a component of the technical documentation production infrastructure that could generate various documents for all the countries worldwide where cars were sold. This component was a huge thesaurus, storing hundreds of thousands of sentences translated into more than 40 languages. Technical documents were represented as an XML structure in Microsoft Word ML format, holding the page layout, the embedded images, and the set of sentence identifiers composing the document. When a document was to be printed, the list of sentence codes was read, and the thesaurus was queried through a web service to return all the translated sentences

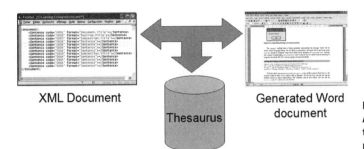

XML Document   Thesaurus   Generated Word document

**Figure 15.6
A general overview of
the documentation
production system**

to build the final readable and localized document. The overall scenario is briefly presented in figure 15.6.

We'll get inspiration from this real-world scenario, and we'll create a document in a custom XML format, holding both the layout of the document and its style, along with the list of sentence codes it contains. The document will be stored on the filesystem in a file named document.xml. The thesaurus will be a simple Excel spreadsheet (thesaurus.xls), with each line representing a sentence and the columns being all the translations available. From those two sources, the XML document and the Excel thesaurus spreadsheet, we'll create a Word file representing the final document through our `producer.groovy` script. We'll look at each of the steps in isolation and then put them together to form the complete application.

Let's start at the beginning, with the document format.

15.3.1 *Designing our document format*

Our document format is simple. It's an XML file that will use only two tags:

- A root element named `Document` holding all the sentences of the document
- Child elements named `Sentence` representing each sentence, with two attributes: a sentence code, and a format string

Let's see an example of that format:

```
<Document>
    <Sentence code="S0001" format="Document.Title"/>
    <Sentence code="S0002" format="Section.Title"/>
    <Sentence code="S0003" format="Subsection.Title"/>
    <Sentence code="S0004" format="Sentence"/>
    <Sentence code="S0005" format="Sentence"/>
    <Sentence code="S0006" format="Subsection.Title"/>
    <Sentence code="S0007" format="Sentence"/>
</Document>
```

In this example, all our codes will be of the form Sxxxx, and the format is just a style to use when rendering each sentence in the final document.

The Groovy groovy.util.XmlParser class makes parsing the document trivial. We need to iterate over all the Sentence elements in the documents, so we use the each method, passing a closure that will initially print out the data so we can check that it looks correct:

```
def xmlDoc = new XmlParser().parse(new File("document.xml"))
xmlDoc.each{ node ->
    println "Code: ${node['@code']}, Format: ${node['@format']}"
}
```

In the final script, we'll replace the logic inside the each{} iteration to output text in the Word document. But now, let's see how we will design our thesaurus.

15.3.2 Designing the thesaurus spreadsheet

The thesaurus is a table of sentence codes and associated translations in all the supported locales. The rows contain a sentence each, whereas the columns give all the translations for a given locale. Our spreadsheet looks like the Excel screenshot shown in figure 15.7.

To look up a particular translated sentence, knowing its code and its locale, we're going to open the thesaurus.xls spreadsheet with Scriptom, read the first row containing the ISO codes of the locales and the first column containing the sentence codes, and retrieve the value of the cell containing the translation.

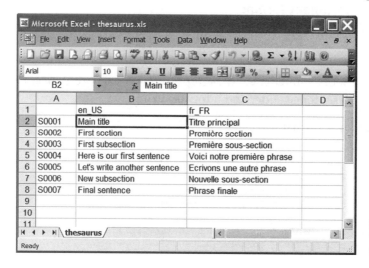

**Figure 15.7
Thesaurus stored as
an Excel spreadsheet**

The first obvious step explained in listing 15.3 is to launch Excel through Scriptom and its `ActiveXProxy` and see how we select the active sheet, and also see how we close and quit the application appropriately.

Listing 15.3 Opening and closing Excel, and selecting the active sheet

```
import org.codehaus.groovy.scriptom.ActiveXProxy

def thesaurus = new File('thesaurus.xls').canonicalPath
def xls = new ActiveXProxy('Excel.Application')
def workbooks = xls.Workbooks
def workbook = workbooks.Open(thesaurus)
def activeSheet = workbook.ActiveSheet

def localeColumns = [:]
for (column in 'B'..'Z') {
    def loc = activeSheet.Range("${column}1").Value.value
    if (!loc) break
    localeColumns[loc] = column
}

def sentenceCodeRows = [:]
for (row in 2..1000) {
    def code = activeSheet.Range("A${row}").Value.value
    if (!code) break
    sentenceCodeRows[code] = row
}

// a few lines further…

workbook.Close()
xls.Quit()
xls.release()
```

❶ Open thesaurus sheet

❷ Find the locales

❸ Find all sentence codes

❹ Clean up

In ❶, after importing the `ActiveXProxy` class and creating the proxy instance, we retrieve the `Workbooks` object to open our thesaurus and select the active sheet containing our translations.

Then, in ❷ and ❸, we create maps containing associations of locales and the columns where they are found, and sentence codes and their rows, respectively. We cache these values to avoid having to traverse the sheet each time we're looking up a locale or code. We use ranges to iterate through the rows and columns, and GStrings to pinpoint the cells we're interested in. We're only interested in a single cell at a time, but as far as Excel is concerned, they're ranges that happen to have only one row and column. These Excel ranges have a `Value` property from which we'll retrieve the equivalent value in Groovy thanks to the value property—getValue could have been used too.

Eventually, in ❹, when we don't need the thesaurus anymore, we close it and close Excel.

> **WARNING** Due to a bug in Jacob, the underlying Java/COM bridge, we noticed certain Excel versions don't always exit gracefully and keep a process running in the background. If this is the case, you should make sure that you call the release method on the ActiveX proxy instance: It tries its best to free all the allocated resources and hence closes the launched process.

Armed with these locale and code associations, we can easily retrieve a translation for a given sentence. Suppose we have a code of S0045 and that we want the French translation with the fr_FR locale. We can write

```
def cell = "${localeColumns['fr_FR']}${sentenceCodeRows['S0045']}"
def translation = activeSheet.Range(cell).Value.value
```

Now, on to drive Word for creating the final document!

15.3.3 *Creating a Word document*

After our Excel manipulations, we have to master Word to make it produce our localized documentation. In our path to COM nirvana, we are going to follow four steps.

First, we create a Word instance, create a new document, and select it as the active file for editing:

```
def word = new ActiveXProxy('Word.Application')
word.Documents.Add()
def doc = word.ActiveDocument
```

Making good-looking documents is not just a matter of style; it's also a matter of formatting the output with the required font, thickness, size, or color. That's why we are creating a map that associates the styles defined in the XML document with formatters defined as closures—another handy usage of closures:

```
def CENTERED = 1
def styleFormatter = [
    'Document.Title':   { it.Font.Size = 24
                          it.Font.Name = 'Arial'
                          it.ParagraphFormat.Alignment = CENTERED },
    'Section.Title':    { it.Font.Size = 18
                          it.Font.Name = 'Arial' },
    'Subsection.Title': { it.Font.Size = 14
```

```
                                 it.Font.Name = 'Arial' },
        'Sentence':              { it.Font.Size = 12 }
   ]
```

For instance, the `styleFormatter` map associates the style `Document.Title` with a closure that will take a Word text range selection, apply a 24-point Arial font, and center the text.

> **NOTE** The magic constant `1` references a centered alignment, whose value in the VBA Object Inspector is *Word.wdAlignParagraphCenter*. Unfortunately, those constants aren't directly available in Scriptom by name. Also note that rather than using our styling closures, you can use the `Style` property to use a style defined in your document.

Let's reuse our XML parsing routine in listing 15.4 to write each localized sentences in our Word document.

Listing 15.4 Write and format localized sentences in the Word document

```
def cursorPos = 0
def xmlDoc = new XmlParser().parse(new File(docName))
xmlDoc.each{ node ->                                        ◁⎤  Iterate over all
    def column = localeColumns[locale]                          the sentences
    def row = sentenceCodeRows[node['@code']]
    def cell = "${column}${row}"                                     ⎤  Retrieve
    def translation = activeSheet.Range(cell).Value.value      ◁⎦  translation

    def range = doc.Range(cursorPos, cursorPos)           ⎤  Insert styled
    range.Text = translation + "\n"                           sentence at
    styleFormatter[node['@format']].call(range)              cursor position
    range.Select()
    cursorPos += translation.size() + 1
}
```

Of particular interest is the somewhat awkward part for inserting each sentence: An empty text range is created, the sentence text is defined as the content of the range, and we then apply our formatter closure on this range. The closure is obtained by retrieving the `format` attribute on the sentence node of the XML document and using it as a key in our `styleFormatter` map. Finally, the `Select` method is called. Although this is not usually required, it is always harmless, and some versions of Word don't apply the style until it is called.

Our last step is to save the produced document and close Word:

```
doc.SaveAs(new File(".\\document-${locale}.doc").canonicalPath)
word.Quit()
```

You have now seen each of the individual pieces of the application, so we just need to put everything together to finish our translation system.

15.3.4 Producing the final document

It's now the magic moment when everything falls into place and we produce our final localized documents with the full script shown in listing 15.5.

Listing 15.5   Script producing Word documents from XML and a spreadsheet

```
import org.codehaus.groovy.scriptom.ActiveXProxy

def docName = args[0]
def locale = args[1]

def thesaurus = new File('thesaurus.xls').canonicalPath
def xls = new ActiveXProxy('Excel.Application')
def workbooks = xls.Workbooks
def workbook = workbooks.Open(thesaurus)
def activeSheet = workbook.ActiveSheet

def word = new ActiveXProxy('Word.Application')
word.Documents.Add()
def doc = word.ActiveDocument

def CENTERED = 1
def styleFormatter = [
    'Document.Title':    { it.Font.Size = 24
                           it.Font.Name = 'Arial'
                           it.ParagraphFormat.Alignment = CENTERED },
    'Section.Title':     { it.Font.Size = 18
                           it.Font.Name = 'Arial' },
    'Subsection.Title':  { it.Font.Size = 14
                           it.Font.Name = 'Arial' },
    'Sentence':          { it.Font.Size = 12 }
]

def localeColumns = [:]
for (column in 'B'..'Z') {
    def loc = activeSheet.Range("${column}1").Value.value
    if (!loc) break
    localeColumns[loc] = column
}

def sentenceCodeRows = [:]
for (row in 2..1000) {
    def code = activeSheet.Range("A${row}").Value.value
    if (!code) break
    sentenceCodeRows[code] = row
}
```

- Open the Excel spreadsheet
- Open Word and create a new document
- Create the style formatter
- Retrieve all the locales
- Retrieve all the sentence codes

```
def cursorPos = 0
def xmlDoc = new XmlParser().parse(new File(docName))
xmlDoc.each{ node ->
    def column = localeColumns[locale]
    def row = sentenceCodeRows[node['@code']]
    def cell = "${column}${row}"
    def translation = activeSheet.Range(cell).Value.value

    def range = doc.Range(cursorPos, cursorPos)
    range.Text = translation + "\n"
    styleFormatter[node['@format']].call(range)
    range.Select()
    cursorPos += translation.size() + 1
}

doc.SaveAs(new File(".\\document-${locale}.doc").canonicalPath)
word.Quit()

workbook.Close()
xls.Quit()
xls.release()
```

Annotations:
- Parse the XML document source file
- Retrieve the translation for the given sentence code and locale
- Write the styled sentences in the Word document
- Save and close the Word document
- Close the spreadsheet and quit Excel

Once you have saved the full script in a file named Producer.groovy, you can run it from the command line with the following command, using two parameters that indicate the XML document to transform and the locale used for the translation:

```
groovy Producer document.xml fr_FR
```

The command will produce a document named document-fr_FR.doc in your local directory. This document is shown in figure 15.8.

You've now successfully created a full script automating two Office applications and benefiting from the Groovy XML APIs. With a concise and clear syntax, you can build useful script glue, which takes only 60 lines of code to parse XML files, look up translations in an Excel spreadsheet, and generate fully styled Word documents.

In the following section, you'll see how you can further integrate Groovy on your desktop to automate some administrative tasks.

15.4 *Further application automation*

You've happily launched and automated native Windows applications, focusing on the generation and manipulation of documents. Although this is helpful and bridges two opposite worlds that usually never meet to create a value-added program, it is only a small part of the Scriptom story.

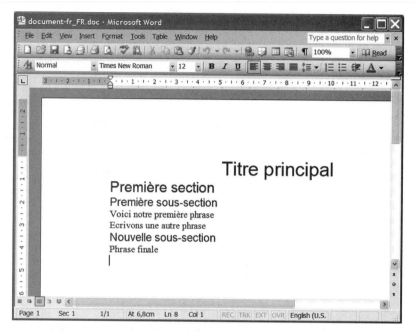

Figure 15.8 The generated Word document

The larger part is using Scriptom to relieve you of repetitive work that involves operating-system-related activities. This can be as simple as opening your corporate timesheet application and submitting today's numbers or letting your scripts conduct a series of actions in an endless loop to make up a self-running presentation. You can even use it for sophisticated tasks such as writing your own application installer or password manager.

From the endless list of possibilities, we show how to interact with the host environment to tweak the Windows registry and how to roll out your own macro system.

15.4.1 *Accessing the Windows registry*

Most Windows applications use the Windows registry to store information such as user preferences, software configurations, or application defaults. The Java Preferences API stores its data in the registry as well. But manipulating the registry directly has never been possible, apart from writing the JNI calls yourself—some third-party libraries provide that feature, though. But again, Scriptom comes to the rescue by allowing you to use the WScript.Shell object to manipulate the registry: You can read, write, or delete keys and values.

To give you a simple example, we'll show you a nice trick we've come across: On some Windows machines, filename and path autocompletion in a DOS console isn't always activated by default, particularly on older machines. However, completion can be enabled thanks to some magic values in the registry. Two keys are responsible for that behavior:

```
HKLM\SOFTWARE\Microsoft\Command Processor\CompletionChar
HKLM\SOFTWARE\Microsoft\Command Processor\PathCompletionChar
```

NOTE   In our code, we're using the abbreviation HKLM, which is short for HKEY_LOCAL_MACHINE. Similarly, HKEY_CURRENT_USER can be abbreviated as HKCU.

By setting the associated values of these keys to the character number, you can define or redefine the key you can use for autocompletion of filenames and paths. The following scripts[2] can do that for you, by setting the Tab key to become the completion key:

```
import org.codehaus.groovy.scriptom.ActiveXProxy

def TAB = 9
def ROOT = /HKLM\SOFTWARE\Microsoft\Command Processor/

def wshell = new ActiveXProxy('WScript.Shell')
wshell.RegWrite(/$ROOT\CompletionChar/,     TAB, 'REG_DWORD')
wshell.RegWrite(/$ROOT\PathCompletionChar/, TAB, 'REG_DWORD')
```

You can write registry keys, but obviously, you can also read them. For example, if Internet Explorer is your default web browser, you can read the browser user agent string like so:

```
import org.codehaus.groovy.scriptom.ActiveXProxy

def wshell = new ActiveXProxy('WScript.Shell')
def key = /HKCU\Software\Microsoft\Windows\CurrentVersion/ +
          /\Internet Settings\User Agent/
println wshell.RegRead(key).value
```

Accessing the registry can be handy, particularly if you wish to customize the default settings of applications that store their preferences or configuration there. Thanks to Scriptom, you can easily create specific software-installation scripts. This is often needed in big companies where the IT department is trying

---

[2] Just like the standard *.reg files do to set registry keys and values.

to commoditize its desktop platforms and computer assets to provide a smoother upgrading mechanism, lowering maintenance costs. Of course, Windows administrators can use VBScript or JavaScript for most of these tasks, but when integrating with Java applications, libraries, or components, Scriptom can help bridge the gap between the native world and the JVM camp.

Another area where Scriptom shines is in automating repetitive tasks. Some applications provide custom macro systems to let users write their own sequences of atomic actions to realize a specific complex job. Let's see how Scriptom can fake user actions by sending keystrokes to running applications.

15.4.2 Rolling out your own automation system

The ubiquitous and almighty `WScript.Shell` object appears yet again and will enable us to roll out our own automation system. We may even consider it to be a macro system, as long as the application being automated supports launching external scripts and assigning shortcuts for these custom commands—some text editors support that feature, for instance.

So far, the interaction with native applications we've dealt with has been done through the COM or ActiveX components exposed by those applications. This time, we are going to use the `WScript.Shell` object to control running applications by sending them keystrokes. To illustrate, you can use Notepad or any other application within which you can enter some text. We'll fill in some text as keystrokes to Notepad, as shown in listing 15.6.

Listing 15.6 Launching Notepad and "ghost typing" in it

```
import org.codehaus.groovy.scriptom.ActiveXProxy

"cmd /c notepad".execute()          ←①  Launch the Notepad process

wsh = new ActiveXProxy("WScript.Shell")    ②  Find and activate
wsh.AppActivate("Notepad")                     Notepad

wsh.sendKeys('First name: Guillaume{TAB}')
wsh.sendKeys('Last name: Laforge{ENTER}')        ③  Send keystrokes to
wsh.sendKeys('Book: Groovy in Action{ENTER}')        the component
wsh.sendKeys('Date: {F5}')
```

Once Notepad is launched at ①—here through Groovy's `execute` method on `String`—we activate the application at ② with the `AppActivate` command to put its window on the forefront. Then, at ③, we can send strings and keystrokes to the application.

All special keys can be entered with their names between curly braces, such as {ENTER} for carriage return, {F1} for the F1 key, and so forth. There are also special characters to represent combined keystrokes: the Shift key corresponds to +, Ctrl maps to ^, and Alt to %. For a more comprehensive list of available keystrokes, please refer to the online documentation: http://msdn.microsoft.com/archive/default.asp?url=/archive/en-us/wsh/htm/wsMthSendKeys.asp.

This is a rather contrived example because we wanted to show you how the sendKeys method can be used, but this means you can control a set of applications to make them collaborate as long as these applications can be operated with keystrokes. With this method, you may cut and paste selected elements from one application to another, create automated GUI test suites as if a robot agent were testing your application, and so on. Furthermore, if the application under control accepts the definition of external commands, you may launch automation tasks from within the application, without having to open a shell and execute a Groovy script manually. For instance, imagine selecting a piece of text and creating a script invocable by Scriptom that would retrieve translations or definitions. Your creativity is the only limit!

15.5 *Where to get documentation*

In the Java world, IDEs are clever enough to propose code completion and Java-Doc pop-ups to help you discover the available methods and properties on a given object and also help you understand how to use them. For dynamic languages, the task is more difficult, because you usually find out the type of an object—and which methods and properties are available—at runtime. Currently, the various Groovy integration plug-ins in the most popular IDEs are not capable of code completion. And the task is even harder when automating native applications, as you might have already experienced if you tried making some slight modifications to the scripts you've written so far!

You might be wondering how you can know which methods and properties are available on a given native object or application. Unfortunately, you will have to dive into the documentation of the application you are driving and see what is available through its exposed APIs. For instance, for Microsoft applications, the best source of information is the *Microsoft Developer Network (MSDN)* web site: http://msdn.microsoft.com/library/.

Although no JavaDoc-like documentation is available, Microsoft does a good job of providing comprehensive online documentation for its applications and components on MSDN. For each application, there is a list of properties, methods, and events for each object, often with snippets of code in Visual Basic, JScript, or C# showing how to use them. It is trivial to translate those examples to Groovy code.

Because finding the relevant documentation is like looking for a needle in a haystack on MSDN's site, in table 15.4 you will find a few pointers for the object model and documentation of the applications we have used throughout this chapter.

Table 15.4   Common applications and their associated documentation

Application	Documentation
Excel	http://msdn.microsoft.com/library/default.asp?url=/library/en-us/vbaxl11/html/xltocOMMap_HV01049651.asp
Internet Explorer	http://msdn.microsoft.com/library/default.asp?url=/workshop/browser/mshtml/reference/ifaces/document2/document2.asp
ScriptControl	http://msdn.microsoft.com/library/default.asp?url=/library/en-us/dnexpvb/html/gettingerrorinformation.asp
Scripting.FileSystemObject	http://msdn.microsoft.com/library/default.asp?url=/library/en-us/script56/html/jsfsotutor.asp
Shell.Application	http://msdn.microsoft.com/library/default.asp?url=/library/en-us/shellcc/platform/shell/programmersguide/shell_basics/shell_basics_programming/objectmap.asp
Windows Media Player	http://msdn.microsoft.com/library/default.asp?url=/library/en-us/wmplay10/mmp_sdk/usingtheversion9objectmodel.asp
Word	http://msdn.microsoft.com/library/default.asp?url=/library/en-us/dv_wrcore/html/wroriautomatingwordusingwordobjectmodel.asp
WScript.Network	http://msdn.microsoft.com/library/en-us/script56/html/wsobjwshnetwork.asp
WScript.Shell	http://msdn.microsoft.com/library/default.asp?url=/library/en-us/script56/html/wsobjwshshell.asp

With a few Office applications such as Word or Excel, and with some of the aforementioned Windows Scripting Host tools, you should be able to find interesting and inventive solutions to common tasks in your everyday life as a developer.

15.6 *Summary*

Although Groovy is a language that runs on top of a multiplatform JVM, you've discovered in this chapter how to leverage Windows native applications through the use of the complimentary Scriptom module, which wraps an API to access native

COM and ActiveX objects through JNI, the Java Native Interface. You learned how to access properties and call methods on these objects, and you also saw how to subscribe to events supported by these applications. You put what you learned into action by creating and running some compelling scripts that automate collaboration between various applications and interact with the host environment.

Groovy and Scriptom are a powerful combination to bridge two worlds: the Java world with its many free libraries and server-side applications, and Microsoft's platform and its end-user-rich native applications. Scriptom allows you to interact almost intuitively with the host environment to create complex automation tasks and control multiple applications and external Java libraries at the same time.

Seeing the Grails light

16

> *Human beings, who are almost unique in having the ability to learn from the experience of others, are also remarkable for their apparent disinclination to do so.*
>
> —Douglas Adams

The book is now officially over, but because you bought the whole album, we'll throw in an additional bonus track for you.

The bonus track is a recording of two developers, Guillaume (G) and Dierk (D), who work together on a full-blown web application in Groovy. By eavesdropping on their conversation and looking at the code they produce, you'll witness the evolution of the application from first ideas until deployment.

G and D work for ACME Software, an independent software vendor. Their boss wants each product to be accompanied by an "interactive tutorial." At least, these were his last words before heading for the golf course. While leaving the room, he grumbled something about "needed by Monday morning" and "only highest quality accepted."

16.1 *Setting the stage*

In which our heroes are given an assignment, make a bold decision, install Grails, and create their first page.

It's Friday afternoon, right after lunch, when Guillaume enters Dierk's office.

G: Hi!

D: Hi, Mr. G. What's up?

G: Didn't you hear the boss? We have to do something about the "interactive tutorial."

D: He can't be serious. I'm not gonna spend the weekend on this.

G: Me neither. We need to find the quickest way to make this happen tonight.

D: You mean "quick and dirty"? Not with me.

G: No, quick and clean. I suggest we use Grails and see how much we can achieve this afternoon.

D: Grails? What's that?

G: Grails is a web application framework.

D: Oh no! Not another one. I've seen so many of them. They all claim to do everything in no time. Please spare me another disappointment.

G: Well, all I'll promise is that it will be fun working with it. I've used it in some other projects, and it worked well. I even think there's a good chance we'll have something running by this evening—and if we don't, what have we got to lose?

D: I wouldn't follow anyone but you after this pitch. *[laughs]* Okay then. We'll give it a try. What's next? Download and install?

16.1.1 *Installing Grails*

Guillaume takes a seat next to Dierk. They start working together at Dierk's machine, sharing the same keyboard, mouse, and monitor.

G: Point your browser to http://grails.codehaus.org. Downloading and installing is explained there. We will go for the latest version, which is 0.3.1 at the moment.

Dierk opens the browser and navigates to the web site.

D: Okay, it needs Java 1.4+ and Ant as prerequisites. I've got them already. Strange that it doesn't need Groovy to be installed. *[raises right eyebrow]*

G: Grails comes with the embeddable *groovy-all.jar* included to avoid any version conflicts.

D: Wise decision. Now how about installation? Aha—setting a GRAILS_HOME environment variable and adding *GRAILS_HOME/bin* to the Path environment variable. So far so good—no surprises. But what's that next thing here: going to *GRAILS_HOME* and typing ant?

G: That means we are *building* Grails from the sources. Isn't that neat?

D: Neat or not, it's a bit odd. But hey—as long as it works, it's fine with me.

G: That was it for installation.

D: Eh—no. Wait. We're gonna need a database.

G: Yep. That's included.

D: And this will be a web application, right? So we also need a web server.

G: No, that's all included. Grails comes with everything you need for development.

D: That can't possibly be right. In the end, we'll have to deploy it on our corporate SphereLogic webserver and the DBacle/2 database! That's all very special. How could we ever develop against a different environment?

G: Well, first of all, Grails will produce a full J2EE-compliant web application as a web archive file. We can throw that into any compliant server. Second, Grails uses Hibernate to take care of the database mapping. That means we have a huge variety of databases that we can choose from.

D: Pretty impressive. Now, how do we start?

16.1.2 *Getting your feet wet*

G: Go to any directory you like, and open a command shell.

D: I'll take one that's already under version control.

G: *[nods]* Sure. Now create a new application by typing

```
grails create-app
```

G: and enter our application name when asked. I think *Tutor* would be appropriate.

D: It's created a lot of directories. Any idea what they all do?

G: Yes, it looks like this. *[produces table 16.1]*

Table 16.1 Directory structure below the Tutor application directory

Directory	Content
grails-app	The grails-specific part of the web application
conf	Configuration data sources and bootstrapping
controllers	All Grails controllers; initially empty
domain	All Grails domain classes (models); initially empty
i18n	Message bundles for internationalization
services	All Grails service classes; initially empty
taglib	All Grails tag libraries
views	All Grails views (GSP or JSP); initially empty
layouts	All sitemesh layouts
grails-tests	All Grails unit tests; initially empty
hibernate	Optional Hibernate configuration and mapping files
lib	Additional libraries as jar files
spring	Spring configuration file(s)
src	
groovy	Additional Groovy sources; initially empty
java	Additional Java sources; initially empty
web-app	Web application document root directory
css	Resource directory for Cascading Style Sheets
images	Resource directory for images
js	Resource directory for JavaScript files
WEB-INF	J2EE meta information (web.xml, and so on)
classes	Target for compiled classes; initially empty
tld	Resource directory for compiled tag libraries

D: Gosh, it's lucky you had that table with you. I see that the layout of the grails-app directory suggests that Grails obeys the good-old Model-View-Controller (MVC) separation or even enforces it.

G: Yes, we will see that throughout the whole project. In general, the model is made by the *domain* objects, which drive the whole process.

D: It's created a whole bunch of files, too.

G: Those are defaults for our application so that we can start right away.

D: You mean we can start the application without having done anything?

G: Yes, we can. *[takes the keyboard]* Go to the application directory

```
cd tutor
```

G: and run the application.

```
grails run-app
```

D: That's a heck of a lot of console output. Is anyone meant to understand that?

G: Well, we're running at warning log level per default. I bet you'd be glad if anything went wrong.

D: Now it waits and says: `watch-context`. What does that mean?

G: That's the Jetty web server, which is included in the distribution. Grails has generated a full-blown J2EE web application and started the server on it.

D: Very helpful. No tinkering with server configuration files. That's a big plus. And where is it running now?

G: http://localhost:8080/tutor/.

D: *[grabs the keyboard]* Here we go. *[figure 16.1 is displayed]*

G: Okay, the setup works.

D: Yes, that's a good installation check. How did you know the URL?

G: `8080` is the default port, but we can of course change it if we want. The */tutor* part comes from the name of the J2EE "application context" that has been created for us.

D: I see. And now we hack away some static HTML pages to create a prototype?

G: Why would we want to write *static* HTML pages? Don't you want to see real data?

D: Of course, eventually, but surely a few dummy pages come first, don't they?

G: No. If we were going to do any more coding right away, we would create domain classes, but I think we should lay out some plans first.

D: *[nods]* Does that mean you're calling a coffee break?

G: Or tea. 15 minutes after lunch is the perfect time for this.

Figure 16.1
Grails welcome page for
the Tutor application

16.2 *Laying out the domain model*

In which our friends learn of requirements and dream up a schema.

Guillaume and Dierk are standing at a round table next to a whiteboard in the coffee corner, with mint tea and cappuccino.

D: This can't be a coincidence.

G: What do you mean?

D: We're working with Grails and standing at a round table...

G: Oh, please. This isn't Camelot.

D: *[grins]* Okay then. What about the "interactive tutorial"?

G: I guess the tutorial needs to consist of at least some text and code examples...

D: ... that we need to create and display.

16.2.1 *Thinking through the use cases*

G: Yes. We have authors who create a tutorial and users who read it. To make the authors' lives easier, it would be nice if they could post tutorial pages through the web application.

D: You mean like posting to a blog or a wiki?

G: Yes, exactly. We'll find out what works best. We'll also need a tree-like structure for the tutorial entries to organize the tutorial and show a table of contents.

D: And where is the interactive part?

G: I talked with our boss about that before. He has the idea that logged-in users should be able to see what tutorial elements they've already worked through so that they can concentrate on the new ones.

D: Hm, that's a bit tricky. A user can scan through the material without reading much of it. That shouldn't count as "reading."

G: Maybe the user clicks a button, indicating that they have visited the page.

D: Hm, sounds doable—with considerable effort.

16.2.2 Designing relations

G: We don't have much time, so we will follow the simplest possible route. Let's see what we have. *[sketches figure 16.2 on the whiteboard]*

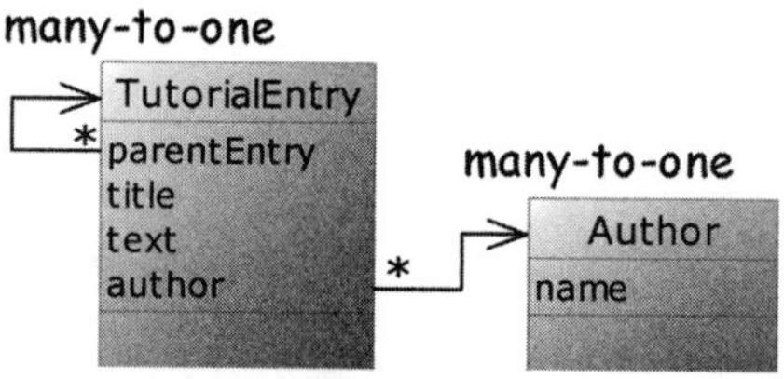

Figure 16.2   Relational design of `TutorialEntry` and `Author` with many-to-one relations

D: That's rather simple.

G: It will become more complex over time. You know: every complex solution that works is based on a simple solution that works.

D: So, what have we got? `TutorialEntry` seems to be the central abstraction.

G: Yes, it holds most of the information and will be the hub of most references. After all, the tutorials are the entities we're doing all this for.

D: And every `TutorialEntry` refers to an `Author`?

G: Yes, each one refers to exactly one `Author`, but many `TutorialEntries` can refer to the same one.

D: Therefore the relation from `TutorialEntry` to `Author` is many-to-one.

G: Right, and it is unidirectional. That means we assume that every `Tutorial-Entry` directly references its `Author`, but a single `Author` doesn't explicitly store a reference to all their `TutorialEntries`.

D: But what if we want to show all `TutorialEntries` of a given `Author`?

G: Then we can query for all `TutorialEntries` where the `author` property matches the given one.

D: Ah, okay. No need to keep track of all the back references, because we can rely on the relational model below the surface.

G: Exactly. It means less work with the bookkeeping but at the expense of performance. A query is always slower than following a reference.

D: Hmm. *[scratches head]* So which is better then: unidirectional or bidirectional?

G: I wish it were that easy. That's an engineering decision. Making such tricky decisions is what we are paid for in the first place—besides knowing the tools and mechanics.

D: You're making me nervous. What if we decide wrong?

G: They will hang us. *[laughs]* No, honestly, the cool thing about Grails is that you can change the design at a later stage without excessive costs. This is where the knowledge of the tools pays off. They give us leeway to defer and correct decisions.

D: Good to know. What about that other reference between the `Tutorial-Entries`? That seems to be the parent-child relationship.

G: All `TutorialEntries` have a parent `TutorialEntry` except the root `Tutorial-Entry`, which has a null parent. Many `TutorialEntries` can have the same parent. They are siblings, so to speak.

D: And the relation is also unidirectional. Every `TutorialEntry` knows its parent but not its children? Is that a wise decision?

G: For the moment, it should be good enough. Introducing back references from the parent to its children is an optimization issue. Grails grants us enough leeway to care about that later, when we have a better idea of what the actual access patterns are.

D: I think I need to see some code to understand all this.

G: All right. Let's go over and get a first version running.

16.3 *Implementing the domain model*

In which Guillaume creates the first domain class, and Dierk is astonished by the scaffolding and testing capabilities of Grails.

Back at Dierk's machine, he unlocks the screensaver.

D: Now, how do we start implementing the domain model? Are we creating POJOs?[1] Do we have to follow any conventions?

---

[1] Plain Old Java Objects.

16.3.1 *Scaffolding domain classes*

G: Both, actually. *[grabs the keyboard]* But Grails gives us all support we need. Let's first create the `Author` class:

```
grails create-domain-class

        [input] Enter domain class name:
author
```

D: Ah, you entered the class name in lowercase?

G: Yes, but that's only because I'm a lazy typist.

D: And Grails says it has created two classes for us: `grails-app/domain/Author.groovy` and `grails-tests/AuthorTests.groovy`.

G: That's a scaffolded domain class and a corresponding unit test to give us something to start with. `Author.groovy` looks like this. *[opens the file in an editor—listing 16.1 is displayed]*

Listing 16.1 Scaffolded domain class `Author.groovy`

```
class Author {

}
```

D: There's not a lot there, really. Is that it?

G: That's all it takes to start with. Grails will inject `id` and `version` properties at runtime for internal purposes. It also adds a `toString` method for the standard display of the object, showing class name and `id`. We should change that to something more meaningful for our domain class.

D: You mean we should make it return something that makes sense to a user rather than to the computer?

G: *[nods]* Exactly. Also, every such class will automatically be persistent—that is, backed by the database and managed by Hibernate.

D: Aha, then let's create the database, the tables, the schema, and the mapping descriptor.

G: No, no, no! That's why I said "automatically." That's all done for us behind the scenes. There's really nothing we have to do.

D: Wow! Very impressive. But how about the `name` attribute that we have to add?

G: That's as simple as this. *[edits the file to make it listing 16.2]*

> **Listing 16.2 Customized domain class `Author.groovy`**
>
> ```
> class Author {
>
>     String name
>
>     String toString() { name }
> }
> ```
> The name is a more useful identifier

D: And no mapping at all?

G: As I said—it's all automatic. Grails follows the "convention over configuration" paradigm, which makes all this possible.

D: I would like to see something tangible before we proceed with the domain model. Can we look at the database?

G: Yes, we can. We can even look at it through the web application.

D: You're kidding! We don't *have* a web application.

16.3.2 *Scaffolding views and controllers*

G: We don't have a web application yet, but we will have one in a minute. See here:

```
grails generate-all

    [input] Enter domain class name:
author
```

D: Lots more screenfuls of output, I see. And this is creating a web application?

G: Start the server with

```
grails run-app
```

G: and point the browser to http://localhost:8080/tutor/author. We need to add "author" to the URL because that is our domain class of interest. *[browsing around, the screens in figure 16.3 are displayed]*

D: Hey, this really works! I can see the initially empty list of authors, create a new one, see it in the list, and edit and delete it. Not bad for having written only two lines of code!

G: Yes, this is called scaffolding. It allows us to get something running quickly.

D: Ah, you mean all these views are scaffolded, as you call it?

G: Not only the views but also the controllers...

D: ... which call the database operations.

G: Kind of. They work on the domain objects rather than calling the database directly. Each change to the domain object gets automatically propagated to the database.

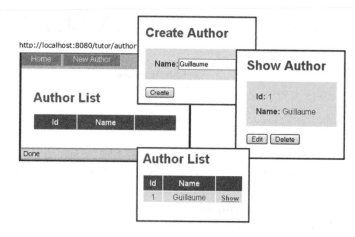

Figure 16.3
Screenshots of scaffolded views to list, create, show, edit, and delete `Authors`

D: Does that mean we can have a campfire with all our SQL reference manuals being burned in a big ceremony?

G: Certainly not. We don't need them for the standard cases any longer, but when times get tough, you'll be glad to have them.

D: Right, right. Now, what's next? Proceed with the other domain classes?

G: Well, we could. But I'd like to show you another feature first.

D: And that is?

G: Functional testing.

16.3.3 *Testing the web application*

D: You mean we can also test the web application automatically?

G: Yes, and it's remarkably easy. Look here. We'll create the webtest, then scaffold the author tests, and finally run it. Creating the webtest support is a one-liner:

```
grails create-webtest
```

G: This fetches Canoo WebTest if necessary and installs it. The download size is pretty big. Luckily we have good network connectivity.

G: Now scaffold a webtest for the `Author` class:

```
grails generate-webtest

    [input] Enter domain class name:
author
```

G: And now we run it:

```
grails run-webtest
```

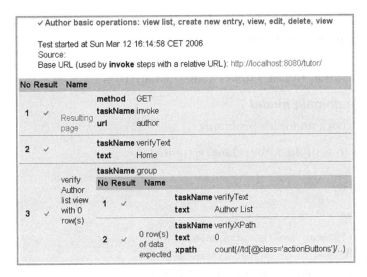

Figure 16.4
Excerpt of the WebTest report for the scaffolded `Author` **CRUD operations**

D: *[as figure 16.4 is displayed]* Ah, it brings up a test report. That's pretty. Does it work by clicking through the web application on my behalf?

G: Yes, and we can run it after every tiny change to the code, asserting that we haven't broken anything.

D: That means the tests will fail if our code doesn't compile?

G: It will even fail if our implementation doesn't add or delete an author properly to the database.

D: Very impressive. That's good-old engineering practice made easy. When we proceed with changing the application logic, do we have to adapt the tests as well?

G: Of course—and the best practice is to adapt the test before we change any functionality. *[smiles]*

D: How do I change the tests, then?

G: See for example `webtest/tests/AuthorTest.groovy`. It specifies the test like in lines like these:

```
clickLink   (label:'New Author')
verifyText  (text: 'Create Author')
clickButton (label:'Create')
verifyText  (text: 'Show Author', description:'Detail page')
clickLink   (label:'List',       description:'Back to list view')
```

D: That reads like a checklist of what to do for manual testing, but it does it automatically.

G: It also is all plain Groovy, which makes it convenient to work with.

D: I feel confident enough to proceed with the domain model.

G: Shall I type?

D: Please let me do it. I think I understand the pattern...

16.3.4 *Completing the domain model*

Guillaume leans back and folds his hands.

D: We're going to scaffold `TutorialEntry`, right?

G: Yep.

D: *[starts typing]*

```
grails create-domain-class

    [input] Enter domain class name:
tutorialEntry
```

D: All fine. Now scaffolding views and controllers?

G: We could do that, but the views are scaffolded from what's available in the domain classes, so we should complete them first.

D: Okay, `Author` is already complete. Now let's do the `TutorialEntry` class. It's stored in the domain directory, if I remember correctly. *[opens the file]* Now what?

G: Add a property for every attribute that we defined in our design: `title`, `text`, `author`, and `parentEntry`.

D: Do we need to declare property types?

G: Yes. Grails uses the type information for building the model. Having the type information available is a big plus.

D: `Title` and `text` are plain `Strings`. Is `author` of type `Author` then?

G: Of course.

D: And `parentEntry` is of type `TutorialEntry`. Very straightforward.

G: *[grabs the keyboard]* Here we go. *[edits `TutorialEntry` to listing 16.3]*

Listing 16.3 Domain class `TutorialEntry`

```
class TutorialEntry {

    String        title
    TutorialEntry parentEntry
    String        text
    Author        author
    String toString() { title }
}
```

D: Can I scaffold the views and controllers now?

G: Go ahead.

D: Piece of cake. *[starts typing]*

```
grails generate-all

    [input] Enter domain class name:
tutorialEntry
```

D: Now starting the server...

```
grails run-app

[wait-forever]:
```

D: ... and open the browser and create a *TutorialEntry*.

G: Every *TutorialEntry* needs an *Author*, so we'd better create one first.

Guillaume opens the browser at the URL http://localhost:8080/tutor/author and creates an *Author*.

G: Now head over to http://localhost:8080/tutor/tutorialEntry/create. *[figure 16.5 is shown]*

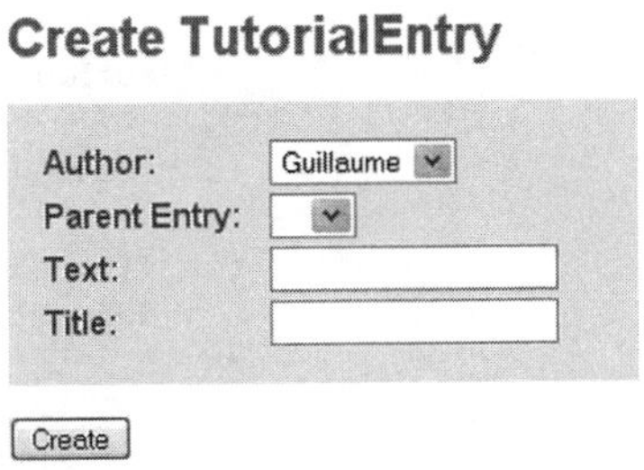

D: Wow! We already have the core of the application. And it's working. We have the full lifecycle for authors and tutorials. The views are still not what we really want, though.

G: Yes. Scaffolding is only to get you started and provide you with something that you can build on. It's not uncommon to progressively replace all scaffolded artifacts in the course of the project.

Create TutorialEntry

Author:	Guillaume ▾
Parent Entry:	▾
Text:	
Title:	

Create

Figure 16.5 Scaffolded create page for tutorial entries

D: Then let's see what we can do about the *TutorialEntry*'s list and details view.

16.4 *Customizing the views*

In which our heroes create some sample data, change a view in GSP, and gain wiki-like formatting using a tag library.

D: We'll need a set of example tutorials that we can test the views with. Shall we create five or so through the interface?

G: We could, but there is an easier way. We can add them to the bootstrapping.

D: Ah, does that mean we write a SQL script that fills the database on server startup?

G: Almost. But not via SQL scripts.

16.4.1 Bootstrapping data

G: We create our domain objects programmatically. Look here.
[creates config/ApplicationBootStrap.groovy—listing 16.4]

Listing 16.4 Creating sample data in `ApplicationBootStrap.groovy`

```
class ApplicationBootStrap {

    Closure init = { servletContext ->

        def guillaume = new Author(name: 'Guillaume')       ⟵ Create a
        guillaume.save()                                       persistent author

        def root = new TutorialEntry(       ⟵ Create a
            title: '1 Root Title',             root entry
            text:  'Root holder for all entries',
            author: guillaume
        )
        root.save()
                                            Create five
        for (i in 1..5) {        ⟵         subentries
            def entry = new TutorialEntry(
                title:       "1.$i Some Title",
                text:        'a very long text ' * i,
                author:      guillaume,
                parentEntry: root
            )
            entry.save()
        }
    }

    Closure destroy = {
    }
}
```

D: You create your objects with references and such, and when you say "save()" it all goes to the database?

G: Isn't that nice? That's the typical Groovy style of having a smart configuration. Just imagine if this were XML like in other systems. Then we wouldn't be able to define any amount of example data as we do in the little *for* loop.

D: Well, then let's display it. *[types]*

```
grails run-app
```

D: Now see what we have in the `TutorialEntry` list. *[web browser displays figure 16.6]*

TutorialEntry List

Id	Author	Parent Entry	Text	Title	
1	Guillaume		"Root" holder for _all_ ~entries~	1 Sample Tutorial	Show
2	Guillaume	1 Sample Tutorial	a very long text	1.1 Some Title	Show
3	Guillaume	1 Sample Tutorial	a very long text a very long text	1.2 Some Title	Show
4	Guillaume	1 Sample Tutorial	a very long text a very long text a very long text	1.3 Some Title	Show
5	Guillaume	1 Sample Tutorial	a very long text a very long text a very long text a very long text	1.4 Some Title	Show
6	Guillaume	1 Sample Tutorial	a very long text a very long text a very long text a very long text a very long text	1.5 Some Title	Show

Figure 16.6 Scaffolded list view for tutorial entries showing bootstrapped data

16.4.2 *Working with Groovy Server Pages*

G: I think the scaffolded list view of tutorials shows too many details. It should only show titles, like in a table of contents, but with indentations.

D: Okay. How do we change it?

G: It's all here. *[opens views/tutorialEntry/list.gsp]*

D: Ah, the directory structure reflects the URL of the view. Very convenient.

G: At least for the standard views as scaffolded. There are alternatives like creating them dynamically, but for our little thing here the standard way is all we need.

D: And this GSP is the Groovy version of JSP?

G: Yes, only better. *[grins]* Look at the snippet here that renders the list of tutorials. *[opens the file, showing listing 16.5]*

Listing 16.5 Snippet of the scaffolded tutorialEntry/list.gsp

```
<table>
    <tr>
        <th>Id</th>
            <th>Author</th>
            <th>Parent Entry</th>
            <th>Text</th>
            <th>Title</th>
        <th></th>
    </tr>
    <g:each in="${tutorialEntryList}">     ⟵  GSP
        <tr>                                    iteration tag
            <td>${it.id}</td>
            <td>${it.author}</td>
```

```
            <td>${it.parentEntry}</td>
            <td>${it.text}</td>
            <td>${it.title}</td>
            <td class="actionButtons">
                <span class="actionButton">
                    <g:link action="show" id="${it.id}">Show</g:link>
                </span>
            </td>
        </tr>
    </g:each>
</table>
```

D: Looks familiar. I know nothing about GSP, but I can guess that this renders a table row for each *TutorialEntry* with table cells for every property. Not surprising. I assume we delete all cells that we don't want to see?

G: Yes. And don't forget the corresponding table header cells.

D: Done. Now restart the server and see what it looks like?

G: No, no. We don't need to restart the server. Just save the file and reload the browser page.

D: Wonderful—very convenient. I like this micro-iteration development.

G: Yes. Instant feedback is really helpful. You do a little change and verify the result without losing your concentration. This is what gets you into the flow of programming.

D: I know what you mean. When everything seems to just fit.

G: That reminds me—our list view doesn't fit yet. It doesn't show indentation.

D: Hm, we need to indent each title as much as its nesting depth counted from root.

G: And that's equivalent to the number of parents it has.

D: Ah, you mean we count the parents and indent by that number? But that's a full-blown tree algorithm that will require a lot of work!

G: Not necessarily. Let me try something. *[grabs the keyboard—edits the file to listing 16.6].*

Listing 16.6   Snippet adapting tutorialEntry/list.gsp with title indentations

```
<g:each var="page" in="${tutorialEntryList}">        ◁─┐  Iterate over each
<tr>                                                   │  page in the list
<%
    depth = 0
    def runner = page
    while (runner.parentEntry) {                          ┐  Calculate the depth from
        runner = runner.parentEntry; depth++    ◁─┘  the root of the tree
```

```
      }
%>
    <td style="padding-left: ${ 5 + depth*20 }px ">      ⊲┘  Indent based
        <g:link action="show" id="${page.id}">${page.title}</g:link>      on the depth
    </td>
    <td style="text-align:right;">${page.id}</td>
    <td style="text-align:center;">${page.author}</td>
    <td>
        ${page.text.size() > 40 ? page.text[0..37]+'...' : page.text}
    </td>
  </tr>
  </g:each>
```

D: Magic, magic. I'm impressed. What's that? A scriptlet?

G: Yes, the same as you would do in Java for JSP but in Groovy. The *depth* variable is calculated in the scriptlet for every *TutorialEntry* before rendering and implicitly stored in the binding. Therefore, we can reuse it in the *padding* argument of the *title* table cell style.

D: It works well, and the output looks nice, but it has a smell. I think a view should never contain logic, and this view does.

G: I'm not so sure. We could easily refactor this code into the *TutorialEntry* domain class or into a tag library. On the other hand, although this scriptlet contains logic, this is only *view* logic. It has nothing to do with the *TutorialEntry* model as such nor with the flow of the application. That makes it justifiable to leave it here.

D: But I don't like the mix of logic here. It doesn't look well factored. I agree it's view logic, but it should go to a separate place.

G: If that's the only thing that makes you feel uneasy, then we can move it into a template. Templates are little view pieces that are reused with changing data.

D: Like a *row* template used for each *TutorialEntry*?

G: In fact, that is a good name. We make a new file *tutorialEntry/_row.gsp* and put all the `<tr>`-enclosed code there.

D: The leading underscore is a naming convention?

G: That separates it from the normal views and suggests that it doesn't produce a full page but only a part of it.

D: And the *tutorialEntry/list.gsp* refers to it by name?

G: Yes, via the *render* method. The old line

```
<g:each var="page" in="${tutorialEntryList}">
```

G: is replaced with

```
<g:render template="row" collection="${tutorialEntryList}" />
```

G: This will pass all entries of the `tutorialEntryList` one after the next into the row template for partial rendering.

D: I like that much better. It clearly shows that the extracted logic affects only one line.

G: It also makes the view logic reusable. Any view that needs to render a `TutorialEntry` in this fashion can refer to the template.

D: What other views need improvement? Ah, the detail view should present tutorial entries in a more readable format. I assume it resides in *views/tutorialEntry/ show.gsp*.

16.4.3 *Working with tag libraries*

D: This looks all very comprehensive. Rearranging the fields a little should be all that's necessary.

G: I have an idea. In addition to having our authors possibly provide HTML tags in their contribution, wouldn't it be nice if they could use some wiki-like markup for the simple cases? We could then display the transformed markup on this page.

D: Hm, sounds complicated.

G: For a start, we allow some simple markup: treating newlines as breaks, two newlines as a paragraph, and support bold, underline, and italic styles.

D: That's still a lot of work—more than we can do in a scriptlet.

G: Yes. That's a job for a taglib.

D: Hm. *[shakes head]* I did some taglib stuff with JSP—lots of configuration and not a lot of fun.

G: I'll show you Grails' no-configuration solution. Go to the taglib dir, and create a new file *WikiTagLib.groovy*.

D: And now?

G: We implement the intended tag as a closure property with the respective name. How about "wikify"? The tag would have a `text` attribute with the raw text that is to be transformed to HTML.

D: And how do we pass the result back?

G: We add it to the `out` result writer. Look here. *[creates taglib/WikiTagLib. groovy, listing 16.7]*

Listing 16.7 Implementing a wiki tag library in taglib/WikiTagLib.groovy

```
class WikiTagLib {

    def replacements = [
        [ "\n"                     , "<br>\n"],          Newlines
                                                          to breaks
        [ "<br>\n\\s*<br>\n"       , "<p/>\n"],          Double breaks
                                                          to paragraphs
        [ /\*(\b[^\*]*?\b)\*/ , '<b>$1</b>' ],    Star-enclosed to bold
        [ /~(\b[^~]*?\b)~/    , '<i>$1</i>' ],    Tilde-enclosed to italic
        [ /\b_([^_]*?)_\b/    ,                    Underscore-
          '<div style="text-decoration:underline">$1</div>' ],  enclosed to
                                                                 underline
    ]

    def wikify = { attributes ->
        def text = attributes.text
        for (pair in replacements) {
            text = text.replaceAll(pair[0], pair[1])
        }
        out << text
    }
}
```

D: Pretty slick. All plain Groovy. But how do we use it?

G: In *show.gsp* we replace

```
${tutorialEntry?.text}
```

G: with

```
<g:wikify text="${tutorialEntry?.text}"/>
```

D: That's all logical. I guess we now have to declare our *WikiTagLib* in the page header and in *web.xml*?

G: No, no. That's all done automatically. Save the files, and reload the page, *[David Copperfield gesture]* et voilà, there it is. *[figure 16.7 appears on the screen]*

D: You know what? This is really how web development should always be: simple and efficient. Why wasn't this invented earlier?

G: *[nods]* I would say: Ruby on Rails invented the idea, and it took the appearance of Groovy to make this possible on the Java platform. The availability of Hibernate

Tutorial 1 Sample Tutorial

Author:	Guillaume
Parent Entry:	
Text:	Root holder for all entries

[Edit]

Figure 16.7 Tutorial entry detail view with wikified text from WikiTagLib

and Spring was also a prerequisite. But it's not the pure power of the Java packages that counts. The dynamic nature of Groovy is just as important.

D: And now the idea can grow.

G: Just like our application. Let's use it a little to see how it feels.

16.5 *Working with controllers and finder methods*

In which Dierk and Guillaume take control of the application and ask searching questions of their database.

D: As a Tutor user, I would like to go through the tutorials in sequence. How about providing Previous and Next links in the detail page?

G: Yes, you're right. That's missing. But how do we determine which tutorial entry is previous or next?

D: We could guess from the containment in the parent/child relationship or from conventions about the title.

G: That's all too shaky. We need to have that in the model itself. After all, the page sequence is a central part of any tutorial, right?

D: But changing the model is always critical.

G: Not necessarily. Let's add this line to `TutorialEntry`

```
TutorialEntry predecessor
```

G: and then restart the server.

D: Changing the domain class requires a restart?

G: Not always. Simple changes don't. Grails tries to avoid making you restart unless it's absolutely essential. However, my personal style is to always do it after changes of the domain classes—just in case, you know.

D: Fair enough. I guess we should also provide our bootstrapped `Tutorial-Entries` with a sensible value for `predecessor`.

G: Ah, right. Thanks. I would have forgotten about that.

D: Okay. All done. The server is restarted.

G: Then let's change the show.gsp to include Previous and Next buttons. I'd say we will use menu buttons for this. *[edits file to listing 16.8]*

> **Listing 16.8   Snippet of views/tutorialEntry/show.gsp introducing Previous and Next menu buttons**

```
<span class="menuButton">
    <g:link action="index">Home</g:link></span>
<span class="menuButton">
```

```
    <g:link action="previous" id="${tutorialEntry?.id}">Previous
    </g:link></span>
  <span class="menuButton">
    <g:link action="next" id="${tutorialEntry?.id}">Next
    </g:link></span>
```

D: And this means?

G: When we click the Previous button, the *previous* action of the *TutorialEntry-Controller* will be invoked. We provide the id of the currently displayed *TutorialEntry* as the *id* attribute.

D: That means we have to extend the *TutorialEntryController* with that action. I can guess where the Controller will be: in the controller directory. Yes, there it is: *TutorialEntryController.groovy*.

G: You see all the scaffolded actions in it? Does it look familiar?

D: They are implemented as closures and assigned to properties—the same way we defined tags for the WikiTagLib. Looks like a pattern to me.

G: *[smiles]* Seems to be more than a coincidence at least. *[takes the keyboard]* Let me try this. *[makes the controller resemble listing 16.9]*

Listing 16.9 Previous action in the `TutorialEntryController`

```
def previous = {
    def entry = TutorialEntry.get( params.id )
    if (entry.predecessor) {
        entry = entry.predecessor
    } else {
        flash.message = "Top of tutorials reached."
    }
    redirect(action: show, id: entry.id)
}
```

D: I don't understand a single line.

G: Well, we first fetch the current *TutorialEntry* instance.

D: Is *get* a database access?

G: Kind of. It "gets" you the instance from the database or from the cache. Chances are that when we reach this point, the instance is already in the cache.

D: And *params.id* is the id we provided in the *<g:link/>* tag?

G: So it is.

D: Then we work with the object references as usual. That's okay. What is the *flash* object?

G: The flash is a scope that lives until the next request and is used for relaying information from one controller call to the next. It is mostly used in situations like this, for relaying messages such as information, warnings, errors, and so on. In the scaffolded views, you will find references to the flash scope to find out whether there are any messages to be shown.

D: Aha—and finally we redirect to the *show* action to render the *show.gsp* as usual but for the predecessor entry.

G: Exactly, possibly showing the flash message if there is no predecessor.

D: After the explanation, it makes sense.

G: I hope so. The *next* action will be even more fun. *[edits the controller to become listing 16.10]*

Listing 16.10 **Next action in the `TutorialEntryController`**

```
def next = {
    def entry = TutorialEntry.get( params.id )
    def nextEntry = TutorialEntry.findByPredecessor(entry)    ←┐  Dynamic
    if (nextEntry) {                                           │  finder
        entry = nextEntry                                      │  method
    } else {
        flash.message = "End of tutorials reached."
    }
    redirect(action: show, id: entry.id)
}
```

D: What's different?

G: Look closely at the second line.

D: *findByPredecessor*? Can that be true? We didn't define any method with that name!

G: No, we didn't, but Grails is smart enough to know what we're after. That's a dynamic finder method made from the domain class information. This expression is roughly equivalent to this pseudo SQL statement:

```
SELECT * FROM TutorialEntry AS te WHERE entry.predecessor.id = te.id
```

D: Why do you say "roughly"?

G: Because strictly speaking, SQL has no notion of "entry" that we used here. Behind the scenes, Hibernate is doing all the work of providing us with nice object-oriented query facilities and optimization. Grails makes them available to us in the most convenient fashion.

D: That is really amazing, but also very unfamiliar. Is there a reference about all these dynamic methods?

G: Yes, it's all on the web under http://grails.org.

D: I know what to read over the weekend, then. Are we finished with the Tutor application?

G: Not yet. The "interactive" part is still missing. We have no model about our users, yet, and how they visit *TutorialEntries*.

D: That sounds like we should have a coffee break for another modeling session.

G: Good idea.

Guillaume and Dierk walk over to the coffee corner.

16.6 *Elaborating the model*

In which Guillaume and Dierk discover a new entity in their midst.

The coffee corner's whiteboard still shows figure 16.2.

D: We should add the new *predecessor* attribute to the picture.

G: *[nods silently]*

D: And we will have a *User* class with a *name* attribute for each *User*.

G: *[nods silently]*

D: You're so quiet. What are you thinking about?

G: About the relation between *User* and *TutorialEntry*. I'm afraid it's a bit complicated.

D: Why? One *User* can visit several *TutorialEntries*. That's a simple one-to-many relation, isn't it?

G: It's not as simple, because many *Users* can visit the same *TutorialEntry*. So it's actually many-to-many.

D: Ah, I see. You're right. If we ask a *TutorialEntry* for all *Users* that have seen it, we will get many *Users*. If we ask one *User* for all *TutorialEntries* he has visited, we will also get many *TutorialEntries*. That's many-to-many. What worries you about it?

G: The rule of thumb is that when you hit a many-to-many relation, you have missed an important concept in your design.

D: Aha. So we know at least there's something missing. Any hint how to find it?

G: The trick is to picture an object that encapsulates the whole many-to-many relationship. If we had an object that takes *TutorialEntries* on the one hand

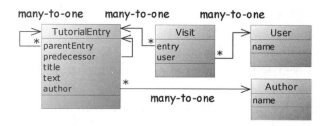

**Figure 16.8
Relational design of the Tutor application completed with User and Visit**

and `User`s on the other hand to care for their relation, what would that object represent?

D: Eureka! I have it! That's a `Visit`! Look here. *[sketches figure 16.8]*

G: Good job! That makes sense. Every time a `User` marks a `TutorialEntry` as visited, we create a new `Visit` for the unique `User`/`TutorialEntry` combination.

D: And the relations become much simpler. Many `Visit`s can refer to the same `TutorialEntry`. That's a standard many-to-one relation.

G: And many visits can be stored for the same `User`. That's many-to-one as well.

D: In other words, we have split the original many-to-many relation into two many-to-one relations. How exciting! We invented a whole new world-changing pattern!

G: I don't like pouring water in your cappuccino, but this pattern isn't new at all. It's as old as relational databases—if not older.

D: Still, I think we did a really good job modeling the domain. I'm impatient to see how that looks in code.

16.7 Working with the session

In which Guillaume and Dierk ask their users to introduce themselves, and allow them to record their visits.

Back on Dierk's machine.

D: Scaffolding `User` and `Visit` is a breeze. Here's the scaffolded `User` class, after customization. *[User class is edited to listing 16.11]*

Listing 16.11   Scaffolded and customized `User` domain class

```
class User {
    String name

    String toString() { name }
}
```

D: And here's the `Visit` class, created and similarly customized. *[Visit class is edited to listing 16.12]*

Listing 16.12   Scaffolded and customized `Visit` domain class

```
class Visit {
    User          user
    TutorialEntry entry

    String toString() { user.toString() + ' : ' + entry.toString() }
}
```

G: The user needs some device to log in.

D: To begin with, they could choose their name from the list of users. Ah, wait—we have scaffolded the user `list` view that we can hijack for that purpose. It's in *views/user/list.gsp.*

G: How should that work?

D: We add a new action button to each table row like so:

```
<span class="actionButton">
    <g:link action="select" id="${it.id}"> That's me </g:link>
</span>
```

G: I see. And we add a *select* action...

D: ... to the scaffolded `UserController`.

G: Okay, let me do it. *[takes the keyboard]* We need get hold of the selected `User` object and store it in the session. I'd suggest the key `user`. *[UserController becomes listing 16.13]*

Listing 16.13   `select` action in `UserController`

```
def select = {
    def user = User.get( params['id'] )       ◁─┐  Load the selected
    if(user) {                                   │  user profile
        session.user = user
        redirect(controller:'tutorialEntry', action:"list")
    } else {                          ◁─┐  Don't assume the id is valid
        flash['message'] =
            "Sorry user ${params['id']} cannot be selected."
        redirect(action:show)
    }
}
```

D: *Session* is a simple map that can store objects?

G: It would be more accurate to say that it can be *used* like a map.

D: And if everything is okay, we forward to the *list* view of the *TutorialEntries*.

G: Yes, via the *TutorialEntryController*.

D: The error handling seems a bit too much. Can it really be that a bad *id* is passed into the *select* action?

G: You're right. It's unlikely, but you never know. Call me paranoid, but in controllers with all the redirections and chaining that might happen, I prefer to keep the code defensive.

D: You're the boss. What's next?

G: Users need some device to mark a *TutorialEntry* as "visited." They could do that best when in the detail view of *TutorialEntry*. Therefore, I'd suggest adding a Visited button to *views/tutorialEntry/show.gsp*.

D: Let me do that GUI stuff. *[keyboard switch]* I will add this line to the *<g:form>* section:

```
<span class="button"><g:actionSubmit value="Visited"/></span>
```

G: If we click this, it will be handled by the *visited* action of the *TutorialEntry-Controller*.

D: Let me try to implement this. I will keep it as defensive as you like it. *[twinkles as he edits to listing 16.14]*

Listing 16.14 *visited* action in *TutorialEntryController*

```
def visited = {
    def entry = TutorialEntry.get( params.id )      Need both an
    if (entry && session.user) {                    entry and a user
        new Visit(entry: entry, user: session.user).save()     Create a new
    }                                                          visit and
    redirect(action: next, id: entry.id)                       save it—all
}                                                              in one line!
```

G: Good. You create the corresponding *Visit* object and save it. Perfect.

D: And I added a convenience feature in the last line. After the button click, there is no point in staying on the same page. We go directly to the next one.

G: Your users will love you.

D: I hope so. Are we done?

G: Almost. We still need to provide a filtered view for the *TutorialEntry* list that only shows links that haven't been visited yet. That's what the boss demanded.

D: That concerns *views/tutorialEntry/list.gsp*. I'd say the simplest solution is to add the filtering functionality as menu buttons in the top row. *[does so to make listing 16.15]*

Listing 16.15 Snippet of menu button section in tutorialEntry/list.gsp for providing filtering views

```
<span class="menuButton">
    <g:link controller="user" action="list">
        <%= (session?.user) ? "${session.user.name}": 'Log in' %>
    </g:link>
</span>
<g:if test="${session?.user}">
    <span class="menuButton">
        <g:link action="listVisited">List visited</g:link>
    </span>
    <span class="menuButton">
        <g:link action="listUnvisited">List unvisited</g:link>
    </span>
</g:if>
```

G: I see you're going to like GSP.

D: Is that too much?

G: You're doing a little more than we need. First, you're displaying the current user.

D: Or "Log in" if there is no user in the session yet. The link behind that button goes to the user list view.

G: And then two filtering buttons to restrict the current view to only the visited of the unvisited links.

D: But only if the user is known. Otherwise there is no point in showing them.

G: Very user-friendly. But none of this will work until we have the *listVisited* and *listUnvisited* actions in the *TutorialEntryController*.

D: Can you help me with this?

G: Sure. Remember, it's all plain Groovy object work. *[edits the controller to listing 16.16]*

Listing 16.16 listVisited and listUnvisited actions in TutorialEntryController

```
def listVisited = {                          Dynamic finder method for user
    def visited = Visit.findAllByUser(session.user).entry  ⟵
    render(view:'list', model:[ tutorialEntryList: visited)
}
```

```
def listUnVisited = {
    def unvisited = TutorialEntry.list() -
        Visit.findAllByUser(session.user).entry
    render(view:'list', model:[ tutorialEntryList: unvisited ])
}
```
> Unvisited =
> all-visited

D: Cool. You use the dynamic finder methods to select all visits for the current user. But why is the simple expression *.entry* working?

G: The finder method returns a list of *Visit* objects, and *.entry* is a GPath expression that returns a list of all *entry* properties of each *Visit*—that is, our list of *TutorialEntries*.

D: And in *listUnvisited*, you subtract this list from the list of all *Tutorial-Entries*. This almost reads as if we were working on an object database!

G: Simple and efficient. That's Grails.

D: I really see the light, now. We're done, aren't we?

G: Yes, we're done with the functionality. But because we still have some time left, I'd suggest doing some spit'n'polish before finally deploying it.

D: You really want to deploy it? Isn't that too much work? All the packaging and so on? Also, I have never before deployed an application that only took an afternoon to create.

G: Why not? It's all good and stable, and deployment will be easy. I promise you can go home early today.

D: Okay then. What do we have to do to finish up?

16.8 Finishing up

In which Guillame and Dierk protect themselves from the forces of evil (well, evil input), deploy the application to a live system, and go their separate ways.

G: Currently, the user needs to know the URL scheme to handle the application. I'd say that's okay for administrators who create new author and user accounts, but not so nice for the casual reader.

D: We need a welcome page in our corporate design with quick links to the frequent entry points. I think a static HTML page would do it.

G: We can store that as *index.html* in the *web-app* directory, and Grails will pick it up automatically.

D: I expected nothing less. *[laughs]* I will copy the start page of our corporate web site for that purpose and change the body to be

```
<a href="tutorialEntry">Tutorials</a>
```

D: That should be okay for the moment. We can refine that later. Anything else for the finishing touch?

G: Well, we could go over the style in *web-app/css/main.css* to adapt it to our corporate style.

D: I think we'll leave that to the web designer. I'm happy with how it is right now.

G: Okay, just in case the designer asks, we can change the whole page layout for all the pages at once by adapting *views/layout/main.jsp*.

D: That's good to know. Anything else?

16.8.1 *Validating constraints*

G: Yep. Finally, I'd like to go over field validation to protect the application from bad user input.

D: I would normally complain that this is too much work, because we have to go over all the affected actions and views, but I guess you have another ace up your sleeve?

G: Well, I haven't—but Grails has. It allows easy declaration of constraints in your model that are automatically used for validation. Let's take the `User` class, for example. The `name` property should never be empty, neither should it be too long or too short. And most importantly, it must be unique in the database.

D: Looks like we have to write some tricky conditionals and database access code here.

G: Or a simple `constraints` property like so that goes directly in *User.groovy*:

```
def constraints = {
    name(length: 5..15, blank: false, unique: true)
}
```

D: Marvelous! And how does it work on the user interface?

G: Let's try to add a user that already exists and see what happens. *[tries it, resulting in figure 16.9]*

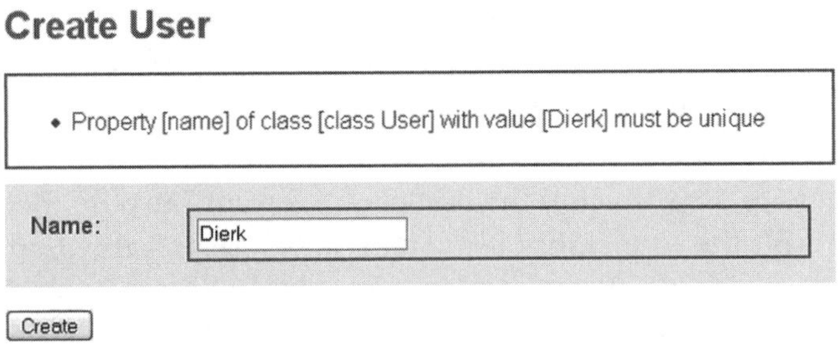

Create User

- Property [name] of class [class User] with value [Dierk] must be unique

Name: Dierk

Create

Figure 16.9
Validation error message when trying to create a new user with a name that already exists in the database

D: Really slick and very intuitive. Can you tell me what kind of validations are available?

G: There's a fairly long list in the online docs. So far, I've been able to do everything I needed, even regular expression matches.

D: That's fine. Regular expressions should at least cover everything we need to validate on the syntactic level. But what if I want to have other error messages?

G: Then you can adapt the file *i18n/defaultErrorMessages.properties* or provide your own localized message bundle. It all goes through the standard Java way of internationalization.

D: Perfect. I'd say we are ready for take-off.

G: So would I.

16.8.2 *Deploying the application*

D: Now, what do we have to do in order to deploy the application?

G: Adapt the database configuration to match the settings of your deployment target, run the `grails prod war` command, and use the production server mechanics to install the generated web archive file.

D: Where is the database configuration?

G: It's in *conf/ProductionDataSource.groovy*, just beneath the data source definitions for testing and development. Look here:

```
class ProductionDataSource {
    boolean pooling = true
    String dbCreate = "update"
    String url = "jdbc:hsqldb:file:prodDb"
    String driverClassName = "org.hsqldb.jdbcDriver"
    String username = "sa"
    String password = ""
}
```

D: I guess we change this to our production settings. What's the purpose of the `dbCreate` property?

G: This mimics what is in Hibernate: the `hibernate.hbm2ddl.auto` property. We can set it to `create`, `create-drop`, or `update`, meaning we want the database schema to be created automatically.

D: Will that mean that all existing data is lost?

G: Not if we set it to `update`, which is the best choice for our purpose. Because we were running with the in-memory test database before, `create-drop` was the fastest solution.

D: Where do we get all the information from?

G: We'd better ask our database administrator, Martin. For production, we'll need his help anyway, because he needs to grant us access rights and provide a user-name and password.

D: And that's all?

G: Martin may have some further advice about the best possible driver to use.

D: Do we need to package that driver class with Grails?

G: If we need to package it, we can store it in the lib directory, and it will be pack-aged with the web archive. However, production systems typically have their drivers installed in a shared library, so we can rely on having it available. All we need to know is the class name, and we can add it to the configuration.

D: I will head over to Martin and ask him.

G: Meanwhile, I'll prepare a text message for the boss, saying that the initial version of the Tutor application is up and running in production. I guess they have Internet access in the clubhouse, and he will be able to connect from there.

D: He will be surprised.

G: Definitely.

Dierk leaves to contact the database administrator and returns with a paper sheet of the configuration details.

D: Here we go. I owe him a beverage.

G: *[smiles]* We'll have one later.

D: Okay, I've fixed up the configuration. What was next? Creating the web archive?

G: Yes. Here it is:

```
grails prod war
```

G: We now have the *tutor.war* web archive ready for deployment.

D: I know how this goes. The server has a web interface where we can upload the file and start the application. That's easy. Just a minute. *[uploads the file]* Okay. Done.

G: Let's do some simple click-through testing to verify it's fine. Open the browser to http://groovy.canoo.com/tutor.

D: Looks okay. *[clicks through the application]* Perfect.

G: Gimme a high five. *[clap]*

D: Okay. Let's invite Martin and call it a day.

16.8.3 *Farewell*

Guillaume, Dierk, and the database administrator Martin assemble in the nearest beer garden.

D: The work with you and Grails was a ton of joy. Thanks for pointing me at it. I think we did an awesome good job this afternoon.

G: Hm, we could have done a little better.

M: I saw your application and used it a little. Really nice. Others need more than a week to achieve anything comparable.

G: Thanks, but I would have liked it better if we'd worked in a more test-driven style. You know: writing unit tests and functional tests as we go along.

D: You're demanding too much. That's hardly possible.

G: With all the scaffolded tests, it's quite easy.

M: And you are testing from a user's perspective?

G: Yes. Those are the so-called webtests. They are testing the view. We did a little of that. But we can also have unit tests for our models and controllers.

D: But we tested the views all the time, because we were constantly switching between coding and using the application.

M: Sounds like an agile programming thing.

D: And the models have no methods at all, so there's no point in testing them.

G: True; they *could* have had some methods, though.

D: I agree that testing the controllers automatically would have been beneficial. They contain the beef of the application logic.

M: Testing controllers is always tricky. You have to set up a server environment for that, because controllers rely on request parameters, session information, and such. That's an awful lot of work.

G: Actually, it's simple. In Grails, all the information is in common maps that you can pass into the controller method when testing.

M: Hm, okay. Then it should be easily possible.

D: I was surprised so many times this afternoon that I believe everything.

G: *[laughs]*

M: You must have had some real fun today.

D: You bet. It felt like everything was just falling in place.

G: Well, almost. Remember how we discussed the design of the domain model? That was the crucial part.

M: The drawings I saw in the coffee corner? They didn't look overly complicated.

G: But that's where the work is: making the complex simple.

D: Yes. I think my first attempt would have been to go for more bidirectional references. Would that have been possible at all?

G: Of course. It's also straightforward. The online docs show how to do it.

M: How about database performance? I certainly don't want you to drag down my db when your application becomes popular. *[twinkles]*

G: We still have room for optimization, whether by using bidirectional references or by optimizing Hibernate usage with direct mappings. However, I expect at least 90% of our database accesses to hit the Hibernate cache anyway.

M: Perfect. I'll look into the database logs to see what you produce, anyway.

G: Thanks. I would have asked you for that favor otherwise. *[grins]*

D: What are we going to do on Monday? I'd like to do some more work with Grails.

G: We'll write some more tests first. After that, I'll say it would make sense to hook in security.

D: That is possible?

G: Of course; Grails is pure J2EE, and we can use every feature of that platform: administration, operation surveillance, logging, load balancing, failover, and so forth, and also security. There is no need to reinvent the wheel just because we're groovy.

M: I can help you with the security setup.

G: Great!

D: The little wiki-like markup we implemented in the WikiTagLib made me think we're re-inventing the wheel, though. Would it be possible to include something like the Radeox Wiki engine?

G: Good idea! Yes, of course, that's possible. We can use any Java library we fancy. We throw its jar file in the lib directory and rework the WikiTagLib to use that functionality!

M: You have so many options that virtually anything is possible.

D: Friends, *[stands up and raises his glass]* I'm afraid the party is over, and I have to leave now. It was an honor to work with you. I know that working with me has not always been easy. I appreciate your forbearance when overlooking my little mistakes. Thank you very much for spending your precious time with me. I hope we will soon meet again and share the joy of dynamic programming.

Cheers!

Installation and documentation

A.1 *Installation*

The only prerequisite for installing Groovy is that you must first have a 1.4 or 1.5 JDK installed (available free from http://java.sun.com/j2se/) and the JAVA_HOME environment variable set to the location of your JDK installation.

To install Groovy:

1   Grab the latest stable release from http://groovy.codehaus.org/Download.

2   Unzip the file to a directory on your filesystem; for example, C:\groovy or /home/username/groovy.

3   We recommend checking whether you have a CLASSPATH variable set in your environment and unsetting it, at least temporarily, to avoid class-path problems, especially if you have any problems running basic Groovy commands.

4   Optionally, set an environment variable GROOVY_HOME whose value is set to the location where you unzipped the distribution zip file. If you are running your Groovy commands from the standard install location, you should not need to set this variable.

5   Optionally, include GROOVY_HOME/bin in your PATH environment variable. This will make all the Groovy command-line tools available in your path.

6   Test your installation by executing groovysh from a command line-shell. You should see output like this:

```
>groovysh
Lets get Groovy!
================
Version: 1.0-RC-01-SNAPSHOT JVM: 1.4.2_05-b04
Type 'exit' to terminate the shell
Type 'help' for command help
Type 'go' to execute the statements

groovy> exit
```

Congratulations! That is it for installing. Type exit to end the groovysh program.

Figure A.1 gives an overview of the contents of GROOVY_HOME, and table A.1 lists the directories and their purpose.

That's all there is. It looks minimal, and that's on purpose. You don't have to deal with any specifics of your operating system, such as messing with the quagmire that is Windows registry. If you decide to "uninstall" Groovy, just delete the GROOVY_HOME directory, and you're done.

Figure A.1 Overview of the GROOVY_HOME directories

Table A.1   Directories in GROOVY_HOME and their contents

Directory	Contents
bin	The executables discussed in this appendix
conf	Startup configuration files
embeddable	A single jar file, which packages Groovy and its dependencies together as a convenience for users embedding Groovy in other applications
lib	The Groovy implementation jars plus all the third-party libraries required for various features

A.2 Obtaining up-to-date documentation

This book aims to provide the necessary documentation for Groovy; however, other sources can provide more detailed, up-to-date, and responsive information. We only list a few starting points here—as the community expands, so will its online output.

A.2.1 Using online resources

Groovy's home page is http://groovy.codehaus.org/. This is where you can find all the latest information, including

- Downloads
- The famous and invaluable Groovy Quick-Reference
- A short language description and the official Groovy Language Specification (GLS), along with the official Groovy grammar in a browsable format
- Links to the CVS and Fisheye, the web view to CVS, together with RSS feeds of latest changes for those who prefer to "live on the edge"
- Links to the continuous integration build server and its feeds
- The JIRA issue tracker
- A number of articles, blogs, and tutorials about Groovy on the Web—for example, the popular "Practically Groovy" series.
- A "Groovy Online Experience" with live running code samples, available soon at http://groovy.canoo.com

A.2.2 Subscribing to mailing lists

For any questions concerning the normal use of Groovy, subscribe to *user-subscribe@groovy.codehaus.org*. Other mailing lists (replace *user* with *dev, jsr,* or *scm*) deal with topics of developing the Groovy core, bringing forward the issues of the Java Specification Request (JSR-241), and getting notifications from the CVS system that is used for Software Configuration Management (SCM).

We're constantly surprised by the responsiveness of these lists and the quality of answers that everybody receives there. All mailing list participants and especially the project manager Guillaume Laforge make this community a fun place to be.

A.2.3 *Connecting to forum and chat*

The core developers meet for chat at irc://irc.codehaus.org/groovy, but everybody else is also welcome. This is like talking with friends in a bar about your favorite programming language. In other words, it's highly addictive.

For questions about this book, there is a forum at Manning at http://www. manning.com/koenig where you can meet the authors.

Groovy language info

Table B.1 lists all the Groovy operators in order of their precedence. Most of these operators can be overridden. See the respective method names and usages in section 3.3, table 3.4.

Table B.1   Groovy operators in order of precedence

Level	Operator	Note

1	`$x`
	`new  ()`
	`()   {}   []`
	`.  ?.  *.`
	`~   !  $  (type)`
		Scope escape
		Explicit parentheses
		Method call, closure, list/map
		Dot, safe dereferencing, spread-dot
		Negate, not, typecast

2	`**`	Power
3	`++ -- + -`	Pre/post increment/decrement, unary sign
4	`* / %`	Multiply, div, modulo
5	`+ -`	Binary
6	`<< >> >>> .. ..<`	Shift, range
7	`< <= > >= instanceof as`	
8	`== != <=>`	
9	`&`	Binary and
10	`^`	Binary xor
11	`|`	Binary or
12	`&&`	Logical and
13	`||`	Logical or
14	`?:`	Ternary conditional
15	`= **= *= /= %= += -= <<= >>= >>>= &=` `^= |=`	Assignments

The list of Groovy language keywords follows. Not all of these keywords are actually used. Some of them are only reserved for future use. However, no keyword is allowed to be used as an identifier, such as a class, method, parameter, or variable name, with the exception of in.

B.1 *Keyword list*

```
abstract, any, as, assert
boolean, break, byte,
case, catch, char, class, continue,
def, default, do, double,
else, enum, extends,
false, final, finally, float, for,
if, import, in,¹ instanceof, int, interface,
long,
native, new, null,
private, protected, public,
return,
short, static, strictfp, super, switch, synchronized,
this, threadsafe, throw, throws, transient, true, try,
void, volatile,
while
```

---

[1] As in for(x in 0..9){}; however, in can still be used as an identifier, as in System.in.

GDK API *quick reference*

C.1 *Arrays and primitives*

Method name	Parameter types	Return type
Array of byte or Byte		
encodeBase64		Writable
Array of primitives		
getAt	int	Object
getAt	Range	Object Returned object is a list of autoboxed items
getAt	Collection	Object Returned object is a list of autoboxed items
putAt	int, Object	void
size		int
toList		List
Array of Object		
getAt	int	Object
getAt	Range	List
getAt	Collection	List
inject	Object, Closure	Object
join	String	String
putAt	int, Object	void
size		int
spread		SpreadList
toArrayString		String
toList		List
toSpreadList		SpreadList
toSpreadMap		SpreadMap
toString		String
Array of String		
execute		Process

continued on next page

Method name	Parameter types	Return type
double, float, long		
downto	Number, Closure	void
upto	Number, Closure	void

C.2 The java.lang package

Method name	Parameter types	Return type
Boolean		
and	Boolean	Boolean
or	Boolean	Boolean
xor	Boolean	Boolean
CharSequence		
getAt	int	CharSequence
getAt	Range	CharSequence Argument may also be an IntRange
getAt	Collection	CharSequence
Character		
compareTo	Character	int Argument may also be a Number
div	Character	Number Argument may also be a Number
intdiv	Character	Number Argument may also be a Number
minus	Character	Number Argument may also be a Number
multiply	Character	Number Argument may also be a Number
next		Number
plus	Character	Number Argument may also be a Number
previous		Number

continued on next page

Method name	Parameter types	Return type
Class		
isCase	Object	boolean
ClassLoader		
getRootLoader		ClassLoader
double, float, long		
abs		double Returns float or long, respectively
downto	Number, Closure	void
round		long
upto	Number, Closure	void
Number		
abs		int
and	Number	Number
compareTo	Number	int Argument may also be a Character
div	Number	Number Argument may also be a Character
downto	Number, Closure	void
intdiv	Number	Number Argument may also be a Character
leftShift	Number	Number
minus	Number	Number Argument may also be a Character
mod	Number	Number
multiply	Number	Number Argument may also be a Character
negate		Number
next		Number
or	Number	Number

continued on next page

Method name	Parameter types	Return type
Number *(continued)*		
plus	Number	Number Argument may also be a Character
plus	String	String
power	Number	Number
previous		Number
rightShift	Number	Number
rightShiftUnsigned	Number	Number
step	Number, Number, Closure	void
times	Closure	void
toBigDecimal		java.math.BigDecimal
toBigInteger		java.math.BigInteger
toDouble		Double
toFloat		Float
toInteger		Integer
toLong		Long
upto	Number, Closure	void
xor	Number	Number
Object		
any	Closure	boolean
collect	Closure	List
collect	Collection, Closure	Collection
dump		String
each	Closure	void
eachWithIndex	Closure	void {item, counter -> ...}
every	Closure	boolean
find	Closure	Object

continued on next page

Method name	Parameter types	Return type
Object *(continued)*		
findAll	Closure	List
findIndexOf	Closure	int
getAt	String	Object Dynamic property access
getMetaPropertyValues		List
getProperties		Map
grep	Object	List
identity	Closure	Object
inspect		String
invokeMethod	String, Object	Object
is	Object	boolean
isCase	Object	boolean
iterator		Iterator
print	PrintWriter	void
print	Object	void
printf	String, Object	void JDK 1.5+
printf	String, [Object]	void JDK 1.5+: varargs version
println	PrintWriter	void
println	Object	void
println		void
putAt	String, Object	void
use	Class, Closure	void
use	List, Closure	void List of classes
use	[Object], Closure	void Variable argument list of classes

continued on next page

Method name	Parameter types	Return type
Process		
consumeProcessOutput		void
getErr		InputStream
getIn		InputStream
getOut		OutputStream
getText		String
leftShift	[byte]	OutputStream
leftShift	Object	Writer
waitForOrKill	long	void
String		
center	Number	String
center	Number, String	String
contains	String	boolean
count	String	int
decodeBase64		[byte]
eachMatch	String, Closure	void
execute		Process
execute	List, File	Process
execute	[String], File	Process
getAt	int	String
getAt	Range	String
getAt	Collection	String
isCase	Object	boolean
leftShift	Object	StringBuffer
minus	Object	String
multiply	Number	String
negate		regex.Pattern
next		String

continued on next page

Method name	Parameter types	Return type
String *(continued)*		
padLeft	Number	String
padLeft	Number, String	String
padRight	Number	String
padRight	Number, String	String
plus	Object	String
previous		String
replaceAll	String, Closure	String
reverse		String
size		int
toBigDecimal		BigDecimal
toBigInteger		BigInteger
toBoolean		Boolean
toCharacter		Character
toDouble		Double
toFloat		Float
toInteger		Integer
toList		List
toLong		Long
toURI		java.net.URI
toURL		java.net.URL
tokenize	String	List
tokenize		List
StringBuffer		
leftShift	Object	StringBuffer
plus	String	String
putAt	IntRange, Object	void
size		int

C.3 The java.math package

Method name	Parameter types	Return type
BigDecimal		
downto	Number, Closure	void
upto	Number, Closure	void
BigInteger		
downto	Number, Closure	void
upto	Number, Closure	void

C.4 The java.util and java.sql packages

Method name	Parameter types	Return type
Collection		
asImmutable		Collection
asList		List
asSynchronized		Collection
collect	Closure	List
collect	Collection, Closure	Collection Add to the given Collection
count	Object	int
disjoint	Collection	boolean
each	Closure	void
find	Closure	Object
findAll	Closure	List
getAt	String	List
groupBy	Closure	Map
inject	Object, Closure	Object

continued on next page

Method name	Parameter types	Return type
Collection *(continued)*		
isCase	Object	boolean
join	String	String
leftShift	Object	Collection
max		Object
max	Closure	Object
max	Comparator	Object
min		Object
min	Closure	Object
min	Comparator	Object
multiply	Number	List
plus	Collection	List
plus	Object	List
sort		List
sort	Closure	List
sort	Comparator	List
sum		Object
sum	Closure	Object
toList		List
toListString		String
toString		String
unique		Collection
unique	Closure	Collection
unique	Comparator	Collection

continued on next page

Method name	Parameter types	Return type
Date (java.util and java.sql)		
minus	int	Date Returns util or sql versions of Date, respectively
next		Date Returns util or sql versions of Date, respectively
plus	int	Date Returns util or sql versions of Date, respectively
previous		Date Returns util or sql versions of Date, respectively
Enumeration		
iterator		Iterator
List		
asImmutable		List
asSynchronized		List
equals	List	boolean
execute		Process
flatten		List
getAt	int	Object
getAt	Collection	List
getAt	IntRange	List
intersect	Collection	List
minus	Collection	List
minus	Object	List
pop		Object
putAt	int, Object	void
putAt	IntRange, Object	void
putAt	List, List	void

continued on next page

Method name	Parameter types	Return type
List *(continued)*		
putAt	List, Object	void
reverse		List
reverseEach	Closure	void
sort		List
sort	Closure	List
sort	Comparator	List
spread		SpreadList
toSpreadList		SpreadList
Map		
asImmutable		Map
asSynchronized		Map
collect	Closure	List
collect	Collection, Closure	Collection Add to the given Collection
each	Closure	void
find	Closure	Object
findAll	Closure	Map
get	Object, Object	Object key, default
getAt	Object	Object
putAt	Object, Object	Object
spread		SpreadMap
subMap	Collection	Map
toMapString		String
toSpreadMap		SpreadMap
toString		String

continued on next page

Method name	Parameter types	Return type
Set		
asImmutable		Set
asSynchronized		Set
SortedMap		
asImmutable		SortedMap
asSynchronized		SortedMap
SortedSet		
asImmutable		SortedSet
asSynchronized		SortedSet
sort		SortedSet
Timer		
runAfter	int, Closure	void

C.5 *The java.util.regex package*

Method name	Parameter types	Return type
Matcher		
each	Closure	void
getAt	int	Object
getAt	Collection	String
getCount		int
hasGroup		boolean
iterator		Iterator
setIndex	int	void
size		long
Pattern		
isCase	Object	boolean

C.6 The java.io package

Method name	Parameter types	Return type
BufferedReader		
getText		String
BufferedWriter		
writeLine	String	void
DataInputStream		
iterator		Iterator Byte-based
File		
append	String	void
append	String, String	void With encoding
asWritable		File
asWritable	String	File With encoding
eachByte	Closure	void
eachDir	Closure	void
eachFile	Closure	void
eachFileMatch	Object, Closure	void isCase() applied to the first argument
eachFileRecurse	Closure	void
eachLine	Closure	void
eachObject	Closure	void
filterLine	Writer, Closure	void
filterLine	Closure	Writable
getText	String	String With encoding

continued on next page

Method name	Parameter types	Return type
File *(continued)*		
getText		String
iterator		Iterator Line-based
leftShift	String	File
newInputStream		BufferedInputStream
newObjectInputStream		ObjectInputStream
newOutputStream		BufferedOutputStream
newPrintWriter		PrintWriter
newPrintWriter	String	PrintWriter With encoding
newReader	String	BufferedReader With encoding
newReader		BufferedReader
newWriter		BufferedWriter
newWriter	boolean	BufferedWriter Append
newWriter	String	BufferedWriter With encoding
newWriter	String, boolean	BufferedWriter With encoding, append
readBytes		[byte]
readLines		List
size		long
splitEachLine	String, Closure	void First argument is the separator to use
withInputStream	Closure	void
withOutputStream	Closure	void
withPrintWriter	Closure	void

continued on next page

Method name	Parameter types	Return type
File *(continued)*		
withReader	Closure	void
withWriter	Closure	void
withWriter	String, Closure	void With encoding
withWriterAppend	String, Closure	Void With encoding
write	String	Void
write	String, String	Void With encoding
InputStream		
eachByte	Closure	Void
eachLine	Closure	Void
filterLine	Writer, Closure	Void
filterLine	Closure	Writable
getText		String
getText	String	String With encoding
iterator		Iterator Byte-based
newReader		BufferedReader
readLine		String
readLines		List
withReader	Closure	void
withStream	Closure	void
ObjectInputStream		
eachObject	Closure	void

continued on next page

Method name	Parameter types	Return type
OutputStream		
leftShift	Object	Writer
leftShift	InputStream	OutputStream
leftShift	[byte]	OutputStream Argument is a byte array
withStream	Closure	void
withWriter	Closure	void
withWriter	String, Closure	void With encoding
Reader		
eachLine	Closure	void
filterLine	Writer, Closure	void
filterLine	Closure	Writable
getText		String
iterator		Iterator Line-based
readLine		String
readLines		List
splitEachLine	String, Closure	void
transformChar	Writer, Closure	void
transformLine	Writer, Closure	void
withReader	Closure	void
Writer		
leftShift	Object	Writer
withWriter	Closure	void
write	Writable	void

C.7 The java.net package

Method name	Parameter types	Return type
ServerSocket		
accept	Closure	Socket
Socket		
leftShift	[byte]	OutputStream
leftShift	Object	Writer
withStreams	Closure	void
URL		
eachByte	Closure	void
eachLine	Closure	void
getText		String
getText	String	String With encoding
withReader	Closure	void

Cheat sheets

Cheat sheets provide you with quick information and examples to get you up and running quickly. For more details about any topic, refer to the corresponding section in the book or on the Groovy web site's wiki.

D.1 Lists

See section 4.2.

```
assert [1,2,3,4]        == (1..4)
assert [1,2,3] + [1]    == [1,2,3,1]
assert [1,2,3] << 1     == [1,2,3,1]
assert [1,2,3,1] - [1] == [2,3]
assert [1,2,3] * 2      == [1,2,3,1,2,3]
assert [1,[2,3]].flatten() == [1,2,3]
assert [1,2,3].reverse()    == [3,2,1]
assert [1,2,3].disjoint([4,5,6])
assert [1,2,3].intersect([4,3,1]) == [3,1]
assert [1,2,3].collect{ it+3 }    == [4,5,6]
assert [1,2,3,1].unique().size()  == 3
assert [1,2,3,1].count(1) == 2
assert [1,2,3,4].min()    == 1
assert [1,2,3,4].max()    == 4
assert [1,2,3,4].sum()    == 10
assert [4,2,1,3].sort()   == [1,2,3,4]
assert [4,2,1,3].findAll{ it%2 == 0 } == [4,2]
def animals = ['cat','kangaroo','koala','dog']
assert animals[2] == 'koala'
def kanimals = animals[1..2]
assert animals.findAll{ it =~ /k.*/ } == kanimals
assert animals.find{ it =~ /k.*/ }    == kanimals[0]
assert animals.grep(~/k.*/)           == kanimals
```

D.2 Closures

See chapter 5.

```
def add  = { x, y -> x + y }
def mult = { x, y -> x * y }
assert add(1,3)   == 4
assert mult(1,3) == 3
def min = { x, y -> [x,y].min() }
def max = { x, y -> [x,y].max() }
def atLeastTen = max.curry(10)
assert atLeastTen(5)  == 10
assert atLeastTen(15) == 15
def pairWise(list, Closure invoke) {
    if (list.size() < 2) return []
    def next = invoke(list[0],list[1])
    return [next] + pairWise(list[1..-1], invoke)
```

```
}
assert pairWise(1..5, add)   == [3, 5, 7, 9]
assert pairWise(1..5, mult)  == [2, 6, 12, 20]
assert pairWise(1..5, min)   == [1, 2, 3, 4]
assert pairWise(1..5, max)   == [2, 3, 4, 5]
assert 'cbaxabc' == ['a','b','c'].inject('x'){
        result, item -> item + result + item }
assert [1,2,3].grep{ it<3 } == [1,2]
assert [1,2,3].any{ it%2 == 0 }
assert [1,2,3].every{ it<4 }
assert (1..9).collect{it}.join()    == '123456789'
assert (1..4).collect{it*2}.join() == '2468'
```

D.3 *Regular expressions*

See section 3.5.

Table D.1   Regular expressions

Symbol	Meaning
.	Any character
^	Start of line (or start of document, when in single-line mode)
$	End of line (or end of document, when in single-line mode)
\d	Digit character
\D	Any character except digits
\s	Whitespace character
\S	Any character except whitespace
\w	Word character
\W	Any character except word characters
\b	Word boundary
()	Grouping
(x|y)	x or y as in (Groovy|Java|Ruby)
\1	Backmatch to group one; for example, find doubled characters with (.)\1
x*	Zero or more occurrences of x

continued on next page

Table D.1 Regular expressions *(continued)*

Symbol	Meaning
x+	One or more occurrences of x
x?	Zero or one occurrence of x
x{m,n}	At least m and at most n occurrences of x
x{m}	Exactly m occurrences of x
[a-f]	Character class containing the characters *a, b, c, d, e, f*
[^a]	Character class containing any character except *a*
[aeiou]	Character class representing lowercase vowels
[a-z&&[^aeiou]]	Lowercase consonants
[a0zA-Z0-9]	Uppercase or lowercase letter or digit
[+|-]?(\d+(\.\d*)?)|(\.\d+)	Positive or negative floating-point number
^[\w-\.]+@([\w-]+\.)+[\w-]{2,4}$	Simple email validation
(?is:x)	Switches mode when evaluating x; i turns on ignoreCase, s is single-line mode
(?=regex)	Positive lookahead
(?<=text)	Positive lookbehind

Examples:

```
def twister = 'she sells sea shells by the sea shore'
// contains word 'shore'
assert twister =~ 'shore'
// contains 'sea' twice (two ways)
assert (twister =~ 'sea').count == 2
assert twister.split(/ /).grep(~/sea/).size() == 2
// words that start with 'sh', \b = word boundary
def shwords = (twister =~ /sh[a-z]*\b/).collect{it}.join(' ')
assert shwords == 'she shells shore'
// four words have three letter, \S = non-Space letter
assert (twister =~ /\b\S{3}\b/).count == 4
// three words start with 's' and have 5 or 6 letters
assert (twister =~ /\bs\S{4}\S?\b/).count == 3
// replace words with 'X', \w = word character
assert twister.replaceAll(/\w+/,'X') == 'X X X X X X X X'
// starts with 'she' and ends with 'shore'
def pattern = ~/she.*shore/
```

```
assert pattern.matcher(twister).matches()
// replace 'sea' with 'ocean' but only if preceded by word 'the'
def ocean = twister.replaceAll('(?<=the )sea','ocean')
assert ocean == 'she sells sea shells by the ocean shore'
// swap 1st and 2nd pairs of words
def pairs = twister =~ /(\S+) (\S+) ?/
assert pairs.hasGroup()
twister = [1, 0, 2, 3].collect{ pairs[it][0] }.join()
assert twister = 'sea shells she sells by the sea shore'
```

D.4 Unit testing

See chapter 14.

Groovy tests may be written in scripts or in classes that extend `GroovyTestCase`, both of which can use the normal `groovy` command or a test runner within your IDE or build environment. One useful method provided by `GroovyTestCase` is `shouldFail`, which lets you easily test failure conditions. You can also use `asserts` within your test scripts.

D.5 Mocks and stubs

See section 14.5.2.

Use stubs when you want to replace an object with one that accepts all the calls of an original object. This is typically done when you want to perform state-based testing. Use mocks when you want to apply stricter expectations on your objects in order to do interaction-based testing.

As an example, suppose you want to test the following class with sufficient tests to reach 100 percent coverage, and either `method1` or `method2` could throw an exception:

```
class MyClass {
    def method() {
        try {
            new Collaborator1().method1()
            new Collaborator2().method2()
        } catch (Exception e) {
            new Collaborator3().method3()
        }
    }
}
```

Here is one way you could write your test code:

```
import groovy.mock.interceptor.MockFor
class MyClassTest extends GroovyTestCase {
    def mock1 = new MockFor(Collaborator1)
```

```
def mock2 = new MockFor(Collaborator2)
def mock3 = new MockFor(Collaborator3)
private static final Closure PASS = {}
private static final Closure FAIL = {
    throw new RuntimeException()
}
void testSuccess() {
    check(PASS, PASS, null)
}
void testCollaborator1Fails() {
    check(FAIL, null, PASS)
}
void testCollaborator2Fails() {
    check(PASS, FAIL, PASS)
}
private check(expected1, expected2, expected3){
    if (expected1) mock1.demand.method1(expected1)
    if (expected2) mock2.demand.method2(expected2)
    if (expected3) mock3.demand.method3(expected3)
    mock1.use { mock2.use { mock3.use {
        new MyClass().method()
    }}}
}
}
```

D.6 XML GPath notation

See chapter 12.

Groovy supports special notation for common XML processing activities. Consider the following XML:

```
def recipeXml = '''
<recipe>
    <ingredients>
        <ingredient amount='2 cups'>Self-raising Flour</ingredient>
        <ingredient amount='2 tablespoons'>Icing sugar</ingredient>
        <ingredient amount='2 tablespoons'>Butter</ingredient>
        <ingredient amount='3/4 - 1 cup'>Milk</ingredient>
    </ingredients>
    <steps>
        <step>Preheat oven to 230 degrees celsius</step>
        <step>Sift flour and icing sugar into a bowl</step>
        <step>Melt butter and mix into dry ingredients</step>
        <step>Gradually add milk to the mixture until moist</step>
        <step>Turn onto floured board and cut into portions</step>
        <step>Bake for 15 minutes</step>
        <step>Serve with jam and whipped cream</step>
    </steps>
</recipe>
'''
```

Using `XmlSlurper`, `XmlParser`, or `DOMCategory`, you can write the following notation to process this XML:

```
assert 4 == recipe.ingredients.ingredient.size()
// should be 14 elements in total
assert 14 == recipe.'**'.findAll{true}.size()
// step 4 (index 3 because we start from 0) involves milk
assert recipe.steps.step[3].text().contains('milk')
assert '2 cups' == recipe.ingredients.ingredient[0].'@amount'.toString()
// two ingredients have '2 tablespoons' amount attribute
def ingredients = recipe.ingredients.ingredient.grep{
    it.'@amount' == '2 tablespoons'
}
assert ingredients.size() == 2
// every step has at least 4 words
assert recipe.steps.step.every{
    step -> step.text().tokenize(' ').size() >= 4
}
```

Initialization for `XmlSlurper` looks like this:

```
def recipe   = new XmlSlurper().parseText(recipeXml)
/* … processing steps … */
```

Initialization for `XmlParser` looks like this:

```
def recipe   = new XmlParser().parseText(recipeXml)
/* … processing steps … */
```

Initialization for `DOMCategory` looks like this:

```
def reader   = new StringReader(recipeXml)
def doc      = groovy.xml.DOMBuilder.parse(reader)
def recipe   = doc.documentElement
use (groovy.xml.dom.DOMCategory) {
    /* … processing steps … */
}
```

index

MORE JAVA TITLES FROM MANNING

Java Persistence with Hibernate
   by Christian Bauer
     and Gavin King
   ISBN: 1-932394-88-5
   880 pages
   $59.99
   November 2006

*iText in Action: Creating and
Manipulating PDF*
   by Bruno Lowagie
   ISBN: 1-932394-79-6
   688 pages
   $49.99
   December 2006

*For ordering information on these and other Manning titles,
please visit www.manning.com*